Acting Out
CULTURE

Reading and Writing

James S. Miller

University of Wisconsin, Whitewater

Bedford/St. Martin's   Boston ◆ New York

For Bedford/St. Martin's

Executive Editors: Leasa Burton and Stephen A. Scipione
Developmental Editor: Adam Whitehurst
Production Editor: Kendra LeFleur
Production Supervisor: Andrew Ensor
Marketing Manager: Molly Parke
Editorial Assistant: Nicholas McCarthy
Production Assistant: Laura Winstead
Copy Editor: Lisa Wehrle
Permissions Manager: Kalina Ingham Hintz
Senior Art Director: Anna Palchik
Text Design: Tom Carling/Carling Design
Cover Design: Billy Boardman
Composition: MPS Limited, a Macmillan Company
Printing and Binding: R. R. Donnelley & Sons Company

President: Joan E. Feinberg
Editorial Director: Denise B. Wydra
Editor in Chief: Karen S. Henry
Director of Marketing: Karen R. Soeltz
Director of Production: Susan W. Brown
Associate Director, Editorial Production: Elise S. Kaiser
Managing Editor: Elizabeth M. Schaaf

Library of Congress Control Number: 2010936408

6   5   4   3   2
f   e   d   c   b

For information, write: Bedford/St. Martin's, 75 Arlington Street, Boston, MA 02116
(617-399-4000)

ISBN-10: 0–312–62429–8

ISBN-13: 978–0–312–62429–3

Acknowledgments

Acknowledgments and copyrights are continued at the back of the book on pages 522–24, which constitute an extension of the copyright page. It is a violation of the law to reproduce these selections by any means whatsoever without the written permission of the copyright holder.

Jessica Bennett, "The Flip Side of Internet Fame" from *Newsweek* 2/22/2008 issue. Reprinted by permission.
Colin Bissett, "Le Vie D'Ennui." Originally printed in *Philosophy Now* issue 77, February/March 2010.

For Henry, Eliza, and Hope

Preface for Instructors

"WHADDAYA GOT?"

In the 1953 film *The Wild One,* Marlon Brando, playing Johnny Strabler, the leather-jacketed leader of a motorcycle gang that invades a small town, utters one of the most famous lines in movie history. Asked "Johnny, what are you rebelling against?" Brando arches an eyebrow and replies, "Whaddaya got?"

Acting Out Culture encourages students to cultivate a "Whaddaya got?" stance toward American culture — although not, of course, in the belligerent and self-destructive vein of Johnny Strabler. Rather, it takes as a given that students have already internalized countless rules, and are bombarded every day with media messages that dictate how they should think, feel, and behave. *Acting Out Culture* urges them to recognize these rules and prescriptions that they may adhere to unthinkingly, probe them, and imagine alternatives. Unlike an actor in a Hollywood movie, students have options. Although scripts for their lives abound, the endings are not written in stone. Working with the readings and assignments in *Acting Out Culture* gives students the opportunity to think critically about the norms and roles handed to or imposed on them and, as it were, devise their own scripts in response to what they discover. On the stage of a composition classroom where popular culture is the subject of inquiry, they have the chance to "act out" through writing that positions them as citizens making informed decisions about their world.

WHY THESE CHAPTERS?

Because they start where students are and encourage them to exceed their own comfort zones of belief and action. The thematic organization of *Acting Out Culture* focuses students' attention not only on *what* our culture tells us but also on *how* it establishes those rules and disseminates those norms. The chapter themes explore questions of what and how we believe, watch, eat, work, learn, and change — questions that get to the heart of who students are and how they behave. Do they count themselves among the "we"s? As students evaluate, negotiate, and resist the roles and stances reflected in the chapters, their "Whaddaya got?" responses begin to emerge.

Moreover, the specific topics and readings within the chapters use students' own knowledge of popular culture as a springboard to deeper analysis. For example, Chapter 2, "How We Watch," covers several types of seeing and makes connections between what it means to watch and be watched. Students are asked to draw on *what* they know about diverse topics such as reality TV, GPS cell phone apps, and TV news as a first step in considering broader questions of *how* this knowledge might connect to the culture at large.

WHY THESE READINGS?

Because they are exceptional models of writing and thinking by contemporary writers who have important things to say about issues students care about. Each chapter includes longer pieces that support sustained reading and model in-depth critical analysis, as well as more popular pieces that go beyond trend-spotting to tackle the question "How does America tick?" — with often surprising conclusions. The writers include academics such as Michael Eric Dyson (writing on the news media's characterization of the African American victims of Hurricane Katrina), journalists such as Barbara Ehrenreich (who finds fault with our culture's insistence on positive thinking), and activists such as Naomi Klein (who objects to sex being sold to women as a form of empowerment). Although the readings approach the book's main themes from different angles, the overall focus on making and breaking the sometimes unspoken rules that govern our everyday lives creates a dialogue that will challenge students' critical thinking skills.

WHY THESE FEATURES IN EACH CHAPTER?

Because they introduce a variety of approaches to thinking and writing about cultural norms and rules. To analyze culture, students need to notice what they often overlook or take for granted, so each chapter opens with a photograph or sign that captures for analysis the rules that often fly beneath students' radar. Another recurring feature that makes the often-invisible visible is **"Everybody Knows That . . . ,"** which appears in the margins of the introductions. These call-outs list common rules that reflect conventional wisdom and invite students to move what's in the margins of their aware-ness to front and center, the better to unpack and examine the assumptions nested in the norms.

Students also need to see that cultural analysis moves beyond binary thinking — the impulse to frame issues in black-and-white terms. Therefore, each chapter introduction closes with a **Rule Maker/Rule Breaker** box, which presents opposing points of view on a cultural issue in the opponents' own words. By looking into debates such as whether the proliferation of mega-retailers like Wal-Mart is beneficial or harmful, and whether the purpose of education is to train thinkers or workers, students can discover that there are more than two sides to every issue, which prepares them for the multiple perspectives and complex dialogues in the ensuing chapter.

Because students increasingly receive their daily doses of popular culture via visual media, *Acting Out Culture* presents advertisements, movies, television, and news photos as objects of analysis. Throughout, the book provides opportunities for students to respond to images as conductors of cultural messages.

The images in **Then and Now** depict popular thinking from the past to the present. Students can compare and contrast the images, but they can also use the accompanying contextual information to think further about what *hasn't* changed over time. In the "How We Believe" chapter, for example, a news photo of a Cold War–era duck-and-cover air raid drill is paired with a recent news photo showing bottles of shampoo and mouthwash being confiscated at the airport. Students are asked to consider, then and now, "What's more important? To feel safe or to be safe?" Do the images suggest similarly futile responses to overwhelming perils? If not, why not? If so, what are some alternatives?

Scenes and Un-Scenes track cultural norms in visual media by juxtaposing images on a central topic. These topics range from patriotic symbols in political speeches to the importance of victory as an American ideal. Students are encouraged to see the images as texts, composed to persuade audiences to interpret the world in a certain way. Discussion and writing prompts then direct students to think about how visual media portray, navigate, and re-frame social rules and norms. What's in the pictures, and what's been left out?

WHY THESE WRITING ASSIGNMENTS?

Because writing is the best way for students to harness their own thinking and take control of what the culture wants them to believe. Writing is one of the most powerful tools we have for participating as active members of society, and the assignments in *Acting Out Culture* help students get a grip on the issues and construct sturdy arguments for action and change. After reading each selection, students are asked to identify the norms the piece addresses, think critically about the issues at hand, and take a stand on these topics by analyzing a writer's argument, examining the point of view, or evaluating the effectiveness of the language.

In particular, the **Putting It into Practice** assignments that close each chapter put students in the driver's seat. Often rooted in field research, these assignments urge students to consider how the issues in a chapter play out in their communities and in their personal lives. For example, in the "How We Work" chapter students are asked to research mean salaries for a range of jobs and write about why we "value" different types of work in different ways, using what they've discovered by reading the chapter selections to frame their own thoughts.

WHAT'S NEW IN THE SECOND EDITION?

*Because American culture evolves at such a rapid pace, there are **28 new readings about extremely current and relevant issues.*** More than half of the reading selections are new, featuring up-and-coming and established voices who think through and challenge established rules and norms, whether these are online, on television, at the dinner table, or at the cash register. The new readings feature the brightest writers, educators, journalists, and activists who challenge our thinking on the issues that matter in America today. From Mike Rose's impassioned defense of blue-collar work, to Mathew Honan's adventures with geolocation apps and the limits of Internet privacy, to Julie Bosman's portrait of one homeless man's resistance to change, each new reading addresses issues students encounter as they move through every role they play in life.

Whether through writing or social interaction, social norms evolve around us every day. **A new chapter, "How We Change,"** explores how we record, respond to, and enact social change, reinforcing *Acting Out Culture*'s overall belief that writing and action give students the power to change their world. The chapter addresses the theme of change on both societal and personal levels, covering topics as timely and engaging as communication in the age of Twitter, Peter Lovenheim's campaign to spend a night in each of his neighbor's homes, and the changing definition of friendship.

Students today are highly culturally attuned. They are surrounded by marketing and are adept at paying attention to huge streams of competing cultural data. In order to help them translate these native skills to the college classroom, the second edition of *Acting Out Culture* provides **more support for doing critical analysis in academic work.** A new, expanded introduction, "How We Read and Write about Culture," gives students a brief crash course in the vocabulary of cultural analysis with extended, real-life examples and an annotated professional essay that walks students step by step through performing cultural analysis. In addition, **a complete student essay in MLA format** in the introduction makes it easier for students to see how to integrate cultural analysis into academic writing.

WHAT RESOURCES ARE AVAILABLE TO SUPPORT TEACHING AND LEARNING?

INSTRUCTOR RESOURCES

Instructor's Edition for *ACTING OUT CULTURE*, 2nd edition
ISBN 978–0–312–67668–1
The instructor's edition for *Acting Out Culture* features an instructor's manual, *Resources for Teaching,* that offers helpful suggestions for integrating the selections into your writing course, including discussion starters and tips for using the book's many special features to get your students thinking about the rules we live by. Also available in PDF that can be downloaded from the Bedford/St. Martin's online catalog, this manual supports every selection in the book and includes overviews, discussion starters, and ideas for clustering the readings into topical or thematic units. To download this manual, visit bedfordstmartins.com/actingout/catalog.

Teaching Central offers the entire list of Bedford/St. Martin's print and online professional resources in one place. You'll find landmark reference works, sourcebooks on pedagogical issues, award-winning collections, and practical advice for the classroom — all free for instructors. Visit bedfordstmartins.com/teachingcentral.

Bits collects creative ideas for teaching a range of composition topics in an easily searchable blog. A community of teachers — leading scholars, authors, and editors — discuss revision, research, grammar and style, technology, peer review, and much more. Take, use, adapt, and pass the ideas around. Then come back to the site to comment or share your own suggestions. Visit blogs.bedfordstmartins.com/bits.

STUDENT RESOURCES

Re:Writing, the best free collection of online resources for the writing class, offers clear advice on citing sources in *Research and Documentation Online* by Diana Hacker, 30 sample papers and designed documents, and over 9000 writing and grammar exercises with immediate feedback and reporting in *Exercise Central.* Updated and redesigned, *Re:Writing* also features 5 free videos from *VideoCentral* and 3 new visual tutorials from our popular *ix visual exercises* by Cheryl Ball and Kristin Arola. *Re:Writing* is completely free and open (no codes required) to ensure access to all students. Visit bedfordstmartins.com/rewriting.

VideoCentral: English is a growing collection of videos for the writing class that captures real-world, academic, and student writers talking about how and why they write. Writer and teacher Peter Berkow interviewed hundreds of people — from Michael Moore to Cynthia Selfe — to produce 50 brief videos about topics such as revising and getting feedback. *VideoCentral* can be packaged with *Acting Out Culture* for free. An activation code is required. To learn more, visit bedfordstmartins.com/videocentral. To order *VideoCentral* packaged with the print book, use **ISBN 978–0–312–58123–7**.

Re:Writing Plus gathers all of Bedford/St. Martin's premium digital content for composition into one online collection. It includes hundreds of model documents, the first-ever peer review game, and *VideoCentral*. *Re:Writing Plus* can be purchased separately or packaged with the print book at a significant discount. An activation code is required. To learn more, visit bedfordstmartins.com/rewriting. To order *Re:Writing Plus* packaged with the print book, use **ISBN 978–0–312–58122–0**.

i-series on CD-ROM presents multimedia tutorials in a flexible format — because there are things you can't do in a book. To learn more, visit bedfordstmartins.com/actingout/catalog.

- *ix visual exercises* helps students put into practice key rhetorical and visual concepts. To order *ix visual exercises* packaged with the print book, use **ISBN 978–0–312–58121–3**.

- *i-claim: visualizing argument* offers a new way to see argument — with 6 tutorials, an illustrated glossary, and over 70 multimedia arguments. To order *i-claim: visualizing argument* packaged with the print book, use **ISBN 978–0–312–58113–8**.

- *i-cite: visualizing sources* brings research to life through an animated introduction, 4 tutorials, and hands-on source practice. To order *i-claim: visualizing sources* packaged with the print book, use **ISBN 978–0–312–58112–1**.

ACKNOWLEDGMENTS

As befits its focus on "acting," this book owes its existence to the contributions of a truly ensemble cast. First, there are the friends and colleagues whose encouragement in the early stages helped keep this project alive when I had little (if any) idea about where it was going. To Alanya Harter, my first friend at Bedford, many thanks for steering this project my way in the first place and for sticking with me through months of initial dithering. Thanks as well to Leasa Burton, whose early insights and guidance helped get this project off the ground, as well as to Joan Feinberg, Denise Wydra, Karen Henry, and Steve Scipione, whose combined wealth of experience and ideas added immeasurable depth and purpose to the book.

I'd like to extend my thanks to the countless students and instructors intrepid enough to have taken a chance on a new cultural studies reader. The anecdotes, reflections, and suggestions I have received over the last three years provided me with exactly the right foundation for thinking about what this book really needs to be. In particular, I would like to single out the contributions of my own students at UW-Whitewater, who never stinted in offering candid and constructive feedback about both what did and did not work. Thank you to the following instructors for their valuable input on the second edition: Richard S. Albright, Harrisburg Area Community College; Tamia Burt, Roger Williams University; Krista E. Callahan-Caudill, University of Kentucky; Liz Canfield, Virginia Commonwealth University; Jason DePolo, North Carolina A&T State University; Stephanie L. Dowdle, Salt Lake Community College; Marie Elliott, Georgia College and State University; Jason D. Fichtel, Joliet Junior College; Robert Forman, St. John's University; Jennifer Hamilton, Modesto Junior College; Virginia Scott Hendrickson, Missouri State University; Ronald Richard Janssen, Hofstra University; Michelle Kaschak, Penn State Lehigh Valley; Thomas W. Kitchen, Montclair State University; Deb Martin, Rowan University; Matthew McMahan, Stony Brook University; Lisa Oldaker Palmer, Quinsigamond Community College; Regina Sakalarios-Rogers, University of West Florida; Charles Shackett, San Ramon Campus of Diablo Valley College; Roy Stamper, North Carolina State University; Karen Stewart, Norwich University; Linda Stewart, Portland Community College; and Lori Vail, English Department, Green River Community College.

To Andrew Hansen and David Zimmerman, my gratitude for allowing themselves to be my sounding board; their feedback about what students might truly want from a book like this — and what they wouldn't — proved invaluable. In the same vein, I want to express my appreciation to the many reviewers whose insight helped shape this book in its first edition:

Amy Braziller, Red Rocks Community College; Cherie Post Dargan, Hawkeye Community College; Daniel L. DeSanto, (formerly) University of Vermont; Danielle Nicole DeVoss, Michigan State University; Robert Dunne, Central Connecticut State University; Heather Eaton, Daytona Beach Community College; Richard Fine, Virginia Commonwealth University; Thomas A. Hamill, Wilkes University; Amy Hawkins, Columbia College, Chicago; Kristina Heiks, Appalachian State University; Tom Henthorne, Pace University; Deborah Kirkman, University of Kentucky; Alison A. Knoblauch, University of New Hampshire; Fern Kupfer, Iowa State University; Matthew Marx, University of Nebraska at Omaha; Randall McClure, Minnesota State University; Geraldine R. McNenny, Chapman University; Terry Nienhuis, Western Carolina University; Jennifer Reich, University of Denver; Rhonda Schlatter, Mesa Community College; Scott Stevens, Western Washington University; Deborah Coxwell Teague, Florida State University; Danica Natalia Vukovic, George Mason University; Cynthia L. Walker, Faulkner University; Christopher Wilkey, Northern Kentucky University; and Lee Zickel, Cleveland State University.

This book would have never made it past manuscript without the careful work of production editor Kendra LeFleur and copyeditor Lisa Wehrle as well as the work of Elizabeth Schaaf and Andrew Ensor. And there'd be very little in it without Linda Winters and Kathleen Karcher to hammer out the text permissions and without Martha Friedman and Connie Gardner applying their expert research skills to the visuals.

Of course *Acting Out Culture* would never have rounded the corner into a second edition were it not for the continuing efforts of my editor, Adam Whitehurst. Adam's keen sense of how to keep the book current, combined with his unfailingly innovative suggestions about prompts, features, and activities, helped to keep this second edition as actively and intimately attuned to the broader culture as the first. Once again, I want to express my affection and gratitude to the crew at EVP Coffee in Madison. When you're lucky enough to have discovered the perfect place for writing a book, why mess with a good thing? And finally, to Emily Hall, whose belief in and support for this project continues to make it all possible. My love and thanks.

Contents

2 How We Watch   99

5   How We Work   363

Introduction: How We Read and Write about Culture

THESE ARE THE RULES

Why do you act differently at a job interview than on a night out with friends? Why do we so rarely see people wearing their pajamas to church? What accounts for the fact that you're far more likely to be on a first-name basis with a classmate than with a professor? Why does your Thanksgiving dinner conversation with a grandparent sound so different from your e-mail exchanges with friends? Whether sitting in class or working an off-campus job, chatting with family on the phone or meeting a roommate for coffee, it's hardly a secret that different situations require different standards of behavior. And while this may seem like a fairly obvious observation, it is also an important one because it raises other questions whose answers aren't nearly as simple or straightforward. Namely, why do we accept *these* standards instead of others? Why do we regard only certain ways of acting, talking, and dressing as acceptable, appropriate, *normal*? Who, or what, teaches us to be normal?

This book invites you to look at and think more deeply about the countless rules that operate in our world: where they come from, how they shape our individual actions and attitudes, and whether ultimately they can be questioned, challenged, or even rewritten. From the shopping mall to the classroom, from the jobs we hold to the parties we attend, from family holidays to first dates, our world abounds with an almost endless array of instructions: different collections of "dos" and "don'ts" that, while generally unspoken, nonetheless play a formative role in influencing how we act. This book asks you to consider writing about the world around you by asking yourself a series of questions:

- *What* is it that producers of popular culture want me to do?

- *How* do they use our common cultural beliefs, identities, or fears to persuade me to do it?

- How do I *really* want to do it?

Unlike other books that focus on popular culture, this book asks you to begin by examining the ordinary details of your daily life. Rather than exploring the texts and products of pop culture in isolation, you will be asked to uncover and make sense of the complex connections between this material and your personal actions. It is the goal of this book to direct your attention not just to what our popular culture *says* but to what it asks you to *do* as well. You probably already know quite a bit about some of the ways that popular culture attempts to influence you. For example, you already have a working understanding of what mass media has as its primary goals: ads exist to sell you products, political commentary wants you to vote a certain way, and TV producers want you to watch their programs. But deciding for yourself which pitches to tune in and which to tune out means looking deeper, beyond *what's* being sold to you to *how* it's being sold. How do writers, advertisers, politicians, and activists use common cultural ideas about normality to influence the ways you believe and behave?

NORMS, SCRIPTS, ROLES, RULES: ANALYZING POPULAR CULTURE

Although you are surrounded by the messages of popular culture every day, the act of talking and writing about it can seem a little foreign. How do we talk about something we all experience, but none of us experience the same way? Because this analysis of popular culture emphasizes how it influences us to "act," this book invites you take up your investigation of culture by using a set of terms borrowed from the theatre as well as cultural studies. What happens, we ask, when we begin looking at our daily actions and choices as if they were highly choreographed *performances*? When we begin thinking about the rules that define the different settings in our world not just as instructions per se, but as *scripts* to be followed? When we start redefining our own individual behavior as *roles* we have been assigned to play? What do we gain, in sum, by thinking about our world as a kind of *stage* on which we are encouraged to *act out* parts written for us in advance?

To get a handle on what this work actually looks like, let's turn to one of those typical or everyday situations we might use as a case study. Imagine for a moment you're sitting in a college composition classroom on the first day of the semester. If we wanted to attempt the kind of analysis of our lives as performances described above, we might begin by itemizing all of the different **rules** that, while often not spelled out explicitly, nonetheless govern within this particular environment: sit attentively, listen to the instructor, write down all the information we are told is especially important, agree to complete the readings, compose the essays, hand in other assignments on firm due dates. Likewise, there are an equal number of rules that set the standard for how we may and may not talk: no interruptions or random interjections; respond on point when questioned by the instructor; speak in a measured tone of voice and make sure to use a formal, more academic vocabulary than you might elsewhere; restrict your conversation to topics and issues that fit the course themes.

Rule:

A spoken or unspoken directive for how people should or should not act in a given situation.

Rather than conclude our investigation here, however, we would next delve more deeply into these rules in search of what ideas they invite us to accept as **norms,** or widely held cultural ideas about what is proper thinking or behavior in a given situation. For example, we might focus on the rules around student speech in order to figure out the more fundamental messages they simultaneously convey, such as "real" learning happens only when power is shared unequally within the classroom or "quality" education requires that instructors lead and students follow. In a similar vein, we could view the rule establishing formal standards for classroom discussion as an effort to impose a value system on different types of talk: one that defines so-called personal stories as being less legitimate than more abstract forms of argumentation. When figuring out what the norms are for a given situation, it is often helpful to think about what they *aren't*. In this case, you might ask yourself what you'd think about a classmate who constantly interrupted others or an instructor who told you you'd be graded solely on your penmanship.

Norm:

A widely held cultural belief about what is appropriate in a given situation.

Conducting this kind of analysis sets us up nicely for the next step in a performative approach: one that involves defining these classroom rules as **social scripts,** the ways that following the rules and accepting the norms require us to behave. Building on the connection uncovered between rules and norms, following a social script in the classroom would be performing a task like reading the assigned selections in this book — both because the rules require it and because the norms tell you that reading the assigned selections will help you in your quest for education. Doing this would then allow us to move to the final phase of this analysis: thinking of your actions and choices within the classroom as if you are performing a **role:** that is, "acting out" a social script for a given situation as part of your relationship to the larger culture. In this class, for example, your role as student means that you will most likely perform the social script of participating in class because the norms tell you that education is valuable and rules of the course require your participation. The relationship between these four terms can be applied to an analysis of any topic in this book, and the more you practice them in your writing, the more second-nature this analysis will become.

Social script:

A set of behavioral instructions reinforced by norms and rules.

Role:

How people act in relation to their standing or environment.

EXERCISE:

Think of two or three roles you are often required to play in your life (for example, student, sibling, friend, consumer) and write a paragraph for each in which you describe the scripts you follow as a part of performing these roles. What norms and rules do you think influence how effectively you play these roles?

How Culture Shapes Us: Rules of the Road

Lest you think the classroom is an isolated example, consider how many other settings in your life are defined and governed by a similar set of rules. Whether in the classroom or on the job, at our computers or riding on the bus, we constantly find ourselves in situations that call on us to navigate the boundary separating what is acceptable to do from what is not. We don't always think about our lives in these terms because, day to day, it's easier to take for granted that the way the world works — the rules we are taught to follow, the roles we are expected to play — is something that just happens. But the truth is that these rules and roles are anything but timeless or universal. They are rather the product of extended, often contested, efforts to define what is normal. Norms, scripts, roles, and rules have been influenced and shaped over time, products of forces that we can learn to recognize.

In December 2009, the debate over healthcare reform seemed to split the country in two. White House Budget Director Peter Orszag stood in front of reporters and faced a firing squad of questions about the mandate contained in the healthcare bill before Congress requiring everyone to buy health insurance. Asked whether this requirement was an affront to American rights and freedoms as guaranteed by the Constitution, Orszag's answer was surprising. He cited social norms as a powerful force that would eventually make us consider having health insurance as much a normal part of American lives as wearing seat belts.

This raises some interesting questions: Have you ever known a time when you weren't aware that you are supposed to wear your seat belt every time you are inside a moving car? Don't most of us think of buckling up as a normal part of our driving? Wasn't it always this way? Among all the rules we (hopefully) follow when we drive — stop on red, go on green, obey the speed limit, use the turn signals — wearing a seat belt sits squarely among them as one of the most important. The 2008 U.S. average for seat belt use was 83 percent, according to the National Highway Traffic Safety Administration.

It might surprise you to learn that although seat belts were invented in the mid-1800s, they first appeared as standard features in the United States in 1958, in cars made by Swedish car manufacter Saab. Only when a federal law was passed in 1968 did it become mandatory for car manufacturers to install seat belts in every car they sold.

And yet, few people wore them. Seat belts were seen as uncomfortable and inconvenient. America's car culture has always used buzz words like *freedom* to describe the experience of driving, and what feels less like being free than being — literally — restrained in your seat? Seat belt laws have always been left to states, and throughout the 1960s and 1970s, attempts to pass mandatory seat belt laws repeatedly failed in many states. New York passed the first law requiring drivers to wear seat belts — after many defeated attempts — in 1984.

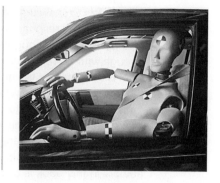

But although seat belt use became the law of the land (currently, New Hampshire is the only state without any seat belt laws), penalizing drivers was not enough to make wearing seat belts seem like a normal thing to do. It would take the passage of time and a concerted public service campaign, including the popular 1980s campaign featuring Vince and Larry, two crash test dummies who walked away from accidents while a voiceover intoned, "You can learn a lot from a dummy. Buckle your safety belt."

In the time since seat belts first appeared in cars many small changes to our car culture have made wearing them seem like a good thing to do. From accident statistics that populate the evening news, to road signs that tell us how many of our fellow drivers are similarly buckled in, to dashboard lights in our cars that blink and beep until we strap ourselves in, reminders to wear our seat belts

shape our thinking and our actions every time we get into a car. Playing the role of good driver now makes wearing seat belts more than a rule we obey or a script we follow. It is a social norm.

Orszag's seat belt analogy highlights another important aspect of the relationship between rules and norms. Framed in historical terms, his comparison reminds us that the process by which a rule transforms itself into a norm is neither seamless nor quick. Rather it happens gradually over time and is always the product of concerted, often contentious, effort. This is important to keep in mind because it reminds us that these norms are actually subject to greater change and influence by us than at first might seem to be the case. As you hear or read debates about issues such as healthcare reform, think about what messages each side is sending out. The more you practice, the better you'll become at understanding how these messages seep in and interact with our larger culture, as well as with our individual lives.

THE WORLD IN WORDS

So, what can we gain by reading about all these rules and norms that we are powerless to change? If we're all cogs in the pop culture machine, what can we gain from learning just how powerless we are? One of the primary goals of this book is to show that we are, in fact, anything *but* helpless. The ways we think about and respond to popular culture are constantly changing, and these changes are often brought about by one common act: questioning the norm through writing. To see examples of how writing helps us question and rewrite what is or should be the norm, you need look no further than the selections in this book. Only by reading and writing about the world we live in can we understand it and learn to navigate it on our own terms.

The selections in this book are designed to challenge the ways many of us think about a wide range of current topics. What they're *not* designed to do is to inspire you to agree with everything their authors say. Each of the authors in this book is using writing as a way to explore, influence, or protest against different aspects of our larger culture. By responding to their ideas with your own writing, you are entering a larger dialogue in which you begin to defend and define your place as part of that culture.

As you read the selections, you may find it helpful to approach each one with a set of questions in mind to assist you in positioning your own opinion.

- **Question the Author:** Who is this author? What is her level of expertise about this topic? What else has she written? Is she an academic, a journalist, an activist, a politician? How do those roles influence the way she communicates her opinions?

- **Question the Audience:** What prompted the author to write this piece? Who is this piece aimed at? What examples in the language or tone tell me about that?

- **Question the Rules:** What rules, norms, or scripts is this author writing about? Is the author writing in support of them or in opposition?

- **Question the Argument:** What are the main points of this piece? How does the author support his point of view? Are his examples scientific, derived from interviews, or part of his own experience? What are the possible counterarguments? How does the author anticipate and refute them?

- **Question Yourself:** How do I react to this piece? Does it support or go against my own experience and exposure to this topic?

GUIDED READING: ANNE TRUBEK'S "STOP TEACHING HANDWRITING"

To figure out how to most effectively analyze this material, let's take a look at a sample essay. The classroom, as we have already seen, offers a perfect example of how forces beyond our immediate control can shape our actions and assumptions. In this setting we are told to obey certain rules, asked to share certain norms, expected to follow certain scripts, and called on to play certain roles. Anne Trubek's "Stop Teaching Handwriting" challenges one of these norms and presents an impassioned plea for changing it. Seeking to question a long-standing classroom practice, Trubek asks: What are the goals this handwriting rule is designed to achieve? What broader assumptions about children and learning do these goals reflect? And are these assumptions valid? This essay is annotated with the sorts of questions you might ask while reading many of the essays in this book, questions about where an essay fits in relation to established norms and how it seeks to question them. As you review the annotations, think about how the questions and observations they raise help you put the essay in perspective.

ANNE TRUBEK

Stop Teaching Handwriting

This title is very direct. How do I feel about this command?

MY SON, WHO IS IN THIRD GRADE, SPENDS MUCH OF HIS SCHOOL day struggling to learn how to form the letter "G." Sometimes he writes it backwards. Sometimes the tail on his lowercase "T" goes the wrong way. His teachers keep telling him he may fail the state assessment standards. We have had several "interventions." Simon now fears taking up a pencil. Repeatedly being told his handwriting is bad (a fine-motor-skill issue) has become, in his mind, proof that he is a bad writer (an expression issue). He now hates writing, period.

The author is revealing herself as a parent. What sort of qualities does the role of "parent" entail?

The state has rules and expectations that students should be able to write a certain way by third grade. Do I agree? Is this rule reasonable?

This is absurd: I am a college professor and a freelance writer, and the only time I pick up a pen is to sign a credit-card receipt. Let's stop brutalizing our kids with years of drills on the proper formation of a cursive capital "S"—handwriting is a historical blip in the long history of writing technologies, and it's time to consign to the trash heap this artificial way of making letters, along with clay tablets, smoke signals, and other arcane technologies.

Other roles. How do these affect how I perceive Trubek as an author? Is she now more of an authority?

Trubek's thesis statement challenges the rule that teaching handwriting is important. She advocates changing it. What would she prefer?

Many will find this argument hard to swallow because we cling to handwriting out of a romantic sense that script expresses identity. But only since the invention of the printing press has handwriting been considered a mark of self-expression. Medieval monks first worried that the invention of printing would be the ruin of books, as presses were more idiosyncratic and prone to human error than manuscripts produced in scriptoriums. And the monks never conceived of handwriting as a sign of identity: For them, script was formulaic, not self-expressive. That concept did not appear until the early 18th century. Still later came the notion that personality and individuality could be deduced by analyzing handwriting. All the while, print became widely available, and handwriting lost its primacy as a vehicle of mass communication.

Trubek makes a claim about what society considers normal. Do I agree that handwriting and identity are linked? Why might we think this way?

The norms have changed over time. How did handwriting go from being considered "formulaic" to "self-expressive"?

7

The typewriter took handwriting down another notch. Henry James took up the then-new writing machine in the 1880s, most likely because he, like my son, had poor handwriting. By the 1890s, James was dictating all his novels to a secretary. And as novelists and businesses were putting down their pens, others started to valorize handwriting as somehow more pure and more authentic, infusing script with nostalgic romanticism. The philosopher Martin Heidegger was particularly guilty of this, writing in 1940 of the losses wrought by typewriters: "In handwriting the relation of Being to man, namely the word, is inscribed in beings themselves. . . . When writing was withdrawn from the origin of its essence, i.e. from the hand, and was transferred to the machine, a transformation occurred in the relation of Being to man."

Meanwhile, back in school, teachers were trying to get student papers to look like typewritten documents: letter characters, the students were told, should look like fonts.

The pattern doesn't change: As writing technologies evolve, we romanticize the old and adapt to the new. This will happen with keyboards, too—some contemporary novelists have ceased using them already. Richard Powers uses voice-recognition software to compose everything, including his novels. "Except for brief moments of duress, I haven't touched a keyboard for years," he says. "No fingers were tortured in producing these words—or the last half a million words of my published fiction." Powers is wonderfully free of technological nostalgia: "Writing is the act of accepting the huge shortfall between the story in the mind and what hits the page. . . . For that, no interface will ever be clean or invisible enough for us to get the passage right," he says to his computer.

That shortfall is exactly how my son describes his writing troubles: "I have it all in my memory bank and then I stop and my memory bank gets wiped out," he explains. Voice-recognition software—judging from the rapid-fire monologues he delivers at dinner about Pokémon and Yu-Gi-Oh!—would help.

No matter what we use to write something will be lost between conception and execution. I have yet to be convinced that making a graphite stick go in certain directions enhances intellectual development. Let us teach our kids to use the best tools at our disposal: There are plenty of cool toys out there. Boys and girls, it is time to put down your pencils.

Margin annotations:

A famous writer. Why does Trubek invoke his name?

Why do people think that handwritten script is more personal than typewritten script? Trubek provides a quote that reinforces this point of view. Do I think that way? Why?

Why might a writer be in favor of these changing norms? What is the purpose of writing, according to Trubek or Powers?

Do I think of writing similarly?

She concludes using a play on words involving classroom rules. Why?

A Student's Response to Trubek

After reading Trubek's essay and considering the questions posed about her argument, you probably have your own reaction to it. Thinking about her essay in terms of the rules it discusses and the way that roles, scripts, and norms influence the way that all of us think can give some shape to your written analysis of an essay. Let's look at a student response to Trubek's essay. As you read, make note of how this student has incorporated cultural analysis into his discussion of her essay.

DON'T ERASE HANDWRITING

Jordan Radziecki

In "Stop Teaching Handwriting," Anne Trubek argues that it's time to stop teaching handwriting and to throw this "historical blip in the long history of writing technologies" on the "trash heap" (7). According to Trubek, new technologies make handwriting instruction unnecessary. She thinks schools still teach it because of a "nostalgic romanticism" (8) and a mistaken belief that "script expresses identity" (7). While she is correct that handwriting has become less important in recent years, Trubek is wrong in her overall argument. It is only when one examines her argument in light of her roles as a freelance writer and professor, and also as the mother of a child who struggles with his handwriting because of poor fine-motor skills, that one begins to see that the roles she plays in her life limit her willingness to see the usefulness of handwriting to others.

While it may be true that Trubek only picks up a pen to "sign a credit-card receipt" (7), she cannot assume that this is true of everyone. The ability to write is fundamental to our society's understanding of what it means to be an educated person. Students must often take quizzes, tests, and exams, and they need to be able to write legibly and with minimal effort. Moreover, how much valuable teachers' time is wasted trying to decipher illegible handwriting? Many classes tend to focus on group work on papers and projects. Trubek doesn't consider the reality that writing for students goes beyond work done outside of class. As a mother, Trubek sees her son struggle with writing and decides based on his difficulties that teaching handwriting is "brutalizing our kids" (7). She sees handwriting as a problem only because it is not her son's strength in school. This doesn't automatically make handwriting useless.

Learning fundamental skills can be difficult, and no one thinks "drills" are fun. Yet, education at the elementary school level is mostly about mastering the basics. After all, you are not learning history, economics, or high-level math at that age. The subject matter is often secondary. Instead, in the third grade you are learning the rules and scripts of the educational process: you are learning how to learn inside a classroom and outside it, too. You are learning how to perform your role as a student. In a sense, knowing how to write is not much different than knowing how to sit still at your desk or knowing how to raise your hand to answer a question rather than just shouting out a response.

When we get out of school or look for work as students, we still must be able to write, even though it's likely that most of our writing will be done on computers, Blackberries, or iPads. Trubek's argument that technology continually advances doesn't mean that we should willingly become dependent on it to do everything for us. For a long, long time, students have been required to learn the three Rs: "reading, writing, and 'rithmatic." Despite Trubek's belief that handwriting's time has passed, educated and capable people are still expected to be able to write legibly. As a professor, Trubek should understand that technology is still too expensive for many students to own. She might see a great advantage to using voice-recognition software, but students, especially in college, will always struggle to keep money in their pockets. Some of us cannot afford to have laptops with us every second, and we shouldn't be denied education because of costly technology.

Like Trubek, I do most of my writing on a computer, at least outside the classroom. I was never taught that handwriting expresses my true identity, nor, as Trubek says, do I "romanticize the old" (8). At the same time, I do like to send handwritten "Thank You" notes: nearly everyone agrees that they are more personal and show more thought. When I write a love note or Valentine to my girlfriend, I do it by hand. Who wants to receive a word-processed love letter? I appreciate the time and care put into such letters on special occasions. I like to know that her pen has pressed down and shaped each letter. But that doesn't mean that I am sentimental about handwriting in general or that I am romanticizing an old technology in a silly way. We all value handmade things, and I am sure that Trubek is no exception to that rule in some aspect of her life. But even if she doesn't, that doesn't make the rest of us hopeless people who live in the past.

While I sympathize with Trubek's son's problems as a third grader and understand Trubek's own frustration as a parent, she takes her argument too far. The answer is for her young son to get the extra help he needs (don't many students struggle with some aspect of elementary school?) to learn a crucial and fundamental skill for school—and for life.

Work Cited

Trubek, Anne. "Stop Teaching Handwriting." *Acting Out Culture: Reading and Writing.* 2nd ed. Ed. James S. Miller. Boston: Bedford/ St. Martin's, 2011. Print.

READING VISUALS

More and more frequently, the messages we receive about popular culture come in visual form. News photos, cartoons, films, and advertisements are composed in much the same way that text is. Subjects are carefully considered and captured in a visual medium in order to communicate a message. With visual art like film or painting, many of these messages are on the surface and can be seen plainly. However, certain images, like advertisements, are often composed for a purpose in which the message is sometimes deeply embedded, even secondary. For example, take a look at the ad below for make-up.

You've probably seen similar ads in magazines before. But how do you go about *reading* the visual messages of an ad as typical as this? Here are a few categories you might consider when analyzing a visual message:

- **Layout:** Think about the different elements of the ad. Here, there is only one figure, a model in close-up. Visually, how does focusing on the model's face help you understand the message of this ad?

- **Audience:** Who is the target audience of this ad? The model in the ad is made up to look like screen icon Audrey Hepburn. Who is likely to see and respond to this resemblance? How does invoking the image of Audrey Hepburn appeal to this audience?

- **Purpose:** Obviously, this is an advertisement, and advertisements are designed to sell products. Can you imagine using this image for another purpose? What would be your response if, instead of in a magazine, you saw this in a museum? How would your reaction be different?

- **Text:** The headline of this ad says, "Inside every woman is a star," and at the bottom of the ad, the text says, "Celebrate glamour. Celebrate 50 years of star-making make-up." How does the addition of text clarify the composition of this image? Without the text, would it be as effective?

- **Message(s):** Of course, as an ad, this image is designed to sell you make-up. But how does it do that? How does the message use some common attitudes about wanting to look like celebrities to convince us to use Max Factor make-up? What do the advertisers gain from associating celebrity with cosmetics?

Most of the images in this book can be read independently or as part of a series. Just like with texts, considering images side by side can show you a larger picture about how our culture depicts as normal any action or belief. Imagine if you were to look at this cosmetics ad, which tells us that using make-up will make any normal woman look like a celebrity, side by side with an image of a celebrity being made up by a team of professionals. If you consider both images as a set, one that examines the topic of beauty, how would looking at the second image influence how you read the first?

MAKING YOURSELF HEARD

The bulk of this book consists of readings from a range of writers who've accepted the job of analyzing the rules we live by. You will be familiar with many of these topics, but some may be new to you. Whether you've had any exposure to these topics or not, each selection is organized into chapters that examine the issues as part of roles we all play: believers, watchers, eaters, learners, workers, and changers. The writing assignments in this book will ask you to take what you know about these topics and consider it side by side with these authors so that you can ultimately decide for yourself how *you* want to play life's roles.

Why should we ultimately care about analyzing popular culture? Consider this: In January 2007, then senators Hillary Rodham Clinton and Barack Obama both announced that they would seek the Democratic nomination for president of the United States. But rather than call a press conference, both politicians did something unprecedented. They posted videos on the Internet. Whereas sites like YouTube and Facebook were once designed for killing time watching clips of strangers' home movies or making new friends across the globe, the power of popular culture has forced contenders for the biggest job in the United States to use the methods of dissemination perfected by popular culture to spread very serious promises about the future of America itself. By writing about popular culture, you become a part of the fabric of cultural conversation. This book will ask you to analyze and write about the world around you, but more important, it will ask you to use that analysis to make a decision about how to rewrite the world on your own terms. You're not only about to read the writing of people who have used words as a way to navigate through thousands of competing media messages. You're about to become one of them.

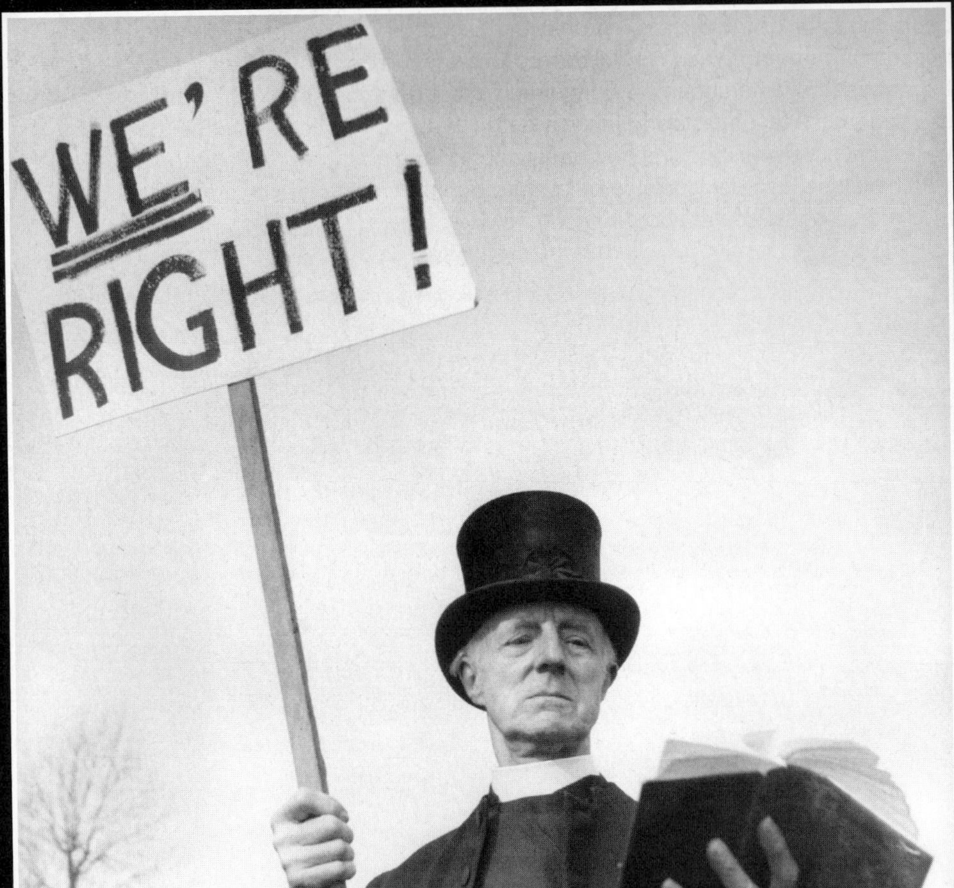
WE'RE
RIGHT!

1 How We BELIEVE

Introduction

BELIEVING IN "BELIEF"

Imagine yourself as the central actor in the following scenarios:

- First-time voter contemplating the choice between candidates in this year's election

- Pacifist member of the National Guard summoned to active duty in Afghanistan

- Graduating senior considering employment offers from both the Peace Corps and Goldman Sachs

- Student in a college physics class who has happened onto the answers to an upcoming midterm exam

- Shopper deciding whether to spend rent money on a new outfit

- Pedestrian on a city street approached by a homeless person asking for money

- Journalist ordered by a judge to divulge a confidential news source

Although these examples touch on different issues, they are alike in one crucial way: Each situation requires you to make a value judgment, to choose between what matters more and what matters less. In other words, each choice hinges on *what you believe*.

The concept of belief turns our attention to what lies *underneath* the choices we make: to the embedded, unspoken, and often subconscious assumptions that make these choices feel natural or normal. It's easy for most of us, given a set of circumstances, to say *what* we believe. But how often do any of us stop to think about *how* we came to hold the beliefs we take for granted? When we really stop to think about it, *how* do we make up our minds about what are the right and wrong things to do? Who or what teaches us to draw these kinds of distinctions? And how do these lessons come to feel so natural to us? Beliefs are not hypotheses. Grounded as they are in faith, in our intuitive or instinctive conviction that something is so, they require no recourse to empirical proof, factual data, or concrete evidence in order to stand in our minds as truth. Indeed, it might be said that belief encompasses all the things in our lives we're convinced are true simply because they *feel* right.

Of course, this is also what makes explaining or defending our beliefs such a tricky matter. If ultimately we can't prove the validity of our beliefs, then how can we ever hope to make others understand, accept, or share them? This dilemma — which in many ways seems hardwired into the very concept of belief — explains in part why our society is marked by so many disputes and controversies over what is and is not proper for us to believe. If beliefs are not hypotheses that can be proved but rather convictions that are "right" because they feel so to their believers, how can different members of society ever establish common ground?

Although it is often assumed that belief applies only to questions of religion, it lies at the heart of some of our most urgent and intractable debates: from gay marriage to abortion to the war in Afghanistan. Belief also underlies countless decisions we confront every day in our personal lives: from how (or even whether) we vote to where we shop, from the work we perform to the money we earn, from the movies and television we watch, the books and magazines we read to the clothes we wear. Whatever the individual focus or context, belief always boils down to the same basic questions: What are the ideas and values we feel most committed to? Which ones end up just feeling right?

If we are not born already hardwired with ingrained assumptions about what is and is not right, then how did it happen that our beliefs feel like second nature to us now? By what process did we learn to regard only certain viewpoints and values as articles of faith?

Everybody Knows That . . .

PERSONAL BELIEFS, CULTURAL NORMS, AND SCRIPTING BELIEF

To pose questions like these is to begin connecting belief to the broader question of social *norms*. Stated differently: It is to wonder about the ways our own assumptions about right and wrong intersect with — perhaps even derive from — the standards and instructions mapped by our larger culture.

Indeed, such questions might even prompt us to rethink the idea of *personal* belief altogether. To be sure, we are far more used to thinking of our personal beliefs as things that belong exclusively to ourselves: those values, ethics, and priorities that, in the final analysis, remain beyond the influence of our larger culture. This definition is an attractive one because it not only reaffirms our faith in our individuality but also seems to confirm our irreducible *agency*: our ability to control and determine the choices we make. But this conceit misrepresents our fundamental relationship to the larger culture around us. Far from being tangential or irrelevant, our culture plays a central role in shaping what we come to believe, suggesting that the values we consider to be our own private domain do not belong to us alone.

Everybody Knows That . . .

"One World, One Dream"

*— Slogan for the
2008 Olympic Games in Beijing, China*

17

Everybody Knows That...

"I believe in ... an America that lives by a Constitution that inspires freedom and democracy around the world. An America with a big, open, charitable heart that reaches out to people in need around the world. ... An America that is still the beacon of light to the darkest corner of the world."

— *Colin Powell, "The America I Believe In"*
from the National Public Radio
series **This I Believe**

We do, after all, live in a world that promotes very specific messages about what is right and what is wrong, a world in which countless instructions get issued telling us what we should and should not care about. From the Patriot Act to the Facebook news feed, from *Cosmopolitan* magazine to the *New York Times* business section, our cultural landscape is littered with sources that tell us, often in very authoritative tones, which things truly matter and which things do not. To compile even so cursory a list as this is to shift the terms of our conversation from individual or personal *choice* to cultural and social *power*; to confront the possibility that our own distinctions and value judgments are better understood as *scripts* we are encouraged, even enjoined, to follow. In attempting to make sense of all this, our goal is less to "pick sides," to vote up or down on the validity of a given belief, than to better understand how beliefs take shape in the first place, how certain ideas come to acquire this special status as unexamined and cherished norms. Stated a bit more abstractly, our job is to assess the process of *legitimation*: the operations through which only select ideas and actions come to be promoted as the proper role models for the rest of us.

"Pledging Allegiance": Acting On and Acting Out Our Commitments

An example from our everyday lives will clarify the kind of work this involves, as well as the implications for us in undertaking it. Virtually all of us are familiar with reciting the Pledge of Allegiance. The Pledge offers an especially useful case study because it underscores how intimately connected belief is to issues of social scripts and role-playing. From the reverential pose we are supposed to maintain toward the flag, to the obligatory "hand-over-the-heart" gesture, to the language itself through which we express our "allegiance," the rules by which this ritual is defined couldn't be more detailed. One way to better apprehend the values underlying this performance is to ask what kind of objectives stand behind this kind of mandatory performance. Why have

Everybody Knows That...

"I pledge allegiance to the Flag of the United States of America, and to the Republic for which it stands: one Nation under God, indivisible, with Liberty and Justice for all."

schoolchildren been required to recite the Pledge as a daily part of their scholastic lives? This line of inquiry leads us to wonder next about the particular assumptions this ritual reinforces — assumptions defining what our proper duties to the nation are supposed to be or the role that such patriotic expressions are supposed to play in our educational system. Building on this, we then consider the implications of endorsing these assumptions. We ponder, for instance, what it means for children to memorize and recite the loyalty oath at the center of the Pledge. What would be different if the words of the Pledge were different, if students were allowed to recite the oath silently or even to opt out from it altogether? Finally, we ask where else in our culture we are presented with opportunities to demonstrate our "allegiance" to the nation.

It is precisely this kind of work that each of the selections included in this chapter invites us to conduct. Referencing a wide range of contemporary issues — from patriotism and consumerism to science and race — this collection shows how complex and overlapping the connection between personal beliefs and social scripts can be. Barbara Ehrenreich starts us off with a critical look at the many ways our culture emphasizes positive thinking and wonders whether it is really good for us. John West recounts his struggle with the social norms governing death and family in a piece about his decision to help his parents end their lives. Catherine Newman, meanwhile, examines a different type of family relationship in her essay about the clichés and assumptions that conventionally define marriage. Recounting her own decision to eschew the traditional rituals and rewards of the "wedding ceremony," she offers a strikingly different way to think not only about marriage, but also about the social and emotional consequences of following this particular social script. Thinking about beliefs that govern American identities, James Twitchell offers an impassioned and surprising defense of consumerism as both an individual and social ideal. Defending shopping both as a quintessentially American undertaking and a laudable personal undertaking, his essay seeks to resuscitate our faith in materialism as a legitimate belief system. Ron Rosenbaum, on the other hand, squares off against traditional American "values" in his argument against reciting the Pledge of Allegiance, making a powerful case that compelling such a recitation runs counter to the American spirit. Finally, this chapter examines race and difference from three surprising angles. Po Bronson and Ashley Merryman highlight important scientific research that seems to argue that babies learn to see racial difference at a very early age, while David Brooks works to reframe our current racial thinking by challenging what he claims is our unthinking embrace of "diversity" as a social ideal. Pursuing her own investigation of what it means to be nonwhite, Debra Dickerson offers a historically rooted challenge to our assumptions of what constitutes "race."

"EVERYBODY KNOWS THAT" EXERCISE

Choose one of the images or quotations featured in the margins on the previous pages and answer the following questions:

1. What does this image or quotation ask you to believe?

2. What are the particular ideas/values/attitudes it invites us to accept as *normal*?

3. What would it feel like to act upon or act out these norms in our personal lives?

Rule *Maker* >>>>>>>>>>> Rule *Breaker*

ʼʼ *Malls begin decorating the first week of November*

The average mall takes about 5 days to decorate for the holidays

Malls will spend an average of 20,000 dollars this year on decorating for the holidays

The holiday that most malls decorate for is Christmas

The most popular holiday song played at malls is Jingle Bells

90% of malls will offer special holiday shopping hours

90% of malls say that their special holiday shopping hours will begin on Black Friday

80% of malls will organize an activity to raise money or merchandise for a charity."

— INTERNATIONAL COUNCIL OF
SHOPPING CENTERS (ICSC)

2009 HOLIDAY FUN FACTS

ʼʼ *Dreading the holiday season? The frantic rush and stress? The to-do lists and sales hype? The spiritless hours trapped in malls?*

This year, why not gather together your loved ones and decide to do things differently? With the simplest of plans you can create a new rhythm, purpose, and meaning for the holidays. Why not take the spirit of Buy Nothing Day and morph it into Buy Nothing Christmas?

With catastrophic climate change looming, we the rich one billion people on the planet have to consume less! And if that's too extreme for grandma and the kids, try for a Buy Less Christmas. And maybe a buy local, buy fairer, buy indie Christmas. Whatever you decide, 'tis the season to reclaim our year-end celebrations and make them our own again."

— BUY NOTHING CHRISTMAS HOMEPAGE,
ADBUSTERS.ORG, 2010

HOLIDAY SHOPPING VS. BUY NOTHING CHRISTMAS

It seems like every holiday season brings a fresh batch of criticism about the pairing of commercialism and seasonal or religious festivities. Many of us gripe about overcommercialization at the same moment a store clerk is swiping our credit card. Television newscasts report on decreases in holiday sales and then air stories on the amount of personal debt the holidays bring. And then they cut to commercial, offering the audience a fresh onslaught of ads urging them to finish their holiday shopping. It could almost be said that holiday shopping is as much a part of our beliefs as the holidays we're shopping for. However, the two quotes above underscore how contested a belief system consumerism actually is. As these examples make clear, we don't all work through these messages in exactly the same way.

In the first quotation, the International Council of Shopping Centers presents some of its "Fun Facts" about holiday shopping (you can find more at factsholiday.icsc.org). What do these tell you about how closely our American "belief" in shopping is tied to our larger religious beliefs? What are the attitudes about shopping that these facts take for granted? What do these facts tell you about holiday shopping as a cultural phenomenon? Compare this quotation to the second, from Adbuster's "Buy Nothing Christmas" initiative, in which we are encouraged to ignore advertisers' calls to buy, buy, buy. How is this second quotation critical of the ideas expressed in the first? How is it critical of us and our roles as holiday shoppers?

FIND THE RULES: Make a list of the different attitudes about consumerism that each of these quotations is expressing. Then write a paragraph for each one that examines how it "sells" its point of view. What does each quotation say, and how does it say it, in order to appeal to its intended audience?

MAKE YOUR OWN RULES: Write a brief essay in which you analyze your own opinions about holiday shopping. Which of the two perspectives in this feature strikes you as most appealing? Why?

Buy Nothing Christmas
RETHINK THE SEASON

ADBUSTERS MEDIA FOUNDATION <www.adbusters.org>

"Introduction," from *Bright-Sided*

From self-help books to empowerment seminars, positivity — the expectation that we always display optimism, cheerfulness, and a sunny smile — is pervasive in our culture. But perhaps the best way to sum up this phenomenon is to say that it operates in this day and age as one of the most powerful and deeply embedded social scripts. Barbara Ehrenreich is a writer and political activist who has written for a wide variety of magazines and newspapers including the *Nation,* the *Atlantic, Ms.,* and the *Progressive.* She has published over a dozen books on journalism and social commentary. *Nickel and Dimed: On Not Getting By in America* (2002) is an undercover investigation of low-wage jobs, and a chapter of it won Ehrenreich a Sydney Hillman Award for Journalism. Among her other books are *Bait and Switch: The (Futile) Pursuit of the American Dream* (2005) and, most recently, *Bright-Sided: How the Relentless Promotion of Positive Thinking Has Undermined America* (2009), in which this selection appears.

AMERICANS ARE A "POSITIVE" PEOPLE. THIS IS OUR REPUTATION as well as our self-image. We smile a lot and are often baffled when people from other cultures do not return the favor. In the well-worn stereotype, we are upbeat, cheerful, optimistic, and shallow, while foreigners are likely to be subtle, world-weary, and possibly decadent. American expatriate writers like Henry James and James Baldwin wrestled with and occasionally reinforced this stereotype, which I once encountered in the 1980s in the form of a remark by Soviet émigré poet Joseph Brodsky to the effect that the problem with Americans is that they have "never known suffering." (Apparently he didn't know who had invented the blues.) Whether we Americans see it as an embarrassment or a point of pride, being positive—in affect, in mood, in outlook—seems to be engrained in our national character.

Who would be churlish or disaffected enough to challenge these happy features of the American personality? Take the business of positive "affect," which refers to the mood we display to others through our smiles, our greetings, our professions of confidence and optimism. Scientists have found that the mere act of smiling can generate positive feelings within us, at least if the smile is not forced. In addition, good feelings, as expressed through our words and smiles, seem to be contagious: "Smile and the world smiles with you." Surely the world would be a better, happier place if we all greeted one another warmly and stopped to coax smiles from babies—if only through the well-known social psychological mechanism of "mood contagion." Recent studies show that happy feelings flit easily through social networks, so that one person's good fortune can brighten the day even for only distantly connected others.

Furthermore, psychologists today agree that positive feelings like gratitude, contentment, and self-confidence can actually lengthen our lives and improve our health. Some of these claims are exaggerated, as we shall see, though positive feelings hardly need to be justified, like exercise or vitamin supplements, as part of a healthy lifestyle. People who report having positive feelings are more likely to participate in a rich social life, and vice versa, and social connectedness turns out to be an important defense against depression, which is a known risk factor for many physical illnesses. At the risk of redundancy or even tautology, we can say that on many levels, individual and social, it is good to be "positive," certainly better than being withdrawn, aggrieved, or chronically sad.

So I take it as a sign of progress that, in just the last decade or so, economists have begun to show an interest in using happiness rather than just the gross national product as a measure of an economy's success. Happiness is, of course, a slippery thing to measure or define. Philosophers have debated what it is for centuries, and even if we were to define it simply as a greater frequency of positive feelings than negative ones, when we ask people if they are happy we are asking them to arrive at some sort of average over many moods and moments. Maybe I was upset earlier in the day but then was cheered up by a bit of good news, so what am I really? In one well-known psychological experiment, subjects were asked to answer a questionnaire on life satisfaction—but only after they had performed the apparently irrelevant task of photocopying a sheet of paper for the experimenter. For a randomly chosen half of the subjects, a dime had been left for them to find on the copy machine. As two economists summarize the results, "Reported satisfaction with life was raised substantially by the discovery of the coin on the copy machine—clearly not an income effect."

In addition to the problems of measurement, there are cultural differences in how happiness is regarded and whether it is even seen as a virtue. Some cultures, like our own, value the positive affect that seems to signal internal happiness; others are more impressed by seriousness, self-sacrifice, or a quiet willingness to cooperate. However hard to pin down, though, happiness is somehow a more pertinent metric for well-being, from a humanistic perspective, than the buzz of transactions that constitute the GDP.

Surprisingly, when psychologists undertake to measure the relative happiness of nations, they routinely find that Americans are not, even in prosperous times and despite our vaunted positivity, very happy at all. A recent meta-analysis of over a hundred studies of self-reported happiness worldwide found Americans ranking only twenty-third, surpassed by the Dutch, the Danes, the Malaysians, the Bahamians, the Austrians, and even the supposedly dour Finns. In another potential sign of relative distress, Americans account for two-thirds of the global market for antidepressants, which happen also to be the most commonly prescribed drugs in the United States. To my knowledge, no one knows how antidepressant use affects people's responses to happiness surveys: do respondents report being happy because the drugs make them feel happy or do they report being unhappy because they know they are dependent on drugs to make them feel better? Without our heavy use of antidepressants, Americans would likely rank far lower in the happiness rankings than we currently do.

When economists attempt to rank nations more objectively in terms of "well-being," taking into account such factors as health, environmental sustainability, and the possibility of upward mobility, the United States does even more poorly than it does when only the subjective state of "happiness" is measured. The Happy Planet Index, to give just one example, locates us at 150th among the world's nations.

> **How can we be so surpassingly "positive" without being the world's happiest and best-off people?**

How can we be so surpassingly "positive" in self-image and stereotype without being the world's happiest and best-off people? The answer, I think, is that positivity is not so much our condition or our mood as it is part of our ideology—the way we explain the world and think we ought to function within it. That ideology is "positive thinking," by which we usually mean two things. One is the generic content of positive thinking—that is, the positive thought itself—which can be summarized as: Things are pretty good right now, at least if you are willing to see silver linings, make lemonade out of lemons, etc., and things are going to get a whole lot better. This is optimism, and it is not the same as hope. Hope is an emotion, a yearning, the experience of which is not entirely within our control. Optimism is a cognitive stance, a conscious expectation, which presumably anyone can develop through practice.

The second thing we mean by "positive thinking" is this practice, or discipline, of trying to think in a positive way. There is, we are told, a practical reason for undertaking this effort: positive thinking supposedly not only makes us feel optimistic but actually makes happy outcomes more likely. If you expect things to get better, they will. How can the mere process of thinking do this? In the rational explanation that many psychologists would offer today, optimism improves health, personal efficacy, confidence, and resilience, making it easier for us to accomplish our goals. A far less rational theory also runs rampant in American ideology—the idea that our thoughts can, in some mysterious way, directly affect the physical world. Negative thoughts somehow produce negative outcomes, while positive thoughts realize themselves in the form of health, prosperity, and success. For both rational and mystical reasons, then, the effort of positive thinking is said to be well worth our time and attention, whether this means reading the relevant books, attending seminars and speeches that offer the appropriate mental training, or just doing the solitary work of concentration on desired outcomes—a better job, an attractive mate, world peace.

There is an anxiety, as you can see, right here in the heart of American positive thinking. If the generic "positive thought" is correct and things are really getting better, if the arc of the universe tends toward happiness and abundance, then why bother with the mental effort of positive thinking? Obviously, because we do not fully believe that things will get better on their own. The practice of positive thinking is an effort to pump up this belief in the face of much contradictory evidence. Those who set themselves up as instructors in the discipline of positive thinking—coaches, preachers, and gurus of various sorts—have described this effort with terms like "self-hypnosis," "mind control," and "thought control." In other words, it requires deliberate self-deception, including a constant effort to repress or block out unpleasant possibilities and "negative" thoughts. The truly self-confident, or those who have in some way made their peace with the world and their destiny within it, do not need to expend effort censoring or otherwise controlling their thoughts. Positive thinking may be a quintessentially American activity, associated in our minds with both individual and national success, but it is driven by a terrible insecurity.

Americans did not start out as positive thinkers—at least the promotion of unwarranted optimism and methods to achieve it did not really find articulation and organized form until several decades after the founding of the republic. In the Declaration of Independence, the founding fathers pledged to one another "our lives, our fortunes, and our sacred honor." They knew that they had no certainty of winning a war for independence and that they were taking a mortal risk. Just the act of signing the declaration made them all traitors to the crown, and treason was a crime punishable by execution. Many of them did go on to lose their lives, loved ones, and fortunes in the war. The point is, they fought anyway. There is a vast difference between positive thinking and existential courage.

Systematic positive thinking began, in the nineteenth century, among a diverse and fascinating collection of philosophers, mystics, lay healers, and middle-class women. By the twentieth century, though, it had gone mainstream, gaining purchase within such powerful belief systems as nationalism and also doing its best to make itself indispensable to capitalism. We don't usually talk about American nationalism, but it is a mark of how deep it runs that we apply the word "nationalism" to Serbs, Russians, and others, while believing ourselves to possess a uniquely superior version called "patriotism." A central tenet of American nationalism has been the belief that the United States is "the greatest nation on earth"—more dynamic, democratic, and prosperous than any other nation, as well as technologically superior. Major religious leaders, especially on the Christian right, buttress this conceit with the notion that Americans are God's chosen people and that America is the designated leader of the world—an idea that seemed to find vivid reinforcement in the fall of Communism and our emergence as the world's "lone superpower." That acute British observer Godfrey Hodgson has written that the American sense of exceptionalism, which once was "idealistic and generous, if somewhat solipsistic," has become "harder, more hubristic." Paul Krugman responded to the prevailing smugness in a 1998 essay entitled "American the Boastful," warning that "if pride goeth before a fall, the United States has one heck of a come-uppance in store."

But of course it takes the effort of positive thinking to imagine that America is the "best" or the "greatest." Militarily, yes, we are the mightiest nation on earth. But on many other fronts, the American score is dismal, and was dismal even before the economic downturn that began in 2007. Our children routinely turn out to be more ignorant of basic subjects like math and geography than their counterparts in other industrialized nations. They are also more likely to die in infancy or grow up in poverty. Almost everyone acknowledges that our health care system is "broken" and our physical infrastructure crumbling. We have lost so much of our edge in science and technology that American companies have even begun to outsource their research and development efforts. Worse, some of the measures by which we do lead the world should inspire embarrassment rather than pride: We have the highest percentage of our population incarcerated, and the greatest level of inequality in wealth and income. We are plagued by gun violence and racked by personal debt.

While positive thinking has reinforced and found reinforcement in American national pride, it has also entered into a kind of symbiotic relationship with American capitalism. There is no natural, innate affinity between capitalism and positive thinking. In fact, one of the classics of sociology, Max Weber's *Protestant Ethic and the Spirit of Capitalism*, makes a still impressive case for capitalism's roots in the grim and punitive outlook of Calvinist Protestantism, which required people to defer gratification and resist

> **While positive thinking has reinforced national pride, it has also entered into a symbiotic relationship with American capitalism.**

all pleasurable temptations in favor of hard work and the accumulation of wealth.

But if early capitalism was inhospitable to positive thinking, "late" capitalism, or consumer capitalism, is far more congenial, depending as it does on the individual's hunger for more and the firm's imperative of growth. The consumer culture encourages individuals to want more— cars, larger homes, television sets, cell phones, gadgets of all kinds—and positive thinking is ready at hand to tell them they deserve more and can have it if they really want it and are willing to make the effort to get it. Meanwhile, in a competitive business world, the companies that manufacture these goods and provide the paychecks that purchase them have no alternative but to grow. If you don't steadily increase market share and profits, you risk being driven out of business or swallowed by a larger enterprise. Perpetual growth, whether of a particular company or an entire economy, is of course an absurdity, but positive thinking makes it seem possible, if not ordained.

In addition, positive thinking has made itself useful as an apology for the crueler aspects of the market economy. If optimism is the key to material success, and if you can achieve an optimistic outlook through the discipline of positive thinking, then there is no excuse for failure. The flip side of positivity is thus a harsh insistence on personal responsibility: if your business fails or your job is eliminated, it must be because you didn't try hard enough, didn't believe firmly enough in the inevitability of your success. As the economy has brought more layoffs and financial turbulence to the middle class, the promoters of positive thinking have increasingly emphasized this negative judgment: to be disappointed, resentful, or downcast is to be a "victim" and a "whiner."

But positive thinking is not only a water carrier for the business world, excusing its excesses and masking its follies. The promotion of positive thinking has become a minor industry in its own right, pro- ducing an endless flow of books, DVDs, and other products; providing employment for tens of thousands of "life coaches," "executive coaches," and motivational speakers, as well as for the growing cadre of profes- sional psychologists who seek to train them. No doubt the growing financial insecurity of the middle class contributes to the demand for these products and services, but I hesitate to attribute the commercial success of positive thinking to any particular economic trend or twist of the business cycle. America has historically offered space for all sorts of sects, cults, faith healers, and purveyors of snake oil, and those that are profitable, like positive thinking, tend to flourish.

At the turn of the twenty-first century, American optimism seemed to reach a manic crescendo. In his final State of the Union address in 2000, Bill Clinton struck a triumphal note, proclaiming that "never before has our nation enjoyed, at once, so much prosperity and social progress with so little internal crisis and so few external threats." But compared with his successor, Clinton seemed almost morose. George W. Bush had been a cheerleader in prep school, and cheerleading—a distinctly American innovation—could be considered the athletically inclined ancestor of so much of the coaching and "motivating" that has gone into the propagation of positive thinking. He took the presidency as an opportunity to continue in that line of work, defining his job as that of inspiring confidence, dispelling doubts, and pumping up the national spirit of self-congratulation. If he repeatedly laid claim to a single adjective, it was "optimistic." On the occasion of his sixtieth birthday, he told reporters he was "optimistic" about a variety of foreign policy challenges, offering as an overview, "I'm optimistic that all problems will be solved." Nor did he brook any doubts or hesitations among his close advisers. According to Bob Woodward, Condoleezza Rice failed to express some of her worries because, she said, "the president almost demanded optimism. He didn't like pessimism, hand-wringing or doubt."

Then things began to go wrong, which is not in itself unusual but was a possibility excluded by America's official belief that things are good and getting better. There was the dot-com bust that began a few months after Clinton's declaration of unprecedented prosperity in his final State of the Union address, then the terrorist attack of September 11, 2001. Furthermore, things began to go wrong in a way that suggested that positive thinking might not guarantee success after all, that it might in fact dim our ability to fend off real threats. In her

> **Things began to go wrong in a way that suggested that positive thinking might dim our ability to fend off real threats.**

remarkable book, *Never Saw It Coming: Cultural Challenges to Envisioning the Worst*, sociologist Karen Cerulo recounts a number of ways that the habit of positive thinking, or what she calls optimistic bias, undermined preparedness and invited disaster. She quotes *Newsweek* reporters Michael Hirsch and Michael Isikoff, for example, in their conclusion that "a whole summer of missed clues, taken together, seemed to presage the terrible September of 2001." There had already been a terrorist attack on the World Trade Center in 1993; there were ample warnings, in the summer of 2001, about a possible attack by airplane, and flight schools reported suspicious students like the one who wanted to learn how to "fly a plane but didn't care about landing and takeoff." The fact that no one—the FBI, the INS, Bush, or Rice—heeded these disturbing cues was later attributed to a "failure of imagination." But actually there was plenty of imagination at work—imagining an invulnerable nation and an ever-booming economy—there was simply no ability or inclination to imagine the worst.

A similar reckless optimism pervaded the American invasion of Iraq. Warnings about possible Iraqi resistance were swept aside by leaders who promised a "cakewalk" and envisioned cheering locals greeting our troops with flowers. Likewise, Hurricane Katrina was not exactly an unanticipated disaster. In 2002, the New Orleans *Times-Picayune* ran a Pulitzer Prize–winning series warning that the city's levees could not protect it against the storm surge brought on by a category 4 or 5 hurricane. In 2001, *Scientific American* had issued a similar warning about the city's vulnerability. Even when the hurricane struck and levees broke, no alarm bells went off in Washington, and when a New Orleans FEMA official sent a panicky e-mail to FEMA director Michael Brown, alerting him to the rising number of deaths and a shortage of food in the drowning city, he was told that Brown would need an hour to eat his dinner in a Baton Rouge restaurant. Criminal negligence or another "failure of imagination"? The truth is that Americans had been working hard for decades to school themselves in the techniques of positive thinking, and these included the reflexive capacity for dismissing disturbing news.

The biggest "come-uppance," to use Krugman's term, has so far been the financial meltdown of 2007 and the ensuing economic crisis. By the late first decade of the twenty-first century, . . . positive thinking had become ubiquitous and virtually unchallenged in American culture. It was promoted on some of the most widely watched talk shows, like *Larry King Live* and the *Oprah Winfrey Show*; it was the stuff of runaway best sellers like the 2006 book *The Secret*; it had been adopted as the theology of America's most successful evangelical preachers; it found a place in medicine as a potential adjuvant to the treatment of almost any disease. It had even penetrated the academy in the form of the new discipline of "positive psychology," offering courses teaching students to pump up their optimism and nurture their positive feelings. And its reach was growing global, first in the Anglophone countries and soon in the rising economies of China, South Korea, and India.

But nowhere did it find a warmer welcome than in American business, which is, of course, also global business. To the extent that positive thinking had become a business itself, business was its principal client, eagerly consuming the good news that all things are possible through an effort of mind. This was a useful message for employees, who by the turn of the twenty-first century were being required to work longer hours for fewer benefits and diminishing job security. But it was also a liberating ideology for top-level executives. What was the point in agonizing over balance sheets and tedious analyses of risks—and why bother worrying about dizzying levels of debt and exposure to potential defaults—when all good things come to those who are optimistic enough to expect them?

I do not write this in a spirit of sourness or personal disappointment of any kind, nor do I have any romantic attachment to suffering as a source of insight or virtue. On the contrary, I would like to see more smiles, more laughter, more hugs, more happiness and, better yet, joy. In my own vision of utopia, there is not only more comfort, and security for everyone—better jobs, health care, and so forth—there are also more parties, festivities, and opportunities for dancing in the streets. Once our basic material needs are met—in my utopia, anyway—life becomes a perpetual celebration in which everyone has a talent to contribute. But we cannot levitate ourselves into that blessed condition by wishing it. We need to brace ourselves for a struggle against terrifying obstacles, both of our own making and imposed by the natural world. And the first step is to recover from the mass delusion that is positive thinking.

DISCUSSION

1. Ehrenreich draws a key distinction between optimism and hope. How does she differentiate between these two? Do you agree with Ehrenreich that each represents a fundamentally different way to be happy? Why or why not?

2. Have you ever felt pressured to "stay positive"? When and where have you felt this pressure most? What kind of role might our culture's emphasis on being positive script for you? What would a typical day in your life look like if you were to try to fulfill this role? Is it one you would like to play? Why or why not?

3. The book from which this essay is excerpted is entitled *Bright-Sided*. How do you respond to this title? What view of positivity does it suggest? Do you share this view?

WRITING

4. For Ehrenreich, cultivating a positive outlook has gone in our culture from being a personal choice to being a mandatory expectation — a social script we are given little choice but to follow. In a brief essay, offer your own assessment of this claim. In your view, do we live in a world where acting and feeling positive have become compulsory? Can you think of an example from our popular culture through which this particular message gets conveyed or enforced?

5. At the heart of our society's emphasis on positivity, notes Ehrenreich, is a profound skepticism toward looking or feeling negative. Write an essay in which you argue for the cultural importance, even the necessity, of negativity. Under what circumstances might there be value in experiencing negative feelings? What larger purpose might such feelings serve?

6. In many respects, John West's account (p. 32) of his father's decision regarding assisted suicide represents a pointed rejection of what Ehrenreich regards as the societal command to stay positive. Write a brief essay in which you use Ehrenreich's argument here to assess West's portrait of his dying father. Based on Ehrenreich's critique of positive thinking, how do you view the father's decision to end his own life? What attitudes toward illness and death does this decision show?

JOHN WEST

Excerpt from *The Last Goodnights:*
Assisting My Parents with Their Suicides

How are we taught to define a "natural" death? And what are the consequences — social, psychological, and moral — when we contemplate, either for ourselves or those we love, alternatives to this definition? John West had to confront this question when his parents, battling terminal illnesses, asked for his help in ending their lives. He agreed and for many years kept his role in his parents' deaths secret until the 2009 publication of *The Last Goodnights: Assisting My Parents with Their Suicides*. Chronicling his own struggle to come to terms with his father's request to die, West's family memoir sheds light on the wrenching and complicated choices our culture's norms concerning death and dying confront us with. West is an attorney who lives in Los Angeles. He runs a consulting firm for people struggling with questions about assisted suicide and is a frequent speaker on the topic at forums, universities, and medical centers across the country.

I DON'T KNOW WHAT MY BOOZE BILL WAS FOR THAT TIME, BUT I'M sure it was big. I had a good reason, though: I had to kill my parents. They asked me to. Actually, they asked me to help them with their suicides, and I did. And if that doesn't justify throwing back an extra glass or three of Jameson's on the rocks, then I don't know what does.

My father was Louis Jolyon "Jolly" West, MD, a world-renowned psychiatrist and former chairman of the department of psychiatry at the University of California, Los Angeles, age seventy-four. My mother was Kathryn "K" West, PhD, a respected clinical psychologist at the West Los Angeles (Brentwood) Veterans Administration Hospital, age seventy-five.

Jolly and K were wonderful people—brilliant, academic medical professionals, highly cultured, and well rounded. Neither was at all religious, but both had deep insight into the human condition. They knew what was what. And they knew what they wanted.

So when they made their wishes clear to me, I wasn't about to argue. I respected my father and mother, and I loved them. And I believe, as they did, in freedom of choice, the right to personal privacy and self-determination—which includes reproductive choice (as the law now recognizes, although it didn't used to), the right to refuse medical treatment (as the law now recognizes, although it didn't used to), and the right to choose death with dignity (as the law does not recognize—not yet—although a few states are getting close).

My father's desire to end his life did not shock me, especially since his newly discovered cancer—a particularly vicious type—was literally eating him up and would take him from playing tennis to lying dead in just five months. Should Jolly have been forced to endure a few more days or weeks of agony just to satisfy some people's notions that death should be "natural"?

> *Should Jolly have been forced to endure agony just to satisfy some people's notions that death should be "natural"?*

And what about my mother? K had midstage Alzheimer's disease, plus osteoporosis and emphysema. Should she have been forced to deteriorate into a walking vegetable, soiling herself, wandering into traffic, hunched over like a crab, and coughing up blood, just because some people say that's how it's always been and always should be?

Jolly and K said no. And I agreed.

THE BEGINNING

I had no idea what my father wanted to talk to me about that afternoon in early November 1998 when he asked me to step into his bedroom for a private chat. But I was used to Jolly's secretiveness, so I didn't find it odd that he would suggest it, particularly with a houseful of visiting relatives and no privacy anywhere but behind a locked door. I assumed he had some additional bad news about the status of his cancer, something he wanted to tell me first, since I would be his successor in the role of what Jolly liked to call "the man of the family." An outdated concept, perhaps, but one that, unfortunately, applied more to our family than I liked. After Jolly's death, I would be the one member of the family who could be called solid, competent, and reliable. My mother had once been an ultra-competent professional, but various illnesses had left her needy and dependent. I had two sisters, both older than I, but Jolly never felt they could properly handle complicated or stressful "real world" matters. Years of experience and many disappointments had informed his opinion.

I sat in the big leather chair by the bookshelves, prepared to wait. Whenever Jolly talked to me about something important, he approached it in a roundabout way.

But not this time. Straight away he said, "John, I need your help."

This startled me—doubly so. He was being direct, which was rare enough. And he was asking for help. Jolly never asked for help. His smoothly contained persona, Mr. Totally In Control, had just popped open right in front of me. Not that any outsider would have noticed, because Jolly's demeanor was exactly the same as it was whenever he discussed anything important: His voice was measured and smooth; he sat squarely on the edge of his bed, leaning forward with his elbows on his knees and his hands clasped; he looked straight at me, seriously and intently, but his face showed little more than mild concern. His face rarely gave anything away. Only his words betrayed him now.

"I'm dying," he said. "That's no secret—everyone knows it. I don't have more than a few months, at most. But I do have something that is very important to me. I have options about how and when my death will occur."

He paused to let this sink in.

"At some point," he continued, "not too long from now, I will decide that enough is enough. By that time I will be full of all sorts of drugs, particularly the morphine that I'm already taking for pain. A little extra of that should do the trick, without anyone having to know and get upset."

He paused again and looked out the window.

I sat up in my chair. I suddenly felt hot and cold at the same time, as I realized what he meant. But as powerfully as his words registered, the idea behind them didn't seem strange at all. It made sense. He was about to die anyway, so why linger in pain? I knew I'd want to do the same thing if I were in his position.

I didn't know what to say, so I kept quiet and waited for him to continue. I don't know if I could have said anything even if I'd wanted to, because I was still somewhat stunned, not only by the intensity of what he'd told me, but also because I'd never expected him to share thoughts like these with me.

Still looking out the window, he continued, "My body is full of cancer. If I knock off a little ahead of schedule, nobody's going to know the difference, and I'll have saved myself a hell of a lot of pain."

Then he looked straight at me. "But I'll need you on board, to help me."

A question was implied, but we both knew what the answer would be. I nodded and said, "You got it."

I didn't register much of what he said right after that, because I was still having trouble processing the whole strange scene. Here we were, my father and I, sitting in his bedroom, calmly talking about his committing suicide. With me "on board," whatever that meant.

What it meant, I soon learned, was more than I had ever imagined. And then some.

Six weeks earlier, Jolly had phoned me at my home in Seattle from his office at UCLA. "I have some bad news, Johnny," he said.

I stopped stirring the soup I had on the stove. My first thought flashed on my mother: K had been declining, with a variety of ailments, for a few years now. Had she taken an unexpected turn for the worse? Or was Jolly just being overdramatic about something else, something relatively innocuous? He often did that.

"What is it?" I asked warily, hoping he wouldn't confirm my fear about K.

"Well," he said, taking a deep breath before continuing, "I had a pain in my hip that I thought was just my arthritis kicking up. I tried to ignore it, but when it got to the point where I needed a cane to get around, I thought I'd better get it looked at."

I was relieved that the bad news wasn't about K, but suddenly realized that it must be extraordinarily bad news about Jolly, because he never talked openly about his own health problems. Never.

"The radiologist took an X-ray of my hip but didn't like what he saw on the film, so he did a full-body bone scan." My stomach sank as I instantly imagined the worst.

"When he put the scan film up on the box, it took me about ten seconds to register what I saw. There were metastases throughout my skeleton. Cancer everywhere. I realized I was looking at a death sentence."

He paused, but I couldn't speak. I was too surprised, completely unprepared for this. He'd been just fine, last I'd heard, and now he was about to die?

He continued, almost casually, "The radiologist said he thought I had about six months to live. I think that's optimistic. I'd say it's closer to four."

I stood there frozen, the phone jammed against my ear. I couldn't believe it. This wasn't possible. Jolly had always been extraordinarily healthy and strong. Hell, he still had more hair than I did. And even though he'd been overweight for many years, he'd never seemed unhealthy—just incredibly big, powerful, sturdy.

Part of what stunned me, surely, was the suddenness of it all, and hearing it over the phone, instead of in person. The soup I'd been making started to boil over on the stove, but I couldn't move. I waited for Jolly to say something else, but the phone was quiet.

I didn't know what to say, so I just blathered the first things that came to mind.

"Jeez, Dad, I'm really sorry. Are you in a lot of pain? What happens next?"

"Well," he said, then sighed heavily, "I'm not in much pain. Not yet. Typically, the next step would be to start a regimen of chemotherapy and radiation, but I'm not sure I want to subject myself to that. I'm going to get additional information over the next few days, and then start making decisions."

Dozens of thoughts jumped through my head, but I tried to focus and concentrate on practical matters. I started to pace, the long phone cord whipping back and forth in my wake.

"What about Mom?" I asked. "How is she holding up?"

"She's okay at the moment, but she's putting on a brave face. I know she's worried as hell, and, of course, I'm worried about her, too. Her health isn't much better than mine. That's something else you and I will have to discuss when you're down here next."

"Of course, of course," I said, the implications of his words starting to ignite in my mind. K's fragile condition could deteriorate rapidly from the stress of Jolly's illness and eventual death.

Then another worry hit me: "What about Anne and Mary? Have you told them about your diagnosis yet?"

"Yes, I've talked with both your sisters."

"How are they taking it?"

"Well," he sighed again, "pretty much true to form—you know how they are. Annie is wound up beyond all reason." He chuckled sadly. "I had to spend almost an hour calming her down and reassuring her that I wasn't already in extremis. Mary was shocked and flustered at first, but put on a good show of acting calm, even though it's obvious she's frightened." He paused and then said pointedly, "You know that both your sisters are going to need your help with what's ahead."

"I know," I said. Both Anne and Mary had had deeply troubled relationships with Jolly and K over the years, and I'd fallen into the role of sometime caretaker. Relative calm seemed to prevail with them at the moment, but Jolly obviously anticipated that would change. At the very least, I knew that Jolly's illness would be extremely difficult for them to cope with.

He continued, "Annie said she's coming to L.A. immediately—to 'help'—which your mother and I are not exactly looking forward to. It'll probably be the other way around, for the most part. And Mary said she'd try to come see me more often, but that damn husband of hers makes it difficult."

"Yeah," I said, "I know."

"What about you?" he asked. "Will your schedule allow you to come down here for a visit? I know you're busy lawyering and helping folks."

"Don't worry," I said, "I'll make arrangements. I'll clear some things off my calendar and come down there as soon as I can."

"No rush," he said. "I'm really not feeling too bad. And I'm not going anywhere. Not yet, anyway."

I could tell by his tone that he was trying to joke about his impending demise, so I chuckled appreciatively and said, "Right." He chuckled too, glad I'd gotten it.

Then I said, "Keep me posted, all right? And if there's anything I can do to help out down there, just let me know."

"Okay, Son," he said. "I'll keep you apprised."

"Okay, Dad. Talk to you soon."

"So long," he said, and hung up.

I stood there staring at the phone, still stunned, until the smell of scorched soup demanded my attention. As I cleaned up the stove, I replayed the phone call over and over in my mind. It didn't make any sense. He sounded healthy, and he was only seventy-four—maybe his doctors had made a mistake and would catch it any day now. But even as I thought that, I knew it was a typical denial reaction. There hadn't been any mistake. The cancer was there. Jolly was dying.

I knew that Jolly had access to hundreds, maybe even thousands, of doctors at UCLA Hospital, where he worked, and that he'd get the absolute best medical care. My offer to help was an instinct, a reflex, what someone says. I didn't know what help I could actually be. But I found out six weeks later, when he called me into his bedroom for that private chat. Jolly's directness and request for help during that conversation had surprised me, but I understood what it meant: all business. He would be as detached, dispassionate, and professional in ending his own life as he had been during any other medical crisis in his fifty-year career. And he would expect me to follow suit. But although I knew (and he did, too) that I could remain calm and professional in a crisis, this was not a professional situation—this was my father, and his suicide, and my participation. I knew I'd have to steel myself like never before in order to handle the pressures that would surely come.

I was used to pressure. A career as a trial lawyer is not for the easily rattled. I could think on my feet, stay calm, and keep a straight face. But assisting Jolly with his suicide promised complexities I wouldn't be able to anticipate. It would be like getting plucked out of my office and tossed into the middle of a jury trial without knowing what the case was about. I'd still be expected to do my job—and maybe I could, to some degree. But this wasn't a court case; it was my father's life.

> **Assisting Jolly with his suicide promised complexities I wouldn't be able to anticipate.**

I knew I couldn't talk about this with anyone, not even my closest friends, because it might put me, and possibly them, in legal jeopardy. They could be forced to testify against me, or one of them might accidentally let it slip to somebody else who might call the cops or possibly . . . I don't know—I just didn't feel that I could run the risk of exposing such intimate and potentially incendiary information to anybody. Keeping professional secrets is stressful enough, but this . . . damn!

Another thing I found troubling was that I had no idea when this business would happen, or how long I would be involved in . . . whatever it turned out to be. Would I have to be in L.A. a lot? How could I schedule my absences from work? It isn't easy to leave a small law firm, or any small business, for more than a few days at a time, particularly when you're the person in charge. Even though I had a partner and support staff, there wasn't much work I could delegate. My specialty—representing victims of employment discrimination and sexual harassment—required an extra level of personal attention because of the intensely personal nature of the harm my clients had suffered. As an attorney I sometimes felt like St. George battling the dragon, particularly when I represented women who had been sexually assaulted in the workplace.

I always put too much of myself into my work. I felt it would be nearly impossible for me to do my job properly if I weren't in the office and able to deal with my clients directly and promptly. All I could think to do, to at least try to lessen the demands on my time and my mind, was stop taking new cases. Maybe that would give me the mental elbow room I knew I'd need to deal with whatever Jolly wanted from me.

JOLLY'S BIRTHDAY

A week after Jolly called and told me about his diagnosis, and five weeks before he asked for my help during that bedroom chat, I flew from Seattle to L.A. for his seventy-fourth birthday. We all knew this would be his last, so my sisters came too: Anne from New York City, and Mary from Northern California. Neither brought her husband.

I felt nervous about seeing Jolly, and not just because of the extreme changes looming over him and the rest of the family. Until he'd phoned me with his bad news, I hadn't planned on attending his birthday party—or any other event involving him—because our recent relationship had not been good. For a long time, Jolly's philandering had been an open secret in our family, but it had never intruded directly on our lives until two years before. Decades of polite, quiet disagreement about Jolly's behavior had finally become pointed conflict when he made the bewildering decision to start bringing into our home, and into the homes of old family friends, his newly admitted illegitimate child—an adolescent boy. I had told Jolly that this was highly inappropriate and painful to the family (and embarrassing to the old family friends), and that it was especially hurtful, insulting, and disrespectful to K. I stood up for K because she was in no position to stand up to Jolly anymore, due to her failing health and increased dependence on him. K and I had always been close, and now that her health and strength were declining, I felt more and more protective of her.

I'd told Jolly that if he wanted to spend time with this boy, there were numerous other places they could go—places on the other side of town, where the boy's mother lived; places that wouldn't be so offensive to basic notions of decency, discretion, and tact. Los Angeles is not a small town; it has plenty such places.

Jolly didn't like my telling him that his flaunting a gross indiscretion was wrong, and he refused to stop it. He even tried to twist the situation on me by saying how sad he was that I "didn't like the kid," but I set things straight immediately: I told Jolly that it wasn't the boy I disliked — I didn't know him well enough to like or dislike him; I'd met him only a time or two, when he was a small child, and long before I'd learned his true lineage. Rather, it was Jolly I didn't like, for behaving in such an astonishingly bad way, especially toward K, his wife of more than fifty years. He'd had no reply to that.

I'd been angry at Jolly for several months afterward, but over time my anger had faded into sadness and disappointment as I mourned the loss of the man I'd once imagined my father to be, and began to know him—and try to accept him—for who he really was.

And now, after learning of his illness and thinking—a lot—about our relationship, I decided to put our recent conflict aside and act like a son, not a judge. Jolly and I hadn't resolved our old business, but life isn't governed by parliamentary procedure, and the new business—end-of-life issues—now took priority.

Besides, until these rough last two years, Jolly and I had had a fine relationship—friendly, warm, adult. Other than the standard turbulence during my teen years, we'd had a smooth trip. I always felt like I could talk to him about anything. (The fact that he was a doctor made some of what we talked about a lot easier, especially when I was struggling through puberty.) We had the kind of understanding that some fathers and sons have, where the son somehow intuits what his father expects and does it naturally—and feels proud to have gotten it right. Behavioral scientists probably have a fancy name for it, but it's a common enough phenomenon: sons learning how to please their fathers. And as much as I always refused to admit it—thinking I had escaped such mundane motivations—I realize now that I'd always had a deep need to make my father notice me and be proud of me.

Of course, when I was a child I thought of Jolly as a deity, and his frequent absences from home only added to his mythology. He would be in Washington, D.C., battling with the National Institute of Mental Health. Or in Tokyo, pontificating at an international medical conference. Or just over at the hospital, working late.

Ah, yes, "working late." Jolly was a doctor—tall, handsome, successful, charming, magnetic, and powerful. Catnip to women. (Picture a young Orson Welles, whom Jolly resembled in his youth.) And so it began, and so it continued—even after he had aged and gained so much weight that, sadly, he'd come to resemble the older, ursine Orson.

Jolly attracted men, too, but in a different way. Men admired him and wanted to be his friend and colleague. This quality made him a formidable recruiter, and over the years he used his persuasive talents to attract many bright young doctors to his department.

Jolly had a true gift for making people feel special. When he wanted to, he could look you in the eye and talk to you and make you feel like you were the most important, fascinating person he'd ever met. Whenever I received this treatment from him, I felt as if Zeus himself had just smiled upon me. He was perhaps the consummate politician. In fact, many have compared him to Bill Clinton because of his powerful charm and intellect (as well as his marital lapses).

Once I arrived at my parents' house and settled into the familiar living room, my earlier nervousness about seeing Jolly subsided. Somehow, everything seemed as normal as ever. Jolly held court from his usual end of the sofa and, surprisingly, showed no sign of his illness. I sat near him, in a chair in front of the fireplace. Mom sat in her usual spot—the opposite end of the sofa from Dad—and tried to keep a poker face, although I could see her fretting. Anne and Mary dealt busily with dinner preparations and last-minute gift wrapping and such, occasionally bouncing in for a quick comment, while I caught up with the folks.

It seemed like old times: The conversation was easy and smooth, the usual rhythms. At one point, Jolly said something a bit too humorous and cavalier about his dire condition, and K gently growled at him, "Jolly, don't exaggerate." He sighed and said, "Yes, dear." She rolled her eyes at his response, then said, "Now knock it off, or you'll scare the children!" And they both chuckled. Classic Jolly-and-K banter.

I finally asked Jolly about his plan for dealing with his rapidly advancing cancer. He replied with great sangfroid. "I'm a physician," he said. "I know when my number's up. It's just a question of how to go through the decline. The 'cure' in a case like this is worse than the goddamn disease. I'm not going to do anything drastic to fight it. What's the point? Maybe I'd live a few more weeks, but I wouldn't be able to do anything except lie in bed and suffer."

> **"The 'cure' in a case like this is worse than the disease."**

I was a bit surprised to hear him say this, because I knew he'd already started chemotherapy and radiation treatments, but I also knew that he often said and did contradictory things. Maybe he felt he needed to "keep up appearances" for his colleagues at the hospital by going through the standard treatment regimen. Or maybe he thought, as he did about so much in his life, that things would go differently for him—that by the sheer force of his considerable will, he could avoid the inevitable side effects of the chemo and radiation.

As Jolly continued, Mom did a good job of remaining stoic. Anne dashed all across the emotional landscape, alternately weeping and vowing grandly to stand by Jolly no matter what, and help him beat the cancer if it was the last thing she ever did. Mary put on a happy face for the most part, although it was obviously forced, and she seemed to shrink in on herself at times, retreating from the intensity of the conversation. I asked questions, remained calm, and tried to be supportive. So we all stayed true to our established familial-behavior patterns.

Dinnertime came and went, Jolly opened his presents with great gusto, and then the party came to an end because I needed to leave for the airport and catch the last flight back to Seattle. I had to be in court with a client the next morning, so I couldn't stay overnight in L.A. I was about to call a cab when Dad volunteered to drive me—another surprise. He usually hated chores like that. Perhaps he felt the need, as I did, for a few minutes of private conversation.

I kissed Mom and my sisters goodbye, and then Jolly and I got into his car and headed down the freeway to LAX. Jolly loved his Cadillac— the fanciest car he'd ever owned. When he'd bought the Caddy only a few years earlier, he'd joked about its being black, saying it would be the last car he'd ever own, and that we could drive him to his funeral in it. Now, as he steered it down the freeway, I realized that the joke would come true. I didn't say anything, though—surely he'd thought of it. I just shook my head at the sad irony.

As we drove along and made small talk, I could tell he had something on his mind—probably our unfinished old business—but I knew it would be hard for him to raise that painful subject. So, as we neared the airport, I waded in.

"Listen, Dad, there's something important I want to talk with you about, and I think it's important that I tell you in person, before I get on the plane."

"Okay," he said; he sounded neutral, but I sensed him bracing himself.

"You and I have been having this big disagreement for a couple of years, but I want you to know that I'm through with it. I've been thinking a lot about the whole situation since you told me your medical news, and, well, life-and-death matters—like what you're facing—are simply more important. So I want you to know that all that other stuff is moot. It's over and done with, as far as I'm concerned."

I heard him exhale slowly, and I thought I could see his shoulders relax. He didn't say anything for a few seconds, but I could tell he was concentrating, thinking how to respond. He glanced at me, then looked back at the road and said very quietly, "Thank you, Johnny. You don't know how much that relieves my mind."

Then we had to stop at a red light, the last light before we entered the LAX causeway for departing passengers. As we sat there waiting, I heard him sigh, and then the sigh turned into a sob, and I looked over and saw a tear roll down his cheek just before he reached up and wiped it away. It was the only time in my life I ever saw him cry.

Then the light turned green and we drove on in silence. I pointed out the terminal, and Jolly maneuvered the car over to the curb and stopped. We both got out and he came around to my side, his eyes still a little moist. He put his arms out and we hugged, and again he said, "Thank you."

I picked up my briefcase. "Well . . . I love you, Dad."

"I love you too," he said.

And then I had to go.

DISCUSSION

1. As he considers his father's request to help him die, West asks himself the following question: "Should Jolly have been forced to endure a few more days or weeks of agony just to satisfy some people's notions that death should be 'natural'?" According to your own belief, what does it mean to die naturally? And how does this differ from what you would term an unnatural death?

2. Growing up, West confides, he tended to regard his father as a larger-than-life figure. "When I was a child," he writes, "I thought of Jolly as a deity." In your estimation, is this kind of admiration typical? When it comes to the ways we are taught in our culture to think about family, does such "worship" constitute a social norm? And how does the father's request challenge or alter this norm? In your view, does this request change the father/son norm for the better or worse? How?

3. How does Jolly West's approach to death compare with the messages about and attitudes toward death modeled by our larger popular culture? Do his attitudes and actions represent a deviation from the script we typically see? How or how not?

WRITING

4. Among other things, West's account represents an attempt to understand not only his father's life and impending death, but his own relationship with his father as well. How would you characterize the role of son that West plays? Does it conform to or differ from what you consider to be the social or cultural norm? And how in particular does his father's request for assistance in dying affect your view of this relationship? Is this the kind of request, in your view, that a father should make to his son? Why or why not?

5. In the essay's opening section, West frames his father's request to die within the context of other human and civil rights, among them the right to reproductive choice and the right to personal privacy. Do you think assisted suicide belongs in this category? Write an essay in which you argue either in favor of or against what West terms "the right to choose death with dignity." In your view, should society create a rule enshrining this right? If so, on what basis is doing so legitimate? If not, what problems does it pose? What norms does it violate?

6. In many ways, West's father evinces an attitude toward his impending death that is in direct opposition to the kind of enforced optimism Barbara Ehrenreich chronicles (p. 22). Write an essay in which you discuss the particular ways West's portrait of his father supports or reinforces Ehrenreich's critique of American cheerfulness. What specific attitudes and assumptions does Jolly West's approach to death reflect? And to what extent do you think these attitudes and assumptions would resonate with Ehrenreich?

JAMES TWITCHELL

Two Cheers for Materialism

How are we taught to define the successful life? And do we create these definitions for ourselves? Taking up these questions, James Twitchell explores how firmly "materialism" has come to anchor our prevailing definitions of "success." Rather than bemoan this fact, however, he offers a spirited defense of this cultural logic, pointing instead to the "creative" and "emancipating" effects of consumerism. Twitchell is a professor of English and advertising at the University of Florida, and he has published several books in each field. His studies on Romantic and Gothic literature include *Living Dead: A Study of the Vampire in Romantic Literature* (1981) and *Dreadful Pleasures: An Anatomy of Modern Horror* (1985). He has also written several books on consumerism, including *Adcult USA: The Triumph of Advertising in America* (1995) and *Living It Up: Our Love Affair with Luxury* (2002). His most recent work is *Shopping for God: How Christianity Moved from in Your Heart to in Your Face* (2007). The following essay is adapted from *Lead Us into Temptation: The Triumph of American Materialism* (1999).

O F ALL THE STRANGE BEASTS THAT HAVE COME SLOUCHING INTO the 20th century, none has been more misunderstood, more criticized, and more important than materialism. Who but fools, toadies, hacks, and occasional loopy libertarians have ever risen to its defense? Yet the fact remains that while materialism may be the most shallow of the 20th century's various -*isms*, it has been the one that has ultimately triumphed. The world of commodities appears so antithetical to the world of ideas that it seems almost heresy to point out the obvious: most of the world most of the time spends most of its energy producing and consuming more and more stuff. The really interesting question may be not why we are so materialistic, but why we are so unwilling to acknowledge and explore what seems the central characteristic of modern life.

When the French wished to disparage the English in the 19th century, they called them a nation of shopkeepers. When the rest of the world now wishes to disparage Americans, they call us a nation of consumers. And they are right. We are developing and rapidly exporting a new material culture, a mallcondo culture. To the rest of the world we do indeed seem not just born to shop, but alive to shop. Americans spend more time tooling around the mallcondo—three to four times as many hours as our European counterparts—and we have more stuff to show for it. According to some estimates, we have about four times as many things as Middle Europeans, and who knows how much more than people in the less developed parts of the world. The quantity and disparity are increasing daily, even though, as we see in Russia and China, the "emerging nations" are playing a frantic game of catch-up.

This burst of mallcondo commercialism has happened recently—in my lifetime—and it is spreading around the world at the speed of television. The average American consumes twice as many goods and services as in 1950; in fact, the poorest fifth of the current population buys more than the average fifth did in 1955. Little wonder that the average new home of today is twice as large as the average house built in the early years after World War II. We have to put that stuff somewhere—quick—before it turns to junk.

Sooner or later we are going to have to acknowledge the uncomfortable fact that this amoral consumerama has proved potent because human beings love things. In fact, to a considerable degree we live for things. In all cultures we buy things, steal things, exchange things, and horde things. From time to time, some of us collect vast amounts of things, from tulip bulbs to paint drippings on canvasses to matchbook covers. Often these objects have no observable use.

Human beings love things.

We live through things. We create ourselves through things. And we change ourselves by changing our things. In the West, we have even developed the elaborate algebra of commercial law to decide how things are exchanged, divested, and recaptured. Remember, we call these things "goods," as in "goods and services." We don't—unless we are academic critics—call them "bads." This sounds simplistic, but it is crucial to understanding the powerful allure of materialism.

Our commercial culture has been blamed for the rise of eating disorders, the spread of "affluenza," the epidemic of depression, the despoliation of cultural icons, the corruption of politics, the carnivalization of holy times like Christmas, and the gnat-life attention span of our youth. All of this is true. Commercialism contributes. But it is by no means the whole truth. Commercialism is more a mirror than a lamp. In demonizing it, in seeing ourselves as helpless and innocent victims of its overpowering force, in making it the scapegoat du jour, we reveal far more about our own eagerness to be passive in the face of complexity than about the thing itself.

Anthropologists tell us that consumption habits are gender-specific. Men seem to want stuff in the latent, arid, post-midlife years. That's when the male collecting impulse seems to be felt. Boys amass playing marbles first, Elgin marbles later. Women seem to gain potency as consumers after childbirth, almost as if getting and spending is part of a nesting impulse.

Historians, however, tell us to be careful about such stereotyping. Although women are the primary consumers of commercial objects today, they have enjoyed this status only since the Industrial Revolution. Certainly in the pre-industrial world men were the chief hunter-gatherers. If we can trust works of art to accurately portray how booty was split (and cultural historians such as John Berger and Simon Schama think we can), then males were the prime consumers of fine clothes, heavily decorated furniture, gold and silver articles, and of course, paintings in which they could be shown displaying their stuff.

Once a surplus was created, in the 19th century, women joined the fray in earnest. They were not duped. The hegemonic phallocentric patriarchy did not brainwash them into thinking goods mattered. The Industrial Revolution produced more and more things not simply because it had the machines to do so, and not because nasty producers twisted their handlebar mustaches and whispered, "We can talk women into buying anything," but because both sexes are powerfully attracted to the world of things.

Karl Marx understood the magnetism of things better than anyone else. In *The Communist Manifesto* (1848), he wrote:

> The bourgeoisie, by the rapid improvement of all instruments of production, by the immensely facilitated means of communication, draws all, even the most barbarian nations into civilization. The cheap prices of its commodities are the heavy artillery with which it batters down all Chinese walls. . . . It compels all nations on pain of extinction, to adopt the bourgeois mode of production; it compels them to introduce what it calls civilization into their midst, i.e. to become bourgeois themselves. In one word, it creates a world after its own image.

Marx used this insight to motivate the heroic struggle against capitalism. But the struggle should not be to deter capitalism and its mad consumptive ways, but to appreciate how it works so its furious energy may be understood and exploited.

Don't turn to today's middle-aged academic critic for any help on that score. Driving about in his totemic Volvo (unattractive and built to stay that way), he can certainly criticize the bourgeois afflictions of others, but he is unable to provide much actual insight into their consumption practices, much less his own. Ask him to explain the difference between "Hilfiger" inscribed on an oversize shirt hanging nearly to the knees and his rear-window university decal (My child goes to Yale, sorry about yours), and you will be met with a blank stare. If you were then to suggest that what that decal and automotive nameplate represent is as overpriced as Calvin Klein's initials on a plain white T-shirt, he would pout that you can't compare apples and whatever. If you were to say next that aspiration and affiliation are at the heart of both displays, he would say that you just don't get it, just don't get it at all.

If you want to understand the potency of American consumer culture, ask any group of teenagers what democracy means to them. You will hear an extraordinary response. Democracy is the right to buy anything you want. Freedom's just another word for lots of things to buy. Appalling perhaps, but there is something to their answer. Being able to buy what you want when and where you want it was, after all, the right that made 1989 a watershed year in Eastern Europe.

Recall as well that freedom to shop was another way to describe the right to be served in a restaurant that provided one focus for the early civil rights movement. Go back further. It was the right to consume freely which sparked the fires of separation of this country from England. The freedom to buy what you want (even if you can't pay for it) is what most foreigners immediately spot as what they like about our culture, even though in the next breath they will understandably criticize it.

The pressure to commercialize — to turn things into commodities and then market them as charms — has always been particularly Western. As Max Weber first argued in *The Protestant Ethic and the Spirit of Capitalism* (1905), much of the Protestant Reformation was geared toward denying the holiness of many things that the Catholic church had endowed with meanings. From the inviolable priesthood to the sacrificial holy water, this deconstructive movement systematically unloaded meaning. Soon the marketplace would capture this off-loaded meaning and apply it to secular things. Buy this, you'll be saved. You deserve a break today. You, you're the one. We are the company that cares about you. You're worth it. You are in good hands. We care. Trust in us. We are there for you.

Materialism, it's important to note, does not crowd out spiritualism; spiritualism is more likely a substitute when objects are scarce. When we have few things we make the next world holy. When we have plenty we enchant the objects around us. The hereafter becomes the here and now.

We have not grown weaker but stronger by accepting the self-evidently ridiculous myths that sacramentalize mass-produced objects; we have not wasted away but have proved inordinately powerful, have not devolved and been rebarbarized, but seem to have marginally improved. Dreaded affluenza notwithstanding, commercialism has lessened pain. Most of us have more pleasure and less discomfort in our lives than most of the people most of the time in all of history.

Commercialism has lessened pain.

As Stanley Lebergott, an economist at Wesleyan University, argues in *Pursuing Happiness* (1993), most Americans have "spent their way to happiness." Lest this sound overly Panglossian, what Lebergott means is that while consumption by the rich has remained relatively steady, the rest of us — the intractable poor (about four percent of the population) are the exception — have now had a go of it. If the rich really are different, as

F. Scott Fitzgerald said, and the difference is that they have longer shopping lists and are happier for it, then we have, in the last two generations, substantially caught up.

The most interesting part of the book is the second half. Here Lebergott unloads reams of government statistics and calculations to chart the path that American consumption has taken in a wide range of products and services: food, tobacco, clothing, fuel, domestic service, and medicine—to name only a few. Two themes emerge strongly from these data. The first, not surprisingly, is that Americans were far better off by 1990 than they were in 1900. And the second is that academic critics—from Robert Heilbroner, Tibor Scitovsky, Robert and Helen Lynd, and Christopher Lasch to Juliet Schor, Robert Frank, and legions of others—who've censured the waste and tastelessness of much of American consumerism have simply missed the point. Okay, okay, money can't buy happiness, but you stand a better chance than with penury.

The cultural pessimists counter that it may be true that materialism offers a temporary palliative against the anxiety of emptiness, but we still must burst joy's grape. Consumption will turn sour because so much of it is based on the chimera of debt. Easy credit = overbuying = disappointment = increased anxiety.

This is not just patronizing, it is wrongheaded. As another economist, Lendol Calder, has argued in *Financing the American Dream* (1999), debt has been an important part of families' financial planning since the time of Washington and Jefferson. And although consumer debt has consistently risen in recent times, the default rate has remained remarkably stable—more than 95.5 percent of consumer debt gets paid, usually on time. In fact, the increased availability of credit to a growing share of the population, particularly to lower-income individuals and families, has allowed many more "have nots" to enter the economic mainstream.

There is, in fact, a special crippling quality to poverty in the modern Western world. For the penalty of intractable, transgenerational destitution is not just the absence of things; it is also the absence of meaning, the exclusion from participating in the essential socializing events of modern life. When you hear that some ghetto kid has killed one of his peers for a pair of branded sneakers or a monogrammed athletic jacket you realize that chronically unemployed poor youths are indeed living the absurdist life proclaimed by existentialists. The poor are truly the selfless ones in commercial culture.

Clearly what the poor are after is what we all want: association, affiliation, inclusion, magical purpose. While they are bombarded, as we all are, by the commercial imprecations of being cool, of experimenting with various presentations of disposable self, they lack the wherewithal to even enter the loop.

The grandfather of today's academic scolds is Thorstein Veblen (1857–1929), the eccentric Minnesotan who coined the phrase "conspicuous consumption" and has become almost a cult figure among critics of consumption. All of his books (save for his translation of the *Lexdaela Saga*) are still in print. His most famous, *The Theory of the Leisure Class,* has never been out of print since it was first published in 1899.

Veblen claimed that the leisure class set the standards for conspicuous consumption. Without sumptuary laws to protect their markers of distinction, the rest of us could soon make their styles into our own—the Industrial Revolution saw to that. But since objects lose their status distinctions when consumed by the hoi polloi, the leisure class must eternally be finding newer and more wasteful markers. Waste is not just inevitable, it is always increasing as the foolish hounds chase the wily fox.

Veblen lumped conspicuous consumption with sports and games, "devout observances," and aesthetic display. They were all reducible, he insisted, to "pecuniary emulation," his characteristically inflated term for getting in with the in-crowd. Veblen fancied himself a socialist looking forward to the day when "the discipline of the machine" would be turned around to promote stringent nationality among the entire population instead of wasted dispersion. If only we had fewer choices we would be happier, there would be less waste, and we would accept each other as equals.

The key to Veblen's argumentative power is that, like Hercules cleaning the Augean stables, he felt no responsibility to explain what happens next. True, if we all purchased the same toothpaste things would be more efficient and less wasteful. Logically we should all read *Consumer Reports,* find out the best brand, and then all be happy using the same product. But we aren't. Procter & Gamble markets 36 sizes and shapes of Crest. There are 41 versions of Tylenol. Is this because we are dolts afflicted with "pecuniary emulation," obsessed with making invidious distinctions, or is the answer more complex? Veblen never considered that consumers might have other reasons for exercising choice in the marketplace. He never considered, for example, that along with "keeping up with the Joneses" runs "keeping away from the Joneses."

Remember in *King Lear* when the two nasty daughters want to strip Lear of his last remaining trappings of majesty? He has moved in with them, and they don't think he needs so many expensive guards. They whittle away at his retinue until only one is left. "What needs one?" they say. Rather like governments attempting to redistribute wealth or like academics criticizing consumption, they conclude that Lear's needs are excessive. They are false needs. Lear, however, knows otherwise. Terrified and suddenly bereft of purpose, he bellows from his innermost soul, "Reason not the need."

Lear knows that possessions are definitions—superficial meanings, perhaps, but meanings nonetheless. And unlike Veblen, he knows those meanings are worth having. Without soldiers he is no king. Without a

BMW there can be no yuppie, without tattoos no adolescent rebel, without big hair no Southwestern glamour-puss, without Volvos no academic intellectual, and, well, you know the rest. Meaning is what we are after, what we need, especially when we are young.

What kind of meaning? In the standard academic view, growing out of the work of the Frankfurt school theorists of the 1950s and '60s (such as Antonio Gramsci, Theodor Adorno, and Max Horkheimer) and later those of the Center for Contemporary Cultural Studies at the University of Birmingham, it is meaning supplied by capitalist manipulators. What we see in popular culture, in this view, is the result of the manipulation of the many for the profit of the few.

For an analogy, take watching television. In academic circles, we assume that youngsters are being reified (to borrow a bit of the vast lexicon of jargon that accompanies this view) by passively consuming pixels in the dark. Meaning supposedly resides in the shows and is transferred to the sponge-like viewers. So boys, for example, see flickering scenes of violence, internalize these scenes, and willy-nilly are soon out Jimmying open your car. This is the famous Twinkie interpretation of human behavior—consuming too much sugar leads to violent actions. Would listening to Barry Manilow five hours a day make adolescents into loving, caring people?

Watch kids watching television and you see something quite different from what is seen by the critics. Most consumption, whether it be of entertainment or in the grocery store, is active. We are engaged. Here is how I watch television. I almost never turn the set on to see a particular show. I am near the machine and think I'll see what's happening. I know all the channels; any eight-year-old does. I am not a passive viewer. I use the remote control to pass through various programs, not searching for a final destination but making up a shopping basket, as it were, of entertainment.

But the academic critic doesn't see this. He sees a passive observer who sits quietly in front of the set letting the phosphorescent glow of mindless infotainment pour over his consciousness. In the hypodermic analogy beloved by critics, the potent dope of desire is pumped into the bleary dupe. This paradigm of passive observer and active supplier, a receptive moron and smart manipulator, is easily transported to the marketplace. One can see why such a system would appeal to the critic. After all, since the critic is not being duped, he should be empowered to protect the young, the female, the foreign, the uneducated, and the helpless from the onslaught of dreck.

In the last decade or so, however, a number of scholars in the humanities and social sciences have been challenging many of the academy's assumptions.[1] What distinguishes the newer thinking is that scholars have left the office to actually observe and question their subjects. Just one example: Mihaly Csikszentmihalyi, a psychology professor at the University of Chicago, interviewed 315 Chicagoans from 82 families, asking them what objects in the home they cherished most. The adult members of the five happiest families picked things that reminded them of other people and good times they'd had together. They mentioned a memento (such as an old toy) from their childhood 30 percent of the time. Adults in the five most dissatisfied families cited such objects only 6 percent of the time.

In explaining why they liked something, happy family members often described, for example, the times their family had spent on a favorite couch, rather than its style or color. Their gloomier counterparts tended to focus on the merely physical qualities of things. What was clear was that both happy and unhappy families derived great meaning from the consumption and interchange of manufactured things. The thesis, reflected in the title of his co-authored 1981 book, *The Meaning of Things: Domestic Symbols and the Self,* is that most of the "work" of consumption occurs after the act of purchase. Things do not come complete; they are forever being assembled.

Twentieth-century French sociologists have taken the argument even further. Two of the most important are Pierre Bourdieu, author of *Distinction: A Social Critique of the Judgement of Taste* (1984), and Jean Baudrillard, whose books include *The Mirror of Production* (1983) and *Simulacra and Simulation* (1994). In the spirit of reader-response theory in literary criticism, they see meaning not as a single thing that producers affix to consumer goods, but as something created by the user, who jumbles various interpretations simultaneously. Essentially, beneath the jargon, this means that the Budweiser you drink is not the same as the one I drink. . . .

The process of consumption is creative and even emancipating. In an open market, we consume the real and the imaginary meanings, fusing objects, symbols, and images together to end up with "a little world made cunningly." Rather than lives, individuals since midcentury have had *lifestyles.* For better or worse, lifestyles are secular religions, coherent patterns of valued things. Your lifestyle is not related to what you do for a living but to what you buy. One of the chief aims of the way we live now is the enjoyment of affiliating with those who share the same clusters of objects as we do.

Mallcondo culture is so powerful in part because it frees us from the strictures of social class. The outcome of material life is no longer preordained by coat of arms, pew seat, or trust fund. Instead, it evolves from a never-ending shifting of individual choice. No one wants to be middle class, for instance. You want to be cool, hip, with it, with the "in" crowd, instead.

Mallcondo culture is so powerful in part because it frees us from the strictures of social class.

One of the reasons terms like *Yuppie, Baby Boomer,* and *GenX* have elbowed aside such older designations as "upper middle class" is that we no longer understand social class as well as we do lifestyle, or what marketing firms call "consumption communities." Observing stuff is the way we understand each other. Even if no one knows exactly how much money it takes to be a yuppie, or how young you have to be, or how upwardly aspiring, everybody knows where yuppies gather, how they dress, what they play, what they drive, what they eat, and why they hate to be called yuppies.

For better or worse, American culture is well on its way to becoming world culture. The Soviets have fallen. Only quixotic French intellectuals and anxious Islamic fundamentalists are trying to stand up to it. By no means am I sanguine about such a material culture. It has many problems that I have glossed over. Consumerism is wasteful, it is devoid of otherworldly concerns, it lives for today and celebrates the body, and it overindulges and spoils the young with impossible promises.

"Getting and spending" has eclipsed family, ethnicity, even religion as a defining matrix. That doesn't mean that those other defining systems have disappeared, but that an increasing number of young people around the world will give more of their loyalty to Nike than to creeds of blood, race, or belief. This is not entirely a bad thing, since a lust for upscale branding isn't likely to drive many people to war, but it is, to say the least, far from inspiring.

It would be nice to think that materialism could be heroic, self-abnegating, and redemptive. It would be nice to think that greater material comforts will release us from racism, sexism, and ethnocentrism, and that the apocalypse will come as it did at the end of romanticism in Shelley's *Prometheus Unbound,* leaving us "Scepterless, free, uncircumscribed . . . Equal, unclassed, tribeless, and nationless."

But it is more likely that the globalization of capitalism will result in the banalities of an ever-increasing worldwide consumerist culture. The French don't stand a chance. The untranscendent, repetitive, sensational, democratic, immediate, tribalizing, and unifying force of what Irving Kristol calls the American Imperium need not necessarily result in a Bronze Age of culture. But it certainly will not produce what Shelley had in mind.

We have not been led into this world of material closeness against our better judgment. For many of us, especially when young, consumerism is our better judgment. We have not just asked to go this way, we have demanded. Now most of the world is lining up, pushing and shoving, eager to elbow into the mall. Getting and spending has become the most passionate, and often the most imaginative, endeavor of modern life. While this is dreary and depressing to some, as doubtless it should be, it is liberating and democratic to many more.

NOTE

[1] This reconsideration of consumption is an especially strong current in anthropology, where the central text is *The World of Goods: Towards an Anthropology of Consumption* (1979), by Mary Douglas and Baron Isherwood. It can also be seen in the work of scholars such as William Leiss in communication studies; Dick Hebdige in sociology; Jackson Lears in history; David Morley in cultural studies; Michael Schudson in the study of advertising; Sidney Levy in consumer research; Tyler Cowan in economics; Grant McCracken in fashion; and Simon Schama in art history. There are many other signs of change. One of the most interesting recent shows at the Museum of Modern Art, "Objects of Desire: The Modern Still Life," actually focused on the salutary influence of consumer culture on high culture.

DISCUSSION

1. Twitchell uses the term "mallcondo commercialism" to define the type of materialism he sees as characteristic of American culture. What vision of consumer society does it imply? Do you have as approving a view of this term as Twitchell? Why or why not?

2. Much of Twitchell's argument rests on what benefits he associates with shopping. What, according to this piece, are the advantages or payoffs of playing the role of shopper? How do these benefits compare to your own experiences as a shopper?

3. While acknowledging the ways in which the pursuit of things can lead to the homogenization or flattening of public life, Twitchell nonetheless concludes on a very optimistic note, going so far as to connect consumerist beliefs to the prospect of living a democratic life. On what basis do you think he draws this conclusion? What does he claim is inherently "democratic" about being a consumer? And are you inclined to draw the same conclusion? Why or why not?

WRITING

4. According to Twitchell, consumer society has gained such ascendancy within our society in part because it has come to function as a kind of "secular religion." Write a brief essay in which you assess the validity of this claim. In your view, does it make sense to think of consumerism as a belief system? If so, what kinds of belief does it promote, and what sorts of religious meaning do they have? If not, what is a more accurate term to describe consumerism, and why?

5. In defending consumerism in his larger work, *Lead Us into Temptation*, Twitchell makes the following claim: "We live through things. We create ourselves through things. And we change ourselves by changing our things." Describe an experience from your life that you think reflects, at least to some degree, the argument Twitchell advances here. What example from your life can you find in which a thing you owned fulfilled this promise? As you look back on this example now, does it seem to warrant the conclusion Twitchell draws? How or how not?

6. Ron Rosenbaum (p. 56) is similarly interested in the ways patriotism gets scripted in contemporary culture. His discussion, however, focuses more on the public and political rituals through which such scripts get enacted. How do you think Rosenbaum's definition of patriotism compares to Twitchell's? Do they view this issue in ways you see as similar or different? How?

Then and Now: *Feeling (In)Secure*

To be sure, belief is partly about those things we've been taught to value and embrace, but it's also about those things we've been taught to fear. When it comes to the threats we are told are most dangerous, what exactly are we supposed to believe? How are we taught to define these threats? What instructions are we issued for how to deal with them? These days, no danger looms more ominously or ubiquitously in our lives than the threat of terrorism. From nightly news broadcasts to political speeches, color-coded government alerts to made-for-TV dramas, it is made clear to us in countless different ways that the world is full of shadowy enemies who

despise "our way of life" and are therefore intent on doing us harm. So ingrained has this belief in the omnipresent terrorist threat become, in fact, that we have reorganized major swaths of our public behavior to accommodate it. There is no more vivid illustration of this fact than in the changes that have reshaped modern air travel. For the millions of Americans who travel by plane, things like long lines at security checkpoints, constantly changing restrictions on what may and may not be brought on board, and random body searches have long since become established facts of life. Less clear, though, are the particular anxieties and fears that these new security rituals have simultaneously normalized. Indeed, it could well be argued that all of these precautions and prohibitions have served to make air travel itself into a kind of extended tutorial in how and what we are supposed to fear. Every time we remove our shoes at the security check-in or dispose of our contraband toothpaste before getting on board, we are acting on (and thereby reinforcing) a particular definition of who and what our enemies are.

When framed as an example of cultural instruction, our modern-day preoccupation with terrorist threats starts to look less new than it first appears. The twentieth century in America was marked by a series of "scares" — from the Palmer raid fears about alien immigrants in the 1920s to the anti-communist "red menace" hysteria of the 1950s — which taught Americans to define and fear the threats to the nation in very specific ways. During the Cold War, for instance, which most historians believe started soon after the end of World War II, these fears revolved largely around the twin specters of Soviet Communism and nuclear weapons. Anticipating in many ways the media coverage we see today, television broadcasts and newspaper headlines of this era were replete with warnings about the "enemies" who might be lurking "in our midst"; politicians regularly enjoined audiences to remain vigilant against "sneak attacks," which, they cautioned, could happen at any time. As a result, countless Americans became convinced that their highest civic duty was to prepare against a Soviet missile attack, digging bomb shelters or stocking basements with canned goods. In contrast to the airport restrictions of today, the rituals through which people acted out these fears centered on the classroom. For elementary schoolchildren of the 1950s, air-raid alerts and "duck and cover" drills came to stand as the norm, the mid-century equivalent to the metal detectors and bomb-sniffing dogs of today.

When we place these two sets of security rituals side by side, what (if any) differences do we see? On the basis of the roles scripted for us in these respective eras, does it seem that we've learned to define and deal with the threats confronting us in new and different ways? Or does it seem instead that we've simply carried old attitudes and anxieties forward?

WRITING

1. Compare the ways that each image demonstrates the concept of safety. How are the rituals depicted in these photos designed to make us *feel* about our own safety?

2. While they may seem at first glance merely to be objective portraits, the images can also be read as depicting *public performances* in which people are shown acting out social scripts that have been written for them. It is from this perspective that such activities can start to seem like tutorials in security, scenarios designed to teach us what and how to fear. For each set of activities shown in the photographs, create instructions that lay out the steps for the safety rituals depicted and state why Americans should perform these steps.

RON ROSENBAUM

In Defense of Obama's Patriotism:
A Dissent on the Pledge

From the national anthem at the start of sporting events to the Pledge of Allegiance, our world is rife with rituals, gestures, and symbols designed to affirm our patriotic feelings. But are all of these things really necessary? Do they create roles or script public performances that truly enhance and enrich our love of country? Posing precisely this question, Ron Rosenbaum makes the case that we all might be better off were we to set these long-standing rituals aside. Rosenbaum is a 1968 graduate of Yale University. Since then, his writing has appeared in the *Village Voice, Harper's, Esquire,* and many other publications. He currently writes a column called "The Spectator" for *Slate* and is the author of the books *Explaining Hitler* (1998) and *The Shakespeare Wars* (2006). The following selection was originally published in *Slate* on November 12, 2007.

YOU'VE PROBABLY READ ABOUT THE VIRAL—AND MISLEADING— e-mail accusing Barack Obama of refusing to put his hand over his heart during the Pledge of Allegiance. (The video, in fact, shows him listening to the national anthem with his hands clasped in front of him, although some consider that a sacrilege, too.)

The widely circulated e-mail seems designed to play upon Obama's previous public decision to stop wearing a flag lapel pin. To suggest there's a pattern there. If so, I would say all these pledge-and-pin, hand-and-heart, loyalty-ritual fetishists are misguided about American history, especially the importance to that history of the challenge to loyalty pledges. If it's a pattern in Obama's behavior, I think it's a courageous challenge to conventional wisdom on firm constitutional grounds (however politically self-destructive it may prove in the short run). When was the last time you saw a politician make that trade-off?

Does anyone else feel the way I do? Glad to be an American, privileged and grateful for its freedoms, but conflicted about pins, pledges, flag worshipping, and other rituals of compulsory or socially enforced patriotism, like the hand over the heart during the national anthem?

I certainly *feel* allegiance, though less to the inanimate flag than to "the republic for which it stands," but, paradoxically, the moment when I feel most rebellious about that allegiance is when I'm being forced by state or social coercion to *pledge* allegiance. The America I feel allegiance to isn't the America that requires compulsory displays of loyalty.

I mean no disrespect for those, especially soldiers and veterans, for whom the flag may be more than a symbol, but I think one of the things they fight for is a nation in which "allegiance" includes the right to dissent.

Maybe it's just that I'm not a demonstrative joiner type, but even back in junior high school, I felt resentful of those who thought that love of country must be recited upon request, with hand to heart, like the ritual kissing of the ring of a feudal liege (the root of "allegiance," after all).

> *The America I feel allegiance to isn't the America that requires compulsory displays of loyalty.*

In fact, the first public political act I ever engaged in was when, for some reason, I was motivated to be the only person who spoke up against a showing of a House Un-American Activities Committee propaganda documentary (*Operation Abolition*) at my high school. I just didn't like the idea of people arrogating to themselves the power to tell me what was American and what wasn't.

The state has the right to define what is legal and illegal, sure, but there's a body of law to define those terms, not mere subjective sentiment as with "American" and "un-American"—especially the way "un-American" has been used to taint any and all dissent.

And even more un-American than the original pledge—and even more patently unconstitutional in my view—is the phrase "under God," which Congress added to the pledge in 1954, to make it "to the republic for which it stands, one nation *under God*, indivisible, with liberty and justice for all."

It was troubling enough as a secular loyalty oath, but adding "under God" made it a religious loyalty test. It's clearly unconstitutional, as is most school prayer, although the Supreme Court has so far avoided what will be an explosive decision by finding procedural grounds to reject the most recent suit against it.

Set aside the term's crass sin against humility in its boast of an implicit *endorsement* from the big guy in the sky, "under God" is an advertising slogan—"we've got God on our side"—rather than a visionary ambition like "liberty and justice for all."

Don't the people who want to force this God-added pledge down our throats realize that America was founded by religious dissidents fleeing a state church that forced religious oaths on them? Mouthing that pledge is truly un-American, an insult to the courage of the Pilgrims!

This is not a critique of the feeling of allegiance, just of the coerced Pledge of Allegiance. So don't accuse me of being un-American or a lesser American than you, just less enthusiastic about an essentially anti-American practice. This was, by the way, something I felt even before I knew the Nazi origins of the famous Supreme Court decisions on Jehovah's Witnesses and the pledge.

For those who may have skipped that day in your constitutional-law class, it's worth repeating that the pledge controversy began in Hitler's Germany when the Nazis sent thousands of Jehovah's Witnesses to concentration camps to punish them for refusing to make the Hitler salute to the Nazi flag on the grounds that they don't believe in swearing allegiance to any worldly government and didn't recognize Adolf as a semi-demi-divinity.

As a result, the American leader of the Witnesses denounced the hand-over-heart flag-salute American Pledge of Allegiance on similar grounds. The flag as false idol. It would seem to me other religions should have joined in.

The clash between the Jehovah's Witness pledge-refusenik parents and children and their school boards led to two landmark Supreme Court decisions. In the first 1940 opinion, *Minnersville School District v. Gobitis*, the court ruled 8-1 against the Witnesses. Justice Frankfurter came up with some constitutional mumbo jumbo about how symbols are supposed to help ensure national unity and loyalty and thus override religious-freedom concerns.

Last time I read the Constitution (I admit it's been a while), I didn't find anything like that, even in the penumbra of the penumbra.

But Justice Harlan Fiske Stone, in what has become a celebrated dissent, treated even the pre-"Under God" pledge as a kind of religious ritual mandated by the state, designed to advance "conformity" rather than "religious liberty."

And then he added this great line:

> History teaches us that there have been but few infringements of personal liberty by the state which have not been justified, as they are here, in the name of righteousness and the public good, and few which have not been directed, as they are now, at politically helpless minorities.

Beautiful!

And then three years later, a different Supreme Court (a couple of new justices) reversed itself in *West Virginia State Board of Education v. Barnette*, and speaking for the new majority, Justice Robert Jackson wrote:

> If there is any fixed star in our constitutional constellation, it is that no official, high or petty, can prescribe what shall be orthodox in politics, nationalism, religion, or other matters of opinion or force citizens to confess by word or act their faith therein.

Yes! The pledge is a kind of forced confession of orthodoxy. No, not water-boarding, but coercion nonetheless. Especially for peer-group-pressured school kids. Even if they have the right to opt out. In past school-prayer cases, the court has resisted the idea that the state should be implicated in even the social coercion or propagation of religion.

Busybody school boards and bombastic anthem peddlers at ball games should let people find their way to allegiance in their own fashion rather than making "allegiance" an implement of state power used to extract oaths.

Is it possible—is it conceivable—that at great risk to his political ambitions Barack Obama is doing things like doffing the flag pin and putting his hands at his sides during the anthem because he is being honest about the inner reservations he may feel at such practices?

Not the pledge. He's told an affecting story about how his grandfather taught him to put his hand over his heart while taking the pledge.

Still, that picture in the viral e-mail of Obama listening to the anthem while standing—looking all casual, with hands clasped—next to two people with hands over their hearts, could be taken two ways. It could suggest that he doesn't think there's anything wrong with the anthem, but it's not as deserving as the pledge of hand over heart. Or it

> *The pledge is a kind of forced confession of orthodoxy.*

could be a way of saying that sacralizing a song with hand to heart is akin in meaningfulness to wearing a flag lapel pin. And that he's not going to disguise his attitude for superficial political considerations. That, in a way, he's saying, "If you reject me for being honest about this, it's your loss as well as mine."

It's probably too much to hope that it's all that deliberate. That he feels it's worth making a point, starting a debate about real patriotism, rather than faking it for the sake of making it. If he does, though, his argument is intellectually superior, however politically inopportune. And not a distraction from "real issues" like the war, because arguments about what is and what isn't "American" and "un-American" are being thrown around indiscriminately in that debate.

Justice Harlan Fiske Stone was in an 8-1 minority when he dissented and called the pledge for what it was. Now we revere his words. As we do Justice Jackson's "fixed star" analogy. I'm sure Obama, a Harvard law school student, is quite familiar with these decisions and the thinking behind them.

Is it too much to hope that's what's going through his mind? Maybe. But Obama's all about the audacity of hope, right?

DISCUSSION

1. Rosenbaum uses the phrase "pledge-and-pin, hand-and-heart, loyalty-ritual fetishists" to describe people who believe it is imperative for public figures to wear an American flag lapel pin. How do you respond to this characterization? What larger point — about current cultural rules regarding flag pins and the norms that underlie this particular script — does this kind of language suggest Rosenbaum is trying to make about these people? What is your own personal reaction to this language? Do you find it troublesome or offensive? Accurate or amusing? Why?

2. Among other historical analogies Rosenbaum draws in this essay is one connecting the Pledge of Allegiance to loyalty oaths imposed by the Nazis. How do you respond to this comparison? In your view, is this a valid or fair parallel to draw? How or how not?

3. Rosenbaum takes particular issue with the religious language ("under God") included in the modern Pledge of Allegiance. What specifically does he find problematic or wrong about the inclusion of such language? Do you agree?

WRITING

4. What is your personal relationship to patriotic rituals like the Pledge of Allegiance? Describe and reflect on your own experiences with reciting the Pledge of Allegiance or singing the "Star-Spangled Banner". Where and when were you called on to follow this kind of social script? How did it feel to play this role? Do your personal experiences challenge or reinforce the argument Rosenbaum is making here about the dangers of what he calls "compulsory patriotism"? Why or why not?

5. Much of Rosenbaum's argument here revolves around an attempt to rethink the notion of dissent. Write an essay in which you describe how Rosenbaum recharacterizes common notions of dissent and allegiance. How does he define each term? How are they related, in his opinion? Does this relationship make sense to you? Why or why not? In what ways is it more accurate to view *dissent* and *allegiance* as opposing terms?

6. Rosenbaum refers to rituals like the Pledge of Allegiance as "socially enforced patriotism." What does he mean by this? Do you agree that institutions and authorities around us can enforce beliefs like patriotism? And how does this understanding of belief as socially enforced compare to the one presented by conservative writer David Brooks (p. 68)? Does Brooks's discussion of diversity reflect a similar conviction that beliefs — rather than personal or private values — can actually be scripted for us by forces beyond our immediate control?

CATHERINE NEWMAN

I Do. Not.:
Why I Won't Marry

In this essay, Catherine Newman offers her views on both the allure and the pitfalls of monogamy. What does it mean, she asks, to choose a "lifelong partner"? In answering this question, she spends a good deal of time exploring the monogamy-marriage paradigm that stands as the norm in our culture. Along the way, Newman tells her personal story as well, describing her own efforts to situate her "unconventional" relationship within the parameters established by this norm. Newman is the author of the memoir *Waiting for Birdy* (2005) and writes a blog about parenting called *Bringing Up Ben and Birdy.* Her essays have appeared in the *New York Times* and have been collected in a number of anthologies, including *The Bitch in the House* (2002), where this essay comes from. She lives in Amherst, Massachusetts, with her partner and their two children.

OF COURSE NOBODY THINKS TO ASK ME AND MICHAEL—MY PARTNER of eleven years and the father of our two-year-old son—why we're not married until we're all at a *wedding,* which is kind of awkward, at best. "Um, maybe because marriage is a tool of the *patriarchy?*" I could say, and smile and take another bite of poached salmon and wink across the table at the bride and groom. But I don't, because I love weddings, and I'm in a borrowed stone-colored outfit, and I probably cried when the bride kissed her parents at the altar and I've just read my special passage from Rumi or Rainer Maria Rilke, and I'm buzzed and happy and eating the entrée I checked off on the reply card months ago. And Michael's terribly handsome in his blazer, and he's probably touching my linen-encased thigh under the table, moony and drunk off of other people's vows. But somebody's father or uncle always has to lean over, all shiny and loose with champagne, and ruin it. "So, how come you two aren't doing this?" he might ask, with a hand gesture that takes in the bride, the cake, the open bar. My best bet is to stall elaborately over a mouthful of fish. There are so many reasons, and they're all only partly true and shot through with contradiction, and I can't say any of them out loud—not here, anyway.

Because marriage is about handing the woman off, like a baton, from her father to her husband. Also known as "traffic in women," this is how men have historically solid̶̶̶̶̶̶̶̶̶̶̶̶̶̶̶̶̶̶̶ic connections to other men (think *empires*; think *in-l̶̶̶̶̶̶̶̶̶̶̶̶̶̶* continuation of their

Seed. The woman has always, of course, been deeply valued for her own sake, hence the *dowry* that required her family to bribe another family with lots of money and cattle and embroidered pillow shams to take her off their hands. Thank goodness we're so much more evolved now. Except, of course, for the embarrassing detail of the bride's family shelling out the ten or fifty thousand dollars for the wedding itself. And the awkward transfer of the veiled woman, father to son-in-law, at the altar. Wives can bear a disconcerting resemblance to

Wives can bear a disconcerting resemblance to objects.

objects. Back in the sixteenth century, adultery was a crime of theft (like making off with your neighbor's snowblower), since wives were no less, or more, than personal property. Thank goodness we're so much more evolved now. Except at a very Catholic wedding we attended recently where the bride was handed a lit candle, which she used to light a candle for her husband. She then had to blow out the first candle, which was supposed to represent her naughty old independent self—the same lucky self that had now been absorbed, and extinguished, by her husband. Hooray for modernity.

Because the Religious Right and their Defense of Marriage Act use marriage as a vehicle for homophobic legislation. Marriage is, of course, a supremely natural and God-given institution and a naturally and God-givenly straight one. But *just in case,* we'd better treat it like it's a fragile and gasping little injured bird, and we'll make it illegal for gay people to even visit a town where there's a bridal boutique. As long as they don't tell us they're gay, though, they can still serve as our Wedding Coordinators, because, let's face it, they really do understand fabrics and color. That's the political version. There's another, less noble version: *Because I'd feel like a real A-hole if I put on a beaded cream bodice and vowed myself away in front of all our gay friends—smiling and polite in their dark silk shirts or gossiping wickedly about our choice of canapés—who cannot themselves marry.* Not that they would all deign to get married, even if they could (see above). But what they're snubbing should certainly be a viable option.

Because I could, myself, have ended up with a woman. Into my mid-twenties, I spent some time in love and in bed with women—a handful of astonishing romances that left me with a lot of steamy memories and a crew cut. You can imagine my horror, then, when I surreptitiously bedded and fell in love with Michael, who played hockey (ice, roller, *and* video) and was relentlessly cheerful. A handsome, athletic, doting guy: not my ideal specimen for a life partner, but there it was. I persist in the knowledge that women are, way more often than not, sexier, funnier, kinder, and more interesting than men. All of my friends certainly are. Do I still think of myself as bisexual? If a tree falls in the forest but you're inside reading *Spotted Yellow Frogs* for the fourth time in five minutes, do you give a shit? If you have ever lived with a two-year-old, then you know that Grappling With Your Sexuality does not tend to make it onto the roster of daily activity goals, like brushing your teeth or not locking the baby in the car with your keys. My mind, it is not such a vibrant organ these days. I can squint past the clogging mass of words like "nasal aspirator" and "glycerin suppositories" and just barely make out the dim shape of a memory of sexual identity, but that's about it. Pulling the crispy skin off of a roast chicken and eating it right there in the kitchen, before the bird even makes it to the table—now *that's* a sensual act worth defending. Especially these days, when our bed is more like a museum of Cheerios artifacts than a place of sexual worship. But it does seem weaselly to participate in a privilege—specifically, marriage—that I would have been denied if I had ended up engaged in a different kind of relationship. Or, really, just a different configuration of wild-thing hydraulics, which is all we're actually talking about here. (I do love the idea that the Law has nothing better to do than referee the naked Hokey Pokey: "No, no—you put *that* in. No! No! Not in *there!* Yes, we know it happens to *fit* there, but that's not where it belongs.")

Because we don't believe in monogamy. At least in theory. Can it possibly be that climbing onto the same exact person for fifty years maximizes the erotic potential of our brief fling here on earth? Especially back in the early days, when I identified more physically and politically as bisexual (*Bisexual People Speak Out!* is a book I had, which makes me want to write, for kids, something more mundanely exuberant like *Bisexual People Buy Bananas!*), it seemed cruel and unusual that one should have to give up so much in order to commit to a man. Open, honest nonmonogamy seemed like the ideal solution. Abstractly, it sounded righteous and right. But in real life, nonmonogamy can sound more like your partner's lover revving a motorcycle right outside your bedroom window, which is just a total bummer. It can look, more or less, like a trampy, selfish bout of sleeping around, talking about it, and hurting everybody's feelings. Beliefs, even strongly held ones, can be somewhat aloof from the world where people actually *feel* things. We are too well trained in the grammar of possession and jealousy, too mired in the blurring of sex and love, to simply turn our backs on convention; we are poorly insulated from the sharp pokes of heartsoreness and humiliation.

And, it turns out, that *third* person inevitably has feelings, too, of all things! Feelings you can't control, not even by chanting "I'll never leave my boyfriend" over and over like a mantra. That third person might even be likely, in fact, to have *extra* feelings, the kind that find expression only in phoning compulsively throughout the night or popping by after supper with an ice pick. Michael and I were ultimately so strained by a few rounds of nondomestic toad-in-the-hole that we gave it up. (A friend of mine who is a famously radical theorist of sexuality once said, tiredly, "Maybe sex just doesn't even *matter* that much.") But we still believe in honesty over the sticky lies of the motel room; we still believe in imagination over living by the available scripts; and we believe, I hope, in treating each other's desires with respect and compassion. We still believe in the *principle* of nonmonogamy, even if we don't have the energy to do it.

Because I will not be possessed. Michael holds everything that comes into his life—our son, a peeled orange, a bath towel, me—as if it is as fragile and fleeting as a soap bubble; he has the lightest, most beautiful touch. And yet—and this is the worst, brattiest king of contradiction—I wish sometimes that he would demand that I marry him, that he would despair so poetically and much about his great love for me that he would have to possess me entirely. (Sometimes, because we share a decade of inside jokes about ourselves, Michael slits his eyes at me over lunch and snarls, "I *must* have you this instant," with his bare foot pressing around in my lap and the baby grinning gamely from his high chair.) Michael is not, how shall I say it, the most passionate tool in the shed. We were recently leafing through our photo album, and there's this glorious picture of me, forty weeks pregnant, which he took himself, and I'm naked and radiant with the gold of the sunset illuminating my huge, ripe belly, two days before the harrowing and miraculous birth of our baby, and Michael says only, about a half-full plastic bottle in the foreground, "Oh, honey, remember how you made that fruit punch? Yum."

You know that kind of romance where your hair is always all matted in the back and you get rug burns on your elbows, and you stay awake all night chain-smoking and watching each other breathe? Everyone has at least one of these. ("Mmmm, the hot dog man," my friend Megan sighed over her passionate interlude with a snack vendor.) Michael's more likely to hop up after sex and say, amiably, "Want a bowl of Golden Grahams? I'm having one." So he would, for instance, never punch someone out over me, like my beautiful and spindly high school boyfriend who once, on the subway, shook his bony, lunatic fist in the face of an innocent bystander and growled, "You staring at my woman?"

But even though I catch myself longing for it sometimes, the truth is that extremes of passion have unnerved me. The people who write poems about your forearm hairs glistening in the moonlight are the same ones who, later, throw beer bottles through your kitchen window from the street and call drunk and weepy every New Year's Eve. They're the same ones who don't always seem to actually *know* you that well—who say baffling, wrong things like, "I just really love how *calm* you are," which send you reeling out to the bookstore to skim *The Complete Idiot's Guide to Zen Meditation.* The best life partner might, I think, be the one who sees you as you are and loves that person—the person who is boring and anxious or blotchy from a weekly scrub mask—not the imaginary one who is poetic and broodingly smart and sexy and ecstatic all the time. The best life partner is exactly the sort of person who doesn't crave possession.

The best life partner is exactly the sort of person who doesn't crave possession.

Because not being married means we get to keep choosing each other. Can married people do this? Of course they can (although one married friend described this as the difference between, in our case, choosing to stay together and, in hers, choosing not to divorce). For us, there's something psychically liberating about that little bit of unmarried space that allows us to move forward, to come toward each other, over and over again. Michael knows me deeply—he sees me truly—and, astonishingly, keeps deciding to stay with me. He can walk into the bathroom while I'm tweezing the hairs on my chin, wrap his arms around my waist, and smile gently at me into the mirror, instead of shouting, "Step right up, folks! See the incredible Bearded Lady!" which is what I would surely do in his place. When I'm not completely infuriated over his occasional bouts of remoteness, or overwhelmed by the frantic dullness that can suck the life out of making a home together, I look at Michael and breathe a huge sigh of relief. I would choose him again this second: his strong shoulders from rocking our baby to sleep every afternoon; his utter lack of unkindness; the way he finds the things I've lost—keys, my cardigan—and then returns them to me as gifts, all wrapped up in fancy paper and ribbons. If you believe, and I do, that people are secretly their truest selves in the middle of the night, then my truest self might be, "Are you going to snore like that until I put a bullet in my head?" Michael's is, "Oh, sweetheart, can't you sleep?" whilst he pats the smooth, cool of his chest for me to crawl onto. I would choose that again in a heartbeat.

Because we have a kid together. So, um, scratch that last paragraph, because I am stuck with Michael forever. What more permanent soul binding can there be than the sharing of a child? This is the real till-death-do-us-part. We could still split up, of course, but only if the benefits seemed distinctly greater than, say, the awkwardness of showing up separately at all the same bar mitzvahs and eighth-grade performances of *Our Town*; and still, we would be ultimately connected. When we were in the hospital, with the baby just born and the three of us in love in our matching plastic ID bracelets like a little nuclear gang, a yearning flitted through me for all of us to have the same last name; I really got it, for a minute—that desire for a united front. (Instead, the baby has my last name. Don't try this unless you want to spend the rest of your life with everybody getting all panicked and sweaty and saying, "Oh, that's so *fascinating!*" about it, as if your kid has an extra limb sprouting from his forehead.) But we are that, anyway—a united front—with or without a shared name or the deed to our relationship. The difference between us and a married couple, apart from some nuances of tax paying and title wielding (Mrs. Michael J. Millner? Who could that possibly be, besides his drag-queen persona?), is slender indeed.

Because we already have rings, is what we always end up saying, and we hold up our hands as proof of commitment. "We got them on our seventh anniversary—seven years is common-law marriage in California."

Common-law marriage? That and three-fifty will get you a latte at Starbucks. We don't even know what it means. But for somebody's father or uncle at a wedding, it tends to settle the issue more often than not. Nobody has to know that we fought like the dickens while we were *getting* the rings—that Michael, instead of gazing at me committedly, was humming a Coors Light jingle (he doesn't even *drink* beer), which enraged me inexplicably much. So much that, in the end, instead of the intimate, beachside vows we had planned, there was merely a "Take your stupid ring!" accompanied by the peevish flinging of velvet boxes.

But I do wear his ring. He is the father of my child. I take Michael in contradiction and in mayhem. In grief and in delight. To cherish, dismay, and split burritos with. For good company and daily comfort. For the tornado of rage and for love. I take him. I do.

DISCUSSION

1. Newman begins by evoking a stereotypical wedding scene. Why do you think she decides to begin her essay this way? What kind of framework does this opening establish for her subsequent discussion of her own unconventional relationship?

2. What are the specific roles that Newman worries the conventional marriage model scripts for her? What specifically does she think is wrong, dangerous, or problematic about following these scripts?

3. What are your experiences with what Newman calls the "marriage paradigm"? Have you or people you know struggled with decisions over how or even whether to marry? How do these experiences compare with the problems and questions posed in this essay? Does Newman's discussion give you any different vantage on your experiences? How or how not?

WRITING

4. Among other things, this essay asks us to look closely at the rituals that have come to define the conventional wedding ceremony. Write an essay in which you analyze the particular messages (for example, about marriage, relationships, gender, monogamy, economics, or the like) you think these conventional rituals are designed to convey.

5. Newman structures her essay very deliberately as a string of *because* statements that all respond to the single question of why she doesn't want to get married. Write your own essay about some common rite of passage that you don't believe is for you (for example, getting an office job, having children, or joining a fraternity or sorority), styling your response after Newman. Then, write a short reflection on why you think Newman chose this particular style for her response and whether you believe it is effective.

6. Newman devotes a good part of her discussion to tracing the unspoken assumptions that have served throughout history to legitimatize the conventional monogamous-marriage model. Write an essay in which you describe and analyze some of the assumptions and ideas that this traditional model has historically excluded. What makes them incompatible with those that have been elevated as the norm? How would our notions about and definitions of marriage change if these alternative assumptions were accorded wider acceptance?

DAVID BROOKS
People Like Us

What norms surround how we think about race? In this essay, David Brooks takes up some of the key terms that currently anchor our public discussions of race, prompting us to think about the assumptions we bring to bear on this question. Do we, he asks, really care about diversity? And even more provocatively, should we? Brooks, a prominent voice for conservative politics, has been a columnist at the *New York Times* since 2003. He has also worked at the *Weekly Standard, Newsweek,* and the *Atlantic Monthly* and is a regular commentator on NPR's *All Things Considered* and PBS's *NewsHour.* He has published two books of commentary on American culture, *Bobos in Paradise: The New Upper Class and How They Got There* (2000) and *On Paradise Drive: How We Live Now (and Always Have) in the Future Tense* (2004). The following essay first appeared in the September 2003 issue of the *Atlantic Monthly.*

MAYBE IT'S TIME TO ADMIT THE OBVIOUS. WE DON'T REALLY CARE about diversity all that much in America, even though we talk about it a great deal. Maybe somewhere in this country there is a truly diverse neighborhood in which a black Pentecostal minister lives next to a white anti-globalization activist, who lives next to an Asian short-order cook, who lives next to a professional golfer, who lives next to a postmodern-literature professor and a cardiovascular surgeon. But I have never been to or heard of that neighborhood. Instead, what I have seen all around the country is people making strenuous efforts to group themselves with people who are basically like themselves.

Human beings are capable of drawing amazingly subtle social distinctions and then shaping their lives around them. In the Washington, D.C., area Democratic lawyers tend to live in suburban Maryland, and Republican lawyers tend to live in suburban Virginia. If you asked a Democratic lawyer to move from her $750,000 house in Bethesda, Maryland, to a $750,000 house in Great Falls, Virginia, she'd look at you as if you had just asked her to buy a pickup truck with a gun rack and to shove chewing tobacco in her kid's mouth. In Manhattan the owner of a $3 million SoHo loft would feel out of place moving into a $3 million Fifth Avenue apartment. A West Hollywood interior decorator would feel dislocated if you asked him to move to Orange County. In Georgia a barista from Athens would probably not fit in serving coffee in Americus.

It is a common complaint that every place is starting to look the same. But in the information age, the late writer James Chapin once told me, every place becomes more like itself. People are less often tied down to factories and mills, and they can search for places to live on the basis of cultural affinity. Once they find a town in which people share their values, they flock there, and reinforce whatever was distinctive about the town in the first place. Once Boulder, Colorado, became known as congenial to politically progressive mountain bikers, half the politically progressive mountain bikers in the country (it seems) moved there; they made the place so culturally pure that it has become practically a parody of itself.

But people love it. Make no mistake—we are increasing our happiness by segmenting off so rigorously. We are finding places where we are comfortable and where we feel we can flourish. But the choices we make toward that end lead to the very opposite of diversity. The United States might be a diverse nation when considered as a whole, but block by block and institution by institution it is a relatively homogeneous nation.

> **We are increasing our happiness by segmenting off so rigorously.**

When we use the word "diversity" today we usually mean racial integration. But even here our good intentions seem to have run into the brick wall of human nature. Over the past generation reformers have tried heroically, and in many cases successfully, to end housing discrimination. But recent patterns aren't encouraging: according to an analysis of the 2000 census data, the 1990s saw only a slight increase in the racial integration of neighborhoods in the United States. The number of middle-class and upper-middle-class African-American families is rising, but for whatever reasons—racism, psychological comfort—these families tend to congregate in predominantly black neighborhoods.

In fact, evidence suggests that some neighborhoods become more segregated over time. New suburbs in Arizona and Nevada, for example, start out reasonably well integrated. These neighborhoods don't yet have reputations, so people choose their houses for other, mostly economic reasons. But as neighborhoods age, they develop personalities (that's where the Asians live, and that's where the Hispanics live), and segmentation occurs. It could be that in a few years the new suburbs in the Southwest will be nearly as segregated as the established ones in the Northeast and the Midwest.

Even though race and ethnicity run deep in American society, we should in theory be able to find areas that are at least culturally diverse. But here, too, people show few signs of being truly interested in building diverse communities. If you run a retail company and you're thinking of opening new stores, you can choose among dozens of consulting firms that are quite effective at locating your potential customers. They can do this because people with similar tastes and preferences tend to congregate by ZIP code.

The most famous of these precision marketing firms is Claritas, which breaks down the U.S population into sixty-two psycho-demographic clusters, based on such factors as how much money people make, what they like to read and watch, and what products they have bought in the past. For example, the "suburban sprawl" cluster is composed of young families making about $41,000 a year and living in fast-growing places such as Burnsville, Minnesota, and Bensalem, Pennsylvania. These people are almost twice as likely as other Americans to have three-way calling. They are two and a half times as likely to buy Light n' Lively Kid Yogurt. Members of the "towns & gowns" cluster are recent college graduates in places such as Berkeley, California, and Gainesville, Florida. They are big consumers of Dove Bars and *Saturday Night Live*. They tend to drive small foreign cars and to read *Rolling Stone* and *Scientific American*.

Looking through the market research, one can sometimes be amazed by how efficiently people cluster—and by how predictable we all are. If you wanted to sell imported wine, obviously you would have to find places where rich people live. But did you know that the sixteen counties with the greatest proportion of imported-wine drinkers are all in the same three metropolitan areas (New York, San Francisco, and Washington, D.C.)? If you tried to open a motor-home dealership in Montgomery County, Pennsylvania, you'd probably go broke, because people in this ring of the Philadelphia suburbs think RVs are kind of uncool. But if you traveled just a short way north, to Monroe County, Pennsylvania, you would find yourself in the fifth motor-home-friendliest county in America.

Geography is not the only way we find ourselves divided from people unlike us. Some of us watch Fox News, while others listen to NPR. Some like David Letterman, and others—typically in less urban neighborhoods—like Jay Leno. Some go to charismatic churches; some go to mainstream churches. Americans tend more and more often to marry people with education levels similar to their own, and to befriend people with backgrounds similar to their own.

My favorite illustration of this latter pattern comes from the first, noncontroversial chapter of *The Bell Curve*. Think of your twelve closest friends, Richard J. Herrnstein and Charles Murray write. If you had chosen them randomly from the American population, the odds that half of your twelve closest friends would be college graduates would be six in a thousand. The odds that half of the twelve would have advanced degrees would be less than one in a million. Have any of your twelve closest friends graduated from Harvard, Stanford, Yale, Princeton, Caltech, MIT, Duke, Dartmouth, Cornell, Columbia, Chicago, or Brown? If you chose your friends randomly from the American population, the odds against your having four or more friends from those schools would be more than a billion to one.

Many of us live in absurdly unlikely groupings, because we have organized our lives that way.

It's striking that the institutions that talk the most about diversity often practice it the least. For example, no group of people sings the diversity anthem more frequently and fervently than administrators at just such elite universities. But elite universities are amazingly undiverse in their values, politics, and mores. Professors in particular are drawn from a rather narrow segment of the population. If faculties reflected the general population, 32 percent of professors would be registered Democrats and 31 percent would be registered Republicans. Forty percent would be evangelical Christians. But a recent study of several universities by the conservative Center for the Study of Popular Culture and the American Enterprise Institute found that roughly 90 percent of those professors in the arts and sciences who had registered with a political party had registered Democratic. Fifty-seven professors at Brown were found on the voter-registration rolls. Of those, fifty-four were Democrats. Of the forty-two professors in the English, history, sociology, and political-science departments, all were Democrats. The results at Harvard, Penn State, Maryland, and the University of California at Santa Barbara were similar to the results at Brown.

What we are looking at here is human nature. People want to be around others who are roughly like themselves. That's called community. It probably would be psychologically difficult for most Brown professors to share an office with someone who was pro-life, a member of the National Rifle Association, or an evangelical Christian. It's likely that hiring committees would subtly—even unconsciously—screen out any such people they encountered. Republicans and evangelical Christians have sensed that they are not welcome at places like

> **People want to be around others who are roughly like themselves. That's called community.**

Brown, so they don't even consider working there. In fact, any registered Republican who contemplates a career in academia these days is both a hero and a fool. So, in a semi-self-selective pattern, brainy people with generally liberal social mores flow to academia, and brainy people with generally conservative mores flow elsewhere.

The dream of diversity is like the dream of equality. Both are based on ideals we celebrate even as we undermine them daily. (How many times have you seen someone renounce a high-paying job or pull his child from an elite college on the grounds that these things are bad for equality?) On the one hand, the situation is appalling. It is appalling that

Americans know so little about one another. It is appalling that many of us are so narrow-minded that we can't tolerate a few people with ideas significantly different from our own. It's appalling that evangelical Christians are practically absent from entire professions, such as academia, the media, and filmmaking. It's appalling that people should be content to cut themselves off from everyone unlike themselves.

The segmentation of society means that often we don't even have arguments across the political divide. Within their little validating communities, liberals and conservatives circulate half-truths about the supposed awfulness of the other side. These distortions are believed because it feels good to believe them.

On the other hand, there are limits to how diverse any community can or should be. I've come to think that it is not useful to try to hammer diversity into every neighborhood and institution in the United States. Sure, Augusta National should probably admit women, and university sociology departments should probably hire a conservative or two. It would be nice if all neighborhoods had a good mixture of ethnicities. But human nature being what it is, most places and institutions are going to remain culturally homogeneous.

It's probably better to think about diverse lives, not diverse institutions. Human beings, if they are to live well, will have to move through a series of institutions and environments, which may be individually homogeneous but, taken together, will offer diverse experiences. It might also be a good idea to make national service a rite of passage for young people in this country: it would take them out of their narrow neighborhood segment and thrust them in with people unlike themselves. Finally, it's probably important for adults to get out of their own familiar circles. If you live in a coastal, socially liberal neighborhood, maybe you should take out a subscription to the *Door*, the evangelical humor magazine; or maybe you should visit Branson, Missouri. Maybe you should stop in at a megachurch. Sure, it would be superficial familiarity, but it beats the iron curtains that now separate the nation's various cultural zones.

Look around at your daily life. Are you really in touch with the broad diversity of American life? Do you care?

DISCUSSION

1. According to Brooks, our good intentions to create a more racially integrated society have failed because they "have run into the brick wall of human nature." Do you agree? Is segregation in America largely or exclusively a matter of human nature? And what kinds of solutions to this problem does such an understanding imply?

2. What do you make of the title of Brooks's essay? What, in his view, makes choosing "people like us" a preferable option to that of integration?

3. One of the main assumptions behind Brooks's argument is that issues like where we live and whom we associate with are fundamentally matters of personal choice. How accurately do you think his discussion treats the issue of choice? Do we all possess this kind of freedom to choose? And if not, what factors or circumstances undermine this possibility?

WRITING

4. Brooks ends his essay by challenging his readers: "Look around at your daily life. Are you really in touch with the broad diversity of American life? Do you care?" Write an essay in which you respond directly to Brooks's questions. How does the organization of your life (for example, by community, by living situation, by leisure activities) either support or refute Brooks's argument? In a hypothetical world that reflected an idealized portrait of diversity, what would need to change in the ways your life is structured to bring you in line with the ideal?

5. What kind of reader do you think would respond most favorably to Brooks's argument? Write an essay in which you sketch out a portrait of the ideal reader for this essay. What background, education, or political beliefs would this ideal reader have? What attitudes, values, or worldview? Make sure to explain, using quotes from Brooks's essay, why you define this reader in the ways you do. In what ways does defining this ideal reader strengthen or diminish Brooks's argument?

6. To what extent does Brooks's discussion of diversity intersect with Debra Dickerson's (p. 86) critique of what could be called "scientific racism," or the notion that race is permanently fixed in biology? Write an assessment of the differing ways these two authors seem to understand the issue of racial difference. What particular features of each author's argument accounts for the contrasting conclusions?

PO BRONSON AND ASHLEY MERRYMAN

See Baby Discriminate

There is little dispute that racial attitudes, rather than being innate or natural, are culturally acquired. But at what age exactly does this acquisition process begin? Is it possible that the scripts teaching us how to think about, view, and value racial difference begin to exert influence before we are even able to walk or talk? Contemplating precisely this possibility, the authors here discuss surprising research about the ways that children perceive racial difference from very young ages. Po Bronson is a novelist and journalist whose writing has appeared in the *New York Times, Wired,* and *Time*, where he wrote a column about American cultural trends and morality. His nonfiction books include *What Should I Do with My Life?* (2002) and *Why Do I Love These People?* (2005). Ashley Merryman is a writer and attorney who lives in Los Angeles. She was a speechwriter for former vice president Al Gore. She currently runs a church-based tutoring program for inner-city children. In 2009, Bronson and Merryman cowrote columns for Newsweek.com about the science of parenting and child development, which they published as a book entitled *NurtureShock: New Thinking about Children.* The following originally appeared in the September 19, 2009, issue of *Newsweek* and is also included in *NurtureShock.*

AT THE CHILDREN'S RESEARCH LAB AT THE UNIVERSITY OF TEXAS, a database is kept on thousands of families in the Austin area who have volunteered to be available for scholarly research. In 2006 Birgitte Vittrup recruited from the database about a hundred families, all of whom were Caucasian with a child 5 to 7 years old.

The goal of Vittrup's study was to learn if typical children's videos with multicultural storylines have any beneficial effect on children's racial attitudes. Her first step was to give the children a Racial Attitude Measure, which asked such questions as:

- How many White people are nice?
  (Almost all) (A lot) (Some) (Not many) (None)

- How many Black people are nice?
  (Almost all) (A lot) (Some) (Not many) (None)

During the test, the descriptive adjective "nice" was replaced with more than 20 other adjectives, like "dishonest," "pretty," "curious," and "snobby."

Vittrup sent a third of the families home with multiculturally themed videos for a week, such as an episode of *Sesame Street* in which characters visit an African-American family's home, and an episode of *Little Bill*, where the entire neighborhood comes together to clean the local park.

In truth, Vittrup didn't expect that children's racial attitudes would change very much just from watching these videos. Prior research had shown that multicultural curricula in schools have far less impact than we intend them to—largely because the implicit message "We're all friends" is too vague for young children to understand that it refers to skin color.

Yet Vittrup figured explicit conversations with parents could change that. So a second group of families got the videos, and Vittrup told these parents to use them as the jumping-off point for a discussion about interracial friendship. She provided a checklist of points to make, echoing the shows' themes. "I really believed it was going to work," Vittrup recalls.

The last third were also given the checklist of topics, but no videos. These parents were to discuss racial equality on their own, every night for five nights.

At this point, something interesting happened. Five families in the last group abruptly quit the study. Two directly told Vittrup, "We don't want to have these conversations with our child. We don't want to point out skin color."

Vittrup was taken aback—these families volunteered knowing full well it was a study of children's racial attitudes. Yet once they were aware that the study required talking openly about race, they started dropping out.

It was no surprise that in a liberal city like Austin, every parent was a welcoming multiculturalist, embracing diversity. But according to Vittrup's entry surveys, hardly any of these white parents had ever talked to their children directly about race. They might have asserted vague principles—like "Everybody's equal" or "God made all of us" or "Under the skin, we're all the same"—but they'd almost never called attention to racial differences.

They wanted their children to grow up colorblind. But Vittrup's first test of the kids revealed they weren't colorblind at all. Asked how many white people are mean, these children commonly answered, "Almost none." Asked how many blacks are mean, many answered, "Some," or "A lot." Even kids who attended diverse schools answered the questions this way.

More disturbing, Vittrup also asked all the kids a very blunt question: "Do your parents like black people?" Fourteen percent said outright, "No, my parents don't like black people"; 38 percent of the kids answered, "I don't know." In this supposed race-free vacuum being created by parents, kids were left to improvise their own conclusions—many of which would be abhorrent to their parents.

Vittrup hoped the families she'd instructed to talk about race would follow through. After watching the videos, the families returned to the Children's Research Lab for retesting. To Vittrup's complete surprise, the three groups of children were statistically the same—none, as a group, had budged very much in their racial attitudes. At first glance, the study was a failure.

Combing through the parents' study diaries, Vittrup realized why. Diary after diary revealed that the parents barely mentioned the checklist items. Many just couldn't talk about race, and they quickly reverted to the vague "Everybody's equal" phrasing.

Of all those Vittrup told to talk openly about interracial friendship, only six families managed to actually do so. And, for all six, their children dramatically improved their racial attitudes in a single week. Talking about race was clearly key. Reflecting later about the study, Vittrup said, "A lot of parents came to me afterwards and admitted they just didn't know what to say to their kids, and they didn't want the wrong thing coming out of the mouth of their kids."

> **In this race-free vacuum, kids were left to improvise their own conclusions— many of which would be abhorrent to their parents.**

We all want our children to be unintimidated by differences and have the social skills necessary for a diverse world. The question is, do we make it worse, or do we make it better, by calling attention to race?

The election of President Barack Obama marked the beginning of a new era in race relations in the United States—but it didn't resolve the question as to what we should tell children about race. Many parents have explicitly pointed out Obama's brown skin to their young children, to reinforce the message that anyone can rise to become a leader, and anyone— regardless of skin color—can be a friend, be loved, and be admired.

Others think it's better to say nothing at all about the president's race or ethnicity—because saying something about it unavoidably teaches a child a racial construct. They worry that even a positive statement ("It's wonderful that a black person can be president") still encourages a child to see divisions within society. For the early formative years, at least, they believe we should let children know a time when skin color does not matter.

What parents say depends heavily on their own race: a 2007 study in the *Journal of Marriage and Family* found that out of 17,000 families with kindergartners, nonwhite parents are about three times more likely to discuss race than white parents; 75 percent of the latter never, or almost never, talk about race.

In our new book, *NurtureShock*, we argue that many modern strategies for nurturing children are backfiring—because key twists in the science have been overlooked. Small corrections in our thinking today could alter the character of society long term, one future citizen at a time. The way white families introduce the concept of race to their children is a prime example.

For decades, it was assumed that children see race only when society points it out to them. However, child-development researchers have increasingly begun to question that presumption. They argue that children see racial differences as much as they see the difference between pink and blue—but we tell kids that "pink" means for girls and "blue" is for boys. "White" and "black" are mysteries we leave them to figure out on their own.

It takes remarkably little for children to develop in-group preferences. Vittrup's mentor at the University of Texas, Rebecca Bigler, ran an experiment in three preschool classrooms, where 4- and 5-year-olds were lined up and given T shirts. Half the kids were randomly given blue T shirts, half red. The children wore the shirts for three weeks. During that time, the teachers never mentioned their colors and never grouped the kids by shirt color.

The kids didn't segregate in their behavior. They played with each other freely at recess. But when asked which color team was better to belong to, or which team might win a race, they chose their own color. They believed they were smarter than the other color. "The Reds never showed hatred for Blues," Bigler observed. "It was more like, 'Blues are fine, but not as good as us.'" When Reds were asked how many Reds were nice, they'd answer, "All of us." Asked how many Blues were nice, they'd answer, "Some." Some of the Blues were mean, and some were dumb—but not the Reds.

Bigler's experiment seems to show how children will use whatever you give them to create divisions—seeming to confirm that race becomes an issue only if we make it an issue. So why does Bigler think it's important to talk to children about race as early as the age of 3?

Her reasoning is that kids are developmentally prone to in-group favoritism; they're going to form these preferences on their own. Children naturally try to categorize everything, and the attribute they rely on is that which is the most clearly visible.

We might imagine we're creating color-blind environments for children, but differences in skin color or hair or weight are like differences in gender—they're plainly visible. Even if no teacher or parent mentions race, kids will use skin color on their own, the same way they use T-shirt colors. Bigler contends that children extend their shared appearances much further—believing that those who look similar to them enjoy the same things they do. Anything a child doesn't like thus belongs to those who look the least similar to him. The spontaneous tendency to assume your group shares characteristics—such as niceness, or smarts—is called essentialism.

Within the past decade or so, developmental psychologists have begun a handful of longitudinal studies to determine exactly when children develop bias. Phyllis Katz, then a professor at the University of Colorado, led one such study—following 100 black children and 100 white children for their first six years. She tested these children and their parents nine times during those six years, with the first test at 6 months old.

How do researchers test a 6-month-old? They show babies photographs of faces. Katz found that babies will stare significantly longer at photographs of faces that are a different race from their parents, indicating they find the face out of the ordinary. Race itself has no ethnic meaning per se—but children's brains are noticing skin-color differences and trying to understand their meaning.

When the kids turned 3, Katz showed them photographs of other children and asked them to choose whom they'd like to have as friends. Of the white children, 86 percent picked children of their own race. When the kids were 5 and 6, Katz gave these children a small deck of cards, with drawings of people on them. Katz told the children to sort the cards into two piles any way they wanted. Only 16 percent of the kids used gender to split the piles. But 68 percent of the kids used race to split the cards, without any prompting. In reporting her findings, Katz concluded: "I think it is fair to say that at no point in the study did the children exhibit the Rousseau type of color-blindness that many adults expect."

The point Katz emphasizes is that this period of our children's lives, when we imagine it's most important to not talk about race, is the very developmental period when children's minds are forming their first conclusions about race.

Several studies point to the possibility of developmental windows— stages when children's attitudes might be most amenable to change. In one experiment, children were put in cross-race study groups, and then were observed on the playground to see if the interracial classroom time led to interracial play at recess. The researchers found mixed study groups worked wonders with the first-grade children, but it made no difference with third graders. It's possible that by third grade, when parents usually recognize it's safe to start talking a little about race, the developmental window has already closed.

The other deeply held assumption modern parents have is what Ashley and I have come to call the Diverse Environment Theory. If you raise a child with a fair amount of exposure to people of other races and cultures, the environment becomes the message. Because both of us attended integrated schools in the 1970s—Ashley in San Diego and, in my case, Seattle—we had always accepted this theory's tenets: diversity breeds tolerance, and talking about race was, in and of itself, a diffuse kind of racism.

But my wife and I saw this differently in the years after our son, Luke, was born. When he was 4 months old, Luke began attending a preschool located in San Francisco's Fillmore/Western Addition neighborhood. One of the many benefits of the school was its great racial diversity. For years our son never once mentioned the color of anyone's skin. We never once mentioned skin color, either. We thought it was working perfectly.

Then came Martin Luther King Jr. Day at school, two months before his fifth birthday. Luke walked out of preschool that Friday before the weekend and started point-ing at everyone, proudly announcing, "That guy comes from Africa. And she comes from Africa, too!" It was embar-rassing how loudly he did this. "People with brown skin are from Africa," he'd repeat. He had not been taught the names for races—he had not heard the

> **For decades, it was assumed that children see race only when society points it out to them.**

term "black" and he called us "people with pinkish-whitish skin." He named every kid in his schoolroom with brown skin, which was about half his class.

My son's eagerness was revealing. It was obvious this was something he'd been wondering about for a while. He was relieved to have been finally given the key. Skin color was a sign of ancestral roots.

Over the next year, we started to overhear one of his white friends talking about the color of their skin. They still didn't know what to call their skin, so they used the phrase "skin like ours." And this notion of ours versus theirs started to take on a meaning of its own. As these kids searched for their identities, skin color had become salient.

Soon, I overheard this particular white boy telling my son, "Parents don't like us to talk about our skin, so don't let them hear you."

As a parent, I dealt with these moments explicitly, telling my son it was wrong to choose anyone as his friend, or his "favorite," on the basis of skin color. We pointed out how certain friends wouldn't be in our lives if we picked friends for their color. Over time he not only accepted but embraced this lesson. Now he talks openly about equal-ity and the wrongfulness of discrimination.

Not knowing then what I do now, I had a hard time understanding my son's initial impulses. Katz's work helped me to realize that Luke was never actually colorblind. He didn't talk about race in his first five years because our silence had unwittingly communicated that race was some-thing he could not ask about.

The Diverse Environment Theory is the core principle behind school desegregation today. Like most people, I assumed that after 30 years of desegregation, it would have a long track record of scientific research proving that the Diverse Environment Theory works. Then Ashley and I began talking to the scholars who've compiled that very research.

In the summer of 2007, led by the Civil Rights Project, a dozen schol-ars wrote an amicus brief to the U.S. Supreme Court supporting school desegregation in Louisville, Ky., and Seattle. By the time the brief reached the court, 553 scientists had signed on in support. However, as much as the scientists all supported active desegregation, the brief is surprisingly circumspect in its advocacy: the benefits of desegregation are qualified with words like "may lead" and "can improve." "Mere school integration is not a panacea," the brief warns.

UT's Bigler was one of the scholars heavily involved in the process of its creation. Bigler is an adamant proponent of desegregation in schools on moral grounds. "It's an enormous step backward to increase social segregation," she says. However, she also admitted that "in the end, I was disappointed with the amount of evidence social psychology could muster [to support it]. Going to integrated schools gives you just as many chances to learn stereotypes as to unlearn them."

The unfortunate twist of diverse schools is that they don't necessarily lead to more cross-race relationships. Often it's the opposite. Duke University's James Moody—an expert on how adolescents form and maintain social networks—analyzed data on more than 90,000 teenagers at 112 different schools from every region of the country. The students had been asked to name their five best male friends and their five best female friends. Moody matched the ethnicity of the student with the race of each named friend, then compared the number of each student's cross-racial friendships with the school's overall diversity.

Moody found that the more diverse the school, the more the kids self-segregate by race and ethnicity within the school, and thus the likelihood that any two kids of different races have a friendship goes down.

Moody included statistical controls for activities, sports, academic tracking, and other school-structural conditions that tend to desegregate (or segregate) students within the school. The rule still holds true: more diversity translates into more division among students. Those increased opportunities to interact are also, effectively, increased opportunities to reject each other. And that is what's happening.

As a result, junior-high and high-school children in diverse schools experience two completely contrasting social cues on a daily basis. The first cue is inspiring—that many students have a friend of another race. The second cue is tragic—that far more kids just like to hang with their own. It's this second dynamic that becomes more and more visible as overall school diversity goes up. As a child circulates through school, she sees more groups that her race disqualifies her from, more lunchroom tables she can't sit at, and more implicit lines that are taboo to cross. This is unmissable even if she, personally, has friends of other races. "Even in multiracial schools, once young people leave the classroom, very little interracial discussion takes place because a desire to associate with one's own ethnic group often discourages interaction between groups," wrote Brendesha Tynes of the University of Illinois at Urbana–Champaign.

All told, the odds of a white high-schooler in America having a best friend of another race is only 8 percent. Those odds barely improve for the second-best friend, or the third-best, or the fifth. For blacks, the odds aren't much better: 85 percent of black kids' best friends are also black. Cross-race friends also tend to share a single activity, rather than multiple activities; as a result, these friendships are more likely to be lost over time, as children transition from middle school to high school.

I can't help but wonder—would the track record of desegregation be so mixed if parents reinforced it, rather than remaining silent? It is tempting to believe that because their generation is so diverse, today's children grow up knowing how to get along with people of every race. But numerous studies suggest that this is more of a fantasy than a fact.

Is it really so difficult to talk with children about race when they're very young? What jumped out at Phyllis Katz, in her study of 200 black and white children, was that parents are very comfortable talking to their children about gender, and they work very hard to counterprogram against boy-girl stereotypes. That ought to be our model for talking about race. The same way we remind our daughters, "Mommies can be doctors just like daddies," we ought to be telling all children that doctors can be any skin color. It's not complicated what to say. It's only a matter of how often we reinforce it.

Shushing children when they make an improper remark is an instinctive reflex, but often the wrong move. Prone to categorization, children's brains can't help but attempt to generalize rules from the examples they see. It's embarrassing when a child blurts out, "Only brown people can have breakfast at school," or "You can't play basketball; you're white, so you have to play baseball." But shushing them only sends the message that this topic is unspeakable, which makes race more loaded, and more intimidating.

To be effective, researchers have found, conversations about race have to be explicit, in unmistakable terms that children understand. A friend of mine repeatedly told her 5-year-old son, "Remember, everybody's equal." She thought she was getting the message across. Finally, after seven months of this, her boy asked, "Mommy, what's 'equal' mean?"

Bigler ran a study in which children read brief biographies of famous African-Americans. For instance, in a biography of Jackie Robinson, they read that he was the first African-American in the major leagues. But only half read about how he'd previously been relegated to the Negro Leagues, and how he suffered taunts from white fans. Those facts—in five brief sentences—were omitted in the version given to the other children.

After the two-week history class, the children were surveyed on their racial attitudes. White children who got the full story about historical discrimination had significantly better attitudes toward blacks than those who got the neutered version. Explicitness works. "It also made them feel some guilt," Bigler adds. "It knocked down their glorified view of white people." They couldn't justify in-group superiority.

Minority parents are more likely to help their children develop a racial identity from a young age. April Harris-Britt, a clinical psychologist and professor at the University of North Carolina at Chapel Hill, found that all minority parents at some point tell their children that discrimination is out there, but they shouldn't let it stop them. Is this good for them? Harris-Britt found that some preparation for bias was beneficial, and it was necessary—94 percent of African-American eighth graders reported to Harris-Britt that they'd felt discriminated against in the prior three months.

> ## *"Parents don't like us to talk about our skin, so don't let them hear you."*

But if children heard these preparation-for-bias warnings often (rather than just occasionally), they were significantly less likely to connect their successes to effort, and much more likely to blame their failures on their teachers—whom they saw as biased against them.

Harris-Britt warns that frequent predictions of future discrimination ironically become as destructive as experiences of actual discrimination: "If you overfocus on those types of events, you give the children the message that the world is going to be hostile—you're just not valued and that's just the way the world is."

Preparation for bias is not, however, the only way minorities talk to their children about race. The other broad category of conversation, in Harris-Britt's analysis, is ethnic pride. From a very young age, minority children are coached to be proud of their ethnic history. She found that this was exceedingly good for children's self-confidence; in one study, black children who'd heard messages of ethnic pride were more engaged in school and more likely to attribute their success to their effort and ability.

That leads to the question that everyone wonders but rarely dares to ask. If "black pride" is good for African-American children, where does that leave white children? It's horrifying to imagine kids being "proud to be white." Yet many scholars argue that's exactly what children's brains are already computing. Just as minority children are aware that they belong to an ethnic group with less status and wealth, most white children naturally decipher that they belong to the race that has more power, wealth, and control in society; this provides security, if not confidence. So a pride message would not just be abhorrent—it'd be redundant.

Over the course of our research, we heard many stories of how people—from parents to teachers—were struggling to talk about race with their children. For some, the conversations came up after a child had made an embarrassing comment in public. A number had the issue thrust on them, because of an interracial marriage or an international adoption. Still others were just introducing children into a diverse environment, wondering when and if the timing was right.

But the story that most affected us came from a small town in rural Ohio. Two first-grade teachers, Joy Bowman and Angela Johnson, had agreed to let a professor from Ohio State University, Jeane Copenhaver-Johnson, observe their classrooms for the year. Of the 33 children, about two thirds were white, while the others were black or of mixed-race descent.

It being December, the teachers had decided to read to their classes *'Twas the Night B'fore Christmas,* Melodye Rosales's retelling of the Clement C. Moore classic. As the teachers began reading, the kids were excited by the book's depiction of a family waiting for Santa to come. A few children, however, quietly fidgeted. They seemed puzzled that this storybook was different: in this one, it was a black family all snug in their beds.

Then there was the famed clatter on the roof. The children leaned in to get their first view of Santa and the sleigh as Johnson turned the page—

And they saw that Santa was black.

"He's black!" gasped a white little girl.

A white boy exclaimed, "I thought he was white!"

Immediately, the children began to chatter about the stunning development. At the ripe old ages of 6 and 7, the children had no doubt that there was a Real Santa. Of that they were absolutely sure. But suddenly there was this huge question mark. Could Santa be black? And if so, what did that mean?

While some of the black children were delighted with the idea that Santa could be black, others were unsure. A couple of the white children rejected this idea out of hand: a black Santa couldn't be real.

But even the little girl the most adamant that the Real Santa must be white came around to accept the possibility that a black Santa could fill in for White Santa if he was hurt. And she still gleefully yelled along with the Black Santa's final "Merry Christmas to All! Y'all Sleep Tight."

Other children offered the idea that perhaps Santa was "mixed with black and white"—something in the middle, like an Indian. One boy went with a two-Santa hypothesis: White Santa and Black Santa must be friends who take turns visiting children. When a teacher made the apparently huge mistake of saying that she'd never seen Santa, the children all quickly corrected her: everyone had seen Santa at the mall. Not that that clarified the situation any.

The debate raged for a week, in anticipation of a school party. The kids all knew Real Santa was the guest of honor.

Then Santa arrived at the party—and he was black. Just like in the picture book.

Some white children said that this black Santa was too thin: that meant that the Real Santa was the fat white one at Kmart. But one of the white girls retorted that she had met the man and was convinced. Santa was brown.

Most of the black children were exultant, since this proved that Santa was black. But one of them, Brent, still doubted—even though he really wanted a black Santa to be true. So he bravely confronted Santa.

"There ain't no black Santas!" Brent insisted.

"Lookit here." Santa pulled up a pant leg.

A thrilled Brent was sold. "This is a black Santa!" he yelled. "He's got black skin and his black boots are like the white Santa's boots."

A black-Santa storybook wasn't enough to crush every stereotype. When Johnson later asked the kids to draw Santa, even the black kids who were excited about a black Santa still depicted him with skin as snowy white as his beard.

But the shock of the Santa storybook was the catalyst for the first graders to have a yearlong dialogue about race issues. The teachers began regularly incorporating books that dealt directly with issues of racism into their reading.

And when the children were reading a book on Martin Luther King Jr. and the civil-rights movement, both a black and a white child noticed that white people were nowhere to be found in the story. Troubled, they decided to find out just where in history both peoples were.

DISCUSSION

1. The experiment depicted in this essay uncovered a surprising fact: that many of the white parents asked to discuss race with their children declined to do so. "They wanted," the authors note, "their children to grow up colorblind." To what extent, in your view, does this attitude represent a social or cultural norm? Is there a prevailing assumption in our world that it is somehow "wrong" to talk about race openly? What is your view of such an assumption? Does it seem appropriate or helpful? Counterproductive and wrong? How?

2. Are you surprised by researchers' findings that adolescents do not typically forge cross-racial friendships? Does this sort of discovery point to an embedded or underlying racial norm in our culture? What might that be?

3. To what extent does this essay offer an alternative way to understand the concept of discrimination? Does the research profiled here give us a different way to think about what discrimination is? How it functions? Where it comes from?

WRITING

4. "We all," these authors write, "want our children to be unintimidated by differences and have the social skills necessary for a diverse world. The question is, do we make it worse, or do we make it better, by calling attention to race?" Write an essay in which you answer this question. In your opinion, does "calling attention to race" help us develop the "skills necessary for a diverse world"? If so, how specifically? If not, how not?

5. Bronson and Merryman write, "For decades, it was assumed that children see race only when society points it out to them. However, child-development researchers have increasingly begun to question that presumption. They argue that children see racial differences as much as they see the difference between pink and blue — but we tell kids that 'pink' means for girls and 'blue' is for boys. 'White' and 'black' are mysteries we leave them to figure out on their own." Write an essay in which you discuss how *you* think children in our society should "figure out" racial and/or color differences. Assume that Bronson and Merryman's assertion is correct, that we currently shy away from discussing race. Should we change this? Why or why not? What sort of social script, in your view, would be most helpful? And why?

6. How does this essay's discussion of diversity compare to the argument advanced by David Brooks (p. 68)? Compare and contrast these essays' respective treatment of this issue. Do you see any overlap or parallels between the findings of the researchers profiled here and Brooks's claims that Americans prefer the company of people "like themselves"? Why or why not?

DEBRA J. DICKERSON

The Great White Way

In this book review, Debra Dickerson questions the status of "whiteness" as our culture's preeminent racial and social norm, the standard against which all other racial and ethnic identity is defined as "different." Challenging the hegemony this term has long exerted over American thought, she offers a succinct historical overview of the ways the boundaries dividing white from nonwhite have shifted in America. Dickerson's work has appeared in many publications, including the *New Republic, Slate,* and *Vibe*, and she writes a regular column for Salon.com. Her memoir, *An American Story* (2001), describes her move from the rough St. Louis neighborhood where she grew up to her success as a Harvard Law School–trained, award-winning journalist. Her most recent book is *The End of Blackness: Returning the Souls of Black Folk to Their Rightful Owners* (2005). The following book review discusses *Working Toward Whiteness: How America's Immigrants Became White* (2005), by David R. Roediger, and *When Affirmative Action Was White: An Untold History of Racial Inequality in Twentieth-Century America* (2005), by Ira Katznelson. It was originally published in the September/ October 2005 issue of *Mother Jones*.

WHEN SPACE ALIENS ARRIVE TO COLONIZE US, RACE, ALONG WITH the Atkins diet and Paris Hilton, will be among the things they'll think we're kidding about. Oh, to be a fly on the wall when the president tries to explain to creatures with eight legs what blacks, whites, Asians, and Hispanics are. Race is America's central drama, but just try to define it in 25 words or less. Usually, race is skin color, but our visitors will likely want to know what a "black" person from Darfur and one from Detroit have in common beyond melanin. Sometimes race is language. Sometimes it's religion. Until recently, race was culture and law: Whites in the front, blacks in the back, Asians and Hispanics on the fringes. Race governed who could vote, who could murder or marry whom, what kind of work one could do and how much it could pay. The only thing we know for sure is that race is not biology: Decoding the human genome tells us there is more difference within races than between them.

Hopefully, with time, more Americans will come to accept that race is an arbitrary system for establishing hierarchy and privilege, good for little more than doling out the world's loot and deciding who gets to kick whose butt and then write epic verse about it. A belief in the immutable nature of race is the only way one can still believe that socioeconomic outcomes in America are either fair or entirely determined by individual effort. [David Roediger's *Working Toward Whiteness* and Ira Katznelson's *When Affirmative Action Was White*] should put to rest any such claims.

If race is real and not just a method for the haves to decide who will be have-nots, then all European immigrants, from Ireland to Greece, would have been "white" the moment they arrived here. Instead, as documented in David Roediger's excellent *Working Toward Whiteness*, they were long considered inferior, nearly subhuman, and certainly not white. Southern and eastern European immi-

> *Race is an arbitrary system for establishing hierarchy and privilege.*

grants' language, dress, poverty, and willingness to do "nigger" work excited not pity or curiosity but fear and xenophobia. Teddy Roosevelt popularized the term "race suicide" while calling for Americans to have more babies to offset the mongrel hordes. Scientists tried to prove that Slavs and "dagoes" were incapable of normal adult intelligence. Africans and Asians were clearly less than human, but Hungarians and Sicilians ranked not far above.

It gives one cultural vertigo to learn that, until the 1920s, Americans from northern Europe called themselves "white men" so as not to be confused with their fellow laborers from southern Europe. Or that 11 Italians were lynched in Louisiana in 1891, and Greeks were targeted by whites during a 1909 Omaha race riot. And curiously, the only black family on the Titanic was almost lost to history because "Italian" was used to label the ship's darker-skinned, nonwhite passengers.

Yet it was this very bureaucratic impulse and political self-interest that eventually led America to "promote" southern and eastern Europeans to "whiteness." The discussion turned to how to fully assimilate these much-needed, newly white workers and how to get their votes. If you were neither black nor Asian nor Hispanic, eventually you could become white, invested with enforceable civil rights and the right to exploit—and hate—nonwhites. World War II finally made all European Americans white, as the "Americans All" banner was reduced to physiognomy alone: Patriotic Japanese Americans ended up in internment camps while fascist-leaning Italian Americans roamed free. While recent European immigrants had abstained from World War I–era race riots, racial violence in the 1940s was an equal-opportunity affair. One Italian American later recalled the time he and his friends "beat up some niggers" in Harlem as "wonderful. It was new. The Italo-American stopped being Italo and started becoming American."

While European immigrants got the racial stamp of approval, the federal government was engaged in a little-recognized piece of racial rigging that resulted in both FDR's New Deal and Truman's Fair Deal being set up largely for the benefit of whites. As Ira Katznelson explains in

When Affirmative Action Was White, these transformative public programs, from Social Security to the GI Bill, were deeply—and intentionally— discriminatory. Faced with a de facto veto by Southern Democrats, throughout the 1930s and 1940s Northern liberals acquiesced to calls for "states' rights" as they drafted the landmark laws that would create a new white middle class. As first-generation white immigrants cashed in on life-altering benefits, black families who had been here since Revolutionary times were left out in the cold.

Disbursement of federal Depression relief was left at the local level, so that Southern blacks were denied benefits and their labor kept at serf status. In parts of Georgia, no blacks received emergency relief; in Mississippi, less than 1 percent did. Agricultural and domestic workers were excluded from the new Social Security system, subjecting 60 percent of blacks (and 75 percent of Southern blacks) to what Katznelson calls "a form of policy apartheid" far from what FDR had envisioned. Until the 1950s, most blacks remained ineligible for Social Security. Even across the North, black veterans' mortgage, education, and housing benefits lagged behind whites'. Idealized as the capstone of progressive liberalism, such policies were as devastatingly racist as Jim Crow.

To remedy this unacknowledged injustice, Katznelson proposes that current discussions about affirmative action refer to events that took place seven, rather than four, decades ago, when it wasn't called affirmative action but business as usual. He's frustrated by the anemic arguments of his liberal allies, who rely on the most tenuous, least defensible of grounds—diversity—while their opponents invoke color blindness, merit, and the Constitution. In short, affirmative action can't be wrong now when it was right—and white—for so long.

Together, these two books indict the notion of race as, ultimately, a failure of the American imagination. We simply can't imagine a world in which skin color does not entitle us to think we know what people are capable of, what they deserve, or their character. We can't imagine what America might become if true affirmative action—not the kind aimed at the Huxtable kids but at poverty and substandard education—was enacted at anywhere near the level once bestowed on those fortunate enough to be seen as white.

DISCUSSION

1. Dickerson opens her essay with a hypothetical scenario in which space aliens are faced with the task of understanding how Americans have perceived and sought to deal with race. Why do you think she chooses to begin her discussion on race by focusing on it from an "alien" perspective? What kind of commentary on race does this particular strategy imply?

2. Dickerson refers to race as the "central drama" of American history. Why do you think she uses the term *drama*? Does her discussion of racial politics and racialist violence invite us in any way to think about this history in terms of role-playing, performance, or social and cultural scripts? If so, how?

3. According to Dickerson, race is best understood as a question of power. "Hopefully, with time," she writes, "more Americans will come to accept that race is an arbitrary system for establishing hierarchy and privilege." What do you make of this claim? To what extent do you share Dickerson's conviction about the arbitrariness of racial categories and racial difference?

WRITING

4. The dominant ways of thinking about race in America, argues Dickerson, are more the product of social fantasy than a reflection of objective reality. In a brief essay, evaluate the validity of this thesis. To what extent is it valid to think of the racial scripts that get taught in our culture as fantastic or fictional? Does this possibility diminish or accentuate the power they can wield?

5. One of the clear goals underlying this essay involves de-naturalizing the racial differences we've been taught to accept. Choose an example from our popular culture (for example, a television show, an advertisement, or a news story) that, in your view, encourages us to accept a view about race and racial difference that you consider artificial. Then, write an essay in which you explain how this product or image goes about promoting this view. How does it endeavor to represent this false view as right or normal? And what do you think are the specific consequences of adopting this view?

6. Dickerson shares with Po Bronson and Ashley Merryman (p. 74) a concern for where our public attitudes about race come from. How do you think Dickerson would respond to or evaluate the findings these two writers document in their essay? In your view, would Dickerson find in this data support for the thesis she advances concerning "scientific racism"? How or how not?

Scenes and Un-Scenes: *Political Protest*

There is a long and storied tradition in America of social or political protest. From the Boston Tea Party to the women's suffrage movement, antisegregation campaigns to abortion rights rallies, our national history is replete with efforts to challenge the practices and beliefs that, at one time or another, have stood as unexamined norms. But how do these public demonstrations actually succeed — if indeed they do — in rewriting beliefs that, for any given era, have become so embedded, entrenched, assumed? The short answer, of course, is that these beliefs were never quite as universal as they may have appeared. Bringing together people who felt marginalized or oppressed by a given societal norm, these demonstrations were designed to challenge the beliefs on which such norms rested, to offer up for scrutiny the embedded practices and unspoken assumptions that justified the status quo. For each of the following examples, how fully would you say this objective is achieved? What particular beliefs does each put on display? What social scripts does each attempt to rewrite?

▲▲ *Even today, the civil rights movement led by Martin Luther King Jr. in the
1960s still stands as a model for how Americans think about social or political
protest. The tradition of public, nonviolent protest that King pioneered persists
within the public imagination as the blueprint for how "the people" can effect not
only tangible changes in public policy, but also meaningful shifts in social attitude.
His famous 1963 March on Washington, for example, marks a watershed both for
efforts to create new civil rights legislation and for the struggle to challenge and
undo long-standing public attitudes about race.*

▲▲ *The Million Man March sought to carry forward King's standard of public,
nonviolent protest into the present day. At the same time, though, such
spectacles make evident how much has changed over the last forty plus years.
In updating King's messages for our contemporary "wired" age, for example, it
reminds us how different the tactics of public protest have become. Availing itself
of the same tools we might find at a sporting event or rock concert, this image
shows how deeply shaped by our media culture political protest is these days.*

≪ *Over the years, in fact, King's legacy has moved well beyond the realm of racial politics, coming to underlie and inform all manner of different causes. His tradition of public, nonviolent protest as well as his rhetoric of civil and social "rights" have long been adopted by a variety of other constituencies and used to advance a host of other interests. Not surprisingly, this tactic has led to the marriage of these tactics to a number of seemingly unlikely causes. We might well wonder, for example, what particular "right" a celebrity-studded, Scientology-sponsored demonstration against the use of antidepressants is meant to advance. When you compare this spectacle to King's March on Washington, how much commonality do you discern?*

>> *Another arena in which King's tradition of public demonstration and civil rights protest has been taken up in recent years is gay rights — in particular, the much publicized and highly contentious issue of gay marriage. In ways large and small, proponents of this movement have sought to model their efforts along the lines of the African American struggle for justice and equality before the law. Deploying some of the same rhetoric, many have framed the demand for legalized marriage as a natural extension of King's work. Do you agree with this analogy?*

▲ *We have even reached the point where technological changes now allow us to alter or fictionalize the historical record itself, a tactic that takes the whole idea of scripting to an entirely new level. In this still image from the film* Forrest Gump, *the title character, played by Tom Hanks, has been inserted into actual footage of a Vietnam War protest. How do you think such an image plays with the idea of social protest?*

DISCUSSION

1. Which of these protests raises an issue that most resonates with your personal experience? Which one touches on an issue or conflict that you feel a personal stake in? To what extent does its embedded or unspoken critique reflect your own views?

2. Choose one of the previous examples. What relationship between public spectacle and societal belief does it showcase? That is, in what ways does this protest seem designed to affect or alter a more fundamental and underlying social norm?

3. What political or social controversy does this collection leave out? What protest would you add to this list, and what in your view would make it worthy of inclusion?

WRITING

4. Choose something from our popular culture (for example, a television show, a commercial, a movie, or the like) that shows an example of a political or social protest that tells the story of how a particular societal rule gets challenged. Describe how this protest gets depicted. How are the protesters presented? What specific issues or ideas are offered up for critique? How do the symbols match or differ from the images you've viewed in this feature? How compelling or convincing do you find this depiction to be? Why?

5. Choose one of the images above that offers a blueprint for social protest that you would not follow yourself. Identify and evaluate the particular aspects of this protest that you find problematic, inadequate, or otherwise ineffective. Then, use this critique to create a model of the kind of protest you would endorse. What different sorts of tactics would this model utilize? What different objectives would it attempt to achieve? And finally, what, in your estimation, makes this alternative more preferable?

6. The role of social protest in our culture has gone a long way toward normalizing certain issues. In what ways can Ron Rosenbaum's (p. 56) discussion of the Pledge of Allegiance be read as its own form of social protest? To what extent does his argument about "compulsory patriotism" constitute a challenge to the prevailing scripts and norms that define this issue?

Putting It into Practice: *Scripting Belief*

Now that you've read the chapter selections, try applying your conclusions to your own life by completing the following exercises.

SURVEYING OURSELVES   How do you think "normal" Americans think? Visit the Gallup Poll website (www.galluppoll.com) and click the link "Topics A-Z" under the "Resources" tab. Here, you will find a long list of survey topics and summaries of how Americans responded to different surveys on these topics. Choose two or three topics and decide how you would answer the survey questions posed. Write an essay in which you compare your beliefs to those of the American majority. Are you "normal" or are you "different"? How do you respond to being categorized in either of those groups?

MARKETING BELIEF   Choose some venue or organization that you think actively works to promote or market a set of beliefs to the general public (for example, a church, a military recruitment center, a campus activist group, or a similar group). Research the ways that this group advertises itself to the larger community. Write an essay in which you explore what tactics the group uses to court new members. What symbols does it use in its advertising? What language do these ads include that is designed to inspire new believers?

SELL IT   Try combining the two activities above. Choose one of the survey topics you wrote about in the first assignment and design an ad you think would be effective in appealing to nonbelievers. This ad could be anything from a speech to a commercial or billboard. What images or language do you believe is most important in convincing others to follow the particular belief you've chosen?

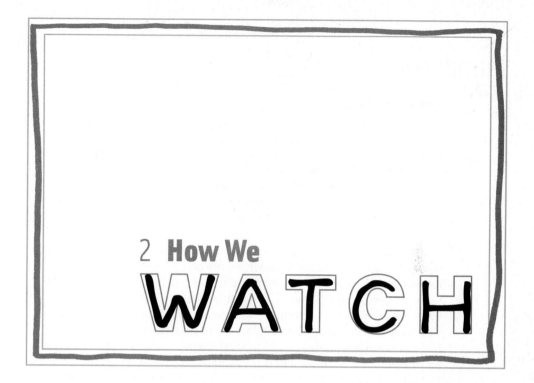

2 **How We**

WATCH

Introduction

SEEING IS BELIEVING?

Do the names Carrie Underwood and Adam Lambert mean anything to you? Do you let your answering machine pick up calls that come in during *Project Runway*? Or do you find yourself regularly debating who should have been voted off the show in the latest episode of *Big Brother*? If so, you are not alone. Reality TV draws millions of viewers like you who enjoy watching everyday people live out certain "realities" in front of the camera. And these viewers, also like you, accurately sense that few other television genres work as hard as reality TV to teach us how to play the *role* of viewer.

As anyone who has seen even an episode or two can attest, very clear but unspoken rules dictate the ways we are and are not supposed to watch reality television. Cardinal among these rules is the presumption that what we see on these shows truly is a snapshot of reality, a window through which we glimpse the personal, private details of real people in real situations feeling real emotions. At the same time, however, we are aware that within the boundaries established by these shows not everything counts equally as reality. If we want to properly perform our role as viewer, we know that our attention needs to remain focused on very specific aspects of what is on display. We must view *selectively.* These shows work only if we suspend disbelief and buy into the idea that what we're seeing is more or less real.

This unspoken message doesn't pertain only to reality television. Indeed, few things abound more plentifully in our world than the opportunity to play the role of watcher. Whether it is the candid photos that pop up on our cell phones, the billboards we drive past on the interstate, the clothing catalogs that litter our mailboxes, or the stories broadcast on the nightly news, we are called constantly to view things. So natural does the experience of watching become, however, that we may miss the larger implication: that at the same time we are being taught how to *watch,* we are also being taught how to *think* about the world around us.

Take, for example, the typical ad for a luxury car. Because we have grown so accustomed to seeing this sort of image in television commercials or magazine ads, we don't really need to be explicitly told how to look at it. Through countless encounters with examples just like it, we have in a sense internalized what the expected form of watching is. And because we have already been schooled about what role to play, we know how we are supposed to think about this image: what associations we are supposed to make, what conclusions we are supposed to draw. We know, for example, that when we come across one of these glossy portraits, there is a very specific type of person we are allowed to imagine sitting behind the wheel, a person with a certain kind of look (young, fit, fashionable); a certain kind of lifestyle (yuppie professional but also rugged and outdoorsy); a particular circle of friends (similarly young, fit and fashionable); and a certain level of income (comfortably upper middle class). And we further know that our job as viewers is not only to accurately define this hypothetical driver, but also to admire him, to see him as a stand-in for ourselves. Once we have taken this step, we are well on our way to accepting and adopting the other messages an image like this conveys (about, for instance, the desirability of wealth, the importance of status, or the proper definition of success).

To a very real degree, it is this same formula that underlies our visual encounters with virtually everything in our popular culture: rules of spectatorship that turn the ever-expanding universe of images, signs, and messages surrounding us into a kind of classroom where we are taught the "true" difference between what matters and what doesn't, what we should aspire to or emulate and what we should spurn. And when this sort of thing happens in places other than our entertainment industry, the stakes involved can be even higher — as, for example, in our news industry. Whether it is a presidential press conference or combat footage from Iraq, a Fox News roundtable on immigration reform or CNN coverage of the photos released of prisoner abuse at Abu Ghraib, every depiction or discussion of current events is underwritten by the same basic requirement: to accept the assumptions and norms being presented as our own. When we catch the tail-end of a Fox News commentator attacking Gulf oil spill protesters or a mock news story on *The Colbert Report* making fun of Sarah Palin, we are no less intimately caught up navigating our culture's ideals and expectations than when we catch a glimpse of A-list celebrities strolling down the red carpet.

Everybody Knows That . . .

Tabloids like *US Weekly* tell us "stars are just like us!"

To return one final time to the example of reality television, think for a moment about what these shows teach us about, say, the importance of not only watching, but also being watched and about the pleasures and payoffs that supposedly result from turning ourselves into an entertainment spectacle. Since we rarely see a cast member on one of these shows expressing annoyance or dismay over having their lives filmed twenty-four hours a day, is it really all that strange

Everybody Knows That . . .

to consider that we might begin to feel the same way—that we might start regarding the prospect of being scrutinized by others as ordinary, unremarkable, just "the way things are"?

To expand this inquiry, in fact, we might note how often this expectation gets reinforced elsewhere in our pop culture. We need only take stock of the growing ubiquity of personal webcam technology, the burgeoning popularity of online sites like Facebook and Twitter, for example, to get a sense of how widespread this norm has become. Is the emergence of popular Internet sites like YouTube an extension of a need to watch ourselves the way we have grown so accustomed to watching others? We certainly don't lack for images that encourage us to think about the private lives of other people as material fit for public consumption. As we've already seen, when we accept this premise — when we look at the websites, television shows, and magazines in the ways prescribed for us — we find ourselves confronting additional expectations as well: from the clothing brands we should wear to the body images we should cultivate to the reasonableness of being watched ourselves.

To sketch out this process does not by itself answer or resolve the thorny questions this introduction poses: Is seeing believing? In a world defined by personal webcams and Photoshop software, Pixar-animated movies and network television "docudramas," how do we know the difference between what is real and what is scripted? How does the role of watcher we're taught affect our assumptions about the world around us? And does this role eventually blur the boundaries between watching and being watched? Given the sheer volume and enormous variety of what we are shown day to day, it should not surprise us that answering these questions gets pretty complicated pretty quickly.

Nonetheless, this task is taken up by each of the following selection authors. The authors in this chapter fall into two basic categories: those exploring some aspect of how we are taught to look, and those addressing some dimension of how we are looked at. Within the first are writers like Ann-Marie Cusac, Naomi Klein, and Trenton Straube. Trying to make sense of the complicated and surprisingly intimate connection between fictional television and real-world events, Cusac's essay explores the degrees to which the public debate in the United States about torture has been scripted by plotlines from the Fox show *24*. In her exploration of corporate branding, Naomi Klein pursues a very similar line of inquiry — pondering how campus activism these days has been co-opted and largely driven by the logic of commercial advertising. Exploring the idea of product placement from a different angle, Trenton Straube argues for more inclusion of safer sex messaging in scripted dramas like *Gossip Girl* and makes a compelling point about programmers' responsibilities to the public. Within the second category are writers like Harriet McBryde Johnson, Ariel Levy, Michael Eric Dyson, Mathew Honan, and Jessica Bennett. In recounting her debate with famed medical ethicist Peter Singer, Johnson, an American with disabilities, offers a startlingly blunt and thought-provoking meditation on what it means to be viewed — and stereotyped — as the "token cripple." Surveying the rise of "raunch culture," Levy examines the phenomenon of stereotyping from a radically different perspective, documenting what she sees as a perplexing eagerness among young American women to make themselves into sexualized spectacles for predominantly male audiences, ironically in the name of female empowerment. Dyson focuses on disaster-as-spectacle, particularly on the way the news media seemed to depict African American victims of Hurricane Katrina. His searing analysis demonstrates the power the media has to frame an event, sometimes unintentionally dragging in old prejudices. Finally, in an era in which the Internet makes us more visible than ever — sometimes even more than we know — two authors offer different stories of the way that constant visibility can affect the way we live. Honan tells of his attempt to be trackable at every moment of the day and shares the unintended consequences of constant visibility. Bennett, on the other hand, portrays the ways that easy fame via viral videos can have a lasting impact on the lives of the reluctantly famous.

Everybody Knows That . . .

While they range widely across the landscape of our modern popular culture, these selections do remain linked in one fundamental way: By questioning some of the key visual roles that get scripted in our world, each in its own way inclines us to wonder whether what we *see* is truly what we *get*.

"EVERYBODY KNOWS THAT" EXERCISE

Choose one of the images or quotations featured in the margins of this introduction and answer the following questions:

1. What does this image or quotation ask you to believe?

2. What are the particular ideas, values, or attitudes it invites us to accept as *normal*?

3. What would it feel like to act on or act out these norms in our personal lives?

Rule *Maker* >>>>>>>>>> Rule *Breaker*

❝ *We thought if you trained cameras on people who were really interesting, and edited that in an interesting way and cut it to music, what do you have? Each person has a unique story and you have to care about them. . . . They are direct with each other about what they are feeling and that comes up clearly. . . . We watch this because it holds a mirror up to ourselves."*

— MARY-ELLIS BUNIM,

CREATOR OF REALITY SERIES *THE REAL WORLD, ROAD RULES*,

AND *STARTING OVER*, ON *LARRY KING LIVE*, JUNE 27, 2000

❝ *Obviously we're entertainers. We are trying to entertain in every aspect of our lives. Whether it's on [MTV's The Hills] or in the tabloids."*

— HEIDI MONTAG

❝ *Anybody who wants to promote our brand, negative or positive, give me a call."*

— SPENCER PRATT,

BOTH QUOTATIONS TAKEN FROM "THE SPEIDI CHRONICLES,"

LOS ANGELES TIMES, MAY 11, 2008

MARY-ELLIS BUNIM VS. HEIDI MONTAG AND SPENCER PRATT

Taken together, these quotations capture what is perhaps the trickiest and most fundamental question about reality television: Is what we are shown, in fact, *real*? The answer, of course, depends on whom you ask. For those who create and produce these shows, the answer could quite easily be "yes." They might acknowledge that those who apply to become cast members are put through a rigorous screening process designed to find specific types of people who viewers will want to root for or revile, people who fit roles and possess character traits that audiences are accustomed to. They might also concede that specific storylines and dramatic conflicts are tailored and polished in the editing room to achieve a show with a more narrative arc. Reality television producers like the late Mary-Ellis Bunim have been pretty upfront that they use the conventional tricks of more traditional scripted television — lighting, music cues, reaction shots from other cast members — to increase dramatic tension. Despite all this, however, reality television producers likely would maintain that what gets broadcast is nonetheless authentic. After all, they might say, reality television still brings viewers into contact with people being *themselves.*

For those on the other side of the camera, however, the answer could be very different. From their vantage point, reality television might easily be less like an opportunity to showcase the "real you" than a job: one that requires you to conform to a role you had no direct hand in creating. It is hardly a secret that shows like these operate according to clear-cut, well-established rules. It doesn't take too many hours of watching before it becomes obvious that only certain character types, certain relationships, and certain kinds of conflict qualify as fit subject matter. Every reality show has its villain, its crybaby, its average Joe. As these shows become more and more popular, the scripts that underline the way they work become more obvious. And those who aspire to be on these shows, who work to find themselves included in these finished portraits of "reality," are also more aware of how these shows are scripted. Does it follow, then, that these reality television participants may be acting a part well before they're even cast to increase their chances of being selected? Are they turning the reality television formula on its head and removing producers' last claim to authenticity?

FIND THE RULES: Spend an evening watching the reality television show of your choice and write a profile of this show. Begin by summarizing the goals of the show. Is there a prize for winning, or does the show instead present itself as an examination of human behavior with no prize in sight? Next, analyze the participants on the show. What roles do they seem to play, and what about their behavior leads you to this conclusion? Finally, which storylines in the show seem to get the most attention? How do the editors seem to script these storylines (pay attention to the music they use, whether prize situations or challenges have anything to do with creating conflict, and so forth)?

MAKE YOUR OWN RULES: Imagine that you are creating your own reality television show, with one catch: Your show must be 100 percent real. In a brief essay, describe what this show would look like. What would its format be? What setting would you choose? What types of characters? Explain how this show would rewrite the rules and norms by which reality television shows are conventionally created. To create your "100 percent real" show, what aspects of the reality format do you think you would have to change?

MATHEW HONAN

I Am Here:
One Man's Experiment with the Location-Aware Lifestyle

Have we reached the point where simply being seen—in whatever state, at whatever time, by whichever audience—counts as an achievement? Abetted by technology, such as Foursquare and Facebook Places, that can now pinpoint and broadcast our every move, at every moment of the day, we seem to have moved into a new cultural moment: one in which being on display 24/7 is not simply desirable but increasingly unremarkable as well. In the following selection, freelance writer Mathew Honan explores what it means to be always trackable. Honan's work has appeared in *Salon, Mother Jones,* and *Runner's World,* among many other publications. During the 2008 presidential election, Honan created the viral Internet site www.barackobamaisyournewbicycle.com, which was published as a book. He is currently a contributing editor to *Wired,* in which the following selection appeared on January 19, 2009.

'M BAFFLED BY WHOSHERE. AND I'M NO NEWBIE. I BUILT MY FIRST Web page in 1994, wrote my first blog entry in 1999, and sent my first tweet in October 2006. My user number on Yahoo's event site, Upcoming.org: 14. I love tinkering with new gadgets and diving into new applications. But WhosHere had me stumped. It's an iPhone app that knows where you are, shows you other users nearby, and lets you chat with them. Once it was installed and running, I drew a blank. What was I going to do with this thing?

So I asked for some help. I started messaging random people within a mile of my location (37.781641 °N, 122.393835 °W), asking what they used WhosHere for.

My first response came from someone named Bridget, who, according to her profile, at least, was a 25-year-old woman with a proclivity for scarves. "To find sex, asshole," she wrote.

"I'm sorry? You mean it's for finding people to have sex with?" I zapped back.

"Yes, I use it for that," she wrote. "It's my birthday," she added.

"Happy birthday," I offered.

"Send me a nude pic for my birthday," she replied.

A friendly offer, but I demurred. Anonymous geoshagging is not what I had in mind when I imagined what the GPS revolution could mean to me.

The location-aware future—good, bad, and sleazy—is here. Thanks to the iPhone 3G and, to a lesser extent, Google's Android phone, millions of people are now walking around with a gizmo in their pocket that not only knows where they are but also plugs into the Internet to share that info, merge it with online databases, and find out what—and who—is in the immediate vicinity. That old saw

> **The location-aware future—good, bad, and sleazy—is here.**

about how someday you'll walk past a Starbucks and your phone will receive a digital coupon for half off on a Frappuccino? Yeah, that can happen now.

Simply put, location changes everything. This one input—our coordinates—has the potential to change all the outputs. Where we shop, who we talk to, what we read, what we search for, where we go—they all change once we merge location and the Web.

I wanted to know more about this new frontier, so I became a geo-guinea pig. My plan: Load every cool and interesting location-aware program I could find onto my iPhone and use them as often as possible. For a few weeks, whenever I arrived at a new place, I would announce it through multiple social geoapps. When going for a run, bike ride, or drive, I would record my trajectory and publish it online. I would let digital applications help me decide where to work, play, and eat. And I would seek out new people based on nothing but their proximity to me at any given moment. I would be totally open, exposing my location to the world just to see where it took me. I even added an Eye-Fi Wi-Fi card to my PowerShot digital camera so that all my photos could be geotagged and uploaded to the Web. I would become the most location-aware person on the Internets!

The trouble started right away. While my wife and I were sipping stouts at our neighborhood pub in San Francisco (37.770401 °N, 122.445154 °W), I casually mentioned my plan. Her eyes narrowed. "You're not going to announce to everyone that you're leaving town without me, are you? A lot of weirdos follow you online."

Sorry, weirdos—I love you, but she has a point. Because of my work, many people—most of them strangers—track my various Flickr, Twitter, Tumblr, and blog feeds. And it's true; I was going to be gone for a week on business. Did I really want to tell the world that I was out of town? It wasn't just leaving my wife home alone that concerned me. Because the card in my camera automatically added location data to my photos, anyone who cared to look at my Flickr page could see my computers, my spendy bicycle, and my large flatscreen TV all pinpointed on an online photo map. Hell, with a few clicks you could get driving directions right to my place—and with a few more you could get black gloves and a lock pick delivered to your home.

To test whether I was being paranoid, I ran a little experiment. On a sunny Saturday, I spotted a woman in Golden Gate Park taking a photo with a 3G iPhone. Because iPhones embed geodata into photos that users upload to Flickr or Picasa, iPhone shots can be automatically placed on a map. At home I searched the Flickr map, and score—a shot from today. I clicked through to the user's photostream and determined it was the woman I had seen earlier. After adjusting the settings so that only her shots appeared on the map, I saw a cluster of images in one location. Clicking on them revealed photos of an apartment interior—a bedroom, a kitchen, a filthy living room. Now I know where she lives.

Geo-enthusiasts will assure you that these privacy concerns are overplayed: Your cell phone can be used to pinpoint your location anyway, and a skilled hacker could likely get that data from your mobile carrier. Heck, in the UK, tracking mobile phone users is as simple as entering their number on a Web site (as long as they give permission). But the truth is, there just aren't that many people who want to prey on your location. Still, I can't help being a little skittish when I start broadcasting my current position and travel plans. I mean, I used to stop newspaper delivery so people wouldn't realize I was out of town. Now I've told everyone on Dopplr that I'm going to DC for five days.

And location info gets around. The first time I saw my home address on Facebook, I jumped—because I never posted it there. Then I realized it was because I had signed up for Whrrl. Like many other geosocial applications, Whrrl lets you cross-post to the microblogging platform Twitter. Twitter, in turn, gets piped to all sorts of other places. So when I updated my location in Whrrl, the message leaped first to Twitter and then to Facebook and FriendFeed before landing on my blog, where Google indexed it. By updating one small app on my iPhone, I had left a giant geotagged footprint across the Web.

> *I used to stop newspaper delivery so people wouldn't realize I was out of town. Now I've told everyone I'm going to DC for five days.*

A few days later I had another disturbing realization. It's a Tuesday and I'm blowing off a work meeting in favor of a bike ride through Golden Gate Park (37.771558 °N, 122.454478 °W). Suddenly it hits me—since I would later post my route online with the date and time, I would be just a Google search ("Mat Honan Tuesday noon") away from getting busted. I'm a freelancer, and these are trying economic times. I can't afford to have the Internet ratting me out like that.

To learn how to deal with this new openness, I met with Tom Coates at Caffe Centro (37.781694 °N, 122.394234 °W). Coates started Fire Eagle, a sort of location clearinghouse: You tell Fire Eagle where you are, and it sends that info to a host of other geoapps, like Outside.in and Bizroof. Not only does Fire Eagle save you from having to update the same information on multiple programs, it also lets you specify the level of detail to give each app—precise location, general neighborhood, or just the city you're in. The idea is that these options will mitigate privacy concerns. In addition to this, as Coates puts it: "You have to have the ability to lie about your location."

Any good social geoapp will let you type in a fake position manually, Coates says. Great news; I didn't need to get busted for missing meetings—or deadlines—ever again.

I was starting to revel in the benefits of location awareness. By trusting an app (iWant) that showed me nearby dining options, I discovered an Iraqi joint in my neighborhood that I'd somehow neglected. Thanks to an app (GasBag) that displayed gas stations with current prices, I was able to find the cheapest petrol no matter where I drove. In Reno, one program (HeyWhatsThat) even gave me the names and elevation profiles of all the surrounding mountains. And another (WikiMe), which displayed Wikipedia entries about local points of interest, taught me a thing or two about the San Francisco waterfront. (Did you know the Marina District exists largely because a land speculator built a seawall in the 1890s?) These GPS tools were making me smarter.

And more social. While working downtown one day, it looked like I was going to have to endure a lonely burrito lunch by myself. So I updated my location and asked for company. My friend Mike saw my post on Twitter and dropped by on his way to the office. Later, I met up with a couple of people I had previously known only online: After learning I would be just around the corner from their office, we agreed to get together for coffee. One of them, it turns out, works in a field I cover and gave me a tip on a story.

But then, two weeks into the experiment, I bumped into my friend Mindy at the Dovre Club (37.749008 °N, 122.420547 °W). She mentioned my constant updates, which she'd noticed on Facebook. "It seems sort of odd," she said with a note of concern. "I've been a little worried about you. I thought, 'Wow, Mat must be really lonely.'"

I explained that I wasn't actually begging for company; I was just telling people where I was. But it's an understandable misperception. This is new territory, and there's no established etiquette or protocol.

This issue came up again while having dinner with a friend at Greens (37.806679 °N, 122.432131 °W), an upscale vegetarian restaurant. Of course, I thought nothing of broadcasting my location. But moments after we were seated, two other friends—Randy and Cameron—showed up, obviously expecting to join us. Randy squatted at the end of the table. Cameron stood. After a while, it became apparent that no more chairs would be coming, so they left awkwardly. I felt bad, but I hadn't really invited them. Or had I?

There were also missed connections—lots of missed connections. Apple doesn't let applications from outside software makers run in the background on the iPhone—for a third-party app to work, it has to be the one currently on the screen. Apple says it does this to prevent random programs from sucking down your battery and degrading your phone's performance. As a result, iPhone location apps can't send out constant updates. This means that people are often showing up where you were, rather than where you are. On a Friday afternoon, for example, I posted an update looking for nearby friends to share a postwork beer downtown (37.787229 °N, 122.387093 °W). A short time later, I heard back from my friend Lisey, who wanted to meet up. But I had already moved on to Zeitgeist (37.770088 °N, 122.422194 °W), a beer garden in San Francisco's Mission District. I again updated my location. But the place was packed, so I decided to split and headed to Toronado (37.771920 °N, 122.431213 °W), a bar closer to home. Just after I left, I heard from Lisey again, who was now on her way to the Mission. I had accidentally dodged her twice. I later discovered that two more pals had shown up at Zeitgeist looking for me.

One way around such snafus is to use the Google phone, T-Mobile's G1. Unlike the iPhone, the G1 lets programs run in the background, so you can launch location-aware apps and keep them humming while you do other things—check email, make calls, take pictures—or just drop the phone in your pocket.

I borrowed a G1 to see what it could do that the iPhone couldn't. One of the first apps I set up, Ecorio, tracked my every movement and used that data to generate a report card on my carbon footprint. Since I get around mostly on foot, bike, or mass transit, this program confirmed my suspicion that I personally was saving the earth. Another app, Locale, kicks in when you enter certain zones—you can set your ringer to go silent when you arrive at work, for instance. I used it to send messages to Twitter automatically when I came within a half mile of home or the *Wired* office. LifeAware not only tracks your phone, it also allows you to connect with other people running the app on their phones, showing you their current location. You can use it to monitor employees, your children, maybe even a spouse. Sadly, I couldn't get anyone to connect with me—for some reason, nobody wanted me to track their every movement.

> **I had gained better location awareness but was losing my sense of place.**

These features were nice, but they didn't completely sell me on the G1. Sure, the iPhone 3G has limitations, but its popularity (6.9 million units sold in its first quarter) means there are more applications available for Apple's handset. One of my favorites is Twinkle, a Twitter widget that lets you see posts from users in your area, even if you don't subscribe to their feeds. Twinkle reminded me of what a great geoapp can do: take an existing service and make it more practical by adding location data. When flames shooting into the night sky appeared to be coming from a nearby hilltop, my Twinkle feed, not the local news, informed me that the fire was actually across the water on Angel Island.

Apps like Twinkle, of course, are just the beginning. The next round of location tools will be even more pervasive, pushy, and predictive. You'll be able to sort through your emails by where you were when you sent them and read blogs written only by writers within your zip code. Everything with an engine is going to be tracked, so you'll know precisely where your bus, taxi, or airplane is at all times. We're going to see more data being pushed to devices as we enter and leave certain areas. And information on who's doing what and where will be crunched for even smarter services.

I was coming to love this new definition of self-centeredness. Then my experiment came to a screeching halt on Interstate 80 just east of Sacramento. I was screaming along at 85 miles an hour in my Civic Hybrid (it can too go that fast), cranking Lil Wayne while scanning for cops. Only I wasn't checking the rearview mirror; I was staring at an app that flags speed traps. Suddenly an object loomed large in my windshield. A jade-colored Prius had slowed almost to a stop in front of me. I stomped the brakes and swerved onto the shoulder to avoid a hybrid mashup. My heart raced.

And that's when it hit me: I had gained better location awareness but was losing my sense of place. Sure, with the proper social filters, location awareness needn't be invasive or creepy. But it can be isolating. Even as we gradually digitize our environment, we should remember to look around the old-fashioned way. I took a deep breath, pulled back onto the highway, and drove home—directed by the Google Maps app on my iPhone, of course. And I didn't get lost once.

DISCUSSION

1. "The location-aware future—good, bad, and sleazy—is here," Honan writes. "Millions of people are now walking around with a gizmo in their pocket that not only knows where they are but also plugs into the Internet to share that info." How do you respond to this portrait of the future? With excitement or open-mindedness? If so, what advantages or benefits do you see? If not, what specific concerns, worries, or problems does this vision of the future suggest?

2. According to Honan, the "GPS revolution" is rapidly ushering in a new type of visual norm, one in which it is considered entirely acceptable, even unremarkable, for countless "strangers" to track the details of our moment-to-moment movements. First, put yourself in the position of a hypothetical viewer of such material. What, in your view, is the appeal of playing this particular role? What is enjoyable or useful about enjoying this kind of visual access? Next, put yourself in the position of a person being watched. What would it feel like to play this role?

3. What does Honan mean when he writes, "I had gained better location awareness but was losing my sense of place"? Do these online devices disconnect us from our experiences and relationships in the "real world"? If so, is this something we should worry about or attempt to change?

WRITING

4. About all the new location-awareness technology, Honan remarks: "This is new territory, and there's no established etiquette or protocol." If you were to create a user's manual for this new technology, what would it include? What specific rules would you create for how this application should be used? In a brief essay, outline the rules you would institute for this particular application. What restrictions would you put on the publication of this "personal-geo" information? What privacy or safety features would you require or recommend? As you describe these rules, spend some time as well explaining why you would choose them. Why do you think these rules are so important or necessary? What larger purpose or goal does each serve?

5. In our increasingly digital age, we face a fundamental question: What (if anything) do we still consider to be truly and exclusively private? Given the explosive rise in technologies granting us access to the most intimate aspects of each others' lives, where do we now draw the line between what we consider public and what we consider private? Write an essay in which you explain where, in your view, the boundary between public and private should be drawn. What guidelines, limits, or restrictions should be placed on what others are allowed to see about us? And why?

6. In many ways, Honan's account of his experiences with location-awareness technology recalls Jessica Bennett's investigation into Internet "fame" (p. 113). In its own way, each essay poses fundamental questions about what it means to put oneself on display: to turn one's life and oneself into a public spectacle for a larger public. Write an essay in which you compare how these two writers address these questions. In your view, does each offer a critique or celebration of this growing trend toward self-display? What benefits or risks does each identify? And which commentary do you find more convincing? Why?

JESSICA BENNETT

The Flip Side of Internet Fame

From YouTube to Facebook to Twitter, we have grown accustomed to the experience of being watched and followed online. Many of us simply take it as a given that our day-to-day activities will be captured and put on display for one audience or another. But is this situation really normal? What are the consequences of living in a world where what we do and what we say automatically become public? Taking up precisely these questions, Jessica Bennett looks more closely at our modern visual culture, examining the effects that such perpetual audienceship has on the ways we think and feel. Bennett is a senior writer for *Newsweek*, where she covers cultural affairs and women's issues. Her reporting about the rise in gay activism after the passage of Proposition 8, which overturned legalized gay marriage in California, earned her a 2009 award from the Gay and Lesbian Alliance Against Defamation (GLAAD). The following selection originally appeared in the February 22, 2008, edition of *Newsweek*.

IN 2002, GHYSLAIN RAZA, A CHUBBY CANADIAN TEEN, FILMED HIMSELF acting out a fight scene from *Star Wars* using a makeshift light saber. His awkward performance was funny, in part because it wasn't meant to be. And it certainly was never meant to be public: for nearly a year the video remained on a shelf in Raza's school's TV studio, where he'd filmed it. Sometime in 2003, though, another student discovered the video, digitized it, and posted it online—and Raza's nightmare began. Within days, "Star Wars Kid" had become a viral frenzy. It was posted on hundreds of blogs, enhanced by music and special effects, and watched by millions. Entire Web sites were dedicated to the subject; one, jedimaster.net, was even named one of *Time*'s 50 best sites of 2003. Had that teenager wanted to be famous, he couldn't have asked for anything better. But in Raza's case it became a source of public humiliation, precisely what every kid fears the most.

Razas of the world take note: among the generation that's been reared online, stories like this are becoming more and more common. They serve as important reminders of a dark side of instant Internet fame: humiliation. Already dozens of Web sites exist solely to help those who would shame others. There are sites for posting hateful rants about ex-lovers (DontDateHimGirl.com) and bad tippers (the S----ty Tipper Database), and for posting cell-phone images of public bad behavior (hollabackNYC.com) and lousy drivers. As a new book makes clear in powerful terms, such sites can make or break a person, in a matter of seconds.

> ## "Anybody can become a celebrity or a worldwide villain in an instant."

"Anybody can become a celebrity or a worldwide villain in an instant," says Daniel Solove, a law professor at George Washington University and author of *The Future of Reputation: Gossip, Rumor and Privacy on the Internet* (Yale). "Some people may revel in that. But others might say that's not the role they wanted to play in life."

"Dog poop girl" wasn't the public role a South Korean student had in mind when, in 2005, she refused to clean up after her dog in the subway in Seoul. A minor infraction, perhaps, but another passenger captured the act on a cell-phone camera, posted it online, and created a viral frenzy. The woman was harassed into dropping out of college. More recently a student at Lewis & Clark University in Portland, Ore., was publicly accused—on Facebook, the social-networking site—of sexually assaulting another student. Normally, such allegations on campus are kept confidential. But in this case a Facebook group revealed his name, with the word "rapist" for the world to see, before the incident was ever even reported to the authorities. The accused teen was never arrested or charged, but he might as well have been: bloggers picked up the story, and a local alt-weekly put it on its cover, revealing graphic details of the encounter as described by the alleged victim, without including the supposed perpetrator's version of events.

Public shaming, of course, is nothing new. Ancient Romans punished wrongdoers by branding them on the forehead—slaves caught stealing got *fur* (Latin for thief) and runaways got *fug* (fugitive). In Colonial America heretics were clamped into stocks in the public square, thieves had their hands or fingers cut off, and adulterers were forced to wear a scarlet A. More recently a U.S. judge forced a mail thief to wear a sign announcing his crime outside a San Francisco post office; in other places sex offenders have to post warning signs on their front lawns.

Although social stigma can be a useful deterrent, "the Internet is a loose cannon," says ethicist Jim Cohen of Fordham University School of Law in New York. Online there are few checks and balances and no due process—and validating the credibility of a claim is difficult, to say the least. Moreover, studies show that the anonymity of the Net encourages people to say things they normally wouldn't. JuicyCampus, a gossip Web site for U.S. college students, has made headlines by tapping into this urge. The site solicits juicy rumors under the protection of anonymity for sources. But what may have begun as fun and games has turned into a venue for bigoted rants and stories about drug use and sex that identify students by name. "Anyone with a grudge can maliciously and sometimes libelously attack defenseless students," Daniel Belzer, a Duke senior, told *Newsweek* in December.

Regulators find sites like JuicyCampus hard to control. Laws on free speech and defamation vary widely between countries. In the United States, proving libel requires the victim to show that his or her persecutor intended malice, while the British system puts the burden on the defense to show that a statement is not libelous (making it much easier to prosecute). A 1996 U.S. law—Section 230 of the Communications Decency Act—specifically protects the operators of Web sites from liability for the speech of their users. As long as the host of a site doesn't post or edit content, it has no liability. (If AOL, say, were held responsible for every poster, it would quickly go out of business.)

So, then, what's to stop a person from posting whatever he wants about you, if he can do so anonymously and suffer no repercussions? For people who use blogs and social-networking sites like diaries, putting their personal information out there for the world to see, this presents a serious risk. "I think young people are seduced by the citizen-media notion of the Internet: that everyone can have their minutes of fame," says Barry Schuler, the former CEO of AOL who is now the coproducer of a new movie, *Look*, about public video surveillance. "But they're also putting themselves out there—forever."

Shaming victims, meanwhile, have little legal recourse. Identifying posters often means having to subpoena an anonymous IP address. But that could lead nowhere. Many people share IP addresses on college networks or Wi-Fi hotspots, and many Web sites hide individual addresses. Even if a victim identifies the defamer, bloggers aren't usually rich enough to pay big damage awards. Legal action may only increase publicity—the last thing a shaming victim wants. "The law can only do so much," warns Solove.

Once unsavory information is posted, it's almost impossible to retrieve. The family of the "Star Wars Kid," who spent time in therapy as a result of his ordeal, filed suit against the students who uploaded his video, and settled out of court. But dozens of versions of his video are still widely available, all over the Net. One of the bad boyfriends featured on Don'tDateHimGirl.com also sued, but his case was dismissed due to lack of jurisdiction. The accused rapist at Lewis & Clark has also hired lawyers. But Google his name today, and the first entry has the word "rapist" in its title. If the "Star Wars Kid" has anything to teach us, it's that shame, like the force, will always be with you.

DISCUSSION

1. Bennett's essay poses fundamental questions about what it means in our culture to watch and be watched. What is the connection between how we view ourselves and how others view us? How does the Internet alter this dynamic? Can you think of a moment in your life when you had to confront a discrepancy between your self-image and the image others held of you? In the face of this discrepancy, what did you do?

2. Take a moment to focus on the title of this essay. To what extent does Bennett's portrait of online shaming challenge prevailing norms regarding fame? What, in your view, are the more typical ways we are taught in our culture to regard the prospect of being famous? What, according to the dominant scripts, is fame supposed to do to and for us? And how does Bennett's discussion uncover the "flip side" of such norms?

3. How do you understand the concept of public shaming? In your view, is this a defensible, even reasonable, practice? Or do its dangers outweigh its benefits?

WRITING

4. Part of the problem posed by online shaming has to do with the ways this behavior bumps up against our belief in free expression. How do we balance a belief in the freedom of speech against our concern for safeguarding peoples' reputation? In a brief essay, identify what limits, if any, you would place on the free exchange of ideas so fundamental to the Internet. If you were given the power to legislate these limits, where would you draw the line? What restrictions or guidelines would you mandate for how a viewer or reader could respond to or use somebody else's personal information? Quote some of Bennett's examples to support your argument.

5. Taken together, the examples Bennett cites amount to a case study in the dangers of our cultural obsession with fame. Write an essay in which you discuss your thoughts on fame and notoriety. How do you understand our society's celebration of being famous? Is this, in your view, a worthwhile ideal to pursue? Does our culture create scripts for how and why to become famous that are worth following? How or how not?

6. How do you think Ariel Levy (p. 143) would respond to Bennett's portrait of online shaming? In a one-page essay, identify and analyze what you see as the parallels between these two essays. Do you think Levy would regard the women profiled in *Girls Gone Wild* as representative examples of how publicity can falsify or malign reputation? Why or why not?

HARRIET MCBRYDE JOHNSON

Unspeakable Conversations

What does it mean to be tokenized, to have the stereotypes based on how we look become the scripts by which others think about and define us? In recounting her two-day experience playing the role of what she calls the "token cripple" on a Princeton University visit, Harriet McBryde Johnson raises a series of provocative questions about the ways in which our physical appearance comes to stand as definitive proof of who and what we are. Johnson practiced law in Charleston, South Carolina. She earned a BS in history from Charleston Southern University (1978), a master's in public administration from the College of Charleston (1981), and a JD from the University of South Carolina (1985). She wrote about political and disability issues for a number of publications, such as *South Carolina Lawyer* and *Review of Public Personnel Administration.* She also wrote a novel titled *Accidents of Nature* (2006). Johnson passed away on June 4, 2008.

HE INSISTS HE DOESN'T WANT TO KILL ME. HE SIMPLY THINKS IT would have been better, all things considered, to have given my parents the option of killing the baby I once was, and to let other parents kill similar babies as they come along and thereby avoid the suffering that comes with lives like mine and satisfy the reasonable preferences of parents for a different kind of child. It has nothing to do with me. I should not feel threatened.

Whenever I try to wrap my head around his tight string of syllogisms, my brain gets so fried it's . . . almost fun. Mercy! It's like *Alice in Wonderland.*

It is a chilly Monday in late March, just less then a year ago. I am at Princeton University.

My host is Prof. Peter Singer, often called—and not just by his book publicist—the most influential philosopher of our time. He is the man who wants me dead. No, that's not at all fair. He wants to legalize the killing of certain babies who

My host is Prof. Peter Singer. . . . He is the man who wants me dead.

might come to be like me if allowed to live. He also says he believes that it should be lawful under some circumstances to kill, at any age, individuals with cognitive impairments so severe that he doesn't consider them "persons." What does it take to be a person? Awareness of your own existence in time. The capacity to harbor preferences as to the future, including the preference for continuing to live.

At this stage of my life, he says, I am a person. However, as an infant, I wasn't. I, like all humans, was born without self-awareness. And eventually, assuming my brain finally gets so fried that I fall into that wonderland where self and other and present and past and future blur into one boundless, formless all or nothing, then I'll lose my personhood and therefore my right to life. Then, he says, my family and doctors might put me out of my misery, or out of my bliss or oblivion, and no one count it murder.

I have agreed to two speaking engagements. In the morning, I talk to 150 undergraduates on selective infanticide. In the evening, it is a convivial discussion, over dinner, of assisted suicide. I am the token cripple with an opposing view.

I had several reasons for accepting Singer's invitation, some grounded in my involvement in the disability rights movement, others entirely personal. For the movement it seemed an unusual opportunity to experiment with modes of discourse that might work with very tough audiences and bridge the divide between our perceptions and theirs. I didn't expect to straighten out Singer's head. But maybe I could reach a student or two. Among the personal reasons: I was sure it would make a great story, first for telling and then for writing down.

By now I've told it to family and friends and colleagues, over lunches and dinners, on long car trips, in scads of e-mail messages and a couple of formal speeches. But it seems to be a story that just won't settle down. After all these tellings, it still lacks a coherent structure; I'm miles away from a rational argument. I keep getting interrupted by questions like these:

Q: Was he totally grossed out by your physical appearance?

A: He gave no sign of it. None whatsoever.

Q: How did he handle having to interact with someone like you?

A: He behaved in every way appropriately and treated me as a respected professional acquaintance and was a gracious and accommodating host.

Q: Was it emotionally difficult for you to take part in a public discussion of whether your life should have happened?

A: It was very difficult. And horribly easy.

Q: Did he get that job at Princeton because they like his ideas on killing disabled babies?

A: It apparently didn't hurt. But he's most famous for animal rights. He's the author of *Animal Liberation*.

Q: How can he put so much value on animal life and so little value on human life?

That last question is the only one I avoid. I used to say I don't know, it doesn't make sense. But now I've read some of Singer's writing, and I admit it does make sense—within the conceptual world of Peter Singer. But I don't want to go there. Or at least, not for long.

So I will start from those other questions and see where the story goes this time.

That first question, about my physical appearance, needs some explaining.

It's not that I'm ugly. It's more that most people don't know how to look at me. The sight of me is routinely discombobulating. The power wheelchair is enough to inspire gawking, but that's the least of it. Much more impressive is the impact on my body of more than four decades of a muscle wasting disease. At this stage of my life, I'm Karen Carpenter thin, flesh mostly vanished, a jumble of bones in a floppy bag of skin. When, in childhood, my muscles got too weak to hold up my spine, I tried a brace for a while, but fortunately a skittish anesthesiologist said no to fusion, plates, and pins—all the apparatus that might have kept me straight. At 15, I threw away the back brace and let my spine reshape itself into a deep twisty S-curve. Now my right side is two deep canyons. To keep myself upright, I lean forward, rest my rib cage on my lap, plant my elbows beside my knees. Since my backbone found its own natural shape, I've been entirely comfortable in my skin.

> **It's not that I'm ugly. It's more that most people don't know how to look at me.**

I am in the first generation to survive to such decrepitude. Because antibiotics were available, we didn't die from the childhood pneumonias that often come with weakened respiratory systems. I guess it is natural enough that most people don't know what to make of us.

Two or three times in my life—I recall particularly one largely crip, largely lesbian cookout halfway across the continent—I have been looked at as a rare kind of beauty. There is also the bizarre fact that where I live, Charleston, S.C., some people call me Good Luck Lady: they consider it propitious to cross my path when a hurricane is coming and to kiss my head just before voting day. But most often, the reactions are decidedly negative. Strangers on the street are moved to comment:

> I admire you for being out; most people would have given up.

> God bless you! I'll pray for you. You don't let the pain hold you back, do you? If I had to live like you, I think I'd kill myself.

I used to try to explain that in fact I enjoy my life, that it's a great sensual pleasure to zoom by power chair on these delicious muggy streets, that I have no more reason to kill myself than most people. But it gets tedious. God didn't put me on this street to provide disability awareness training to the likes of them. In fact, no god put anyone anywhere for any reason, if you want to know.

But they don't want to know. They think they know everything there is to know, just by looking at me. That's how stereotypes work. They don't know that they're confused. That they're really expressing the discombobulation that comes in my wake.

So. What stands out when I recall first meeting Peter Singer in the spring of 2001 is his apparent immunity to my looks. His apparent lack of discombobulation, his immediate ability to deal with me as a person with a particular point of view.

Then, 2001. Singer has been invited to the College of Charleston not two blocks from my house. He is to lecture on "Rethinking Life and Death." I have been dispatched by Not Dead Yet, the national organization leading the disability-rights opposition to legalized assisted suicide and disability based killing. I am to put out a leaflet and do something during the Q and A.

On arriving almost an hour early to reconnoiter, I find the scene almost entirely peaceful; even the boisterous display of South Carolina spring is muted by gray wisps of Spanish moss and mottled oak bark.

I roll around the corner of the building and am confronted with the unnerving sight of two people I know sitting on a park bench eating veggie pitas with Singer. Sharon is a veteran activist for human rights. Herb is South Carolina's most famous atheist. Good people, I've always thought—now sharing veggie pitas and conversation with a proponent of genocide. I try to beat a retreat, but Herb and Sharon have seen me. Sharon tosses her trash and comes over. After we exchange the usual courtesies she asks, "Would you like to meet Professor Singer?" She doesn't have a clue. She probably likes his book on animal rights. "I'll just talk to him in the Q and A." But Herb, with Singer at his side, is fast approaching. They are looking at me and Herb is talking, no doubt saying nice things about me. He'll be saying that I'm a disability rights lawyer and that I gave a talk against assisted suicide at his secular humanist group a while back. He didn't agree with everything I said, he'll say, but I was brilliant. Singer appears interested, engaged. I sit where I'm parked. Herb makes an introduction.

Singer extends his hand.

I hesitate. I shouldn't shake hands with the Evil One. But he is Herb's guest, and I simply can't snub Herb's guest at the college where Herb teaches. Hereabouts, the rule is that if you're not prepared to shoot on sight, you have to be prepared to shake hands. I give Singer the three fingers on my right hand that still work. "Good afternoon, Mr. Singer. I'm here for Not Dead Yet." I want to think he flinches just a little. Not Dead Yet did everything possible to disrupt his first week at Princeton. I sent a check to the fund for the 14 arrestees, who included comrades in power chairs. But if Singer flinches, he instantly recovers. He answers my questions about the lecture format. When he says he looks forward to an interesting exchange, he seems entirely sincere.

It is an interesting exchange. In the lecture hall that afternoon, Singer lays it all out. The "illogic" of allowing abortion but not infanticide, of allowing withdrawal of life support but not active killing. Applying the basic assumptions of preference utilitarianism, he spins out his bone-chilling argument for letting parents kill disabled babies and replace them with nondisabled babies who have a greater chance at happiness. It is all about allowing as many individuals as possible to fulfill as many of their preferences as possible.

As soon as he's done, I get the microphone and say I'd like to discuss selective infanticide. I'm a lawyer. I disagree with his jurisprudential assumptions. Logical inconsistency is not a sufficient reason to change the law. As an atheist, I object to his using religious terms (the doctrine of the sanctity of human life) to characterize his critics. Singer takes a note pad out of his pocket and jots down my points, apparently eager to take them on, and I proceed to the heart of my argument: that the presence or absence of a disability doesn't predict quality of life. I question his replacement-baby theory, with its assumption of "other things equal," arguing that people are not fungible. I draw out a comparison of myself and my nondisabled brother Mac (the next-born after me), each of us with a combination of gifts and flaws so peculiar that we can't be measured on the same scale.

He responds to each point with clear and lucid counterarguments. He proceeds with the assumption that I am one of the people who might rightly have been killed at birth. He sticks to his guns, conceding just enough to show himself open-minded and flexible. We go back and forth for 10 long minutes. Even as I am horrified by what he says and by the fact that I have been sucked into a civil discussion of whether I ought to exist, I can't help being dazzled by his verbal facility. He is so respectful, so free of condescension, so focused on the argument, that by the time the show is over, I'm not exactly angry with him. Yes, I am shaking, furious, enraged—but it's for the big room, 200 of my fellow Charlestonians who have listened with polite interest, when in decency they should have run him out of town on a rail.

My encounter with Peter Singer merits a mention in my annual canned letter that December. I decide to send Singer a copy. In response, he sends me the nicest possible e-mail message. Dear Harriet (if he may) . . . Just back from Australia where he's from. Agrees with my comments on the world situation. Supports my work against institutionalization. And then some pointed questions to clarify my views on selective infanticide.

I reply. Fine, call me Harriet, and I'll reciprocate in the interest of equality, though I'm accustomed to more formality. Skipping agreeable preambles, I answer his questions on disability-based infanticide and pose some of my own. Answers and more questions come back. Back and forth over several weeks it proceeds, an engaging discussion of baby killing, disability prejudice, and related points of law and philosophy. Dear Harriet. Dear Peter.

Singer seems curious to learn how someone who is as good an atheist as he is could disagree with his entirely reasonable views. At the same time, I am trying to plumb his theories. What has him so convinced it would be best to allow parents to kill babies with severe disabilities, and not other kinds of babies if no infant is a "person" with a right to life? I learn it is partly that both biological and adoptive parents prefer healthy babies. But I have trouble with basing life-and-death decisions on market considerations when the market is structured by prejudice. I offer a hypothetical comparison: "What about mixed-race babies, especially when the combination is entirely nonwhite, who I believe are just about as unadoptable as babies with disabilities? Wouldn't a law allowing the killing of these undervalued babies validate race prejudice?" Singer agrees there is a problem. "It would be horrible," he says, "to see mixed-race babies being killed because they can't be adopted, whereas white ones could be." What's the difference? Preferences based on race are unreasonable. Preferences based on ability are not. Why? To Singer, it's pretty simple: disability makes a person "worse off."

Are we "worse off?" I don't think so. Not in any meaningful sense. There are too many variables. For those of us with congenital conditions, disability shapes all we are. Those disabled later in life adapt. We take constraints that no one could choose and build rich and satisfying lives within them. We enjoy pleasures other people enjoy, and pleasures peculiarly our own. We have something the world needs.

Pressing me to admit a negative correlation between disability and happiness, Singer presents a situation: imagine a disabled child on the beach, watching the other children play.

It's right out of the telethon. I expected something more sophisticated from a professional thinker. I respond: "As a little girl playing on the beach, I was already aware that some people felt sorry for me, that

I wasn't frolicking with the same level of frenzy as other children. This annoyed me, and still does." I take the time to write a detailed description of how I, in fact, had fun laying on the beach, without the need of standing, walking, or running. But, really, I've had enough. I suggest to Singer that we have exhausted our topic, and I'll be back in touch when I get around to writing him.

He responds by inviting me to Princeton. I fire off an immediate maybe.

Of course, I'm flattered. Mama will be impressed. But there are things to consider. Not Dead Yet says—and I completely agree—that we should not legitimate Singer's views by giving them a forum. We should not make disabled lives subject to debate. Moreover, any spokesman chosen by the opposition is by definition a token. But even if I'm a token, I won't have to act like one. Anyway, I'm kind of stuck. If I decline, Singer can make some hay: "I offered them a platform, but they declined rational discussion." It's an old trick, and I've laid myself wide open.

Imagine a disabled child on the beach, watching the other children play.

My invitation is to have an exchange of views with Singer during his undergraduate course. He also proposes a second "exchange," open to the whole university later in the day. This sounds a lot like debating my life—and on my opponent's turf, with my opponent moderating, to boot. I offer a counterproposal, to which Singer proves amenable. I will open the class with some comments on infanticide and related issues and then let Singer drill me as hard as he likes before we open it up for the students. Late in the day, I might take part in a discussion of some other disability issues in a neutral forum. Singer suggests a faculty-student discussion group sponsored by his department but with cross-departmental membership. The topic I select is "Assisted Suicide, Disability Discrimination, and the Illusion of Choice: A Disability Rights Perspective." I inform a few movement colleagues of this turn of events, and advice starts rolling in. I decide to go with the advisers who counsel me to do the gig, lie low, and get out of Dodge.

I ask Singer to refer me to the person who arranges travel at Princeton. I imagine some capable and unflappable woman like my sister, Beth, whose varied job description at a North Carolina University includes handling visiting artists. Singer refers me to his own assistant, who certainly seems capable and unflappable enough. However, almost immediately Singer jumps back in via e-mail. It seems the nearest hotel has only one wheelchair-accessible suite available with two rooms for $600 per night. What to do? I know I shouldn't be so accommodating, but I say I can make do with an inaccessible room if it has certain features. Other logistical issues come up. We go back and forth. Questions and answers. Do I really need a lift-equipped vehicle at the airport? Can't my assistant assist me into a conventional car? How wide is my wheelchair?

By the time we're done, Singer knows that I am 28 inches wide. I have trouble controlling my wheelchair if my hand gets cold. I am accustomed to driving on rough, irregular surfaces, but I get nervous turning on steep slopes. Even one step is too many. I can swallow purees, soft bread, and grapes. I use a bedpan, not a toilet. None of this is a secret: none of it cause for angst. But I do wonder whether Singer is jotting down my specs in his little note pad as evidence of how "bad off" people like me really are.

I realize I must put one more issue on the table: etiquette. I was criticized within the movement when I confessed to shaking Singer's hand in Charleston, and some are appalled that I have agreed to break bread with him in Princeton. I think they have a very good point, but again, I'm stuck. I'm engaged for a day of discussion, not a picket line. It is not in my power to marginalize Singer at Princeton; nothing would be accomplished by displays of personal disrespect. However, chumminess is clearly inappropriate. I tell Singer that in the lecture hall it can't be Harriet and Peter, it must be Ms. Johnson and Mr. Singer.

He seems genuinely nettled. Shouldn't it be Ms. Johnson and Professor Singer, if I want to be formal? To counter, I invoke the ceremonial low country usage. Attorney Johnson and Professor Singer, but point out that Mr./Ms. is the custom in American political debates and might seem more normal in New Jersey. All right, he says. Ms./Mr. it will be.

I describe this awkward social situation to the lawyer in my office who has served as my default lunch partner for the past 14 years. He gives forth a full body shudder.

"That poor, sorry son of a bitch! He has no idea what he's in for."

Being a disability rights lawyer lecturing at Princeton does confer some cachet at the Newark airport. I need all the cachet I can get. Delta Airlines has torn my power chair. It is a fairly frequent occurrence for any air traveler on wheels.

When they inform me of the damage in Atlanta, I throw a monumental fit and tell them to have a repair person meet me in Newark with new batteries to replace the ones inexplicably destroyed. Then I am told no new batteries can be had until the morning. It's Sunday night. On arrival in Newark, I'm told of a plan to put me up there for the night and get me repaired and driven to Princeton by 10 A.M.

"That won't work. I'm lecturing at 10. I need to get there tonight, go to sleep, and be in my right mind tomorrow."

"What? You're lecturing? They told us it was a conference. We need to get you fixed tonight!"

Carla, the gate agent, relieves me of the need to throw any further fits by undertaking on my behalf the fit of all fits.

Carmen, the personal assistant with whom I'm traveling, pushes me in my disabled chair around the airport in search of a place to use the bedpan. However, instead of diaper-changing tables, which are functional, though far from private, we find a flip-down plastic shelf that doesn't look like it would hold my 70 pounds of body weight. It's no big deal: I've restricted my fluids. But Carmen is a little freaked. It is her first adventure in power-chair air travel.

I keep forgetting that even people who know me well don't know much about my world.

I thought I prepared her for the trip, but I guess I neglected to warn her about the probability of wheelchair destruction. I keep forgetting that even people who know me well don't know much about my world.

We reach the hotel at 10:15 P.M., four hours late.

I wake up tired. I slept better than I would have slept in Newark with an unrepaired chair, but any hotel bed is a near guarantee of morning crankiness. I tell Carmen to leave the TV off. I don't want to hear the temperature.

I do the morning stretch. Medical people call it passive movement but it's not really passive. Carmen's hands move my limbs following my precise instructions, her strength giving effect to my will. Carmen knows the routine, so it is in near silence that we begin easing slowly into the day. I let myself be propped up to eat oatmeal and drink tea. Then there's the bedpan and then bathing and dressing, still in bed. As the caffeine kicks in, silence gives way to conversation about practical things. Carmen lifts me into my chair and straps a rolled towel under my ribs for comfort and stability. She tugs at my clothes to remove wrinkles that could cause pressure sores. She switches on my motors and gives me the means of moving without anyone's help. They don't call it a power chair for nothing.

I drive to the mirror. I do my hair in one long braid. Even this primal hairdo requires, at this stage of my life, joint effort. I undo yesterday's braid. Fix the part and comb the hair in front. Carmen combs where I can't reach. I divide the mass into three long hanks and start the braid just behind my left ear. Section by section, I hand it over to her—and her unimpaired young fingers pull tight. Crisscross, until the braid is fully formed.

A big polyester scarf completes my costume. Carmen lays it over my back. I tie it the way I want it. But Carmen starts fussing with it trying to tuck it down in the back. I tell her that it's fine, and she stops.

On top of the scarf, she wraps the two big shawls that I hope will substitute for an overcoat. I don't own any real winter clothes. I just stay out of the cold, such cold as we get in Charleston.

We review her instructions for the day. Keep me in view and earshot; be instantly available but not intrusive. Be polite, but don't answer any questions about me. I am glad that she has agreed to come. She's strong, smart, adaptable, and very loyal. But now she is digging under the shawl, fussing with that scarf again.

"Carmen. What are you doing?" "I thought I could hide this furry thing you sit on." "Leave it, Singer knows lots of people eat meat. Now he'll know some crips sit on sheepskin."

The walk in is cold but mercifully short. The hotel is just across the street from Princeton's wrought-iron gate and a few short blocks from the building where Singer's assistant shows us to the elevator. The elevator doubles as the janitor's closet—the cart with the big trashcan and all the accouterments is rolled aside so I can get in. Evidently, there aren't a lot of wheelchair people using this building.

We ride the broom closet down to the basement and are led down a long passageway to a big lecture hall. As the students drift in, I engage in light badinage with the sound technician. He is squeamish about touching me but I insist that the cordless lavaliere is my mike of choice. I invite him to clip it to the big polyester scarf.

The students enter from the rear door, way up at ground level and walk down stairs to their seats. I feel like an animal in the zoo. I hadn't reckoned on the architecture, those tiers of steps that separate me from a human wall of apparent physical and mental perfection, that keep me confined down here in my pit.

It is 5 before 10. Singer is loping down the stairs. I feel like signaling to Carmen to open the door, summon the broom closet, and get me out of here. But Singer greets me pleasantly and hands me Princeton's check for $500, the fee he offered with apologies for its inadequacy.

So. On with the show.

My talk to the students is pretty Southern. I've decided to pound them with heart, hammer them with narrative and say "y'all" and "folks." I play with the emotional tone, giving them little peaks and valleys, modulating three times in one 45-second patch. I talk about justice. Even beauty and love. I figure they haven't been getting much of that from Singer.

Of course, I give them some argument too. I mean to honor my contractual obligations. I lead with the hypothetical about mixed-race, non-white babies and build the ending around the question of who should have the burden of proof as to the quality of disabled lives. And woven through the talk is the presentation of myself as a representative of a minority group that has been rendered invisible by prejudice and oppression, a participant in a discussion that would not occur in a just world.

I let it go a little longer than I should. Their faces show they're going where I'm leading, and I don't look forward to letting them go. But the clock on the wall reminds me of promises I mean to keep, and I stop talking and submit myself to examination and inquiry.

Singer's response is surprisingly soft. Maybe after hearing that this discussion is insulting and painful to me, he doesn't want to exacerbate my discomfort. His reframing of the issues is almost pro forma, abstract, entirely impersonal. Likewise, the students' inquiries are abstract and fairly predictable: anencephaly, permanent unconsciousness, eugenic abortion. I respond to some of them with stories, but mostly I give answers I could have e-mailed in.

I call on a young man near the top of the room.

"Do you eat meat?" "Yes, I do." "Then how do you justify—"

"I haven't made any study of animal rights, so anything I could say on the subject wouldn't be worth everyone's time." The next student wants to work the comparison of disability and race, and Singer joins the discussion until he elicits a comment from me that he can characterize as racist. He scores a point, but that's all right. I've never claimed to be free of prejudice, just struggling with it.

Singer proposes taking me on a walk around campus, unless I think it would be too cold. What the hell? "It's probably warmed up some. Let's go out and see how I do." He doesn't know how to get out of the building without using the stairs, so this time it is my assistant leading the way. Carmen has learned of another elevator, which arrives empty. When we get out of the building, she falls behind a couple of paces, like a respectful chaperone.

In the classroom, there was a question about keeping alive the unconscious. In response, I told a story about a family I knew as a child, which took loving care of a nonresponsive teenage girl, acting out their unconditional commitment to each other, making all the other children, and me as their visitor, feel safe. This doesn't satisfy Singer. "Let's assume we can prove, absolutely, that the individual is totally unconscious and that we can know, absolutely, that the individual will never regain consciousness." I see no need to state an objection with no stenographer present to record it; I'll play the game and let him continue.

"Assuming all that," he says, "don't you think continuing to take care of that individual would be a bit weird?" "No. Done right, it could be profoundly beautiful."

"But what about the caregiver, a woman typically, who is forced to provide all this service to a family member, unable to work, unable to have a life of her own?" "That's not the way it should be. Not the way it has to be. As a society, we should pay workers to provide that care, in the home. In some places, it's been done that way for years. That woman shouldn't be forced to do it, any more than my family should be forced to do my care."

Singer takes me around the architectural smorgasbord that is Princeton University by a route that includes not one step, unramped curb, or turn on a slope. Within the strange limits of this strange assignment, it seems Singer is doing all he can to make me comfortable.

He asks what I thought of the students' questions.

"They were fine, about what I expected. I was a little surprised by the question about meat eating."

"I apologize for that. That was out of left field. But—I think what he wanted to know is how you can have such high respect for human life and so little respect for animal life."

"People have lately been asking me the converse, how you can have so much respect for animal life and so little respect for human life."

"And what do you answer?"

"I say I don't know. It doesn't make a lot of sense to me."

"Well, in my view—"

"Look, I have lived in blissful ignorance all these years, and I'm not prepared to give that up today."

"Fair enough," he says and proceeds to recount bits of Princeton history. He stops. "This will be of particular interest to you, I think. This is where your colleagues with Not Dead Yet set up their blockade." I'm grateful for the reminder. My brothers and sisters were here before me and behaved far more appropriately than I am doing.

A van delivers Carmen and me early for the evening forum. Singer says he hopes I had a pleasant afternoon.

Yes, indeed. I report a pleasant lunch and a very pleasant nap, and I tell him about the Christopher Reeve Suite in the hotel which has been remodeled to accommodate Reeve, who has family in the area.

"Do you suppose that's the $600 accessible suite they told me about?" "Without doubt. And if I'd known it was the Christopher Reeve Suite, I would have held out for it." "Of course you would have!" Singer laughs. "And we'd have had no choice, would we?"

We talk about the disability rights critique of Reeve and various other topics. Singer is easy to talk to, good company. Too bad he sees lives like mine as avoidable mistakes.

I'm looking forward to the soft vegetarian meal that has been arranged; I'm hungry. Assisted suicide, as difficult as it is, doesn't cause the kind of agony I felt discussing disability-based infanticide. In this one, I understand, and to some degree can sympathize with, the opposing point of view, misguided though it is.

My opening sticks to the five-minute time limit. I introduce the issue as framed by academic articles Not Dead Yet recommended for my use. Andrew Batavia argues for assisted suicide based on autonomy, a principle generally held high in the disability rights movement. In general, he says, the movement fights for our right to control our own lives; when we need assistance to effect our choices, assistance should be available to us as a matter of right. If the choice is to end our lives, he says, we should have assistance then as well. But Carol Gill says that it is differential treatment—disability discrimination—to try to prevent most suicides while facilitating the suicides of ill and disabled people. The social-science literature suggests that the public in general, and physicians in particular, tend to underestimate the quality of life of disabled people, compared with our own assessments of our lives. The case for assisted suicide rests on stereotypes that our lives are inherently so bad that it is entirely rational if we want to die.

> **The case for assisted suicide rests on stereotypes.**

I side with Gill. What worries me most about the proposals for legalized assisted suicide is their veneer of beneficence—the medical determination that, for a given individual, suicide is reasonable or right. It is not about autonomy but about nondisabled people telling us what's good for us.

In the discussion that follows, I argue that choice is illusory in a context of pervasive inequality. Choices are structured by oppression. We shouldn't offer assistance with suicide until we all have the assistance we need to get out of bed in the morning and live a good life. Common causes of suicidality—dependence, institutional confinement, being a burden—are entirely curable. Singer, seated on my right, participates in the discussion but doesn't dominate it. During the meal, I occasionally ask him to put things within my reach and he competently complies.

I feel as if I'm getting to a few of them. When a student asks me a question, the words are all familiar, but they're strung together in a way so meaningless that I can't even retain them—it's like a long sentence in Tagalog. I can only admit my limitations. "That question's too abstract for me to deal with. Can you rephrase it?" He indicates that it is as clear as he can make it, so I move on.

A little while later my right elbow slips out from under me. This is awkward. Normally I get whoever is on my right to do this sort of thing. Why not now? I gesture to Singer. He leans over, and I whisper, "Grasp this wrist and pull forward one inch, without lifting." He follows my instructions to the letter. He sees that now I can again reach my food with my fork. And he may now understand what I was saying a minute ago, that most of the assistance disabled people need does not demand medical training.

A philosophy professor says, "It appears that your objections to assisted suicide are essentially tactical."

"Excuse me?"

"By that I mean they are grounded in current conditions of political, social, and economic inequality. What if we assume that such conditions do not exist?"

"Why would we want to do that?"

"I want to get to the real basis for the position you take."

I feel as if I'm losing caste. It is suddenly very clear that I'm not a philosopher. I'm like one of those old practitioners who used to visit my law school, full of bluster about life in the real world. Such a bore! A once-sharp mind gone muddy! And I'm only 44—not all that old.

The forum is ended, and I've been able to eat very little of my pureed food. I ask Carmen to find the caterer and get me a container. Singer jumps up to take care of it. He returns with a box and obligingly packs my food to go.

When I get home, people are clamoring for the story. The lawyers want the blow-by-blow of my forensic triumph over the formidable foe; when I tell them it wasn't like that, they insist that it was. Within the disability rights community, there is less confidence. It is generally assumed that I handled the substantive discussion well, but people worry that my civility may have given Singer a new kind of legitimacy. I hear from Laura, a beloved movement sister. She is appalled that I let Singer provide even minor physical assistance at the dinner. "Where was your assistant?" she wants to know. How could I put myself in a relationship with Singer that made him appear so human, even kind?

I struggle to explain. I didn't feel disempowered; quite the contrary, it seemed a good thing to make him do some useful work. And then, the hard part: I've come to believe that Singer actually is human, even kind in his way. There ensues a discussion of good and evil and personal assistance and power and philosophy and tactics for which I'm profoundly grateful.

I e-mail Laura again. This time I inform her that I've changed my will. She will inherit a book that Singer gave me, a collection of his writings with a weirdly appropriate inscription: "To Harriet Johnson, So that you will have a better answer to questions about animals. And thanks for coming to Princeton. Peter Singer. March 25, 2002." She responds that she is changing her will, too. I'll get the autographed photo of Jerry Lewis she received as an M.D.A. poster child. We joke that each of us has given the other a "reason to live."

I have had a nice e-mail message from Singer, hoping Carmen and I and the chair got home without injury, relaying positive feedback from my audiences—and taking me to task for a statement that isn't supported by a relevant legal authority, which he looked up. I report that we got home exhausted but unharmed and concede that he has caught me in a generalization that should have been qualified. It's clear that the conversation will continue.

I am soon sucked into the daily demands of law practice, family, community, and politics. In the closing days of the state legislative session, I help get a bill passed that I hope will move us one small step toward a world in which killing won't be such an appealing solution to the "problem" of disability. It is good to focus on this kind of work. But the conversations with and about Singer continue. Unable to muster the appropriate moral judgments, I ask myself a tough question: am I in fact a silly, little lady whose head is easily turned by a man who gives her a kind of attention she enjoys? I hope not, but I confess that I've never been able to sustain righteous anger for more than about 30 minutes at a time. My view of life tends more toward tragedy.

The tragic view comes closest to describing how I now look at Peter Singer. He is a man of unusual gifts, reaching for the heights. He writes that he is trying to create a system of ethics derived from fact and reason, that largely throws off the perspectives of religion, place, family, tribe, community, and maybe even species—to "take the point of view of the universe." His is a grand, heroic undertaking.

But like the protagonist in a classical drama, Singer has his flaw. It is his unexamined assumption that disabled people are inherently "worse off," that we "suffer," that we have lesser "prospects of a happy life." Because of this all-too-common prejudice and his rare courage in taking it to its logical conclusion, catastrophe looms. Here in the midpoint of the play, I can't look at him without fellow-feeling.

I am regularly confronted by people who tell me that Singer doesn't deserve my human sympathy. I should make him an object of implacable wrath, to be cut off, silenced, destroyed absolutely. And I find myself lacking an argument to the contrary.

I am talking to my sister Beth on the phone. "You kind of like the monster, don't you?" she says.

I find myself unable to evade, certainly unwilling to lie. "Yeah, in a way. And he's not exactly a monster." "You know, Harriet, there were some very pleasant Nazis. They say the SS guards went home and played on the floor with their children every night."

She can tell that I'm chastened; she changes the topic, lets me off the hook. Her harshness has come as a surprise. She isn't inclined to moralizing; in our family, I'm the one who sets people straight.

When I put the phone down, my argumentative nature feels frustrated. In my mind, I replay the conversation but this time defend my position. "He's not exactly a monster. He just has some strange ways of looking at things." "He's advocating genocide." "That's the thing. In his mind, he isn't. He's only giving parents a choice. He thinks the humans he is talking about aren't people, aren't 'persons.'"

"But that's the way it always works, isn't it? They're always animals or vermin or chattel goods. Objects, not persons. He's repacking some old ideas. Making them acceptable." "I think his ideas are new, in a way. It's not old-fashioned hate. It's a twisted, misinformed, warped kind of beneficence. His motive is to do good."

"What do you care about motives?" she asks. "Doesn't this beneficent killing make disabled brothers and sisters just as dead?"

"But he isn't killing anyone. It's just talk."

"Just talk? It's talk with an agenda, talk aimed at forming policy. Talk that's getting a receptive audience. You of all people know the power of that kind of talk."

"Well, sure, but—"

"If talk didn't matter, would you make it your life's work?"

"But," I say, "his talk won't matter in the end. He won't succeed in reinventing morality. He stirs the pot, brings things out into the open. But ultimately, we'll make a world that's fit to live in, a society that has room for all its flawed creatures. History will remember Singer as a curious example of the bizarre things that can happen when paradigms collide."

"What if you are wrong? What if he convinces people that there's no morally significant difference between a fetus and a newborn, and just as disabled fetuses are routinely aborted now, so disabled babies are routinely killed? Might some future generation take it further than Singer wants to go? Might some say there's no morally significant line between a newborn and a 3-year-old child?"

"Sure. Singer concedes that a bright line cannot be drawn. But he doesn't propose killing anyone who prefers to live."

"That overarching respect for the individual's preference for life—might some say it's a fiction, a fetish, a quasi-religious belief?"

"Yes," I say. "That's pretty close to what I think. As an atheist, I think all preferences are moot once you kill someone. The injury is entirely to the surviving community."

"So what if that view wins out, but you can't break disability prejudice? What if you wind up in a world where the disabled person's 'irrational' preference to live must yield to society's 'rational' interest in reducing the incidence of disability? Doesn't horror kick in somewhere? Maybe as you watch the door close behind whoever has wheeled you into the gas chamber?"

"That's not going to happen."

"Do you have empirical evidence?" she asks. "A logical argument?"

"Of course not. And I know it's happened before, in what was considered the most progressive medical community in the world. But it won't happen. I have to believe that."

Belief. Is that what it comes down to? Am I a person of faith after all? Or am I clinging to foolish hope that the tragic protagonist, this one time, will shift course before it's too late?

DISCUSSION

1. Johnson devotes a good deal of time acquainting her readers with the facts about her disability, itemizing the various things that, as a result of her physical condition, she can and cannot do. Why do you think she does this? How does this tactic help her advance her argument about the ways disabled people are seen in our culture?

2. Look again at the photograph of Johnson that begins the essay. What were your initial assumptions about her based on her picture? In what ways does our popular culture encourage us both to see and *not* see people with disabilities? That is to say, how do the images of and stories about disability that we typically see encourage us to think about people with disabilities?

3. To what extent is it valid to think of Johnson's account here as expanding or enlarging the scope of the ways disabled people are conventionally seen? What quotes can you find from her essay to support your opinion?

WRITING

4. Take a moment to look at the photo that Johnson includes of herself in this essay. What are your immediate reactions? What does it feel like to be shown this picture? In a short essay, describe the particular cultural or social norms you think the portrait is designed to challenge or violate. How does this image differ from those we typically see? What alternative messages (for example, about disabled experience itself, about how it gets represented) do you think it is intended to convey? What quotes from Johnson's essay support your reading of this image? Finally, argue either for or against the validity of showing this kind of image.

5. Have you ever felt "tokenized" because of your physical or external appearance? When people first meet you, what assumptions do you think they make about you based on your appearance? Write a personal essay in which you recount what the experience of being seen in this particular way is like. What perceptions of you did people have? What conclusions did they draw? And in what ways were they inaccurate, unfair, or otherwise limiting? Use quotes from Johnson's essay to pinpoint both the parallels and the key differences between your own experience and what Johnson recounts in her essay.

6. Johnson and Michael Eric Dyson (p. 147) both draw a clear connection between watching and stereotyping. Each of their essays points centrally to the ways that being "misread" by the public at large can lead to being marginalized, disenfranchised, and oppressed. Write an essay in which you compare and contrast the differences in the ways these two writers explore this connection. Despite their shared concern over stereotyping, how and where do their discussions diverge?

TRENTON STRAUBE

Viewer Discretion

Can entertainment television do more than merely entertain us? Is it possible for things like sitcoms and reality shows to serve as vehicles for serious political discussion? Trenton Straube certainly thinks so, arguing for the powerful role pop culture might play in the fight against HIV. Straube is an editor and a writer for the gay news outlet the *New York Blade.* His writing has appeared in the gay publications *HX* and *POZ,* a magazine that specializes in HIV/AIDS education. He lives in New York City. The following selection was originally published in the December 2009 issue of *POZ.*

THE "POST-AIDS SEXUAL REVOLUTION" IS HERE! IT'S HAPPENING right now, every Tuesday night on the new *Melrose Place.* That's according to the show's executive director Todd Slavkin. When describing the updated series to E! Entertainment, he said: "We feel that there is a current sexual revolution going on. Kind of post-AIDS—where the boundaries are off." Unlike their sexually shackled parents, today's twentysomethings residing in the new Melrose want to explore their wild sides.

Sounds fun! But will those explorations include condoms or real-world consequences? If the "post-AIDS" attitude is any indication, then no. And that's more than irresponsible. It's a wasted opportunity. One of the most underused and overlooked resources in the fight against AIDS is right in front of our eyes: the stories and characters on today's hit television shows.

"It can be especially powerful when [sexual health] messaging is incorporated in a show," explains Victoria Rideout, MA, who studies health and media at the Kaiser Family Foundation. "The advantage is that it's less preachy and in the context of drama and characters you already know and care about." (Not to mention, you can't fast-forward them like commercials.)

Plus, the messages sink in. Kaiser proved this last year when it worked with the writers of *Grey's Anatomy* to create an episode in which an HIV-positive woman discovers she is pregnant and is informed that she has a 98 percent chance of giving birth to a healthy, HIV-negative baby if she takes the proper meds. Polling the show's viewers, researchers found that one week before the show, 15 percent understood the correct risk of mother-to-child transmission. A week after the show, 61 percent remembered the proper risk—which translated to more than 8 million people absorbing the HIV message—and six weeks later, 45 percent had retained the information.

Unfortunately, references on TV to condoms and safe-sex messages seem to be going the way of analog broadcasts. "Among the 20 most highly rated shows for teen viewers, only one in 10 of those with sexual content includes a reference to sexual risks or responsibilities at some point in the episode," found a separate Kaiser study that examined TV programs from 1997 to 2005. And those references were often in passing and incidental.

Additionally, the number of sex scenes on television doubled during the same period, and a total of one out of every nine shows (excluding news, sports, and children's shows) depicted or strongly implied sexual intercourse.

The average 8- to 18-year old watches three hours of television a day, and the average adult watches 5.5 hours a day—that's a lot of sex scenes. And RAND studies have proved that adolescents who were exposed to a high level of sexual content were twice as likely to initiate sex in the next year, compared with peers who watched fewer such shows.

Given that television remains the most popular entertainment media among youths, even a smart fifth-grader could realize that the most direct route to viewers is advertisements and public service announcements (PSAs). But aside from their expense, commercials must be approved by the networks and cable affiliates. (And their logic can sometimes be as head-scratching as an episode of *Lost*.)

The AIDS Healthcare Foundation (AHF) discovered the challenge of delivering safe-sex messages via a PSA when it created a commercial starring Sheryl Lee Ralph, who implored viewers to talk about HIV, practice safe sex, and get tested. AHF planned to air the spot during the animated series *Family Guy*—but, according to AHF president Michael Weinstein, Fox rejected the ad because it talked about and showed a condom.

> *Products with preventative claims—especially preventing pregnancy—are not allowed.*

Trojan, the nation's largest condom manufacturer, runs into a similar wall. "With restrictions [on TV marketing], we can only reach about 50 to 60 percent of our target audience in a year," says Jim Daniels, Trojan's vice president of marketing. He recounts asking a network lawyer, "Why is it that we can see advertisements for herpes medications, but I can't advertise for the very product that will prevent it?" That network's rationale, Daniels says, was that it's OK to advertise products that diagnose or treat a preexisting condition, but products with preventive claims—especially preventing pregnancy—are not allowed.

Groups like AHF, Kaiser, and The National Campaign to Prevent Teen and Unplanned Pregnancy are finding ways to navigate television's rules by creating PSAs and web content directly related to TV shows. And in the case of MTV's *16 and Pregnant*, even helping to create and market an entire program. But more needs to be done. A Trojan study found that 50 percent of Americans between 18 and 34 claim they didn't receive condom education. And according to the CDC, more HIV infections occurred in 2006 among people ages 13 to 29 than any other age group, confirming that HIV is an epidemic primarily of young people.

Imagine how these numbers might change if more advocates focused on embedding safe-sex information in television programs. It could be done in an organic manner that's consistent with and honors the show. After all, *Seinfeld* found a way to talk about condoms and the Sponge—and we're still laughing about it 14 years later. If more programs could follow suit, then maybe one day, when we talk about a post-AIDS world, it won't be as far-fetched as an episode of *Melrose Place*.

DISCUSSION

1. Straube's central argument is that TV, our most pervasive disseminator of pop culture, constitutes an almost entirely overlooked resource in our fight against AIDS. How do you respond to this claim? Does our pop culture strike you as a valuable opportunity to generate discussions of contentious social or political issues? Is this the sort of thing you already see happening? How? If not, why not?

2. One of the assumptions on which Straube's argument relies is the premise that media images help shape peoples' actual behavior. Do you see the media in the same way? Does it create scripts that we live out directly? Or do you see media influence expressing itself in other ways? If so, how?

3. While the number of sex scenes on mainstream television has doubled over the last decade, Straube reports, only one in ten of the most highly rated shows "includes a reference to sexual risks or responsibilities." What point is Straube trying to make by including these statistics? What do these statistics suggest about the sexual norms being promulgated within the media?

WRITING

4. "*Seinfeld*," Straub observes, "found a way to talk about condoms and the Sponge—and we're still laughing about it 14 years later. If more programs could follow suit, then maybe one day, when we talk about a post-AIDS world, it won't be as far-fetched as an episode of *Melrose Place*." Choose a TV show that, in your view, offers a useful vehicle for advancing either an AIDS-aware or any other social message. Then write a brief essay outlining how such a message might be integrated into this show's existing format. What sort of script would you use to rewrite this show's depiction of and messages about sex? What new story line might you create? What new characters might you introduce? Why?

5. What are the more typical ways we are taught in our popular culture to look at and think about HIV/AIDS? In a brief essay, present an overview of the images of and messages about HIV/AIDS our media tends to present. What attitudes toward this disease and those who live with it are we typically encouraged to form? Are these views, in your estimation, accurate? Fair? Why or why not?

6. Ariel Levy (p. 143) is another writer interested in the ways our pop culture can influence prevailing public attitudes about sex. Write a one-page essay in which you assess Straube's strategy for creating HIV/AIDS-conscious television in the context of Levy's portrait of *Girls Gone Wild*. To what extent does Levy's exposé complicate or undermine Straube's call for a more "responsible" depiction of sex? Do these two authors, taken together, illustrate a larger problem about the depiction of sex in popular culture?

ANNE-MARIE CUSAC
Watching Torture in Prime Time

Foremost among our pop culture's signature features is its striking confluence of fiction and reality. To what extent, we could well ask, is our understanding of real-world events conditioned and mediated by the entertainment spectacles, shows, and images that we watch? For Anne-Marie Cusac, this very possibility poses a fundamental and troubling question: When it comes to the news and current events, how do we ever know the real story? Cusac is an investigative reporter and an assistant professor in the Department of Communication at Roosevelt University. Her magazine articles have won several prizes, including the George Polk Award. She has also published poems in a number of journals, and her work has been nominated twice for the Pushcart Prize. She has published two books of poems, *The Mean Days* (2001) and *Silkie* (2007). The following essay first appeared in the August 2005 issue of the *Progressive*.

IN THE SAME WEEK AS THE ONE-YEAR ANNIVERSARY OF ABU GHRAIB, an episode of the Fox hit show 24 opened with a scene of the Counter Terrorism Unit medical clinic. Lying in a hospital bed, attended to by physicians, was the terrorism suspect who, in the last seconds of the previous episode, had screamed as the show's hero, Jack Bauer, broke the bones in his hand.

As Fox pumped out advertisements for 24's season finale, the newspapers boiled over with revelations of more real torture by U.S. officers. Then the finale came, and Jack and company saved Los Angeles from a nuclear bomb thanks to a wild series of strategies that included brutal torture.

In the days that followed, Amnesty International issued what amounted to an all-points bulletin for Bush Administration officials: "The officials implicated in these crimes are . . . subject to investigation and possible arrest by other nations while traveling abroad." Like Jack Bauer, the 24 star who in the final scene of the last episode flees to Mexico, Donald Rumsfeld and George W. Bush were suddenly wanted men, accused of breaking international law.

Rarely in my days has fictional television seemed so entwined with our national political life.

Unlike most current cop shows, 24 is concerned with crime prevention. In 24, the would-be crimes are so huge and so imminent that the anti-terrorism team believes it does not have the luxury of playing by the rules. Anxiety—which the show manipulates with exaggerated plot twists—explains some of 24's appeal. Among other explanations is 24's proximity to real events and public fears. The shadow of 9/11 hangs over the show. And then there is torture itself, which has a unique power to horrify.

Kiefer Sutherland, an executive producer on the show as well as the star who plays Jack Bauer, seems driven to address the places where his show intersects with American guilt. "Do I personally believe that the police or any of these other legal agencies that are working for this government should be entitled to interrogate people and do the things that I do on the show? No, I do not," he said in an interview with Charlie Rose.

Joel Surnow, also an executive producer, has connected 24's realism with an appearance of conservatism. "Doing something with any sense of reality to it seems conservative," he told the rightwing paper the *Washington Times,* which praised the show. Surnow also told the paper that 24's writers are both liberal and conservative, that 24 doesn't "try to push an agenda," but is "committed to being non-PC." He also offered a defense of torture under extreme circumstances, the sort that characterize the world of 24. "If there's a bomb about to hit a major U.S. city and you have a person with information . . . if you don't torture that person, that would be one of the most immoral acts you could imagine," he told the *Washington Times.* Surnow doesn't admit this, but the continual regurgitation of situations involving imminent bombings and torture separates 24 from reality and renders it a fantasy show. Impending disaster has rarely, if ever, accompanied the real tortures that get into our newspapers.

> **Rarely in my days has fictional television seemed so entwined with our national political life.**

Torture on 24 is as contradictory as the statements of its producers. In this past season, 24 depicted torture and terrorism as married. The show's logic ran like this: A nuclear bomb launched from Iowa was in the air on its way to . . . no one knew exactly where. The target was almost certainly a large coastal city. The hardworking counter-terrorism employees who never ate, used the toilet, or slept, whose cell phone batteries never died, needed to stop the explosion from killing millions of innocent people. They had no information on the bomb. They did, however, have a suspect in custody.

It's an unfair competition. If you place torture of a few people, innocent or not, next to an imminent nuclear holocaust, torture seems like a necessity.

But 24's voyeuristic interest in torture is an uncomfortable one. For one thing, and I count this as a detail in the show's favor, 24 differs from many cop shows in that it does not mince around pain. Physical hurt is audible and visible on this show and often difficult to watch. The pain is a harsh contrast to the "happy violence" (which avoids realistic depictions of suffering) that critics of TV have complained about for decades. That 24 insists on rendering pain with such clarity is disturbing in light of the fact that, in this past season, the torturers caused extreme hurt to the wrong people several times. The possibility of torturing an innocent is a hovering concern of the show.

On the other hand, 24 also depicts torture as a useful tool as long as the torturers manage to choose the correct victim. Both those who know a lot and those who know a little spill important information within seconds after the pain starts—which is not a common occurrence.

But efficacy doesn't have the only vote here. Some of those who disagree with Jack's action are straw men, but one voice of reason and goodness belongs to Audrey, who loves Jack and whose own personality and situation are compelling. When she starts to wonder about her love for him, Jack starts to seem monomaniacal and dangerous. After Audrey sees the man with broken fingers lying in the CTU hospital bed, for instance, she turns on the man she loves. "Jack, you cannot keep working outside the law and not expect consequences," she says.

One big consequence is that, by season's end, Jack has lost Audrey's love. After seeing Jack torture her estranged husband, Paul, using a lamp's electrical wires, Audrey also watches as he commands the medical personnel who are trying to save Paul's life to disconnect him from the machines. As Paul begins to die, Jack forces the doctor to save another man so that Jack can interrogate him. "You killed him," accuses Audrey. "I hate you."

But Audrey, who represents, among other things, an ineffectual President, U.S. law, and human love, is not the only indication that Jack's behavior has been criminal. Equally revealing is the post-torture scene, where the victim lies in a hospital bed getting torture aftercare—a physical position often occupied by victims of crime in police dramas.

Those humanistic messages bump up against others that depict Jack as a hero. When Audrey, who is the daughter of the Defense Secretary, tells her dad that she no longer sees the humane Jack, he responds, "We need men like that." And the season finale's very last scene shows Jack in sunglasses walking off into (really!) the sunset.

These multiple meanings suggest why both Amnesty International (which sees torture in the show as "educational") and the conservative magazine *National Review* (which compared the show's conflicts to Greek tragedy) have praised 24. But some critics read the torture scenes as advocating the practice rather than questioning it.

Some critics read the torture scenes as advocating the practice rather than questioning it.

In a May 22 article in the *New York Times*, Adam Green asks: "Has 24 descended down a slippery slope in portraying acts of torture as normal and there-fore justifiable?" His article bears the unsubtle title, "Normalizing Torture, One Rollicking Hour at a Time." He wonders whether the audience of the show, "and the public more generally," is "reworking the rules of war to the point where the most expedient response to terrorism is to resort to terror." How that debate "plays out on 24 may say a great deal about what sort of society we are in the process of becoming," he writes.

But in certain parts of American society, torture is already normal. The cultural conditions and political decisions that created Abu Ghraib and widespread torture of detainees by American forces happened before 24. We are already a society that tortures—evidently we became that long ago. What is left to us now as a public is a decision we can make or avoid. We can deal with torture or ignore it. Television does not deter-mine the outcome of that decision; we do.

The more our government sanctions torture, the more that high-level officials do not face censure, the more our democracy erodes. When our highest officials are not held to account, it is often tempting to feel apathetic about torture, as if we have nothing to do with its existence. Intentional disregard seems to be the way we are dealing with this, though few of us are saying so.

In bringing its loudmouthed depictions of extreme cruelty into a show as otherwise attractive and suspense-driven as 24, the show's writers are giving their often fervent fans something to trouble them.

DISCUSSION

1. "Rarely in my days," writes Cusac, "has fictional television seemed so entwined with our national political life" as in the case of the popular television show *24*. Can you think of another example from our current pop culture that fictionalizes current events? Another show where the line between fact and fiction seems similarly blurred?

2. In your view, is there a clear connection between the images of and stories about violence we see and our own personal behavior? What is the best way to understand the relationship between the things we look at and the things we do?

3. *24*'s depiction of torture remains compelling, Cusac argues, in part because the show is able to instill in its viewers an almost palpable feeling of fear. "Anxiety," she writes, "which the show manipulates . . . explains some of *24*'s appeal." Do you agree with this argument? Do we live in a world where the pleasure of watching is tied in some way to the prospect of being frightened? How or how not?

WRITING

4. Cusac contrasts the ways torture gets depicted on *24* to the countless examples elsewhere on television of what she calls "happy violence," violence where the terrible and tangible are largely erased. Choose one such example from our current pop culture and describe the particular ways this show works to expunge the consequences of violence from its presentation. And as you sketch out how this process works, make sure that you address what you think this process means, what the consequences are of rendering the effects of violence invisible and what this trend suggests about the ways we are taught to think about violence in our culture more generally. What attitude toward violence does this kind of portrayal seem designed to normalize?

5. Under what conditions can something even as shocking and taboo as torture come to seem like an unremarkable norm? Make a list of all the things about torture that you think are wrong: all the aspects of this practice that render it outside the bounds of our conventional (social, political, ethical) norms. Then create a second list of the particular circumstances (political crisis, catastrophic event, and so on) under which somebody could argue for the validity, even the necessity, of torture. Write an essay in which you argue how Cusac sees the role of television as normalizing torture. Do you agree or disagree?

6. Cusac shares with Naomi Klein (p. 160) a common concern over the ways our entertainment media can shape public attitudes regarding current events, especially the political. What aspects of Cusac's thinking do you think Klein would most likely endorse? Where might the two part ways? Offer a response to Cusac's argument that, in your view, Klein herself would write, using quotes from both writers to support your argument.

ARIEL LEVY

Women and the Rise of Raunch Culture

What does it feel like to be a consumer in the world of "raunch culture"? A world where, according to Ariel Levy, sexual self-exhibition has for women become not merely a norm but a perverse kind of social ideal? Focusing on the rise of such things as *Girls Gone Wild* and the Howard Stern radio show, Levy wonders about the new and troubling ways we have learned to think about gender equity, feminist politics, and the pursuit of civil rights. Levy studied literature at Wesleyan University and worked briefly at Planned Parenthood before starting her career as a journalist. Her articles have been published in the *New York Times,* the *Washington Post, Vogue,* and *Slate.* She is currently a staff writer at the *New Yorker.* Her first book, published in 2005, is *Female Chauvinist Pigs: Women and the Rise of Raunch Culture.*

I FIRST NOTICED IT SEVERAL YEARS AGO. I WOULD TURN ON THE television and find strippers in pasties explaining how best to lap dance a man to orgasm. I would flip the channel and see babes in tight, tiny uniforms bouncing up and down on trampolines. Britney Spears was becoming increasingly popular and increasingly unclothed, and her undulating body ultimately became so familiar to me I felt like we used to go out.

Charlie's Angels, the film remake of the quintessential jiggle show, opened at number one in 2000 and made $125 million in theaters nationally, reinvigorating the interest of men and women alike in leggy crime fighting. Its stars, who kept talking about "strong women" and "empowerment," were dressed in alternating soft-porn styles—as massage parlor geishas, dominatrixes, yodeling Heidis in alpine bustiers. (The summer sequel in 2003—in which the Angels' perilous mission required them to perform stripteases—pulled in another $100 million domestically.) In my own industry, magazines, a porny new genre called the Lad Mag, which included titles like *Maxim, FHM,* and *Stuff,* was hitting the stands and becoming a huge success by delivering what *Playboy* had only occasionally managed to capture: greased celebrities in little scraps of fabric humping the floor.

This didn't end when I switched off the radio or the television or closed the magazines. I'd walk down the street and see teens and young women—and the occasional wild fifty-year-old—wearing jeans cut so low they exposed what came to be known as butt cleavage paired with miniature tops that showed off breast implants and pierced navels alike. Sometimes, in case the overall message of the outfit was too subtle, the shirts would be emblazoned with the Playboy bunny or say PORN STAR across the chest.

Some odd things were happening in my social life, too. People I knew (female people) liked going to strip clubs (female strippers). It was sexy and fun, they explained; it was liberating and rebellious. My best friend from college, who used to go to Take Back the Night marches on campus, had become captivated by porn stars. She would point them out to me in music videos and watch their (topless) interviews on *Howard Stern*. As for me, I wasn't going to strip clubs or buying *Hustler* T-shirts, but I was starting to show signs of impact all the same. It had only been a few years since I'd graduated from Wesleyan University, a place where you could pretty much get expelled for saying "girl" instead of "woman," but somewhere along the line I'd started saying "chick." And, like most chicks I knew, I'd taken to wearing thongs.

What was going on? My mother, a shiatsu masseuse who attended weekly women's consciousness-raising groups for twenty-four years, didn't own makeup. My father, whom she met as a student radical at the University of Wisconsin, Madison, in the sixties was a consultant for Planned Parenthood, NARAL, and NOW. Only thirty years (my lifetime) ago, our mothers were "burning their bras" and picketing Playboy, and suddenly we were getting implants and wearing the bunny logo as supposed symbols of our liberation. How had the culture shifted so drastically in such a short period of time?

> *Suddenly we were getting implants and wearing the bunny logo as supposed symbols of our liberation.*

What was almost more surprising than the change itself were the responses I got when I started interviewing the men and—often—women who edit magazines like *Maxim* and make programs like *The Man Show* and *Girls Gone Wild*. This new raunch culture didn't mark the death of feminism, they told me; it was evidence that the feminist project had already been achieved. We'd *earned* the right to look at *Playboy*; we were *empowered* enough to get Brazilian bikini waxes. Women had come so far, I learned, we no longer needed to worry about objectification or misogyny. Instead, it was time for us to join the frat party of pop culture, where men had been enjoying themselves all along. If Male Chauvinist Pigs were men who regarded women as pieces of meat, we would outdo them and be Female Chauvinist Pigs: women who make sex objects of other women and of ourselves.

When I asked female viewers and readers what they got out of raunch culture, I heard similar things about empowering miniskirts and feminist strippers, and so on, but I also heard something else. They wanted to be "one of the guys"; they hoped to be experienced "like a man." Going to strip clubs or talking about porn stars was a way of showing themselves and the men around them that they weren't "prissy little women" or "girly-girls." Besides, they told me, it was all in fun, all tongue-in-cheek, and for me to regard this bacchanal as problematic would be old-school and uncool.

I tried to get with the program, but I could never make the argument add up in my head. How is resurrecting every stereotype of female sexuality that feminism endeavored to banish *good* for women? Why is laboring to look like Pamela Anderson empowering? And how is imitating a stripper or a porn star—a woman whose *job* is to imitate arousal in the first place—going to render us sexually liberated?

Despite the rising power of Evangelical Christianity and the political right in the United States, this trend has only grown more extreme and more pervasive in the years that have passed since I first became aware of it. A tawdry, tarty, cartoonlike version of female sexuality has become so ubiquitous, it no longer seems particular. What we once regarded as a *kind* of sexual expression we now view *as* sexuality. As former adult film star Traci Lords put it to a reporter a few days before her memoir hit the bestseller list in 2003, "When I was in porn, it was like a back-alley thing. Now it's everywhere." Spectacles of naked ladies have moved from seedy side streets to center stage, where everyone—men and women—can watch them in broad daylight. *Playboy* and its ilk are being "embraced by young women in a curious way in a postfeminist world," to borrow the words of Hugh Hefner.

> **Just because we are post doesn't automatically mean we are feminists.**

But just because we are post doesn't automatically mean we are feminists. There is a widespread assumption that simply because my generation of women has the good fortune to live in a world touched by the feminist movement, that means everything we do is magically imbued with its agenda. It doesn't work that way. "Raunchy" and "liberated" are not synonyms. It is worth asking ourselves if this bawdy world of boobs and gams we have resurrected reflects how far we've come, or how far we have left to go.

DISCUSSION

1. Levy's essay tries to pinpoint what she sees as a contradiction between the tactics of sexual or "porny" self-exhibition and the kind of liberation these acts of display supposedly enable. For Levy, there is something wrong with believing that miniskirts can be empowering or that stripping can be viewed as a feminist act. Do you agree? If so, what in your view makes this kind of association problematic? If not, why not?

2. For the women Levy interviews, there are clear rewards for displaying themselves in the ways they do — payoffs that, in their eyes, make putting on these particular acts well worth doing. How do you assess these so-called benefits? What, specifically, are they? And in your view are they adequate rewards for putting on this kind of role?

3. Choose one of the examples of so-called raunchy behavior described in this essay. Where else (either in the media or in your own experiences) have you seen this same kind of role acted out? What sort of statement about female empowerment do you think this performance made?

WRITING

4. Choose a product (for example, a show, an image, or an object) from our larger popular culture that, in your view, is designed to promote an empowering or liberating message for women. What role does it script, and how does this role compare to the examples cited by Levy? Write an analytical essay in which you argue the benefits and/or pitfalls of these two respective roles.

5. According to Levy, one of the signature aspects of raunch culture is the idea that women are encouraged to participate in it and, in many ways, to control it. Indeed, she writes, "What we once regarded as a *kind* of sexual expression we now view *as* sexuality." Write an essay in which you explore what you think Levy means by this statement. What are her criticisms of this conflation of sex and sexuality? In your opinion, what are some possible ways to address the problem as Levy sees it? How do you think she would respond to your suggestions?

6. Both Levy and Jessica Bennett (p. 113) are interested in examining the consequences of self-exhibitionism. Write an essay in which you compare the way each writer critiques cultural scripts that concern self-display. What does each writer identify as the harm or damage that can result from following this script? And which critique do you find more compelling or convincing? Why?

MICHAEL ERIC DYSON
Frames of Reference

How do media outlets shape, perhaps even create, our impressions of the news? Using the coverage of the Hurricane Katrina disaster as his case study, noted public intellectual Michael Eric Dyson explores some of the consequences of the contrasting ways in which the media "framed" white and black experiences of this event. Dyson is professor of sociology at Georgetown University as well as an ordained Baptist minister. He is the author of sixteen nonfiction books, many of which address race in American society, including *Between God and Gangsta Rap: Bearing Witness to Black Culture* (1996), *Why I Love Black Women* (2003), and *Debating Race* (2007). A number of his essays, speeches, and interviews are collected in *The Michael Eric Dyson Reader* (2004). "Frames of Reference" is from Dyson's *Come Hell or High Water: Hurricane Katrina and the Color of Disaster* (2006).

I F THE MILITANT ADVOCATES HELPED TO FRAME FOR THEIR GENERA-
tion the racial consequences of a natural and economic disaster, the media was critical in framing perceptions of people and events surrounding the catastrophe. This was painfully evident with a set of photos, and their accompanying captions (parts of which I will italicize for emphasis), that were widely circulated on the Internet the day after the storm struck. In the first photo, a young black man clasps items in each arm as he forges through the flood waters. The caption to the AP (Associated Press) photo of him reads: "A young man walks through chest deep flood water after *looting a grocery store* in New Orleans on Tuesday, Aug. 20, 2005. Flood waters continue to rise in New Orleans after Hurricane Katrina did extensive damage when it made landfall on Monday."[1] In the second photo, also from AP, a young white man and woman tote food items in their hands as they carry backpacks and slush through the flood waters. The caption accompanying their photograph reads: "Two residents wade through chest-deep water after *finding bread and soda from a local grocery store* after Hurricane Katrina came through the area in New Orleans, Louisiana."[2]

In this case, the captions say it all: the young black man *loots* his groceries, the white youth *find* theirs. With no stores open, the white youth clearly couldn't have found their groceries, and would have had to obtain them the same way the young black man did. It didn't appear in either photo that someone's charity was responsible for any of the people pictured receiving food, which probably means that the young black man and the white youth stormed a store to get groceries, a quite understandable move under the circumstances. While the white youth's move is rendered "quite understandable" by the language—what else were they to do, after all, and the language lessens the obvious means of their acquiring groceries—the black youth's move is rendered as legally and morally questionable. If he has "looted" then he has broken the legal and moral codes of society.

He is further alienated from his civic standing by simply being described as "a young man" while his white peers are cited as citizens—"two residents." The value judgment communicated by the photo and its caption is largely implicit, though strongly implied by the language. The captions help lend value, and a slant, to essentially neutral photographs, pictures that, on their own, suggest solidarity of circumstance between the black and white youth. But the identical character of their experience is shattered by the language, which casts their actions in contrasting lights: the white youth have been favored by serendipity and thus "naturally" exploit their luck in "finding" food, a gesture that relieves them of culpability; the black youth, by comparison, has interrupted the natural order of things to seize what didn't belong to him and thus remains responsible for his behavior.

> **The captions help lend value, and a slant, to essentially neutral photographs.**

To be sure, none of this is expressly articulated; the existing framework of racial reference suggests its meaning. Such a framework, one that weaves white innocence and black guilt into the fabric of cultural myths and racial narratives, is deeply embedded in society and affects every major American institution, including the media. How black folk are "framed"—how we are discussed, pictured, imagined, conjured to fit a negative idea of blackness, or called on to fill a slot reserved for the outlaw, thug, or savage—shapes how we are frowned on or favored in mainstream society. Words help to interpret images; language and pictures in combination reinforce ideas and stories about black identity. The words that accompany these photos, like the reams of words that accompany the images of black folk in society throughout history, help to underscore hidden bias and sleeping bigotry, often in the most innocent, gentle, and subtle form imaginable. Hence, plausible deniability is critical to such maneuvers, allowing invested parties to reply when called to account: "I didn't mean it that way"; "You're too sensitive"; "You're exaggerating"; or "You're reading too much into things." Thus, the burden to explain or justify behavior is shifted from offender to victim.

The media's role in framing blacks as outlaws and savages achieved a rare blatancy when it endlessly looped on television the same few frames of stranded blacks "looting" food and other items, largely for survival.

The repetition of the scenes of black "looting" contains its own indictment: there wasn't enough film of vandalizing behavior to feature several
instances. By repeating the same few scenes the media helped to spread
the notion that black folk were in a state of social anarchy and were
tearing violently at the fabric of civility and order. The framework didn't
allow for blacks to receive the benefit of the doubt extended to the white
couple that "found" food. Neither was the compelling imagery often
accompanied by commentary to suggest that people who had been abandoned by their government had a right to help themselves—a theme
that surely ought to have pleased the bootstrapping Republicans at the
helm of the federal government. Instead, many critics bitterly lamented
the actions of people who did what they had to do to survive.

To be sure, besides taking food and items to survive—as did local
officials and authorities, including aides to the mayor and the police, who
were given the sort of pass that the masses would never receive—black
folk took clothes and appliances, and a few took guns. These blacks
were drowned in a second flood of media and social criticism that
vilified them for their inexcusable behavior. Even those critics who
were sympathetic to the urgent conditions of the abandoned blacks felt
pressured to embrace the frame of reference of black criminality before
otherwise defending poor blacks. Such critics had to acknowledge that
yes, these were awful and heinous acts, but still, distinctions must be
made between acts of survival and acts of greed, wanton cynicism, or
reckless morality. In order to defend them, their supporters had to prove
that they were willing to establish a hierarchy of the "good Negro" and
the "bad Negro." They often failed to realize that such moral ordering is
futile in a society where the inclination to misbehavior is viewed as true
of black folk in general. Although separating "worthy" from "unworthy"
blacks is supposed to strengthen the cause of the "good Negro," such
distinctions ultimately make all blacks more vulnerable because they
grant legitimacy to a distorted racial framework. Thus, the looting for
looting's sake, versus the looting for survival's sake, may appear to be
a legitimate ordering of black morality, but it is just as likely to obscure
how black identity is seen though a muddy lens. The very act of black folk
taking food, even when conditions are oppressive, generates the sort of
suspicion that white folk will not as a rule be subject to—as in the case
of "looting" versus "finding" food.

Thus, when a moral distinction is made between taking food and
taking other items, it denies the stigma already attached to blacks who
simply sought to survive. I am not arguing that because of the ethical
distortion found in drawing faulty distinctions among black folk, one
cannot thereby condemn immoral behavior. I am simply suggesting that
what constitutes "immoral" black behavior conveniently shifts in reference to black folk to suit the social or racial purposes of a given moment,

or crisis, in the culture. Katrina was one of those moments of crisis. By exaggerating the crisis, the media proved it was caught in a crisis of exaggeration.

Moreover, the hand wringing over poor black folk "looting" exposes the ugly reality that may explain the apparent glee with which some black folk "looted": that property matters more than poor and black people in many quarters of the culture. Some people took clothing items because they needed to change from their soiled clothing where they had to urinate or defecate on themselves. Some people took televisions to barter for food. Some saw luxury items as capital to purchase momentary relief from their misery, whether through exchanging those for food or for money that might, however illusorily, get them and their families free of their situation. Perhaps they could pay somebody with a car to drive them to safety on higher ground. And some of them must have learned their seemingly illogical behavior—that is, for those critics who suggest the black poor couldn't do anything practical or purposeful with the items they filched—from a culture of consumption from which they had been barred. The lesson of that culture seemed to be: have it because you want it.

Of course some were greedy, but that greed wasn't any different—in fact, was its naked face in miniature—than the greed that passed as normal and desirable when it showed up in the upper, richer, whiter classes. To begrudge poor people a gleeful moment of rebellion against property—by taking it, by possessing it, by hoarding it, and by having a taste of things they had been denied all their lives, nice things that they saw the people for whom they slaved routinely enjoy and treasure, even more than they did the poor black folk who stoked their leisure, is an act of arrogant and self-righteous indifference to the plight of the black poor, most of whom, mind you, would never in a million years take anything that didn't belong to them. But desperate people do in desperation what capitalist and political and cultural looters do daily—steal and give little thought to its moral consequence. In a comparative ethical framework, the black poor come out looking a lot more justified than do the disingenuous critics who lambaste them.

That is why New Orleans rapper Juvenile expressed compassion for the black poor and called into question the sanctification of property that would be washed away anyhow. "I don't call it looting," the rapper said. "They stole everything from out of my house, and I'm not mad at the person that stole out of my house. Because the hurricane was gonna hit and the house was gonna get hit with 25 feet of storm surging. It was gonna be damaging. I couldn't do nothing with it anyway. . . . And I think the looting in New Orleans, I don't call it looting, I call it survival."[3] Juvenile explains the logic of folk stealing televisions in order to better their chances of survival. "I might could get this TV and sell it to somebody and get some money. They talking about the TVs and VCRs, 'Why would you take that?' There's still people that got money that could buy where money was still useful. We don't know. The average person don't know. They wasn't down there in the waters. They had people who just wanted some herb to calm they damn nerves."[4]

As journalist Jordan Flaherty argues, the real criminal activity in Katrina can't be laid at the feet of the black poor, but at those who benefited from unjust economic and racial arrangements long before the storm struck. More-over, the media framed black sur-

> *The media framed black survivors as lawless thugs while ignoring the social conditions that made their lives hell.*

vivors as lawless thugs while ignoring the social conditions that made their lives hell.

> While the rich escaped New Orleans, those with nowhere to go and no way to get there were left behind. Adding salt to the wound, the local and national media have spent the last week demonizing those left behind. As someone that loves New Orleans and the people in it, this is the part of this tragedy that hurts me the most, and it hurts me deeply. No sane person should classify someone who takes food from indefinitely closed stores in a desperate, starving city as a "looter," but that's just what the media did over and over again. Sheriffs and politicians talked of having troops protect stores instead of perform rescue operations. Images of New Orleans' hurricane-ravaged population were transformed into black, out-of-control, criminals. As if taking a stereo from a store that will clearly be insured against loss is a greater crime than the governmental neglect and incompetence that did billions of dollars of damage and destroyed a city. This media focus is a tactic, just as the eighties focus on "welfare queens" and "super-predators" obscured the simultaneous and much larger crimes of the Savings and Loan scams and mass layoffs, the hyper-exploited people of New Orleans are being used as a scapegoat to cover up much larger crimes.[5]

The media also framed the black poor when it helped to spread rumors about violent and animalistic black behavior in the shelters to which they fled. Television reports and newspaper accounts brimmed with the unutterable horror of what black folk were doing to each other and their helpers in the Superdome and the convention center: the rape of women and babies, sniper attacks on military helicopters, folk killed for food and water, armed gang members assaulting the vulnerable, dozens of bodies being shoved into a freezer.[6] As the *Times-Picayune* reported, the "picture that emerged was one of the impoverished masses of flood victims resorting to utter depravity, randomly attacking each other, as well as the police trying to protect them and the rescue workers trying to save them."[7] Nearly every one of the allegations proved to be baseless rumor. Of course, the mayor and police commissioner of New Orleans helped spread the rumors as well in famous interviews on *Oprah*. Police commissioner Eddie Compass broke down crying while describing "the little babies getting raped," and Mayor Nagin spoke of the mayhem of people "in that frickin' Superdome for five days watching dead bodies, watching hooligans killing people, raping people."[8]

But hyperbole pervaded the media as well. A day before evacuations began at the Superdome, *Fox News* television issued an "alert" warning of "robberies, rapes, carjackings, riots, and murder. Violent gangs are roaming the streets at night, hidden by the cover of darkness." The *Los Angeles Times* featured a lead news story that dramatically reported National Guard troops taking "positions on rooftops, scanning for snipers and armed mobs as seething crowds of refugees milled below, desperate to flee. Gunfire crackled in the distance." Although the *New York Times* was more cautious in its reporting, noting that reports couldn't be verified, it still repeated stories and reports about widespread violence and unrest. And neither was the exaggeration quarantined to the states. The *Ottawa Sun*, a Canadian tabloid, reported unverified news of "a man seeking help gunned down by a National Guard Soldier" and "a young man run down and then shot by a New Orleans police officer." And the *Evening Standard*, a London newspaper, compared the carnage and chaos to the Mel Gibson futuristic film *Mad Max* and to the novel *Lord of the Flies*.[9]

Most of the information reported by the media proved to be urban legends and cultural myths that swirled in the toxic stew unleashed by Katrina. "It just morphed into this mythical place where the most unthinkable deeds were being done," said National Guard spokesman Major Ed Bush. As government help failed to arrive, a conceptual vacuum opened up that was filled with a powerful mix of lies and legends. There were reports that an infant's body was found in a trash can, that there were sharks unschooled from Lake Pontchartrain swimming through the city's business district, and that hundreds of bodies had been stashed in the basement of the Superdome.[10] A physician from FEMA arrived at the Superdome after international reports of the killings, rapes, murders, and gang violence, expecting a huge cache of bodies. "I've got a report of 200 bodies," National Guard Colonel Thomas Beron recalls the doctor saying to him. "The real total was six."[11] Four people had died of natural causes, one overdosed on drugs, and the other committed suicide by jumping to his death.

Eddie Jordan, the Orleans Parish District Attorney, was outraged by the media's glaring inaccuracies in framing the shelter survivors

> **"It just morphed into this mythical place where the most unthinkable deeds were being done."**

as animals. "I had the impression that at least 40 or 50 murders had occurred at the two sites," Jordan said. "It's unfortunate we saw these kinds of stories saying crime had taken place on a massive scale when that wasn't the case. And they [national media outlets] have done nothing to follow up on any of these cases, they just accepted what people [on the street] told them. . . . It's not consistent with the highest standards of journalism."[12]

Of course, given the nature of rape—a crime that is dramatically underreported under normal conditions—it is likely that such crimes indeed did occur, but, it seems, with nothing near the frequency as reported. Neither has there been any verification of widespread reports of murder—in fact, only one person in the convention center appears to have been a victim of homicide, by stabbing, but even that case is murky. It is likely that there were indeed some thugs present, but it seems clear that they were Antediluvian Thugs—thugs before the flood. But they didn't have much of an impact on the crowds at the Superdome and the convention center. Later, before he was asked to resign by Mayor Nagin, Compass admitted that he was wrong, adding, "The information I had at the time, I thought it was credible." Nagin, too, acknowledged that he didn't have, and probably never would have, an accurate picture of the alleged anarchy that prevailed. "I'm having a hard time getting a good body count."[13]

The *Times-Picayune* captured the remarkable dignity of the crowds and the grossly exaggerated nature of the reports of social disarray that occurred among the evacuees when it concluded that

> Few of the widely reported atrocities have been backed with evidence. The piles of bodies never materialized, and soldiers, police officers, and rescue personnel on the front lines say that although anarchy reigned at times and people suffered unimaginable indignities, most of the worst crimes reported at the time never happened. Military, law enforcement, and medical workers agree that the flood of evacuees—about 30,000 at the Dome and an estimated 10,000 to 20,000 at the Convention Center—overwhelmed their security personnel. The 400 to 500 soldiers in the Dome could have been easily overrun by increasingly agitated crowds, but that never happened, said Col. James Knotts, a midlevel commander there. Security was nonexistent at the Convention Center, which was never designated as a shelter. Authorities provided no food, water, or medical care until troops secured the building the Friday after the storm. While the Convention Center saw plenty of mischief, including massive looting and isolated gunfire, and many inside cowered in fear, the hordes of evacuees for the most part did not resort to violence, as legend has it.[14]

What fed the rumors? It seems that poor communications fostered by the breakdowns of telephones made it nearly impossible for reporters to get accurate information. But the major reason seems to

> *Journalists outdid each other in the competitive urge to describe and remythologize the sheer horror of the huddled black masses.*

be—as *Times-Picayune* editor Jim Amass admitted—a matter of race and class. "If the dome and Convention Center had harbored large numbers of middle class white people," Amoss said, "it would not have been a fertile ground for this kind of rumor-mongering."[15] It is safe to say that the media's framework was ready to receive and recycle rumors of vicious black behavior because such rumors seemed to confirm a widely held view about poor blacks. The more outrageous the reports, the juicier the alleged details, the more poetic and breathless the news reports became. Journalists outdid each other in the competitive urge to describe and remythologize the sheer horror of the huddled black masses. No adjective or metaphor seemed alien to reporters seeking to adequately conjure the chaos of blackness being unleashed on the world in all of its despotic wizardry and evil inventiveness. The cruelty, and crudity, of the poor black evacuees seemed to be a necessary analogue to the environmental misery they endured.

Besides, the media's framing of the black poor seemed to exonerate those who hadn't gotten there quickly enough to help them. The message seemed to be: "If this is how they act, if this is who they are, then their inhumanity is a justification for not rushing to their rescue." The government seemed to be let off the hook. Other folk may have argued that such negative actions among poor blacks could have been arrested had the government arrived on time. Still others thought that the government should have gotten there earlier to arrest the folk themselves. Law and order was a recurring motif of the criticism lobbed at the black evacuees: there was simply no excuse—not even one of the worst natural disasters in the nation's history—for them to misbehave in such fashion. It seems that the status quo and the powers that be needed precisely the sociological framework of the poor that the media presented.

How ironic, then, that the media should have gathered such kudos for locating again that part of their skeletal structure that threads down their backs. It is really doubly ironic. First, because it was at the expense of black suffering—which television reporters and cameras undoubtedly brought home to America in full color—that journalists got credit for regaining their voice. The edifying skepticism displayed by nearly the entire crew of frontline reporters, and on occasion those stationed at a safer distance at their home studios, was a lively and refreshing departure from the predictable banter that sadly passes for refined suspicion. It may have not been very refined, but the outright combativeness that frequently flared for a few days in the media was positively bracing. But the fact that it took such an utter tragedy for the media to stop pretending it was neutral—and to find a way between disingenuous claims of objectivity and crushing bias dressed up as fairness—is ultimately sad. That means that unless another crisis comes along—and already, despite protests to the contrary, America, and the media, have largely moved on past the tragic revelations of Katrina—the media will slink back into spineless endorsements of black pathology, especially for the poor, in one form or another.

The celebration of the media during Katrina is perhaps ultimately ironic since it is the media that has largely been responsible for communicating the culture's spleenful bigotry toward the black poor. To be championed as the defenders of the very population the media has harmed so much, whether intending to or not, should provide more than one occasion of intense discomfort and squirming for journalists. Unless the media reframe their very reference to blackness and poverty, which is not likely to occur without intense pressure, they will have not only failed to earn the encomiums they've received, but worse, they will have set back the quest to truly expose the problems the black poor face by pretending to have done so. As framers of black life, the media can either illumine for the world our complexity or shutter the dizzying dynamism of our identities behind stale stereotypes and callous clichés.

The media framed the evacuees at first as refugees, a term that caused denunciations by black leaders because it seemed to deny that black folk were citizens of the nation. A few critics responded by suggesting that, technically, the black poor could be considered refugees because they were fleeing a catastrophe and seeking refuge away from their homes. But what such clarifications missed is the spiritual truth of black identity that rested more in connotation than denotation, more in signification than grammar. Black folk felt that they had already, for so long, been treated as foreigners in their own land. We desperately sought to claim the rights and privileges that our bitterly fought-for membership in the society should provide.

I saw flashes of this when I visited one of the shelters in Houston for the black displaced, dislocated, and dispersed. When I stepped into the Reliant Center, where thousands of mostly black and poor folk from New Orleans, Mississippi, and Alabama had been chased by Hurricane Katrina's ugly force, I felt the hurt and desperation of a people whose middle name throughout history has been exile. A sea of green nylon cots was all that separated displaced bodies from pavement floors. Some of the folk needed medicine and healing talk. Their ailments of flesh and mind were indifferent to their current plight, as indifferent, it seems, as the government that miserably failed them in their hour of need. Grown men openly wept; resourceful women were emotionally depleted; younger folk had whatever innocence remained from childhoods already battered by poverty cruelly washed away. They were desperate for a glimpse of hope beyond the hell and high water into which they had been plunged. Instead, the richest nation in the world shuttled them to harsh makeshift quarters. But many of the evacuees called upon their faith to see them through. And some of them undoubtedly wondered where God was in all of this. Perhaps they even believed that this was God's will. Could it be that God caused Katrina?

NOTES

[1]"Black People Loot, White People Find?" *Boingboing: A Directory of Wonderful Things*, August 30, 2005, http://www.boingboing.net/2005/08/30/black_people_loot_wh.html.

[2]Ibid.

[3]Satten, "Still Lives Through," *XXL*, December 2005, pp. 112, 114.

[4]Ibid.

[5]Jordan Flaherty, "Notes from Inside New Orleans," *New Orleans Independent Media Center*, September 2, 2005, http://neworleans.indymedia.org/news/2005/09/4043.php.

[6]Susannah Rosenblatt and James Rainey, "Katrina Takes a Toll on Truth, News Accuracy," *Los Angeles Times*, September 27, 2005, p. A16; Brian Thevenot and Gordon Russell, "Rape. Murder. Gunfights. For Three Anguished Days the World's Headlines Blared that the Superdome and Convention Center Had Descended into Anarchy," *The Times-Picayune*, September 26, 2005, p. A01.

[7]Thevenot and Russell, "Rape. Murder. Gunfights."

[8]Rosenblatt and Rainey, "Katrina Takes a Toll."

[9]Ibid.

[10]Ibid.

[11]Thevenot and Russell, "Rape. Murder. Gunfights."

[12]Ibid.

[13]Ibid.

[14]Ibid.

[15]Rosenblatt and Rainey, "Katrina Takes a Toll."

DISCUSSION

1. According to Dyson, the tendency to associate African Americans with "lawlessness," "irresponsibility," "immorality," and "animalism" is one of our culture's most long-standing norms. Do you agree that this kind of thing reflects an ingrained cultural pattern? Can you think of another example where this same kind of association gets reinforced?

2. For Dyson, the term *media framing* has a double meaning, referring both to how an image can be selectively presented and to the ways such selection can lead viewers to form inaccurate or unfair opinions about what it is they see. To what extent do you see one or both of these meanings applying to the general depiction of African Americans in our contemporary culture?

3. In your opinion, how might the media coverage of the Katrina disaster have been different if the majority of the victims were not African American? Do you think Dyson would find himself swayed by your hypothesis?

WRITING

4. Dyson writes, "How black folk are 'framed' — how we are discussed, pictured, imagined, conjured to fit a negative idea of blackness, or called on to fill a slot reserved for the outlaw, thug, or savage — shapes how we are frowned on or favored in mainstream society." Write an essay that analyzes Dyson's argument. What are his main points, and what evidence or statements does he use to support his point of view? As a writer, how does Dyson use words to incite action in the reader?

5. In this essay, Dyson gives us examples of what he argues are the typical responses to the charge of race-specific media bias that he levels: " 'You're too sensitive,' " " 'You're exaggerating,' " " 'You're reading too much into things.' " Indeed, these statements are often employed as a defense against thinking deemed too "politically correct," whether the topic is race, gender, sexuality, or politics. Pick a current event in the news where you see bias in the way a certain class of people has been characterized (illegal immigrants or gay marriage proponents, for example). Write an essay in which you summarize what characterizations of these people you see in the news stories about them. Pay careful attention to the words chosen to describe them or the debate. In what ways do these groups themselves address stories being written about them? Finally, argue whether you see media bias as existing in these cases, using quotes from Dyson's essay to support your argument.

6. Jessica Bennett's essay (p. 113) is another piece that takes a critical look at how mass media technologies can distort or misrepresent what we think of as the truth about ourselves. How does Bennett's assessment of the Internet compare to Dyson's discussion of media framing? Despite the different types of media each investigates, would you say there are parallels that link their respective arguments together? What are they?

Then and Now: *Wearing Your Identity on Your Sleeve*

Merchandisers have long sought to sell their goods by appealing to our sense of personal style: by flattering our desire to make an impression or cultivate an image that reflects our unique individuality. For years, this goal revolved around a strategy known as niche marketing, a tactic designed to associate a given product with the interests, hobbies, or "look" of a particular group. To wear a specific brand of clothing, drive a certain model of car, drink a particular variety of soda was (according to this formulation) to demonstrate your membership within a cohort of people who wear, drive, and drink the same thing — in effect, to make a statement about the *type* of person you truly are. Niche marketing, in other words, encourages us to treat commercial marketing as a viable blueprint for *self*-marketing. When you think of 1950s fashion, one word that might first come to mind is *conformity*,

and indeed the picture at the left shows a group of teenage girls wearing more-or-less the teenage girl uniform of the 1950s. Fashions are often designed to appeal to members of a certain group, even as we talk about fashion as a way to express individual identity. These days, however, niche marketing is giving way to a new sales strategy, one that seems at first glance to resolve this contradiction. No longer content with associating their goods with a consumer type, many merchandisers nowadays promote products that they claim are tailored to nonconformist consumers. A website like Threadless.com, for example, allows artists to create designs that are then voted on by Threadless members, with the most popular designs being printed and sold by the company. For many, this change not only heralds the demise of niche marketing but also signals a movement beyond the outmoded ideas of self-marketing and image-creation. With the advent of customized marketing, we are told, it is now possible for shopping to serve as a truly legitimate means of self-expression, a vehicle for defining and displaying our true individuality.

But how much has *really* changed? Just because merchandisers now market customized products, after all, doesn't necessarily mean they've gotten out of the business of creating and marketing different images. No matter how personalized the messages on these design-your-own T-shirts are, they are still logos. We could well ask whether all of this so-called customized design is simply a different, admittedly more sophisticated, form of branding. At the end of the day, after all, customers who wear these products are still engaging in the same operation that customers always have, one in which they use brand images and logos to make statements about the types of people they are. Do we find ourselves drawn to these kinds of products because they really do help us showcase our genuine selves? Or do we respond to this come-on for the same old reasons — because these products promise to supply us with a genuine self that is made for us?

WRITING

1. In a brief essay, compare the different directions each image lays out for how and why we should shop. What role for the average consumer does each example seem to create? What parallels or similarities do you note? What differences? Which is a more effective way to market clothing? Why?

2. Naomi Klein (p. 160) takes up the issue of consumerism, exploring the ways that commercial culture influences some of our personal attitudes and beliefs. Put yourself in the position of Klein for a moment and write out a description of the ways you think she would evaluate or respond to the notion of "personalized marketing." What aspects of this promotional campaign do you think Klein would focus most attention on? How would she evaluate the messages about shopping and identity these products encourage us to accept?

NAOMI KLEIN

Patriarchy Gets Funky:
The Triumph of Identity Marketing

To what extent do we turn to the world of commercial advertising for guidance about how to think through social and political questions? Tracking the growing phenomenon of identity marketing, Naomi Klein tells the story of how such companies as Benetton and MTV have learned to use mass-produced and mass-marketed models of racial and ethnic diversity as brand names for the products they sell. Wondering about and worrying over the growing indistinguishability between our political and commercial lives, Klein shows how intimately corporate iconography has insinuated itself into the ways we view not just the issue of social activism but the idea of social justice as well. Klein, a writer and activist, was born into a political family in Montreal, Quebec, and currently lives in Toronto. She has worked as the editor of *THIS Magazine* and as a weekly columnist for the *Toronto Star,* and she is currently a columnist for the *Nation* and the *Guardian.* Her books *No Logo* (2000), where this selection comes from, and *Fences and Windows* (2002) discuss globalization and its countermovement. Her latest book is *The Shock Doctrine: The Rise of Disaster Capitalism* (2007).

AS AN UNDERGRADUATE IN THE LATE EIGHTIES AND EARLY NINE-ties, I was one of those students who took a while to wake up to the slow branding of university life. And I can say from personal experience that it's not that we didn't notice the growing corporate presence on campus—we even complained about it sometimes. It's just that we couldn't get particularly worked up about it. We knew the fast-food chains were setting up their stalls in the library and that profs in the applied sciences were getting awfully cozy with pharmaceutical companies, but finding out exactly what was going on in the board-rooms and labs would have required a lot of legwork, and, frankly, we were busy. We were fighting about whether Jews would be allowed in the racial equality caucus at the campus women's center, and why the meeting to discuss it was scheduled at the same time as the lesbian and gay caucus—were the organizers implying that there were no Jewish lesbians? No black bisexuals?

In the outside world, the politics of race, gender, and sexuality remained tied to more concrete, pressing issues, like pay equity, same-sex spousal rights, and police violence, and these serious movements were—and continue to be—a genuine threat to the economic and social order. But somehow, they didn't seem terribly glamorous to students on many university campuses, for whom identity politics had evolved by the late eighties into something quite different. Many of the battles we fought were over issues of "representation"—a loosely defined set of grievances mostly lodged against the media, the curriculum, and the English language. From campus feminists arguing over "representation" of women on the reading lists to gays wanting better "representation" on television, to rap stars bragging about "representing" the ghettos, to the question that ends in a riot in Spike Lee's 1989 film *Do the Right Thing*—"Why are there no brothers on the wall?"—ours was a politics of mirrors and metaphors.

These issues have always been on the political agendas of both the civil-rights and the women's movements, and later, of the fight against AIDS. It was accepted from the start that part of what held back women and ethnic minorities was the absence of visible role models occupying powerful social positions, and that media-perpetuated stereo-types—embedded in the very fabric of the language—served to not so subtly reinforce the supremacy of white men. For real progress to take place, imaginations on both sides had to be decolonized.

But by the time my generation inherited these ideas, often two or three times removed, representation was no longer one tool among many, it was the key. In the absence of a clear legal or political strategy, we traced back almost all of society's problems to the media and the curriculum, either through their perpetuation of negative stereotypes or simply by omission. Asians and lesbians were made to feel "invisible," gays were stereotyped as deviants, blacks as criminals, and women as weak and inferior: a self-fulfilling prophecy responsible for almost all real-world inequalities. And so our battlefields were sitcoms with gay neighbors who never got laid, newspapers filled with pictures of old white men, magazines that advanced . . . "the beauty myth," reading lists that we expected to look like Benetton ads, Benetton ads that trivialized our reading-list demands. So outraged were we media children by the narrow and oppressive portrayals in magazines, in books, and on television that we convinced ourselves that if the typecast images and loaded language changed, so too would the reality. We thought we would find salvation in the reformation of MTV, CNN, and Calvin Klein. And why not? Since media seemed to be the source of so many of our problems, surely if we could only "subvert" them to better represent us, they could save us instead. With better collective mirrors, self-esteem would rise and prejudices would magically fall away, as society became suddenly inspired to live up to the beautiful and worthy reflection we had retouched in its image.

For a generation that grew up mediated, transforming the world through pop culture was second nature. The problem was that these fixations began to transform us in the process. Over time, campus identity politics became so consumed by personal politics that they all but eclipsed the rest of the world. The slogan "the personal is political" came

Transforming the world through pop culture was second nature.

to replace the economic as political and, in the end, the Political as political as well. The more importance we placed on representation issues, the more central a role they seemed to elbow for themselves in our lives—perhaps because, in the absence of more tangible political goals, any movement that is about fighting for better social mirrors is going to eventually fall victim to its own narcissism.

Soon "outing" wasn't about AIDS, but became a blanket demand for gay and lesbian "visibility"—all gays should be out, not just right-wing politicians but celebrities as well. By 1991, the radical group Queer Nation had broadened its media critique: it didn't just object to portrayals of homicidal madmen with AIDS, but any non-straight killer at all. The group's San Francisco and L.A. chapters held protests against *The Silence of the Lambs,* objecting to its transvestite serial-killer villain, and they disrupted filming on *Basic Instinct* because it featured ice-pick-wielding killer lesbians. GLAAD (Gay and Lesbian Alliance Against Defamation) had moved from lobbying the news media about its use of terms like "gay plague" to describe AIDS, and had begun actively pushing the networks for more gay and lesbian characters in TV shows. In 1993, Torie Osborn, a prominent U.S. lesbian rights activist, said that the single biggest political issue facing her constituency was not same-sex spousal benefits, the right to join the military, or even the right of two women to marry and adopt children. It was, she told a reporter, "Invisibility. Period. End of sentence."[1]

Much like a previous generation of anti-porn feminists who held their rallies outside peep shows, many of the political demonstrations of the early nineties had shifted from the steps of government buildings and courthouses to the steps of museums with African art exhibits that were deemed to celebrate the colonial mindset. They massed at the theater entrances showing megamusicals like *Showboat* and *Miss Saigon,* and they even crept right up to the edge of the red carpet at the 1992 Academy Awards.

These struggles may seem slight in retrospect, but you can hardly blame us media narcissists for believing that we were engaged in a crucial battle on behalf of oppressed people everywhere: every step we took sparked a new wave of apocalyptic panic from our conservative foes. If we were not revolutionaries, why, then, were our opponents saying that a revolution was under way, that we were in the midst of a "culture war"? "The transformation of American campuses is so sweeping that it is no exaggeration to call it a revolution," Dinesh D'Souza, author of *Illiberal Education,* informed his readers. "Its distinctive insignia can be witnessed on any major campus in America today, and in all aspects of university life."[2]

Despite their claims of living under Stalinist regimes where dissent was not tolerated, our professors and administrators put up an impressively vociferous counteroffensive: they fought tooth and nail for the right to offend us thin-skinned radicals; they lay down on the tracks in front of every new harassment policy, and generally acted as if they were fighting for the very future of Western civilization. An avalanche of look-alike magazine features bolstered the claim that ID politics constituted an international emergency: "Illiberal Education" (*Atlantic Monthly*), "Visigoths in Tweed" (*Fortune*), "The Silences" (*Maclean's*), "The Academy's New Ayatollahs" (*Outlook*), "Taking Offense" (*Newsweek*). In *New York* magazine, writer John Taylor compared my generation of campus activists with cult members, Hitler Youth, and Christian fundamentalists.[3] So great was the threat we allegedly posed that George Bush even took time out to warn the world that political correctness "replaces old prejudices with new ones."

THE MARKETING OF ID

The backlash that identity politics inspired did a pretty good job of masking for us the fact that many of our demands for better representation were quickly accommodated by marketers, media makers, and pop-culture producers alike—though perhaps not for the reasons we had hoped. If I had to name a precise moment for this shift in attitude, I would say August of 1992: the thick of the "brand crisis" that peaked with Marlboro Friday. That's when we found out that our sworn enemies in the "mainstream"—to us a giant monolithic blob outside of our known university-affiliated enclaves—didn't fear and loathe us but actually thought we were sort of interesting. Once we'd embarked on a search for new wells of cutting-edge imagery, our insistence on extreme sexual and racial identities made for great brand-content and niche-marketing strategies. If diversity is what we wanted, the brands seemed to be saying, then diversity was exactly what we would get.

> *If diversity is what we wanted, the brands seemed to be saying, then diversity was exactly what we would get.*

And with that, the marketers and media makers swooped down, airbrushes in hand, to touch up the colors and images in our culture.

The five years that followed were an orgy of red ribbons, Malcolm X baseball hats, and Silence = Death T-shirts. By 1993, the stories of academic Armageddon were replaced with new ones about the sexy wave of "Do-Me Feminism" in *Esquire* and "Lesbian Chic" in *New York* and *Newsweek*. The shift in attitude was not the result of a mass political conversion but of some hard economic calculations. According to *Rocking the Ages,* a book produced in 1997 by leading U.S. consumer researchers Yankelovich Partners, "Diversity" was the "defining idea" for Gen-Xers, as opposed to "Individuality" for boomers and "Duty" for their parents.

> Xers are starting out today with pluralistic attitudes that are the strongest we have ever measured. As we look towards the next twenty-five years, it is clear that acceptance of alternative lifestyles will become even stronger and more widespread as Xers grow up and take over the reins of power, and become the dominant buying group in the consumer marketplace. . . . *Diversity is the key fact of life for Xers, the core of the perspective they bring to the marketplace.* Diversity in all of its forms—cultural, political, sexual, racial, social—is a hallmark of this generation [italics theirs]. . .[4]

The Sputnik cool-hunting agency, meanwhile, explained that "youth today are one big sample of diversity" and encouraged its clients to dive into the psychedelic "United Streets of Diversity" and not be afraid to taste the local fare. Dee Dee Gordon, author of *The L. Report,* urged her clients to get into Girl Power with a vengeance: "Teenage girls want to see someone who kicks butt back";[5] and, sounding suspiciously like me and my university friends, brand man Tom Peters took to berating his corporate audiences for being "OWMs—Old White Males."

As we have seen, this information was coming hot on the heels of two other related revelations. The first was that consumer companies would only survive if they built corporate empires around "brand identities." The second was that the ballooning youth demographic held the key to market success. So, of course, if the market researchers and cool hunters all reported that diversity was the key character trait of this lucrative demographic, there was only one thing to be done: every forward-thinking corporation would have to adopt variations on the theme of diversity as their brand identities.

Which is exactly what most brand-driven corporations have attempted to do. In an effort to understand how Starbucks became an overnight household name in 1996 without a single national ad campaign, *Advertising Age* speculated that it had something to do with its tie-dyed, Third World aura. "For devotees, Starbucks' 'experience' is about more than a daily espresso infusion; it is about immersion in a politically correct, cultured refuge. . . ."[6] Starbucks, however, was only a minor player in the P.C. marketing craze. Abercrombie & Fitch ads featured guys in their underwear making goo-goo eyes at each other; Diesel went further, showing two sailors kissing; and a U.S. television spot for Virgin Cola depicted "the first-ever gay wedding featured in a commercial," as the press release proudly announced. There were also gay-targeted brands like Pride Beer and Wave Water, whose slogan is "We label bottles not people," and the gay community got its very own cool hunters—market researchers who scoured gay bars with hidden cameras.[7]

The Gap, meanwhile, filled its ads with racially mixed rainbows of skinny, childlike models. Diesel harnessed frustration at that unattainable beauty ideal with ironic ads that showed women being served up for dinner to a table of pigs. The Body Shop harnessed the backlash against both of them by refusing to advertise and instead filled its windows with red ribbons and posters condemning violence against women. The rush to diversity fitted in neatly with the embrace of African-American style and heroes that companies like Nike and Tommy Hilfiger had already pinpointed as a powerful marketing source. But Nike also realized that people who saw themselves as belonging to oppressed groups were ready-made market niches: throw a few liberal platitudes their way and, presto, you're not just a product but an ally in the struggle. So the walls of Nike Town were adorned with quotes from Tiger Woods declaring that "there are still courses in the U.S. where I am not allowed to play, because of the color of my skin." Women in Nike ads told us that "I believe 'babe' is a four-letter word" and "I believe high heels are a conspiracy against women."

And everyone, it seemed, was toying with the fluidity of gender, from the old-hat story of MAC makeup using drag queen RuPaul as its spokesmodel to tequila ads that inform viewers that the she in the bikini is really a he; from Calvin Klein's colognes that tell us that gender itself is a construct to Sure Ultra Dry deodorant that in turn urges all the gender benders to chill out: "Man? Woman? Does it matter?"

OPPRESSION NOSTALGIA

Fierce debates still rage about these campaigns. Are they entirely cynical or do they indicate that advertisers want to evolve and play more positive social roles? Benetton's mid-nineties ads careened wildly between witty and beautiful challenges to racial stereotypes on the one hand, and grotesque commercial exploitation of human suffering on the other. They were, however, indisputably part of a genuine attempt to use the company's vast cultural real estate to send a message that went beyond "Buy more sweaters"; and they played a central role in the fashion world's embrace of the struggle against AIDS. Similarly, there is no denying that the Body Shop broke ground by proving to the corporate sector that a multinational chain can be an outspoken and controversial political player, even while making millions on bubble bath and body lotion. The complicated motivations and stark inconsistencies inside many of these "ethical" businesses [are] explored [elsewhere]. But for many of the activists who had, at one point not so long ago, believed that better media representation would make for a more just world, one thing had become abundantly clear: identity politics weren't fighting the system, or even subverting it. When it came to the vast new industry of corporate branding, they were feeding it.

The crowning of sexual and racial diversity as the new superstars of advertising and pop culture has understandably created a sort of Identity Identity Crisis. Some ex-ID warriors are even getting nostalgic about the good old days, when they were oppressed, yes, but the symbols of their radicalism weren't for sale at Wal-Mart. As music writer Ann Powers observed of the much-vaunted ascendancy of Girl Power, "at this intersection between the conventional feminine and the evolving Girl, what's springing up is not a revolution but a mall . . . Thus, a genuine movement devolves into a giant shopping spree, where girls are encouraged to purchase whatever identity fits them best off the rack."[8] Similarly, Daniel Mendelsohn has written that gay identity has dwindled into "basically, a set of product choices . . . At least culturally speaking, oppression may have been the best thing that could have happened to gay culture. Without it, we're nothing."

The nostalgia, of course, is absurd. Even the most cynical ID warrior will admit, when pressed, that having Ellen Degeneres and other gay characters out on TV has some concrete advantages. Probably it is good for the kids, particularly those who live outside of larger urban settings—in rural or small-town environments, where being gay is more likely to confine them to a life of self-loathing. (The attempted suicide rate in 1998 among gay and bisexual male teens in America was 28.1 percent, compared with 4.2 percent among straight males of the same age group.)[9] Similarly, most feminists would concede that although the Spice Girls' crooning, "If you wanna be my lover, you have to get with my friends" isn't likely to shatter the beauty myth, it's still a step up from Snoop Dogg's 1993 ode to gang rape, "It ain't no fun if my homies can't have none."

And yet, while raising teenagers' self-esteem and making sure they have positive role models is valuable, it's a fairly narrow achievement, and from an activist perspective, one can't help asking: Is this it? Did all our protests and supposedly subversive theory only serve to provide great content for the culture industries, fresh new lifestyle imagery for Levi's new "What's True" ad campaign and girl-power-charged record sales for the music business? Why, in other words, were our ideas about political rebellion so deeply non-threatening to the smooth flow of business as usual?

The question, of course, is not Why, but Why on earth not? Just as they had embraced the "brands, not products" equation, the smart businesses quickly realized that short-term discomfort—whether it came from a requirement to hire more women or to more carefully vet the language in an ad campaign—was a small price to pay for the tremendous market share that diversity promised. So while it may be true that real gains have emerged from this process, it is also true that Dennis Rodman wears dresses and Disney World celebrates Gay Day less because of political progress than financial expediency. The market has seized upon multiculturalism and gender-bending in the same ways that it has seized upon youth culture in general—not just as a market niche but as a source of new carnivalesque imagery. As Robert Goldman and Stephen Papson note, "White-bread culture will simply no longer do."[10] The $200 billion culture industry—now America's biggest export—needs an ever-changing, uninterrupted supply of street styles, edgy music videos, and rainbows of colors. And the radical critics of the media clamoring to be "represented" in the early nineties virtually handed over their colorful identities to the brandmasters to be shrink-wrapped.

The need for greater diversity—the rallying cry of my university years—is now not only accepted by the culture industries, it is the mantra of global capital. And identity politics, as they were practiced in the nineties, weren't a threat, they were a gold mine. "This revolution," writes cultural critic Richard Goldstein in *The Village Voice*, "turned out to be the savior of late capitalism."[11] And just in time, too.

NOTES

[1]Jeanie Russell Kasindorf, "Lesbian Chic," *New York*, 10 May 1993, 35.

[2]Dinesh D'Souza, "Illiberal Education," *Atlantic Monthly*, March 1991, 51.

[3]John Taylor, "Are You Politically Correct?" *New York*, 21 January 1991.

[4]J. Walker Smith and Ann Clurman, *Rocking the Ages* (New York: HarperCollins, 1997), 88.

[5]*Vogue*, November 1997.

[6]"Starbucks Is Ground Zero in Today's Coffee Culture," *Advertising Age*, 9 December 1996.

[7]Jared Mitchell, "Out and About," *Report on Business Magazine*, December 1996, 90.

[8]Ann Powers, "Everything and the Girl," *Spin*, November 1994, 74.

[9]Gary Remafedi, Simone French, Mary Story, Michael D. Resnick, and Robert Blum, "The Relationship between Suicide Risk and Sexual Orientation: Results of a Population-Based Study," *American Journal of Public Health*, January 1998, 88, no. 1, 57–60.

[10]Robert Goldman and Stephen Papson, *Sign Wars*, (New York: Guilford Press, 1996), v.

[11]Richard Goldstein, "The Culture War Is Over! We Won! (For Now)," *Village Voice*, 19 November 1996.

DISCUSSION

1. How do you respond to the term *identity marketing* as Klein defines it? What kinds of images or associations does it evoke? Is identity something you naturally think of as marketable? How or how not?

2. Among the many problems with commercial marketing, Klein argues, is its tendency to define ethnic and racial difference in very limited ways. Choose one of the ad campaigns Klein references in her essay. In what particular ways might you alter the portrait of diversity so that it offers a more accurate or realistic depiction? In your view, would doing so enhance or inhibit the marketability of the product being sold?

3. In our culture, is there any social or political issue that could never be marketed? What would this issue be? And what aspect of it would make it impervious to commercial or corporate uses?

WRITING

4. Choose a commercial image you've come across recently, one that you think attempts to sell a particular definition of diversity. First, describe what definition or model this image endeavors to convey. Next, analyze the ways this definition seems connected to the particular product this commercial is also trying to sell. How (if at all) does this image of diversity shape viewer attitudes toward the product itself?

5. Klein asks whether identity marketing campaigns are "entirely cynical or do they indicate that advertisers want to evolve and play more positive social roles?" Write an essay in which you take a position on this question, using examples from ad campaigns you remember or those Klein discusses in her writing. Make sure that you consider both sides of the question in your argument.

6. Klein and Michael Eric Dyson (p. 147) are concerned with the ways our contemporary media teaches us both to see and not to see racial and ethnic difference. Write an essay in which you analyze how each writer discusses the idea of diversity and how it is portrayed in popular culture. What aspects of diversity are of particular concern to Klein? How do you think Dyson would respond to her argument that diversity sells?

Scenes and Un-Scenes: *Picturing Disaster*

Whether it is a television commercial or a news broadcast, a web image or blockbuster movie, virtually everything we see has been selectively shaped for our inspection. While it may purport to show us "the way things are," the truth is that every image bears traces of some slant or bias, intentional or not. And yet while it may be inevitable, this doesn't mean it is automatically excusable — that such bias doesn't warrant our attention, doesn't deserve to be challenged, critiqued, or changed. Certainly when it comes to something as politically important and personally catastrophic as Hurricane Katrina, it is no small matter to know whether the images we are shown tell the true or whole story.

▼▼ *In the hours before it made landfall, media coverage tended to treat Hurricane Katrina as an entirely natural phenomenon. Tracking its movements from the supposedly objective vantage of outer space, for example, satellite photos like the one below reinforced an initial perception among many in the general public that no one was really to blame for this disaster.*

▲▲ *The following caption originally accompanied this image: "A young man walks through chest deep flood water after looting a grocery store in New Orleans on Tuesday, Aug. 30, 2005. Flood waters continue to rise in New Orleans after Hurricane Katrina did extensive damage when it made landfall on Monday."*

In the days immediately following the breach of the levees in New Orleans, news organizations ran countless images documenting local residents' struggles to survive. Despite their shared focus, however, not all such records invited viewers to think about this struggle in the same way. Take, for example, the two pictures featured above and on the facing page. Although taken on the same day and picturing virtually identical circumstances, the captions accompanying these images encouraged viewers to draw very different conclusions about what they were being shown. In the first, we are told, a "young man walks through chest deep flood water after looting a grocery store." In the second, we are told, "Two residents wade through chest deep water after finding bread and soda at a local grocery store." Bloggers across the Internet were quick to point out that the captions fed into possible racial biases, and although both photo agencies defended their methods for captioning the photos, the images were subsequently pulled from syndication.

▲▲ *The following caption originally accompanied this*
image: "Two residents wade through chest-deep
water after finding bread and soda from a local grocery
store after Hurricane Katrina came through the area in
New Orleans, Louisiana."

Another hallmark of the Katrina coverage involved what we might call the "sympathetic celebrity" story, in which a famous person toured the aftermath of the flooding in New Orleans to showcase her or his "personal" anguish or outrage at what was transpiring. What is the effect of casting Katrina as this type of human-interest story? What kind of reaction does it seem designed to elicit from viewers?

Unlike much of the media coverage nationally, headlines such as the one on the facing page presented a view of the disaster informed by a far more thorough and realistic understanding of the local conditions. Does this local perspective seem different from that modeled in other examples?

KATRINA: THE STORM WE'VE ALWAYS FEARED

The Times-Picayune

50 CENTS 169th year No. 221 | WEDNESDAY, AUGUST 31, 2005 | HURRICANE EDITION

UNDER WATER

LEVEE BREACH SWAMPS CITY FROM LAKE TO RIVER

Population urged to leave; years of cleanup ahead

STAFF PHOTO BY TED JACKSON

NEW ORLEANS: Gravess at Greenwood and Metairie cemeteriesmark the waterlineof the sheet of water that covered the city from Lake Pontchartrain to nearly the French Quarter on Tuesday.

Daylong efforts to repair levee fail

By Dan Shea
Staff writer

New Orleans became an unimaginable scene of water, fear and suffering Tuesday after a levee breach in the 17th Street Canal sent billions of gallons of Lake Pontchartrain coursing through the city.

As the day wore on, the only dry land was a narrow band from the French Quarter and parts of Uptown, the same small strip that was settled by Bienville amid the swamps.

On Tuesday night, it appeared the city was returning to swamp when a daylong effort to shore the levee near the Hammond Highway failed. Mayor Ray Nagin said pumps were being overwhelmed and warned that a new deluge would bury the city in up to 15 feet of water.

With solid water from the lake to the French Quarter, the inundation and depopulation of an entire American city was at hand.

"Truth to tell, we're not to far from filling in the bowl," said Terry Ebbert, the city's director of homeland security. The waters were still rising at 3 inches per hour, and eventually could move close to the French Quarter levee.

Although the breach occurred on the Orleans side of the canal, it did not spare the Jefferson side. Water found its way into much of the east bank, meeting the flow that came in from the west from Hurricane Katrina's storm surge Monday.

An accurate tally of death was hard to determine. Five deaths related to Katrina have been confirmed in Jefferson Parish, officials said. There also are seven people missing who decided to ride out Katrina on Grand Isle.

Gov. Kathleen Blanco spoke of "many deaths," but there were only rumors and anecdotes of firefighters tying floating bodies to trees.

"We have some bodies floating," Ebbert said. "Not like thousands, but we have seen some."

As to the living, with the absence of cars and electric motors in the powerless city, a sad tableau played itself out in an eerie quiet.

All day, a weary army of storm victims trodged through waist-deep muddy water toward the Superdome, where more than 20,000 people took refuge. The next problem is what to do with them. Late Tuesday Gov. Blanco ordered them out, saying the facility was too damaged to house people and the atmosphere too dangerous. Officials said the National Guard soon would begin driving them out to dry ground, then airlift them out of southeast Louisiana.

In other areas, lawlessness took hold.

See KATRINA, A-2

STAFF PHOTO BY ALEX BRANDON

MID-CITY: A New Orleans Police officer ferries refugees out of the danger zone as floodwaters rose Tuesday.

Flooding will only get worse

By Mark Schleifstein
Staff writer

The catastrophic flooding that filled the bowl that is New Orleans on

Monday and Tuesday will only get worse over the next few days because

rainfall from Hurricane Katrina continues to flow into Lake Pontchartrain from north shore rivers and streams, and east winds and a 17.5-foot storm crest on the Pearl River block the outflow water through the Rigolets and Chef Menteur Pass.

The lake is normally 1 foot above sea level, while the city of New Orleans is an average of 6 feet below sea level. But a combination of storm surge and rainfall from Katrina have raised the lake's surface to 6 feet above sea level, or more.

All of that water moving from the lake has found several holes in the lake's banks - all pouring into New Orleans. Water that crossed St. Charles Parish in an area where the lakefront levee has not yet been completed, and that backed up from the lake in Jefferson Parish canals, is funneling into Kenner and Metairie.

A 500-yard and growing breach in the eastern wall of the 17th Street Canal separating New Orleans from Metairie is pouring hundreds of thousands of gallons of lake water per second into the New Orleans

See WATER, A-4

▲ By contrast, this New Yorker cover demonstrates how drastically
▲ public opinion about Katrina had shifted a month later. Referencing
the "flood" of criticism leveled against the Bush administration for its
supposed indifference and inaction, this cartoon treats the issues of
causation and responsibility quite differently — representing the Katrina
disaster less as a natural event than a political and moral crime.

DISCUSSION

1. Are we always fully aware of the ways an image's bias shapes the conclusions we draw? Does it really matter? Would anything change if we were? How or how not?

2. In your view, does the racial identity of the viewer make any difference in what these images show or say? How might a white viewer draw different conclusions than an African American viewer? Why?

3. Is the Katrina coverage an isolated or idiosyncratic example of media bias, or do you think it reflects a more wide-ranging pattern? Can you think of another news event or controversy that ended up being defined by such contrasting sorts of images?

WRITING

4. The above portfolio makes abundantly clear that bias is a question not only of (mis)representation, but also of omission. That is, bias reveals itself not simply in terms of what an image shows, but also by virtue of what it leaves out. Choose one of the images showcased in the preceding pages and write a one-page assessment of the things it does not show. What key aspects of its portrait are left out? How do these omissions influence the conclusions viewers are encouraged to draw?

5. As discussed throughout this chapter, our culture's visual rules teach us not only how to watch but also how to think. Choose one of the images shown on the preceding pages and write a one-page script for how the image is supposed to make us think about race. What sorts of ideas concerning racial difference and racial conflict does it encourage viewers to adopt? Is this script different based on what race the viewer belongs to?

6. As Michael Eric Dyson (p. 147) reports, media bias within the Hurricane Katrina coverage revealed itself in both subtle and explicit ways. Choose three of the images previously listed and in two or three sentences write the kind of caption you think Dyson would create for each. What aspect of each image would Dyson focus on? What specific sort of bias or slant would he identify? Then, write a second set of captions you think accurately describes what is happening in the photos you've chosen. How does your perspective compare to Dyson's?

Putting It into Practice: *Keep an Eye Out*

Now that you've read the chapter selections, try applying your conclusions to your own life by completing the following exercises.

WINDOW SHOPPING   Pay a visit to the retail store of your choice. Based on the décor and marketing images inside the store, what sort of customer do you think it is trying to attract? How does the store's layout, products, and signage stereotype this customer? Do your fellow patrons appear to fit the image of the store's ideal customer? How? Imagine that you are creating a store designed to attract a certain type of person, whether it is the soccer mom, macho guy, or urban hipster. Describe what your customer looks like, and then decide what sort of marketing images you would use to draw the customer into your store.

RATING THE HEADLINES   In television news, stories are typically covered in the order that news producers deem most important to least important. Watch a broadcast of the national evening news and keep a running record of the order in which the stories of the day are covered. What images stand out in your mind that characterize each story? Write a brief essay in which you discuss why you think certain stories are given more weight or are broadcast earlier than others, and be sure to include examples from the broadcast you've just watched. If you were a news producer, in what order would you broadcast the same stories? Why?

THE REAL YOU   Make a photo collage of images you think express facets of your identity, whether they are personal photos, advertisements for products you like, or pieces of art you find important. In class, swap collages with a peer and write a brief characterization of him or her based on the collage you've been given. Based on your collage, what do your classmates have to say about you? How closely does their description of you match what you had in mind? How might you have portrayed yourself differently to get them to describe you more accurately?

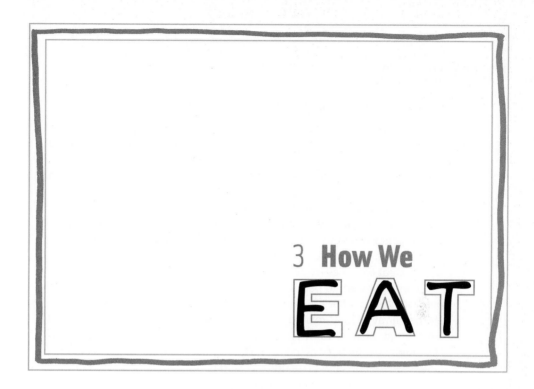

3 **How We**
EAT

Introduction

SCRIPTING THE PERFECT MEAL

Few activities seem as straightforward as eating. We do it so regularly and for such apparently obvious reasons, it's hard at first to take seriously the idea that there's all that much to it. We're hungry, we eat. What's so complicated about that? Because we tend to treat eating as such a given, such an essential and unexamined part of our lives, it's easy to believe that the choices we make about it are entirely our own. Some people like Chicken McNuggets while others prefer sushi; some of us are die-hard vegetarians while others fall into the meat-and-potatoes camp. Whichever way we slice it, however, the underlying assumption is the same: How and what we eat are, in every sense of the word, matters of personal taste.

We might want to pause, however, before too quickly accepting this premise. We do, after all, live in a world that presents us with an almost endless array of food-related choices. For starters, there's the question of *what* to eat. Meat or tofu? Homemade or takeout? Organic or processed? High carb, low carb, or no carb? Following this, there is the question of *how* to eat. Alone or with friends? Driving in our cars or sitting in front of the TV? Fresh from a wok or out of a microwave? And then, there are those questions concerning the economics of eating: Do we shop at 7-11 or Whole Foods? Do we need to buy what's on sale, or can we splurge instead? When we really stop to think about it, how *do* we make up our minds?

In answering these questions, we would do well to start by acknowledging a basic (if often overlooked) fact about our modern food culture: No matter how instinctive our individual eating choices feel to us, they aren't, in the strictest sense, personal at all. We don't make our decisions about food all by ourselves; we get a lot of help. From diet books to FDA guidelines, fast-food commercials to gourmet magazines, we are surrounded by images and instructions, messages and advice — all of which aim to fix our "proper" relationship to food. Our culture has rules for what types of food we are supposed to eat, when we are supposed to eat them, and in what amounts. We have rules for how different meals should be prepared, and others for how they should be hosted. And rules dictate how much all of these different things cost. Whether these rules take the form of government-issued

Everybody Knows That . . .

66 Atkins Diet: The Rules of Induction

Rule 4. Eat nothing that isn't on the Acceptable Foods list. And that means absolutely nothing. Your 'just this one taste won't hurt' rationalization is the kiss of failure during this phase of Atkins."

— *Atkins Nutritional Approach, www.atkins.com*

regulations about growth hormones, diet fads proscribing our daily allowance of carbohydrates, fast-food commercials instructing us to supersize our selections, or websites extolling the benefits of going vegan, every one of these rules reminds us of the same inescapable truth: Our food choices are framed long before we ever set foot in the kitchen, the grocery store, or the restaurant.

FOOD FOR THOUGHT

Nor are these rules concerned solely with how we *act*. They play just as formative a role in shaping how we *think* as well. Whether this means following the 15 percent tipping rule or memorizing Dr. Phil's ten steps to a slimmer waistline, every time we live up to one of our culture's food-related instructions we simultaneously endorse the value or ideas that underlie it. To illustrate, let's compare two representative but quite distinct eating experiences: a Thanksgiving dinner and a McDonald's meal. Even if our own experiences sometimes deviate from the stereotype, few of us would argue that there aren't well-entrenched and universally recognized rules dictating how these two meals are supposed to unfold. In each of these settings, only a few select items may properly appear on the menu: We are far more likely to come across turkey and cranberry sauce at the Thanksgiving table than veggie kabobs or tuna salad, and burgers and fries at the fast-food counter rather than tofu stir-fry. Very different dress codes apply in each case too. Cut-off jeans are far more appropriate when we are sitting in a plastic booth at McDonald's than when we are sitting at a holiday dinner table. Very different social rituals prevail also: Napkins go on laps and pleases and thank-yous accompany requests for food at a Thanksgiving gathering, while at McDonald's it is OK to eat with your hands and to throw away plates, containers, and napkins once the meal is finished.

These sorts of differences, as we've already begun to see, are not terribly difficult to list. A bit trickier to discern, however, are the ways these instructions simultaneously function as social scripts. When we live up to the more formal edicts of a traditional Thanksgiving dinner, we are doing more than playing the role of a particular kind of diner. In donning this costume and adhering to this script, we are just as firmly giving our assent to a number of related notions: about the importance of tradition, about the special role that home and family should play in commemorating national holidays, even about which version of American history to accept as right. Similarly, when we assume the role of the typical fast-food consumer,

Everybody Knows That...

MyPyramid.gov
STEPS TO A HEALTHIER YOU

— U.S. Department of Agriculture,
www.mypyramid.gov

181

our performance registers our tacit acceptance of a number of unspoken priorities: processed over "whole" foods, speed and efficiency over patience, convenience over nutrition.

This particular relationship — between the eating roles we take on and the eating rules we follow on the one hand and the social norms that underlie them on the other — links all of the readings in this chapter. Because our eating habits offer such a sensitive barometer of our current ideals and anxieties, each of the following selections uses its portrait of eating as a jumping-off point for investigating a larger issue or controversy to which food is connected. In several cases, writers focus their attention on the ways our contemporary system of food production and consumption is organized. Pursuing just this line of inquiry, Michael Pollan writes an open letter to President Barack Obama in which he outlines just how important sound food policy is to the continued development of American culture. Sara Dickerman considers the role that food safety, or perhaps food fear, plays in shaping the way we eat, while Tara Lohan shares her experiences of cutting out that middle man by engaging in the practice of urban foraging, or eating only what she finds in her own environment. Another proponent of the eating local movement, Makenna Goodman, poses the blunt and disarming question, "Could you kill what you eat?" and causes us to rethink not only how our food gets on our tables, but also our proper relationship with what we eat. Other selections focus on some of the different cultural attitudes embedded within our current eating practices. In what ways and for what reasons, these writers ponder, have we learned to differentiate ideal from taboo forms of eating? And what are the consequences of trying to live up to these distinctions? Surveying the cultural history of "gluttony," Francine Prose indicts our contemporary society for its long-standing demonization of overeating, a tradition that has led so many of us to stigmatize our overweight population as victims of food, social misfits, or pariahs. Addressing what we might consider the flip side of this issue, Caroline Knapp chronicles her own decade-long struggle with anorexia, a struggle that revolved around an effort

Everybody Knows That . . .

❝How do I prepare my TOMBSTONE FOR ONE Pizza?

Toaster Oven/Conventional Oven Cooking Directions: Preheat the oven to 400 degrees Fahrenheit. Remove pizza from box and overwrap. Discard silver cooking circle. Place pizza directly on oven rack in Center Position (8 to 10 inches from bottom of oven). Bake according to the table below, or until the cheese is melted and edges are golden brown. Oven temperatures vary, so adjust baking time and oven temperature as necessary. Supreme: 12 to 16 minutes. Extra Cheese: 9 to 12 minutes. Pepperoni: 9 to 12 minutes. CAUTION: Do not use silver circle in toaster oven or conventional oven."

— *Frequently Asked Questions, www.kraftfoods.com*

to make sense of our culture's treacherous and contradictory injunctions to be "slim" and "beautiful." In his journalistic account of "professional eating," Jason Fagone draws a different set of conclusions about our culture's imperatives regarding food, detecting within the surprising popularity of such events as the National Hot Dog Eating Contest the outlines of the classic American dream. And finally, Frederick Kaufman encourages us to think about the ways we view ourselves by exploring what we feed our pets.

"EVERYBODY KNOWS THAT" EXERCISE

Choose one of the images or quotations featured in the margins on the preceding pages and answer the following questions:

1. What does this image or quotation ask you to believe?
2. What are the particular ideas, values, or attitudes it invites us to accept as *normal*?
3. What would it feel like to act on or act out these norms in our personal lives?

Rule *Maker* >>>>>>>>>> Rule *Breaker*

❝ *I am not sure if merely because of our size and success Whole Foods Market deserves the pejorative label 'Big Organic' or 'Industrial Organic,' or even to be linked to those categories. I would argue instead that organic agriculture owes much of its growth and success over the past 20 years to Whole Foods Market's successful growth and commitment to organic. As an organization we continually challenge ourselves to be responsible and ethical tenants of the planet. Through our stores, large and small organic farmers, both local and international, can offer their products to an increasingly educated population that is more interested in organics every day. . . . Whole Foods Market is one of the 'good guys' in this story about the 'industrialization of agriculture.'"*

— JOHN MACKEY,
CEO WHOLE FOODS, 2006

❝ *[T]he trickiest contradiction Whole Foods attempts to reconcile is the one between the industrialization of organic food and the pastoral ideals on which that industry has been built. The organic movement, as it was once called, has come a remarkably long way in the last thirty years, to the point where it now looks considerably less like a movement than a big business. . . . So is an industrial organic food chain finally a contradiction in terms? It's hard to escape the conclusion it is. . . . As in so many other realms, nature's logic has proven no match for the logic of capitalism."*

— MICHAEL POLLAN,
THE OMNIVORE'S DILEMMA, 2006

WHOLE FOODS VS. MICHAEL POLLAN

Since the 1960s and 1970s, the organic food industry has played a major role in reshaping how millions of Americans think about, shop for, and (of course) eat their food. Pioneered by a small cadre of local farmers, grocery co-op proprietors, and eco-conscious consumers, the organic movement cast itself in its early years as a revolutionary alternative to what was often termed the "corporate" or "industrial" food economy, a system typified by the giant, chain grocery store, with its row after row of frozen TV dinners, pesticide-coated oranges, canned vegetables, and potato chips. Organizing their efforts around the twin ideals of *naturalness* and *community,* these early proponents supported weaning the general public from its reliance on mass-produced, artificially preserved, chemically altered foodstuffs.

And yet, while organic grocery stores have seen both the public enthusiasm for their goals and their own market shares rise steadily over the years, this very success has also raised some uncomfortable questions about whether these ventures remain true to the movement's original "green" ideals. As enormously popular and profitable stores like Whole Foods and Trader Joe's have become national chains, and as wholesale distributors like Harmony Valley or Cascadian Farms have adopted corporate-style growing and distribution practices, many have begun to wonder whether any meaningful differences still exist between industrial and organic food. In a world where even Wal-Mart has begun marketing organic selections to its shoppers, does it still make sense to talk about this movement as a kind of anticorporate revolution? For observers like food critic Michael Pollan, the answer is "not really." For people like Whole Foods CEO John Mackey, on the other hand, such doubts are shortsighted and unfair, overlooking the ways that the organic industry has succeeded in rewriting the rules by which countless Americans eat.

FIND THE RULES: Next time you're at the grocery store (whether it is an organic chain like Whole Foods or another corporate chain with an organic section), takes notes on the way the store presents itself to you. In what ways is the décor designed to appeal to an organic foods shopper? What assumptions about the typical shopper does the store's design make? Pay attention to the types of products the store keeps in stock. How does the labeling of something like organic macaroni and cheese differ from a brand like Kraft's? How do the nutritional facts about each compare? What about their prices? If you are unable to visit a store in person, you can find information about Whole Foods products on its website (www.wholefoodsmarket.com). After you have collected your observations, write a one-page summary describing your trip.

MAKE YOUR OWN RULES: Proponents of organic farming and markets list many reasons for favoring these methods, including better nutrition, more responsible use of land, and reduced pollution from trucks that bring conventional products a long way to market. According to Michael Pollan, however, large organic grocery chains sometimes, to continue operating, resort to practices that are against their founding ideals. Write a one-page essay in which you propose a happy medium — that is, the type of shopping scenario that would preserve the organic ideals while allowing consumers to buy everything they needed. What complications might arise from the scenario you've proposed?

MICHAEL POLLAN
Farmer in Chief

While it can often feel like an entirely personal activity, the truth is that eating is connected to some of the most pressing social, cultural, and political questions of our day. It plays a role in shaping how we think about health and nutrition, about social class and the state of the environment, even about gender, racial, and ethnic differences. Taking this insight as his starting point, noted food writer Michael Pollan offers then-President-elect Barack Obama some pointed recommendations about what our future food policy should look like — and in the process he offers readers a more expansive way of understanding the place of food in our everyday lives. Pollan is the John S. and James L. Knight Professor of Journalism at the University of California Berkeley's Graduate School of Journalism. A contributing writer to the *New York Times Magazine*, he has published extensively on food and food culture. His books include *The Omnivore's Dilemma* (2006), *In Defense of Food: An Eater's Manifesto* (2008), and most recently *Food Rules: An Eater's Manual* (2009). The following selection appeared in the *New York Times Magazine* on October 9, 2008.

DEAR MR. PRESIDENT-ELECT,

It may surprise you to learn that among the issues that will occupy much of your time in the coming years is one you barely mentioned during the campaign: food. Food policy is not something American presidents have had to give much thought to, at least since the Nixon administration—the last time high food prices presented a serious political peril. Since then, federal policies to promote maximum production of the commodity crops (corn, soybeans, wheat, and rice) from which most of our supermarket foods are derived have succeeded impressively in keeping prices low and food more or less off the national political agenda. But with a suddenness that has taken us all by surprise, the era of cheap and abundant food appears to be drawing to a close. What this means is that you, like so many other leaders through history, will find yourself confronting the fact—so easy to overlook these past few years—that the health of a nation's food system is a critical issue of national security. Food is about to demand your attention.

Complicating matters is the fact that the price and abundance of food are not the only problems we face; if they were, you could simply follow Nixon's example, appoint a latter-day Earl Butz as your secretary of agriculture and instruct him or her to do whatever it takes to boost production. But there are reasons to think that the old approach won't work this time around; for one thing, it depends on cheap energy that we can no longer count on. For another, expanding production of industrial agriculture today would require you to sacrifice important values on which you did campaign. Which brings me to the deeper reason you will need not simply to address food prices but to make the reform of the entire food system one of the highest priorities of your administration: unless you do, you will not be able to make significant progress on the health care crisis, energy independence, or climate change. Unlike food, these are issues you did campaign on—but as you try to address them you will quickly discover that the way we currently grow, process, and eat food in America goes to the heart of all three problems and will have to change if we hope to solve them. Let me explain.

After cars, the food system uses more fossil fuel than any other sector of the economy—19 percent. And while the experts disagree about the exact amount, the way we feed ourselves contributes more greenhouse gases to the atmosphere than anything else we do—as much as 37 percent, according to one study. Whenever farmers clear land for crops and till the soil, large quantities of carbon are released into the air. But the 20th-century industrialization of agriculture has increased the amount of greenhouse gases emitted by the food system by an order of magnitude; chemical fertilizers (made from natural gas), pesticides (made from petroleum), farm machinery, modern food processing and packaging, and transportation have together transformed a system that in 1940 produced 2.3 calories of food energy for every calorie of fossil-fuel energy it used into one that now takes 10 calories of fossil-fuel energy to produce a single calorie of modern supermarket food. Put another way, when we eat from the industrial-food system, we are eating oil and spewing greenhouse gases. This state of affairs appears all the more absurd when you recall that every calorie we eat is ultimately the product of photosynthesis—a process based on making food energy from sunshine. There is hope and possibility in that simple fact.

In addition to the problems of climate change and America's oil addiction, you have spoken at length on the campaign trail of the health care crisis. Spending on health care has risen from 5 percent of national income in 1960 to 16 percent today, putting a significant drag on the economy. The goal of ensuring the health of all Americans depends on getting those costs under control. There are several reasons health care has gotten so expensive, but one of the biggest, and perhaps most tractable, is the cost to the system of preventable chronic diseases. Four of the top 10 killers in America today are chronic diseases linked to diet: heart disease, stroke, Type 2 diabetes, and cancer. It is no coincidence that in the years national spending on health care went from 5 percent to 16 percent of national income, spending on food has fallen by a comparable amount—from 18 percent of household income to less than 10 percent.

While the surfeit of cheap calories that the U.S. food system has produced since the late 1970s may have taken food prices off the political agenda, this has come at a steep cost to public health. You cannot expect to reform the health care system, much less expand coverage, without confronting the public-health catastrophe that is the modern American diet.

The impact of the American food system on the rest of the world will have implications for your foreign and trade policies as well. In the past several months more than 30 nations have experienced food riots, and so far one government has fallen. Should high grain prices persist and shortages develop, you can expect to see the pendulum shift decisively away from free trade, at least in food. Nations that opened their markets to the global flood of cheap grain (under pressure from previous administrations as well as the World Bank and the I.M.F.) lost so many farmers that they now find their ability to feed their own populations hinges on decisions made in Washington (like your predecessor's precipitous embrace of biofuels) and on Wall Street. They will now rush to rebuild their own agricultural sectors and then seek to protect them by erecting trade barriers. Expect to hear the phrases "food sovereignty" and "food security" on the lips of every foreign leader you meet. Not only the Doha round, but the whole cause of free trade in agriculture is probably dead, the casualty of a cheap food policy that a scant two years ago seemed like a boon for everyone. It is one of the larger paradoxes of our time that the very same food policies that have contributed to overnutrition in the first world are now contributing to undernutrition in the third. But it turns out that too much food can be nearly as big a problem as too little—a lesson we should keep in mind as we set about designing a new approach to food policy.

> **The way we feed ourselves contributes more greenhouse gases to the atmosphere than anything else we do.**

Rich or poor, countries struggling with soaring food prices are being forcibly reminded that food is a national-security issue. When a nation loses the ability to substantially feed itself, it is not only at the mercy of global commodity markets but of other governments as well. At issue is not only the availability of food, which may be held hostage by a hostile state, but its safety: as recent scandals in China demonstrate, we have little control over the safety of imported foods. The deliberate contamination of our food presents another national-security threat. At his valedictory press conference in 2004, Tommy Thompson, the secretary of health and human services, offered a chilling warning, saying, "I, for the life of me, cannot understand why the terrorists have not attacked our food supply, because it is so easy to do."

This, in brief, is the bad news: the food and agriculture policies you've inherited—designed to maximize production at all costs and relying on cheap energy to do so—are in shambles, and the need to address the problems they have caused is acute. The good news is that the twinned crises in food and energy are creating a political environment in which real reform of the food system may actually be possible for the first time in a generation. The American people are paying more attention to food today than they have in decades, worrying not only about its price but about its safety, its provenance, and its healthfulness. There is a gathering sense among the public that the industrial-food system is broken. Markets for alternative kinds of food—organic, local, pasture-based, humane—are thriving as never before. All this suggests that a political constituency for change is building and not only on the left: lately, conservative voices have also been raised in support of reform. Writing of the movement back to local food economies, traditional foods (and family meals), and more sustainable farming, *The American Conservative* magazine editorialized last summer that "this is a conservative cause if ever there was one."

There are many moving parts to the new food agenda I'm urging you to adopt, but the core idea could not be simpler: we need to wean the American food system off its heavy 20th-century diet of fossil fuel and put it back on a diet of contemporary sunshine. True, this is easier said than done—fossil fuel is deeply implicated in everything about the way we currently grow food and feed ourselves. To put the food system back on sunlight will require policies to change how things work at every link in the food chain: in the farm field, in the way food is processed and sold, and even in the American kitchen and at the American dinner table. Yet the sun still shines down on our land every day, and photosynthesis can still work its wonders wherever it does. If any part of the modern economy can be freed from its dependence on oil and successfully resolarized, surely it is food.

HOW WE GOT HERE

Before setting out an agenda for reforming the food system, it's important to understand how that system came to be—and also to appreciate what, for all its many problems, it has accomplished. What our food system does well is precisely what it was designed to do, which is to produce cheap calories in great abundance. It is no small thing for an American to be able to go into a fast-food restaurant and to buy a double cheeseburger, fries, and a large Coke for a price equal to less than an hour of labor at the minimum wage—indeed, in the long sweep of history, this represents a remarkable achievement.

It must be recognized that the current food system—characterized by monocultures of corn and soy in the field and cheap calories of fat, sugar, and feedlot meat on the table—is not simply the product of the free market. Rather, it is the product of a specific set of government policies that sponsored a shift from solar (and human) energy on the farm to fossil-fuel energy.

Did you notice when you flew over Iowa during the campaign how the land was completely bare—black—from October to April? What you were seeing is the agricultural landscape created by cheap oil. In years past, except in the dead of winter, you would have seen in those fields a checkerboard of different greens: pastures and hayfields for animals, cover crops, perhaps a block of fruit trees. Before the application of oil and natural gas to agriculture, farmers relied on crop diversity (and photosynthesis) both to replenish their soil and to combat pests, as well as to feed themselves and their neighbors. Cheap energy, however, enabled the creation of monocultures, and monocultures in turn vastly increased the productivity both of the American land and the American farmer; today the typical corn-belt farmer is single-handedly feeding 140 people.

This did not occur by happenstance. After World War II, the government encouraged the conversion of the munitions industry to fertilizer—ammonium nitrate being the main ingredient of both bombs and chemical fertilizer—and the conversion of nerve-gas research to pesticides. The government also began subsidizing commodity crops, paying farmers by the bushel for all the corn, soybeans, wheat, and rice they could produce. One secretary of agriculture after another implored them to plant "fence row to fence row" and to "get big or get out."

The chief result, especially after the Earl Butz years, was a flood of cheap grain that could be sold for substantially less than it cost farmers to grow because a government check helped make up the difference. As this artificially cheap grain worked its way up the food chain, it drove down the price of all the calories derived from that grain: the high-fructose corn syrup in the Coke, the soy oil in which the potatoes were fried, the meat and cheese in the burger.

Subsidized monocultures of grain also led directly to monocultures of animals: since factory farms could buy grain for less than it cost farmers to grow it, they could now fatten animals more cheaply than farmers could. So America's meat and dairy animals migrated from farm to feedlot, driving down the price of animal protein to the point where an American can enjoy eating, on average, 190 pounds of meat a year—a half pound every day.

But if taking the animals off farms made a certain kind of economic sense, it made no ecological sense whatever: their waste, formerly regarded as a precious source of fertility on the farm, became a pollutant—factory farms are now one of America's biggest sources of pollution. As Wendell Berry has tartly observed, to take animals off farms and put them on feedlots is to take an elegant solution—animals replenishing the fertility that crops deplete—and neatly divide it into two problems: a fertility problem on the farm and a pollution problem on the feedlot. The former problem is remedied with fossil-fuel fertilizer; the latter is remedied not at all.

What was once a regional food economy is now national and increasingly global in scope—thanks again to fossil fuel. Cheap energy—for trucking food as well as pumping water—is the reason New York City now gets its produce from California rather than from the "Garden State" next door, as it did before the advent of Interstate highways and national trucking networks. More recently, cheap energy has underwritten a globalized food economy in which it makes (or rather, made) economic sense to catch salmon in Alaska, ship it to China to be filleted, and then ship the fillets back to California to be eaten; or one in which California and Mexico can profitably swap tomatoes back and forth across the border; or Denmark and the United States can trade sugar cookies across the Atlantic. About that particular swap the economist Herman Daly once quipped, "Exchanging recipes would surely be more efficient."

Whatever we may have liked about the era of cheap, oil-based food, it is drawing to a close. Even if we were willing to continue paying the environmental or public-health price, we're not going to have the cheap energy (or the water) needed to keep the system going, much less expand production. But as is so often the case, a crisis provides opportunity for reform, and the current food crisis presents opportunities that must be seized.

In drafting these proposals, I've adhered to a few simple principles of what a 21st-century food system needs to do. First, your administration's food policy must strive to provide a healthful diet for all our people; this means focusing on the quality and diversity (and not merely the quantity) of the calories that American agriculture produces and American eaters consume. Second, your policies should aim to improve the resilience, safety, and security of our food supply. Among other things, this means promoting regional food economies both in America and around the world. And lastly, your policies need to reconceive agriculture as part of the solution to environmental problems like climate change.

These goals are admittedly ambitious, yet they will not be difficult to align or advance as long as we keep in mind this One Big Idea: most of the problems our food system faces today are because of its reliance on fossil fuels, and to the extent that our policies wring the oil out of the system and replace it with the energy of the sun, those policies will simultaneously improve the state of our health, our environment, and our security.

I. RESOLARIZING THE AMERICAN FARM

What happens in the field influences every other link of the food chain on up to our meals—if we grow monocultures of corn and soy, we will find the products of processed corn and soy on our plates. Fortunately for your initiative, the federal government has enormous leverage in determining exactly what happens on the 830 million acres of American crop and pasture land.

Today most government farm and food programs are designed to prop up the old system of maximizing production from a handful of subsidized commodity crops grown in monocultures. Even food-assistance programs like WIC and school lunch focus on maximizing quantity rather than quality, typically specifying a minimum number of calories (rather than maximums) and seldom paying more than lip service to nutritional quality. This focus on quantity may have made sense in a time of food scarcity, but today it gives us a school-lunch program that feeds chicken nuggets and Tater Tots to overweight and diabetic children.

Your challenge is to take control of this vast federal machinery and use it to drive a transition to a new solar-food economy, starting on the farm. Right now, the government actively discourages the farmers it subsidizes from growing healthful, fresh food: farmers receiving crop subsidies are prohibited from growing "specialty crops"—farm-bill speak for fruits and vegetables. (This rule was the price exacted by California and Florida produce growers in exchange for going along with subsidies for commodity crops.) Commodity farmers should instead be encouraged to grow as many different crops—including animals—as possible. Why? Because the greater the diversity of crops on a farm, the less the need for both fertilizers and pesticides.

The power of cleverly designed polycultures to produce large amounts of food from little more than soil, water, and sunlight has been proved, not only by small-scale "alternative" farmers in the United States but also by large rice-and-fish farmers in China and giant-scale operations (up to 15,000 acres) in places like Argentina. There, in a geography roughly comparable to that of the American farm belt, farmers have traditionally employed an ingenious eight-year rotation of perennial pasture and annual crops: after five years grazing cattle on pasture (and producing the world's best beef), farmers can then grow three years of grain without applying any fossil-fuel fertilizer. Or, for that matter, many pesticides: the weeds that afflict pasture can't survive the years of tillage, and the weeds of row crops don't survive the years of grazing, making herbicides all but unnecessary. There is no reason—save current policy and custom—that American farmers couldn't grow both high-quality grain and grass-fed beef under such a regime through much of the Midwest. (It should be noted that today's sky-high grain prices are causing many Argentine farmers to abandon their rotation to grow grain and soybeans exclusively, an environmental disaster in the making.)

Federal policies could do much to encourage this sort of diversified sun farming. Begin with the subsidies: payment levels should reflect the number of different crops farmers grow or the number of days of the year their fields are green—that is, taking advantage of photosynthesis, whether to grow food, replenish the soil, or control erosion. If Midwestern farmers simply planted a cover crop after the fall harvest, they would significantly reduce their need for fertilizer, while cutting down on soil erosion. Why don't farmers do this routinely? Because in recent years fossil-fuel-based fertility has been so much cheaper and easier to use than sun-based fertility.

In addition to rewarding farmers for planting cover crops, we should make it easier for them to apply compost to their fields—a practice that improves not only the fertility of the soil but also its ability to hold water and therefore withstand drought. (There is mounting evidence that it also boosts the nutritional quality of the food grown in it.) The U.S.D.A. estimates that Americans throw out 14 percent of the food they buy; much more is wasted by retailers, wholesalers, and institutions. A program to make municipal composting of food and yard waste mandatory and then distributing the compost free to area farmers would shrink America's garbage heap, cut the need for irrigation and fossil-fuel fertilizers in agriculture, and improve the nutritional quality of the American diet.

Right now, most of the conservation programs run by the U.S.D.A. are designed on the zero-sum principle: land is either locked up in "conservation" or it is farmed intensively. This either-or approach reflects an outdated belief that modern farming and ranching are inherently destructive, so that the best thing for the environment is to leave land untouched. But

> **The era of cheap, oil-based food is drawing to a close.**

we now know how to grow crops and graze animals in systems that will support biodiversity, soil health, clean water, and carbon sequestration. The Conservation Stewardship Program, championed by Senator Tom Harkin and included in the 2008 Farm Bill, takes an important step toward rewarding these kinds of practices, but we need to move this approach from the periphery of our farm policy to the very center. Longer term, the government should back ambitious research now under way (at the Land Institute in Kansas and a handful of other places) to "perennialize" commodity agriculture: to breed varieties of wheat, rice, and other staple grains that can be grown like prairie grasses—without having to till the soil every year. These perennial grains hold the promise of slashing the fossil fuel now needed to fertilize and till the soil, while protecting farmland from erosion and sequestering significant amounts of carbon.

But that is probably a 50-year project. For today's agriculture to wean itself from fossil fuel and make optimal use of sunlight, crop plants and animals must once again be married on the farm—as in Wendell Berry's elegant "solution." Sunlight nourishes the grasses and grains, the plants nourish the animals, the animals then nourish the soil, which in turn nourishes the next season's grasses and grains. Animals on pasture can also harvest their own feed and dispose of their own waste—all without our help or fossil fuel.

If this system is so sensible, you might ask, why did it succumb to Confined Animal Feeding Operations, or CAFOs? In fact there is nothing inherently efficient or economical about raising vast cities of animals in confinement. Three struts, each put into place by federal policy, support the modern CAFO, and the most important of these—the ability to buy grain for less than it costs to grow it—has just been kicked away. The second strut is F.D.A. approval for the routine use of antibiotics in feed, without which the animals in these places could not survive their crowded, filthy, and miserable existence. And the third is that the government does not require CAFOs to treat their wastes as it would require human cities of comparable size to do. The F.D.A. should ban the routine use of antibiotics in livestock feed on public-health grounds, now that we have evidence that the practice is leading to the evolution of drug-resistant bacterial diseases and to outbreaks of E. coli and salmonella poisoning. CAFOs should also be regulated like the factories they are, required to clean up their waste like any other industry or municipality.

It will be argued that moving animals off feedlots and back onto farms will raise the price of meat. It probably will—as it should. You will need to make the case that paying the real cost of meat, and therefore eating less of it, is a good thing for our health, for the environment, for our dwindling reserves of fresh water, and for the welfare of the animals. Meat and milk production represent the food industry's greatest burden on the environment; a recent U.N. study estimated that the world's livestock alone account for 18 percent of all greenhouse gases, more than all forms of transportation combined. (According to one study, a pound of feedlot beef also takes 5,000 gallons of water to produce.) And while animals living on farms will still emit their share of greenhouse gases, grazing them on grass and returning their waste to the soil will substantially offset their carbon hoof prints, as will getting ruminant animals off grain. A bushel of grain takes approximately a half gallon of oil to produce; grass can be grown with little more than sunshine.

It will be argued that sun-food agriculture will generally yield less food than fossil-fuel agriculture. This is debatable. The key question you must be prepared to answer is simply this: Can the sort of sustainable agriculture you're proposing feed the world?

There are a couple of ways to answer this question. The simplest and most honest answer is that we don't know, because we haven't tried. But in the same way we now need to learn how to run an industrial economy without cheap fossil fuel, we have no choice but to find out whether sustainable agriculture can produce enough food. The fact is, during the past century, our agricultural research has been directed toward the goal of maximizing production with the help of fossil fuel. There is no reason to think that bringing the same sort of resources to the development of more complex, sun-based agricultural systems wouldn't produce comparable yields. Today's organic farmers, operating for the most part without benefit of public investment in research, routinely achieve 80 to 100 percent of conventional yields in grain and, in drought years, frequently exceed conventional yields. (This is because organic soils better retain moisture.) Assuming no further improvement, could the world—with a population expected to peak at 10 billion—survive on these yields?

First, bear in mind that the average yield of world agriculture today is substantially lower than that of modern sustainable farming. According to a recent University of Michigan study, merely bringing international yields up to today's organic levels could increase the world's food supply by 50 percent.

The second point to bear in mind is that yield isn't everything—and growing high-yield commodities is not quite the same thing as growing food. Much of what we're growing today is not directly eaten as food but processed into low-quality calories of fat and sugar. As the world epidemic of diet-related chronic disease has demonstrated, the sheer quantity of calories that a food system produces improves health only up to a point, but after that, quality and diversity are probably more important. We can expect that a food system that produces somewhat less food but of a higher quality will produce healthier populations.

The final point to consider is that 40 percent of the world's grain output today is fed to animals; 11 percent of the world's corn and soybean crop is fed to cars and trucks, in the form of biofuels. Provided the developed world can cut its consumption of grain-based animal protein and ethanol, there should be plenty of food for everyone—however we choose to grow it.

In fact, well-designed polyculture systems, incorporating not just grains but vegetables and animals, can produce more food per acre than conventional monocultures, and food of a much higher nutritional value. But this kind of farming is complicated and needs many more hands on the land to make it work. Farming without fossil fuels—performing complex rotations of plants and animals and managing pests without petrochemicals—is labor intensive and takes more skill than merely "driving and spraying," which is how corn-belt farmers describe what they do for a living.

To grow sufficient amounts of food using sunlight will require more people growing food—millions more. This suggests that sustainable agriculture will be easier to implement in the developing world, where large rural populations remain, than in the West, where they don't. But what about here in America, where we have only about two million farmers left to feed a population of 300 million? And where farmland is being lost to development at the rate of 2,880 acres a day? Post-oil agriculture will need a lot more people engaged in food production—as farmers and probably also as gardeners.

The sun-food agenda must include programs to train a new generation of farmers and then help put them on the land. The average American farmer today is 55 years old; we shouldn't expect these farmers to embrace the sort of complex ecological approach to agriculture that is called for. Our focus should be on teaching ecological farming systems to students entering land-grant colleges today. For decades now, it has been federal policy to shrink the number of farmers in America by promoting capital-intensive monoculture and consolidation. As a society, we devalued farming as an occupation and encouraged the best students to leave the farm for "better" jobs in the city. We emptied America's rural counties in order to supply workers to urban factories. To put it bluntly, we now need to reverse course. We need more highly skilled small farmers in more places all across America—not as a matter of nostalgia for the agrarian past but as a matter of national security. For nations that lose the ability to substantially feed themselves will find themselves as gravely compromised in their international dealings as nations that depend on foreign sources of oil presently do. But while there are alternatives to oil, there are no alternatives to food.

Can the sort of sustainable agriculture you're proposing feed the world?

National security also argues for preserving every acre of farmland we can and then making it available to new farmers. We simply will not be able to depend on distant sources of food, and therefore need to preserve every acre of good farmland within a day's drive of our cities. In the same way that when we came to recognize the supreme ecological value of wetlands we erected high bars to their development, we need to recognize the value of farmland to our national security and require real-estate developers to do "food-system impact statements" before development begins. We should also create tax and zoning incentives for developers to incorporate farmland (as they now do "open space") in their subdivision plans; all those subdivisions now ringing golf courses could someday have diversified farms at their center.

The revival of farming in America, which of course draws on the abiding cultural power of our agrarian heritage, will pay many political and economic dividends. It will lead to robust economic renewal in the countryside. And it will generate tens of millions of new "green jobs," which is precisely how we need to begin thinking of skilled solar farming: as a vital sector of the 21st-century post-fossil-fuel economy.

II. REREGIONALIZING THE FOOD SYSTEM

For your sun-food agenda to succeed, it will have to do a lot more than alter what happens on the farm. The government could help seed a thousand new polyculture farmers in every county in Iowa, but they would promptly fail if the grain elevator remained the only buyer in town and corn and beans were the only crops it would take. Resolarizing the food system means building the infrastructure for a regional food economy—one that can support diversified farming and, by shortening the food chain, reduce the amount of fossil fuel in the American diet.

A decentralized food system offers a great many other benefits as well. Food eaten closer to where it is grown will be fresher and require less processing, making it more nutritious. Whatever may be lost in efficiency by localizing food production is gained in resilience: regional food systems can better withstand all kinds of shocks. When a single factory is grinding 20 million hamburger patties in a week or washing 25 million servings of salad, a single terrorist armed with a canister of toxins can, at a stroke, poison millions. Such a system is equally susceptible to accidental contamination: the bigger and more global the trade in food, the more vulnerable the system is to catastrophe. The best way to protect our food system against such threats is obvious: decentralize it.

Today in America there is soaring demand for local and regional food; farmers' markets, of which the U.S.D.A. estimates there are now 4,700, have become one of the fastest-growing segments of the food market. Community-supported agriculture is booming as well: there are now nearly 1,500 community-supported farms, to which consumers pay an annual fee in exchange for a weekly box of produce through the season. The local-food movement will continue to grow with no help from the government, especially as high fuel prices make distant and out-of-season food, as well as feedlot meat, more expensive. Yet there are several steps the government can take to nurture this market and make local foods more affordable. Here are a few:

Four-Season Farmers' Markets. Provide grants to towns and cities to build year-round indoor farmers' markets, on the model of Pike Place in Seattle or the Reading Terminal Market in Philadelphia. To supply these markets, the U.S.D.A. should make grants to rebuild local distribution networks in order to minimize the amount of energy used to move produce within local food sheds.

Agricultural Enterprise Zones. Today the revival of local food economies is being hobbled by a tangle of regulations originally designed to check abuses by the very largest food producers. Farmers should be able to smoke a ham and sell it to their neighbors without making a huge investment in federally approved facilities. Food-safety regulations must be made sensitive to scale and marketplace, so that a small producer selling direct off the farm or at a farmers' market is not regulated as onerously as a multinational food manufacturer. This is not because local food won't ever have food-safety problems—it will—only that its problems will be less catastrophic and easier to manage because local food is inherently more traceable and accountable.

Local Meat-Inspection Corps. Perhaps the single greatest impediment to the return of livestock to the land and the revival of local, grass-based meat production is the disappearance of regional slaughter facilities. The big meat processors have been buying up local abattoirs only to close them down as they consolidate, and the U.S.D.A. does little to support the ones that remain. From the department's perspective, it is a better use of shrinking resources to dispatch its inspectors to a plant slaughtering 400 head an hour than to a regional abattoir slaughtering a dozen. The U.S.D.A. should establish a Local Meat-Inspectors Corps to serve these processors. Expanding on its successful pilot program on Lopez Island in Puget Sound, the U.S.D.A. should also introduce a fleet of mobile abattoirs that would go from farm to farm, processing animals humanely and inexpensively. Nothing would do more to make regional, grass-fed meat fully competitive in the market with feedlot meat.

Establish a Strategic Grain Reserve. In the same way the shift to alternative energy depends on keeping oil prices relatively stable, the sun-food agenda—as well as the food security of billions of people around the world—will benefit from government action to prevent huge swings in commodity prices. A strategic grain reserve, modeled on the Strategic Petroleum Reserve, would help achieve this objective and at the same time provide some cushion for world food stocks, which today stand at perilously low levels. Governments should buy and store grain when it is cheap and sell when it is dear, thereby moderating price swings in both directions and discouraging speculation.

Regionalize Federal Food Procurement. In the same way that federal procurement is often used to advance important social goals (like promoting minority-owned businesses), we should require that some minimum percentage of government food purchases—whether for school-lunch programs, military bases, or federal prisons—go to producers located within 100 miles of institutions buying the food. We should create incentives for hospitals and universities receiving federal funds to buy fresh local produce. To channel even a small portion of institutional food purchasing to local food would vastly expand regional agriculture and improve the diet of the millions of people these institutions feed.

Create a Federal Definition of "Food." It makes no sense for government food-assistance dollars, intended to improve the nutritional health of at-risk Americans, to support the consumption of products we know to be unhealthful. Yes, some people will object that for the government to specify what food stamps can and cannot buy smacks of paternalism.

Yet we already prohibit the purchase of tobacco and alcohol with food stamps. So why not prohibit something like soda, which is arguably less nutritious than red wine? Because it is, nominally, a food, albeit a "junk food." We need to stop flattering nutritionally worthless foodlike substances by calling them "junk food"—and instead make clear that such products are not in fact food of any kind. Defining what constitutes real food worthy of federal support will no doubt be controversial (you'll recall President Reagan's ketchup imbroglio), but defining food upward may be more politically palatable than defining it down, as Reagan sought to do. One approach would be to rule that, in order to be regarded as a food by the government, an edible substance must contain a certain minimum ratio of micronutrients per calorie of energy. At a stroke, such a definition would improve the quality of school lunch and discourage sales of unhealthful products, since typically only "food" is exempt from local sales tax.

A *few other ideas*: Food-stamp debit cards should double in value whenever swiped at farmers' markets—all of which, by the way, need to be equipped with the Electronic Benefit Transfer card readers that supermarkets already have. We should expand the WIC program that gives farmers'-market vouchers to low-income women with children; such programs help attract farmers' markets to urban neighborhoods where access to fresh produce is often nonexistent. (We should also offer tax incentives to grocery chains willing to build supermarkets in underserved neighborhoods.) Federal food assistance for the elderly should build on a successful program pioneered by the state of Maine that buys low-income seniors a membership in a community-supported farm. All these initiatives have the virtue of advancing two objectives at once: supporting the health of at-risk Americans and the revival of local food economies.

III. REBUILDING AMERICA'S FOOD CULTURE

In the end, shifting the American diet from a foundation of imported fossil fuel to local sunshine will require changes in our daily lives, which by now are deeply implicated in the economy and culture of fast, cheap, and easy food. Making available more healthful and more sustainable food does not guarantee it will be eaten, much less appreciated or enjoyed. We need to use all the tools at our disposal—not just federal policy and public education but the president's bully pulpit and the example of the first family's own dinner table—to promote a new culture of food that can undergird your sun-food agenda.

Changing the food culture must begin with our children, and it must begin in the schools. Nearly a half-century ago, President Kennedy announced a national initiative to improve the physical fitness of American children. He did it by elevating the importance of physical education, pressing states to make it a requirement in public schools. We need to bring the same commitment to "edible education"—in Alice Waters's phrase—by making lunch, in all its dimensions, a mandatory part of the curriculum. On the premise that eating well is a critically important life skill, we need to teach all primary-school students the basics of growing and cooking food and then enjoying it at shared meals.

Eating well is a critically important life skill.

To change our children's food culture, we'll need to plant gardens in every primary school, build fully equipped kitchens, train a new genera-tion of lunchroom ladies (and gentlemen) who can once again cook, and teach cooking to children. We should introduce a School Lunch Corps program that forgives federal student loans to culinary-school graduates in exchange for two years of service in the public-school lunch program. And we should immediately increase school-lunch spending per pupil by $1 a day—the minimum amount food-service experts believe it will take to underwrite a shift from fast food in the cafeteria to real food freshly prepared.

But it is not only our children who stand to benefit from public education about food. Today most federal messages about food, from nutrition labeling to the food pyramid, are negotiated with the food industry. The surgeon general should take over from the Department of Agriculture the job of communicating with Americans about their diet. That way we might begin to construct a less equivocal and more effective public-health message about nutrition. Indeed, there is no reason that public-health campaigns about the dangers of obesity and Type 2 dia-betes shouldn't be as tough and as effective as public-health campaigns about the dangers of smoking. The Centers for Disease Control estimates that one in three American children born in 2000 will develop Type 2 diabetes. The public needs to know and see precisely what that sentence means: blindness; amputation; early death. All of which can be avoided by a change in diet and lifestyle. A public-health crisis of this magnitude calls for a blunt public-health message, even at the expense of offending the food industry. Judging by the success of recent antismoking cam-paigns, the savings to the health care system could be substantial.

There are other kinds of information about food that the government can supply or demand. In general we should push for as much transpar-ency in the food system as possible—the other sense in which "sunlight" should be the watchword of our agenda. The F.D.A. should require that every packaged-food product include a second calorie count, indicating how many calories of fossil fuel went into its production. Oil is one of the most important ingredients in our food, and people ought to know just how much of it they're eating. The government should also throw its support behind putting a second bar code on all food products that, when scanned either in the store or at home (or with a cellphone), brings up on a screen the whole story and pictures of how that product was produced: in the case of crops, images of the farm and lists of agrochemicals used in its production; in the case of meat and dairy, descriptions of the animals' diet and drug regimen, as well as live video feeds of the CAFO where they live and, yes, the slaughterhouse where they die. The very length and complexity of the modern food chain breeds a culture of ignorance and indifference among eaters. Shortening the food chain is one way to create more conscious consumers, but deploying technology to pierce the veil is another.

Finally, there is the power of the example you set in the White House. If what's needed is a change of culture in America's thinking about food, then how America's first household organizes its eating will set the national tone, focusing the light of public attention on the issue and communicating a simple set of values that can guide Americans toward sun-based foods and away from eating oil.

The choice of White House chef is always closely watched, and you would be wise to appoint a figure who is identified with the food movement and committed to cooking simply from fresh local ingredients. Besides feeding you and your family exceptionally well, such a chef would demonstrate how it is possible even in Washington to eat locally for much of the year, and that good food needn't be fussy or complicated but does depend on good farming. You should make a point of the fact that every night you're in town, you join your family for dinner in the Executive Residence—at a table. (Surely you remember the Reagans' TV trays.) And you should also let it be known that the White House observes one meatless day a week—a step that, if all Americans followed suit, would be the equivalent, in carbon saved, of taking 20 million mid-size sedans off the road for a year. Let the White House chef post daily menus on the Web, listing the farmers who supplied the food, as well as recipes.

Since enhancing the prestige of farming as an occupation is critical to developing the sun-based regional agriculture we need, the White House should appoint, in addition to a White House chef, a White House farmer. This new post would be charged with implementing what could turn out to be your most symbolically resonant step in building a new American food culture. And that is this: tear out five prime south-facing acres of the White House lawn and plant in their place an organic fruit and vegetable garden.

When Eleanor Roosevelt did something similar in 1943, she helped start a Victory Garden movement that ended up making a substantial contribution to feeding the nation in wartime. (Less well known is the fact that Roosevelt planted this garden over the objections of the U.S.D.A., which feared home gardening would hurt the American food industry.)

By the end of the war, more than 20 million home gardens were supplying 40 percent of the produce consumed in America. The president should throw his support behind a new Victory Garden movement, this one seeking "victory" over three critical challenges we face today: high food prices, poor diets, and a sedentary population. Eating from this, the shortest food chain of all, offers anyone with a patch of land a way to reduce their fossil-fuel consumption and help fight climate change. (We should offer grants to cities to build allotment gardens for people without access to land.) Just as important, Victory Gardens offer a way to enlist Americans, in body as well as mind, in the work of feeding themselves and changing the food system—something more ennobling, surely, than merely asking them to shop a little differently.

I don't need to tell you that ripping out even a section of the White House lawn will be controversial: Americans love their lawns, and the South Lawn is one of the most beautiful in the country. But imagine all the energy, water, and petrochemicals it takes to make it that way. (Even for the purposes of this memo, the White House would not disclose its lawn-care regimen.) Yet as deeply as Americans feel about their lawns, the agrarian ideal runs deeper still, and making this particular plot of American land productive, especially if the First Family gets out there and pulls weeds now and again, will provide an image even more stirring than that of a pretty lawn: the image of stewardship of the land, of self-reliance, and of making the most of local sunlight to feed one's family and community. The fact that surplus produce from the South Lawn Victory Garden (and there will be literally tons of it) will be offered to regional food banks will make its own eloquent statement.

You're probably thinking that growing and eating organic food in the White House carries a certain political risk. It is true you might want to plant iceberg lettuce rather than arugula, at least to start. (Or simply call arugula by its proper American name, as generations of Midwesterners have done: "rocket.") But it should not be difficult to deflect the charge of elitism sometimes leveled at the sustainable-food movement. Reforming the food system is not inherently a right-or-left issue: for every Whole Foods shopper with roots in the counterculture you can find a family of evangelicals intent on taking control of its family dinner and diet back from the fast-food industry—the culinary equivalent of home schooling. You should support hunting as a particularly sustainable way to eat meat—meat grown without any fossil fuels whatsoever. There is also a strong libertarian component to the sun-food agenda, which seeks to free small producers from the burden of government regulation in order to stoke rural innovation. And what is a higher "family value," after all, than making time to sit down every night to a shared meal?

Our agenda puts the interests of America's farmers, families, and communities ahead of the fast-food industry's. For that industry and its apologists to imply that it is somehow more "populist" or egalitarian to hand our food dollars to Burger King or General Mills than to support a struggling local farmer is absurd. Yes, sun food costs more, but the reasons why it does only undercut the charge of elitism: cheap food is only cheap because of government handouts and regulatory indulgence (both of which we will end), not to mention the exploitation of workers, animals, and the environment on which its putative "economies" depend. Cheap food is food dishonestly priced—it is in fact unconscionably expensive.

Your sun-food agenda promises to win support across the aisle. It builds on America's agrarian past, but turns it toward a more sustainable, sophisticated future. It honors the work of American farmers and enlists them in three of the 21st century's most urgent errands: to move into the post-oil era, to improve the health of the American people, and to mitigate climate change. Indeed, it enlists all of us in this great cause by turning food consumers into part-time producers, reconnecting the American people with the American land, and demonstrating that we need not choose between the welfare of our families and the health of the environment—that eating less oil and more sunlight will redound to the benefit of both.

DISCUSSION

1. How does addressing the president-elect as "Farmer in Chief" differ from the more conventional honorific "Commander in Chief"? How does this title challenge the norms that typically define how we think about this office? Why do you think Pollan chooses this title? What larger point is he trying to make about government policy and the industrial food chain?

2. Pollan spends a good deal of time detailing the process through which agricultural policy gets formulated. What, in his view, are the principal problems with this process? What specifically does he object to? In your view, is Pollan correct? Are there counterarguments to his critique that could be made? If so, what?

3. Addressing Barack Obama directly, Pollan speaks of "the power of the example you set in the White House. If what's needed is a change of culture in America's thinking about food, then how America's first household organizes its eating will set the national tone." How would you recommend the president go about "setting the national tone" when it comes to eating? What sorts of initiatives and practices would you like to see? And why?

WRITING

4. Much of Pollan's critique here revolves around the ways our industrial food system has skewed, even warped, contemporary eating habits — in his view rendering our relationship to food increasingly unnatural. Choose a type of food that you think supports Pollan's contention. How, specifically, does this food and the messages that surround it script a relationship to eating and/or food that is in some way unnatural? Next, choose a food that, in your view, challenges or refutes Pollan's contention. What sort of relationship to eating does it script? And how does this differ from your first example?

5. Create an instruction manual that lays out a diet that you think would help remedy some of the eating-related problems Pollan identifies in this essay: a diet that challenges our current overreliance on unhealthy eating habits and unsustainable agricultural practices. What steps does it map? What foods does it proscribe and in what amounts? And how would this particular diet succeed in fostering some of the changes Pollan calls for?

6. Makenna Goodman's essay (p. 246) offers perhaps the starkest counterpoint to the portrait of industrial food that Pollan sketches here. In a brief essay, reflect on the key differences in the way these two authors talk about food and eating. To what extent does Goodman's account of "killing what you eat" outline a set of attitudes toward eating that are different from the ones Pollan examines? Which set of norms do you find more appealing? Why?

SARA DICKERMAN
Food Fright

As we all know from personal experience, today's food products often come firmly affixed with countless health warnings — from doctor recommendations to FDA guidelines. But do these warnings provide us with information we truly need? Or that do us any good? Taking a look at the myriad dietary restrictions relating to pregnancy, Sara Dickerman wonders whether our modern-day obsession with food safety might not be contributing to a new and dangerous anxiety, one that teaches us to be afraid of virtually everything we eat. Dickerman is a freelance food writer and former food editor at the Seattle newspaper the *Stranger*. Her writing has appeared in *Chow*, the *New York Times*, and *Seattle Magazine*. The following selection originally appeared in *Slate* on September 15, 2004.

I'VE GOT TO CONFESS: I'M IN MY EIGHTH MONTH OF PREGNANCY, AND so far I have sheepishly eaten several slivers of air-dried Serrano ham, a few crumbles of blue cheese, and one shimmering piece of yellowtail nigiri. Then, there's the red wine. It started with furtive thimblefuls (just to taste a new wine at the restaurant where I work!) but has spiraled out of control into a biweekly half-glass. All of these items are on the do-not-consume list for pregnant women, but no one seems to be able to tell me how much of a risk occasional lapses like mine pose to my baby. Food, which has always been my great delight in life, has now begun to freak me out.

I'm clearly not alone. As Alex Kuczynski observed in the *New York Times*, incessant warnings from doctors, friends, and the Internet tend to give the modern pregnant woman a nasty case of "pregnancy paranoia." The list of sketchy comestibles is almost comically long. Alcohol is an obvious no-no even though it's unclear whether or how moderate drinking could lead to fetal alcohol syndrome or miscarriage. We are also told to avoid deli meats (listeria risk), sushi (parasite risk), coffee (possible miscarriage risk), soft and blue cheeses (listeria again), peanut butter (allergy risk), tuna (mercury risk), liver (retinol poisoning risk), aioli (salmonella risk), herbal teas (untested medicinal effects), and any meats cooked less than shoe-leather tough (toxemia risk). It's understandable that modern women think they live in a time when it's particularly stressful to be pregnant. But are the vigilance and anxiety that accompany pregnant women to the dinner table really all that new?

As long as women have been carrying children, they have received advice, often dour, often from men, about what to eat and drink. Even Plato had his rather common-sense saying: "Children shouldn't be made in bodies saturated with drunkenness." But alcohol hasn't remained off-limits throughout history: According to historian Janet Golden, in the eighteenth and nineteenth centuries, alcohol was prescribed to pregnant women as a tonic to treat "deranged stomachs" (the contemporary term for morning sickness). Even though nutrients had not yet been discovered, women were still directed to eat or avoid certain foods. It was believed that a mother who consumed sour, spicy food might produce an ill-tempered baby, and mothers were sometimes urged to eat "young meats" like lamb and veal in the interest of their own young offspring.

Childbirth, of course, used to be a more deadly business for mothers and newborns—one that may have stoked apprehension in many new mothers but may have also prompted a certain fatalistic repose. In the 1880s German Dr. L. Prochownick developed a high-protein, calorie-restricted diet intended to help expecting mothers limit the weight that they—and thus their fetuses—would gain during pregnancy. The theory was that a smaller baby would make for an easier delivery. We now know, of course, that low-birth-weight babies have a harder time surviving. But low-pregnancy-weight gain remained a major recommendation even as modern obstetrics (prenatal consultations, C-sections, antibiotics) helped maternal mortality rates shoot downward in the midcentury. Doctors worried about the effects of substantial weight gain on a mother's overall health. The low-weight-gain imperative was supported by the spurious view, popular through the 1960s, that the fetus was a "perfect parasite," siphoning off its nutritional needs from the mother's body, regardless of her diet (a notion that no doubt set a mother's mind at ease when it came to her prenatal eating habits).

Although eating too much was long discouraged, the role of dietary nutrients became clearer throughout the twentieth century; doctors began to recognize that a good diet could have a positive impact on maternal and newborn health, even if they did not agree on specifics. As the century progressed, supplements and vitamin-rich foods, like cod-liver oil and liver, became more commonly recommended for mothers to be. Moderate alcohol use was not forbidden, but liquor was shunned as a source of "empty calories" not worth the potential weight gain. It has only been since the 1980s or so that, in the United States, the hazard of a malnourished baby has trumped the potential complications of the postpartum mother's being overweight, and women are given more workable guidelines for weight gain: 25 to 35 pounds for an average woman, 15 to 25 for an overweight one. (In the midcentury the recommendation for an average woman maxed out at about 20 pounds, and some overweight women were even encouraged to lose weight.)

But as weight became less of an obsession, the relative safety of everything a mother consumed became more of an issue. In the 1980s the popular mothering-advice business exploded with the publication of the best-selling *What To Expect When You're Expecting* series. (WTEWYE itself has sold over 10 million copies since its 1984 debut.) The books, which continue to be an essential part of the pregnancy library, exposed women to a wealth of information about pregnancy, but they were also notorious for their puritanical tone, particularly on issues of nutrition. The *WTEWYE* "best odds diet" demanded not only increased vitamin, protein, and iron consumption from expecting mothers, but urged them, while they were at it, to seriously restrict salt and fat intake and to give up refined flours and sugars. The nutritional companion to *What To Expect*, called *What To Eat When You're Expecting*, scolded, "Nothing offers your baby less to grow on than sugar. Every calorie refined sugar supplies could better come from foods that yield a nutritional return, which is reason enough to offer it to your baby as rarely as possible." At the core of this thinking is the overwhelming notion that no action a mother takes is without direct consequence for the baby. "Your baby equals what you eat." (The times have changed a bit: A recent third edition of *What To Eat* boasts an "all-new (guilt-free!) attitude.")

> **At the core of this thinking is the notion that no action a mother takes is without direct consequence for the baby.**

The *WTEWYE* books were not so much the cause of pregnancy paranoia as the crystallization of a trend that was already in the works. One reason for the new parental vigilance might have been the newly available images of unborn children. Until the late twentieth century, Americans had never been so aware of the prenatal life of a fetus: The spread of ultrasounds and amniocentesis in the '70s and '80s gave women a glimpse of their babies in utero while *Roe v. Wade* sparked the legal movement toward what Golden calls "fetal personhood." At the same time, childbirth professionals became increasingly legally liable for anything that went wrong with a child's delivery, so instead of offering common-sense advice, many health-care professionals were understandably inclined to tell women how to avoid all possible risks. The surgeon general's 1989 warning about alcohol use during pregnancy, for example, called for absolute abstention, even though fetal alcohol syndrome develops almost exclusively in the offspring of alcoholic women.

In the wake of WTEWYE's success, dozens of pregnancy guides sprang up in print and on the Internet, many with "don't" lists outnumbering "do" lists. And this is a key problem with contemporary pregnancy advice, on culinary matters and otherwise—the emphasis on fears of a poisonous environment, rather than on positive steps that can help the baby's development. On babycenter.com, the massive Web site for parents and parents-to-be, for example, the paid content, which is presumably the site's most desirable, consists largely of anxiety-focused information: baby equipment recall alerts and a long list of "Is it safe" questions and their heavily qualified answers.

Before the window into the womb opened up, pregnancy's anxieties stemmed more from a lack of information than its overabundance. As my mother, who was pregnant in the '60s and '70s, said: "We certainly knew something could go very wrong, but there was not too much we could do about it." A woman who made the effort to eat liver and onions once a week was pretty proactive in those days. But thanks to a surfeit of information, today's expecting mothers have a sense of culpability about every bite they eat and sip they take—even if they don't know precisely how risky such behavior is. As much as I wish some of the information available were more conclusive, I have come to accept that there will probably never be a double-blind study on the effects of raw yellowtail on fetal development. I do know I'm looking forward to the sushi party I'm going to have in celebration of my baby's birth. Or do I have to wait until I'm done breast-feeding?

DISCUSSION

1. Dickerman begins her essay by offering a confession of all the different things she has eaten while pregnant. Why do you think she chooses to begin this way? What does her confession suggest about the larger argument Dickerman is making about food and food safety when it comes to pregnancy?

2. Does it make sense to you that so many of our culture's warnings and proscriptions around food focus on women — in particular, pregnant women? Does this bias seem understandable? Reasonable? What does this fact suggest about the gender norms that might underlie our cultural messages about food?

3. Dickerman includes a quick overview of some historical assumptions about pregnant women and food. Why do you think she includes this information? Does this historical context give you a different way of thinking about the food safety norms that govern today? How or how not?

WRITING

4. Choose a food that, in your view, exemplifies Dickerman's larger point about our culture's obsession with food safety. Then write an essay in which you explain how your example helps support or advance her argument. What sorts of warnings typically accompany this food? What particular dangers typically are associated with it? How do these warnings function as a kind of social script, teaching consumers to "fear" this food? And how, finally, do you respond to this script? Is it a sensible one to follow? How or how not?

5. The "key problem with contemporary pregnancy advice," Dickerman declares, is "the emphasis on fears of a poisonous environment, rather than on positive steps that can help the baby's development." Choose a food that, in your view, could be made to fulfill Dickerman's suggestion. Then write a one-page essay in which you outline what, for this food, such "positive" advice would look like. What instructions or script might you create for how one might think about and eat this food?

6. Another writer who looks at the gendered implications of our culture's eating-related norms is Caroline Knapp (p. 232). Write a brief essay comparing the argument each makes about food, eating, and gender. How does Dickerman's critique of our food safety mania also function as a commentary about embedded social stereotypes regarding women? To what extent does Knapp's account of her struggles with anorexia uncover and critique gender stereotypes as well? What are the key differences and similarities between these critiques?

Then and Now: *How to Make Meatloaf*

Far more than a list of ingredients and steps, each of these recipes offers a quick snapshot of the sorts of attitudes toward eating that, at two different moments in our food culture's recent history, passed for the norm. Meatloaf is a classic American dish that first became popular on family dinner tables during the Great Depression. It's a dish families could make on a budget because the recipe relied on cheaper cuts of meat and included bread or cracker crumbs as a way to create more servings. The first recipe is a classic meatloaf recipe from the Heinz ketchup company. Looking at it we may learn more about what the prevailing food attitudes were by focusing on what the recipe does *not* say — that is, on the things it simply takes for granted. The instructions are much less explicit than what we're used to today: no temperature setting for the oven, no specifications for the size of baking dish,

Circa 1956

HEINZ KETCHUP MEATLOAF RECIPE

> 2 lbs. ground beef
> ½ lb. bologna
> 1 tablespoon grated onion
> 1 cup moist cracker crumbs
> 1 egg
> 1 teaspoon salt
> ½ cup Heinz Tomato Ketchup
> Pepper

Chop bologna finely and add to the meat. Add other ingredients, adding Tomato Ketchup last, and bake in a moderate oven, basting frequently.

and no order for the ingredients added. The recipe also omits nutritional information — no discussion of calories or cholesterol here, or references to recommended daily allowances of fiber or calcium. These omissions stem in part from ingrained assumptions about eating that people of this era simply regarded as *common sense.* To put it mildly, any dish whose list of ingredients goes no further than pepper, ground beef, and bologna didn't achieve popularity at a historical moment that placed a terribly high premium on physical health. The point of eating, this recipe all but says out loud, is not to make us live longer; it is to put things into our bodies that conform to a particular standard of good taste or smart spending — a standard that in this case appears to have revolved primarily around adding flavor using the least expensive ingredients possible.

Contrast the second recipe, which transforms the all-American dish. The tofu meatloaf recipe carefully acquaints its readers with the particular facts about the ingredients it assembles, a tactic exemplified in its references to "light miso," "tahini," and "dried dill." This difference underscores how much more diversified our culture's prevailing definitions of American cuisine have grown since the Depression era. But perhaps even more important, it suggests how much more worried we are about what we put into our bodies. This recipe is meat-free and includes all-natural ingredients and exotic flavors. Indeed, if this Moosewood Restaurant recipe is a reliable guide, we could well argue that ours has become a food culture in which concerns over physical health (as well as its corollary, physical appearance) and ideology now supplant expense as the primary standard by which we judge the quality of our food.

These recipes may represent night and day in terms of what goes in them, but both represent a certain anxiety over eating. The first recipe includes just a few inexpensive ingredients (and relies on ketchup to provide the zing), while the second includes numerous fresh and healthy ingredients that are tough to find in some areas and cost considerably more than a bottle of ketchup. While the first recipe's author is conscious of the cook's pocketbook, the second is conscious of his or her health and lifestyle. Each recipe provides a revealing glimpse into how meatloaf can reflect our cultural concerns.

2001

Tofu Meatloaf

Serves 8
Prep time: 30 minutes
Baking time: 25–30 minutes

> 2 cakes firm tofu (16 ounces each)
> 2 tablespoons vegetable oil
> 2 cups diced onions
> 1 cup peeled and grated carrots
> 1 cup diced bell peppers
> 1 teaspoon dried oregano
> 1 teaspoon dried basil
> 1 teaspoon dried dill
> ⅔ cups chopped walnuts
> 1 cup bread crumbs
> 2 tablespoons tahini
> 2 tablespoons light miso
> 2 tablespoons soy sauce
> 1-2 tablespoons Dijon mustard

Press the tofu between two plates and rest a heavy weight on the top plate. Press for 15 minutes, then drain the liquid.

Meanwhile, heat the oil in a frying pan and sauté the onions, carrots, peppers, oregano, basil, and dill for about 7 minutes, until the vegetables are just tender. Crumble the pressed tofu into a large bowl, or grind it through a food processor. Stir in the walnuts, bread crumbs, tahini, miso, soy sauce, and mustard. Add the sautéed vegetables and mix well.

Preheat the oven to 350 or 375 degrees. Press the mix into an oiled casserole dish, and bake for about 30 minutes, until lightly browned.

— Reprinted from Moosewood Restaurant New Classics, Copyright © 2001 by the Moosewood Collective, Clarkson N. Potter, New York, publishers.

WRITING

1. How does each recipe seem to define "good" eating? What is supposed to make each dish worth eating? What does each recipe seem to define its standards of good eating against? Why? Write a one-page essay in which you analyze and evaluate the key differences between these two scripts. In what ways have the norms around eating changed since the first recipe was popular?

2. Both Michael Pollan (p. 186) and Tara Lohan (p. 250) write about food and economics. What do you think each author would have to say about these meatloaf recipes? Do they accord with Pollan's critique of our "industrial food complex"? Do they seem in concert with the ethic of "localism" Lohan describes? How or how not?

FRANCINE PROSE
The Wages of Sin

When it comes to eating, how much is too much? And where do we learn to draw this line? Taking aim at our current fixation on food, dieting, and body image, Francine Prose contemplates whether ours has become a culture in which overeating now stands as the preeminent sign of our moral and physical failure. Prose graduated from Radcliffe College in 1968 and currently lives and writes in New York City. She is the author of nine novels, including *The Blue Angel* (2001), a finalist for the National Book Award, and *A Changed Man* (2005), which won the Dayton Literary Peace Prize. She has also published several nonfiction books, including *Gluttony* (2003), from which the following is excerpted, and *Reading Like a Writer* (2006). Her most recent works are the novel *Goldengrove* (2008) and the nonfiction book *Anne Frank: The Book, the Life, the After Life* (2009).

MORE AND MORE OFTEN, WE READ ARTICLES AND HEAR TV commentators advocating government intervention to protect us from the greed of a corporate culture that profits from our unhealthy attraction to sugary and fatty foods. Legal experts discuss the feasibility of mounting class action suits—on the model of the recent and ongoing litigation against so-called big tobacco companies—against fast-food restaurants, junk-food manufacturers, and advertisers who target children with ads for salty fried snacks and brightly colored candy masquerading as breakfast cereal.

What's slightly more disturbing is the notion that not only do fat people need to be monitored, controlled, and saved from their gluttonous impulses, but that we need to be saved from them—that certain forms of social control might be required to help the overweight resist temptation. Writing in the *San Francisco Chronicle*, essayist Ruth Rosen has suggested that such actions might be motivated by compassion for such innocent victims as the parents of a child whose overweight helped lead to diabetes, or the child of a parent who died from weight-related causes. Of course the bottom line is concern for our pocketbooks, for the cost—shared by the wider population—of treating those who suffer from obesity-related ailments. As a partial remedy, Rosen proposes that schools and employers might forbid the sale of junk food on campus and in offices. Finally, she suggests that, in a more glorious future, the host who serves his guests greasy potato chips and doughnuts will incur the same horrified disapproval as the smoker who lights up—and blows smoke in our faces.

Rosen is not alone in her belief that legislation may be required to regulate the social costs of overeating. A recent item on CBS worriedly considered the alarming growth in the number of overweight and obese young people—a group that now comprises 14 percent of American children. According to the news clip, overweight was soon expected to surpass cigarette smoking as the major preventable cause of death: each year, 350,000 people die of obesity-related causes. Thirteen billion dollars is spent annually on food ads directed at children, and four out of five ads are for some excessively sugary or fatty product. The problem is undeniable, but once more the projected solution gives one pause; several interviewees raised the possibility of suing the purveyors of potato chips and candy bars. How far we have come from Saint Augustine and John Cassian and Chrysostom, taking it for granted that the struggle against temptation would be waged in the glutton's heart and mind—and not, presumably, in the law courts.

> You're so fat when they pierced your ears, they had to use a harpoon.
> You're so fat you've got to put on lipstick with a paint roller.

In studies that have examined the causes and motives behind the stigmatization of the overweight, such prejudice has been found to derive from the widely accepted notion that fat people are at fault, responsible for their weight and appearance, that they are self-indulgent, sloppy, lazy, morally lax, lacking in the qualities of self-denial and impulse control that our society (still so heavily influenced by the legacy of Puritanism) values and rewards. In a 1978 book, *The Seven Deadly Sins: Society and Evil*, sociologist Stanford M. Lyman takes a sociocultural approach to the reasons why we are so harsh in our condemnation of the so-called glutton.

> The apparently voluntary character of food gluttony serves to point up why it is more likely to seem "criminal" than sick, an act of moral defalcation rather than medical pathology. Although gluttony is not proscribed by the criminal law, it partakes of some of the social sanctions and moral understandings that govern orientations toward those who commit crimes. . . . Gluttony is an excessive *self*-indulgence. Even in its disrespect for the body it overvalues the ego that it slavishly satisfies.[1]

Most of us would no doubt claim that we are too sensible, compassionate, and enlightened to feel prejudice against the obese. We would never tell the sorts of cruel jokes scattered throughout this chapter. But let's consider how we feel when we've taken our already cramped seat in coach class on the airplane and suddenly our seatmate appears—a man or woman whose excessive weight promises to make our journey even more uncomfortable than we'd anticipated. Perhaps, contemplating a trip of this sort, we might find ourselves inclined to support Southwest

Airline's discriminatory two-seats-per-large-passenger rule. Meanwhile, as we try not to stare at our sizable traveling companion, we might as well be the medieval monks glaring at the friar who's helped himself to an extra portion. For what's involved in both cases is our notion of one's proper share, of surfeit and shortage—not enough food in one case, not enough space in the other.

"The glutton is also noticeable as a defiler of his own body space. His appetite threatens to engulf the spaces of others as he spreads out to take more than one person's ordinary allotment of territory. If he grows too large, he may no longer fit into ordinary chairs . . . and require special arrangements in advance of his coming."[2] The glutton's "crime" is crossing boundaries that we jealously guard and that are defined by our most primitive instincts: hunger, territoriality—that is to say, survival.

> **The glutton's "crime" is crossing boundaries that we jealously guard and that are defined by our most primitive instincts: hunger, territoriality—that is to say, survival.**

So we come full circle back to the language of crime and innocence, sin and penance, guilt and punishment—a view of overweight frequently adopted and internalized by the obese themselves. "Many groups of dieters whom I studied," writes Natalie Allon, "believed that fatness was the outcome of immoral self-indulgence. Group dieters used much religious language in considering themselves bad or good dieters—words such as sinner, saint, devil, angel, guilt, transgression, confession, absolution, diet Bible—as they partook of the rituals of group dieting."[3] Nor does the association between gluttony and the language of religion exist solely in the minds of dieters, the obese, and the food-obsessed. In fact it's extremely common to speak of having overeaten as having "been bad"; rich, fattening foods are advertised as being "sinfully delicious"; and probably most of us have thought or confessed the fact that we've felt "guilty" for having eaten more than we should have.

Like the members of other Twelve-Step programs, and not unlike the medieval gluttons who must have felt inspired to repent and pray for divine assistance in resisting temptation, the members of Overeaters Anonymous employ the terminology of religion. *Lifeline,* the magazine of Overeaters Anonymous, is filled with stories of healing and recovery, first-person accounts in which God was asked to intercede, to provide a spiritual awakening, and to remove the dangerous and destructive flaws from the recovering overeater's character.

Routinely, the capacity to achieve sobriety and abstinence—which for OA members means the ability to restrict one's self to three healthy and sensible meals a day—is credited to divine mercy and love, and to the good effects of an intimate and sustaining relationship with God. In one testimonial, a woman reports that coming to her first meeting and identifying herself as a recovering compulsive eater was more difficult for her than to say that she was a shoplifter, a serial killer, or a prostitute. Only after admitting that she was powerless over food and asking for the help of a higher power was she at last able to end her unhappy career as a "grazer and a binger."

For perhaps obvious reasons, the term "gluttony" is now rarely used as a synonym for compulsive eating. Yet Stanford Lyman conflates the two to make the point that our culture's attitude toward the obese is not unlike an older society's view of the gluttonous sinner:

> Societal opposition to gluttony manifests itself in a variety of social control devices and institutional arrangements. Although rarely organized as a group, very fat individuals at times seem to form a much beset minority, objects of calculating discrimination and bitter prejudice. Stigmatized because their addiction to food is so visible in its consequences, the obese find themselves ridiculed, rejected, and repulsed by many of those who do not overindulge. Children revile them on the streets, persons of average size refuse to date, dance, or dine with them, and many businesses, government, and professional associations refuse to employ them. So great is the pressure to conform to the dictates of the slimness culture in America that occasionally an overweight person speaks out, pointing to the similarities of his condition to that of racial and national minorities.[4]

Indeed, the overweight have found a forum in which to speak out, at the meetings, conventions, and in the bimonthly newsletter sponsored by NAAFA—the National Association to Advance Fat Acceptance. A recent issue of the newsletter, available on the internet, calls for readers to write to the government to protest the National Institute of Health's ongoing studies of normal-sized children to find out if obesity might have a metabolic basis. There are directions for giving money and establishing a living trust to benefit NAAFA, reviews of relevant new books, a report on the Trunk Sale at a NAAFA gathering in San Francisco, an update on the struggle to force auto manufacturers to provide seat belts that can save the lives of passengers who weigh over 215 pounds, and an article on the problems—the fear of appearing in public in a bathing suit, the narrow ladders that often provide the only access to swimming pools—that make it more difficult for the overweight to get the exercise that they need. There is a brief discussion of how obesity should be defined, and another about the effectiveness of behavioral psychotherapy in helping patients lose weight. Finally, there are grateful letters from readers whose lives have been improved by the support and sustenance they gain from belonging to NAAFA.

Equally fervent—if somewhat less affirmative and forgiving—are the gospel tracts, also available on-line. One of the most heartfelt and persuasive is the work of a preacher identified only as George Clark:

> After conducting healing campaigns and mailing out thousands of anointed handkerchiefs—since 1930—I have learned that the greatest physical cause of sickness among the people of God is coming from this lust for over-indulgence in eating. . . . Tens of thousands of truly converted people are sick and are suffering with heart trouble coming from high blood pressure and other ailments which result from overeating. . . . Did you ever wonder why artists have never depicted any of Jesus' disciples as being overweight or of the fleshy type? No one could have followed Jesus very long and remained overweight. . . . If eating too much has brought on high blood pressure, heart trouble, or many of the other diseases which come from being overweight, then God requires a reduction in your eating.

Given our perhaps misguided sense of living in a secular society, it's startling to find that our relationship with food is still so commonly translated directly into the language of God and the devil, of sin and repentance. But why should we be surprised, when we are constantly being reminded that our feelings about our diet and our body can be irrational, passionate, and closer to the province of faith and superstition than that of reason and science?

NOTES

[1] Stanford M. Lyman, *The Seven Deadly Sins: Society and Evil* (New York: St. Martin's Press, 1978), 220.

[2] Ibid., 223.

[3] Benjamin Wolman, ed., *Psychological Aspects of Obesity: A Handbook* (New York: Van Nostrand Reinhold, 1982), 148.

[4] Lyman, *Seven Deadly Sins,* 218.

BIBLIOGRAPHY

Albala, Ken. *Eating Right in the Renaissance.* Berkeley: University of California Press, 2002.

Augustine, Saint. *The Confessions of Saint Augustine,* trans. Edward B. Pusey, D. D. New York: The Modern Library, 1949.

Bell, Rudoph M. *Holy Anorexia.* Chicago: University of Chicago Press, 1985.

Chaucer, Geoffrey. *The Works of Geoffrey Chaucer,* ed. F. N. Robinson. Boston: Houghton Mifflin, 1957.

Chernin, Kim. *The Obsession.* New York: Harper Perennial, 1981.

Chesterton, G. K. *Saint Thomas Aquinas.* New York: Image Books, Doubleday, 2001.

Fielding, Henry. *Tom Jones.* New York: The Modern Library, 1994.

Fisher, M. F. K. *The Art of Eating.* New York: Vintage, 1976.

Lyman, Stanford M. *The Seven Deadly Sins: Society and Evil.* New York: St. Martin's Press, 1978.

Petronius. *The Satyricon,* trans. William Arrowsmith. New York: Meridian, 1994.

Pleij, Herman. *Dreaming of Cockaigne,* trans. Diane Webb. New York: Columbia University Press, 2001.

Rabelais, François. *Gargantua and Pantagruel,* trans. Burton Raffel. New York: W. W. Norton, 1991.

Roth, Geneen. *When Food Is Love.* New York: Plume, 1991.

Schwartz, Hillel. *Never Satisfied: A Cultural History of Fantasies and Fat.* New York: The Free Press, 1986.

Shaw, Teresa M. *The Burden of the Flesh: Fasting and Sexuality in Early Christianity.* Minneapolis: Fortress Press, 1996.

Spenser, Edmund. *The Faerie Queene.* New York: E. P. Dutton & Company, 1964.

Wolman, Benjamin, ed., with Stephen DeBerry, editorial associate. *Psychological Aspects of Obesity: A Handbook.* New York: Van Nostrand Reinhold, 1982.

DISCUSSION

1. Elsewhere in this essay Prose writes, "The so-called glutton is a walking rebuke to our self-control, our self-denial, and to our shaky faith that if we watch ourselves, then surely death cannot touch us." What exactly does she mean by this? Do you think she is right? In what ways do we use the images and examples of those body types that are regarded in our culture as deficient or abnormal as role models for what *not* to be ourselves?

2. From diet books to exercise videos, there is no shortage of material that scripts the ways we are and are not supposed to eat. Choose one such example from our current culture and describe the specific steps it itemizes. What does this list imply is the right attitude we should have toward food? How does it endeavor to get readers to adopt this view? What incentives does it offer? What punishments does it threaten?

3. There is, according to Prose, a close and complex connection between gluttony and guilt. Whether in the form of FDA warnings or ad copy for "sinfully delicious desserts," overeating is regularly associated in our culture with some kind of misbehavior or even moral failing. What do you make of this connection? Choose an example from our pop culture that you think is designed to teach this kind of guilt.

WRITING

4. Choose some venue (for example, a fast-food restaurant, health club, doctor's office, or similar place) that in your view endeavors to teach us specific attitudes about overeating. Spend a couple of hours there. First, write out as comprehensive a description of this place as you can. What kind of people do you observe? What sorts of equipment or décor? Next, write a short essay in which you speculate about the rules for eating that this venue attempts to instill. What relationship to food are people here encouraged to form? How does this relationship get presented or packaged as the norm?

5. One of the hallmarks of our contemporary culture, according to Prose, is that overeating is no longer viewed as a vice or sin but as an illness. Do you agree? What are some of the ways this change in thinking is communicated in popular culture or in the media? Write an essay in which you argue for or against gluttony as a moral issue.

6. Prose and Jason Fagone (p. 219) address the issue of gluttony in different ways. Write an essay in which you compare how each writer uses the idea of overeating to talk about larger cultural issues. How does each piece use food and appetite as a metaphor to comment on other social rules? Do you think this metaphor is effective? Why or why not?

JASON FAGONE
In Gorging, Truth

There is nothing within our media culture, it would seem, that can't be made into a competition — even eating. Recounting his experiences following the "competitive eating" circuit, Jason Fagone wonders about what our newfound enthusiasm for events like the National Hot Dog Eating Contest say not only about the current state of popular culture, but also about the American dream. Fagone is a journalist who has written for the city magazines *Cincinnati* and *Philadelphia.* In 2002, *Columbia Journalism Review* named him one of "Ten Young Writers on the Rise." His first book, *Horsemen of the Esophagus: Competitive Eating and the Big Fat American Dream,* from which "In Gorging, Truth" was taken, was published in 2006.

THE DAY AFTER GEORGE W. BUSH WON HIS SECOND TERM, A FRIEND OF mine e-mailed me, "How about this as a possible theme for your book?"

americans are big, fat, infantile, stupid assholes who love to shovel shit down their throats, and so to shovel more shit down one's throat than any other is to be truly king of america.

At that point I had been covering eating contests for three months. In the thick of a nasty presidential election and a dumb bloody war fueled by certain American appetites, I had been humping around the country on Southwest Airlines, taking notes on the exploits of professional gluttons. It was hard not to make the connection. One Saturday in October, I flew to Jackson, Mississippi, for a Krystal-brand hamburger contest. When I woke up the next morning in my Red Roof Inn in an asphalt no-man's-land next to a Whataburger franchise (TRY OUR TRIPLE MEAT AND TRIPLE CHEESE), an anonymous Bush adviser informed me, via the online *New York Times,* "We're an empire now," and anyone who didn't agree was "in what we call the reality-based community." The adviser said that "when we act, we create our own reality. . . . We're history's actors . . . and you, all of you, will be left to just study what we do." Pass the gravy, suckers. I walked fifty yards to the Waffle House and ate my reality-based eggs along with fifteen or twenty other Jacksonians, all of them non-historical actors like me. Somebody had left a *Clarion-Ledger* on the counter, with headlines like N. KOREAN NUKES LIKELY POWELL TOPIC and UTAH BIOWEAPONS TEST SITE TO GROW. I walked to the fair, where the Federation's gurgitators[1] visited terrible indignities upon their hamburgers under a sweltering sun. In the bleachers, I talked to a man with one tooth who said he eats all day and never gets full. I met two men from Texas who'd driven eleven hours to compete here. "I think it's sort of a celebration," said one. "A celebration of our prosperity. We're able to do this, so we might as well do it, I guess." After the contest, the TV cameras descended upon Nick Blackburn, a roly-poly local who had placed third. I interviewed his loudest supporter, a youngish guy with black spiky hair, who said he was Nick's pastor. If Christ happened upon an eating contest, I asked, what would Jesus do? "God knows our heart," the pastor said. "He judges what's in our hearts, not the stupid things we do." He laughed. "If he did that, we'd *all* be in trouble."

The Federation's critics are easy to find, having left a trail of acerbic, disapproving quotes in thousands of newspaper and wire stories about competitive eating. Food historians like Barbara Haber ("It's the fall of Rome, my dear") and physicians like the Harvard Medical School's George Blackburn ("This is sick, abnormal behavior") have lined up to take a whack, as have foreign critics such as the *Guardian*, which in the same 2002 article that quoted Blackburn called competitive eating "a sport for our degraded times" and connected its rise to "an unprecedented boom in the American economy fuelled by rampant consumption." In 2003, consumer advocate Ralph Nader sounded the alarm about four "signs of societal decay": three involved corporate greed and congressional gerrymandering, and the fourth was competitive eating. The Federation's chairman, George Shea, responded to Nader by talking up his Turducken contest. A Turducken is a chicken stuffed into a duck stuffed into a turkey. Shea called his contest "the first real advancement in Thanksgiving since the Indians sat down with the Pilgrims." Shea's counterattacks tend to mix deadpan charm and gentle mockery: "There are those who object to our sport," Shea told me when I asked if it was wise to promote gluttony in the fattest nation on earth,[2] "and for the moment I'd like to refer to them as," and Shea's voice sped up and dropped a half-octave to let me in on the joke, "knee-jerk reactionaries and philistines." He continued, normal-voiced, "A lot of people have had trouble separating this superficial visual of people stuffing their faces with large quantities of food with the stereotype of the Ugly American. That is not where I am. I see beauty. I see physical poetry."

Poetry, exactly. Shea's eating contests were poetic in their blatancy, their brazen mixture of every American trait that seemed to terrify the rest of the planet: our hunger for natural resources that may melt the ice caps and flood Europe, our hunger for cheap thrills that turns Muslim swing voters into car bombers.[3] If anti-American zealots anywhere in the world wanted to perform a minstrel show of our culture, this is what they'd come up with. Competitive eating was

> **Competitive eating was a symbolic hairball coughed up by the American id.**

a symbolic hairball coughed up by the American id. It was meaningful like a tumor was meaningful. It seemed to have a purpose, a message, and its message was this: Look upon our gurgitators, ye Mighty, and despair. Behold these new supergluttons, these ambassadors of the American appetite, these horsemen of the esophagus.

There was a time, of course—a year and fifteen pounds ago—when I didn't watch people gorge themselves in public and try to figure out what it meant, or if it meant anything at all. I was a serious journalist with a good job. I wrote for a magazine in Philadelphia. I wrote about doctors, developers, politicians, and the occasional eccentric who wanted to change the world. I had never heard of the Belt of Fat Theory. I couldn't tell the difference between "Hungry" Charles Hardy and Hungry Hungry Hippo. I couldn't rap a single verse of competitive-eating-themed hip-hop. The only thing I knew about competitive eating was what everybody else knows: that every year, some skinny Japanese guy kicks all of our American asses in hot dogs.

I was okay with all of that.

Then, one day in the summer of 2004, while using my magazine's Internet connection to distract myself from thinking about my doctors and developers and politicians and eccentrics who wanted to change the world, I came across the Federation's website, ifoce.com.

The outer rim of the donut hole.

Across the top of the page, a banner spelled out INTERNATIONAL FEDERATION OF COMPETITIVE EATING. The site's design was unremarkable except for an illustration on the page's upper left: a heraldic seal with two facing lions. Upon closer inspection, the lions were eating a hot dog from both ends while pawing tubes of mustard and ketchup that crossed, like swords, to form an X. A Latin inscription read IN VORO VERITAS.

In Gorging, Truth.

I clicked "Media Inquiries."

Within a day or two I got a call back from Rich Shea, younger brother of George Shea. In the meantime I had done some more reading. I had discovered that my hometown, Philly, hosted an annual chicken-wing contest called Wing Bowl. A couple of times since I had moved to Philly, friends and strangers had tried to tell me about Wing Bowl, but I must have blown them off. On the phone, Rich Shea explained the significance of Wing Bowl's greatest champion, a truck driver named Bill "El Wingador" Simmons. "Wingador's done a lot for competitive eating, certainly in Philly," Rich said. "So, you know, he could be the Moses Malone — did Moses Malone play for the Sixers? He could be the Doctor J"—he paused, thought of something better—"the *G. Love and Special Wing Sauce* of competitive eating." He laughed.

Rich talked quickly and thought quickly. He explained that he and his brother maintained a public relations firm in New York—Shea Communications—and their bread-and-butter clients were legitimate types like detectives and commercial real estate managers. The Federation was a separate track of the business, run from the same loft office in Chelsea. The Sheas got into the eating game in the late eighties, when both of them graduated from college, one after the other, and went to work in New York City for two old-school PR guys from the era when PR guys were called "press agents." The two old-school PR guys were the ones who invented the biggest eating contest in the world, the Nathan's Famous Hot Dog contest, back in the 1970s. The brothers eventually took over the Nathan's account and formed the Federation in 1997 with the goal of extruding that single hot dog contest into a gluttonous empire.

And they were getting close. The Federation claimed to have 300 active eater-members. Rich said that by the end of 2004, the Federation would have sanctioned about seventy-five contests that year, anywhere from three to ten per month. This was in addition to a handful of non-Federation contests that came in two flavors: indie and bootleg. The indie contests—one or two per month—were organized under the umbrella of an offshoot league called the Association of Independent Competitive Eaters, or AICE. Because AICE was newer, its contests were far smaller than the Federation's. As for the bootleg contests, they were harder to characterize: dozens, maybe hundreds, of minor spectacles at low-rent venues, at America's crummy bars, small-town carnivals, drive-time radio stations.

Eaters had options, but there was a catch. They couldn't mix and match. The Federation required its top talent to sign exclusive eighteen-month management contracts, and it had not been reluctant to shoot off cease-and-desist letters to wayward eaters it suspected of breaching the contract. Ambitious eaters—those who desired the imprimatur of a league—were therefore forced to pick either AICE or the Federation. Most eaters went with the Federation because it was bigger in every way: bigger stage, bigger money, bigger media. The Federation contests were sponsored by food companies, mostly, but also by municipal festivals and casinos on Indian reservations. The Sheas earned a per-contest fee from each sponsor, usually in the mid-four to low-five figures. The sponsors also put up the prize money, which Rich described as "a thousand dollars here, a thousand dollars there." In 2004, the total cash prize money was more than $60,000, of which the top American eater, Sonya Thomas, took home at least $17,000, plus a car—but the prizes, the number of contests, and the fan base were all growing; in 2005, sponsors would dole out more than $160,000, and Sonya would double her cash winnings. "It appeals to our competitive nature," Rich told me, adding, "You could also argue it's packaging and promotion and marketing. We've been very careful with how we've presented it." The Shea brothers had targeted "that guy demo," landing the horny eighteen-to-thirty-four set that loved *Maxim* and *FHM*. Capturing the guy demo allowed them to pitch eating specials to the Travel Channel, the Food Network, the Discovery Channel, and even such bigger fish as Fox. In 2004, ESPN scored 765,000 household viewers for its first live broadcast of the Nathan's contest.

Eventually, said Rich, he and his brother hoped to convert eating from a hobby into a professional sport, like bass fishing. "That's sort of the curve we're looking at," Rich said.

He didn't mention it, but in 2001, the B.A.S.S. league sold to ESPN for a purported $35 million.

Eating contests weren't invented by the Shea brothers or their mentors, or even by Americans. Anthropological studies and old copies of scurrilous newspapers suggest that the will to gorge is universal. Speed and volume competitions pop up in Greek myth, in the *Eddas* of Norse myth,[4] and even in what may be mankind's first novel, Apuleius's *Golden Ass*, written in the second century A.D.: "Last night at supper, I was challenged to an eating race by some people at my table and tried to swallow too large a mouthful of polenta cheese." (Choking ensued.) Ethnographies show that eating contests were regular events at lavish Native American potlatch feasts, and there's historical evidence of rice contests in Japan, beefsteak contests in Britain, mango contests in India. Even in France, that supposed bastion of foody sanity, *les goinfres* (pigs) compete to pound *le fromage* at seasonal festivals.

We're different because we have more of it, more types of contests in more places. We do it broader and bigger, and unlike the British, the French, and the Germans—whose health ministry explicitly condemned the German variation of eating contests, called *Wettessen*, in a letter to a researcher of mine—we make no apologies. We unabashedly marry the public-gorging impulse to our most sacred American rituals (the catching of the greased pig followed by the pie contest followed by the reading of the Declaration of Independence on the Fourth of July) and give organized gluttony an iconic role in our most iconic movies. One of the feel-good pinnacles of *Cool Hand Luke*, Paul Newman's epic prison flick, is the scene in which Luke wins over his fellow prisoners by declaring, casually, that he can eat fifty hardboiled eggs—"Yeah, well, it'll be somethin' to do," says Luke—commencing days of fevered speculation, betting, logistical preparation, training meals, and exercise leading up to the eventual eating performance itself. Luke eats the fifty eggs, winning his buddy Dragline a ton of cash and triumphing existentially over his captors by making prison seem like fun. Also uplifting, though in a different sense, is the infamous blueberry-pie-eating scene in *Stand by Me*. A young boy in a small town, cruelly nicknamed "Lardass" and taunted by classmates and adults alike, gets revenge by entering a pie contest and vomiting on one of his competitors. Lardass ignites a chain reaction: "Girlfriends barfed on boyfriends. Kids barfed on their parents. A fat lady barfed in her purse. The Donnelly twins barfed on each other. And the Women's Auxiliary barfed all over the Benevolent Order of Antelopes . . ."

I never found a newspaper clipping that described a "total barf-o-rama" like the one in *Stand by Me*, but minus the barf-o-rama, it could be any contest in any small town. Prison masculinity tests like the one in *Cool Hand Luke* also have a basis in reality, if my interview with a Baltimore gurgitator nicknamed Tony Hustle, formerly incarcerated in the state of Maryland for armed robbery, is any indication. When it comes to contest lore, fact trumps fiction. The great Damon Runyon, the bard of 1920s Broadway, staged a fictional eating contest for his short story "A Piece of Pie," but for my money, his nonfiction account of an eating contest in the March 5, 1920, *New York American* is more pleasurable. Runyon, reporting from the Yankees training camp in Florida, describes preparations for a "gustatory grapple" between the sportswriters (especially a top eater-scribe named Irwin Cobb) and the ballplayers (primarily Babe Ruth, for obvious reasons):

> It was decided that Mr. Cobb should start from scratch with Ruth, and that they shall spot their competitors one Virginia ham each, and a double porterhouse. George Mogridge, who is managing Ruth, insisted on a rule that Mr. Cobb shall not be permitted to tell any stories during the encounter, as George says his man cannot do a menu justice if he has to stop and laugh, while Mr. Cobb's ability to laugh and eat at the same time is well known. He can emit a raucous guffaw and chamber a Dill pickle simultaneously.

Maybe because of the nature of the subject, it's impossible to find a boring account of an eating contest, even if you go all the way back to the beginning—back as far as 1793, when a newspaper in York, Pennsylvania, noted that "two young men of this County, an hour after dining, undertook to eat twenty-four ginger Cakes each, to have them gratis provided they accomplished it." In sclerotic nineteenth-century New York City, fat mayors and even fatter aldermen settled bets with their jaws while corrupt Tammany Hall racketeers treated their armies of tenement dwellers to pie-eating contests at lavish picnics. On the ambrosial frontier of pre-smog Los Angeles, a gold-rusher's daughter challenged her friends to "an eating race" of peaches, while on the mean, fallen frontier, in the mining town of Galena, Montana, the Fourth of July "was ushered in by the booming of giant powder which shook the buildings from roof to basement," followed by "the soup eating contest between Sperindo Perrcri, superintendent of the Savage mine, and Defenbaugh, watchman at the Red Cloud, for the championship of the Hills and a silver-striking hammer." The contests belched out the fierce impulses of a new country. By the turn of the century, every town from Rolla, Missouri, to Bountiful, Utah, speed-ate pies on the Fourth. Contests attracted chowhounds from the most dignified institutions (academia, the church, the military[5]) and lifted nobodies to mythic heights.[6] An eating contest was a natural icebreaker for picnics, summer camps, and county fairs because it swallowed people's differences in its broad, low humor—though there was a certain breed of contest that did

> *An eating contest . . . swallowed people's differences in its broad, low humor.*

the exact opposite, that heightened differences, and cruelly so. From the late nineteenth century through the Great Depression, whites recruited blacks—often little kids—to eat watermelons. The supposed voracity of the black appetite had its roots in the minstrel-show tradition. NO MINSTREL SHOW, IF YOU PLEASE, protested one conservative[7] black newspaper in 1922: "The comic supplement Negro, the water melon eating Negro, is the one which our enemies would have us resemble."

As America grew more body-conscious, the stigma of public gluttony spread to whites. In 1946, the wife of the Army's top eater, PFC Chester Salvatori, divorced him "on grounds of cruelty" because she was "humiliated by the publicity that came from her husband's feats in eating," according to a wire story. Once the occasion for manly pride, eating contests now faded into the hidden recesses of personal biography, to be trotted out later for laughs should the person become famous, as in the case of Colonel Parker (whose biographer notes that he promoted a contest, once, before he met Elvis), and the segregationist George Wallace (who is shown at a pie contest in an old college snapshot, gazing "pensively at the floor," according to a biographer), and even Al Gore Jr., whose eventual political profilers couldn't resist noting that a young Al Gore, working as a cub reporter in Tennessee, once reported on a Whopper-eating contest at Burger King.[8]

Eating contests lost their swagger. Adults ceded the competition table to little kids and frat boys. Contests grew stunty and tame.

And then the Federation came along, and eating contests became big and dangerous and wild again. Into the delicate ecosystem of American gurgitation, the Federation introduced several new elements: first, a full-time promoter—the Shea brothers—and second, a core group of pioneering gurgitators, the first people in history to self-identify as professional eaters. "We did all the footwork years ago," as "Hungry" Charles Hardy told me. "Traveling here, traveling there. We didn't really make no kinda money. We pretty much took it to where it was today."

I started calling eaters in September 2004, starting with the veterans like Hardy and Ed "Cookie" Jarvis and Don "Moses" Lerman. They all said they were amazed by eating's trajectory, its quick-rising legitimacy: "The life has been a lot better, eating on the circuit," Hardy said, owing to the uptick in prize pots. Ed Jarvis said, "Let's face it. We're on ESPN. If that's not professional sports, I don't know what is." Don Lerman said, "I think in three years it'll be as big as PGA golf. In five years it may be in the Olympics."[9] The one eater to offer me a reality check was Arnie

"Chowhound" Chapman, the renegade with the league of his own. He told me he wanted eating to be chilled-out and shticky, not corporate. Arnie was the bizarro-world version of the Federation guys, believing them all delusional and the Federation morally depraved. "The elite eaters," Arnie said, "they're addicted to adulation, they're addicted to publicity."

Arnie was half right. There were definite hints of pride and obsession in those early calls, not least in Arnie's own anti-Federation spiel. Ed said he maintained a trophy room. "It's like a shrine," Ed said. "I mean, people look in and they're like, 'God.'" Don had a trophy room, too. And a weight problem. "Since I'm thirty, I've been fighting obesity," Don said. Ed was pushing four hundred and also trying to lose weight.[10] The day I talked to him, he was pondering an upcoming cannoli contest. Ed was the cannoli champ, but was thinking about not defending his title. "It's rough on the body," he said. "One, you're eating 11,000 calories. Two, there's no money. Three, all that said, the bottom line is 'What am I doing this for?' I'm basically putting 11,000 calories into my body with the chance I could get hurt. What for? There's gotta be a cause." Even Arnie admitted, "I'm even a little concerned about myself. I'm now 245 pounds. I've never been that heavy before."

Slander, rivalry, hubris, recklessness: that was half of the Shakespearean palette, the exact half you'd expect to find in a group of pro gluttons. But the more eaters I called, and the more I pushed past their immediate need to impress upon me that they weren't a bunch of freaks, the more I saw that they really weren't. I got a sense of the other half of the palette, the subtler shades. With a few conspicuous exceptions, the eaters didn't seem to be lifelong publicity hounds or career eccentrics. They had wives and kids. They had jobs as construction workers, social workers, bankers, engineers, lawyers. I would come to know them as genuinely sweet and generous guys, most of them. Except for their collective waist size, they were as averagely American as the Americans in campaign commercials. They had to know that competitive eating was a marketing ploy, and yet—out of some psychic contortion it was too soon for me to guess at—rarely spoke of it that way. Eating, to them, wasn't a ploy. It was fun. It was a chance to compete, to travel the country and make a little money, or at least break even. It was a chance to be on ESPN.

How many people get to be on ESPN?

And beyond the obvious rewards were the intangibles, borne of the fact that eating was a community, one with its own distinct interior culture, its own goals and sacred controversies. (The controversies, if anything, legitimize the community, as sociologist Gary Alan Fine told me: "It means . . . there are some things that matter.") Charles Hardy, who in a few months would tattoo the letters "IFOCE" on his right bicep, said, "We're like one big family." Ed Jarvis said, "I'm with a group, not by myself . . . It's nice to have a group." They readily talked trash and bestowed compliments, too. He's fast (said Don of Ed), he's got capacity, he's got technique, "he believes in what he does." Belief/believes/believer. The eaters kept con-jugating that word. I talked to another eater, twenty-seven-year-old Tim "Eater X" Janus, who told me the story of the first time George Shea offered to pay for his hotel room at an out-of-state contest. "I was pretty flattered, actually," Tim said. "I knew it could lead to big things . . . I don't know, it's just neat to see people believe in you, for anything, really."

It didn't seem that it could be so welcoming, this weird little corner of the culture, but there it was, warm and cozy, teeming with improb-ably hopeful activity. In *The Control of Nature*, John McPhee writes that the founders of New Orleans built a city "where almost any camper would be loath to pitch a tent." Here on the pro gluttony circuit, atop the same cultural terrain that made me feel, in my bitterest moments, ashamed to be an American, the eaters were planting their dearest desires—for fair and honest competition, for a pat on the back, to get noticed, to prove themselves, to make their kids and spouses proud.

Life/liberty/pursuit of happiness by way of eating/shitting/vomiting/ shilling.

In Gorging, Truth.

Could it work?

Could the eaters really draw blood from this stone? Could they extract, from this grotesque spectacle, meaning? And if they could, did that mean the spectacle wasn't as grotesque as it seemed to someone like me, looking in from the outside? Was there something nourishing hidden within American trash culture?

Look, to be clear: these were my own existential questions. Not the eat-ers'. The eaters weren't staying up nights wondering if they could extract meaning from the grotesque. Eating wasn't grotesque, it was cool, and if the eaters did stay up nights, it was to trade stomach-stretching techniques on the phone or check the latest eating gossip on beautifulbrian.com.

This is where we converged. Seriousness. The eaters took eating seriously—they trained, they spent their money and time, risked their health and their relationships—and I felt like I should take eating as seri-ously as they did. That didn't mean adopting a persona and joining the circuit as a gurgitator, although once, at a pastrami contest at New York's Second Avenue Deli, I did step up to the competition table myself, about which the less said the better.[11]

No: serious, to me, meant, on a basic level, going to a ton of contests. Starting with a Krystal hamburger qualifier in Knoxville, Tennessee, on September 19, 2004, and ending with a blueberry pie contest in Machias, Maine, on August 20, 2005, I would eventually attend twenty-seven eat-ing contests in thirteen states and two continents, including seventeen Federation contests, five AICE contests, two local TV contests, one sports radio contest, one contest sponsored by a United Church of Christ con-gregation, and one contest organized by a Japanese weatherman. I would attend, for instance, four Krystal hamburger events and five Nathan's hot-dog events. I would attend the Gameworks World Tex Mex Roll-Eating Championship Presented by Great Lakes Crossing at the Great Lakes Crossing Mall in Auburn Hills, Michigan. The World's Greatest Shoo-Fly Pie-Eating Championship at the Rockvale Outlets in Lancaster, Pennsylvania. The ACME World Oyster Eating Championship in Metairie, Louisiana. The World Cheesecake-Eating Championship in Brooklyn. The Entenmann's Pies Thanksgiving Invitational in the Chelsea district of New York City. The Ball Park Fiesta Bowl National Hot Dog Eating Championship in Tempe, Arizona. The Third Annual International Chili Society's World Championship Chili Eating Contest at Mandalay Bay Hotel and Casino in Las Vegas. And after enough contests, after filling enough notebooks with columns of numbers signifying quantities of meats and sweets, I would become akin to an actual serious beat reporter covering an actual serious beat—which was my goal starting out. I wanted the coverage *itself*, not just the effort, to be serious. I wanted to cover eating as if it were important. Not mock-important.[12] Truly important.

It was possible, of course, that it wasn't important—that it was all just empty calories, signifying nothing. It was possible that the eaters weren't harbingers of the coming apocalypse, just an excuse for headline writers to make bad puns. Appetite for Destruction. Cool Hand Puke. Lord of the Wings.[13] Wing Eaters Peck for Position. Frankly Speaking. Great Balls of Matzo. Getting Stuffed.[14] A Competitor With Guts. Big Eater Can Stomach the Competition.

> **A cross-section of the promise and the threat we represent to the world and to ourselves.**

Man Bites Dogs, Over and Over. She Meats Expectations. This isn't a knock on reporters—I am one—but, for most of us, an eating piece isn't a project, it's a blessed break from *other* projects, which is why eating always gets shoehorned into a few standard and easy-to-pull-off formats: (1) the shlocky thirty-second "brite" segment at the end of a local newscast; (2) the half-playful, half-serious newspaper feature; (3) the puffy, sprawling alt-weekly profile of the alt-weekly's town's most prominent eater; or (4) the stripped-down News of the Weird brief sandwiched contextless between other, wildly unrelated briefs.[15]

And they fail. They all fail to capture the mad galumphing experience of an eating contest, a really good one, when the crowd's into it, gawking, screaming, and the food's detonated on contact with a merciless line of teeth and jaws, and Shea's on his game—*we cannot SEE, we cannot HEAR, we need something MORE!*—and when, scanning the crowd's faces, I can tell that we're all feeling something, something intense, maybe revulsion, maybe joy, maybe just a deep curiosity, but it's more than can be expressed in a thirty-second brite or a fifty-word brief. Whatever's happening doesn't feel shabby or small, but instead—I swear to the Virgin Mary Grilled Cheese—broad and big and consequential, as though America has vomited up its deepest hope and deepest dread in one place and now something worthwhile having to do with this *big, fat, infantile, stupid* country can be learned, or accomplished. The whole goopy range of it, everything that makes America so undeniably great and infuriating, loved and hated, everything that makes me want to buy a ranch in Montana one day and move to Scandinavia the next: a cross-section of the promise and the threat we represent to the world and to ourselves.

I wanted to capture that range. And I wanted to do it by writing about the eaters, who were living it. That meant I needed eaters of a certain type. Eaters who embodied eating's risks (meaning they competed often enough to strain their bodies) and also its rewards (meaning they were talented and high-ranked). I needed eaters with a good chance of transcending the pro circuit's intrinsic comedy, tragedy, slander, and bad food to achieve true athletic grace, maybe even redemption.

I found three of the lucky ones, and latched on.

I'm talking about Bill "El Wingador" Simmons, chicken-wing champion of the world. I'm talking about Tim "Eater X" Janus, tiramisu-eating champion of the world.

I'm talking, especially, about David "Coondog" O'Karma, tag-team bratwurst champion of Canton, Ohio.

NOTES

[1]The word "gurgitator" is actually a registered trademark of the Federation, but, perhaps owing to its dull-edged awkwardness, the competitors preferred to call themselves "eaters." The fan site trencherwomen.com later made the term gendered, separating "gurgitators" (men) from "gurgitrices" (women), though the proper word probably should have been "gurgitatrices."

[2]Now that residents of several E.U. countries have been found to be more obese than Americans, and obesity panics have taken hold in Britain and France, any Europeans who mock the girth of our nation are merely throwing stones at fat houses. Luckily for them, American-style eating contests are still totally mockable.

[3]Not to mention the contests' wankish indifference to the 800 million global hungry and also the 12 percent of American households our own Department of Agriculture considers "food-insecure."

[4]The god Loki loses to a giant. Both eat all of their meat, but the giant eats his plate, too, proving that competitive eating really does have a strategic component.

[5]U.S. troops have battled with food on navy battleships and inside Trident nuclear submarines; they have staged eating contests while stationed in Paris in 1918 (pie), Italy in 1945 (pie), Vietnam in 1968 (eggs), and Beirut in 1984 (dog biscuits).

[6]The eating prowess of "Honest Red" Dugan, a poor Lower Manhattan cabdriver who died in 1911, scored him a *Times* obituary longer than that of most congressmen.

[7]So conservative, in fact, that it had refused to criticize the governor of Missouri when he vetoed an anti-lynching bill.

[8]Gore's fastidious coverage of the event ("one of the contestants regurgitated his first three Whoppers on the table and dampened the morale of his competitors") was later interpreted by one profiler as proof of Gore's resolve not to skate by on merely his "pedigree" and his "cum laude Ivy League diploma," and to get his hands dirty by taking on what the profiler called "stories like that." It was seen to be revealing of his inner character which is probably why it was so much fun to learn, from the *Los Angeles Times* in early 2006, that the disgraced lobbyist Jack Abramoff, who elevated mere conflict of interest to a lucrative criminal art, once organized "a Quarter Pounder–eating contest at a McDonald's, with some proceeds going to the American Cancer Society"—a fundraising effort that the Wonkette weblog called "uniquely ironic."

[9]As a publicity stunt for a Spam-eating contest, George Shea once arranged an Olympic-style "torch run" using a can of Spam mounted on a chair leg. He later told the *Washington Post* it was "the first-ever meat-based torch run in the United States, if not the world." He also claimed to have lobbied unsuccessfully for eating's inclusion in the Olympics: "I strongly believe that we have overtaken curling in the overall pantheon of sports," he told the *McGill Daily* (whose interviewer, by the way, had decided to call Shea after "musing about what could be accomplished in the world if all the money spent on eating contests in the U.S. per year were to be diverted toward, say, treating preventable disease in sub-Saharan Africa," only to be wooed by Shea's deadpan savvy into publishing a full Q&A of their exchange), "and I think tennis is next."

[10]Caveat: pinning down an eater's poundage is more difficult than it may seem. One reason is that the eaters' weights fluctuate significantly; Don "Moses" Lerman has weighed as much as 250 pounds and as little as 142. Also, the official "weigh-in" ceremonies have been known to produce odd numbers, and the IFOCE's "bib sheets," which list eaters' weights and heights, are rarely updated. Absent any canonical source, I tend to trust what the eaters tell me. Still, all weights in this book should be considered estimates.

[11]Okay, I'll say this: prior to the contest, I agonized about how far I should push myself—i.e., whether it was the better part of valor to stop if I felt like I was about to vomit, or to keep going, so as to more fully empathize with the discomfort my subjects often endure. As it turned out, owing to the chewiness of the meat and also my inability to resist the urge, every ten seconds or so, to pick up a napkin and wipe my face, I ended up eating one sandwich in ten minutes. One.

[12]The *New York Post*'s Gersh Kuntzman, writing in the IFOCE's newsletter *The Gurgitator* ("Life on the Circuit"): ". . . the Land of the Rising Bun is the one remaining breeding ground for the next generation of gustatory gladiators. Whether it's in their elementary schools, where kids learn about the legendary eaters like Nakajima, Shirota, and Arai, or in the buffet academies, where potential stars are groomed for eating greatness, Japan prepares while the rest of the world errs . . . "

[13]The title, I'm sad to say, of my own article about the Philadelphia Wing Bowl.

[14]There's a definite and creepy sexual subtext to some of the headlines, a gleeful, violative aggression; somebody once told a friend of mine that he hated this book's title because it seemed like someone was "getting orally raped."

[15]Page 6 news briefs, *Ottawa Sun*, November 27, 2005: (1) Toronto boy falls off a building and dies; (2) Colorado teen faces a year in prison for hitting and killing a bicyclist "while text-messaging"; (3) Sonya Thomas eats a Thanksgiving turkey in twelve minutes; (4) tribal leaders in South Africa oppose government's outlawing of virginity tests for young girls.

DISCUSSION

1. What do you make of the title "professional eater"? What kind of person does it conjure in your mind? Is there anything surprising or odd (that is, against the norm) about joining these two terms? Does it make sense to think of eating as a professional undertaking?

2. Fagone reports one eating contest mogul as saying that competitive eating "'appeals to our competitive nature.'" In your view, is this true? Does it make more sense to think of competition as something natural or as something we are trained or taught to regard as a norm? To what extent would you describe the types of competition featured in these eating contests to be natural?

3. How does competitive eating compare to the forms of eating we regard as the norm? Are there any similarities between the eating showcased in events like the World Oyster Eating Championship or the National Hot Dog Eating Championship and the ways you typically eat? And if so, what do these parallels tell us about the messages or scripts around eating purveyed by our larger culture?

WRITING

4. One of this essay's underlying premises is that our individual eating practices are a kind of societal mirror, reflecting the values, ideals, and norms purveyed within our larger culture. Write an essay in which you analyze this argument. How does Fagone use evidence to support it? Can you find additional evidence from your own experience that confirms what Fagone is proposing? Evidence against it?

5. Consider the title of Fagone's essay: "In Gorging, Truth." What do you think he means by this? Write an essay in which you discuss the explicit ways that Fagone connects the metaphor of competitive eating with larger American culture. Do you agree with his conclusion? Why or why not?

6. Fagone and Caroline Knapp (p. 232) in many ways write about eating from opposite ends of a spectrum. Yet both writers connect the topic of eating to larger cultural phenomena. Write an essay in which you compare the ways both writers look at eating as a symptom of or reaction to larger cultural influences. How is it possible for these two very different perspectives to coexist?

CAROLINE KNAPP

Add Cake, Subtract Self-Esteem

When are our appetites about more than just food? Detailing her own
struggle with anorexia, Caroline Knapp offers some pointed observations
about the ways our contemporary culture fosters "disorders of the appetite"
in women, creating an environment in which it has become normal to define
questions of female self-worth and female power in relation to what one
does (or does not) eat. Knapp was a columnist for the *Boston Phoenix*.
Some of the pieces she wrote as the anonymous "Alice K." are collected
in *Alice K.'s Guide to Life* (1994). Her other books include *Drinking: A Love
Story* (1996) and *Pack of Two: The Intricate Bond Between People and
Dogs* (1998). She died in 2002 from complications of lung cancer, just after
completing her last book, *Appetites: Why Women Want* (2003), the book in
which the following essay appears.

THE LURE OF STARVING—THE BAFFLING, SEDUCTIVE HOOK—WAS
that it soothed, a balm of safety and containment that seemed to
remove me from the ordinary, fraught world of human hunger and place
me high above it, in a private kingdom of calm.

This didn't happen immediately, this sense of transcendent solace, and
there certainly wasn't anything blissful or even long-lived about the state;
starving is a painful, relentless experience, and also a throbbingly dull one,
an entire life boiled down to a singular sensation (physical hunger) and a
singular obsession (food). But when I think back on those years, which lasted
through my mid-twenties, and when I try to get underneath the myriad
meanings and purposes of such a bizarre fixation, that's what I remember
most pointedly—the calm, the relief from an anxiety that felt both oceanic
and nameless. For years, I ate the same foods everyday, in exactly the same
manner, at exactly the same times. I devoted a monumental amount of
energy to this endeavor—thinking about food, resisting food, observing other
people's relationships with food, anticipating my own paltry indulgences in
food—and this narrowed, specific, driven rigidity made me feel supremely
safe: one concern, one feeling, everything else just background noise.

Disorders of appetite—food addictions, compulsive shopping, pro-
miscuous sex—have a kind of semiotic brilliance, expressing in symbol
and metaphor what women themselves may not be able to express in
words, and I can deconstruct anorexia with the best of them. Anorexia
is a response to cultural images of the female body—waiflike, angular—
that both capitulates to the ideal and also mocks it, strips away all the

ancillary signs of sexuality, strips away breasts and hips and butt and leaves in their place a garish caricature, a cruel cartoon of flesh and bone. It is a form of silent protest, a hunger strike that expresses some deep discomfort with the experience of inhabiting an adult female body. It is a way of co-opting the traditional female preoccupation with food and weight by turning the obsession upside down, directing the energy not toward the preparation and provision and ingestion of food but toward the shunning of it, and all that it represents: abundance, plenitude, caretaking. Anorexia is this, anorexia is that. Volumes have been written about such symbolic expressions, and there's truth to all of them, and they are oddly comforting truths: They help to decipher this puzzle; they help to explain why eating disorders are the third most common chronic illness among females in the United States, and why fifteen percent of young women have substantially disordered attitudes and behaviors toward food and eating, and why the incidence of eating disorders has increased by thirty-six percent every five years since the 1950s. They offer some hope—if we can understand this particularly devastating form of self-inflicted cruelty, maybe we can find a way to stop it.

I, too, am tempted to comfort and explain, to look back with the cool detachment of twenty years and offer a crisp critique: a little cultural commentary here, a little metaphorical analysis there. But what recedes into the background amid such explanations—and what's harder to talk about because it's intangible and stubborn and vast—is the core, the underlying drive, the sensation that not only made anorexia feel so seductively viable for me some two decades ago but that also informs the central experience of appetite for so many women, the first feeling we bring to the table of hunger: anxiety, a sense of being overwhelmed.

There is a particular whir of agitation about female hunger, a low-level thrumming of shoulds and shouldn'ts and can'ts and wants that can be so chronic and familiar it becomes a kind of feminine Muzak, easy to dismiss, or to tune out altogether, even if you're actively participating in it. Last spring, a group of women gathered in my living room to talk about appetite, all of them teachers and administrators at a local school and all of them adamant that this whole business—weight, food, managing hunger—troubles them not at all. "Weight," said one, "is not really an issue for me." "No," said another, "not for me, either." And a third: "I don't really think about what I'm going to eat from day to day. Basically, I just eat what I want."

This was a cheerful and attractive group, ages twenty-two to forty-one, and they were all so insistent about their normalcy around food that, were it not for the subtle strain of caveat that ran beneath their descriptions, I might have believed them.

The caveats had to do with rules, with attitudes as ingrained as reflexes, and with a particularly female sense of justified reward: They are at the center of this whir, an anxious jingle of mandate and restraint. The woman who insisted that weight is "not really an issue," for instance, also noted that she only allows herself to eat dessert, or second helpings at dinner, if she's gone to the gym that day. No workout, no dessert. The woman who agreed with her (no, not an issue for her, either) echoed that sentiment. "Yeah," she nodded, "if I don't work out, I start to feel really gross about food and I'll try to cut back." A third said she eats "normally" but noted that she always makes a point of leaving at least one bite of food on her plate, every meal, no exceptions. And the woman who said she "basically just eats what she wants" added, "I mean, if someone brings a cake into the office, I'll have a tiny slice, and I might not eat the frosting, but it's not like a big deal or anything. I just scrape the frosting off."

> ## That one has great thighs, this one's gained weight, who's thin, who's fat, how do I compare?

Tiny slices, no frosting, forty-five minutes on the StairMaster: These are the conditions, variations on a theme of vigilance and self-restraint that I've watched women dance to all my life, that I've danced to myself instinctively and still have to work to resist. I walk into a health club locker room and feel an immediate impulse toward scrutiny, the kneejerk measuring of self against other: *That one has great thighs, this one's gained weight, who's thin, who's fat, how do I compare?* I overhear snippets of conversation, constraints unwittingly articulated and upheld in a dollop of lavish praise here *(You look fabulous, have you lost weight?)*, a whisper of recriminating judgment there *(She looks awful, has she gained weight?)*, and I automatically turn to look: Who looks fabulous, who looks awful? I go to a restaurant with a group of women and pray that we can order lunch without falling into the semi-covert business of collective monitoring, in which levels of intake and restraint are aired, compared, noticed: *What are you getting? Is that all you're having? A salad? Oh, please.* There's a persistent awareness of self in relation to other behind this kind of behavior, and also a tacit nod to the idea that there are codes to adhere to, and self-effacing apologies to be made if those codes are broken. *I'm such a hog,* says the woman who breaks rank, ordering a cheeseburger when everyone else has salad.

Can't, shouldn't, I'm a moose. So much of this is waved away as female vanity—this tedious nattering about calories and fat, this whining, shallow preoccupation with surfaces—but I find it poignant, and painful in a low-level but chronic way, and also quite revealing. One of the lingering cultural myths about gender is that women are bad at math—they lack confidence for it, they have poor visual-spatial skills, they simply don't excel at numbers the way boys do. This theory has been widely challenged over the years, and there's scant evidence to suggest that girls are in any way neurologically ill-equipped to deal with algebra or calculus. But I'd challenge the myth on different grounds: Women are actually superb at math; they just happen to engage in their own variety of it, an intricate personal math in which desires are split off from one another, weighed, balanced, traded, assessed. These are the mathematics of desire, a system of self-limitation and monitoring based on the fundamental premise that appetites are at best risky, at worst impermissible, that indulgence must be bought and paid for. Hence the rules and caveats: Before you open the lunch menu or order that cheeseburger or consider eating the cake with the frosting intact, haul out the psychic calculator and start tinkering with the budget.

Why shouldn't you? I asked a woman that question not long ago while she was demurring about whether to order dessert at a restaurant.

Immediate answer: "Because I'll feel gross."

Why gross?

"Because I'll feel fat."

And what would happen if you felt fat?

"I hate myself when I feel fat. I feel ugly and out of control. I feel really un-sexy. I feel unlovable."

And if you deny yourself the dessert?

"I may feel a little deprived, but I'll also feel pious," she said.

So it's worth the cost?

"Yes."

These are big trade-offs for a simple piece of cake—add five hundred calories, subtract well-being, allure, and self-esteem—and the feelings behind them are anything but vain or shallow. Hidden within that thirty-second exchange is an entire set of mathematical principles, equations that can dictate a woman's most fundamental approach to hunger. Mastery over the body—its impulses, its needs, its size—is paramount; to lose control is to risk beauty, and to risk beauty is to risk desirability, and to risk desirability is to risk entitlement to sexuality and love and self-esteem. Desires collide, the wish to eat bumping up against the wish to be thin, the desire to indulge conflicting with the injunction to restrain. Small wonder food makes a woman nervous. The experience of appetite in this equation is an experience of anxiety, a burden and a risk; yielding to hunger may be permissible under certain conditions, but mostly it's something to be Earned or Monitored and Controlled. $E = mc^2$.

During the acute phases of my starving years, I took a perverse kind of pleasure in these exhibitions of personal calculus, the anxious little jigs that women would do around food. Every day at lunchtime, I'd stand in line at a café in downtown Providence clutching my 200-calorie yogurt, and while I waited, I'd watch the other women deliberate. I'd see a woman mince edgily around the glass case that held muffins and cookies, and I'd recognize the look in her eye, the longing for something sweet or gooey, the sudden flicker of *No*. I'd overhear fragments of conversation: debates between women (*I can't eat that, I'll feel huge*), and cajolings (*Oh, c'mon, have the fries*), and collaborations in surrender (*I will if you will*). I listened for these, I paid attention, and I always felt a little stab of superiority when someone yielded (*Okay, fuck it, fries, onion rings, PIE*). I would not yield—to do so, I understood, would imply lack of restraint, an unseemly, indulgent female greed—and in my stern resistance I got to feel coolly superior while they felt, or so it seemed to me, anxious.

But I knew that anxiety. I know it still, and I know how stubbornly pressing it can feel, the niggling worry about food and calories and size and heft cutting to the quick somehow, as though to fully surrender to hunger might lead to mayhem, the appetite proven unstoppable. If you plotted my food intake on a graph from that initial cottage cheese purchase onward, you wouldn't see anything very dramatic at first: a slight decline in consumption over my junior and senior years, and an increasing though not yet excessive pattern of rigidity, that edgy whir about food and weight at only the edges of consciousness at first. I lived off campus my senior year with a boyfriend, studied enormously hard, ate normal dinners at home with him, but permitted myself only a single plain donut in the morning, coffee all day, not a calorie more. The concept of "permission" was new to me—it heralded the introduction of rules and by-laws, a nascent internal tyrant issuing commands—but I didn't question it. I just ate the donut, drank the coffee, obeyed the rules, aware on some level that the rigidity and restraint served a purpose, reinforced those first heady feelings of will and determination, a proud sensation that I was somehow beyond ordinary need. I wrote a prize-winning honors thesis on two hundred calories a day.

The following year, my first out of college, the line on the graph would begin to waver, slowly at first, then peaking and dipping more erratically: five pounds up, five pounds down, six hundred calories here, six thousand there, the dieting female's private NASDAQ, a personal index of self-torture.

This was not a happy time. I'd taken a job in a university news bureau, an ostensible entree into writing and a fairly hefty disappointment (I was an editorial assistant in title, a glorified secretary in fact, bored nearly senseless from day one). The boyfriend had left for graduate school in California, and I was living alone for the first time, missing him with the particularly consuming brand of desperation afforded by long-distance love. I was restless and lonely and full of self-doubt, and the low-level tampering I'd been doing with my appetite began to intensify, my relationship with food thrown increasingly out of whack. This is familiar territory to anyone with a long history of dieting: a fundamental severing between need and want begins to take place, eating gradually loses its basic associations with nourishment and physical satisfaction and veers onto a more complex emotional plane in which the whole notion of hunger grows loaded and confusing. Sometimes I was very rigid with my diet during this period, resolving to consume nothing but coffee all day, only cheese and crackers at night. Other times I ate for comfort, or because I was bored, or because I felt empty, all reasons that frightened and confused me. I'd make huge salads at night, filled with nuts and cubes of cheese and slathered in creamy dressings; I'd eat big bowls of salty soups, enormous tuna melts, hideously sweet oversized chocolate chip cookies, purchased in little frenzies of preservation (should I? shouldn't I?) from a local bakery. I started drinking heavily during this period, too, which weakened my restraint; I'd wake up feeling bloated and hungover and I'd try to compensate by eating nothing, or next to nothing, during the day.

For a year, I gained weight, lost weight, gained the weight back, and I found this deeply unnerving, as though some critical sense of bodily integrity were at risk, my sense of limits and proportion eroding. I'd feel my belly protrude against the waistband of my skirt, or one thigh chafing against another, and I'd be aware of a potent stab of alarm: *Shit, the vigilance has been insufficiently upheld, the body is growing soft and doughy, something central and dark about me*—a lazy, gluttonous, insatiable second self—*is poised to emerge.* Women often brought pastries into the office where I worked. Sometimes I'd steadfastly avoid them, resolve not even to look; other times I'd eye the pastry box warily from across the room, get up periodically and circle the table, conscious of a new sensation of self-mistrust, questions beginning to flitter and nag. *Could I eat one pastry, or would one lead to three, or four, or six? Was I actually hungry for a Danish or a croissant, or was I trying to satisfy some other appetite? How hungry—how rapacious, greedy, selfish, needy—was I?* The dance of the hungry woman—two steps toward the refrigerator, one step back, that endless loop of hunger and indulgence and guilt—had ceased to be a game; some key middle ground between gluttony and restraint, a place that used to be easily accessible to me, had grown elusive and I didn't know how to get back there.

This, of course, is one of appetite's insidious golden rules: The more you meddle with a hunger, the more taboo and confusing it will become. Feed the body too little and then too much, feed it erratically, launch that maddening cycle of deprivation and overcompensation, and the sensation of physical hunger itself becomes divorced from the body, food loaded with alternative meanings: symbol of longing, symbol of constraint, form of torture, form of reward, source of anxiety, source of succor, measure of self-worth. And thus the

> **The more you meddle with a hunger, the more taboo and confusing it will become.**

simple experience of hunger—of wanting something to eat—becomes frightening and fraught. What does it mean this time? Where will it lead? Will you eat *everything* if you let yourself go? Will you prove unstoppable, a famished dog at a garbage bin? Young and unsure of myself and groping for direction, I was scared of many things that year—leaving the structure of college was scary, entering the work world was scary, living on my own was scary, the future loomed like a monumental question mark—but I suspect I was scared above all of hunger itself, which felt increasingly boundless and insatiable, its limits and possible ravages unknown.

I suspect, too, that this feeling went well beyond the specific issue of food, that anxiety about caloric intake and body size were merely threads in a much larger tapestry of feeling that had to do with female self-worth and power and identity—for me and for legions of other women. This time period—late 1970s, early 1980s—coincided with the early stages of the well-documented shift in the culture's collective definition of beauty, its sudden and dramatically unambiguous pairing with slenderness. There is nothing new about this today; the pressure (internal and external) to be thin is so familiar and so widespread by now that most of us take it for granted, breathe it in like air, can't remember a time when we weren't aware of it, can't remember how different the average model or actress or beauty pageant contestant looked before her weight began to plummet (in the last twenty-five years, it's dropped to twenty-five percent below that of the average woman), can't remember a world in which grocery store shelves didn't brim with low-cal and "lite" products, in which mannequins wore size eight clothes instead of size two, in which images of beauty were less wildly out of reach.

But it's worth recalling that all of this—the ratcheted-up emphasis on thinness, the aesthetic shift from Marilyn Monroe to Kate Moss, the concomitant rise in eating disorders—is relatively recent, that the emphasis on diminishing one's size, on miniaturizing the very self, didn't really heat up until women began making gains in other areas of their lives. By the time I started to flirt with anorexia, in the late 1970s, women had gained access to education, birth control, and abortion, as well as widespread protection from discrimination in most areas of their lives. At the same time, doctors were handing out some ten billion appetite-suppressing amphetamines per year, Weight Watchers had spread to forty-nine states, its membership three million strong, and the diet-food business was about to eclipse all other categories as the fastest-growing segment of the food industry.

This parallel has been widely, and sensibly, described as the aesthetic expression of the backlash against feminist strength that Susan Faludi would document in 1992. At a time when increasing numbers of women were demanding the right to take up more space in the world, it is no surprise that they'd be hit with the opposite message from a culture that was (and still is) both male-dominated and deeply committed to its traditional power structures. Women get psychically larger, and they're told to grow physically smaller. Women begin to play active roles in realms once dominated by men (schools, universities, athletic fields, the workplace, the bedroom), and they're countered with images of femininity that infantilize them, render them passive and frail and non-threatening. "The female body is the place where this society writes its messages," writes Rosalind Coward in *Female-Desires*, and its response to feminism was etched with increasing clarity on the whittled-down silhouette of the average American model: Don't get too hungry, don't overstep your bounds.

The whispers of this mandate, audible in the 1970s and 1980s, have grown far louder today; they are roars, howls, screams. The average American, bombarded with advertisements on a daily basis, will spend approximately three years of his or her lifetime watching television commercials, and you don't have to look too closely to see what that deluge of imagery has to say about the female body and its hungers. A controlled appetite, prerequisite for slenderness, connotes beauty, desirability, worthiness. An uncontrolled appetite—a fat woman—connotes the opposite, she is ugly, repulsive, and so fundamentally unworthy that, according to a *New York Times* report on cultural attitudes toward fat, sixteen percent of adults would choose to abort a child if they knew he or she would be untreatably obese.

Hatred of fat, inextricably linked to fear of fat, is so deeply embedded in the collective consciousness it can arouse a surprising depth of discomfort and mean-spiritedness, even among people who consider themselves to be otherwise tolerant and sensitive to women. Gail Dines, director of women's studies and professor of sociology at Wheelock College in Boston and one of the nation's foremost advocates of media literacy, travels around the country giving a slide show/lecture called "Sexy or Sexist: Images of Women in the Media." The first half of the presentation consists of images, one after the other, of svelte perfection: a sultry Brooke Shields clad in a blue bikini on a *Cosmo* cover, an achingly slender leg in an ad for Givenchy pantyhose, a whisper-thin Kate Moss. Then, about halfway into the presentation, a slide of a postcard flashes onto the screen, a picture of a woman on a beach in Hawaii. The woman is clad in a bright blue two-piece bathing suit, and she is very fat; she's shown from the rear, her buttocks enormous, her thighs pocked with fleshy folds, and the words on the postcard read: HAVING A WHALE OF A TIME IN HAWAII. The first time I saw this, I felt a jolt of something critical and mean—part pity, part judgment, an impulse to recoil—and I felt immediately embarrassed by this, which is precisely the sensation Dines intends to flush out. At another showing before a crowd at Northeastern University, the image appears on the screen and several people begin to guffaw, nervous titters echo across the room. Dines stops and turns to the audience. "Now why is this considered funny?" she demands. "Explain that to me. Does she not have the right to the dignity that you and I have a right to? Does having extra pounds on your body deny you that right?" The crowd falls silent, and Dines sighs. There it is: This obese woman, this object of hoots and jeers, is a tangible focus of female anxiety, a 350-pound picture of the shame and humiliation that will be visited upon a woman if her hunger is allowed to go unchecked.

Dines, among many others, might identify culture as the primary protagonist in this narrative, a sneering villain cleverly disguised as Beauty who skulks around injecting women with an irrational but morbid fear of fat. There is certainly some truth to that—a woman who isn't affected to some degree by the images and injunctions of fat-and-thin is about as rare as a black orchid. But I also think the intensity of the struggle around appetite that began to plague me twenty years ago, that continues to plague so many women today, speaks not just to cultural anxiety about female hunger, profound though it may be, but also to deep reservoirs of personal anxiety. Fear of fat merely exists on the rippled surface of that reservoir; mass-market images are mere reflections upon it. Underneath, the real story—each woman in her own sea of experience—is more individual and private; it's about what happens when hunger is not quite paired with power, when the license to hunger is new and unfamiliar, when a woman is teased with freedom—to define herself as she sees fit, to attend to her own needs and wishes, to fully explore her own desires—but may not quite feel that freedom in her bones or believe that it will last.

Once, several months into that first year of weight gain and weight loss, I met some friends for Sunday brunch, an all-you-can-eat buffet at a local hotel restaurant. All-you-can-eat buffets terrify me to this day—I find them sadistic and grotesque in a particularly American way, the emphasis on quantity and excess reflecting something insatiably greedy and short-sighted about the culture's ethos—and I date the onset of my terror to that very morning. Such horrifying abundance! Such potential for unleashed gluttony! The buffet table seemed to stretch out for a mile: at one station, made-to-order omelets and bacon and sausage; at another, waffles and pancakes and crêpes; at another, bagels and muffins and croissants and pastries; at yet another, an entire array of desserts, cakes and pies and individual soufflés. If you're confused about hunger, if the internal mechanisms that signal physical satiety have gone haywire, if food has become symbolically loaded, or a stand-in for other longings, this kind of array can topple you. I couldn't choose. More to the point, I couldn't trust myself to choose moderately or responsibly, or to stop when I was full, or even to know what I wanted to begin with, what would satisfy and how much. And so I ate everything. The suppressed appetite always rages just beneath the surface of will, and as often happened during that period, it simmered, then bubbled up, then boiled over. I ate. I ate eggs and bacon and waffles and slabs of cake. I ate knowing full well that I'd feel bloated and flooded with disgust later on and that I'd have to make restitution—I'd starve the next day, or go for a six-mile run, or both. I ate without pleasure. I ate until I hurt.

Years later, I'd see that brunch in metaphorical terms, a high-calorie, high-carbohydrate testament to the ambiguous blessings of abundance, its promise and its agonizing terror. As a rule, women of my generation were brought up without knowing a great deal about how to understand hunger, with very little discussion about how to assess and respond adequately to our own appetites, and with precious few examples of how to negotiate a buffet of possibility, much less embrace one. Eating too much—then as now—was a standard taboo, a mother's concern with her own body and weight handed down to her daughter in a mantle of admonishments: *Always take the smallest portion; always eat a meal before you go on a date lest you eat too much in front of him; don't eat that, it'll go straight to your hips.* Sexual hunger was at best undiscussed, at worst presented as a bubbling cauldron of danger and sin, potentially ruinous; the memory banks of women my age are riddled with images of scowling mothers, echoes of recriminating hisses (*Take that off, you look like a slut!*), fragments of threat-laden lectures about the predatory hunger of boys. And the world of ambition was in many ways uncharted territory, one that required qualities and skills—ego strength, competitiveness, intellectual confidence—that were sometimes actively discouraged in girls (*Don't brag, don't get a swelled head, don't be so smart*), rarely modeled.

This is a complicated legacy to bring to a world of blasted-open options, each *yes* in potential collision with an old *no*, and it makes for a great deal of confusion. The underlying questions of appetite, after all, are formidable—What *would* satisfy? How much *do* you need, and of what? What *are* the true passions, the real hungers behind the ostensible goals of beauty or slenderness?—and until relatively recently, a lot of women haven't been encouraged to explore them, at least not in a deep, concerted, uniform, socially supported way. We have what might be called post-feminist appetites, whetted and encouraged by a generation of opened doors and collapsed social structures, but not always granted unequivocal support or license, not always stripped of their traditional alarm bells and warnings, and not yet bolstered by a deeper sense of entitlement.

Freedom, it is important to note, is not the same as power; the ability to make choices can feel unsettling and impermanent and thin if it's not girded somehow with the heft of real economic and political

strength. Women certainly have more of that heft than they did a generation ago; we are far less formally constrained, far more autonomous, and
far more politically powerful, at least potentially so. Forty-three million
women—forty percent of all adult women—live independently today,
without traditional supports. Women make the vast majority of consumer
purchases in this country—eighty-three percent—and buy one fifth of all
homes. We have an unprecedented amount of legal protection, with equality on the basis of sex required by law in virtually every area of American
life. We are better educated than the women of any preceding generation,
with women representing more than half of full-time college enrollments.
By all accounts, we ought to feel powerful, competent, and strong—and
many women no doubt do, at least in some areas and at some times.

But it's also true that an overwhelming majority of women—estimates
range from eighty to eighty-nine percent—wake up every morning aware
of an anxious stirring of self-disgust, fixated on the feel of our thighs as
we pull on our stockings, the feel of our bellies and hips as we zip up our
pants and skirts. Women are three times as likely as men to feel negatively
about their bodies. Eighty percent of women have been on a diet, half are
actively dieting at any given time, and half report feeling dissatisfied with
their bodies all the time. There is no doubt that this negativity is a culturally mediated phenomenon, that culture gives the female preoccupation
with appearance (which in itself is nothing new) its particular cast, its
particularly relentless focus on slenderness. But the sheer numbers, which
indicate an unprecedented depth and breadth of anxiety about appearance in general and weight in particular, suggest that something more
complex than imagery is at work, that our collective sense of power and
competence and strength hasn't quite made it to a visceral level.

To be felt at that level, as visceral and permanent and real, entitlement must exist beyond the self; it must be known and acknowledged on
a wider plane. And this is where women still get the short end of the stick;
for all the gains of the last forty years, we are hardly ruling the world out
there. Congress is still ninety percent male, as are ninety-eight percent of
America's top corporate officers. Ninety-five percent of all venture capital
today flows into men's bank accounts. The two hundred highest-paid
CEOs in America are all men. Only three women head Fortune 500 companies, a number that hasn't budged in twenty years. We also have less
visibility than men; women—our lives, issues, concerns—are still featured in only fifteen percent of page-one stories, and when we do make
front-page news, it is usually only as victims or perpetrators of crime.
And we still have less earning power: Women continue to make eighty-
four cents for every dollar a man makes; women who take time off from
work to have children make seventeen percent less than those who don't
even six years after they return; men with children earn the most money
while women with children earn the least.

This gap, I think—this persistent imbalance between personal freedom on the one hand and political power on the other—amps up the anxiety factor behind desire; it can leave a woman with a sense that something does not quite compute; it can give choices a partial, qualified feel. A woman, today, can be a neurosurgeon, or an astrophysicist; she can marry or not marry, leave her spouse, pack up, and move across the country at will. But can she take such choices a step further, or two or ten? Can a woman be not just an astrophysicist, but a big, powerful, lusty astrophysicist who feels unequivocally entitled to food and sex and pleasure and acclaim? Can she move across the country and also leave behind all her deeply ingrained feelings about what women are really supposed to look and act and be like? External freedoms may still bump up against a lot of ancient and durable internal taboos; they may still collide with the awareness, however vague, that women still represent the least empowered portion of the population, and these collisions help explain why appetites are so particularly problematic today; they exist in a very murky context, and an inherently unstable one, consistently pulled between the opposing poles of possibility and constraint, power and powerlessness.

The world mobilizes in the service of male appetite; it did during my upbringing and it does still. Whether or not this represents the actual experience of contemporary boys and men, our cultural stereotypes of male desire (and stereotypes exist precisely because they contain grains of truth) are all about facilitation and support: Mothers feed (Eat! Eat!), fathers model assertion and unabashed competitiveness, teachers encourage outspoken bravado. At home and at work, men have helpers, usually female, who clean and cook and shop and type and file and assist. And at every turn—on billboards, magazine covers, in ads—men are surrounded by images of offering, of breasts and parted lips and the sultry gazes of constant availability: Take me, you are entitled, I exist to please you. For all the expansion of opportunity in women's lives, there is no such effort on behalf of female appetite, there are no comparable images of service and availability, there is no baseline expectation that a legion of others will rush forward to meet our needs or satisfy our hungers. The striving, self-oriented man is adapted to, cut slack, his transgressions and inadequacies explained and forgiven. *Oh, well, you wouldn't expect him to cook or take care of his kids, who cares if he's put on a few pounds, so what if he's controlling or narcissistic, he's busy, he gets things done, he's running the show, he's running the company, he's running the COUNTRY.* That litany of understanding does not apply to women; it sounds discordant and artificial if you switch the genders, and if you need a single example of the double standard at work here, think about Bill and Hillary Clinton. Bill's pudginess and fondness for McDonald's was seen as endearing; his sexual appetite criticized but ultimately forgiven by most Americans, or at least considered irrelevant to his abilities on the job; Hillary got no such latitude, the focus on her appearance (hairstyle, wardrobe, legs) was relentless, the hostility released toward her ambition venomous.

The one exception to this rule, the one area where a legion of others might, in fact, rush forward in service to a woman's needs, is shopping, particularly high-end retail shopping, but in itself, that merely underscores how lacking the phenomenon is in other areas, and how constricted the realm of appetite is for women in general: We can want, and even expect, the world to mobilize on our behalf when we're equipped with an American Express gold card and an appetite for Armani. But beyond the world of appearances and consumer goods, expressions of physical hunger and selfish strivings rarely meet with such consistent support. Instead, the possibility of risk can hang in the air like a mildly poisonous mist; for every appetite, there may be a possible backlash, or a slap or a reprimand or a door that opens but has caveats stamped all over the welcome mat. A novelist tells me in a whisper about a glowing review she's received; she can barely get the words out, so strong are the chastising echoes of her family: *Now, don't you let it go to your head*, her mother used to say, and it took her decades to realize how truly defeating that phrase was. ("Where's it supposed to go," she asks today, "someone else's head?") A scientist, brilliant and respected, secures a major grant for a project she's dreamed of taking on for years and later describes what an emotional hurdle it was to fully take pride in the accomplishment, to really revel in it: "I couldn't say it aloud, I just couldn't get the words out," she says. "I don't think a man would *get* that." An educator, who's taught high school for thirteen years and is now pursuing a PhD in education, tells me, "For years, I've carried around the feeling that if I really allow myself to follow my passions, something bad will happen." She can't follow that line of thought to any logical conclusion; rather, it expresses an amalgam of worries, some specific (she's apprehensive about being consumed by work, and about making sacrifices in her personal life), but more of them generic, as though the admission of hunger and ambition is in itself a dangerous thing, quite likely a punishable offense.

This quiet, dogged anxiety, this internalized mosquito whine of caveat, may explain why the memory of that hotel brunch would stick with me for so long; the experience seemed to capture something about the times, about the onset of a complicated set of conflicts between an expansive array of options on the one hand and a sense of deep uncertainty on the other, a feeling that this freedom was both incomplete and highly qualified, full of risks. Certainly that's how I felt in those early unformed twentysomething years, as though I were standing before an enormous table of possibilities with no utensils, no serving spoons, no real sense that I was truly entitled to sample the goods, to experiment or indulge or design my own menu.

DISCUSSION

1. Knapp begins her personal account of anorexia by referring to the "lure of starving." How do you react to this provocative phrase? In your view, is it possible for something as harrowing and harmful as self-starvation to feel so compelling or desirable? If so, how?

2. For Knapp, anorexia is both a personal and a societal disease, starkly registering the ways women can be taught to internalize and act on destructive gender stereotypes. How valid does this hypothesis seem to you? Does it make sense to think about this illness as a blueprint for the scripts that get written out and imposed on women?

3. As Knapp relates, denying herself food felt for so long like the right thing to do in part because it gave her an enhanced sense of "being in control." Choose one of the diets Knapp describes having followed during her anorexic years and evaluate it as a recipe for achieving a particular form of control. In your view, does the diet achieve this objective?

WRITING

4. Much of Knapp's writing of her own hunger centers around imaginary conversations or internal dialogue that expresses common embedded attitudes about eating and appetite. Write an essay in which you analyze how effective this approach to writing about appetite is. Who is Knapp talking to in these conversations, and how does she use this dialogue to highlight her own attitudes toward eating?

5. Here is a partial list of the words Knapp tells us she learned to associate with her own hunger: *rapacious*, *greedy*, *selfish*, *needy*, *unsexy*, *bad*. Write an essay in which you propose what scripts about food and eating have given rise to these kinds of associations. What scripts in food advertising, nutritional guidelines, or the popular media do you think reinforce this type of thinking? In your opinion, are these scripts intentional? How might you approach communicating messages about health or beauty without triggering the negative associations that Knapp discusses?

6. For Knapp, cultural attitudes about food formed "a low-level thrumming of shoulds and shouldn'ts and can'ts and wants," or what the author calls a kind of "feminine Muzak." In your view, does this analogy do a good or bad job of capturing the ways we learn to absorb or internalize cultural norms around eating? Write an essay in which you compare these messages and this process of internalization to what Francine Prose (p. 212) has to say in her piece on gluttony. Does Prose seem to share Knapp's view of where our norms vis-à-vis food typically come from and the ways they come to feel so normal? How or how not?

MAKENNA GOODMAN

Ever Wonder if You Could Kill What You Eat? We Did the Other Night

For most us, our connection to the food we eat extends no further than the container in which it is packaged or the label with which it is affixed. For others, however, this connection goes much deeper, all the way back to our food's former existence as a living thing. Sketching the way these connections work in her own life, Makenna Goodman invites readers to think about the repercussions of "killing what you eat." And in doing so, she offers a pointed challenge to the norms that typically define our relationship to food. Goodman is assistant editor at Chelsea Green Publishing, a publisher of books about politics and sustainable living. Her writing has appeared in *Grist* and the *Huffington Post*. The following selection was originally posted on *Alternet* on August 28, 2009.

LAST NIGHT, WE HAD FOURTEEN PEOPLE OVER FOR DINNER. AND THEY wanted chicken. Good thing we had some . . . but they were running around. And so it was—all in the name of well balanced meals—farm life came down to its grittiest.

I live and work on a farm in central Vermont, and there's always family around. That means a lot of emotional turmoil (and joy, ehem), a lot of secretly chugging whiskey in the closet (not really, but really), and best of all—extra hands. No one visits without pitching in. And now that it's late August, the farm work is at its peak. Harvesting, preserving food for winter, and chicken killing.

While some may balk (bawwwk) at the idea of taking a life on the grounds of a homestead, we do it for the sake of food—not sport—and when it comes down to it, for the sake of the chicken itself. It's not indulging in sadism, nor for power over an animal, nor an image of something hardcore and awesome to impress the neighbors. It's about being connected to the very foundations of self sufficiency, and understanding that meat does not simply fall from the sky, packaged on a shelf in a supermarket; it comes from a living, breathing being. Chicken killing at home is deep. Emotional. Ethical. As Joel Salatin says in his book *Pastured Poultry Profit$*, it's *necessary*:

> Animal rights activists, for all their misdirection, are right on target when pushing for animal slaughter as close to the point of production as possible. Not only does it relieve [the chicken's] stress, a direct cause of tough meat, but is far more environmentally sensible.

Joel Salatin is at the forefront of the farming movement. His name is becoming household, and his practices are emulated across the country. He's the farmer who changed Michael Pollan's life, in *The Omnivore's Dilemma*, remember? He's the farmer young farmers want to be; he makes money farming, but he does it right—his animals live according to their "ness," which means closest to their nature. And while most chicken producers send their birds long distances to slaughter houses (which really stresses out the chickens in their final days), like us—and many other small farmers in Vermont—Salatin supports the at-home processing method. To him, it represents the very foundation of his respect for his animals. He says:

> We have customers who occasionally like to come out and "get connected" to their food . . . If one of our ultimate goals is to reconnect the urban and rural sectors of our culture, on-farm processing affords us a technique to accomplish that goal.

My fella's stepmom was intent on killing one of the two broilers for last night's dinner. She's a foodie from Brooklyn, and wanted to honor this chicken by taking its life as sweetly and quickly as possible. She wanted to get more connected to her food. She was nervous, but determined. We all gathered to watch, including Clara, the seven-year-old aspiring artist/farmer, whose eyes were glued to the scene. It's not an easy

She wanted to honor this chicken by taking its life as sweetly and quickly as possible.

thing to watch a chicken slaughter. While it may be common knowledge there's post-mortem thrashing—ever heard of "like a chicken with its head cut off"?—seeing it live can be a bit gruesome. But unlike a public prisoner execution, we were there to celebrate the chicken's life, and what it had to offer us. And what better way to experience death for the first time. There was no: "take that, you sucker!" No proving our cultural masculinity, nor prowess. Therese was as careful and as kind as could be as she cooed to the bird, and quick as a wink in her execution with the knife. There was no suffering or stress on the bird, and it died in a habitat it's come to know quite well, with familiar smells and familiar views. Frida the dog sat quietly through it all, and afterward buried her treat: the feet.

Were we traumatized? Did we feel sorry for the chicken? Are we dreading this weekend, where (without family around for help) we'll have to kill 150 more? Here's why not.

I've been feeding, pasturing, watering, and talking to these guys since the spring. They wander around all day in grass, pecking for bugs. So I know they've had a good life when they make it to that cone; as far as a chicken goes, they've seen the best there is to offer. Of course there's something to say for one being taking another being's life—and to be honest, I'll probably be dealing with that emotionally for the rest of my life. It's not *easy*.

Did we feel more connected to our dinner, because of the kill? Surprisingly, the guests' reaction varied. Clara was ravenous for the meat. Another young woman couldn't touch it: "Too soon!" And Therese didn't wind up feeling a closer connection to her food, the opposite of what she thought would happen. Perhaps it was her adrenaline, or maybe the ambiance of "this happens every day" farms tend to have. But maybe feeling connected to her food, in the end, wasn't as important as being connected to the *animal* during its life and final moments. Which is the nobler goal for us local food eating, small-scale farm supporting folk? I know since moving to a farm, I'm much less concerned with labels like Organic, Local, and Farm-Fresh. I want to know how that animal *lived*, not just what it ate, or where it came from. Local chicken could come from next door, and been raised in a cage. Organic chicken could have been pumped with feed, and not a blade of grass. Foodie labels don't excite me anymore. I want to know the amount of sun, fresh air, and forage that animal got during its life. Organic, shmorganic, in other words. Give me the backstory.

I ate up the meat just like any other dinner—I felt no urge to pat myself on the back. It was almost like being numbed, until I realized—farming gets you as close to death as one can get. We see the composting of bodies, of soil, and the process by which an animal is born and leaves the world. We facilitate their birth and their death. We offer our animals a good life, in exchange for their bodies. And in time (the amount of which we'll never know, for we will never be able to control it), we'll offer up our own to the earth. But, at the same time . . . what if robots descended upon earth and decided to farm *us*? I might not like it.

DISCUSSION

1. How would you answer the question posed in this essay's title? What is your reaction to the prospect of killing what you eat? Does it seem shocking, even unimaginable? Does it strike you as offensive or off-putting? Or does it suggest the possibility of something more positive, useful, even perhaps necessary?

2. Killing what you eat, Goodman writes, is "about being connected to the very foundations of self sufficiency, and understanding that meat does not simply fall from the sky, packaged on a shelf in a supermarket; it comes from a living, breathing being." According to the norms around food in our culture, how typical would you say this view of eating is? To what extent does it model a different set of attitudes, a different set of values, than the ones that conventionally prevail? And do you find these alternatives preferable to the norm? How or how not?

3. What would happen if the practice of killing what you eat were to become a more widely accepted social norm? What rules would you suggest for how this practice should be carried out? What guidelines? What limitations? And why?

WRITING

4. Goodman describes in detail what is actually involved in slaughtering a chicken. Write an assessment of this particular decision. Why do you think Goodman chooses to include this description? What is her larger goal in doing so? Next, explain how it felt to read this section. What were your reactions? In what ways did this description influence your views about killing what you eat?

5. Near the end of the essay, Goodman summarizes her newfound attitudes toward food this way: "Foodie labels don't excite me anymore. I want to know the amount of sun, fresh air, and forage that animal got during its life. Organic, shmorganic, in other words. Give me the backstory." Write an essay in which you analyze these claims more closely. What, for Goodman, is the key difference between the information provided by a label and the information gained by raising and killing an animal on your own? What makes knowing this backstory so important? And do you share this view?

6. Goodman's essay, like Michael Pollan's (p. 186), takes a rather dim view of what often gets termed the *industrial food chain*. In a two-page essay, discuss the ways each of these essays can be read as extended critiques of industrial food. What aspects of this conventional system do these two writers agree need to be reformed? And where do you see their critiques deviating?

TARA LOHAN

The Ultimate in Eating Local:
My Adventures in Urban Foraging

For most of us, roaming the aisles of our local supermarket is as close as we get to the experience of foraging for our own food. For others, however, foraging is a much more immediate and ongoing aspect of their everyday eating lives. Chronicling the activities of one such forager, Tara Lohan prompts us to rethink the social norms that render us so disconnected from the food we eat. Lohan is a senior editor for the website *Alternet*, where the following selection was posted on September 5, 2009. She writes primarily about food and the environment. She lives in the San Francisco Bay area.

AFTER SPENDING AN AFTERNOON WITH ISO RABINS, IT HAS COME to my attention that I have no useful skills. And by useful, I mean the kind that could save my life if I was plucked out of the warm embrace of industrial, consumer society.

I can type with all 10 fingers, but Rabins can do me one better, much better: He can find food.

Having been successfully able to grow one, tiny Meyer lemon, in the last year-and-a-half, I have a fond appreciation for people with fruited vines tangled in their backyard, and green arms, heavy with tomatoes coming out of their pots, and a windowsill alive with herbs.

To be a farmer, even if only on the crammed fire escape of your city nest, is something special and ancient.

But Rabins is another breed, and an older one—he doesn't grow food, he finds it, and he does so mostly around the city of San Francisco and its neighboring towns and shores.

He's also among a growing band of urban foragers who have been sprouting through sidewalk cracks all across the country as the economy tightens belts and the local-foods movement gains popularity. And thanks to Rabins, I got to spend a day seeing what's it's like to start looking at your neighborhood as a potential meal.

GATHERING THE BOUNTY

I always assumed that if I was lost in the woods, a safe bet would be to eat acorns, one thing I think I could identify for certain. But Rabins, who knows a delicious recipe for acorn ice cream, helps save me from a potentially sickening experience.

On a recent walk through San Francisco's Golden Gate Park, he explains that acorns have a lot of tannins and are poisonous if you eat too many raw. You have to take them out of their shell, and then the nut meat needs to be soaked—either submerged in the cold water of a rushing stream for weeks as the indigenous people did, or boiled in numerous baths on the stove, a process that could take all day or longer.

But this is just passing advice—we are not out to gather acorns. Rabins runs Forage SF, a group he started a year ago to provide foodies in the Bay area with a box of locally foraged foods.

Similar to the popular CSA (community-supported agriculture) model that allows people to buy a subscription to a farmer's regular bounty, Rabins' CSF provides members with a monthly box of foraged goodies that range from mushrooms to fruit to herbs to sea beans to fish.

Some of the foraging he does himself, and the rest is contracted from other foragers (or fishermen). Rabins is still working out the kinks and trying to get a reliable group of foragers together, which, it seems, is a lot like herding cats. For the time being though, he's stuck with me, a total beginner.

I had hoped that maybe I'd come home from my first foraging outing with pink-stained fingers from berry picking, but instead we are peering underneath long green leaves looking for snails. Snails!

I'm not even sure I want to find a snail, let alone think about anyone eating it. My parents gave up on me eating any kind of meat products around the age of 12, and I'm pretty sure snails fall somewhere in the meatlike category.

These snails, Rabins says, will be used for an escargot he is planning for another one of his ventures—monthly foraged-food dinners that he serves to groups of

> **Rabins doesn't grow food, he finds it.**

up to about 30 and include an ambitious six courses that are probably as close as you can get to actually eating the city of San Francisco.

In jeans and hoodies, we look more like urban hipsters than foragers. But I guess that's a good thing, because we are wandering the paths of one of the city's gardens (which will remain nameless).

We've slipped past the groups of toddlers wobbling on the front lawn and the vacationing families dutifully reading all the informational signs. We head to the winding, dirt paths, farther from the crowds, passing the occasional photographer hunched over a tripod.

Rabins looks like your average young Mission District guy—which he is. He lives in the hip 'hood, has a film degree, shaggy brown hair, and a bit of a beard. He has learned foraging from books and other people who know what they are doing, and a bit of trial and error. He doesn't own a car, so he takes the bus around the city or bums rides from other aspiring foragers.

Of course, if you're in a city garden like the one we're in, you're not suppose to actually take anything out. But we're not taking plants—just the snails hiding in their midst, and the snails, Rabins says, are pests. So, I guess we're doing the garden a favor.

Rabins has shown me the kind of plant we're looking for, although he doesn't know it by name, he just knows the snails prefer them. The plants grow in clumps and sport long, flat green leaves. Some have tall spears that shoot from the middle, armed with clusters of light purple flowers. We run our hands through the leaves, parting them to see others further inside.

I get a quick burst of excitement when I point out my first snail to Rabins, who plucks it from its green berth, making a slight sucking sound as it is pulled free. He opens his backpack and drops it in a plastic container that looks like it was probably intended for take-out soup. Just one snail, and I'm hooked. It feels incredibly rewarding and also a bit risky.

Rabins used to find huge swaths of Miner's lettuce in an area called the Presidio, which is both a neighborhood and a park and is technically a National Historic Landmark, with architecture dating back to the Spanish forts.

An article about Rabins in a local paper mentioned his foraging ventures there, and the Presidio establishment decided to nip his picking in the bud. I guess they were afraid hordes of San Franciscans would descend on the area like a pack of starved goats and eat all the vegetation.

But certainly there are some legal hazards when you're in urban areas. Just ask "Wildman" Steve Brill. He's probably the country's most well known forager who has been leading foraging trips in the New York area since 1982.

Brill got his big break in 1986, when the New York City parks commissioner planted undercover agents on one of his tours in Central Park. When Brill popped a dandelion in his mouth, he was handcuffed and arrested. The incident made national, and even international, news and the city was forced to not only drop the charges but then hire him to lead foraging tours through the parks department.

Brill spent four years as a parks naturalist before he went back to freelancing. Now he leads tours for all kinds of groups—schools, birthday parties, garden clubs, and anyone else interested in learning what you can find to eat in New York City and its environs.

It turns out there is a lot. Brill tells me some of it: wild watercress, mulberries, wild persimmons, raspberries, Juneberries, various species of bramble, parsnips, burdock root, wild carrot, giant puffballs, chicken mushrooms, honey mushrooms, white oak acorns, black walnuts, lambs quarters, and even kelp if you venture out to the shores of the Long Island Sound, which is where I grew up.

GETTING THE GOODS FOR FREE

That's the beauty of foraging. It's like getting a new lens on life. All of a sudden, you can see things—food—where there wasn't any before. The weed you might be stepping over on the sidewalk without even noticing—that's purslane, and its stems and leaves are great in salad or you can cook it up. It's packed with iron, beta carotene, Vitamin C, and other healthy stuff. It's also a secret source of omega-3 fatty acids. Forget fish pills, just look beneath your feet.

> **When Brill popped a dandelion in his mouth, he was handcuffed and arrested.**

Foraging has its benefits for sure and beats the supermarket in many ways.

"It's a lot more fun, it's less expensive, the food tastes better, and there are more nutrients," Brill said. "It is also a good way of getting in touch with your planet, especially if you have kids who love learning about nature."

Urban foraging has become a nice complement to the "freegans," who popularized Dumpster diving and have reminded us that one person's trash is another's dinner.

"Freeganism (a conjunction of 'free' and 'vegan') is the philosophy that participation in our capitalist economy makes a person complicit in the exploitative practices that are used to create consumer goods," Becca Tucker wrote about her exploits living off what her fellow New Yorkers had tossed.

Of course, when I think of Dumpster diving, I think first of the folks whose association with garbage isn't a philosophical arrangement, but a necessity. Having the skills to get by on the streets when you're homeless or jobless or both is quite a feat.

But over the years, as our society has grown more and more attached to "more," we've created a consumer culture where most of the stuff we kick to the curb is totally usable—from TVs to shoes to muffins. So why not live off the bounty of discards?

The same is true for food that's growing in our midst. While I imagine that finding still-edible cheesecake in a Dumpster behind a bakery feels like an incredible score—probably even topping my glee at finding my first snail—foraging offers food that is super-fresh and nutritious. And well, clean—that is, if you're foraging in the right places (like not beside highways and railroads, Brill warns).

Even in our most populated urban environments like New York City or Los Angeles, as people hurry to Whole Foods or Safeway, they're passing by food as they go—things that can fill their plate for free.

Thankfully, more and more people are seeing the beauty of foraging.

"Urban foraging in the United States is more a choice than a necessity," *Reuters* reported. "Most foragers see both the health and environmental benefits to eating a more natural diet."

Of course in a tight economy, where clipping coupons has fallen back into practice for many, the free aspect doesn't hurt either. And lots of people are also experiencing a cultural shift when it comes to their food.

The backlash to fast food and processed food has grown as people are embracing not just organic, but locally grown food. And increasingly, people have a desire to not just understand where their food comes from, but to actively participate in that food system.

GROWING COMMUNITY

Where I live on the West Coast, the trees are heavy with fruit, so much of which goes to waste, even while people in the city go hungry. Thankfully, several groups have stepped up to help with this problem.

Across the bay from San Francisco is the group Forage Oakland, pioneered by Asiya Wadud. The effort creates maps of Oakland's fruit trees to share and has helped to form a food network among neighbors. Wadud explains on Forage Oakland's Web site that their mission is much larger than just helping you access those ripe plums on the other side of the fence:

> Imagine gathering several friends for morning, midday, evening or weekend foraged city bicycle rides through your neighborhood. Rough maps are drawn, noting the forageables that can be found at each location, and "cold calls" are made to your neighbors asking if you can sample a fruit from their backyard tree. You have the courage to introduce yourself (despite the pervasiveness and acceptance of urban anomie), and they reward your neighborliness with a sample of Santa Rosa plums, for example.
>
> Later, when you find yourself with a surplus of Persian mulberries, you—in turn—deliver a small basket to said neighbor. With time, and in this fashion, a community of people who care for and know one another is built, and rather than being the exception, this could be the norm. This is not idealistic, rather it is necessary, pragmatic and creative—especially in times when much of the world is suffering from lack of access to healthful and satisfying fresh food.
>
> Forage Oakland is a project that works to construct a new model—and is one of many neighborhood projects that will eventually create a network of local resources that address the need and desire for neighborhoods to be more self-sustaining in meeting their food needs.

Groups like this exists across the country—Fallen Fruit in Los Angeles and Santa Fe, New Mexico; Urban Edibles in Portland, Oregon; and North Berkeley Harvest and SF Glean around the San Francisco Bay Area. There are also tons of links on Brill's Web site to various other foragers.

Iso Rabins also includes gleaned fruit in his foraged boxes. The day we were out snail gathering (we found 10!) we made a trip across town to scavenge some plums from a woman with an overloaded tree in her backyard.

When we arrived, and she led us around to her backyard, it was like there had been a plum storm. Many still hung overhead, but lots had fallen to the ground, were squished into the patio, or had been sampled by birds, rats, or other lucky urbanites.

Rabins worked the picker to reach the higher branches and plucked the tree nearly bare in about 20 minutes, leaving some of the smaller, less-ripe fruit and the ones out of reach all the way at the top. Occasionally there would be a solid thump as a plum missed the picking basket and fell to the ground.

The whole thing seemed symbiotic—just as Wadud described on her Forage Oakland Web site. We got some plums, the woman got her yard cleaned up a bit, and all the while she and Rabins chatted about his foraged-food dinners, and she offered her place to host one of his upcoming meals.

By the end of it, there were the makings for some good plum pudding and the cultivation of community, which is a different kind of cultivation than what farmers experience.

"When I talk to farmers, they don't quite get the foraging stuff," said Rabins. "They think it's neat, and then they say, 'Why don't you save the seeds from what you find and then grow it yourself.' But of course, that's not really what I'm interested in. People have this idea that food is some-

> **"People don't see food as something that grows on its own."**

thing that you make happen—you grow it—they don't see it as something that grows on its own, that is out there in the world. I like foraging because it is a different kind of way of looking at nature and being in it."

GET OUT THERE AND DO IT

It doesn't take a special kind of naturalist to forage, it's really just something you have to learn.

"This is no [more] difficult than any other skill that people tend to pick up, from mastering Photoshop to learning ballroom dancing to swimming," said Brill. "It is a skill, it takes steps, it takes persistence, but it is very rewarding."

Of course, you have to be careful. Never eat anything you haven't identified with 100 percent certainty, said Brill.

"You can eat any wild plant once, but you might not be around to eat it twice," he said. The best way to start, he advises, is to learn a small number of common plants really well that have no poisonous look-alikes and follow them through a whole year before you eat any of them.

"Wild plants and instant gratification don't always mix," he wrote in his book *Identifying and Harvesting Edible and Medicinal Plants in Wild (and Not So Wild) Places*. Once you've got a few down, slowly add to what you're collecting year after year.

Brill's book is a good place to start if you're interested in getting your foraging feet wet. Of course, finding the edibles is only part of it. Thankfully Brill has a cookbook to help you figure out what to do with the stuff once you've gotten it home. His Web site also has links from resources and foraging experts that might be in your neck of the woods.

Since my outing with Rabins, I've picked up copies of both Brill's books, and I keep spotting snails everywhere I go. I haven't yet had the desire to pluck them from where they're parked, but I'm just glad that I can finally see one more thing that's right in front of me.

And, thanks to Rabins I know a little of their story—the journey from European delicacy to American garden pest. I've also been eyeing the blackberry bushes that seem far enough out of the spray of the dogs that frequent the hill behind my house.

A few weeks ago, with some friends, I picked delicious berries from along a riverbank north of San Francisco, and they made our pancakes taste like summer.

Wild food and community are ingredients for a perfect meal.

"An edible landscape can be formed that is interactive, a bit different every day as fruit ripens and falls and as the seasons change," wrote Wadud. "The barter can translate to other areas of urban living and can create a community of people who'd rather do it for themselves and play an active role in their consumerism. When there are plums in your neighbor's backyard, enjoy them with your neighbor."

It's really true what they say: The best things in life are free.

DISCUSSION

1. How do you understand the phrase "urban foraging"? Are these terms you are used to seeing together? What sort of images does this phrase evoke?

2. How do you understand the distinction between "grown" food and "found" food? What images or ideas do you associate with each? When it comes to eating, which term comes closer to the cultural norm? Why?

3. According to Lohan, the appeal of urban foraging lies partly in the way it offers people a chance to "actively participate in the food system." Do you agree? In what particular ways does urban foraging offer greater opportunities for "active participation" than is typical? And what are the specific advantages or benefits that result?

WRITING

4. "Foraging," writes Lohan, "has its benefits for sure and beats the supermarket in many ways." Do you agree? Use Lohan's description of urban foraging to assess the ways it compares to more conventional ways of acquiring, cultivating, and consuming food. In what ways does this practice rewrite the traditional scripts that define what it means to play the role of food consumer in our culture? And in your view, are these changes for the better? How or how not?

5. The impetus underlying urban foraging, Lohan notes, is as much philosophical as it is practical. "Over the years, as our society has grown more and more attached to 'more,' we've created a consumer culture where most of the stuff we kick to the curb is totally usable — from TVs to shoes to muffins. So why not live off the bounty of discards?" Write an essay in which you analyze the ways that urban foraging challenges prevailing cultural norms around consumerism. To what extent does this practice offer a rebuke to the societal assumptions that "more" is automatically "good"? What alternative to this assumption does urban foraging represent? And in your view, is this alternative preferable? How or how not?

6. What are the differences between *finding* your food and *killing* your food? Do foraging and hunting model comparable or antithetical relationships to food and eating? In a two-page essay, compare the ways Lohan's portrait of urban foraging compares to Makenna Goodman's (p. 246) account of killing what she eats. What goals underlie and motivate these respective practices? What larger attitude toward our prevailing food norms does each reflect? And which do you find more compelling? Why?

FREDERICK KAUFMAN
They Eat What We Are

When we look at the eating habits of our pets, to what extent do they reflect our own? What do we learn about our own views and values, our own aspirations and anxieties, when we track how and what the animals around us eat? Taking seriously the proposition that pet cuisine can serve as a cultural mirror, Frederick Kaufman documents some of the more representative ways we cater to animals in order to serve ourselves. Kaufman has written for *Harper's, Gourmet,* and the *New York Times,* where the following selection was originally published on September 2, 2007. He teaches at the City University of New York's Graduate School of Journalism and is the author of the book *A Short History of the American Stomach* (2008).

I HAD BEEN TOLD THAT IN THE BASEMENT OF THE ANIMAL-SCIENCE laboratory building at the University of Illinois, Dr. George Fahey kept a colony of strange-looking dogs. At Fahey's orders, each of the dogs had undergone a surgical procedure to string a length of tubing from its intestinal tract to a clear plastic spout that stuck out its side. Fahey, a professor of animal and nutritional sciences, could open a spout by hand, fill a bag with whatever happened to ooze out, and calculate how much the dog had digested before whatever it had not digested could move farther through its body. The plastic tubing was inserted in the ileum—the exact spot where food absorption ends and fermentation by the microflora and bacteria of the lower bowel begins. Given a large enough sample of any dog food, George Fahey could calculate how much vitamin or mineral or fat or sugar would enter a dog's bloodstream and how much would be irretrievably lost. Fahey has spent his career investigating the metabolism of domestic animals, and his research has helped define the nature of pet food.

In addition to his dog colony, Fahey supervised a number of other nutrition laboratories in the university's department of animal sciences, and for the most part his workaday hardware consisted of the various contrivances necessary to measure how much food a pet might or might not digest. Thus the baroque collections of viscometers, desiccators, and pulverizers, the vials brimming with dog excreta laced with acid, the racks of test tubes filled with cat urine, the containers of canine and feline gastric fluid, and the retorts of dog and cat blood. The largest of his labs contained a walk-in refrigerator holding glass jars of secret-coded dog and cat diets, experimental feeds of the future that in their present states resembled nothing more than heaps of brown dust. Piled nearby were stacks and stacks of the commercial pet foods the researchers give to animals in the control groups of their experiments—brands Fahey did not want specified in this article.

I had come to Urbana-Champaign to tour Fahey's nutrition laboratories and to catch a glimpse behind the scenes of the canine- and feline-nutrition business. I had geared myself up to see those plugged dogs in the basement, but first we had to spend an hour or so strolling the upper floors of offices and laboratories. As we did, Fahey outlined the evolution of the canine habitat, from the wild to the barnyard to the front yard to the front porch, then from the front porch to the living room, from the living room to the bedroom, and from the bedroom to the bed—and under the sheets. He described how, to people who live alone or couples without children, a dog or a cat becomes an object of love. And an object of love must be civilized.

Civilized means different things to different people, and it does not necessarily have anything to do with a pet's nutritional requirements. Dogs can get along just fine on a daily ration of corn and soybeans. "That's about the cheapest diet you could put together," Fahey said, and it provides all the vitamins, minerals, protein, fat, and carbohydrates a dog needs. But it wouldn't sell to broad segments of the modern market.

"People buy diets on the basis of two things," Fahey said. "The first is palatability. You put it on the floor and the dogs clean up the bowl." He lifted a pencil from a desk and held it in the air. The second thing, he explained, is the appearance of the stool. "It should be half as long as this pencil, picked up as easily as this pencil, Ziplocked—and away we go." He added, "We have to have that if they're keeping the dog in the condo on the 34th floor and they have a white carpet." All the more so if the dog is in bed, under the sheets.

The reason Fahey has spent his scientific career investigating all manner of starch, carbohydrate, and fiber, the reason he has put tubes inside dogs to analyze what they have digested before they have finished digesting it—that reason suddenly became clear: George Fahey has been confronting the myriad challenges of controlling canine bowel movements. Premium dog foods contain at least 30 percent protein and 20 percent fat, he said. "Do we need to feed that much? No. But this way, you have a total tract digestibility of 88 percent, which is good if you don't want that dog to go in your house when you're out for the day. A corn-soy diet can't do that. The dog can't hold it."

For all the apparent variety—store shelves stocked with everything from Alpo to ZiwiPeak—pet food is a business of behemoths and bottom lines, with sales approaching $15 billion last year. Procter & Gamble acquired Iams for more than $2 billion in 1999, and two years later Nestlé purchased Ralston Purina for $11 billion. A single multinational, Mars Petcare, sells not only Whiskas and Pedigree but also Royal

Canin, Sheba, Kitekat, Frolic, Trill, Aquarian, and many other brands. In 2005, the big companies in the industry spent nearly $300 million on advertising.

With his academic status and independent financing, George Fahey's research spares pet-food manufacturers the negative publicity they might attract if they ran their own experiments on surgically altered dogs. Even so, the industry giants operate proprietary research centers, like the 60,000-square-foot facility in St. Louis where Nestlé Purina scientists conduct investigations into molecular biology, immunology, and aroma chemistry. But as the pet-food titans pour millions into developing and mass-producing chow, biscuits, and treats, they have been challenged by manifold new marketers of high-end animal diets that pride themselves on their organic suppliers, sustainable packaging, human-food-grade ingredients, and revolutionary philosophy.

The recall this spring of 60 million packages of pet food contaminated with melamine from China highlighted what was already an obsessive focus on what our dogs and cats eat. In recent years, the relative merits of low-cholesterol diets, high-protein diets, low-fat diets, and the BARF program of bones and raw food have generated arguments among pet-food zealots as enduring and bitter as Atkins versus Pritikin among human dieters. Web sites like BalanceIt.com offer astounding arrays of pet food recipes that mimic human cuisine and use human-grade ingredients: lasagna, spaghetti and meatballs, lamb stew. Numerous sellers offer doggy doughnuts, cannoli, and even wedding cakes.

In fact, the lines of human and companion-animal nutrition have been tightly interwoven ever since the domestication of the dog some 12,000 years ago. Our culinary ambitions for our pets have defined something of a utopian project, and its refinements have mirrored our own relationship with food. The increasing specialization of the pet-food industry today may well reflect not just our desire to keep our pets healthy but also our continuing urge to shape them in our own image.

The first commercial dog comestible appeared soon after James Spratt, a Cincinnati electrician, traveled to London in 1860 to market lightning rods, then changed his mind and entered the business of retailing a feed inspired by his own dog's diet of discarded ship's biscuits. In the early 20th century, Chappel Brothers of Rockford, Illinois, supplied canned horse meat to the hungry citizens of France, Holland, and Italy—and exported the scraps back to the United States as dog food. Chappel Brothers marketed Ken-L Ration and at its apex slaughtered more than 50,000 horses a year.

But as the desire for purity and health spread to growing numbers of Americans, it influenced their hopes and dreams for their pets. In the book *The Ralston Brain Regime*, a turn-of-the-century human-diet guru named Webster Edgerly presented "a course of conduct, exercises and study designed to develop perfect health in the physical brain." The name Ralston was itself an acronym of Edgerly's seven life principles: Regime, Activity, Light, Strength, Temperation, Oxygen, and Nature. One of the 800,000 "Ralstonite" acolytes Edgerly eventually attracted happened to be William H. Danforth, a young fitness fanatic and animal-feed entrepreneur who had begun to shovel together a mix of grain, molasses, and salt that he sold under the brand name Purina, "where purity is paramount." When Danforth approached Edgerly, the diet celebrity granted Purina an endorsement from "Dr. Ralston," and the company took on a new name.

Despite the emphasis on health, food for animals has long been prone to potentially lethal adulteration. In the 1920s and '30s, industrial processing generated a number of newfangled carbohydrate byproducts that entered the food stream, and a terrible ailment known as canine hysteria began to torment dogs. "The animal behaves in a thoroughly panic-stricken manner," noted a report by Food and Drug Administration scientists in 1948, "throwing itself against the sides of the cage, clawing the air and howling piteously. If unconfined, it will run wildly about bumping into all objects in its path." In acute cases the disease culminated in convulsions and death, and the culprit turned out to be a chemical wheat-bleaching agent used in processing flour. Of course, there would have been no panic-stricken dogs if there had been no processed flour in their food, and no processed flour in their food if there had been no processed flour in human food.

> *George Fahey has been confronting the myriad challenges of controlling canine bowel movements.*

Notwithstanding such occasional defilements, research into pet food and human food continued to follow parallel paths. In 1954, a pair of Ralston Purina visionaries borrowed an extruder from the human breakfast cereal group at Purina, where the apparatus was being used to produce a variety of new breakfast cereals like Chex. The investigators cleaned out the rice flour, salt, and sugar; packed the machine with emulsified livers, buttermilk, soy meal, and other ingredients; mixed everything together; and let the slurry dry on an asphalt lot. "It tasted similar to popcorn," one of its creators later wrote—and dogs loved it. When the marketing meetings began, Purina executives decided that instead of distributing the product to the company's nationwide web of feed stores, this new pet food, code-named X-24, would go to supermarkets, where it could be bought and sold next to human groceries. Within four years, Purina Dog Chow had become the best-selling dry dog food in the world.

The vast majority of America's 75 million dogs and 88 million cats continue to feed on scraps from the human food industry's table: pet-food ingredients like ground chicken bones, pig blood, and distillers byproducts. Indeed, when an agriculture-processing company encounters an industrial leftover—corn fiber, let's say, from its production of ethanol—it might put in a call to George Fahey's lab. Fahey has done a great deal of work with corn fiber and is exploring its potential as a source of fiber in the canine diet.

Although pet nutrition has generally followed trends in human nutrition, sometimes that order has been reversed. "We will see corn fiber in human foods like cereals and snacks," Fahey told me. "There's no reason that it should not be able to be used." Such adaptations have occurred before. In the 1980s, for instance, the experimental meals Fahey fed to the dogs in his lab sometimes included hydrogen-peroxide-treated wheat straw. A major manufacturer of baked goods for humans, he said, picked up on the idea of using hydrogen-peroxide-treated fiber and experimented with mixing the substance into some of its breads.

Experiments with cats and dogs have long been used as a key to the scientific mysteries of the human diet. For obvious reasons, scientists cannot test human digestion by delivering experimental meals that lack vital nutriments. Dogs, however, have metabolisms similar to ours, they are widely available, and their internal organs are larger than those of rats, which makes them well suited to examination. In 1816, a French physiologist, François Magendie, fed groups of dogs only a single food, like sugar or olive oil. The animals died, but Magendie helped identify the dietary requirement for protein. In 1921, Edward Mellanby, a British pharmacologist, conducted an experiment in which he raised hundreds of puppies indoors. In the total absence of sunlight, and eating nothing but oats, the dogs developed skeletal deformities associated with rickets, but Sir Mellanby laid the groundwork for the discovery of vitamin D. In fact, some of the vitamins sold at your local supermarket or health food store were discovered thanks to deficiency studies that left experimental colonies of domesticated animals emaciated or comatose.

Paradoxically, the same nutrition experiments that caused disease or death have led to pioneering advances in animal health care. Because nutritional biochemists have measured almost everything about the canine and feline diets—from energy densities to intestinal transit times—they know what to do when something goes wrong. The latest word in digestibility studies may have cost lab animals a score of nasty symptoms, but the data gathered will help save many sick pets down the road.

The William R. Pritchard Veterinary Medical Teaching Hospital at the University of California, Davis, houses what was the first therapeutic pet nutrition center in America when it opened in 2003. Today the hospital treats more than 25,000 small animals every year, and the nutrition center does much of its work on the clinical frontier where sustenance meets medication. Here, on a wall outside the Nutrition Support Service,

I noted a plaque announcing that the center had been backed by money from the Nestlé Purina PetCare Company and Hill's Pet Nutrition Inc. "There's virtually no national funding out of the federal government for research on the health and well-being of cats and dogs," said Bennie Osburn, the dean of the university's School of Veterinary Medicine. "We have not seen N.I.H. show interest. The U.S.D.A. has not shown interest. The federal government will provide basic funding for ornamental flowers, but not companion animals."

In the hospital's hallways, white-coated doctors walked sick and bandaged pets, while weaker animals reclined on low gurneys. Inside the nutrition center, staff members were formulating individualized diets for the patients. Along one wall of the room ran a line of more than 30 clear plastic dispensers of various kibbles in every shade of ocher, and next to the standard brands of cat food sat jumbo packs of GastroENteric Feline Formula, Kidney Function Feline Formula, and Diabetes Management Feline Formula. There were jars of oral electrolyte solution, milk replacers for neonates, protein supplements made from whey, and synthetic diets for critically ill animals on life support. Above the provisions and extracts sat two rice steamers for those patients whose gastrointestinal upset would allow them only bland foods like white rice. In fact, human food pervaded the pet nutrition center, from Chicken of the Sea tuna to Betty Crocker's Potato Buds, not to mention Metamucil and Fibersure.

"The clinical nutrition program will spread across the country," Osburn predicted. Some of his confidence was surely an administrator's pride in his university, but it didn't seem like a stretch to imagine that the nutritional products and procedures developed here—including cancer-care diets and high-fat regimens for anorectic pets—could soon become successful on the mass market. Dogs and cats are living longer and growing fatter and more dyspeptic, and, like their owners, they have to watch the calories.

In 2003, scientists published the genome of a standard poodle named Shadow, followed two years later by the full genetic sequence of a boxer named Tasha. Today, as geneticists close in on the cat genome, researchers and pet-food marketers are rushing to find ways to make high-end pet diets even more customized.

"This is part of a larger trend in nutrition: complexity and individualization," says Marion Nestle, a professor of nutrition, food studies, and public health at New York University. "In the future someone is likely to do a genetic profile of your animal and prescribe accordingly. How accurate or useful this will be is an open question." Genome-based animal feed may evolve into the ultimate personalized diet for pets, or it may meet the same fate as the unsuccessful collaboration by Carnation and Upjohn in 1985 to market birth-control dog food.

Professor Nestle perceives two tracks for the future feeding of America's cats and dogs, tracks that parallel the nutrition trends of their owners: The wealthiest 5 to 8 percent of pet owners, those with college educations, annual household incomes in excess of $70,000, and an expanding human diet of organic, locally grown, and luxury food products, will provide ever better, fresher, and more delicious food for their pets. The other 92 to 95 percent of pets compose a second track that will consume increasingly industrialized diets. Even today these diets commonly consist of byproducts cooked into sterile and viscous masses, sheared into the simulacrum of a bone or a patty, and then, according to a report by the National Research Council in Washington, spray-dried with minuscule beadlets of fat, protein, and calibrated savor. Kind of like the industrial, increasingly synthetic, and processed diets of their owners.

> *Pet-food marketers are rushing to find ways to make high-end pet diets even more customized.*

Nestle's research for her next book, *What Pets Eat*, has also brought to her attention the enormous numbers of emerging pet-food companies. ("I just met with this guy in Colorado who's doing a high-end bison pet food," she says.) As these pet-food start-ups edge their way into the market, many entrepreneurs appear to have concluded that there must be a way to feed dogs and cats without relying on the rendering industry, the surgical procedures of academic research, or the detritus of alternative-fuel manufacturing. They have begun to speak of a pet-food revolution.

According to Nestle, the push to reform pet food is part of the broader movement to transform the way human beings eat. The pet-food movement "is grass roots, and it is a combination of the so-called good, clean, fair movement, the slow-food movement, the locally grown movement and the farm-animal welfare movement. These social movements are about changing the industrialized food system," she says. The latest trends in pet food emphasize not only natural and organic ingredients but also an increased obligation to identify the precise origins of those ingredients. Nestle says, "This will place enormous pressure on standard industrialized pet-food companies to say where their stuff comes from."

Typical of the grass-roots, slow-food, socially responsible pet-food campaign are Miya Gowdy and Vivian Outlaw, who cooked 5,000 pounds of dog food in Gowdy's TriBeCa loft last year. They simmered the stews of their Righteous Dog Food brand on a four-burner stove top that, when I visited a few months ago, sat amid Gowdy's collection of her own abstract paintings, bookshelves stocked with back issues of the Buddhist magazine *Tricycle,* and an array of other companies' pet-food packaging that ranged from Buddy Biscuits to Chompions Super Premium Breakfast

Formula. "Our artistic proclivities have made us perfectly suited to lead this revolution," Gowdy said. Her intense painter's gaze beamed from behind horn-rimmed glasses. "Artists think in process."

Righteous Dog Food retails for $7.50 a pound, compared with around $1 a pound for an inexpensive commercial brand. Gowdy and Outlaw envision a time when they will sell 12,000 pounds of food each month in the New York metropolitan area, enough to feed 600 dogs—and to make a profit. For now, demand has outstripped the capacity of Gowdy's General Electric range, so the partners have begun to prepare their products at an industrial kitchen called Hudson Valley Foodworks, in upstate New York. Righteous Dog Food shares the kitchen's 25,000 square feet with 40 other food companies, among them the makers of Hot Dog Charlie's Chili Meat Sauce and Spacey Tracy's Sweet Sunshine Pickles. A company manufacturing dog biscuits, which, like Righteous Dog Food, only uses human-grade ingredients, has also joined the roster.

On the sweltering morning the partners invited me to visit their operation, Gowdy and Outlaw planned on cooking two 500-pound batches of a chicken recipe and one 500-pound batch of beef-based fare. Eight cooks in clear plastic gloves and hairnets met them when the partners walked into the plant at 8:30. The crew members cored apples, chopped parsnips, and chattered in Spanish while one of them fiddled with a CD remote wrapped in cellophane. Soon, the sweet chords of ranchera music joined the whirring, the grinding, and the sudden bangs and crashes.

In the back of the kitchen stood two massive stainless-steel steam kettles of seething ingredients hooked up to a byzantine arrangement of pipes, pressure valves, and a variable-speed transmission. Sweat dripped down the outside of each 150-gallon kettle, while inside revolved the 14 teeth of the mixing blade. Unlike standard industrial pet-food operations, the cooking processes of Righteous Dog Food involved no gelatinizing, no solubilizations, no extrusion, and no spray coating. Nor did Righteous Dog Food rely on computerized spreadsheets to measure its ingredients. On a table next to a steam kettle sat a handwritten production chart: Take 24 quarts of chicken broth and add carrots and garlic (mix 10 minutes); add potatoes and yams (mix 15 minutes); add rosemary and apples, then pour in the bone meal and the raw eggs, the certified organic alfalfa, the red rose hips and the nettles, the safflower and salmon oils, the barley and the chicken meat, the burdock and the parsley, the dandelion greens, the cilantro, and the liquefied beef hearts.

A heavyset production manager named Mike Perez stood next to the tanks and checked items off the ingredient list. A former truck driver from Brooklyn, Perez went into the commercial baking business in 2000, when he joined a friend who was producing a line of cookies, brownies, blondies, and biscotti. "And now dog food," he said. He beamed a searchlight into a steam kettle. "I never thought I'd be cooking dog food."

Perez poked a stainless-steel shovel into the simmering mixture and extracted some tidbits. Gowdy crushed the vegetables with her fingers and popped the gray mass into her mouth. She chewed, nodded, smiled, and invited the rest of us to try it. Perez ripped open a 50-pound bag of organic rolled oats and shook his head. "It's probably too healthy for me," he said.

If you are what you eat, is it also true that you are what your pet eats? Tim Phillips, the editor of *Petfood Industry* magazine, says that animal owners tend to think so, and even more often they tend to think, This is what I like, so my dog or cat must like the same things. If a cat owner wants takeout, her cat can have takeout, too; if she watches TV while she dines, her cat can have its own TV dinner. Vegetarians offer their animals vegetarian meals, and if you happen to be allergic to beef, perhaps your pet should eat only kibble based on protein from rabbit, venison, or kangaroo. Observant Jewish pet owners may select Evanger's Super Premium Gold Dinners, which have been certified kosher by the Chicago Rabbinical Council. The dogs and cats of athletes crunch energy bars. "It's a quasi religion," Phillips says.

The installation of plastic plumbing into a living hound did not seem much like spoiling.

Whether religion, science, or business, pet food is booming. Today about a third of the animal-science graduate students studying at the University of Illinois with George Fahey and other professors devote themselves to nutrition, and according to Fahey the industry brims with job opportunities for them. "It's as good a time as ever in the 30 years I've been doing this," he told me.

As we neared the end of Fahey's tour of the laboratories at Urbana-Champaign, I wasn't exactly eager to see the animals in the basement that had been mutilated for the sake of science—however much their surgically attached plugs may have contributed to the research Fahey and his colleagues had published on the digestibility of beet pulp and citrus pulp, potato starch, and wood cellulose. But there seemed to be little choice. "Let's go out and see the dogs," he said.

When we came to the Authorized Access sign, the professor swept his electronic pass card over a pad, and the metal door swung open. "This is a very secure building," he said. Accompanied by one of his lab technicians, we passed a set of bright red cattle gates, then continued down a long corridor of pink portals, behind which resided colonies of rats, rabbits, hens, swine, and cats. We passed a disease quarantine room and a chamber marked Surgery.

Fahey stopped at a green door. Another swipe of the pass card and we stood before seven immaculate kennels, each of which held a short-haired, mixed-breed hound. From the side of each hound emerged a clear, plastic spout.

"Hello, girls," Fahey said. They looked at him with calm, bright eyes and wagged their tails.

Wiggles came up to us and sniffed my fingers. She had a wet nose and sleek white fur. Above her black-barred kennel hung a plastic clipboard marked with a number, courtesy of the U.S.D.A. "We get inspected," Fahey said.

Wiggles's sign read:

USDA #348643

Canine, Hound Mix, Female DOB 8/25/00

Received 8/28/01 Butler Farms

Dr. Fahey Protocol 06222

Protocol 06222 turned out to be a test of something called an oligosaccharide. Fahey would not reveal the precise origin and nature of this particular carbohydrate, but given his record it was possible to imagine that the mystery molecule might one day turn up in Iams dog food, or perhaps your seven-grain bread.

We inspected Wiggles's cage, then the cages of Bo, Teeny, Dutchess, Flick, Shai, and Todd. Every floor sparkled, every stainless-steel feed bowl shone. The hounds were gentle and sociable, Fahey said, "ideal animals to work with."

The dogs appeared content within their temperature-controlled environment, where the lights go on at 6 every morning and off at 8 every evening, where regulated supplies of air enter and exit the ventilation system, where they can play with their toys and listen to AM radio all day. Fahey said that the kennels exceeded federal guidelines for size and that the lab assistants took the dogs outside twice a week to exercise, romp, and catch some rays. "If you had this much money spent on you, you'd be happy, too," he said.

"They're spoiled brats," the lab technician said.

Of course, the installation of plastic plumbing into a living hound did not seem much like spoiling. And in fact there was another way—a more precise way—to determine how much energy a dog or a cat had acquired from its food. Unfortunately, it turned out to be a research method called "total carcass analysis," which, as the name implies, required the animal to be dead. "You need to have a darned good reason to do a terminal case," Fahey said to me earlier. "It's too expensive." And it is not for the squeamish. "It's a helluva job," he said. "You have to grind, you have to sieve, you have to grind again. It's a good technique, but it's very labor-intensive." I cringed.

Now Fahey pointed to the spout sticking out of Wiggles's side. "There," he said. "You see the cannula."

The plugs did not seem to irritate the dogs. "If it is put in correctly, it becomes part of them," he said. "It heals very nicely, and becomes a part of their anatomy." The ports must be opened and inspected at least once a week and flushed at least once a month, and when Fahey or his colleagues collect samples they simply unplug a stopper, attach a plastic bag, and let the dogs run around, which pushes out the digesta.

As Fahey described the lab's procedures, the room grew quiet, and by the end of his monologue the dogs sat in total silence, their eyes plaintive. Clearly, they were begging, but begging for what? Perhaps they expected to be fed. Perhaps they longed for an end to their captivity. Fahey grinned and said nothing, but the moment we left the room and shut the green metal door, it sounded as if some evil doctor had begun to torture the poor animals. They howled and blubbered and brayed and whined, and their pathetic ululations followed us as we traced our way back down the yellow cinder-block hallway, past the cattle gates, through the final door, and out to the light of a hot Midwestern afternoon.

"What made them so upset?" I asked.

"They thought you were going to take them out to play," Fahey said. "Look what you did."

DISCUSSION

1. "The increasing specialization of the pet-food industry today," Kaufman declares, "may well reflect not just our desire to keep our pets healthy but also our continuing urge to shape them in our own image." What do you think he means by that? Do you agree? Is there a widespread tendency in our culture to treat pets as mirrors of our self-image? Can you think of an example that either confirms or challenges this view?

2. Can you think of a particular product that gets marketed in the ways Kaufman describes? How does this marketing strategy define the proper or normal relationship between pets and owners? Does it describe the relationship you have with pets?

3. When it comes to nutrition, should there be differences in the standards we apply to animals and those we apply to ourselves? Does it seem more or less "normal" to think of our eating practices and nutritional needs as similar or different?

WRITING

4. Kaufman writes, "For all the apparent variety — store shelves stocked with everything from Alpo to ZiwiPeak — pet food is a business of behemoths and bottom lines, with sales approaching $15 billion last year." How do you understand this statistic? What does the proliferation of these various brands tell us about the place that pets occupy in our lives? What, in your view, are the dominant scripts that teach us how to think about and interact with the pets in our lives? And do these scripts seem sensible to you?

5. Here's how Kaufman summarizes the prevailing attitude toward pets and food: "If a cat owner wants takeout, her cat can have takeout, too; if she watches TV while she dines, her cat can have its own TV dinner. Vegetarians offer their animals vegetarian meals, and if you happen to be allergic to beef, perhaps your pet should eat only kibble based on protein from rabbit, venison, or kangaroo. Observant Jewish pet owners may select Evanger's Super Premium Gold Dinners, which have been certified kosher by the Chicago Rabbinical Council. The dogs and cats of athletes crunch energy bars." In an essay, identify and evaluate the assumptions or norms that underlie this form of behavior. What do we learn about peoples' attitudes toward their pets, their attitudes toward themselves, by looking at this approach to eating?

6. Makenna Goodman's essay (p. 246) maps the outlines of a very different relationship between humans and animals. How does her discussion of killing what you eat compare to Kaufman's profile of pet food research and pet food marketing? To what extent do these essays give us different models for understanding human/animal interaction? What similarities or parallels do you see between them?

Scenes and Un-Scenes: *Giving Thanks*

Thanksgiving stands out as one of our few genuinely American holidays. Its rituals are rooted in American myth, one that is separate from religious doctrine. Regardless of who we are, where we come from, or what we do, virtually all Americans celebrate this holiday in one way or another. Of course, what makes things tricky is the fact that we don't all share a single view of how this meal should go or what it means. We may all be familiar with the classic Thanksgiving stereotype (the harmonious and homogeneous nuclear family gathered around the well-stocked dinner table), but this doesn't mean our own holiday experiences conform to this standard. It is precisely this question of difference, in fact, that the portraits assembled here highlight. Representing Thanksgiving dinner from a range of vantage points, the following images underscore various ways Americans observe and think about this national holiday. In each case, we can pose two related sets of questions. First, what vision of the typical holiday meal does it present? What typical ways of eating? What typical American family? What typical American values? And second, how does this depiction serve to either challenge or reinforce those traditional ideals this meal is supposed to symbolize?

▶▶ *Painted at the height of World War II, Norman Rockwell's* Freedom from Want *remains arguably the most well-known and influential depiction of Thanksgiving dinner ever created. For decades, its old-fashioned, homespun portrait has succeeded in setting the boundaries around how we are supposed to think about this particular holiday. Connecting this meal to one of the nation's core freedoms, it has encouraged countless Americans over the years to regard Thanksgiving as a celebration of the values (such as comfort, security, and abundance) universally available to all Americans. Given how this picture defines the typical American family and the typical American meal, however, do these values seem as universal as they are intended?*

▼ *Created over a half century later, John Currin's* Thanksgiving
▼ *rewrites Rockwell's portrait in dramatic ways. Replacing* Freedom's
*vision of comfort and plenitude with a darker and more anxiety-ridden
image of thwarted desire and unfulfilled appetite, Currin makes this
holiday meal into an occasion for critiquing our long-standing emphasis
on excessive consumption. As one reviewer puts it, "We've come a long
way from Norman Rockwell."*

For artists of color, the effort to revise the Rockwell Thanksgiving vision has frequently revolved around challenging its assumptions about who gets to count as a typical American — a definition that treats being white as an unexamined given. Seeking to enlarge the boundaries of this definition, John Holyfield's Blessing II does more than merely recapitulate the basic terms of the Thanksgiving myth; it also subtly alters them. What sort of messages (about comfort and security, about family and tradition) would you say this image conveys? And to what extent do they either resemble or rework the messages discernible in the Rockwell portrait?

The stereotypical Thanksgiving scene is so familiar to most Americans that it has become shorthand for visual artists seeking to comment on current events. This cartoon by Oliphant adopts the traditional Thanksgiving scene in order to make a satirical point about paranoia surrounding recent news reports about possible bird flu outbreaks in the United States.

⋀ *Not every modern portrayal of Thanksgiving, of course, adopts such an ironic,*
⋀ *skeptical, or dismissive perspective. It could be argued, for example, that this*
image from the 1990s sitcom Friends presents us with simply an updated version
of the same ideals promoted by Rockwell. What do you think of this proposition?
Does this portrait define the typical American family in the same ways? The typical
American meal?

▶▶ *Many of these old-fashioned*
Thanksgiving ideals have proved so
enduring, in fact, that they have become
woven into the fabric of our political life as
well. No politician these days passes up an
opportunity to be pictured celebrating this
holiday meal with one or another group of
"regular" Americans — a ritual designed to
promote the same vision of America that we
see in Norman Rockwell's painting. How
well would you say this photo-op does this?
Does it offer a similarly convincing portrait
of community?

DISCUSSION

1. Which of these portraits most closely resembles your typical Thanksgiving experience? Which least resembles your experience? Why?

2. What does each of these images define its portrait of Thanksgiving against? In your view, which of these visions (ideal or anti-ideal) strikes you as more legitimate? How so?

3. As these pictures make clear, our eating attitudes and habits can serve as a revealing metaphor for the other kinds of things we think and care about. Based on the preceding portfolio, which cultural issues and debates would you say eating gets connected to most often in our culture?

WRITING

4. First, focus on how eating is being represented in one of the images you've just reviewed. What stands out? What seems most important or noteworthy? And what, by contrast, seems noticeably absent? Then, analyze the ways you think this image uses its dining portrait to define the typical or ideal American family. What behaviors and attitudes does it seem to present as normal? And what values, beliefs, or ideas does this portrait seem to endorse as right?

5. Taken together, the images assembled here make clear what boundaries exist around how we are and are not allowed to think about eating. On the basis of what this portfolio includes, where do these boundaries seem to get drawn? Write an essay in which you speculate about the kinds of activities, attitudes, assumptions, and values that this collection of images implies lies outside the norm. Make sure you argue either in favor of or against drawing the boundary in these particular ways, using details from these images and your own experience to reinforce your point of view.

6. Choose one of the preceding examples. How does its depiction of the typical meal compare to the eating practices by Jason Fagone (p. 219) or Caroline Knapp (p. 232)? In a page, evaluate how the norms promoted by this image compare to those profiled in one of these two essays. What similarities? What differences? To what extent do you think either Fagone or Knapp would subscribe to or choose to emulate them? Why or why not?

Putting It into Practice: *Consumer Profiling*

Now that you've read the chapter selections, try applying your conclusions to your own life by completing the following exercises.

FOOD JOURNAL For one week, keep a written account of all your meals, including what you eat, what time you ate, where you ate, how healthy you believed your meal was, and how much it cost. At the end of the week, write a brief essay in which you reflect on the reasons or motives behind *why* you made these particular choices. Identify and evaluate the different scripts, rules, and norms you think may have played a part in your eating habits. How many of your choices were simply prompted by cravings and how many by nutritional concerns? How much did your physical appearance influence your choices? How much was determined by non-food-related factors (such as your time schedule or financial budget)? Do any of your decisions line up with the topics discussed by the authors in this chapter? How?

LOCAL CUISINES, LOCAL CULTURES In her essay, Tara Lohan (p. 250) references a growing concern in the culture with eating locally. Indeed, as you have seen, what and how we eat are greatly influenced by the cultures in which we're raised. Pick a region of the world that you are unfamiliar with and research its eating customs: what foods are most popular, how they are eaten, the settings in which meals take place, and the significance of food within the larger culture (for example, in religious rituals or festivals). Pick one dish of particular significance from that culture and make a list the ways it parallels a familiar American dish. Write a brief essay in which you discuss how learning about the foods of another culture has shed light on the way you view eating as a cultural exercise in your own culture. Be sure to cite your research in your discussion.

WHOLESALE MESSAGES For this exercise, find some examples of the ways that food and eating are advertised: how restaurants, food brands, or diet gurus try to sell you on their products and the experiences of consuming them as positive ones. What elements of these products seem to have the most weight in terms of marketing? Taste? Fitness? Fun? Family? Write an essay in which you discuss which key elements seem to occur most often. Why do you think that is? Do you feel like food and eating are sold as part of a larger package? That is, when you are being sold the idea of eating, what other norms are you also buying, according to these advertisers?

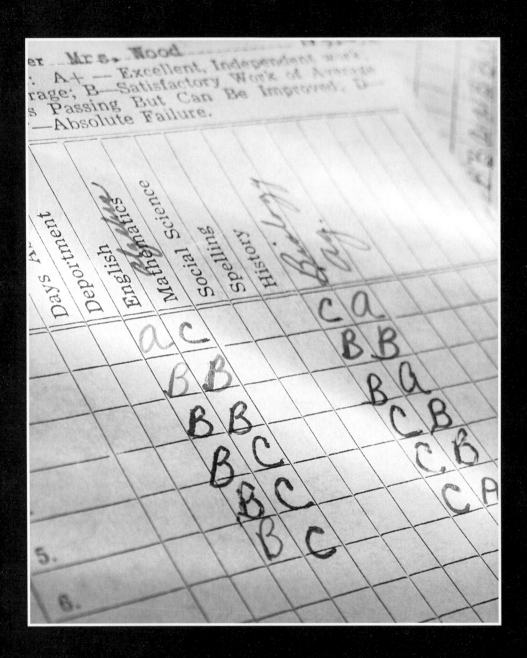

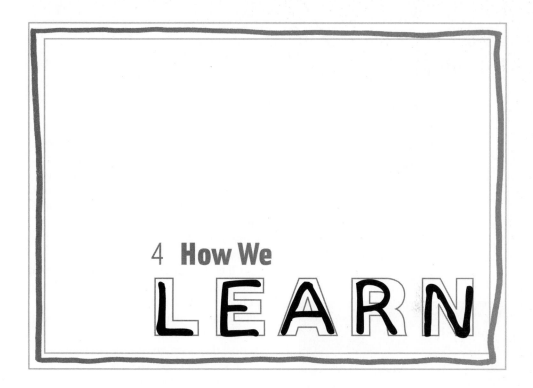

4 **How We**

LEARN

Introduction

SCHOOL RULES

If you were to create your own school, what would it look like? What kinds of courses would get taught? What kind of work would get assigned, and how would it be evaluated? What sorts of activities and routines would organize daily classroom life? What roles would you script for teachers and students? As you consider all this, think too about what such a school would *not* look like: what sorts of lessons would never get taught, what rules would never get written, what kinds of teachers and students you would never see. After you've considered these questions, ask yourself a final one: How much of your experience at school has ever measured up to this ideal?

Everybody Knows That...

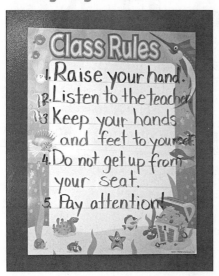

— *Detroit, Michigan, rules posted on a classroom door at Guyton Elementary School, part of the Detroit public school system*

It is difficult to think of an environment in contemporary life more rule-bound than school. If you doubt the validity of this claim, take a moment to compile a mental list of all regulations by which a typical school day is organized. We all know firsthand that once we walk into the classroom, precious few activities are really up for debate. In ways that are perhaps a bit more explicit than elsewhere, school is a world defined by very firm boundaries and governed by very clear requirements. Rules tell us what kinds of homework we have to complete and what kinds of tests we have to take, decree which courses are mandatory and which ones are optional, mandate the number of hours per week and the number of weeks per semester we need to spend at school. In some cases, in fact, rules even set standards for what we can wear or how we can talk. Underlying and justifying these many regulations is one final expectation: that we look on the rigid organization of school life as something both indispensable and nonnegotiable, an essential component of a quality education. Without things like homework and pop quizzes, standardized testing and attendance policies, graduation requirements and semester schedules, P.E. and recess, we are supposed to believe, real learning simply wouldn't happen.

But what exactly is *real* learning? And who should be given the authority to decide this? Do all the expectations and instructions we are called on to follow at school really turn us into better educated people? While school is one of the few genuine touchstones in our lives — one of only a handful of institutions with which we all have had some degree of personal experience — it remains one of the most problematic as well. Because so many of the day-to-day decisions are taken out of our hands, it doesn't always feel as if the education we spend so many years pursuing actually belongs to us. We may wonder whether there is a logical connection between the tests we take and the grades we receive or between our personal opinions about a poem or short story and the views espoused by a professor in lecture, but given the way school is typically set up, there isn't a whole lot we can do about it. No matter what ideas we have about what rules should and should not govern our school experiences, we also know that subordinating these decisions to somebody else is part of our jobs.

For a particularly vivid illustration, take the example of grading. Grades are absolutely essential, so goes the conventional thinking, because they alone offer educators a reliable and verifiable way of assessing students' work. Without grades, how would we ever know if students were measuring up? But notice the unspoken assumptions that lie beneath this anxious query, most prominently among them the conviction that grades are accurate barometers of student ability and achievement. To believe in the validity and necessity of grading, we also have to believe that the standards on which they rest — the standards that differentiate, say, A work from C work — are grounded in a fair and universally applicable understanding of what good work involves. Nor do the assumptions stop here. We could easily probe the implications of this grading norm even further,

Everybody Knows That...

a. The Honor Code is an undertaking of the students, individually and collectively:

1. that they will not give or receive aid in examinations; that they will not give or receive unpermitted aid in class work, in the preparation of reports, or in any other work that is to be used by the instructor as the basis of grading;

2. that they will do their share and take an active part in seeing to it that others as well as themselves uphold the spirit and letter of the Honor Code.

— From the Stanford University Honor Code

Everybody Knows That...

"I recognize the great work that some of our urban districts are doing, in fact I cited them in my remarks today. They are blazing the trail, they're the folks that are not in denial; they are working hard to close the achievement gap and are seeing some of the best progress.

But I would say that no small part of that is due to No Child Left Behind, to this annual measurement, to paying attention to every child, every year, and to prescribing a cure, an instructional cure if you will, so that we can get kids on grade level by 2013–14, as the law requires."

— Secretary of Education Margaret Spellings on The NewsHour with Jim Lehrer, PBS, April 7, 2005

posing questions about the ultimate wisdom of any system that so conspicu-ously emphasizes competition and rank. Does an arrangement that compels students to focus so much attention on the external markers of achievement really offer the best way to encourage meaningful learning? This question might well lead us to rethink the kinds of authority that typically get vested in teachers: the authority not only to grade student work, but also to evaluate, assess, and judge more generally. Posing these kinds of questions not only challenges some of the rules by which school conventionally operates, but, even more fundamentally, also starts the process of unlearning the core les-sons that have taught us what a worthwhile education is.

In many ways, this unlearning process is already taking place. Educa-tion is one of the most contentiously debated issues of our time. We argue over the merits of public versus private schooling, over the limits of free speech on campus, over the place of religious belief in the classroom, over how to best utilize the educational resources of the Internet. Educational issues anchor our debates about multiculturalism, about economic and social class, about free speech. Whether it involves a court case adjudicating the merits of teaching intelligent design or a state initiative to require school uniforms, a dispute over online university accreditation or protests regarding a col-lege's financial ties to companies that exploit their workers, school-related issues and controversies remain at the very center of our national life. So engrossing and encom-passing a topic has education become that we could easily extend the scope of this investigation well beyond the walls of the classroom. The other chapters in this book help illustrate the argument that our larger culture itself is a classroom in which we are all pupils.

Everybody Knows That...

"This textbook contains material on evolution. Evolution is a theory, not a fact, regarding the origin of living things. This material should be approached with an open mind, studied carefully, and critically considered."

Approved by
Cobb County Board of Education
Thursday, March 28, 2002

— *Sticker added to Cobb County, Georgia, science textbooks*

Taken together, the readings assembled in this chapter provide some sense of how richly diverse and broadly encompassing the issue of educa-tion is. Mike Rose argues passionately about the assumptions we make about a link between education and intellect. Several writers examine some discrete aspect of our contemporary schooling practices. Alfie Kohn, for example, calls into question the conventional wisdom regarding grades and grading. Colin Bisset offers a defense of boredom, explaining what we have to learn from boredom and why we should consider embracing it. From a scientific angle, Nicholas Wade's report on new research into natural selec-tion raises a lot of questions about whether our ability to shape our world has also shaped our evolution. Whereas Kohn criticizes specific aspects of formal schooling, former teacher John Taylor Gatto argues that we ought to dismantle the entire system. In a personal comment on the educational system, bell hooks recounts her experiences navigating the educational and the social boundaries she encountered as a working-class student of color. Looking at the role of technology in education, reporter Brigid Schulte writes an eye-opening account of plagiarism that surveys the online resources students so often use these days and how drastically this material has altered the ways students think about and define cheating. Jonathan Kozol's essay catalogs the insidious ways that business language and business logic has come to underlie much of what happens in our elementary classrooms.

"EVERYBODY KNOWS THAT" EXERCISE

Choose one of the images or quotations featured in the margins on the preceding pages and answer the following questions:

1. What does this image or quotation ask you to believe?

2. What are the particular ideas, values, or attitudes it invites us to accept as *normal*?

3. What would it feel like to act on or act out these norms in our personal lives?

Rule **Maker** >>>>>>>>>>> Rule **Breaker**

❝❞ *The United States increasingly needs what the best of higher education has to offer:* graduates who contribute positively to economic development through increased private and public revenues, greater productivity, increased consumption, more workforce flexibility, and decreased reliance on government financial support.... 'What do students really learn?' and 'What's the value-added?' are questions increasingly being asked across America."

— CHARLES MILLER AND CHERYL OLDHAM, THE SECRETARY OF EDUCATION'S COMMISSION ON THE FUTURE OF HIGHER EDUCATION, 2005

❝❞ *Is this, really, what it all comes down to? Is future productivity, from this point on, to be the primary purpose of the education we provide our children? Is this to be the way in which we decide if teachers are complying with their obligations to their students and society?... [T]here must be something more to life as it is lived by six-year-olds or ten-year-olds, or by teenagers for that matter, than concerns about 'successful global competition.'"*

— JONATHAN KOZOL, EDUCATION WRITER AND ACTIVIST, 2005

Miami, Florida, Little Haiti Edison Park Elementary School Career Day student uniforms

THE U.S. DEPARTMENT OF EDUCATION VS. JONATHAN KOZOL

When it comes to something as fundamental as education, it would be reassuring if there were a consensus on exactly what our national priorities and objectives should be. Unfortunately, though, this is far from the case. Over the last several years, in fact, the public discussion of this question has increasingly pitted two antithetical educational models against each other. The quotation from the Secretary of Education's Commission on the Future of Higher Education articulates the first model: The goal of schooling is to prepare students to become productive workers and contributors to America's market-driven economy. Jonathan Kozol sums up the second model: The goal of education is to make students into critical thinkers, to foster a familiarity with a diverse range of viewpoints, and to instill an appreciation for how varied and complex the world around us truly is. While terms such as *critical thinking* and *intellectual inquiry* loom large for defenders of the liberal arts ideal, the most prominent catchwords in the market-based lexicon include *productivity, workforce preparedness*, and *efficiency.* Within these competing vocabularies, we can get a fairly clear sense of the ways each side defines what education is as well as what it is for. Envisioning school as a kind of preprofessional training ground, the first model defines education as an economic resource, a set of discrete skills whose value is measured in terms of usefulness in the marketplace. Casting school as the setting for disinterested inquiry, the liberal arts model defines the nature and value of learning intrinsically, independent of any vocational purpose to which it might be put. What does it mean to be truly educated? How do we define legitimate or valuable knowledge? What are the rules by which our competence and skills, our abilities and intelligence, should really be measured?

FIND THE RULES: Write a brief essay in which you list all the ways you normally hear education described — in the news, in your classes, in your personal relationships with friends and families. Which of the two models represented by the quotations in this feature do these descriptions seem to align with?

MAKE YOUR OWN RULES: Write an essay in which you argue in favor of one of the characterizations of education featured here. Is there any way to reconcile these points of view so that a definition of education can encompass both models? How is that possible?

ALFIE KOHN

From Degrading to De-grading

Are grades really necessary? Do they truly offer us an accurate, meaningful measure of student ability or achievement? Couldn't we have a quality education without them? Answering this final question with an emphatic "yes!," Alfie Kohn makes the case that grades are not only irrelevant but actually antithetical to learning. Kohn has published eleven books on education and parenting, including *No Contest: The Case against Competition* (1986), *Unconditional Parenting: Moving from Rewards and Punishments to Love and Reason* (2005), and, most recently, *The Homework Myth: Why Our Kids Get Too Much of a Bad Thing* (2006). His articles have appeared in *Phi Delta Kappan*, the *Journal of Education*, the *Nation*, and the *Harvard Business Review*. As a public speaker he has lectured school groups and corporations against competition in education. He has also appeared on the *Today* show and *The Oprah Winfrey Show*. The essay that follows was originally published in *High School Magazine*.

YOU CAN TELL A LOT ABOUT A TEACHER'S VALUES AND PERSONALITY just by asking how he or she feels about giving grades. Some defend the practice, claiming that grades are necessary to "motivate" students. Many of these teachers actually seem to enjoy keeping intricate records of students' marks. Such teachers periodically warn students that they're "going to have to know this for the test" as a way of compelling them to pay attention or do the assigned readings—and they may even use surprise quizzes for that purpose, keeping their grade books at the ready.

Frankly, we ought to be worried for these teachers' students. In my experience, the most impressive teachers are those who despise the whole process of giving grades. Their aversion, as it turns out, is supported by solid evidence that raises questions about the very idea of traditional grading.

THREE MAIN EFFECTS OF GRADING

Researchers have found three consistent effects of using—and especially, emphasizing the importance of—letter or number grades:

1. **Grades tend to reduce students' interest in the learning itself.** One of the best-researched findings in the field of motivational psychology is that the more people are rewarded for doing something, the more they tend to lose interest in whatever they had to do to get the reward (Kohn 1993). Thus, it shouldn't be surprising that when students are told they'll

need to know something for a test—or, more generally, that something they're about to do will count for a grade—they are likely to come to view that task (or book or idea) as a chore.

While it's not impossible for a student to be concerned about getting high marks and also to like what he or she is doing, the practical reality is that these two ways of thinking generally pull in opposite directions. Some research has explicitly demonstrated that a "grade orientation" and a "learning orientation" are inversely related (Beck, Rorrer-Woody, and Pierce 1991; Milton, Pollio, and Eison 1986). More strikingly, study after study has found that students—from elementary school to graduate school, and across cultures—demonstrate less interest in learning as a result of being graded (Benware and Deci 1984; Butler 1987; Butler and Nisan 1986; Grolnick and Ryan 1987; Harter and Guzman 1986; Hughes, Sullivan, and Mosley 1985; Kage 1991; Salili et al. 1976). Thus, anyone who wants to see students get hooked on words and numbers and ideas already has reason to look for other ways of assessing and describing their achievement.

2. Grades tend to reduce students' preference for challenging tasks. Students of all ages who have been led to concentrate on getting a good grade are likely to pick the easiest possible assignment if given a choice (Harter 1978; Harter and Guzman 1986; Kage 1991; Milton, Pollio, and Eison 1986). The more pressure to get an A, the less inclination to truly challenge oneself. Thus, students who cut corners may not be lazy so much as rational; they are adapting to an environment where good grades, not intellectual exploration, are what count. They might well say to us, "Hey, you told me the point here is to bring up my GPA, to get on the honor roll. Well, I'm not stupid: The easier the assignment the more likely that I can give you what you want. So don't blame me when I try to find the easiest thing to do and end up not learning anything."

3. Grades tend to reduce the quality of students' thinking. Given that students may lose interest in what they're learning as a result of grades, it makes sense that they're also apt to think less deeply. One series of studies, for example, found that students given numerical grades were significantly less creative than those who received qualitative feedback but no grades. The more the task required creative thinking, in fact, the worse the performance of students who knew they were going to be graded. Providing students with comments in addition to a grade didn't help: The highest achievement occurred only when comments were given *instead* of numerical scores (Butler 1987; Butler 1988; Butler and Nisan 1986).

In another experiment, students told they would be graded on how well they learned a social studies lesson had more trouble understanding the main point of the text than did students who were told that no grades would be involved. Even on a measure of rote recall, the graded group remembered fewer facts a week later (Grolnick and Ryan 1987). And students who tended to think about current events in terms of what they'd need to know for a grade were less knowledgeable than their peers, even after taking other variables into account (Anderman and Johnston 1998).

MORE REASONS TO JUST SAY NO TO GRADES

The preceding three results should be enough to cause any conscientious educator to rethink the practice of giving students grades. But there's more.

Grades aren't valid, reliable, or objective. A B in English says nothing about what a student can do, what she understands, where she needs help. Moreover, the basis for that grade is as subjective as the result is uninformative. A teacher can meticulously record scores for one test or assignment after another, eventually calculating averages down to a hundredth of a percentage point, but that doesn't change the arbitrariness of each of these individual marks. Even the score on a math test is largely a reflection of how the test was written: what skills the teacher decided to assess, what kinds of questions happened to be left out, and how many points each section was "worth."

> **A B in English says nothing about what a student can do, what she understands, where she needs help.**

Moreover, research has long been available to confirm what all of us know: Any given assignment may well be given two different grades by two equally qualified teachers. It may even be given two different grades by a single teacher who reads it at two different times (for example, see some of the early research reviewed in Kirschenbaum, Simon, and Napier 1971). In short, what grades offer is spurious precision—a subjective rating masquerading as an objective evaluation.

Grades distort the curriculum. A school's use of letter or number grades may encourage a fact- and skill-based approach to instruction because that sort of learning is easier to score. The tail of assessment thus comes to wag the educational dog.

Grades waste a lot of time that could be spent on learning. Add up all the hours that teachers spend fussing with their grade books. Then factor in the (mostly unpleasant) conversations they have with students and their parents about grades. It's tempting to just roll our eyes when confronted with whining or wheedling, but the real problem rests with the practice of grading itself.

Grades encourage cheating. Again, we can either continue to blame and punish all the students who cheat—or we can look for the structural reasons this keeps happening. Researchers have found that the more students are led to focus on getting good grades, the more likely they are to cheat, even if they themselves regard cheating as wrong (Anderman, Griesinger, and Westerfield 1998; Milton, Pollio, and Eison 1986).

Grades spoil teachers' relationships with students. Consider this lament, which could have been offered by a teacher in your district: "I'm getting tired of running a classroom in which everything we do revolves around grades. I'm tired of being suspicious when students give me compliments, wondering whether or not they are just trying to raise their grade. I'm tired of spending so much time and energy grading your papers, when there are probably a dozen more productive and enjoyable ways for all of us to handle the evaluation of papers. I'm tired of hearing you ask me, 'Does this count?' And, heaven knows, I'm certainly tired of all those little arguments and disagreements we get into concerning marks which take so much fun out of the teaching and the learning . . ."(Kirschenbaum, Simon, and Napier 1971, p. 115).

Grades spoil students' relationships with one another. The quality of students' thinking has been shown to depend partly on the extent to which they are permitted to learn cooperatively (Johnson and Johnson 1989; Kohn 1992). Thus, the ill feelings, suspicion, and resentment generated by grades aren't just disagreeable in their own right; they interfere with learning.

The most destructive form of grading by far is that which is done "on a curve," such that the number of top grades is artificially limited: No matter how well all the students do, not all of them can get an A. Apart from the intrinsic unfairness of this arrangement, its practical effect is to teach students that others are potential obstacles to their own success. The kind of collaboration that can help all students to learn more effectively doesn't stand a chance in such an environment. Sadly, even teachers who don't explicitly grade on a curve may assume, perhaps unconsciously, that the final grades "ought to" come out looking more or less this way: a few very good grades, a few very bad grades, and the majority somewhere in the middle.

The competition that turns schooling into a quest for triumph and ruptures relationships among students doesn't only happen within classrooms, of course. The same effect is witnessed schoolwide when kids are not just rated but ranked, sending the message that the point isn't to learn, or even to perform well, but to defeat others. Some students might be motivated to improve their class rank, but that is completely different from being motivated to understand ideas. (Wise educators realize that it doesn't matter how motivated students are; what matters is *how* students are motivated. It is the type of motivation that counts, not the amount.)

EXCUSES AND DISTRACTIONS

Most of us are directly acquainted with at least some of these disturbing consequences of grades, yet we continue to reduce students to letters or numbers on a regular basis. Perhaps we've become inured to these effects and take them for granted. This is the way it's always been, we assume,

> *It's rather like people who have spent all their lives in a terribly polluted city and have come to assume that this is just the way air looks.*

and the way it has to be. It's rather like people who have spent all their lives in a terribly polluted city and have come to assume that this is just the way air looks—and that it's natural to be coughing all the time.

Oddly, when educators are shown that it doesn't have to be this way, some react with suspicion instead of relief. They want to know why you're making trouble, or they assert that you're exaggerating the negative effects of grades (it's really not so bad—cough, cough), or they dismiss proven alternatives to grading on the grounds that our school could never do what other schools have done.

The practical difficulties of abolishing letter grades are real. But the key question is whether those difficulties are seen as problems to be solved or as excuses for perpetuating the status quo. The logical response to the arguments and data summarized here is to say: "Good heavens! If even half of this is true, then it's imperative we do whatever we can, as soon as we can, to phase out traditional grading." Yet, many people begin and end with the problems of implementation, responding to all this evidence by saying, in effect, "Yeah, yeah, yeah, but we'll never get rid of grades because . . ."

It is also striking how many educators never get beyond relatively insignificant questions, such as how many tests to give, or how often to send home grade reports, or what number corresponds to what letter. Some even reserve their outrage for the possibility that too many students are ending up with good grades, a reaction that suggests stinginess with A's is being confused with intellectual rigor.

COMMON OBJECTIONS

Let's consider the most frequently heard responses to the above arguments — which is to say, the most common objections to getting rid of grades.

First, it is said that students expect to receive grades and even seem addicted to them. This is often true; I've taught high school students who reacted to the absence of grades with what I can only describe as existential vertigo. (*Who am I if not a B+?*) But as more elementary and even some middle schools move to replace grades with more informative (and less destructive) systems of assessment, the damage doesn't begin until students get to high school. Moreover, elementary and middle schools that *haven't* changed their practices often cite the local high school as the reason they must get students used to getting grades regardless of their damaging effects—just as high schools point the finger at colleges.

Even when students arrive in high school already accustomed to grades, already primed to ask teachers, "Do we have to know this?" or "What do I have to do to get an A?", this is a sign that something is very wrong. It's more an indictment of what has happened to them in the past than an argument to keep doing it in the future.

Perhaps because of this training, grades can succeed in getting students to show up on time, hand in their work, and otherwise do what they're told. Many teachers are loath to give up what is essentially an instrument of control. But even to the extent this instrument works (which is not always), we are obliged to reflect on whether mindless compliance is really our goal. The teacher who exclaims, "These kids would blow off my course in a minute if they weren't getting a grade for it!" may be issuing a powerful indictment of his or her course. Who would be more reluctant to give up grades than a teacher who spends the period slapping transparencies on the overhead projector and lecturing endlessly at students about Romantic poets or genetic codes? Without bribes (A's) and threats (F's), students would have no reason to do such assignments. To maintain that this proves something is wrong with the kids—or that grades are simply "necessary"—suggests a willful refusal to examine one's classroom practices and assumptions about teaching and learning.

"If I can't give a child a better reason for studying than a grade on a report card, I ought to lock my desk and go home and stay there." So wrote Dorothy De Zouche, a Missouri teacher, in an article published in February . . . of 1945. But teachers who *can* give a child a better reason for studying don't need grades. Research substantiates this: When the curriculum is engaging—for example, when it involves hands-on, interactive learning activities—students who aren't graded at all perform just as well as those who are graded (Moeller and Reschke 1993).

Another objection: It is sometimes argued that students must be given grades because colleges demand them. One might reply that "high schools have no responsibility to serve colleges by performing the sorting function for them"—particularly if that process undermines learning (Krumboltz and Yeh 1996, p. 325). But in any case the premise of this argument is erroneous: Traditional grades are not mandatory for admission to colleges and universities.

MAKING CHANGE

A friend of mine likes to say that people don't resist change—they resist being changed. Even terrific ideas (like moving a school from a grade orientation to a learning orientation) are guaranteed to self-destruct if they are simply forced down people's throats. The first step for an administrator, therefore, is to open up a conversation—to spend perhaps a full year just encouraging people to think and talk about the effects of (and alternatives to) traditional grades. This can happen in individual classes, as teachers facilitate discussions about how students regard grades, as well as in evening meetings with parents, or on a website—all with the help of relevant books, articles, speakers, videos, and visits to neighboring schools that are further along in this journey.

The actual process of "de-grading" can be done in stages. For example, a high school might start by freeing ninth-grade classes from grades before doing the same for upperclassmen. (Even a school that never gets beyond the first stage will have done a considerable service, giving students one full year when they can think about what they're learning instead of their GPAs.)

Another route to gradual change is to begin by eliminating only the most pernicious practices, such as grading on a curve or ranking students. Although grades, per se, may continue for a while, at least the message will be sent from the beginning that all students can do well, and that the point is to succeed rather than to beat others.

Anyone who has heard the term *authentic assessment* knows that abolishing grades doesn't mean eliminating the process of gathering information about student performance—and communicating that information to students and parents. Rather, abolishing grades opens up possibilities that are far more meaningful and constructive. These include narratives (written comments), portfolios (carefully chosen collections of students' writings and projects that demonstrate their interests, achievements, and improvement over time), student-led parent-teacher conferences, exhibitions, and other opportunities for students to show what they can do.

Of course, it's harder for a teacher to do these kinds of assessments if he or she has 150 or more students and sees each of them for forty-five to fifty-five minutes a day. But that's not an argument for continuing to use traditional grades; it's an argument for challenging these archaic remnants of a factory-oriented approach to instruction, structural aspects of high schools that are bad news for reasons that go well beyond the issue of assessment. It's an argument for looking into block scheduling, team teaching, interdisciplinary courses—and learning more about schools that have arranged things so each teacher can spend more time with fewer students (e.g., Meier 1995).

> **The real problem is that almost all kids . . . will come to focus on grades and, as a result, their learning will be hurt.**

Administrators should be prepared to respond to parental concerns, some of them completely reasonable, about the prospect of edging away from grades. "Don't you value excellence?" You bet—and here's the evidence that traditional grading *undermines* excellence. "Are you just trying to spare the self-esteem of students who do poorly?" We are concerned that grades may be making things worse for such students, yes, but the problem isn't just that some kids won't get A's and will have their feelings hurt. The real problem is that almost all kids (including yours) will come to focus on grades and, as a result, their learning will be hurt.

If parents worry that grades are the only window they have into the school, we need to assure them that alternative assessments provide a far better view. But if parents don't seem to care about getting the most useful information or helping their children become more excited learners—if they demand grades for the purpose of documenting how much better their kids are than everyone else's—then we need to engage them in a discussion about whether this is a legitimate goal, and whether schools exist for the purpose of competitive credentialing or for the purpose of helping everyone to learn (Kohn 1998; Labaree 1997). Above all, we need to make sure that objections and concerns about the details don't obscure the main message, which is the demonstrated harm of traditional grading on the quality of students' learning and their interest in exploring ideas.

High school administrators can do a world of good in their districts by actively supporting efforts to eliminate conventional grading in elementary and middle schools. Working with their colleagues in these schools can help pave the way for making such changes at the secondary school level.

IN THE MEANTIME

Finally, there is the question of what classroom teachers can do while grades continue to be required. The short answer is that they should do everything within their power to make grades as invisible as possible for as long as possible. Helping students forget about grades is the single best piece of advice for those who want to create a learning-oriented classroom.

When I was teaching high school, I did a lot of things I now regret. But one policy that still seems sensible to me was saying to students on the first day of class that, while I was compelled to give them a grade at the end of the term, I could not in good conscience ever put a letter or number on anything they did during the term—and I would not do so. I would, however, write a comment—or, better, sit down and talk with them—as often as possible to give them feedback.

At this particular school I frequently faced students who had been prepared for admission to Harvard since their early childhood—a process I have come to call "Preparation H." I knew that my refusal to rate their learning might cause some students to worry about their marks all the more, or to create suspense about what would appear on their final grade reports, which of course would defeat the whole purpose. So I said that anyone who absolutely had to know what grade a given paper would get could come see me and we would figure it out together. An amazing thing happened: As the days went by, fewer and fewer students felt the need to ask me about grades. They began to be more involved with what we were learning, because I had taken responsibility as a teacher to stop pushing grades into their faces, so to speak, whenever they completed an assignment.

What I didn't do very well, however, was to get students involved in devising the criteria for excellence (what makes a math solution elegant, an experiment well designed, an essay persuasive, a story compelling) or in deciding how well their projects met those criteria. I'm afraid I unilaterally set the criteria and evaluated the students' efforts. But I have seen teachers who were more willing to give up control, more committed to helping students participate in assessment and turn that into part of the learning. Teachers who work with their students to design powerful alternatives to letter grades have a replacement ready to go when the school finally abandons traditional grading—and are able to minimize the harm of such grading in the meantime.

ADDENDUM: MUST CONCERNS ABOUT COLLEGE DERAIL HIGH SCHOOL LEARNING?

Here is the good news: College admissions practices are not as rigid and reactionary as many people think. Here is the better news: Even when that process doesn't seem to have its priorities straight, high schools don't have to be dragged down to that level.

Sometimes it is assumed that admissions officers at the best universities are eighty-year-old fuddy-duddies peering over their spectacles and muttering about "highly irregular" applications. In truth, the people charged with making these decisions are often just a few years out of college themselves, and after making their way through a pile of interchangeable applications from 3.8-GPA, student-council-vice-president, musically accomplished hopefuls from high-powered traditional suburban high schools, they are desperate for something unconventional. Given that the most selective colleges have been known to accept homeschooled children who have never set foot in a classroom, secondary schools have more latitude than they sometimes assume. It is not widely known, for example, that hundreds of colleges and universities don't require applicants to take either the SAT or the ACT.

Admittedly, large state universities are more resistant to unconventional applications than are small private colleges simply because of economics: It takes more time, and therefore more money, for admissions officers to read meaningful application materials than it does for them to glance at a GPA or an SAT score and plug it into a formula. But I have heard of high schools approaching the admissions directors of nearby universities and saying, in effect, "We'd like to improve our school by getting rid of grades. Here's why. Will you work with us to make sure our seniors aren't penalized?" This strategy may well be successful for the simple reason that not many high schools are requesting this at present and the added inconvenience for admissions offices is likely to be negligible. Of course, if more and more high schools abandon traditional grades, then the universities will have no choice but to adapt. This is a change that high schools will have to initiate rather than waiting for colleges to signal their readiness.

> *It takes more time ... for admissions officers to read meaningful application materials than it does for them to glance at a GPA or an SAT score.*

At the moment, plenty of admissions officers enjoy the convenience of class ranking, apparently because they have confused being better than one's peers with being good at something; they're looking for winners rather than learners. But relatively few colleges actually insist on this practice. When a 1993 survey by the National Association of Secondary School Principals asked eleven hundred admissions officers what would happen if a high school stopped computing class rank, only 0.5 percent said the school's applicants would not be considered for admission, 4.5 percent said it would be a "great handicap," and 14.4 percent said it would be a "handicap" (Levy and Riordan 1994). In other words, it appears that the absence of class ranks would not interfere at all with students' prospects for admission to four out of five colleges.

Even more impressive, some high schools not only refuse to rank their students but refuse to give any sort of letter or number grades. Courses are all taken pass/fail, sometimes with narrative assessments of the students' performance that become part of a college application. I have spoken to representatives and all assure me that, year after year, their graduates are accepted into large state universities and small, highly selective colleges. *Even the complete absence of high school grades is not a barrier to college admission*, so we don't have that excuse for continuing to subject students to the harm done by traditional grading.

REFERENCES

Anderman, E. M., T. Griesinger, and G. Westerfield. 1998. "Motivation and Cheating During Early Adolescence." *Journal of Educational Psychology* 90: 84–93.

Anderman, E. M., and J. Johnston. 1998. "Television News in the Classroom: What Are Adolescents Learning?" *Journal of Adolescent Research* 13: 73–100.

Beck, H. P., S. Rorrer-Woody, and L. G. Pierce. 1991. "The Relations of Learning and Grade Orientations to Academic Performance." *Teaching of Psychology* 18: 35–37.

Benware, C. A., and E. L. Deci. 1984. "Quality of Learning With an Active Versus Passive Motivational Set." *American Educational Research Journal* 21: 755–65.

Butler, R. 1987. "Task-Involving and Ego-Involving Properties of Evaluation: Effects of Different Feedback Conditions on Motivational Perceptions, Interest, and Performance." *Journal of Educational Psychology* 79: 474–82.

Butler, R. 1988. "Enhancing and Undermining Intrinsic Motivation: The Effects of Task-Involving and Ego-Involving Evaluation on Interest and Performance." *British Journal of Educational Psychology* 58: 1–14.

Butler, R., and M. Nisan. 1986. "Effects of No Feedback, Task-Related Comments, and Grades on Intrinsic Motivation and Performance." *Journal of Educational Psychology* 78: 210–16.

De Zouche, D. 1945. "'The Wound Is Mortal': Marks, Honors, Unsound Activities." *The Clearing House* 19: 339–44.

Grolnick, W. S., and R. M. Ryan. 1987. "Autonomy in Children's Learning: An Experimental and Individual Difference Investigation." *Journal of Personality and Social Psychology* 52: 890–98.

Harter, S. 1978. "Pleasure Derived from Challenge and the Effects of Receiving Grades on Children's Difficulty Level Choices." *Child Development* 49: 788–99.

Harter, S., and M. E. Guzman. 1986. "The Effect of Perceived Cognitive Competence and Anxiety on Children's Problem-Solving Performance, Difficulty Level Choices, and Preference for Challenge." Unpublished manuscript, University of Denver.

Hughes, B., H. J. Sullivan, and M. L. Mosley. 1985. "External Evaluation, Task Difficulty, and Continuing Motivation." *Journal of Educational Research* 78: 210–15.

Johnson, D. W., and R. T. Johnson. 1989. *Cooperation and Competition: Theory and Research.* Edina, Minn.: Interaction Book Co.

Kage, M. 1991. "The Effects of Evaluation on Intrinsic Motivation." Paper presented at the meeting of the Japan Association of Educational Psychology, Joetsu, Japan.

Kirschenbaum, H., S. B. Simon, and R. W. Napier. 1971. *Wad-Ja-Get?: The Grading Game in American Education.* New York: Hart.

Kohn, A. 1992. *No Contest: The Case Against Competition.* Rev. ed. Boston: Houghton Mifflin.

Kohn, A. 1993. *Punished by Rewards: The Trouble with Gold Stars, Incentive Plans, A's, Praise, and Other Bribes.* Boston: Houghton Mifflin.

Kohn, A. 1998. "Only for My Kid: How Privileged Parents Undermine School Reform." *Phi Delta Kappan,* April: 569–77.

Krumboltz, J. D., and C. J. Yeh. 1996. "Competitive Grading Sabotages Good Teaching." *Phi Delta Kappan,* December: 324–26.

Labaree, D. F. 1997. *How to Succeed in School Without Really Learning: The Credentials Race in American Education.* New Haven, Conn.: Yale University Press.

Levy, J., and P. Riordan. 1994. *Rank-in-Class, Grade Point Average, and College Admission.* Reston, Va.: NASSP. (Available as ERIC Document 370988.)

Meier, D. 1995. *The Power of Their Ideas: Lessons for America from a Small School in Harlem.* Boston: Beacon.

Milton, O., H. R. Pollio, and J. A. Eison. 1986. *Making Sense of College Grades.* San Francisco: Jossey-Bass.

Moeller, A. J., and C. Reschke. 1993. "A Second Look at Grading and Classroom Performance: Report of a Research Study." *Modern Language Journal* 77: 163–69.

Salili, F., M. L. Maehr, R. L. Sorensen, and L. J. Fyans Jr. 1976. "A Further Consideration of the Effects of Evaluation on Motivation." *American Educational Research Journal* 13: 85–102.

DISCUSSION

1. Kohn has some pointed things to say about the connection that is often presumed to exist between traditional grading and student motivation. More specifically, he questions the long-standing educational norm that says students who do not receive grades have no incentive to work. What do you think of this claim? Is it valid? How does your own view compare to Kohn's?

2. Kohn's critique of conventional grading practices rests in part on his assertion that, no matter how minutely calculated, every letter or number grade is a subjective and arbitrary assessment. Do you agree? Can you think of an example from your own school experiences that either confirms or confounds this argument?

3. "Perhaps," Kohn speculates, "we've become inured to [the] effects [of grades] and take them for granted. This is the way it's always been, we assume, and the way it has to be. It's rather like people who have spent all their lives in a terribly polluted city and have come to assume that this is just the way air looks — and that it's natural to be coughing all the time." What do you make of this analogy? To what extent does it seem valid to think of our contemporary approach to grading as a kind of pollution? Does this analogy capture any aspect of your own educational experiences?

WRITING

4. Write a personal essay in which you either support or refute Kohn's argument about grading using anecdotes from your experience as a student. Do you view grading in a negative or positive light? Why or why not? Make sure to structure your argument by addressing Kohn's multiple points directly.

5. Kohn writes about the need to move a school "from a grade orientation to a learning orientation." What do you think he means by labeling the shift this way? How, according to Kohn, does grading make it harder to focus on learning? Write an essay in which you discuss what the characteristics of these two orientations are. Do you think it's possible to have an educational system that emphasizes both?

6. Write an essay in which you discuss how Kohn might use Brigid Schulte's "The Case of the Purloined Paper" (p. 325) as evidence for his argument against grading. How do you think Kohn would argue that non-grade-based assignments would help solve the problem of plagiarism?

Then and Now: *Encyclopedic Knowledge*

For generations, the classic multivolume encyclopedia has epitomized what it means to be an educated person. Studded with dense descriptions and overviews of countless subjects — from astronomy to anatomy, geography to world history — these leather-bound tomes have long stood as vivid and material symbols of what we consider legitimate knowledge. Supporting

these compendia of information were a number of unspoken assumptions: not only about the things we were expected to know, but also about the proper way we were expected to go about acquiring this knowledge. Widely respected as the arbiter of learning, the encyclopedia drew boundaries around what is and is not a worthwhile subject of study; and even more fundamentally, it conveyed a clear message about who was in charge of setting these boundaries. Legitimate knowledge, these monumental volumes implied, was not something we were allowed to define on our own; this task, rather, remained the purview of those with greater expertise and authority — namely, the experts and editors deemed educated enough to write the encyclopedia.

With the explosion of digital technologies, however, many of these cherished norms have been turned on their head. Case in point: Wikipedia. As the latter half of the name implies, this site is designed to function as a comprehensive collection of entries on subjects of importance. On closer inspection, however, it becomes clear that the wiki does a good deal more than simply transpose old practices and old assumptions into a new century. Unlike the traditional encyclopedia, Wikipedia sets very different parameters around what constitutes legitimate knowledge. Rather than a collection of facts culled by a cadre of faceless experts, wikis offer themselves as clear-inghouses for information to which virtually anyone — regardless of training, background, or expertise — can contribute. The prerogative to weigh in on a given subject — to present information — is not confined to so-called experts; it is an invitation, rather, for collaborative writing about subjects important to culture, revisable almost in real time. The result is not just a more democratic definition of knowledge, but also one that is far more fluid and dynamic — one that is constantly undergo-ing change as more and more contributors add to the body of information.

But are these changes for the better? To be sure, Wikipedia goes a long way toward broaden-ing the range of information and perspectives that are allowed to be included: It makes great strides in reconfiguring research and knowledge sharing as col-laborative undertakings, and it's interactive in ways that traditional encyclopedias aren't. But these

changes give rise to important questions having to do with credibility and reliability of the information this new technology makes available. Are there adequate standards in place for determining what gets defined as legitimate knowledge? Have we lost a belief in the value of experts and expertise that perhaps we shouldn't have? What are the new norms, the new definitions, of education these sorts of changes have ushered in? Does this exciting new technology actually improve the ways we learn?

WRITING

1. How does technology such as Wikipedia redefine what it means to conduct research? Does knowing that the information contributed in a Wikipedia article comes from many anonymous sources change the way you value its contents? Write a brief evaluation of the pros and cons of using Wikipedia versus a more traditional research source.

2. Pull up a Wikipedia article for a subject of your choosing that also has an entry in a traditional encyclopedia. Write a comparison of how each source treats the subject. Which is more useful to you, and why? What are the shortcomings of each source? In the end, does either source provide adequate information for research? Why or why not?

JOHN TAYLOR GATTO
Against School

Does boredom define the modern experience of being a student? And if so, who or what is to blame for this? Posing the provocative question "do we really need school?" long-time educator and educational critic John Taylor Gatto offers a stinging rebuke to the practices and assumptions that underlie what passes for modern education. Gatto was born in Monongahela, Pennsylvania, and before becoming a schoolteacher and educational critic he held a number of jobs, including scriptwriter, taxi driver, and hot dog vendor. In 1991 he was named New York State Teacher of the Year. His books include *Dumbing Us Down: The Hidden Curriculum of Compulsory Schooling* (1992), *Different Kind of Teacher: Solving the Crisis of American Schooling* (2000), *The Underground History of American Education* (2001), and, most recently, *Weapons of Mass Instruction: A Schoolteacher's Journey through the Dark World of Compulsory Schooling* (2009). He is now retired from teaching and is working on a documentary about compulsory education called *The Fourth Purpose*. The following piece originally appeared in the September 2003 issue of *Harper's*.

TAUGHT FOR THIRTY YEARS IN SOME OF THE WORST SCHOOLS IN Manhattan, and in some of the best, and during that time I became an expert in boredom. Boredom was everywhere in my world, and if you asked the kids, as I often did, why they felt so bored, they always gave the same answers: They said the work was stupid, that it made no sense, that they already knew it. They said they wanted to be doing something real, not just sitting around. They said teachers didn't seem to know much about their subjects and clearly weren't interested in learning more. And the kids were right: their teachers were every bit as bored as they were.

Boredom is the common condition of schoolteachers, and anyone who has spent time in a teachers' lounge can vouch for the low energy, the whining, the dispirited attitudes, to be found there. When asked why they feel bored, the teachers tend to blame the kids, as you might expect. Who wouldn't get bored teaching students who are rude and interested only in grades? If even that. Of course, teachers are themselves products of the same twelve-year compulsory school programs that so thoroughly bore their students, and as school personnel they are trapped inside structures even more rigid than those imposed upon the children. Who, then, is to blame?

We all are. My grandfather taught me that. One afternoon when I was seven I complained to him of boredom, and he batted me hard on the head. He told me that I was never to use that term in his presence again, that if I was bored it was my fault and no one else's. The obligation to amuse and instruct myself was entirely my own, and people who didn't know that were childish people, to be avoided if possible. Certainly not to be trusted. That episode cured me of boredom forever, and here and there over the years I was able to pass on the lesson to some remarkable students. For the most part, however, I found it futile to challenge the official notion that boredom and childishness were the natural state of affairs in the classroom. Often I had to defy custom, and even bend the law, to help kids break out of this trap.

The empire struck back, of course; childish adults regularly conflate opposition with disloyalty. I once returned from a medical leave to discover that all evidence of my having been granted the leave had been purposely destroyed, that my job had been terminated, and that I no longer possessed even a teaching license. After nine months of tormented effort I was able to retrieve the license when a school secretary testified to witnessing the plot unfold. In the meantime my family suffered more than I care to remember. By the time I finally retired in 1991, I had more than enough reason to think of our schools—with their long-term, cell-block-style, forced confinement of both students and teachers—as virtual factories of childishness. Yet I honestly could not see why they had to be that way. My own experience had revealed to me what

Do we really need school?

many other teachers must learn along the way, too, yet keep to themselves for fear of reprisal: if we wanted to we could easily and inexpensively jettison the old, stupid structures and help kids take an education rather than merely receive a schooling. We could encourage the best qualities of youthfulness—curiosity, adventure, resilience, the capacity for surprising insight—simply by being more flexible about time, texts, and tests, by introducing kids to truly competent adults, and by giving each student what autonomy he or she needs in order to take a risk every now and then.

But we don't do that. And the more I asked why not, and persisted in thinking about the "problem" of schooling as an engineer might, the more I missed the point: What if there is no "problem" with our schools? What if they are the way they are, so expensively flying in the face of common sense and long experience in how children learn things, not because they are doing something wrong but because they are doing something right? Is it possible that George W. Bush accidentally spoke the truth when he said we would "leave no child behind"? Could it be that our schools are designed to make sure not one of them ever really grows up?

Do we really need school? I don't mean education, just forced schooling: six classes a day, five days a week, nine months a year, for twelve years. Is this deadly routine really necessary? And if so, for what? Don't hide behind reading, writing, and arithmetic as a rationale, because 2 million happy homeschoolers have surely put that banal justification to rest. Even if they hadn't, a considerable number of well-known Americans never went through the twelve-year wringer our kids currently go through, and they turned out all right. George Washington, Benjamin Franklin, Thomas Jefferson, Abraham Lincoln? Someone taught them, to be sure, but they were not products of a school system, and not one of them was ever "graduated" from a secondary school. Throughout most of American history, kids generally didn't go to high school, yet the unschooled rose to be admirals, like Farragut; inventors, like Edison; captains of industry, like Carnegie and Rockefeller; writers, like Melville and Twain and Conrad; and even scholars, like Margaret Mead. In fact, until pretty recently people who reached the age of thirteen weren't looked upon as children at all. Ariel Durant, who co-wrote an enormous, and very good, multivolume history of the world with her husband, Will, was happily married at fifteen, and who could reasonably claim that Ariel Durant was an uneducated person? Unschooled, perhaps, but not uneducated.

We have been taught (that is, schooled) in this country to think of "success" as synonymous with, or at least dependent upon, "schooling," but historically that isn't true in either an intellectual or a financial sense. And plenty of people throughout the world today find a way to educate themselves without resorting to a system of compulsory secondary schools that all too often resemble prisons. Why, then, do Americans confuse education with just such a system? What exactly is the purpose of our public schools?

Mass schooling of a compulsory nature really got its teeth into the United States between 1905 and 1915, though it was conceived of much earlier and pushed for throughout most of the nineteenth century. The reason given for this enormous upheaval of family life and cultural traditions was, roughly speaking, threefold:

1. To make good people.

2. To make good citizens.

3. To make each person his or her personal best.

These goals are still trotted out today on a regular basis, and most of us accept them in one form or another as a decent definition of public education's mission, however short schools actually fall in achieving them. But we are dead wrong. Compounding our error is the fact that the national literature holds numerous and surprisingly consistent statements of compulsory schooling's true purpose. We have, for example, the great H. L. Mencken, who wrote in the *American Mercury* for April 1924 that

the aim of public education is not to fill the young of the species with knowledge and awaken their intelligence.... Nothing could be further from the
truth. The aim ... is simply to reduce as many individuals as possible to the
same safe level, to breed and train a standardized citizenry, to put down dissent and originality. That is its aim in the United States ... and that is its aim
everywhere else.

Because of Mencken's reputation as a satirist, we might be tempted
to dismiss this passage as a bit of hyperbolic sarcasm. His article, however, goes on to trace the template for our own educational system
back to the now vanished, though never to be forgotten, military state
of Prussia. And although he was certainly aware of the irony that we
had recently been at war with Germany, the heir to Prussian thought
and culture, Mencken was being perfectly serious here. Our educational system really is Prussian in origin, and that really is cause for
concern.

The odd fact of a Prussian provenance for our schools pops up
again and again once you know to look for it. William James alluded to
it many times at the turn of the century. Orestes Brownson, the hero of
Christopher Lasch's 1991 book, *The True and Only Heaven*, was publicly
denouncing the Prussianization of American schools back in the 1840s.
Horace Mann's "Seventh Annual Report" to the Massachusetts State
Board of Education in 1843 is essentially a paean to the land of Frederick
the Great and a call for its schooling to be brought here. That Prussian
culture loomed large in America is hardly surprising, given our early
association with that utopian state. A Prussian served as Washington's
aide during the Revolutionary War, and so many German-speaking
people had settled here by 1795 that Congress considered publishing a
German-language edition of the federal laws. But what shocks is that we
should so eagerly have adopted one of the very worst aspects of Prussian
culture: an educational system deliberately designed to produce mediocre
intellects, to hamstring the inner life, to deny students appreciable
leadership skills, and to ensure docile and incomplete citizens in order
to render the populace "manageable."

It was from James Bryant Conant—president of Harvard for twenty
years, WWI poison-gas specialist, WWII executive on the atomic-bomb
project, high commissioner of the American zone in Germany after WWII,
and truly one of the most influential figures of the twentieth century—that
I first got wind of the real purposes of American schooling. Without
Conant, we would probably not have the same style and degree of
standardized testing that we enjoy today, nor would we be blessed with
gargantuan high schools that warehouse 2,000 to 4,000 students at a
time, like the famous Columbine High in Littleton, Colorado. Shortly after
I retired from teaching I picked up Conant's 1959 book-length essay, "The
Child, the Parent, and the State," and was more than a little intrigued to

see him mention in passing that the modern schools we attend were the result of a "revolution" engineered between 1905 and 1930. A revolution? He declines to elaborate, but he does direct the curious and the uninformed to Alexander Inglis's 1918 book, *Principles of Secondary Education*, in which "one saw this revolution through the eyes of a revolutionary."

Inglis, for whom a lecture in education at Harvard is named, makes it perfectly clear that compulsory schooling on this continent was intended to be just what it had been for Prussia in the 1820s: a fifth column into the burgeoning democratic movement that threatened to give the peasants and the proletarians a voice at the bargaining table. Modern, industrialized, compulsory schooling was to make a sort of surgical incision into the prospective unity of these underclasses. Divide children by subject, by age-grading, by constant rankings on tests, and by many other more subtle means, and it was unlikely that the ignorant mass of mankind, separated in childhood, would ever re-integrate into a dangerous whole.

Inglis breaks down the purpose—the actual purpose—of modern schooling into six basic functions, any one of which is enough to curl the hair of those innocent enough to believe the three traditional goals listed earlier:

1. The adjustive or adaptive function. Schools are to establish fixed habits of reaction to authority. This, of course, precludes critical judgment completely. It also pretty much destroys the idea that useful or interesting material should be taught, because you can't test for reflexive obedience until you know whether you can make kids learn, and do, foolish and boring things.

2. The integrating function. This might well be called "the conformity function," because its intention is to make children as alike as possible. People who conform are predictable, and this is of great use to those who wish to harness and manipulate a large labor force.

3. The diagnostic and directive function. School is meant to determine each student's proper social role. This is done by logging evidence mathematically and anecdotally on cumulative records. As in "your permanent record." Yes, you do have one.

4. The differentiating function. Once their social role has been "diagnosed," children are to be sorted by role and trained only so far as their destination in the social machine merits—and not one step further. So much for making kids their personal best.

5. The selective function. This refers not to human choice at all but to Darwin's theory of natural selection as applied to what he called "the favored races." In short, the idea is to help things along by consciously attempting to improve the breeding stock. Schools are meant to tag the unfit—with poor grades, remedial placement, and other punishments— clearly enough that their peers will accept them as inferior and effectively

bar them from the reproductive sweepstakes. That's what all those little humiliations from first grade onward were intended to do: wash the dirt down the drain.

6. The propaedeutic function. The societal system implied by these rules will require an elite group of caretakers. To that end, a small fraction of the kids will quietly be taught how to manage this continuing project, how to watch over and control a population deliberately dumbed down and declawed in order that government might proceed unchallenged and corporations might never want for obedient labor.

That, unfortunately, is the purpose of mandatory public education in this country. And lest you take Inglis for an isolated crank with a rather too cynical take on the educational enterprise, you should know that he was hardly alone in championing these ideas. Conant himself, building on the ideas of Horace Mann and others, campaigned tirelessly for an American school system designed along the same lines. Men like George Peabody, who funded the cause of mandatory schooling throughout the South, surely understood that the Prussian system was useful in creating not only a harmless electorate and a servile labor force but also a virtual herd of mindless consumers. In time a great number of industrial titans came to recognize the enormous profits to be had by cultivating and tending just such a herd via public education, among them Andrew Carnegie and John D. Rockefeller.

There you have it. Now you know. We don't need Karl Marx's conception of a grand warfare between the classes to see that it is in the interest of complex management, economic or political, to dumb people down, to demoralize them, to divide them from one another, and to discard them if they don't conform. Class may frame the proposition, as when Woodrow Wilson, then president of Princeton University, said the following to the New York City School Teachers Association in 1909: "We want one class of persons to have a liberal education, and we want another class of persons, a very much larger class, of necessity, in every society, to forgo the privileges of a liberal education and fit themselves to perform specific difficult manual tasks." But the motives behind the disgusting decisions that bring about these ends need not be class-based at all. They can stem purely from fear, or from the by now familiar belief that "efficiency" is the paramount virtue, rather than love, liberty, laughter, or hope. Above all, they can stem from simple greed.

> **School didn't have to train kids in any direct sense to think they should consume nonstop, because it did something even better: it encouraged them not to think at all.**

There were vast fortunes to be made, after all, in an economy based on mass production and organized to favor the large corporation rather than the small business or the family farm. But mass production required mass consumption, and at the turn of the twentieth century most Americans considered it both unnatural and unwise to buy things they didn't actually need. Mandatory schooling was a godsend on that count. School didn't have to train kids in any direct sense to think they should consume nonstop, because it did something even better: it encouraged them not to think at all. And that left them sitting ducks for another great invention of the modem era—marketing.

Now, you needn't have studied marketing to know that there are two groups of people who can always be convinced to consume more than they need to: addicts and children. School has done a pretty good job of turning our children into addicts, but it has done a spectacular job of turning our children into children. Again, this is no accident. Theorists from Plato to Rousseau to our own Dr. Inglis knew that if children could be cloistered with other children, stripped of responsibility and independence, encouraged to develop only the trivializing emotions of greed, envy, jealousy, and fear, they would grow older but never truly grow up. In the 1934 edition of his once well-known book *Public Education in the United States*, Ellwood P. Cubberley detailed and praised the way the strategy of successive school enlargements had extended childhood by two to six years, and forced schooling was at that point still quite new. This same Cubberley—who was dean of Stanford's School of Education, a textbook editor at Houghton Mifflin, and Conant's friend and correspondent at Harvard—had written the following in the 1922 edition of his book *Public School Administration*: "Our schools are . . . factories in which the raw products (children) are to be shaped and fashioned. . . . And it is the business of the school to build its pupils according to the specifications laid down."

It's perfectly obvious from our society today what those specifications were. Maturity has by now been banished from nearly every aspect of our lives. Easy divorce laws have removed the need to work at relationships; easy credit has removed the need for fiscal self-control; easy entertainment has removed the need to learn to entertain oneself; easy answers have removed the need to ask questions. We have become a nation of children, happy to surrender our judgments and our wills to political exhortations and commercial blandishments that would insult actual adults. We buy televisions, and then we buy the things we see on the television. We buy computers, and then we buy the things we see on the computer. We buy $150 sneakers whether we need them or not, and when they fall apart too soon we buy another pair. We drive SUVs and believe the lie that they constitute a kind of life insurance, even when we're upside-down in them. And, worst of all, we don't bat an eye when Ari Fleischer tells us to "be careful what you say," even if we remember having been told somewhere back in school that America is the land of the free. We simply buy that one too. Our schooling, as intended, has seen to it.

Now for the good news. Once you understand the logic behind modern schooling, its tricks and traps are fairly easy to avoid. School trains children to be employees and consumers; teach your own to be leaders and adventurers. School trains children to obey reflexively; teach your own to think critically and independently. Well-schooled kids have a low threshold for boredom; help your own to develop an inner life so that they'll never be bored. Urge them to take on the serious material, the grown-up material, in history, literature, philosophy, music, art, economics, theology—all the stuff schoolteachers know well enough to avoid. Challenge your kids with plenty of solitude so that they can learn to enjoy their own company, to conduct inner dialogues. Well-schooled people are conditioned to dread being alone, and they seek constant companionship through the TV, the computer, the cell phone, and through shallow friendships quickly acquired and quickly abandoned. Your children should have a more meaningful life, and they can.

First, though, we must wake up to what our schools really are: laboratories of experimentation on young minds, drill centers for the habits and attitudes that corporate society demands. Mandatory education serves children only incidentally; its real purpose is to turn them into servants. Don't let your own have their childhoods extended, not even for a day. If David Farragut could take command of a captured British warship as a preteen, if Thomas Edison could publish a broadsheet at the age of twelve, if Ben Franklin could apprentice himself to a printer at the same age (then put himself through a course of study that would choke a Yale senior today), there's no telling what your own kids could do. After a long life, and thirty years in the public school trenches, I've concluded that genius is as common as dirt. We suppress our genius only because we haven't yet figured out how to manage a population of educated men and women. The solution, I think, is simple and glorious. Let them manage themselves.

DISCUSSION

1. Gatto repeatedly associates conventional compulsory schooling with entrapment. To what extent does this reflect your feelings and experiences? Has school ever made you feel trapped?

2. Gatto draws a distinction between helping children "take an education" and "receive a schooling." How do you understand the difference between the two? In your view, which of these phrases defines the superior model of education? Why?

3. "Childishness and boredom," writes Gatto, are too often "the natural state of affairs in the classroom." To what extent do you think this is true? And what factors account for why these things have come to stand as our current educational norms? What, in your view, would it take to denaturalize them — to get teachers and students to regard them as something other than "just the way school is"?

WRITING

4. At the heart of the problems around contemporary schooling, argues Gatto, is its compulsory nature. Think back on your experiences in school. How much of what typically defined your role was compulsory? What are some of the scripts (for how to act, talk, even think) that were required? Write an essay that argues in favor of or against the validity of implementing these particular requirements. What educational goals did they seem designed to accomplish, and were they worth it?

5. Gatto lists the three objectives that, he contends, we typically assume underlie contemporary education: "to make good people," "to make good citizens," "to make each person his or her personal best." Create a lesson plan that, in your view, would actually help fulfill these goals. What activities or assignments would it include? What would be the roles for teachers and students? Then, in an additional paragraph, sketch out an analysis or assessment of the ways this lesson plan would rewrite the script that you think more typically characterizes the modern classroom.

6. Much of Gatto's critique revolves around the charge of standardization. Modern American schools, he says, have become "factories" bent on mass-producing unimaginative, conformist, mediocre students. How do you think Alfie Kohn (p. 286) would respond to such a statement? Write an essay in which you compare each author's opinion on the state of education. What are the key problems each sees? Do you ultimately agree with their assessments of the education system? Why or why not?

MIKE ROSE

Blue-Collar Brilliance

Among the many stereotypes that shape cultural attitudes toward manual or blue-collar work is the assumption that such work is not intellectually challenging. Working with your head and working with your hands, the social script would have us believe, are fundamentally different, even incompatible, endeavors. Challenging this thinking, noted educator Mike Rose presents us with a portrait of blue-collar work that flouts this narrow view. Rose has spent his career studying literacy and the relationship of working-class Americans to the educational system. His books include *Possible Lives: The Promise of Public Education in America* (1995), *The Mind at Work: Valuing the Intelligence of the American Worker* (2004), and *An Open Language: Selected Writing on Literacy, Learning, and Opportunity* (2006). He is currently professor of social research methodology at the UCLA Graduate School of Education and Information Studies. This essay originally appeared in the September 2009 edition of the *American Scholar.*

MY MOTHER, ROSE MERAGLIO ROSE, SHAPED HER ADULT IDENTITY as a waitress in coffee shops and family restaurants. When I was growing up in Los Angeles during the 1950s, my father and I would occasionally hang out at the restaurant until her shift ended, and then we'd ride the bus home with her. Sometimes she worked the register and the counter, and we sat there; when she waited booths and tables, we found a booth in the back where the waitresses took their breaks.

There wasn't much for a child to do at the restaurants, and so as the hours stretched out, I watched the cooks and waitresses and listened to what they said. At mealtimes, the pace of the kitchen staff and the din from customers picked up. Weaving in and out around the room, waitresses warned *behind you* in impassive but urgent voices. Standing at the service window facing the kitchen, they called out abbreviated orders. *Fry four on two*, my mother would say as she clipped a check onto the metal wheel. Her tables were *deuces*, *four-tops*, or *six-tops* according to their size; seating areas also were nicknamed. The *racetrack*, for instance, was the fast-turnover front section. Lingo conferred authority and signaled know-how.

Rosie took customers' orders, pencil poised over pad, while fielding questions about the food. She walked full tilt through the room with plates stretching up her left arm and two cups of coffee somehow cradled in her right hand. She stood at a table or booth and removed a plate for this person, another for that person, then another, remembering who had the hamburger, who had the fried shrimp, almost always getting it right. She would haggle with the cook about a returned order and rush by us, saying, *He gave me lip, but I got him*. She'd take a minute to flop down in the booth next to my father. *I'm all in*, she'd say, and whisper something about a customer. Gripping the outer edge of the table with one hand, she'd watch the room and note, in the flow of our conversation, who needed a refill, whose order was taking longer to prepare than it should, who was finishing up.

I couldn't have put it in words when I was growing up, but what I observed in my mother's restaurant defined the world of adults, a place where competence was synonymous with physical work. I've since studied the working habits of blue-collar workers and have come to understand how much my mother's kind of work demands of both body and brain. A waitress acquires knowledge and intuition about the ways and the rhythms of the restaurant business. Waiting on seven to nine tables, each with two to six customers, Rosie devised memory strategies so that she could remember who ordered what. And because she knew the average time it took to prepare different dishes, she could monitor an order that was taking too long at the service station.

Like anyone who is effective at physical work, my mother learned to work smart, as she put it, *to make every move count*. She'd sequence and group tasks: What could she do first, then second, then third as she circled through her station? What tasks could be clustered? She did everything on the fly, and when problems arose—technical or human—she solved them within the flow of work, while taking into account the emotional state of her coworkers. Was the manager in a good mood? Did the cook wake up on the wrong side of the bed? If so, how could she make an extra request or effectively return an order?

And then, of course, there were the customers who entered the restaurant with all sorts of needs, from physiological ones, including the emotions that accompany hunger, to a sometimes complicated desire for human contact. Her tip depended on how well she responded to these needs, and so she became adept at reading social cues and managing feelings, both the customers' and her own. No wonder, then, that Rosie was intrigued by psychology. The restaurant became the place where she studied human behavior, puzzling over the problems of her regular customers and refining her ability to deal with people in a difficult world. She took pride in being among the public, she'd say. *There isn't a day that goes by in the restaurant that you don't learn something*.

Intelligence is closely associated with formal education, and most people seem to move comfortably from that notion to a belief that work requiring less schooling requires less intelligence. These assumptions run through our cultural history, from the post–Revolutionary War period, when mechanics were characterized by political rivals as illiterate and therefore incapable of participating in government, until today. Generalizations about intelligence, work, and social class deeply affect our assumptions about ourselves and each

Most people seem to move . . . to a belief that work requiring less schooling requires less intelligence.

other, guiding the ways we use our minds to learn, build knowledge, solve problems, and make our way through the world.

Although writers and scholars have often looked at the working class, they have generally focused on the values such workers exhibit rather than on the thought their work requires—a subtle but pervasive omission. Our cultural iconography promotes the muscled arm, sleeve rolled tight against biceps, but no brightness behind the eye, no image that links hand and brain.

One of my mother's brothers, Joe Meraglio, left school in the ninth grade to work for the Pennsylvania Railroad. From there he joined the Navy, returned to the railroad, which was already in decline, and eventually joined his older brother at General Motors, where, over a 33-year career, he moved from working on the assembly line to supervising the paint-and-body department. When I was a young man, Joe took me on a tour of the factory. The floor was loud—in some places deafening—and when I turned a corner or opened a door, the smell of chemicals knocked my head back. The work was repetitive and taxing, and the pace was inhumane.

Still, for Joe the shop floor was a school. He learned the most efficient way to use his body by acquiring a set of routines that were quick and preserved energy. Otherwise he never would have survived on the line.

As a foreman, Joe constantly faced new problems and became a consummate multitasker, evaluating a flurry of demands quickly, parceling out physical and mental resources, keeping a number of ongoing events in his mind, returning to whatever task had been interrupted, and maintaining a cool head under the pressure of grueling production schedules. In the midst of all this, Joe learned more and more about the auto industry, the technological and social dynamics of the shop floor, the machinery and production processes, and the basics of paint chemistry and of plating and baking. With further promotions, he not only solved problems but also began to find problems to solve: Joe initiated the redesign of the nozzle on a paint sprayer, thereby eliminating costly and unhealthy overspray. And he found a way to reduce the energy costs of the baking ovens without affecting the quality of the paint. He lacked formal knowledge of how the machines under his supervision worked, but he had direct experience with them, hands-on knowledge, and was savvy about their quirks and operational capabilities. He could experiment with them.

In addition, Joe learned about budgets and management. Coming off the line as he did, he had a perspective of workers' needs and management's demands, and this led him to think of ways to improve efficiency on the line while relieving some of the stress on the assemblers. He had each worker in a unit learn his or her coworkers' jobs so they could rotate across stations to relieve some of the monotony. He believed that rotation would allow assemblers to get longer and more frequent breaks. It was an easy sell to the people on the line. The union, however, had to approve any modification in job duties, and the managers were wary of the change. Joe had to argue his case on a number of fronts, providing him a kind of rhetorical education.

Biographical accounts of the lives of scientists, lawyers, entrepreneurs, and other professionals are rich with detail about the intellectual dimension of their work. But the life stories of working-class people are few and are typically accounts of hardship and courage or the achievements wrought by hard work.

Eight years ago I began a study of the thought processes involved in work like that of my mother and uncle. I catalogued the cognitive demands of a range of blue-collar and service jobs, from waitressing and hair styling to plumbing and welding. To gain a sense of how knowledge and skill develop, I observed experts as well as novices. From the details of this close examination, I tried to fashion what I called "cognitive biographies" of blue-collar workers.

Our culture—in Cartesian fashion—separates the body from the mind, so that, for example, we assume that the use of a tool does not involve abstraction. We reinforce this notion by defining intelligence solely on grades in school and numbers on IQ tests. And we employ social biases pertaining to a person's place on the occupational ladder. The distinctions among blue, pink, and white collars carry with them attributions of character, motivation, and intelligence. Although we rightly acknowledge and amply compensate the play of mind in white-collar and professional work, we diminish or erase it in considerations about other endeavors—physical and service work particularly. We also often ignore the experience of everyday work in administrative deliberations and policymaking.

Here's what we find when we get in close. The plumber seeking leverage in order to work in tight quarters and the hair stylist adroitly handling scissors and comb manage their bodies strategically. Though work-related actions become routine with experience, they were learned at some point through observation, trial and error, and, often, physical or verbal assistance from a coworker or trainer.

The use of tools requires the studied refinement of stance, grip, balance, and fine-motor skills. Workers must also know the characteristics of the material they are engaging—how it reacts to various cutting or compressing devices, to degrees of heat, or to lines of force. Some of these things demand judgment, the weighing of options, the consideration of multiple variables, and, occasionally, the creative use of a tool in an unexpected way.

Carpenters have an eye for length, line, and angle; mechanics troubleshoot by listening; hair stylists are attuned to shape, texture, and motion. Sensory data merge with concept, as when an auto mechanic relies on sound, vibration, and even smell to understand what cannot be observed.

Planning and problem solving have been studied since the earliest days of modern cognitive psychology and are considered core elements in Western definitions of intelligence. To work is to solve problems. The big difference between the psychologist's laboratory and the workplace is that in the former the problems are isolated and in the latter they are embedded in the real-time flow of work with all its messiness and social complexity.

Verbal and mathematical skills drive measures of intelligence in the Western Hemisphere, and many of the kinds of work I studied are thought to require relatively little proficiency in either. Compared to certain kinds of white-collar occupations, that's true. But written symbols flow through physical work.

Numbers are rife in most workplaces: on tools and gauges, as measurements, as indicators of pressure or concentration or temperature, as guides to sequence, on ingredient labels, on lists and spreadsheets, as markers of quantity and price. Certain jobs require workers to make, check, and verify calculations, and to collect and interpret data. Basic math can be involved, and some workers develop a good sense of numbers and patterns. Consider, as well, what might be called material mathematics: mathematical functions embodied in materials and actions, as when a carpenter builds a cabinet or a flight of stairs.

A simple mathematical act can extend quickly beyond itself. Measuring, for example, can involve more than recording the dimensions of an object. As I watched a cabinetmaker measure a long strip of wood, he read a number off the tape out loud, looked back over his shoulder to the kitchen wall, turned back to his task, took another measurement, and paused for a moment in thought. He was solving a problem involving the molding, and the measurement was important to his deliberation about structure and appearance

In the blue-collar workplace, directions, plans, and reference books rely on illustrations, some representational and others, like blueprints, that require training to interpret. Esoteric symbols—visual jargon—depict switches and receptacles, pipe fittings, or types of welds. Workers themselves often make sketches on the job. I frequently observed them grab a pencil to sketch something on a scrap of paper or on a piece of the material they were installing.

Though many kinds of physical work don't require a high literacy level, more reading occurs in the blue-collar workplace than is generally thought, from manuals and catalogs to work orders and invoices, to lists, labels, and forms. With routine tasks, for example, reading is integral to understanding production quotas, learning how to use an instrument, or applying a product. Written notes can initiate action, as in restaurant orders or reports of machine malfunction, or they can serve as memory aids.

True, many uses of writing are abbreviated, routine, and repetitive, and they infrequently require interpretation or analysis. But analytic moments can be part of routine activities, and seemingly basic reading and writing can be cognitively rich. Because workplace language is used in the flow of other activities, we can overlook the remarkable coordination of words, numbers, and drawings required to initiate and direct action.

If we believe everyday work to be mindless, then that will affect the work we create in the future. When we devalue the full range of everyday cognition, we offer limited educational opportunities and fail to make fresh and meaningful instructional connections among disparate kinds of skill and knowledge. If we think that whole categories of people— identified by class or occupation—are not that bright, then we reinforce social separations and cripple our ability to talk across cultural divides.

> **If we think that whole categories of people—identified by class or occupation—are not that bright, then we reinforce social separations.**

Affirmation of diverse intelligence is not a retreat to a softhearted definition of the mind. To acknowledge a broader range of intellectual capacity is to take seriously the concept of cognitive variability, to appreciate in all the Rosies and Joes the thought that drives their accomplishments and defines who they are. This is a model of the mind that is worthy of a democratic society.

DISCUSSION

1. Take a closer look at this essay's title. How do you interpret the phrase "blue-collar brilliance"? To what extent does this phrase challenge or rewrite the norms we are taught to use when thinking about blue-collar work? What alternative vision of such work does a phrase like this suggest?

2. Using his mother's experiences on the job as a kind of case study, Rose presents readers with a list of the particular skills and knowledge that one blue-collar job requires. His mother, Rose tells us, "took customers' orders, pencil poised over pad, while fielding questions about the food. She walked full tilt through the room with plates stretching up her left arm and two cups of coffee somehow cradled in her right hand. She stood at a table or booth and removed a plate for this person, another for that person, then another, remembering who had the hamburger, who had the fried shrimp, almost always getting it right." Does this list, in your view, successfully make the case that blue-collar jobs can call on and foster brilliance in workers? Do the skills, talents, and knowledge necessary to perform this job fit your definition of *brilliance*? How or how not?

3. Can you think of an example of blue-collar work that fits Rose's definition of *brilliance*? What kind of job is it? What aptitudes and skills does it require? How are these skills and aptitudes typically viewed?

WRITING

4. This essay asks you to think about the relationship between blue- and white-collar work. Write an essay in which you compare the particular rules, scripts, roles, and norms that teach us how to think about each of these two categories. How is each type of work typically defined? What tasks, skills, or abilities are we told each conventionally involves? And, perhaps most important, how are we taught to value these types of work differently? In your view, are these value distinctions fair? Accurate? How or how not?

5. What would a school curriculum look like that values and teaches the skills and abilities Rose showcases in this essay? What types of work would it require? What assignments or tests would it include? How would teachers evaluate these? Assess how this curriculum would differ from the one typically seen operating in schools. How do its rules differ? What role does it script for students? What are the underlying norms it is designed to support? And which do you find preferable? Why?

6. How do you think Rose's dissection of "blue-collar brilliance" relates to John Taylor Gatto's (p. 300) critique of school? Does Rose's attempt to rewrite the conventional norms regarding class, learning, and "smarts" seem similar to Gatto's attempt to rewrite the conventional scripts regarding school? In your view, would Gatto's plan for changing the rules for school better accommodate the types of aptitudes, skills, and knowledge described by Rose? How or how not?

Learning in the Shadow of Race and Class

How does one's race and class affect one's experience of school? To what extent is modern education shaped by the unspoken norms connected to these two questions? Recounting her own experiences at one of America's elite institutions of higher education, bell hooks examines some of the core assumptions, ideals, and double standards that go into scripting the ideal "minority" student. As a writer and scholar, hooks focuses on the intersections of race, class, and gender. She is the author of over thirty books, including *Talking Back: Thinking Feminist, Thinking Black* (1989), *Teaching to Transgress* (1994), *Rock My Soul: Black People and Self-Esteem* (2002), and *Outlaw Culture: Resisting Representations* (2006). Most recently, hooks published a book of poems, *When Angels Speak of Love* (2007). She was born Gloria Jean Watkins in Hopkinsville, Kentucky. Currently, hooks is a Distinguished Professor of English at City College in New York. The following essay first appeared in the November 17, 2000, issue of the *Chronicle of Higher Education*.

A S A CHILD, I OFTEN WANTED THINGS MONEY COULD BUY THAT MY parents could not afford and would not get. Rather than tell us we did not get some material thing because money was lacking, mama would frequently manipulate us in an effort to make the desire go away. Sometimes she would belittle and shame us about the object of our desire. That's what I remember most. That lovely yellow dress I wanted would become in her storytelling mouth a really ugly mammy-made thing that no girl who cared about her looks would desire. My desires were often made to seem worthless and stupid. I learned to mistrust and silence them. I learned that the more clearly I named my desires, the more unlikely those desires would ever be fulfilled.

I learned that my inner life was more peaceful if I did not think about money, or allow myself to indulge in any fantasy of desire. I learned the art of sublimation and repression. I learned it was better to make do with acceptable material desires than to articulate the unacceptable. Before I knew money mattered, I had often chosen objects to desire that were costly, things a girl of my class would not ordinarily desire. But then I was still a girl who was *unaware of class*, who did not think my desires were stupid and wrong. And when I found they were, I let them go. I concentrated on *survival*, on making do.

When I was choosing a college to attend, the issue of money surfaced and had to be talked about. While I would seek loans and scholarships, even if everything related to school was paid for, there would still be transportation to pay for, books, and a host of other hidden costs. Letting me know that there was no extra money to be had, mama urged me to attend any college nearby that would offer financial aid. My first year of college, I went to a school close to home. A plain-looking white woman recruiter had sat in our living room and explained to my parents that everything would be taken care of, that I would be awarded a full academic scholarship, that they would have to pay nothing. They knew better. Still they found this school acceptable.

After my parents dropped me at the predominately white women's college, I saw the terror in my roommate's face that she was going to be housed with someone black, and I requested a change. She had no doubt also voiced her concern. I was given a tiny single room by the stairs—a room usually denied a first-year student—but I was a first-year black student, a scholarship girl who could never in a million years have afforded to pay her way or absorb the cost of a single room. My fellow students kept their distance from me. I ate in the cafeteria and did not have to worry about who would pay for pizza and drinks in the world outside. I kept my desires to myself, my lacks, and my loneliness; I made do.

I rarely shopped. Boxes came from home, with brand-new clothes mama had purchased. Even though it was never spoken, she did not want me to feel ashamed among privileged white girls. I was the only black girl in my dorm. There was no room in me for shame. I felt contempt and disinterest. With their giggles and their obsession to marry, the white girls at the women's college were aliens. We did not reside on the same planet. I lived in the world of books. The one white woman who became my close friend found me there reading. I was hiding under the shadows of a tree with huge branches, the kinds of trees that just seemed to grow effortlessly on well-to-do college campuses. I sat on the "perfect" grass reading poetry, wondering how the grass around me could be so lovely, and yet, when daddy had tried to grow grass in the front yard of Mr. Porter's house, it always turned yellow or brown and then died. Endlessly, the yard defeated him, until finally he gave up. The outside of the house looked good, but the yard always hinted at the possibility of endless neglect. The yard looked poor.

Foliage and trees on the college grounds flourished. Greens were lush and deep. From my place in the shadows, I saw a fellow student sitting

> *I was still a girl who was unaware of class, who did not think my desires were stupid and wrong.*

alone weeping. Her sadness had to do with all the trivia that haunted our day's classwork, the fear of not being smart enough, of losing financial aid (like me she had loans and scholarships, though her family paid some), and boys. Coming from an Illinois family of Czechoslovakian immigrants, she understood class.

When she talked about the other girls who flaunted their wealth and family background, there was a hard edge of contempt, anger, and envy in her voice. Envy was always something I pushed away from my psyche. Kept too close for comfort, envy could lead to infatuation and on to desire. I desired nothing that they had. She desired everything, speaking her desires openly, without shame. Growing up in the kind of community where there was constant competition to see who could buy the bigger better whatever, in a world of organized labor, of unions and strikes, she understood a world of bosses and workers, of haves and have-nots.

White friends I had known in high school wore their class privilege modestly. Raised, like myself, in church traditions that taught us to identify only with the poor, we knew that there was evil in excess. We knew rich people were rarely allowed into heaven. God had given them a paradise of bounty on earth, and they had not shared. The rare ones, the rich people who shared, were the only ones able to meet the divine in paradise, and even then it was harder for them to find their way. According to the high-school friends we knew, flaunting wealth was frowned upon in our world, frowned upon by God and community.

The few women I befriended my first year in college were not wealthy. They were the ones who shared with me stories of the other girls flaunting the fact that they could buy anything expensive—clothes, food, vacations. There were not many of us from working-class backgrounds; we knew who we were. Most girls from poor backgrounds tried to blend in, or fought back by triumphing over wealth with beauty or style or some combination of the above. Being black made me an automatic outsider. Holding their world in contempt pushed me further to the edge. One of the fun things the "in" girls did was choose someone and trash their room. Like so much else deemed cute by insiders, I dreaded the thought of strangers entering my space and going through my things. Being outside the in crowd made me an unlikely target. Being contemptuous made me first on the list. I did not understand. And when my room was trashed, it unleashed my rage and deep grief over not being able to protect my space from violation and invasion. I hated the girls who had so much, took so much for granted, never considered that those of us who did not have mad money would not be able to replace broken things, perfume poured out, or talcum powder spread everywhere—that we did not know everything could be taken care of at the dry cleaner's, because we never took our clothes there. My rage fueled by contempt was deep, strong, and long lasting. Daily it stood as a challenge to their fun, to their habits of being.

Nothing they did to win me over worked. It came as a great surprise. They had always believed black girls wanted to be white girls, wanted to possess their world. My stony gaze, silence, and absolute refusal to cross the threshold of their world was total mystery; it was for them a violation they needed to avenge. After trashing my room, they tried to win me over with apologies and urges to talk and understand. There was nothing about me I wanted them to understand. Everything about their world was overexposed, on the surface.

One of my English professors had attended Stanford University. She felt that was the place for me to go—a place where intellect was valued over foolish fun and games and dress up, and finding a husband did not overshadow academic work. I had never thought about the state of California. Getting my parents to agree to my leaving Kentucky to attend a college in a nearby state had been hard enough. They had accepted a college they could reach by car, but a college thousands of miles away was beyond their imagination. Even I had difficulty grasping going that far away from home. The lure for me was the promise of journeying and arriving at a destination where I would be accepted and understood.

All the barely articulated understandings of class privilege that I had learned my first year of college had not hipped me to the reality of class shame. It still had not dawned on me that my parents, especially mama, resolutely refused to acknowledge any difficulties with money because her sense of shame around class was deep and intense. And when this shame was coupled with her need to feel that she had risen above the low-class backwoods culture of her family, it was impossible for her to talk in a straightforward manner about the strains it would put on the family for me to attend Stanford.

All I knew then was that, as with all my desires, I was told that this desire was impossible to fulfill. At first, it was not talked about in relation to money, it was talked about in relation to sin. California was an evil place, a modern-day Babylon where souls were easily seduced away from the path of righteousness. It was not a place for an innocent young girl to go on her own. Mama brought the message back that my father had absolutely refused to give permission.

I expressed my disappointment through ongoing unrelenting grief. I explained to mama that other parents wanted their children to go to good schools. It still had not dawned on me that my parents knew nothing about "good" schools. Even though I knew mama had not graduated from high school, I still held her in awe.

When my parents refused to permit me to attend Stanford, I accepted the verdict for awhile. Overwhelmed by grief, I could barely speak for weeks. Mama intervened and tried to change my father's mind, as folks she respected in the outside world told her what a privilege it was for me to have this opportunity, that Stanford University was a good school for a smart girl. Without their permission, I decided I would go. And even though she did not give her approval, mama was willing to help.

My decision made conversations about money necessary. Mama explained that California was too far away, that it would always "cost" to get there, that if something went wrong, they would not be able to come and rescue me, that I would not be able to come home for holidays. I heard all this, but its meaning did not sink in. I was just relieved I would not be returning to the women's college, to the place where I had truly been an outsider.

There were other black students at Stanford. There was even a dormitory where many black students lived. I did not know I could choose to live there. I went where I was assigned. Going to Stanford was the first time I flew somewhere. Only mama stood and waved farewell as I left to take the bus to the airport. I left with a heavy heart, feeling both excitement and dread. I knew nothing about the world I was journeying to. Not knowing made me afraid, but my fear of staying in place was greater.

I had no idea what was ahead of me. In small ways, I was ignorant. I had never been on an escalator, a city bus, an airplane, or a subway. I arrived in San Francisco with no understanding that Palo Alto was a long drive away—that it would take money to find transportation there. I decided to take the city bus. With all my cheap overpacked bags, I must have seemed like just another innocent immigrant when I struggled to board the bus.

This was a city bus with no racks for luggage. It was filled with immigrants. English was not spoken. I felt lost and afraid. Without words the strangers surrounding me understood the universal language of need and distress. They reached for my bags, holding and helping. In return, I told them my story—that I had left my village in the South to come to Stanford University and that, like them, my family were workers.

On arriving, I called home. Before I could speak, I began to weep as I heard the faraway sound of mama's voice. I tried to find the words to slow down, to tell her how it felt to be a stranger, to speak my uncertainty and longing. She told me this is the lot I had chosen. I must live with it. After her words, there was only silence. She had hung up on me—let me go into this world where I am a stranger still.

Stanford University was a place where one could learn about class from the ground up. Built by a man who believed in hard work, it was to have been a place where students of all classes would come, women and men, to work together and learn. It was to be a place of equality and communalism. His vision was seen by many as almost communist. The fact that he was rich made it all less threatening. Perhaps no one really believed the vision could be realized. The university was named after his son, who had died young, a son who had carried his name but who had no future money could buy. No amount of money can keep death away. But it could keep memory alive.

Everything in the landscape of my new world fascinated me, the plants brought from a rich man's travels all over the world back to this place of water and clay. At Stanford University, adobe buildings blend with Japanese plum trees and leaves of kumquat. On my way to study medieval literature, I ate my first kumquat. Surrounded by flowering cactus and a South American shrub bougainvillea of such trailing beauty it took my breath away, I was in a landscape of dreams, full of hope and possibility. If nothing else would hold me, I would not remain a stranger to the earth. The ground I stood on would know me.

Class was talked about behind the scenes. The sons and daughters from rich, famous, or notorious families were identified. The grown-ups in charge of us were always looking out for a family who might give their millions to the college. At Stanford, my classmates wanted to know me, thought it hip, cute, and downright exciting to have a black friend. They invited me on the expensive vacations and ski trips I could not afford. They offered to pay. I never went. Along with other students who were not from privileged families, I searched for places to go during the holiday times when the dormitory was closed. We got together and talked about the assumption that everyone had money to travel and would necessarily be leaving. The staff would be on holiday as well, so all students had to leave. Now and then the staff did not leave, and we were allowed to stick around. Once, I went home with one of the women who cleaned for the college.

Now and then, when she wanted to make extra money, mama would work as a maid. Her decision to work outside the home was seen as an act of treason by our father. At Stanford, I was stunned to find that there were maids who came by regularly to vacuum and tidy our rooms. No one had ever cleaned up behind me, and I did not want them to. At first I roomed with another girl from a working-class background—a beautiful white girl from Orange County who looked like pictures I had seen on the cover of *Seventeen* magazine. Her mother had died of cancer during her high-school years, and she had since been raised by her father. She had been asked by the college officials if she would find it problematic to have a black roommate. A scholarship student like myself, she knew her preferences did not matter and, as she kept telling me, she did not really care.

Like my friend during freshman year, she shared the understanding of what it was like to be a have-not in a world of haves. But unlike me, she was determined to become one of them. If it meant she had to steal nice clothes to look the same as they did, she had no problem taking these risks. If it meant having a privileged boyfriend who left bruises on her body now and then, it was worth the risk. Cheating was worth it. She believed the world the privileged had created was all unfair—all one big cheat; to get ahead, one had to play the game. To her, I was truly an innocent, a lamb being led to the slaughter. It did not surprise her one bit when I began to crack under the pressure of contradictory values and longings.

Like all students who did not have seniority, I had to see the school psychiatrists to be given permission to live off campus. Unaccustomed to being around strangers, especially strangers who did not share or understand my values, I found the experience of living in the dorms difficult. Indeed, almost everyone around me believed working-class folks had no values. At the university where the founder, Leland Stanford, had imagined different classes meeting on common ground, I learned how deeply individuals with class privilege feared and hated the working classes. Hearing classmates express contempt and hatred toward people who did not come from the right backgrounds shocked me.

To survive in this new world of divided classes, this world where I was also encountering for the first time a black bourgeois elite that was as contemptuous of working people as their white counterparts were, I had to take a stand, to get clear my own class affiliations. This was the most difficult truth to face. Having been taught all my life to believe that black people were inextricably bound in solidarity by our struggles to end racism, I did not know how to respond to elitist black people who were full of contempt for anyone who did not share their class, their way of life.

> **I did not know how to respond to elitist black people who were full of contempt for anyone who did not share their class, their way of life.**

At Stanford, I encountered for the first time a black diaspora. Of the few black professors present, the vast majority were from African or Caribbean backgrounds. Elites themselves, they were only interested in teaching other elites. Poor folks like myself, with no background to speak of, were invisible. We were not seen by them or anyone else. Initially, I went to all meetings welcoming black students, but when I found no one to connect with, I retreated. In the shadows, I had time and books to teach me about the nature of class—about the ways black people were divided from themselves.

Despite this rude awakening, my disappointment at finding myself estranged from the group of students I thought would understand, I still looked for connections. I met an older black male graduate student who also came from a working-class background. Even though he had gone to the right high school, a California school for gifted students, and then to Princeton as an undergraduate, he understood intimately the intersections of race and class. Good in sports and in the classroom, he had been slotted early on to go far, to go where other black males had not gone. He understood the system. Academically, he fit. Had he wanted to, he could have been among the elite, but he chose to be on the margins, to hang with an intellectual artistic avant-garde. He wanted to live in a world of the mind where there was no race or class. He wanted to worship at the throne of art and knowledge. He became my mentor, comrade, and companion.

Slowly, I began to understand fully that there was no place in academe for folks from working-class backgrounds who did not wish to leave the past behind. That was the price of the ticket. Poor students would be welcome at the best institutions of higher learning only if they were willing to surrender memory, to forget the past and claim the assimilated present as the only worthwhile and meaningful reality.

Students from nonprivileged backgrounds who did not want to forget often had nervous breakdowns. They could not bear the weight of all the contradictions they had to confront. They were crushed. More often than not, they dropped out with no trace of their inner anguish recorded, no institutional record of the myriad ways their take on the world was assaulted by an elite vision of class and privilege. The records merely indicated that, even after receiving financial aid and other support, these students simply could not make it, simply were not good enough.

At no time in my years as a student did I march in a graduation ceremony. I was not proud to hold degrees from institutions where I had been constantly scorned and shamed. I wanted to forget these experiences, to erase them from my consciousness. Like a prisoner set free, I did not want to remember my years on the inside. When I finished my doctorate, I felt too much uncertainty about who I had become. Uncertain about whether I had managed to make it through without giving up the best of myself, the best of the values I had been raised to believe in—hard work, honesty, and respect for everyone no matter their class—I finished my education with my allegiance to the working class intact. Even so, I had planted my feet on the path leading in the direction of class privilege. There would always be contradictions to face. There would always be confrontations around the issue of class. I would always have to reexamine where I stand.

DISCUSSION

1. Take a few moments to consider the title of this piece. What are the shadows that, according to hooks, most directly affect or shape her experiences of school? To what extent do these shadows operate in her life as powerful, unspoken scripts, drawing the lines around the particular role she felt allowed to play?

2. As hooks relates, she became familiar with the standards and expectations being placed on her in college largely by indirection and inference. The norms and scripts to which she was expected to conform, she makes clear, remained invisible and unspoken. How would you put some of these norms and scripts into words? What script would you write?

3. For hooks, the prospect of succeeding in school revolved around the experience of loss: giving up connections and relationships that had formerly defined how she viewed herself. In your experience, has anything similar defined your relationship to school?

WRITING

4. Race and class, hooks argues, are the unspoken norms that structure everyday college life, the invisible scripts that set the boundaries around what different types of students are encouraged or allowed to expect from school. Write an essay in which you analyze how hooks makes this argument. How does she present her own experience as a student as an example? What unspoken (or spoken) scripts about schooling, education, race, or class does hooks expose in her writing?

5. For hooks, there is a complicated relationship between education and desire. Write an essay in which you analyze how this relationship works, according to hooks. Describe the particular role imposed on hooks as a black working-class student, and assess the particular ways this role seems designed to set boundaries around the educational designs and desires she was allowed to have.

6. On pages 304–05, John Taylor Gatto lists Alexander Inglis's six basic functions of modern schooling. Write an essay in which you analyze these functions with regard to whether any of them also appear in hooks' assessment of education. How do you think hooks would respond to Gatto's critique of the educational system? Would any of Gatto's suggestions alleviate the issues of race and class that hooks faced?

BRIGID SCHULTE
The Case of the Purloined Paper

When it comes to plagiarism, where does borrowing end and cheating begin? And what do we do when students and teachers retain widely different conceptions of what plagiarism involves? Taking up this tricky question, journalist Brigid Schulte offers an overview of current attitudes about academic "cheating" — how we define it, why and when we argue over it, and what this entire discussion says about the changing nature of our educational norms. Brigid Schulte is a journalist who writes for the Metro section of the *Washington Post*. Her work has also appeared in *American Journalism Review*. The selection that follows first appeared in the *Washington Post* on September 23, 2002.

NANCY ABESHOUSE IS EXCITED ABOUT TEACHING HER ADVANCED Placement literature class at Springbrook High School in Montgomery County, Maryland. These are her best students, the class is rigorous enough to count for college credit, and the activity she has planned is one of the intellectual highlights of the year: She's had the class read Henry James's *The Turn of the Screw*. They've had to write a paper on whether the main character, the governess, really saw ghosts or was just imagining things.

But it turns out not to be such a highlight. The discussion falls flat. Everyone in the class has the same opinion—that James didn't believe in ghosts and was parodying sexually repressed Victorian society. And most of the papers include variations on the same sentence: "Unable to express her desires, she imagines that she sees the ghosts of luckier souls who did express their desires."

After the students file out, Abeshouse is more than suspicious. She goes to her computer, logs on to the Internet, and types bits of the telltale sentence into the search engine Google. Up it comes on SparkNotes.com, a hipper, online version of Cliffs Notes. "I wanted them to go through an intellectual exercise. And they just wanted the answer," Abeshouse says later. "By our standards, it's cheating. By theirs, it's efficiency."

A teacher for 22 years, Abeshouse has battled the run-of-the-mill copiers and cheaters, and in recent years even the ones who merely change the typeface and turn in their friend's homework. Usually she gives students zeros or sends them to the principal's office for a lecture on plagiarism. This time, since these students are among the best, she wants to teach them a lesson. She downloads the SparkNotes summary of *The Turn of the Screw*—which, she says, has an "anti-intellectual, cynical, what's-the-bottom-line tone." Then she prints copies of an analysis from a top journal, using letters James wrote to his publisher about the book and historical references to the era. She gives them both to her students and hopes they notice the difference. Or care.

Lately, Abeshouse has become nearly obsessed with how easy the Internet makes it for students to cheat and get away with it. "I've just found a Web site that posts International Baccalaureate–style essays. In different languages," she says, sadly triumphant. But what she may not realize is that the *Turn of the Screw* incident is just one skirmish in the ongoing cold war of high-tech cheating. "It's like an arms race," says Joe Howley, a student in an elite Montgomery County magnet program who says he watched widespread cheating from the sidelines. "And teachers are always playing catch-up."

Donald McCabe is the founding president of the Center for Academic Integrity at Rutgers University, and his research shows that "academic integrity" is fast becoming an oxymoron. And not just in colleges, where cheating is rampant, he says.

McCabe is finding that cheating is starting younger—in elementary school, in fact. And by the time students hit middle and high school, cheating is, for many, like gym class and lunch period, just part of the fabric of how things are. It isn't that students have become moral reprobates. What has changed, says McCabe, is technology. It has made cheating so easy. The vast realms of information on the Web are so readily available. Who could resist?

> **Cheating is, for many, like gym class and lunch period, just part of the fabric of how things are.**

Not many do. In McCabe's 2001 survey of 4,500 high school students from 25 high schools around the country, 74 percent said they had cheated at least once on a big test. Seventy-two percent reported serious cheating on a written work. And 97 percent reported at least one questionable activity, such as copying someone else's homework or peeking at someone else's test. More than one-third admitted to repetitive, serious cheating.

And few appeared to feel shame. "You do what it takes to succeed in life," wrote one student. "Cheating is part of high school," said another. Fifteen percent had turned in a paper bought or copied from Internet sources. More than half said they had copied portions of a paper from the Web without citing the source. And 90 percent were indiscriminate copiers, plagiarizing from the Net, from books, magazines, even the old low-tech standard, the World Book encyclopedia.

"Students were certainly cheating before the Internet became available. But now it's easier. Quicker. More anonymous," McCabe says. "I can't tell you how many high school students say they cheat because others do and it goes unpunished. Being honest disadvantages them."

Besides, most people get away with it. It's easy for students to stay at least one step ahead of their teachers. When teachers began noticing that students would copy from the Internet or from one another and simply change the typeface, students quickly moved on. They discovered the wonders of Microsoft Word's AutoSummarize feature, which can take an entire page and shorten it to highlight the key points.

They think "that we don't know as much about technology as they do," says Carol Wansong, who just retired from teaching high school. "And, of course, we don't. They were born with it."

Even if students are caught, the consequences can be negligible. At some colleges, students who plagiarize are expelled. But a high school student caught plagiarizing may just get a zero for that particular assignment. Often, he or she will be given a chance to make it up for at least partial credit. And there's no mention of it on the all-important transcript that gets sent to colleges. At Bardstown High School in Kentucky last year, 118 seniors were caught copying and pasting from the Internet. Sometimes entire short stories were lifted. The punishment? One essay on the evils of plagiarism. No National Honor Society memberships were pulled, and one of those caught cheating remained the class valedictorian.

Plagiarism—a derivative of the Latin word for kidnapping—literally means to steal someone else's words or credit for them. According to the rules of scholarship, if you borrow someone else's words, you put them in quotation marks. If you use someone else's idea, you acknowledge it in your essay or in a footnote.

All this cheating raises an uncomfortable question: Are successful, educated parents putting too much pressure on their children in the belief that going to an elite school buys entree into the good life and attending a lesser school will leave you at a disadvantage?

At Walt Whitman High School in Bethesda, Maryland, students answered the question for themselves after a low-tech cheating scandal—the student government president was caught with 150 answers to a final exam hidden in his baseball cap—raised the issue. A junior who wasn't involved in the scandal told the school newspaper that some parents "are under the impression that if you don't do well and your grades aren't top, you'll be lying in a gutter somewhere for the rest of your life."

To Wansong, who taught rigorous International Baccalaureate classes, it's not just that parents put pressure on their children to achieve, it's the attitude that the end justifies whatever means necessary. In the past, she says, she would find one or two students plagiarizing their research project. But in recent years, with the advent of the Internet, it's been more like 12 or 14. "They showed no remorse when they were caught," she says.

"I had students look me right in the eye and say, 'I don't see what the big deal is.' And their parents didn't, either."

That attitude echoed loudly in Kansas last year. When teacher Christine Pelton failed more than two dozen students for plagiarizing from the Internet, their parents complained. The students were given credit for the work. And Pelton quit. (The superintendent who had told Pelton to restore the grades, however, recently resigned.)

One Washington area high school magnet program student who plagiarized multiple sources for an essay on *Macbeth* said he knew what he did was wrong but that he didn't feel bad about it. "Remorse," he said, "just slows you down."

John Barrie, a Berkeley biophysics graduate student, wrote software he intended to help students peer-review each other's work. Instead, they were selling each other's papers on the quad. So he rewrote the program to catch plagiarism. And now, that program has become a booming business, with some of the toniest names in public and private schools paying for its services. Turnitin.com scans 10,000 papers a day, half of them from middle and high school students. One-third are plagiarized from the Web. And most, Barrie says, come from high-achieving kids in top-performing schools.

Students responded by shifting tactics. They began taking a sentence here, a paragraph there, in what Barrie calls "mosaic" plagiarism. The students in Abeshouse's class need not have relied solely on SparkNotes. A quick Net search on Henry James and *The Turn of the Screw* yields obscure essays such as "A Ghost Story" or a "Delve into a Neurotic Mind?"

Barrie says Turnitin.com's software can detect anything copied from the Net down to an eight-word string. What it won't catch is students who crib the ideas, not the words.

One Maryland high school student was stuck on the Hamlet paper due in her AP lit class. So she went to the Internet and found the perfect essay from a site that offered them for free. "I took a good idea that wasn't given much effort in the online paper and put it into my paper with correct grammar and clear sentence structure. Added a little quote. Touched up the final thought. And took credit for it," she wrote in an e-mail. "Is that wrong?"

> **"I took a good idea that wasn't given much effort in the online paper and put it into my paper with correct grammar and clear sentence structure. . . . Is that wrong?"**

Well, yes. "If all a student has done is taken big quotes or paraphrased and more or less pasted together others' opinions, by academic standards, that's plagiarism," Abeshouse says.

For teachers like Abeshouse, the next tactical move in the cheating war is to change the way they teach. Abeshouse has students write more during class. She asks for rough drafts of term papers, annotated bibliographies, summaries of contents, evaluation of sources. "We don't ask them to summarize a book anymore. Now we ask for comparisons, personal responses, evidence of themes," she says. "Any teacher that says, 'The term paper is due four weeks from now' is asking for the kiss of death."

But who will win the wider conflict in the cheating game is anyone's guess. "It's naive to think that once a student has a high school or a Harvard diploma that all of a sudden they become an ethical person," Barrie says. "Where that leads you to is a very ugly society in the future."

His stolen *Macbeth* paper long forgotten, the magnet student eagerly packs to go off to a top university. He had applied to six universities, and, with his high grades, had been accepted at all six. With scholarships. "It's highly conceivable I'll cheat," he says matter-of-factly. He has no qualms that he will do whatever it takes to succeed.

DISCUSSION

1. The original derivation for plagiarism, Schulte informs us, is "kidnapping": literally, to "steal someone else's words." How valid is it to define contemporary plagiarism in terms of this original meaning?

2. Cast yourself in the role of a teacher or an administrator whose job is to devise a new policy for dealing with online plagiarism. What should this policy be? How should *cheating* get defined? What punishments or consequences would you assign for these infractions? And what incentives, conversely, would you proffer to encourage students to "do the right thing"?

3. One of Schulte's central premises is that the rise in incidents of plagiarism reflects less a decline in the morality of current students than the influence of new technology designed to make the copying and borrowing of others' work easier to do. Do you agree with this contention?

WRITING

4. As Schulte writes, there are clear differences in the ways that teachers and students define plagiarism. Write a list of all the "borrowings" you think should be considered permissible. Then, write a second list of "borrowings" that you think cross the line into cheating. Write an essay in which you analyze the different levels of borrowing, and explain what principles or rules you used in making your distinction between borrowing and cheating.

5. One of the most enduring norms of contemporary schooling involves what Schulte calls the bottom-line approach to classroom work: an approach that forgoes the real intellectual work of critical thinking in favor of finding only the so-called right answer. Write an essay in which you describe some type of school assignment that, in your view, encourages or even requires this kind of approach. What does the assignment look like? What work does it require students to undertake? And in what particular ways does it seem designed to discourage critical thinking? How would you change this assignment to foster a more satisfying approach to learning?

6. One of the points Schulte emphasizes is that what most teachers see as cheating, students see as efficiency. How do you think Jonathan Kozol (p. 331) would respond to this statement? Write an essay in which you look at Schulte's examination of cheating as part of the larger issue Kozol writes about.

JONATHAN KOZOL

Preparing Minds for Markets

Whether we want to admit it, many of our public schools play a formative role in shaping how children come to see themselves as workers. Presenting an eye-opening account of the ways that corporate logos and workplace terminology have permeated our modern classrooms, Jonathan Kozol offers a spirited critique of the work-related scripts children today are often compelled to take up. Kozol is a writer and educator best known for his works on inequality in American education. He graduated from Harvard University and was awarded a Rhodes Scholarship to study at Magdalen College, Oxford. Rather than finishing at Oxford, however, he moved to Paris to work on a novel. When he returned to the United States, he began teaching in the Boston public schools, but he was fired for teaching a Langston Hughes poem that was not in the curriculum. His experiences in Boston's segregated classrooms led to his first book, *Death at an Early Age* (1967), which won the National Book Award. His other books include *Savage Inequalities* (1991), *Amazing Grace* (1995), and, most recently, *Letters to a Young Teacher* (2007). The following selection is from *The Shame of the Nation*, published in 2006.

THREE YEARS AGO, IN COLUMBUS, OHIO, I WAS VISITING A SCHOOL IN which the stimulus-response curriculum that Mr. Endicott was using in New York had been in place for several years.[1] The scripted teaching method started very early in this school. ("Practice Active Listening!" a kindergarten teacher kept repeating to her children.) So too did a program of surprisingly explicit training of young children for the modern marketplace. Starting in kindergarten, children in the school were being asked to think about the jobs that they might choose when they grew up. The posters that surrounded them made clear which kinds of jobs they were expected to select.

"Do you want a manager's job?" the first line of a kindergarten poster asked.

"What job do you want?" a second question asked in an apparent effort to expand the range of choices that these five-year-olds might wish to make.

But the momentary window that this second question seemed to open into other possible careers was closed by the next question on the wall. "How will you do the manager's job?" the final question asked.

The tiny hint of choice afforded by the second question was eradicated by the third, which presupposed that all the kids had said yes to the first. No written question asked the children: "Do you want a lawyer's job? a nurse's job? a doctor's job? a poet's job? a preacher's job? an engineer's job? or an artist's job?" Sadly enough, the teacher had not even thought to ask if anybody in the class might someday like to be a teacher.

In another kindergarten class, there was a poster that displayed the names of several retail stores: JCPenney, Wal-Mart, Kmart, Sears, and a few others. "It's like working in a store," a classroom aide explained. "The children are learning to pretend that they're cashiers."

Work-related themes and managerial ideas were carried over into almost every classroom of the school. In a first grade class, for instance, children had been given classroom tasks for which they were responsible. The names of children and their tasks were posted on the wall, an ordinary thing to see in classrooms everywhere. But in this case there was a novel twist: All the jobs the kids were given were described as management positions!

There was a "Coat Room Manager" and a "Door Manager," a "Pencil Sharpener Manager" and a "Soap Manager," an "Eraser, Board, and Marker Manager," and there was also a "Line Manager." What on earth, I was about to ask, is a "Line Manager"? My question was answered when a group of children filing in the hallway grew a bit unruly and a grown-up's voice barked out, "Who is your line manager?"

In the upper grades, the management positions became more sophisticated and demanding. In a fourth grade, for example, I was introduced to a "Time Manager" who was assigned to hold the timer to be sure the teacher didn't wander from her schedule and that everyone adhered to the prescribed number of minutes that had been assigned to every classroom task.

Turning a corner, I encountered a "HELP WANTED" sign. Several of these signs, I found, were posted on the walls at various locations in the school. These were not advertisements for school employees, but for children who would be selected to fill various positions as class managers. "Children in the higher grades are taught to file applications for a job," the principal explained—then "go for interviews," she said, before they can be hired. According to a summary of schoolwide practices she gave me, interviews "for management positions" were intended to teach values of "responsibility for . . . jobs."

> "Children in the higher grades are taught to file applications for a job."

In another fourth grade class, there was an "earnings chart" that had been taped to every child's desk, on which a number of important writing skills had been spelled out and, next to each, the corresponding earnings that a child would receive if written answers he or she provided in the course of classroom exercises such as mini-drills or book reports displayed the necessary skills.

"How Much Is My Written Answer Worth?" the children in the class were asked. There were, in all, four columns on the "earnings charts" and children had been taught the way to fill them in. There was also a Classroom Bank in which the children's earnings were accrued. A wall display beneath the heading of the Classroom Bank presented an enticing sample of real currency—one-dollar bills, five-dollar bills, ten-dollar bills—in order to make clear the nexus between cash rewards and writing proper sentences.

Ninety-eight percent of children in the school were living in poverty, according to the school's annual report card; about four-fifths were African-American. The principal said that only about a quarter of the students had been given preschool education.

At another elementary school in the same district, in which 93 percent of children were black or Hispanic, the same "HELP WANTED" posters and the lists of management positions were displayed. Among the positions open to the children in this school, there was an "Absence Manager," a "Form-Collector Manager," a "Paper-Passing Manager," a "Paper-Collecting Manager," a "Paper-Returning Manager," an "Exit Ticket Manager," even a "Learning Manager," a "Reading Manager," a "Behavior Manager," and a "Score-Keeper Manager." Applications for all management positions, starting with the second graders, had to be "accompanied by references," according to the principal.

On a printed application form she handed me—"Consistency Management Manager Application"[2] was its title—children were instructed to fill in their name, address, phone number, teacher, and grade level, and then indicate the job that they preferred ("First job choice. . . . Why do you want this job? Second job choice. . . . Why do you want this job?"), then sign and date their application. The awkwardly named document, the principal explained, originated in a program aimed at children of minorities that had been developed with financial backing from a businessman in Texas.

The silent signals I'd observed in the South Bronx and Hartford were in use in this school also. As I entered one class, the teacher gave his students the straight-arm salute, with fingers flat. The children responded quickly with the same salute. On one of the walls, there was a sign that read "A Million Dollars Worth of Self-Control." It was "a little incentive thing," the teacher told me when I asked about this later in the afternoon.

As I was chatting with the principal before I left, I asked her if there was a reason why those two words "management" and "manager" kept popping up throughout the school. I also summoned up my nerve to tell her that I was surprised to see "HELP WANTED" signs within an elementary school.

"We want every child to be working as a manager while he or she is in this school," the principal explained. "We want to make them understand that, in this country, companies will give you opportunities to work, to prove yourself, no matter what you've done."

I wasn't sure of what she meant by that—"no matter what you've done"—and asked her if she could explain this. "Even if you have a felony arrest," she said, "we want you to understand that you can be a manager someday."

I told her that I still did not quite understand why management positions were presented to the children as opposed to other jobs—being a postal worker, for example, or construction worker, or, for that matter, working in a field of purely intellectual endeavor—as a possible way to earn a living even if one once had been in trouble with the law. But the principal was interrupted at this point and since she had already been extremely patient with me, I did not believe I had the right to press her any further. So I left the school with far more questions in my mind than answers.

When I had been observing Mr. Endicott at P.S. 65, it had occurred to me that something truly radical about the way that inner-city children are perceived was presupposed by the peculiar way he spoke to students and the way they had been programmed to respond. I thought of this again here in these classes in Ohio. What is the radical perception of these kids that underlies such practices? How is this different from the way most educated friends of mine would look at their own children?

"Primitive utilitarianism"—"Taylorism in the classroom"—were two of the terms that Mr. Endicott had used in speaking of the teaching methods in effect within his school. "Commodification"—"of the separate pieces of the learning process, of the children in themselves"—is the expression that another teacher uses to describe these practices. Children, in this frame of reference, are regarded as investments, assets, or productive units—or else, failing that, as pint-sized human deficits who threaten our competitive capacities. The package of skills they learn, or do not learn, is called "the product" of the school. Sometimes the educated child is referred to as "the product" too.

These ways of viewing children, which were common at the start of the last century, have reemerged over the past two decades in the words of business leaders, influential educators, and political officials. "We must start thinking of students as workers . . . ," said a high official of one of the nation's teachers unions at a forum convened by *Fortune* magazine in 1988.[3] I remember thinking when I read these words: Is this, really, what it all comes down to? Is future productivity, from this point on, to be the primary purpose of the education we provide our children? Is this to be the way in which we will decide if teachers are complying with their obligations to their students and society? What if a child should grow ill and die before she's old enough to make her contribution to the national economy? Will all the money that our government has spent to educate that child have to be regarded as a bad investment?

Admittedly, the economic needs of a society are bound to be reflected to some rational degree within the policies and purposes of public schools. But, even so, most of us are inclined to ask, there must be *something* more to life as it is lived by six-year-olds or ten-year-olds, or by teenagers for that matter, than concerns about "successful global competition." Childhood is not merely basic training for utilitarian adulthood. It should have some claims upon our mercy, not for its future value to the economic interests of competitive societies but for its present value as a perishable piece of life itself.

Listening to the stern demands we hear for inculcating worker ideologies in the mentalities of inner-city youth—and, as we are constantly exhorted now, for "getting tough" with those who don't comply—I am reminded of a passage from the work of Erik Erikson, who urged us to be wary of prescriptive absoluteness in the ways we treat and think about our children. "The most deadly of all possible sins" in the upbringing of a child, Erikson wrote, derive too frequently from what he called "destructive forms of conscientiousness."[4] Erikson's good counsel notwithstanding, the momentum that has led to these utilitarian ideas about the education of low-income children has been building for a long, long time and, at least in public discourse as it is presented in the press and on TV, has not met with widespread opposition. Beginning in the early 1980s and continuing with little deviation right up to the present time, the notion of producing "products" who will then produce more wealth for the society has come to be embraced by many politicians and, increasingly, by principals of inner-city schools that have developed close affiliations with the representatives of private business corporations.

> **The notion of producing "products" who will then produce more wealth for the society has come to be embraced by many politicians and . . . principals.**

"Dismayed by the faulty products being turned out by Chicago's troubled public schools," the *Wall Street Journal* wrote in 1990, "some 60 of the city's giant corporations have taken over the production line themselves," a reference to the efforts that these corporations had invested in creation of a model school in a predominantly black neighborhood that was intended to embody corporate ideas of management and productivity. "I'm in the business of developing minds to meet a market demand," the principal of the school announced during a speech delivered at "a power breakfast" of the top executives of several of these corporations. "If you were manufacturing Buicks, you would have the same objectives," said a corporate official who was serving as the school's executive director.[5]

Business jargon has since come to be commonplace in the vocabularies used within the schools themselves. Children in the primary grades are being taught they must "negotiate" with one another for a book or toy or box of crayons or a pencil-sharpener—certainly not a normal word for five- or six-year-olds to use. In many schools, young children have been learning also to "sign contracts" to complete their lessons rather than just looking up and telling Miss O'Brien they will "try real hard" to do what she has asked.

Learning itself—the learning of a skill, or the enjoying of a book, and even having an idea—is now defined increasingly not as a process or preoccupation that holds satisfaction of its own but in proprietary terms, as if it were the acquisition of an object or stock-option or the purchase of a piece of land. "Taking ownership" is the accepted term, which now is used both by the kids themselves and also by their teachers. Most people like to think they "get" ideas, "understand" a process, or "take pleasure" in the act of digging into a good book. In the market-driven classroom, children are encouraged to believe they "own" the book, the concept, the idea. They don't *engage* with knowledge; they possess it.

In the Columbus schools, as we have seen, children are actively "incentivized" (this is another term one hears in many inner-city schools) by getting reimbursements for the acquisition of a skill in terms of simulated cash. At P.S. 65 in the South Bronx, I was shown another Classroom Bank, out of which a currency called "Scholar Dollars" was disbursed. Some of these things may be dismissed as little more than modern reembodiments of ordinary rituals and phrases known to schoolchildren for decades. We all got gold stars in my elementary school if we brought in completed homework; many teachers give their students sticky decals with a picture of a frog or mouse or cat or dog, for instance, as rewards for finishing a book report or simply treating one another with politeness. Most Americans, I think, would smile at these innocent and pleasant ways of giving children small rewards. But would they smile quite so easily if their own children were provided earnings charts to calculate how much they will be paid for learning to write sentences?

Some of the usages that I have cited here ("ownership," "negotiate," for instance) have filtered into the vocabularies of suburban schools as well, but in most of these schools they are not introduced to children as the elements of acquisitional vocabulary and are more likely to be used, unconsciously perhaps, as borrowings from language that has come to be familiar in the world of pop psychology—"learning to 'take ownership' of one's emotions," for example. It is a different story when they are incorporated into a much broader package of pervasive corporate indoctrination.

Very few people who are not involved with inner-city schools have any idea of the extremes to which the mercantile distortion of the purposes and character of education have been taken or how unabashedly proponents of these practices are willing to defend them. The head of a Chicago school, for instance, who was criticized by some for emphasizing rote instruction which, his critics said, was turning children into "robots," found no reason to dispute the charge. "Did you ever stop to think that these robots will never burglarize your home?" he asked, and "will never snatch your pocket books. . . . These robots are going to be producing taxes. . . ."[6]

Would any educator feel at ease in using terms like these in reference to the children of a town like Scarsdale or Manhasset, Glencoe or Winnetka, or the affluent suburban town of Newton, Massachusetts, in which I attended elementary school and later taught? I think we know this is unlikely. These ways of speaking about children and perceiving children are specific to the schools that serve minorities. Shorn of unattractive language about "robots" who will be producing taxes and not burglarizing homes, the general idea that schools in ghettoized communities must settle for a different set of goals than schools that serve the children of the middle class and upper middle class has been accepted widely. And much of the rhetoric of "rigor" and "high standards" that we hear so frequently, no matter how egalitarian in spirit it may sound to some, is fatally belied by practices that vulgarize the intellects of children and take from their education far too many of the opportunities for cultural and critical reflectiveness without which citizens

> **These ways of speaking about children and perceiving children are specific to the schools that serve minorities.**

become receptacles for other people's ideologies and ways of looking at the world but lack the independent spirits to create their own.

Perhaps the clearest evidence of what is taking place is seen in schools in which the linkage between education and employment is explicitly established in the names these schools are given and the work-related goals that they espouse. When badly failing schools are redesigned—or undergo "reconstitution," as the current language holds—a fashionable trend today is to assign them names related to the world of economics and careers. "Academy of Enterprise" or "Corporate Academy" are two such names adopted commonly in the renaming of a segregated school. Starting about ten years ago, a previously unfamiliar term emerged to specify the purposes these various academies espouse. "School-to-work" is the unflinching designation that has since been used to codify these goals, and "industry-embedded education" for the children of minorities has now become a term of art among practitioners.

Advocates for school-to-work do not, in general, describe it as a race-specific project but tend instead to emphasize the worth of linking academic programs to the world of work for children of all backgrounds and insisting that suburban children too should be prepared in school for marketplace demands, that children of all social classes ought to have "some work experience" in high school, for example. But the attempt at even-handedness in speaking of the ways that this idea might be applied has been misleading from the start. In most suburban schools, the school-to-work idea, if educators even speak of it at all, is little more than seemly decoration on the outer edges of a liberal curriculum. In many urban schools, by contrast, it has come to be the energizing instrument of almost every aspect of instruction.

Some business leaders argue that this emphasis is both realistic and humane in cases, for example, where a sixteen-year-old student lacks the skills or motivation to pursue a richly academic course of study or, indeed, can sometimes barely write a simple paragraph or handle elementary math. If the rationale for this were so defined in just so many words by the administrators of our schools, and if it were not introduced until the final years of secondary education at a point when other options for a student may appear to be foreclosed, an argument could certainly be made that school-to-work is a constructive adaptation to the situation many teenage students actually face.

But when this ethos takes control of secondary education almost from the start, or even earlier than that, before a child even enters middle school, as is the case in many districts now, it's something very different from an adaptation to the needs of students or the preferences they may express. It's not at all an "adaptation" in these cases; it's a prior legislation of diminished options for a class of children who are not perceived as having the potential of most other citizens. It's not "acceding" to their preferences. It's manufacturing those preferences and, all too frequently, it's doing this to the direct exclusion of those options other children rightly take as their entitlement.

There are middle schools in urban neighborhoods today where children are required, in effect, to choose careers before they even enter adolescence. Children make their applications to a middle school when they're in the fifth grade. . . . [A] South Bronx middle school [bears] Paul Robeson's name. "Robeson," however, as I subsequently learned, wasn't the complete name of this school. "The Paul Robeson School for Medical Careers and Health Professions" was the full and seemingly enticing designation that it bore; and, sadly enough, this designation and the way the school described itself in a brochure that had been given to the fifth grade students in the local elementary schools had led these girls into believing that enrolling there would lead to the fulfillment of a dream they shared: They wanted to be doctors.

"An understanding and embracement of medical science and health," said the brochure in a description of the school's curriculum, "is developed through powerful learning opportunities....To be successful at the Paul Robeson School..., a student is expected to be highly motivated to broaden their horizons." Not many ten-year-olds in the South Bronx would likely know that this description represented an outrageous over-statement of the academic offerings this middle school provided. Unless they had an older sibling who had been a student there, most would have no way of knowing that the Robeson School, perennially ranking at the lowest level of the city's middle schools, sent very few students into high schools that successfully prepared a child for college and that any likelihood of moving from this school into a medical career, as these girls understood the term, was almost nonexistent.

"It's a medical school," another child, named Timeka, told me when I asked her why she had applied there. "I want to be a baby doctor," she explained, a goal that a number of the girls had settled on together, as children often do in elementary school. But the program at the Robeson School did not provide the kind of education that could lead her to that goal. A cynic, indeed, might easily suspect it was designed instead to turn out nursing aides and health assistants and the other relatively low-paid personnel within a hospital or nursing home, for instance, all of which might be regarded as good jobs for children with no other options, if they continued with their education long enough to graduate; but even this was not the usual pattern for a child who had spent three years at Robeson.

Timeka went from Robeson to another of those "industry-embedded" schools,[7] a 97 percent black and Hispanic school called "Health Opportu-nities," in which only one in five ninth graders ever reached twelfth grade and from which Timeka dropped out in eleventh grade.[8] I had known Timeka since she was a jubilant and energetic eight-year-old. I used to help her with her math and reading when she was in the fourth grade. She was smart and quick and good with words, and very good in math. If she had gone to school in almost any middle-class suburban district in this nation, she'd have had at least a chance of realizing her dream if she still wanted to when she completed high school. And if she changed her mind and settled on a different dream, or many different dreams, as adolescents usually do, she would have been exposed to an array of options that

> **The choice of a career means virtually nothing if you do not know what choices you may actually have.**

would have permitted her to make a well-informed decision. The choice of a career means virtually nothing if you do not know what choices you may actually have.

"In recent years, business has taken ownership of school-to-work...," according to an advocate for these career academies.[9] National and regional industry associations, he reports, are "linking students" to "standards-driven, work-based learning opportunities while they are in school" and then, he says, providing students with job offers from participating businesses. One such program has taken place for several years at a high school in Chicago where an emphasis on "Culinary Arts" has been embedded in curriculum.[10] A teacher at the school, where 98 percent of students are black or Hispanic (many of Mexican descent), told me of a student she had grown attached to when she taught her in eleventh grade. The student, she said, showed academic promise—"I definitely thought that she was capable of going on to college"—so she recommended her to be admitted to a senior honors class.

It was a big school (2,200 students) and the teacher said she didn't see this girl again until the following September when she happened to run into her during a class break on an escalator in the building, and she asked her if she'd been admitted to the honors class. The student told her, "No," she said. "I couldn't figure out why." Then, she said, "I realized she'd been placed in Culinary Arts."

Students, she explained, were required "to decide on a 'career path' at the end of freshman year," and "once you do this, your entire program is determined by that choice." Technically, she said, a student could select a college education as "career path," but this option, she reported, wasn't marketed to many of the students at the school as forcefully as were the job-related programs. The career programs in the upper-level grades, moreover, were blocked out "as a double period every day," the teacher said, which made it harder for the students in these programs who so wished to take an honors class or other academic classes that appealed to them.[11]

The program in culinary arts, in which the students were prepared to work in restaurant kitchens, had been set up in coordination with Hyatt Hotels, which offered jobs or internships to students on completion of their education.[12] The program was promoted to the students so effectively that many who initially may have had academic goals "appear to acquiesce in this"—"they will defend it, once they've made the choice," she said—even though some recognize that this will lead them to a relatively lower economic role in later years than if they somehow found the will to keep on and pursue a college education. "If you talk with them of college options at this point," and "if they trust you," said the teacher, "they will say, 'Nobody ever told me I could do it.' If you tell them, 'You could do it,' they will say, 'Why didn't someone tell me this before?'"

She told me she felt torn about expressing her concern that college education as a possible career path for such students was, in her words, either "not presented" or else "undersold," because she said there were outstanding teachers in the work-related programs and she did not want to speak of them with disrespect or compromise their jobs. At the same time, she clearly was upset about this since she spoke with deep emotion of the likelihood that "we may be trapping these young ones" in "low-paying jobs."

The teacher's story of her brief encounter with her former student reminded me of the disappointment I had felt about Timeka. The teacher seemed to blame herself to some degree, wishing, I guess, that she could have remained in closer touch with this bright student in the months since she had been a pupil in her class, perhaps believing that she might have intervened somehow on her behalf. The teacher didn't speak of a career in cooking in a restaurant, or work in a hotel, with any hint of condescension or disparagement. She was simply cognizant of other possibilities her student might have entertained; and she was saddened by this memory.

NOTES

[1] I visited these schools in November 2002, following a preliminary visit in October 2001.

Poverty and racial data for both schools described: School Year Report Cards, Columbus City School District, 2003–2004 (race and poverty data from 2002–2003).

[2] This document, part of a self-described "comprehensive classroom management program" known as "Consistency Management and Cooperative Discipline," is published by Project Grad USA, based in Houston, Texas.

[3] Albert Shanker, American Federation of Teachers, cited in *Fortune*, November 7, 1988.

[4] *Young Man Luther*, by Erik Erikson (New York: Norton, 1962).

[5] *Wall Street Journal*, February 9, 1990.

[6] "Learning in America," a MacNeil/Lehrer Production, PBS, April 3, 1989.

[7] Clara Barton High School for Health Professionals (95 percent black and Hispanic) had 633 ninth graders and 301 twelfth graders in 2002–2003). Graphic Arts Communications High School (94 percent black and Hispanic) had 1,096 ninth graders and 199 twelfth graders. Metropolitan Corporate Academy (98 percent black and Hispanic) had 90 ninth graders and 55 twelfth graders, of whom 34 graduated in 2003. Metropolitan Corporate Academy was conceived as a partnership with the financial firm Goldman Sachs, which provided mentors and internships for students. A school's reliance on resources from the private sector carries risks of instability, however. After serious layoffs at Goldman Sachs in 2002, according to Insideschools, an online service of Advocates for Children, "the number of mentors was cut in half." (Annual School Reports for all three schools, New York City Public Schools, 2002–2003 and 2003–2004; Insideschools 2002.)

[8] Of 294 ninth graders in the fall of 1999, only 60 remained as twelfth graders in 2003. White students made up 1.6 percent of the school's enrollment of 665. (Annual School Report for Health Opportunities High School, New York City Public Schools, 2002–2003; Common Core of Data, National Center for Education Statistics, U.S. Department of Education, 1999–2000 and 2002–2003.)

[9] Tim Barnicle, director of the Workforce Development Program at the National Center on Education and the Economy, Washington, D.C., in a letter to *Education Week*, February 3, 1999. "The most viable school-to-work partnerships," Mr. Barnicle writes, are "tied to high academic standards . . . , supported by business and industry partners that provide students with technical skills needed to succeed in

a job. . . ." He concedes that "too often school-to-work" has not been "viewed as being connected to higher academic performance in the classroom," but nonetheless believes that career-embedded schools, if properly conceived, can improve retention and increase "access to postsecondary education."

[10] The program is sited at the Roberto Clemente High School. For racial demographics, see Illinois School Report Card for Roberto Clemente Community High School, 2002, and Roberto Clemente Community High School Profile 2003–2004, Chicago Public Schools, 2004.

[11] Interview with teacher (unnamed for privacy concerns), July 2003, and subsequent correspondence in 2004 and 2005.

[12] "Project Profile, Roberto Clemente Community Academy," Executive Service Corps of Chicago, 2002–2003. An early evaluation of the program is provided in "The Millennium Breach: The American Dilemma, Richer and Poorer," a report by the Milton S. Eisenhower Foundation and the Corporation for What Works, Washington, D.C., 1998.

DISCUSSION

1. For many minority or low-income children in the United States today, school is primarily a dress rehearsal for one's future life on the job — what Kozol refers to as "vocational" or "utilitarian" learning. What do you think of this educational model? Are the market-driven roles Kozol describes the ones best for children to practice and master in school?

2. What do you make of the phrase "school-to-work"? In your view, does it suggest an approach to education that is legitimate or even useful? Does it reflect the way we're usually taught to think about education? Can you think of an alternative term that would suggest an educational approach that is preferable?

3. Kozol describes visiting one kindergarten classroom in which posters of different retail stores (JCPenney, Wal-Mart, Kmart, Sears) were displayed. "'It's like working in a store,' a classroom aide explained. 'The children are learning to pretend that they're cashiers.'" What, in your opinion, is either good or bad about this kind of educational setting? This particular lesson? Are these types of roles worth modeling?

WRITING

4. Here is a list of the job titles to which the students in the classroom Kozol observes can aspire: coat room manager; door manager; pencil sharpener manager; soap manager; eraser, board, and marker manager; line manager. Write an essay in which you assess the particular kind of learning environment this classroom seems to offer. What rules and what roles are present for students and teachers alike? Do you find anything redeeming about this classroom model? Why or why not?

5. "A fashionable trend today," Kozol writes, "is to assign [schools] names related to the world of economics and careers" — names like "Academy of Enterprise" or "Corporate Academy." Write an essay in which you analyze how this might or might not represent a shift in the way we think about the purposes of education. How would you go about arguing in favor of this market-oriented approach to education? What advantages or benefits of this model would you play up?

6. From very different perspectives, Kozol and Mike Rose (p. 309) invite readers to take a closer look at the way cultural stereotypes about different jobs can influence how we define legitimate or valid intelligence. Write an essay in which you identify and assess how these writers' respective commentaries compare. How does each understand the connection between work and learning? What sort of conclusions or critique does each offer? And which do you find more convincing or compelling? Why?

Human Culture, an Evolutionary Force

Long-standing logic has held that cultural change is unalterably opposed to evolutionary change, helping to shield people from the forces of natural selection. After all, if we're able to shape our world according to our needs, wouldn't we cease to evolve in order to meet the demands nature places upon us? According to Nicholas Wade, however, many scientists have begun to rethink this orthodoxy, reenvisioning culture as a powerful evolutionary force in its own right. Wade writes about science for the *New York Times,* where this piece originally appeared on March 1, 2010. He is also the author of the books *Before the Dawn: Recovering the Lost History of Our Ancestors* (2006) and, most recently, *The Faith Instinct: How Religion Evolved and Why It Endures* (2009).

A S WITH ANY OTHER SPECIES, HUMAN POPULATIONS ARE SHAPED by the usual forces of natural selection, like famine, disease, or climate. A new force is now coming into focus. It is one with a surprising implication—that for the last 20,000 years or so, people have inadvertently been shaping their own evolution.

The force is human culture, broadly defined as any learned behavior, including technology. The evidence of its activity is the more surprising because culture has long seemed to play just the opposite role. Biologists have seen it as a shield that protects people from the full force of other selective pressures, since clothes and shelter dull the bite of cold and farming helps build surpluses to ride out famine.

Because of this buffering action, culture was thought to have blunted the rate of human evolution, or even brought it to a halt, in the distant past. Many biologists are now seeing the role of culture in a quite different light.

Although it does shield people from other forces, culture itself seems to be a powerful force of natural selection. People adapt genetically to sustained cultural changes, like new diets. And this interaction works more quickly than other selective forces, "leading some practitioners to argue that gene-culture co-evolution could be the dominant mode of human evolution," Kevin N. Laland and colleagues wrote in the February issue of *Nature Reviews Genetics.* Dr. Laland is an evolutionary biologist at the University of St. Andrews in Scotland.

The idea that genes and culture co-evolve has been around for several decades but has started to win converts only recently. Two leading proponents, Robert Boyd of the University of California, Los Angeles, and Peter J. Richerson of the University of California, Davis, have argued for years that genes and culture were intertwined in shaping human evolution. "It wasn't like we were despised, just kind of ignored," Dr. Boyd said. But in the last few years, references by other scientists to their writings have "gone up hugely," he said.

> *Culture was thought to have blunted the rate of human evolution. . . . Many biologists are now seeing the role of culture in a quite different light.*

The best evidence available to Dr. Boyd and Dr. Richerson for culture being a selective force was the lactose tolerance found in many northern Europeans. Most people switch off the gene that digests the lactose in milk shortly after they are weaned, but in northern Europeans—the descendants of an ancient cattle-rearing culture that emerged in the region some 6,000 years ago—the gene is kept switched on in adulthood.

Lactose tolerance is now well recognized as a case in which a cultural practice—drinking raw milk—has caused an evolutionary change in the human genome. Presumably the extra nutrition was of such great advantage that adults able to digest milk left more surviving offspring, and the genetic change swept through the population.

This instance of gene-culture interaction turns out to be far from unique. In the last few years, biologists have been able to scan the whole human genome for the signatures of genes undergoing selection. Such a signature is formed when one version of a gene becomes more common than other versions because its owners are leaving more surviving offspring. From the evidence of the scans, up to 10 percent of the genome—some 2,000 genes—shows signs of being under selective pressure.

These pressures are all recent, in evolutionary terms—most probably dating from around 10,000 to 20,000 years ago, in the view of Mark Stoneking, a geneticist at the Max Planck Institute for Evolutionary Anthropology in Leipzig, Germany. Biologists can infer the reason for these selective forces from the kinds of genes that are tagged by the genome scans. The roles of most of the 20,000 or so genes in the human genome are still poorly understood, but all can be assigned to broad categories of likely function depending on the physical structure of the protein they specify.

By this criterion, many of the genes under selection seem to be responding to conventional pressures. Some are involved in the immune system, and presumably became more common because of the protection they provided against disease. Genes that cause paler skin in Europeans or Asians are probably a response to geography and climate.

345

But other genes seem to have been favored because of cultural changes. These include many genes involved in diet and metabolism and presumably reflect the major shift in diet that occurred in the transition from foraging to agriculture that started about 10,000 years ago.

Amylase is an enzyme in the saliva that breaks down starch. People who live in agrarian societies eat more starch and have extra copies of the amylase gene compared with people who live in societies that depend on hunting or fishing. Genetic changes that enable lactose tolerance have been detected not just in Europeans but also in three African pastoral societies. In each of the four cases, a different mutation is involved, but all have the same result—that of preventing the lactose-digesting gene from being switched off after weaning.

Many genes for taste and smell show signs of selective pressure, perhaps reflecting the change in foodstuffs as people moved from nomadic to sedentary existence. Another group under pressure is that of genes that affect the growth of bone. These could reflect the declining weight of the human skeleton that seems to have accompanied the switch to settled life, which started some 15,000 years ago.

A third group of selected genes affects brain function. The role of these genes is unknown, but they could have changed in response to the social transition as people moved from small hunter-gatherer groups a hundred strong to villages and towns inhabited by several thousand, Dr. Laland said. "It's highly plausible that some of these changes are a response to aggregation, to living in larger communities," he said.

Though the genome scans certainly suggest that many human genes have been shaped by cultural forces, the tests for selection are purely statistical, being based on measures of whether a gene has become more common. To verify that a gene has indeed been under selection, biologists need to perform other tests, like comparing the selected and unselected forms of the gene to see how they differ.

Dr. Stoneking and his colleagues have done this with three genes that score high in statistical tests of selection. One of the genes they looked at, called the EDAR gene, is known to be involved in controlling the growth of hair. A variant form of the EDAR gene is very common in East Asians and Native Americans, and is probably the reason that these populations have thicker hair than Europeans or Africans.

Still, it is not obvious why this variant of the EDAR gene was favored. Possibly thicker hair was in itself an advantage, retaining heat in Siberian climates. Or the trait could have become common through sexual selection, because people found it attractive in their partners.

A third possibility comes from the fact that the gene works by activating a gene regulator that controls the immune system as well as hair growth. So the gene could have been favored because it conferred protection against some disease, with thicker hair being swept along as a side effect. Or all three factors could have been at work. "It's one of the cases we know most about, and yet there's a lot we don't know," Dr. Stoneking said.

The case of the EDAR gene shows how cautious biologists have to be in interpreting the signals of selection seen in the genome scans. But it also points to the potential of the selective signals for bringing to light salient events in human prehistory as modern humans dispersed from the ancestral homeland in northeast Africa and adapted to novel environments. "That's the ultimate goal," Dr. Stoneking said. "I come from the anthropological perspective, and we want to know what the story is."

With archaic humans, culture changed very slowly. The style of stone tools called the Oldowan appeared 2.5 million years ago and stayed unchanged for more than a million years. The Acheulean stone tool kit that succeeded it lasted for 1.5 million years. But among behaviorally modern humans, those of the last 50,000 years, the tempo of cultural change has been far brisker. This raises the possibility that human evolution has been accelerating in the recent past under the impact of rapid shifts in culture.

> *Human evolution may be accelerating as people adapt to pressures of their own creation.*

Some biologists think this is a possibility, though one that awaits proof. The genome scans that test for selection have severe limitations. They cannot see the signatures of ancient selection, which get washed out by new mutations, so there is no base line by which to judge whether recent natural selection has been greater than in earlier times. There are also likely to be many false positives among the genes that seem favored.

But the scans also find it hard to detect weakly selected genes, so they may be picking up just a small fraction of the recent stresses on the genome. Mathematical models of gene-culture interaction suggest that this form of natural selection can be particularly rapid. Culture has become a force of natural selection, and if it should prove to be a major one, then human evolution may be accelerating as people adapt to pressures of their own creation.

DISCUSSION

1. According to recent scientific research, Wade writes, it looks as if over the past several millennia "people have inadvertently been shaping their own evolution." What does Wade mean by this? How do we typically think about evolution, and how does this claim challenge that norm?

2. One of Wade's key contentions is that, relative to the pace of change 10,000 years ago, human evolution today is accelerating at a rapid pace. Does this argument seem plausible to you? Would you define the pace of change in today's world as "accelerated"? And if so, do these changes seem powerful enough to shape our evolution?

3. What, in your view, do we gain by thinking about human evolution in cultural terms? What does this shift in our understanding actually teach us that we didn't know before? And is this knowledge useful? Valuable? How or how not?

WRITING

4. Evolution generally occurs over time through a process of "natural selection." Write an essay in which you reflect on the ways Wade's essay attempts to redefine this term. To what extent is evolution shown here to be something other than an exclusively natural process? How does the inclusion of cultural factors within this definition change the way you think about evolution and selection overall? Are these changes, in your view, for the better? How or how not?

5. "The idea that genes and culture co-evolve has been around for several decades," Wade writes, "but has started to win converts only recently." In an essay, speculate about why there may have been such resistance to this particular theory. What assumptions or norms (about who we are, where we come from, how we change) does this idea of gene/culture "co-evolution" challenge?

6. A number of the other selections in this chapter emphasize the role that culture can play in shaping the direction our lives take. One of the implications of the research Wade showcases here is that individuals may have more power to influence or shape the larger world around them than had previously been thought, right down to the genetic level. Choose another writer from this chapter who you think would be especially drawn to this insight. Why, in your view, would this writer find this argument so compelling? How does it relate to or reinforce the argument he or she is attempting to make?

COLIN BISSET
La Vie D'Ennui

Does boredom get a bad rap? Colin Bisset thinks so. Derided by parents, pundits, and educators as the signature malady of contemporary society, boredom has long stood as a barometer of what is lacking or deficient in modern life. But this view, contends Bisset, overlooks the myriad and subtle pleasures of boredom. Rather than evidence of a pervasive cultural crisis, he argues, boredom may well be a necessary precondition for the kinds of learning that are most valuable. Bisset is a British writer living in Australia. This essay originally appeared in the February/March 2010 edition of *Philosophy Now.*

A FRIEND AND I ARE WANDERING THROUGH THE LUSH GARDENS OF A grand country home. "Wouldn't it be wonderful to live somewhere like this?" I ask, stopping to admire the view of the house over its lake. "Summer days on the lawn, grand parties, cocktails." My friend mutters something about having a social conscience, but I'm not listening. "Lazing about," I continue. "Wonderfully bored." My friend's face swivels toward me like the ventriloquist's dummy in *Magic*. "Bored? How could you be bored if you had all that?" he exclaims.

I have always fancied being bored on a huge and stylish scale. I'm talking Great Gatsby boredom, with everyone lying around in white clothes and floppy hats, sipping long drinks with cooling names, and being utterly and divinely bored. How sophisticated can one get, goes my thinking, that even when surrounded by the best things in life, it's not enough? Boredom wins through.

There's something exquisite about boredom. Like melancholy and its darker cousin sadness, boredom is related to emptiness and meaninglessness, but in a perfectly enjoyable way. It's like wandering though the National Gallery, being surrounded by all those great works of art, and deciding not to look at them because it's a pleasure just walking from room to room enjoying the squeak of your soles on the polished floor. Boredom is the no-signal sound on a blank television, the closed-down monotone of a radio in the middle of the night. It's an uninterrupted straight line.

Actually, my idea of boredom has little to do with wealthy surroundings. It's about a certain mindset. Perfect boredom is the enjoyment of the moment of stasis that comes between slowing down and speeding up—like sitting at a traffic light for a particularly long time. It's at the cusp of action, because however enjoyable it may be, boredom is really not a long-term aspiration. It's for an afternoon before a sociable evening. It marks that point in a holiday when you've shrugged off all the concerns of work and home, explored the hotel and got used to the swimming pool, and everything has become totally familiar. "I'm bored" just pops into your mind one morning as you're laying your towel over the sunlounger before breakfast, and then you think "How lovely." It's about the stillness and familiarity of that precise moment before the inevitable anxiety about packing up and heading back to God-knows-what.

Like everyone, I've been bored in the way often linked with death, but that was mainly as a child, and as you get older you become more resilient in dealing with it. As an adult, you can choose between luxuriating in your boredom or eliminating it by getting up and doing something. The choice is yours.

> **You can choose between luxuriating in your boredom or eliminating it by getting up and doing something.**

Being observed to be bored stirs up judgment from others, especially parents. "Haven't you got anything better to do?" they ask. Do they expect the truth? That you do have nothing better to do than lie around listening to music, but that you're also perfectly happy doing this? And when did being told to tidy your room constitute an interesting alternative?

As a child boredom is a bleak prospect. It was my regular companion when my family stayed with my grandparents in Scotland for the summer holidays. Their house faced the sea, which meant that there was a rocky seashore to explore. But after five or six years of that it was beginning to pall. Ruby splats of jellyfish were no longer regarded as terrifying, and there was a limit to how many times you could yell "I just saw something move in the water!" and run screaming from the water's edge. There was also the fact that my sister was now grown up enough to find it demeaning to hang out with someone my age who wanted to play. My parents and grandparents seemed delighted to sit and conduct endlessly dull conversations.

And so I would sit and think. I would sit at the top of the garden looking out over the roof of the house to the water beyond, and wonder what it would be like to live on a boat. And I would sit on the rocks on the seashore and watch the birds foraging for food, and wonder what it would be like to fly. And I would sit in the sunroom listening to the rain on the roof, and wonder what it would be like to be old enough to have holidays on your own, in proper hotels with swimming pools and waiters and organized amusements. And sometimes it was lovely just to be sitting and thinking like that for hours on end.

At other times my thoughts took more perplexing turns. I would wonder if everything I was looking at wasn't actually there, that it was just an illusion. Or what if everything was pitch black but only I thought it was light and colorful? Or what if what I heard didn't match what I thought I was seeing? These were not the sort of thoughts I felt able to own up to at the afternoon tea table, and so I ended up for quite some time believing that nothing could be trusted because my eyes were certainly being deceived. I'm not sure why a ten-year-old boy was experiencing philosophical angst, but it certainly shows that I had an awful lot of time on my hands.

And that's the point of boredom, isn't it? Wasn't Newton sitting underneath an apple tree staring into space, and Archimedes wallowing in the bath, when clarity struck? In my own insignificant way, I think I have always understood that doing nothing is the key to getting somewhere. As a writer, it takes a while to convince others that you are working hard whilst appearing to be lying on

> **As a writer, it takes a while to convince others that you are working hard whilst appearing to be lying on the sofa staring at the ceiling.**

the sofa staring at the ceiling, but once this is accomplished it can be very useful, especially If you are enjoying staring at the ceiling and hear, "I'm sorry, he can't come to the phone at the moment, he's working"—which suggests a genius on the cusp of a plot breakthrough rather than someone deciding whether to have poached or scrambled eggs for lunch.

Living in a surfing suburb, I am often aware of groups of people of all ages who gather ostensibly to watch the surf. The bigger and more dangerous the surf, the more people will gather and watch it. But there's a limit to how long you can focus on huge waves crashing near the shore. Isn't the reality that these people have completely zoned out and are simply using the surf as an excuse to stare into space? If you asked them why they're staring at the sea they'd come up with a host of answers, many of which might have the ring of truth. Sure, the color and drama of a roiling ocean is a sight to behold, but who's going to admit that really, they've been loafing on the beach with an empty thought bubble hovering over their heads?

Boredom in the workplace is something else, of course. Here every moment has hovering over it the question-mark of time passing.

This kind of boredom sucks the life from you. It has none of the hallmarks of the grand boredom that I'm after—the sort with a rousing soundtrack as you emerge from the darkness of sloth into the light of inspiration. The sort that illuminates new questions: Why not go and live in another country? Why shouldn't I write a novel? That sort of boredom is the equivalent of a long bath with French soap and frangipani flowers floating on the surface; something so relaxing and pleasurable that you really don't want it to end. And yet, when the bathwater has cooled and the flowers have gone mushy, you're happy to lift your glowing self from the tub and move forward into the stream of life with renewed vigor. Such is *la vie d'ennui*.

Okay, so sometimes you might wrap your bathrobe around you and snuggle into the sofa and think, I'll tackle the future just as soon as I've caught up with these old episodes of *The West Wing*. But that's how boredom works. Eventually you will step out into the brave new world. You have to move. That's what boredom is for; and perhaps why God invented cramps and bed sores.

DISCUSSION

1. As Bisset reminds us, we are taught to associate boredom with emptiness and meaninglessness. Is this the way you typically think about boredom? How do you define this term? How does it compare to the more typical definition that Bisset offers?

2. For Bisset, boredom is valuable because it creates opportunities for thinking about issues and experience in ways that might not otherwise be possible. Do you share this view? Can you think of a moment in your own life when being bored served this purpose?

3. Bisset believes there is a crucial distinction between the way boredom functions in our personal lives and how it functions at work. "Boredom in the workplace is something else, of course. Here every moment has hovering over it the question-mark of time passing." How do you understand this distinction? Do the rules and scripts around work create an environment in which boredom means something different?

WRITING

4. Bisset's celebration of boredom invites itself to be read as a challenge to the prevailing social scripts around education—scripts that emphasize the importance of qualities like energy, drive, focus, and ambition. Write an essay in which you speculate about how a typical school classroom or curriculum might look if it were redesigned with Bisset's argument about boredom in mind. How might this different understanding of boredom lead to particular changes in what students and teachers were expected to do? In your view, would these changes be for the better? Why or why not?

5. Consider how Bisset describes some of the pleasures of boredom: "Boredom is the no-signal sound on a blank television, the closed-down monotone of a radio in the middle of the night. It's an uninterrupted straight line." Write an essay in which you evaluate these and other metaphors in Bisset's essay. Do they appeal to you? Why or why not? In what other ways would you describe boredom?

6. For John Taylor Gatto (p. 300), boredom is the enemy of real learning. "I found it futile," he writes, "to challenge the official notion that boredom and childishness were the natural state of affairs in the classroom." In an essay, assess the ways that Gatto's conception of boredom compares to Bisset's. What are the key claims that each makes about the nature of boredom and the effect it has on us? What do you think accounts for the different conclusions each draws about this phenomenon? Which writer's view resonates more with your own? Why?

Scenes and Un-Scenes: *Looking at Learning*

How do we define what learning looks like? What a good education looks like? Underneath every definition of the ideal school, every vision of the perfect teacher or model student, there lies an even more fundamental vision: of what it means to be truly educated. Think for a moment about all of the different material that gets proffered and promoted in our culture that, in one way or another, claims to answer this question. There are all of the advice books, offering parents and educators "expert" instruction on how to enhance kids' learning. There are all of the "enrichment" games, toys, and programs currently on the market. There are all of the TV shows — from *Sesame Street* to *Mr. Rogers* — that model the proper way of "doing school." Whatever its individual purview, each of these can be understood as an effort to script out for us the standards and ideals that define "real" education. Each of the following examples invites you to conduct this kind of analysis: to decode the vision of learning, the model of schooling each presents.

>> *Though school environments like the one pictured here are less and less the norm (with the advent of pods and grouping), nonetheless this stereotype of school remains relevant. How many scripts can you spot here regarding teacher authority, student interaction, learning styles, and so on?*

▲▲ Much debate on U.S. education focuses not only on what is taught, but also on the environment in which it is taught including concerns about school security. What do images like this make you think about learning environments today? How does this shift the norm from the previous photo?

▲▲ We are much more likely today to think of educational environments as diverse. This photo shows a mother homeschooling her children. What strikes you as inherently different about this environment versus those that we more commonly associate with school?

▲▲ *Films for teenagers such as* **Mean Girls** *(2005) have always used school as a central locale for their stories to unravel. Why do you think this is? How closely do the portrayals of school made in television or film reflect your experiences as a student? How do these movies present education? What factors of education do they ignore?*

◄◄ *Photos like this one show how our culture values even the youngest children learning before they enter formal schooling. How does this photo present the learning process? Are there any elements of this photo you would alter to reflect criticism of pushing children into formal learning too soon?*

357

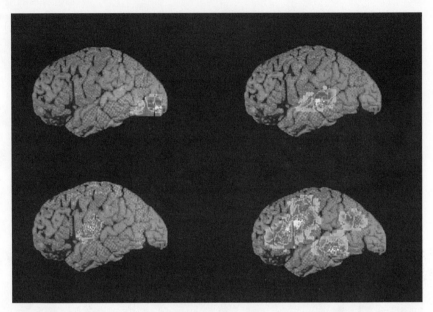

▲ This photo shows activity in the brain during the learning process.
▲ Without being able to see an environment or a context for the
learning process shown here, how does this change your impression
of what learning looks like?

DISCUSSION

1. Which of these images best captures your experiences in school? Which of them would you most want to use as a model or template for rewriting the scripts by which your experiences as a student unfolded?

2. Do you think any of these depictions promote messages that are problematic or dangerous to follow?

3. Are there any educational ideals that you think this collection of images leaves out? If so, what are they? And what, in your view, makes them so valuable?

WRITING

4. Choose a television show or movie that sketches a portrait of modern school life. How does it depict school? What specific aspects of schooling (for example, school rules, teacher or student behavior, and so on) get idealized? Which satirized? Write an essay in which you analyze the practices and standards this portrait presents as the ideal. How do they compare with the images of school or learning shown in this feature?

5. Make a list of all the different aspects of contemporary education that you think this collection could critique. Then write an essay in which you identify a particular question or issue that does not get raised or referenced in this collection. What is it, and what in your view makes it an important aspect of our educational life to focus on? Can you find an image of this issue that you would include to better balance this set?

6. Choose one of the images above, one whose depiction clearly lays out an alternative model of schooling. Then choose the writer in this chapter whose own critique of conventional education most closely mirrors this model. Write an essay in which you compare and contrast the specific features within each of these alternative visions.

Putting It into Practice: *Educational Scripts*

Now that you've read the chapter selections, try applying your conclusions to your own life by completing the following exercises.

QUIZZING TEACHERS   Prepare an interview questionnaire about attitudes toward teaching and education, and ask an instructor, teacher, or education major you know to complete it. Here are some suggested questions: *What do you like most about teaching? Least? What are the biggest challenges you face as an educator? What do you believe is the purpose of education? What do you believe is most important for your students to know?* Feel free to ask any other questions you might think of. When you get his or her answers, write an essay in which you analyze the responses based on what you think are the most common ways we think of education in our culture. How do the answers reflect this common thinking? Where do they differ? Do any of the responses echo the critiques or anxieties of any of the authors in this chapter?

DOING YOUR HOMEWORK   Choose some educational issue or controversy that is currently being publicly debated: school board election, referendum on funding, and so on. First, research this issue as thoroughly as you can. What are the key points of disagreement? What questions or issues does it involve? What people, organizations, or interest groups are on each side? If you were asked to pick a side in the debate, which would it be, and why? Then attend one of the public meetings in which this debate is being conducted and write up a description of your observations.

GRADE THE IMPACT   Choose one of the educational issues discussed by the writers included in this chapter and write a personal essay in which you discuss how this issue has impacted your life as a student. What new insight have you gained by reading further about this issue? How do you view your education differently? If you could, what would you change about your education?

5 **How We**
WORK

Introduction

RULES AND ROLES/REWARDS AND PUNISHMENTS

Think back to your last job. Was it waiting tables? Making cold calls as a telemarketer? Perhaps you gave guided tours at a museum or worked construction. Or maybe you delivered pizzas, sold insurance, or interned at a nonprofit. Whatever type of job it was, chances are it didn't take you very long to discover that it had some basic and nonnegotiable rules in place — rules laying out in fairly specific detail the things you were and were not permitted to do. Whether white-collar, blue-collar, or no-collar, every job is defined by certain regulations and instructions, some of which are spelled out explicitly and others of which remain unspoken. Usually, for example, we are told up front what tasks we have to perform and how much we're going to get paid to complete them. Other expectations are laid out less overtly: the norms, for instance, about how employees interact with bosses or dress appropriately for their jobs. Whether formal or informal, overt or implied, however, all of these rules share one thing: They are set in stone long before we ever step behind the counter, sit down at a desk, pick up a shovel, or type our first word on the computer.

Why do so many of us adhere to rules like these written by somebody else? Is this the normal cost of "doing business"? The short answer, of course, is because we *have* to. Adhering to the rules governing a given job, common sense tells us, is required to keep it. And although undoubtedly true, this explanation is incomplete. The rules of work are more than just marching orders, commands we have no choice but to obey simply because we can't think of any alternative. It is more accurate, in fact, to think of these rules as *propositions* or *bargains* in which we choose to adopt a particular role or conform to a particular script in exchange for a payoff that we've decided makes doing so worth it. From the perks or promotions dangled in front of us to the threats of reprimand or dismissal we face, the truth is that our day-to-day lives on the job are shaped less by a set of abstract rules per se than by a set of very tangible rewards and punishments. When we go along with the office mandate to wear "standard business attire" or accede to our supervisor's reminder to "always wear a smile," we're doing so not because we are mindless robots or powerless pawns, but rather because we have made the calculation that such compliance is in our better interest. When reframed in these kinds of cost/benefit terms, we confront a slightly different set of questions: On what basis do we decide to make these choices? Where do we learn which standards are the right ones to employ?

Everybody Knows That . . .

364

SELLING SUCCESS, SCRIPTING FAILURE

It is tempting to answer this last question by saying simply "ourselves." However, as with so many other aspects of our daily lives, it is far more likely that the standards and priorities we use as we navigate our work lives have their origins at least partly in the popular culture that surrounds us. And if you doubt this contention, just think back to all the different television shows, movies, and commercials you've seen in the last few months that convey one message or another about work. Even if we sample this kind of material only sporadically, it's difficult not to come away with a clear sense of the attitudes toward work that it's our "job" to adopt. We quickly learn, for example, that we should covet certain jobs and spurn others. We become adept at identifying, almost instinctively, the things that make one career choice advantageous and another altruistic. We learn that being, say, a corporate CEO is a more "legitimate" undertaking than being a nurse, a social worker, or a high school teacher. The work it involves, the contribution it makes, and therefore the rewards it garners are supposedly far superior. Whether we embrace these lessons or resist them, whether they accurately reflect our personal views and experiences or drastically misrepresent them, one thing seems indisputable: Our culture's tutorial vis-à-vis work goes on constantly.

To be sure, our world abounds with messages and markers that tell us how to measure not only a job's desirability but also its fundamental worthiness as well as our worthiness in taking it. Perhaps the most obvious of these has to do with money. If we are looking for the quickest way to see where certain jobs rank within the official hierarchy of American employment, we need look no further than at the disparity in salary between them. And this difference is closely related to other, nonmonetary kinds of distinctions we are encouraged to draw between different jobs — between, for instance, the relative respectability or social status accorded to each. All of this thinking gets reinforced and elaborated by the ways these jobs get depicted in our popular media as well — by the clichés and stereotypes that typically attach themselves to each. If you had to write profiles of fictional wall street bankers, you could, because you've seen the same depictions of them over and over again on the nightly news.

Everybody Knows That . . .

❝ I'm not a doctor, but I play one on TV"

— Aspirin commercial from the 1970s featuring Robert Young, who played the title character on the popular show Marcus Welby, M.D.

And the more familiar this instruction becomes, the easier it is to believe that we really do know the difference between worthy and unworthy work. What makes all this more than a little dangerous, of course, is that the conclusions we are encouraged to draw are often wildly off the mark. Put simply, they are cultural stereotypes rather than objective facts. Pointing this out, however, doesn't necessarily diminish their influence. Indeed, we may be drawn to these generalizations precisely *because* they're stereotypes — because they take a situation that otherwise would feel complicated and messy, and render it disarmingly simple. It's no easy task to figure out what really makes work meaningful, to decide what is valid about certain jobs and not valid about others. While commercials depict corporate boardrooms filled with zany pranksters and free-thinking individuals, construction sites populated by truck-driving he-men, and insurance offices staffed with empathetic, dedicated salespeople, we know on some level that these images don't supply us with scripts that adequately explain the true meaning or value of work.

It is precisely this question of valuation that the selections in this chapter invite you to ponder. How is it, their authors ask, that work has come to stand as our culture's preeminent marker of self-worth? What does it mean that we so often turn to our jobs as definitive expressions of who and what we are? To delve into the assumptions and norms around work is to confront one of the key places in our world where we learn to draw distinctions between success and failure, to differentiate being a "winner" from being a "loser." Our job, of course, is hardly to take such distinctions for granted. Rather, it is to make sense of what these instructions mean and what they do: whether these scripts are helpful or harmful, whether they crowd out other, more valid ways to measure our personal value. In doing so, we will devote our energy not only to examining some of the different jobs available in our world, but also to expanding our understanding of what exactly work is.

One of the most versatile, encompassing terms in our modern vocabulary, *work* really describes any activity or undertaking — from doing algebra homework to taking out the garbage — that involves a degree of effort. Because of its very capaciousness, in fact, work offers us an especially resonant metaphor for understanding our relationship to popular culture in general. The term *work* underscores the degree to which the cultural messages conveyed to us, the standards mapped for us, the scripts written for us are presented not as optional things but as requirements. Like a job, our pop culture calls on us to take up particular tasks and perform particular roles. And as with a job, these expectations or rules get enforced in terms of the rewards and punishments facing us for following along or rebelling against. And finally, there is the double meaning of using this term in a cultural context, referring not only to the work our pop culture assigns to us, but also to the ways we respond to these expectations, the ways, that is, we "work out" our individual relationship to these scripts. The term reminds us that pop culture, like the jobs we hold, is not just a task master, but also a testing ground. It is the place where we assess whether these rules and roles really "work" for us.

Despite their differences, each of the essays collected here is informed by this particular understanding. Each selection author invites us to look more closely at the places where work and culture most powerfully intersect. Some pieces accomplish this goal by chronicling the ways different kinds of work gets done day to day, detailing the real-world pressures and rules that dictate how different jobs are performed. Anthony DePalma, for example, tells the story of Mexican restaurant workers in New York City, whose struggles to remain gainfully employed in a volatile job market underscore how factors like race and class can drastically skew the sorts of opportunities available. Also looking through the lens of racial experience, Lynette Clemetson explores what it means to have no choice but to take on the dual role of "working mother." As an exercise in contrast, Judith Warner also looks at the world of parenting, posing hard questions about what it means that motherhood itself is often talked about as its own kind of job. At the heart of this chapter is an exploration of the question "Do we work to live, or live to work?" Because work and identity are linked, Louis Uchitelle analyzes under- and unemployment trends in contemporary America to critique some of our most deeply embedded assumptions and beliefs about success and self-worth. Addressing the contradictions among our culture's success myths from a decidedly ironic perspective, Robert Sullivan's essay lays out instructions for how "not to become rich and famous" — a satiric how-to list that gleefully skewers the work-related values and priorities we are so often encouraged to embrace. In a similar vein, Matthew Crawford champions manual labor and the way our culture values it in relation to sitting behind a desk. But this chapter would not be complete without a look at our capitalist values in action, and Matt Taibbi presents a jaw-dropping and

> ## *Everybody Knows That...*
>
> ## ❝ 'Nice to meet you. What do you do?'
>
> **For many, this is one of the first conversations we have when meeting someone new. But our jobs are more than simply a topic of conversation — they are an important part of our lives. They can be an extension of us and a matter of pride. What we 'do' is part of who we are."**
>
> — *Hilda Solis, Secretary of Labor, May 11, 2010*

timely exposé on the restrained money-making practices of financial firm Goldman Sachs, where out-of-control bankers took their belief in capitalism and free markets to the brink and almost brought the American economy down in the process. Finally, Frank Deford advocates for ditching the altruistic, school-spirited view of college athletics, arguing that such a big business should pay its workers what they're worth.

"EVERYBODY KNOWS THAT" EXERCISE

Choose one of the images or quotations featured in the margins on the preceding pages and answer the following questions:

1. What does this image or quotation ask you to believe?
2. What are the particular ideas, values, or attitudes it invites us to accept as *normal*?
3. What would it feel like to act on or act out these norms in our personal lives?

Rule *Maker* >>>>>>>>> Rule *Breaker*

" *Give me a W!*
Give me an A!
Give me an L!
Give me a squiggly!
Give me an M!
Give me an A!
Give me an R!
Give me a T!

What's that spell?
Wal-Mart!

Whose Wal-Mart is it?
It's my Wal-Mart!

Who's number one?
The customer! Always!"

— THE WAL-MART CHEER

" *Wal-Mart, the recidivist criminal, is*
back in trouble with the law. Jesse
James, Bonnie & Clyde, and Al Capone
had nothing on this notorious violator
of our nation's laws and moral code of
behavior. It routinely robs its nearly one
million workers, depriving them of a fair
wage and a fair chance. For example:
Wal-Mart illegally compels employees to
work an extra hour or so without pay after
their shift is over. More than 30 states
have filed class-action suits against the
company for requiring this 'off the clock'
work."

— JIM HIGHTOWER,
"WAL-MART RIDES AGAIN,"
NOVEMBER 11, 2003

WAL-MART VS. JIM HIGHTOWER

How does the promise of work compare to the reality? How often do the jobs we take actually live up to the ways they've been promoted? Whether in television commercials or magazine spreads, Internet job sites or help-wanted ads, it is hardly a secret that virtually every job gets hyped in ways calculated to cast it in the best possible light. No matter what the position being offered, we can pretty much rest assured we'll be told it offers "stimulating challenges" and "opportunities for advancement," that employees are fairly compensated for the work they perform, and that relations between management and labor are entirely harmonious. As many of us know from personal experience, however, sooner or later most such rosy predictions bump up against the kinds of pressures and limitations that these promotions rarely mention. We know, for example, that in the "real world" discrepancies in economic and educational background or barriers of race and class can drastically restrict the opportunities available to people looking for work. Or that when we actually find ourselves in a given job, the interests of employers and rights of employees are not always in sync. Take, for instance, the controversy surrounding Wal-Mart's employment practices. While it may be commonplace for corporate boosters to describe their workforce as one big, happy family, it is also true that such feel-good language can serve to direct attention away from more serious and pressing discussions: about things like fair wages, hiring discrimination, or unionization. In this case, the gap between the promise and the reality suggests that we may need to rethink the ways we talk about work. Should we rewrite the scripts that teach us what to expect from our jobs? And if so, what would these new scripts look like?

FIND THE RULES: What attitudes about working for Wal-Mart does the "Wal-Mart Cheer" seem designed to promote? Make a list of these attitudes and write a one-page essay in which you discuss how this cheer helps script the idea of working for Wal-Mart in a certain light.

MAKE YOUR OWN RULES: How do you think Jim Hightower or others critical of Wal-Mart's employment practices would respond to the "Wal-Mart Cheer"? Rewrite the cheer to reflect such criticism of Wal-Mart, and write a brief response explaining why you rewrote the cheer the way you did.

LOUIS UCHITELLE
The Consequences—Undoing Sanity

Chronicling what he calls the "psychiatric aspects of layoffs," Louis Uchitelle uses a focus on joblessness to better understand the social messages and cultural values that teach Americans to connect their work to their self-worth. In a world ever more frequently marked by downsizing and layoffs, Uchitelle asks whether it's still possible to treat such cherished notions as job security and the dignity of work as indisputable facts of life. Uchitelle writes about business and economics for the *New York Times*, and he won a George Polk Award for the *Times* series "The Downsizing of America," an investigation of layoffs that ran in 1996. He addressed the subject again in his book *The Disposable American: Layoffs and Their Consequences* (2006), from which the following selection is taken. Before moving to the *Times*, he worked at the Associated Press as a foreign correspondent, reporter, and editor. He has taught at Columbia University and in 2002–2003 was a visiting scholar at the Russell Sage Foundation in New York.

HARD AS SHE TRIED, STACY BROWN COULD NOT REKINDLE IN HER husband, Erin, the passion for work that he lost when United Airlines laid him off as a mechanic at its giant aircraft maintenance center in Indianapolis. She loved Erin; that is, she loved the engaged and energetic young man she had married three years earlier. "He was just going a million miles a minute before this all happened," she said. She wanted that Erin back, and soon. Not for the income. If need be, she could support the family quite handsomely herself, as a litigator at a white-shoe Indianapolis law firm. But as we talked in late 2004, she was six months pregnant with their second child, and it was time to embrace the roles they had planned for themselves when they married: she as the mother and care-giver, he as the really skilled engineer, mechanic, and craftsman rising adventurously in the corporate world, or going out on his own as an entrepreneur. The layoff had destroyed all this and her distress was unrestrained.[1]

"I think the layoff destroyed his self-esteem," Stacy said, her words coming rapidly and intensely. "I don't think he will ever admit that but I think it has. That is a hard thing to overcome and I don't know how you overcome it to get back into the working world, which is what I think he is going to have to do. When he fills out résumés and applies for jobs, you can see it is not with the extreme belief that he is going to get one. He waits until the last minute and gets the résumé in, but maybe doesn't get it in completely. I think that is because he is probably depressed."

Two years after Erin Brown lost his job at United Airlines, his wife was attempting, in a drastic, risky way, to jump-start her husband's self-confidence—to puncture his inertia and bring him quickly to the point that he would once again want to step into a career and take on the risks involved in pursuing uncertain goals. She had insisted on the purchase of a rundown three-bedroom house half a block from their

> **"I think the layoff destroyed his self-esteem."**

own home in their once splendid Victorian-era neighborhood, which was now coming back as a downtown enclave for young professionals and executives. Erin had balked at the purchase, as he had balked at earlier opportunities to acquire and renovate rundown houses in the neighborhood, then flip them at a profit. Too risky, he insisted. This time, ignoring her husband's reluctance, Stacy put in a bid anyway, winning the house for a rock-bottom $95,000 at a mortgage foreclosure sale. She closed the deal by doing all the paperwork herself, moving forward decisively once Erin assured her that the eighty-four-year-old dwelling with its spacious front veranda was structurally sound.

They paid cash, drawing on their savings, and immediately put the house up for sale at $165,000, untouched. They were ready in their own minds, or at least Stacy was, to accept a counteroffer of $140,000 for this handyman special. Gentrification alone would bring them a sufficient profit, she reasoned, and that success would rebuild in Erin some of the self-esteem and energy that the layoff had destroyed. Or, faced with ownership—having been pushed by his wife into a gamble—Erin would renovate the house and they would then resell it for at least $195,000, an even greater success for him. Mainly, however, Stacy hoped for the quick resale. She doubted that Erin possessed the self-confidence to carry out the renovation. "He's going to want to start this and then he's not going to be able to finish it in a very timely manner," she said, "so we will end up hanging on to two houses, which is okay, but what it doesn't do is give him that sense of accomplishment and purpose and financial reward, which is what he needs to function effectively again."

In the cataloging of damage that results from layoffs, incapacitating emotional illness almost never appears on the lists that economists, politicians, sociologists, union leaders, business school professors, management consultants, and journalists compile. There is much discussion of income loss, downward mobility, a decrease in family cohesion, a rise in the divorce rate, the unwinding of communities, the impact on children, the impact on survivors who dodge a layoff but are left feeling insecure and guilty that they kept their jobs while colleagues did not.[2] Extended periods of unemployment bring a cascade of damages, including depression, and these too are documented. One study, for example, found that for every percentage point change in the unemployment rate, up or down, the national suicide rate rose or fell in tandem, and so did the frequency of strokes, heart attacks, crime, and accidents.[3]

The layoff, however, is seldom singled out as damaging in itself, quite apart from the unemployment that follows. But the trauma of dismissal—the "acuteness of the blow," as Dr. Theodore Jacobs, the New York psychoanalyst, put it—unwinds lives in its own right, damaging self-esteem, undoing normal adaptive mechanisms, and erecting the sort of emotional barriers that have prevented Erin Brown and thousands of others, perhaps millions of others, from returning energetically to the workforce in jobs that draw productively on their education and skills. "There are many people who do not want to face that trauma again and to some degree they lose a sense of reality," Dr. Jacobs said. "They give themselves a lot of conscious reasons why they cannot accept this job or that job, but deeper down they don't want to face the rigors and anxieties of work and the fears they won't be up to it and they will be dropped again."[4]

I did not think in the early stages of the reporting for this book that I would be drawn so persistently into the psychiatric aspect of layoffs. But a surprisingly high number of the laid-off people with whom I talked described from every angle and over and over again what, in their minds, had been done to them, the mistakes they had made, their bad luck in being caught in the particular situation that cost them their jobs, the shortsightedness or outright evil of the bosses who failed to protect them or did not want to do so, how cut adrift they felt, or, hiding their loss and hurt in elaborate rationalizations, how comfortable they insisted they were in some new way of life, safely separated from challenging work.

The emotional damage was too palpable to ignore. Whenever I insisted that layoffs were a phenomenon in America beyond their control, they agreed perfunctorily and then went right back to describing their own devaluing experiences, and why it was somehow their fault or their particular bad luck. When I turned to psychiatrists and psychologists for an explanation of what I was finding, they offered similar observations of their own. "Chipping away at human capital," Dr. Jacobs called it. "Even when a person accurately realizes that he has done a good job, that the company is in a bad way, that it has to lay off a lot of people and it is not about me, there is always some sense of diminishment. Others at the company are not laid off, so why me? And that sense of having been judged and found wanting dovetails with older feelings of inadequacy about one's self that were acquired growing up."

Dr. Kim Cameron, an organizational psychologist at the University of Michigan's business school, focuses in his work on developing ways for corporate managers to carry out layoffs benignly, the goal being to limit the damage to the victims and in doing so soften the blow to morale among the survivors. In the same vein, management consultants and business school professors write end-lessly about the various techniques for finessing layoffs. Dr. Cameron has con-cluded, however, that no matter how sophisticated the technique, there is not much balm: layoffs are destructive psy-chologically for the individuals who lose their jobs.

Layoffs are destructive psychologically for the individuals who lose their jobs.

I told him Brown's story, including the conflicts with his manager at United Airlines over his inspection reports and the related setback in his application to advance to the engineering department at United's main-tenance center, and Dr. Cameron replied that Brown seemed to be an example of a "fundamental in-the-bones blow to ego and self-worth."[5]

"You can have all kinds of people like spouses and friends say you are terrific, you are wonderful, you are great," Dr. Cameron said, "but in the core you say, I am not, and I have big evidence that I am not. Layoffs diminish the ability to restart. They are the opposite of life giving; they literally deplete life." In Brown's case and in many others, Dr. Cameron said, the damage is hard to observe. "It is subversive in that it limits all kinds of other activities—for example, the ability to form emotional bonds with people, the ability to be energized and aggressive in pursuing a new job or position, and the ability to try new things. Trial-and-error learning is diminished. If I am feeling awful about myself, I don't want one more failure. If you try new things, the probability seems higher that you will fail, so you don't try them."[6]

Psychiatrists and psychologists uncover these hidden linkages in therapy. Living with Erin, Stacy also gradually saw them, although her husband tried to hide what he was feeling from her, and from him-self. The emotional damage from layoffs varies, of course, from case to case. Brown had to contend with his wife's success as a lawyer and her earning power. His parents' divorce when he was a boy may have also undermined his sense of himself as an effective worker. But who among us does not have contributing factors embedded in our lives waiting for a catalyst, like a layoff, to set them off? At age thirty, Erin was frozen, unable to act, not just in home renovation but in elbowing his way back into a job that would draw on his considerable skills. Denial and anger justified his inaction and hid its deeper causes.

A year after her husband's layoff, Stacy prodded him into applying for a job at a Rolls-Royce engine plant in Indianapolis. The opening was for a technical specialist in the engineering department, a job involving research on jet engines that Erin later said he wanted. But his description of his encounter with the human resources manager who interviewed him was laced with resentment and insult, and the manager must have noticed. "I was well-qualified and I went through a lot of effort to get that one," Erin said, "and it turns out the guy who was doing the hiring had not bothered to understand the nature of the job he was in charge of filling."

In Brown's view, the candidate finally selected was inferior to him in education and know-how. "He had no bachelor's degree in engineering and he lacked the analytical skill that the job required," Erin asserted, berating the interviewer for bureaucratically placing too much importance on a relatively insignificant aspect of the job description: shop-floor experience in machining. The winning candidate had that experience and that made the difference, Erin said, despite his plea to the interviewer that he could come up to speed as a machinist in two weeks. "I said to this guy, 'Hey, look, I have the training, I just don't have the experience in the field, but I'll do whatever you want me to do on my own time to get it.' No interest on his part. They want everything exactly according to the specifications. . . . And then, even if you are among the top applicants, they don't have the decency to get back to you and say, 'Thanks, but no thanks.' I mean you have to call them and hound them to see what happened with the position."

His account of the purchase of the house down the street from their home differed alarmingly from his wife's subsequent explanation. He did not mention her decisive role in making the purchase or that she was trying to prod him out of what she described as a mild but incapacitating depression. Instead, he left the impression that he had taken the initiative in making the purchase. If the house did not resell quickly—and it was already on the market—then he would remodel the kitchen and add a garage to increase the resale value. None of Stacy's anguish came through in the optimistic plans that Erin described. Before doing any of the remodeling, he said, sounding sure of himself, he just might move his family into the new dwelling while he completed the long-drawn-out renovation of his own home. The Rolls-Royce debacle, he said, he had put behind him. He had made no further attempt to apply for challenging jobs in big corporations. Henceforth, he said, he would go the entrepreneurial route, relying on himself. As evidence of his determination and effectiveness, he declared that he had finally completed construction of the two-story carriage house behind his and Stacy's home. It was ready to be sold or rented as office space, he said.

This was the project that Erin had started while Stacy was on maternity leave in the winter and spring of 2003, shortly after he lost his job at United. Birth, layoff, and maternity leave melded. During Stacy's leave, Erin did 60 percent of the construction work and then, when she went back to her job, he stopped, not touching the carriage house again for more than a year; caring for Kyle took up too much of his time, he said. Now, after all those months of inactivity, Erin told me by phone that he had completed the project, the work carried out in what appeared to be a spurt of energy and activity despite the time consumed in child care. He e-mailed me a photo of the exterior, freshly painted green and white. But he had not finished the interior. Inside that cozy two-story house, wiring and electricity were yet to be installed and studs were still exposed.

Stacy set me straight on the status of the carriage house. Her husband had indeed completed the exterior, she said. "He did beautiful work." But he had acted because he had no choice: either he used the materials he had purchased or they would "sit there and rot." As for the interior, Erin found reasons to put off doing that essential work, and Stacy saw the postponements as a signal from her husband—a signal whose true meaning he suppressed—that he did not want to take the risk of actually finishing the carriage house and then somehow having that achievement, too, taken from him.

She had finally concluded that Erin's emotional damage had become a barrier to the family life they both seemed to want. "Our hope is that . . . there will be a time for me to stay home with our children for a while," Stacy told me. "But at the same time, just this morning, we were talking that it was time to make elections next year for my work and my contributions to the medical savings account and things like that, and he says, 'What happens if you have to go back to work?' And I thought, What do you mean what happens if I have to go back to work? I thought the plan was that you were going to go to work. So I think at the same time he's just such an optimistic soul, but I think in the back of his mind, I think he is doubting. I mean, I think he is doubting his ability to get gainful employment and employment that supports our family. I mean, all along, even though he wanted to be laid off in the sense that he thought he was ready to leave United, I firmly believe the layoff impacted him very much. To think back to the person he was when I met him—he enjoyed his job, he really thought he had a career going. And to watch the person that he is today, so averse to employment and so averse to being a worker."

Stacy asked me for help. She had appealed to Erin's father, but father and son did not communicate easily, and Erin resisted taking advice from members of her family. "He talks to you," she said. So I waited a couple of weeks and called Erin. I said that he had misled me at times, without meaning to, and that Stacy and I were concerned about his inaction. I suggested that he see a therapist, that therapy might help him get through this crisis. He did not respond directly to my suggestion, nor did he veer from amiability. "What worries Stacy and you is that I am not really concerned about working to my potential," he replied.

That did worry us, but Erin would not be swayed. He had just completed a two-evening-a-week course in air-conditioner repair, learning very little that he did not already know, to get the necessary certification for a $13- or $14-an-hour dead-end job. Driving about in a panel truck making repairs to air-conditioning units would give him health insurance and some income for the family, once Stacy left her law firm, he explained to me. Most important, he would have a nondemanding, unthreatening platform from which to branch out and ample spare time for truly challenging work: renovating and reselling rundown homes, for example. "I know that I will be overqualified for the next position that I take," he said.

Not everyone has as much difficulty as Erin Brown in shaking off the emotional setback that layoffs produce. Some of those whose stories have been told earlier managed to move on to a next stage in their lives with their mental health more or less intact. But the majority did not. Psychiatrists and psychoanalysts view layoffs as catalysts for emotional damage. There is no mechanism, however, for collecting and disseminating what they know so that the consequences of corporate layoffs can be publicly flagged. The Centers for Disease Control and Prevention in Atlanta track the number of cases of flu, AIDS, measles, polio, Lyme disease, and other physical illnesses, and when the number spikes for one of these ailments, the center alerts us that an epidemic may be brewing, one that requires stepped-up medical treatment and a concerted public effort to shrink the number of cases. While doctors and hospitals funnel data about physical illness to the Centers for Disease Control, psychiatrists and psychologists do not similarly report the incidence among their patients of disabling neuroses connected to layoffs. Nor do the organizations that represent them adopt resolutions that declare layoffs to be a source of mental illness and therefore a menace to public health.

The American Psychiatric Association, whose 35,000 members are likely to treat mental illness related to layoffs, has never formally declared that the modern American layoff is hazardous to health. The president of the association, Dr. Steven S. Sharfstein, readily acknowledges the linkage as do other leaders of the organization.[7] Divorce, however, also damages mental health, Dr. Sharfstein said. So does the death of a spouse or a parent, not to mention the trauma of war. For psychiatry to oppose these events on public health grounds would be futile, he argued, and in the case of layoffs very possibly counterproductive. "If a company refrains from a layoff and then, as a result, is forced out of business, everyone would end up laid off," he said. So the American Psychiatric Association acquiesces in the practice and pushes instead to expand treatment of the victims. It lobbies business, for example, to expand coverage for mental illness. "We do see there are major shortcomings with employer health insurance in terms of access to mental health care," Dr. Sharfstein said, "and that is how we go at this issue."

Only one group of psychiatrists that I could find had singled out the layoff, the act in which a worker is sent away, as damaging in itself to mental health. The alert had come from the three hundred members of the Group for the Advancement of Psychiatry, or more specifically from the dozen or so in the group's Committee on Psychiatry in Industry.

These were psychiatrists whose practices focused on working with companies as consultants. Their client companies engaged in layoffs and they had first-hand knowledge of what people went through. In 1982, when the modern layoff was still a raw American experience, they published a monograph, *Job Loss—a Psychiatric Perspective,* in which they declared: "Our experience in industry and with patients suggests that those who lose their functional role as workers may behave as if their society no longer values them. Because they accept that as true, they suffer a consequent loss in the perception of their value in their families and to themselves."[8]

They distributed that study, with its straightforward, unpleasant observation, and eight years later, three psychiatrists on the committee expanded their findings into a book, *The Psychosocial Impact of Job Loss.*[9] Neither drew any attention. "Company managers were more interested in talking about the coping skills of those who remained on the job than they were about the damage to those they had laid off," Dr. Stephen Heidel, a consultant to businesses and a clinical professor of psychiatry at the University of California, San Diego, told me. I asked the doctors why, in their opinion, they had had so little success in publicizing the message in their monograph and book.[10] Various possibilities were mentioned, but all seemed to agree with Dr. Heidel's observation that managers don't want to be told about damage to mental health that results from a layoff they initiated. "If a psychiatrist goes out and says, I am an expert in job loss, the manager does not want to hear that and the psychiatrist won't be consulted about other services he can provide to a corporation," Dr. Heidel said. "If you lead with that, the door will be shut. You need to put a positive spin on things."

> **"Company managers were more interested in talking about the coping skills of those who remained on the job."**

While the nation's psychiatrists remain all but silent as a group, psychologists and sociologists in academic research seldom spot the sorts of debilitating neuroses that are evident in one-on-one therapy. Academics place much more faith in what they can document through empirical studies. They seek quantifiable evidence and shun the diagnostic judgment that is unavoidable in psychotherapy, whose raw material is narrative and free association. Their work, in consequence, relies heavily on surveys that blend together layoffs and unemployment and correlate the undifferentiated experience with measurable reactions: elevated blood pressure; an increased incidence of stomach problems, headaches, and insomnia; noticeably greater anxiety; a tendency to drink and smoke more; an increase in hospital admissions for ostensibly physical ailments. No survey of observable symptoms would pick up Brown's malady.

Psychoanalysts like Dr. Jacobs are also reluctant to single out layoffs publicly as damaging to mental health. By way of explanation, Dr. Jacobs said that people who seek psychoanalysis do so because of "long-standing character problems and in the course of analysis they mention a layoff, which has magnified what is already there or latently there." As a result, the layoff is not a central issue for the 2,500 members of the American Psychoanalytic Association. None of the numerous sessions at the association's four-day semiannual conferences have focused on layoffs and mental health. When I posted a request at the winter meeting in January 2005 to interview psychoanalysts concerned about the linkage, the only response came from Dr. Alexandra K. Rolde, a psychiatrist and psychoanalyst in private practice in Boston and a clinical instructor in psychiatry at Harvard Medical School.[11] For some of her patients, layoffs were indeed a central theme.

Dr. Rolde, a Czech immigrant in her late sixties, lived through the German occupation of Prague during World War II, in "semihiding" with her mother, as she puts it, to escape deportation and death as Jews. It was an experience that familiarized her with trauma, which is now her specialty in psychiatry. After the war she moved to Canada with her mother and stepfather, and the parents thrived in the jewelry business, first in Montreal and then in Toronto. When they moved the business from one city to the other, acting out of concern that Quebec's separatist movement might isolate the province from the rest of Canada, all fifty of the employees moved, too. No one was laid off, Dr. Rolde said, proud of the loyalties that kept her parents and their workers together. She has treated roughly thirty patients over the past twenty years for layoff-related ailments, she said, and she considers the layoffs to have been life-changing for them. Like Dr. Jacobs, she sees children as well as adults, and they, too, are often damaged.

"It is a trauma to the entire family," she said. "You have a parent working at a prestigious full-time job. All of a sudden the parent sits at home and can't find a job and is depressed. And suddenly the child's role model sort of crumbles. Instead of feeling admiration for the parent, the child eventually begins to feel disrespect. Because the children identify with their parents, they begin to doubt that they can accomplish anything. They feel they won't be successful in life and their self-esteem plummets. This of course is a long-term thing. We call it transgenerational trauma; it is similar to what we used to see with Holocaust survivors and their children. The children feel as damaged as their parents, even though they did not experience the trauma directly themselves."

She told me about a woman she had treated for years after the woman was laid off from an executive job at General Electric. "She got back into the workforce quickly enough, but in a job she did not like, yet she clung to it anyway," Dr. Rolde said. "She was so traumatized by the layoff that she did not have the self-confidence to risk moving on to more suitable work."

NOTES

[1] Interview with Stacy Brown, December 27, 2004.

[2] Concerning children, some studies show that children in two-parent families react differently to a father's job loss than to a mother's. In a study of 4,500 school-age children, for example, Ariel Kalil and Kathleen M. Ziol-Guest of the University of Chicago found that "mothers' employment is never significantly associated with children's academic progress. In contrast, we found significant adverse associations between fathers' job losses [and] children's probability of grade repetition and school suspension/expulsion."

[3] M. Merva and R. Fowles, "Effects of Diminished Economic Opportunities on Social Stress: Heart Attacks, Strokes and Crime," Salt Lake City Economic Policy Institute, University of Utah, 1992. The study covered fifteen metropolises over a twenty-year period. For other studies of the effects of unemployment on health, see "Links in the Chain of Adversity Following Job Loss: How Financial Strain and Loss of Personal Control Lead to Depression, Impaired Functioning and Poor Health," by Richard H. Price, Jin Nam Choi, and Amiram D. Vinokur, *Journal of Occupational Health Psychology* 7 (2002).

[4] Interview with Dr. Theodore Jacobs, August 5, 2004. In addition to his posts as a clinical professor of psychiatry at New York University School of Medicine and at the Albert Einstein College of Medicine, Dr. Jacobs is also the supervising analyst at the Psychoanalytic Institute at New York University and at the New York Psychoanalytic Institute.

[5] Interviews with Kim Cameron, January 17, 2005, and February 2, 2005.

[6] Interview with Kim Cameron, February 2, 2005.

[7] Interview with Dr. Steven Sharfstein, January 17, 2005. Dr. Sharfstein's one-year term as president of the APA began in May 2005. He is president and chief executive of Sheppard Pratt Health Care System, a nonprofit organization in Baltimore that provides mental health care for drug addicts and education for mentally disturbed children, among other services. He has a private psychiatric practice in Baltimore and has been a clinical professor of psychiatry at the University of Maryland.

[8] *Job Loss—a Psychiatric Perspective*, published by Mental Health Materials Center, New York, 1982.

[9] Nick Kates, Barrie S. Grieff, and Duane Hagen, *The Psychosocial Impact of Job Loss* (American Psychiatric Press, 1990).

[10] The conversation took place on April 8, 2005, during and after a session of the Committee on Psychiatry and Industry at the spring meeting of the Group for the Advancement of Psychiatry.

[11] The request was posted at the winter meeting, January 2005, at the Waldorf-Astoria. Dr. Rolde is also on the faculty of the Psychoanalytic Institute of New England East (PINE) and is a member of the Psychoanalytic Society of New England East (PSNE) as well as the Boston Psychoanalytic Society and Institute (BPSI).

DISCUSSION

1. It is far more conventional to speak about layoffs in economic rather than emotional terms. How does Uchitelle challenge this convention? In what ways does his examination of the psychiatric aspects of joblessness rewrite the scripts by which we are taught to think about unemployment?

2. "'You can have all kinds of people like spouses and friends say you are terrific, you are wonderful, you are great,'" Uchitelle quotes one medical expert as saying, "'but in the core you say, I am not, and I have big evidence that I am not. Layoffs diminish the ability to restart.'" Why are layoffs so often considered such convincing evidence of our self-worth? What does it tell us about the kind of importance we are taught to place on the work we do?

3. "In the cataloging of damage that results from layoffs," writes Uchitelle, "incapacitating emotional illness almost never appears on the lists that economists, politicians, sociologists, union leaders, business school professors, management consultants, and journalists compile." Why doesn't it? What would you say are the assumptions or norms that keep us from viewing emotional illness as a legitimate consequence of unemployment?

WRITING

4. One of the costs of layoffs, according to Uchitelle, is that they deprive people of a primary way to define their self-worth. Write an essay in which you reflect on the role that work plays in anchoring and validating your views of yourself. Can you think of a job you've held or a career path you've pursued (or one you would like to) that you've used to define your self-worth? What would the effect be of having this particular work outlet taken away?

5. Some of the psychological or emotional effects of being laid off that Uchitelle lists are low self-esteem, nervousness, inability to form close bonds, and fear of trying new things. Do you think it is reasonable for employers to consider the emotional costs of layoffs in determining whether to let workers go? How might an employer address the criticisms that Uchitelle is making? Ultimately, is an employer responsible for the emotional well-being of its employees? Why or why not?

6. Their many differences aside, Uchitelle does share with Matthew Crawford (p. 395) an interest in exploring what we might call the emotional life of work. Both writers ask us to consider what effects working (or not working) can have on our happiness, contentment, and self-esteem. Write an essay in which you compare how each writer explores this issue. To what extent does Uchitelle's argument about the psychological damage wrought by unemployment recall or help reinforce Crawford's claims about the emotional satisfactions afforded by working with your hands?

ANTHONY DePALMA

Fifteen Years on the Bottom Rung

America, it is said, is the "land of opportunity." Depending on where you're born, what pressures you face, or what circumstances you find yourself in, however, this myth can play itself out in radically different ways. Anthony DePalma focuses on one group of workers for whom the supposedly universal promise of opportunity bumps up against the hard realities that often confront those on the lower rungs of the socioeconomic ladder. DePalma is the author of The *Man Who Invented Fidel* (2006), a study of the *New York Times* reporter who helped to create the myth surrounding Castro. He has also published *Here: A Biography of the New American Continent* (2001). DePalma was a staff writer for the *New York Times*, and as bureau chief for Mexico and Canada, he covered political events such as the Zapatista uprising, economic news such as the crisis of the peso, and natural disasters such as the Quebec ice storm. He has also worked as a business correspondent in both the Metropolitan and National divisions. The following essay is from *Class Matters* (2005), by correspondents of the *New York Times*.

IN THE DARK BEFORE DAWN, WHEN MADISON AVENUE WAS ALL BUT deserted and its pricey boutiques were still locked up tight, several Mexicans slipped quietly into 3 Guys, a restaurant that the Zagat guide once called "the most expensive coffee shop in New York."

For the next ten hours they would fry eggs, grill burgers, pour coffee, and wash dishes for a stream of customers from the Upper East Side of Manhattan. By 7:35 A.M., Eliot Spitzer, attorney general of New York, was holding a power breakfast back near the polished granite counter. In the same burgundy booth a few hours later, Michael A. Wiener, cofounder of the multibillion-dollar Infinity Broadcasting, grabbed a bite with his wife, Zena. Just the day before, Uma Thurman slipped in for a quiet lunch with her children, but the paparazzi found her and she left.

More Mexicans filed in to begin their shifts throughout the morning, and by the time John Zannikos, one of the restaurant's three Greek owners, drove in from the north Jersey suburbs to work the lunch crowd, Madison Avenue was buzzing. So was 3 Guys.

"You got to wait a little bit," Zannikos said to a pride of elegant women who had spent the morning at the Whitney Museum of American Art, across Madison Avenue at 75th Street. For an illiterate immigrant who came to New York years ago with nothing but $100 in his pocket and a willingness to work etched on his heart, could any words have been sweeter to say?

With its wealthy clientele, middle-class owners, and low-income work-force, 3 Guys is a template of the class divisions in America. But it is also the setting for two starkly different tales about breaching those divides.

The familiar story is Zannikos's. For him, the restaurant—don't dare call it a diner—with its twenty-dollar salads and elegant décor represents the American promise of upward mobility, one that has been fulfilled countless times for generations of hardworking immigrants.

But for Juan Manuel Peralta, a thirty-four-year-old illegal immigrant who worked there for five years until he was fired in May 2004, and for many of the other illegal Mexican immigrants in the back, restaurant work today is more like a dead end. They are finding the American dream of moving up far more elusive than it was for Zannikos. Despite his efforts to help them, they risk becoming stuck in a permanent underclass of the poor, the unskilled, and the uneducated.

That is not to suggest that the nearly five million Mexicans who, like Peralta, are living in the United States illegally will never emerge from the shadows. Many have, and undoubtedly many more will. But the sheer size of the influx—over 400,000 a year, with no end in sight—creates a problem all its own. It means there is an ever-growing pool of interchangeable workers, many of them shunting from one low-paying job to another. If one moves on, another one—or maybe two or three—is there to take his place.

> **There is an ever-growing pool of interchangeable workers, many of them shunting from one low-paying job to another.**

Although Peralta arrived in New York almost forty years after Zannikos, the two share a remarkably similar beginning. They came at the same age to the same section of New York City, without legal papers or more than a few words of English. Each dreamed of a better life. But monumental changes in the economy and in attitudes toward immigrants have made it far less likely that Peralta and his children will experience the same upward mobility as Zannikos and his family.

Of course, there is a chance that Peralta may yet take his place among the Mexican-Americans who have succeeded here. He realizes that he will probably not do as well as the few who have risen to high office or who were able to buy the vineyards where their grandfathers once picked grapes. But he still dreams that his children will someday join the millions who have lost their accents, gotten good educations, and firmly achieved the American dream.

Political scientists are divided over whether the twenty-five million people of Mexican ancestry in the United States represent an exception to the classic immigrant success story. Some, like John H. Mollenkopf at the City University of New York, are convinced that Mexicans will eventually do as well as the Greeks, Italians, and other Europeans of the last century who were usually well assimilated after two or three generations. Others, including Mexican-Americans like Rodolfo O. de la Garza, a professor at Columbia, have done studies showing that Mexican-Americans face so many obstacles that even the fourth generation trails other Americans in education, home ownership, and household income.

The situation is even worse for the millions more who have illegally entered the United States since 1990. Spread out in scores of cities far beyond the Southwest, they find jobs plentiful but advancement difficult. President Vicente Fox of Mexico was forced to apologize in the spring of 2005 for declaring publicly what many Mexicans say they feel, that the illegal immigrants "are doing the work that not even blacks want to do in the United States." Resentment and race subtly stand in their way, as does a lingering attachment to Mexico, which is so close that many immigrants do not put down deep roots here. They say they plan to stay only long enough to make some money and then go back home. Few ever do.

But the biggest obstacle is their illegal status. With few routes open to become legal, they remain, like Peralta, without rights, without security, and without a clear path to a better future.

"It's worrisome," said Richard Alba, a sociologist at the State University of New York, Albany, who studies the assimilation and class mobility of contemporary immigrants, "and I don't see much reason to believe this will change."

Little has changed for Peralta, a cook who has worked at menial jobs in the United States for fifteen years. Though he makes more than he ever dreamed of in Mexico, his life is anything but middle class and setbacks are routine. Still, he has not given up hope. "*Querer es poder*," he sometimes says—want something badly enough and you will get it.

But desire may not be enough anymore. That is what concerns Arturo Sarukhan, Mexico's consul general in New York. In early 2005, Sarukhan took an urgent call from New York's police commissioner about an increase in gang activity among young Mexican men, a sign that they were moving into the underside of American life. Of all immigrants in New York City, officials say, Mexicans are the poorest, least educated, and least likely to speak English.

The failure or success of this generation of Mexicans in the United States will determine the place that Mexicans will hold here in years to come, Sarukhan said, and the outlook is not encouraging.

"They will be better off than they could ever have been in Mexico," he said, "but I don't think that's going to be enough to prevent them from becoming an underclass in New York."

DIFFERENT RESULTS

There is a break in the middle of the day at 3 Guys, after the lunchtime limousines leave and before the private schools let out. That was when Zannikos asked the Mexican cook who replaced Peralta to prepare some lunch for him. Then Zannikos carried the chicken breast on pita to the last table in the restaurant.

"My life story is a good story, a lot of success," he said, his accent still heavy. He was just a teenager when he left the Greek island of Chios, a few miles off the coast of Turkey. World War II had just ended, and Greece was in ruins. "There was only rich and poor, that's it," Zannikos said. "There was no middle class like you have here." He is seventy now, with short gray hair and soft eyes that can water at a mention of the past.

Because of the war, he said, he never got past the second grade, never learned to read or write. He signed on as a merchant seaman, and in 1953, when he was nineteen, his ship docked at Norfolk, Virginia. He went ashore one Saturday with no intention of ever returning to Greece. He left behind everything, including his travel documents. All he had in his pockets was $100 and the address of his mother's cousin in the Jackson Heights–Corona section of Queens.

Almost four decades later, Juan Manuel Peralta underwent a similar rite of passage out of Mexico. He had finished the eighth grade in the poor southern state of Guerrero and saw nothing in his future there but fixing flat tires. His father, Inocencio, had once dreamed of going to the United States, but never had the money. In 1990, he borrowed enough to give his firstborn son a chance.

Peralta was nineteen when he boarded a smoky bus that carried him through the deserted hills of Guerrero and kept going until it reached the edge of Mexico. With eight other Mexicans he did not know, he crawled through a sewer tunnel that started in Tijuana and ended on the other side of the border, in what Mexicans call El Norte.

He had carried no documents, no photographs, and no money except what his father gave him to pay his shifty guide and to buy an airline ticket to New York. Deep in a pocket was the address of an uncle in the same section of Queens where John Zannikos had gotten his start. By 1990, the area had gone from largely Greek to mostly Latino.

Starting over in the same working-class neighborhood, Peralta and Zannikos quickly learned that New York was full of opportunities and obstacles, often in equal measure. On his first day there, Zannikos, scared and feeling lost, found the building he was looking for, but his mother's cousin had moved. He had no idea what to do until a Greek man passed by. Walk five blocks to the Deluxe Diner, the man said. He did.

The diner was full of Greek housepainters, including one who knew Zannikos's father. On the spot, they offered him a job painting closets, where his mistakes would be hidden. He painted until the weather turned cold. Another Greek hired him as a dishwasher at his coffee shop in the Bronx.

It was not easy, but Zannikos worked his way up to short-order cook, learning English as he went along. In 1956, immigration officials raided the coffee shop. He was deported, but after a short while he managed to sneak back into the country. Three years later he married a Puerto Rican from the Bronx. The marriage lasted only a year, but it put him on the road to becoming a citizen. Now he could buy his own restaurant, a greasy spoon in the South Bronx that catered to a late-night clientele of prostitutes and undercover police officers.

Since then, he has bought and sold more than a dozen New York diners, but none have been more successful than the original 3 Guys, which opened in 1978. He and his partners own two other restaurants with the same name farther up Madison Avenue, but they have never replicated the high-end appeal of the original.

"When employees come in, I teach them, 'Hey, this is a different neighborhood,'" Zannikos said. What may be standard in some other diners is not

> ### "I'm in the middle and I'm happy."

tolerated here. There are no Greek flags or tourism posters. There is no television or twirling tower of cakes with cream pompadours. Waiters are forbidden to chew gum. No customer is ever called "Honey."

"They know their place and I know my place," Zannikos said of his customers. "It's as simple as that."

His place in society now is a far cry from his days in the Bronx. He and his second wife, June, live in Wyckoff, a New Jersey suburb where he pampers fig trees and dutifully looks after a bird feeder shaped like the Parthenon. They own a condominium in Florida. His three children all went far beyond his second-grade education, finishing high school or attending college.

They have all done well, as has Zannikos, who says he makes about $130,000 a year. He says he is not sensitive to class distinctions, but he admits he was bothered when some people mistook him for the caterer at fund-raising dinners for the local Greek church he helped build.

All in all, he thinks immigrants today have a better chance of moving up the class ladder than he did fifty years ago.

"At that time, no bank would give us any money, but today they give you credit cards in the mail," he said. "New York still gives you more opportunity than any other place. If you want to do things, you will."

He says he has done well, and he is content with his station in life. "I'm in the middle and I'm happy."

A DIVISIVE ISSUE

Juan Manuel Peralta cannot guess what class John Zannikos belongs to. But he is certain that it is much tougher for an immigrant to get ahead today than fifty years ago. And he has no doubt about his own class.

"*La pobreza*," he says. "Poverty."

It was not what he expected when he boarded the bus to the border, but it did not take long for him to realize that success in the United States required more than hard work. "A lot of it has to do with luck," he said during a lunch break on a stoop around the corner from the Queens diner where he went to work after 3 Guys.

"People come here, and in no more than a year or two they can buy their own house and have a car," Peralta said. "Me, I've been here fifteen years, and if I die tomorrow, there wouldn't even be enough money to bury me."

In 1990, Peralta was in the vanguard of Mexican immigrants who bypassed the traditional barrios in border states to work in far-flung cities like Denver and New York. The 2000 census counted 186,872 Mexicans in New York, triple the 1990 figure, and there are undoubtedly many more today. The Mexican consulate, which serves the metropolitan region, has issued more than 500,000 ID cards just since 2001.

Fifty years ago, illegal immigration was a minor problem. Now it is a divisive national issue, pitting those who welcome cheap labor against those with concerns about border security and the cost of providing social services. Though newly arrived Mexicans often work in industries that rely on cheap labor, like restaurants and construction, they rarely organize. Most are desperate to stay out of sight.

Peralta hooked up with his uncle the morning he arrived in New York. He did not work for weeks until the bakery where the uncle worked had an opening, a part-time job making muffins. He took it, though he didn't know muffins from crumb cake. When he saw that he would not make enough to repay his father, he took a second job making night deliveries for a Manhattan diner. By the end of his first day he was so lost he had to spend all his tip money on a cab ride home.

He quit the diner, but working there even briefly opened his eyes to how easy it could be to make money in New York. Diners were everywhere, and so were jobs making deliveries, washing dishes, or busing tables. In six months, Peralta had paid back the money his father gave him. He bounced from job to job and in 1995, eager to show off his new-found success, went back to Mexico with his pockets full of money, and married. He was twenty-five then, the same age at which Zannikos married. But the similarities end there.

When Zannikos jumped ship, he left Greece behind for good. Though he himself had no documents, the compatriots he encountered on his first days were here legally, like most other Greek immigrants, and could help him. Greeks had never come to the United States in large numbers—the 2000 census counted only 29,805 New Yorkers born in Greece—but they tended to settle in just a few areas, like the Astoria section of Queens, which became cohesive communities ready to help new arrivals.

Peralta, like many other Mexicans, is trying to make it on his own and has never severed his emotional or financial ties to home. After five years in New York's Latino community, he spoke little English and owned little more than the clothes on his back. He decided to return to Huamuxtitlán, the dusty village beneath a flat-topped mountain where he was born.

"People thought that since I was coming back from El Norte, I would be so rich that I could spread money around," he said. Still, he felt privileged: his New York wages dwarfed the $1,000 a year he might have made in Mexico.

He met a shy, pretty girl named Matilde in Huamuxtitlán, married her, and returned with her to New York, again illegally, all in a matter of weeks. Their first child was born in 1996. Peralta soon found that supporting a family made it harder to save money. Then, in 1999, he got the job at 3 Guys.

"Barba Yanni helped me learn how to prepare things the way customers like them," Peralta said, referring to Zannikos with a Greek title of respect that means Uncle John.

The restaurant became his school. He learned how to sauté a fish so that it looked like a work of art. The three partners lent him money and said they would help him get immigration documents. The pay was good.

But there were tensions with the other workers. Instead of hanging their orders on a rack, the waiters shouted them out, in Greek, Spanish, and a kind of fractured English. Sometimes Peralta did not understand, and they argued. Soon he was known as a hothead.

Still, he worked hard, and every night he returned to his growing family. Matilde, now twenty-seven, cleaned houses until their second child, Heidi, was born in 2002. Now Matilde tries to sell Mary Kay products to other mothers at Public School 12, which their son Antony, who is eight, attends.

Most weeks, Peralta could make as much as $600. Over the course of a year that could come to over $30,000, enough to approach the lower middle class. But the life he leads is far from that and uncertainty hovers over everything about his life, starting with his paycheck.

To earn $600, he has to work at least ten hours a day, six days a week, and that does not happen every week. Sometimes he is paid overtime for the extra hours, sometimes not. And, as he found out, he can be fired at any time and bring in nothing, not even unemployment, until he lands another job. In 2004, he made about $24,000.

Because he is here illegally, Peralta can easily be exploited. He cannot file a complaint against his landlord for charging him $500 a month for a nine- by nine-foot room in a Queens apartment that he shares with nine other Mexicans in three families who pay the remainder of the $2,000-a-month rent. All thirteen share one bathroom, and the established pecking order means the Peraltas rarely get to use the kitchen. Eating out can be expensive.

Because they were born in New York, Peralta's children are United States citizens, and their health care is generally covered by Medicaid. But he has to pay out of his pocket whenever he or his wife sees a doctor. And forget about going to the dentist.

As many other Mexicans do, he wires money home, and it costs him $7 for every $100 he sends. When his uncle, his nephew, and his sister asked him for money, he was expected to lend it. No one has paid him back. He has middle-class ornaments, like a cellphone and a DVD player, but no driver's license or Social Security card.

He is the first to admit that he has vices that have held him back; nothing criminal, but he tends to lose his temper and there are nights when he likes to have a drink or two. His greatest weakness is instant lottery tickets, what he calls "*los scratch,*" and he sheepishly confesses that he can squander as much as $75 a week on them. It is a way of preserving hope, he said. Once he won $100. He bought a blender.

Years ago, he and Matilde were so confident they would make it in America that when their son was born they used the American spelling of his name, Anthony, figuring it would help pave his passage into the mainstream. But even that effort failed.

"Look at this," his wife said one afternoon as she sat on the floor of their room near a picture of the Virgin of Guadalupe. Peralta sat on a small plastic stool in the doorway, listening. His mattress was stacked against the wall. A roll of toilet paper was stashed nearby because they dared not leave it in the shared bathroom for someone else to use.

She took her pocketbook and pulled out a clear plastic case holding her son's baptismal certificate, on which his name is spelled with an H. But then she unfolded his birth certificate, where the H is missing.

"The teachers won't teach him to spell his name the right way until the certificate is legally changed," she said. "But how can we do that if we're not legal?"

PROGRESS, BUT NOT SUCCESS

An elevated subway train thundered overhead, making the afternoon light along Roosevelt Avenue blink like a failing fluorescent bulb. Peralta's daughter and son grabbed his fat hands as they ran some errands. He had just finished a ten-hour shift, eggs over easy and cheeseburgers since 5:00 A.M. It had been especially hard to stand the monotony that day. He kept thinking about what was going on in Mexico, where it was the feast day of Our Lady of the Rosary. And, oh, what a feast there was—sweets and handmade tamales, a parade, even a bullfight. At night, fireworks, bursting loud and bright against the green folds of the mountains. Paid for, in part, by the money he sends home.

But instead of partying, he was walking his children to the Arab supermarket on Roosevelt Avenue to buy packages of chicken and spare ribs, and hoping to get to use the kitchen. And though he knew better, he grabbed a package of pink and white marshmallows for the children. He needed to buy tortillas, too, but not there. A Korean convenience store a few blocks away sells La Maizteca tortillas, made in New York.

The swirl of immigrants in Peralta's neighborhood is part of the fabric of New York, just as it was in 1953, when John Zannikos arrived. But most immigrants then were Europeans, and though they spoke different languages, their Caucasian features helped them blend into New York's middle class.

> *In 1953, . . . most immigrants . . . were Europeans, and . . . their Caucasian features helped them blend into New York's middle class.*

Experts remain divided over whether Mexicans can follow the same route. Samuel P. Huntington, a Harvard professor of government, takes the extreme view that Mexicans will not assimilate and that the separate culture they are developing threatens the United States.

Most others believe that recent Mexican immigrants will eventually take their place in society, and perhaps someday muster political clout commensurate with their numbers, though significant impediments are slowing their progress. Francisco Rivera-Batiz, a Columbia University economics professor, says that prejudice remains a problem, that factory jobs have all but disappeared, and that there is a growing gap between the educational demands of the economy and the limited schooling that the newest Mexicans have when they arrive.

But the biggest obstacle by far, and the one that separates newly arrived Mexicans from Greeks, Italians, and most other immigrants—including earlier generations of Mexicans—is their illegal status. Rivera-Batiz studied what happened to illegal Mexican immigrants who became legal after the last national amnesty in 1986. Within a few years, their incomes rose 20 percent and their English improved greatly.

"Legalization," he said, "helped them tremendously."

Although the Bush administration talks about legalizing some Mexicans with a guest worker program, there is opposition to another amnesty, and the number of Mexicans illegally living in the United States continues to soar. Desperate to get their papers any way they can, many turn to shady storefront legal offices. Like Peralta, they sign on to illusory schemes that cost hundreds of dollars but almost never produce the promised green cards.

Until the 1980s, Mexican immigration was largely seasonal and mostly limited to agricultural workers. But then economic chaos in Mexico sent a flood of immigrants northward, many of them poorly educated farmers from the impoverished countryside. Tighter security on the border made it harder for Mexicans to move back and forth in the traditional way, so they tended to stay here, searching for low-paying unskilled jobs and concentrating in barrios where Spanish, constantly replenished, never loses its immediacy.

"*Cuidado!*" Peralta shouted when Antony carelessly stepped into Roosevelt Avenue without looking. Although the boy is taught in English at school, he rarely uses anything but Spanish at home.

Even now, after fifteen years in New York, Peralta speaks little English. He tried English classes once, but could not get his mind to accept the new sounds. So he dropped it, and has stuck with Spanish, which he concedes is "the language of busboys" in New York. But as long as he stays in his neighborhood, it is all he needs.

It was late afternoon by the time Peralta and his children headed home. The run-down house, the overheated room, the stacked mattress, and the hoarded toilet paper—all remind him how far he would have to go to achieve a success like John Zannikos's.

Still, he says, he has done far better than he could ever have done in Mexico. He realizes that the money he sends to his family there is not enough to satisfy his father, who built stairs for a second floor of his house made of concrete blocks in Huamuxtitlán, even though there is no second floor. He believes Juan Manuel has made it big in New York and he is waiting for money from America to complete the upstairs.

His son has never told him the truth about his life up north. He said his father's images of America came from another era. The older man does not know how tough it is to be a Mexican immigrant in the United States now, tougher than any young man who ever left Huamuxtitlán would admit. Everything built up over fifteen years here can come apart as easily as an adobe house in an earthquake. And then it is time to start over, again.

A CONFLICT ERUPTS

It was the end of another busy lunch at 3 Guys in the late spring of 2003. Peralta made himself a turkey sandwich and took a seat at a rear table. The Mexican countermen, dishwashers, and busboys also started their breaks, while the Greek waiters took care of the last few diners.

It is not clear how the argument started. But a cross word passed between a Greek waiter and a Mexican busboy. Voices were raised. The waiter swung at the busboy, catching him behind the ear. Peralta froze. So did the other Mexicans.

Even from the front of the restaurant, where he was watching the cash register, Zannikos realized something was wrong and rushed back to break it up. "I stood between them, held one and pushed the other away," he said. "I told them: 'You don't do that here. Never do that here.'"

Zannikos said he did not care who started it. He ordered both the busboy and the waiter, a partner's nephew, to get out.

But several Mexicans, including Peralta, said that they saw Zannikos grab the busboy by the head and that they believed he would have hit him if another Mexican had not stepped between them. That infuriated them because they felt he had sided with the Greek without knowing who was at fault.

Zannikos said that was not true, but in the end it did not matter. The easygoing atmosphere at the restaurant changed. "Everybody was a little cool," Zannikos recalled.

What he did not know then was that the Mexicans had reached out to the Restaurant Opportunities Center, a workers' rights group. Eventually six of them, including Peralta, cooperated with the group. He did so reluctantly, he said, because he was afraid that if the owners found out, they would no longer help him get his immigration papers. The labor group promised that the owners would never know.

The owners saw it as an effort to shake them down, but for the Mexicans it became a class struggle pitting powerless workers against hard-hearted owners.

> **For the Mexicans it became a class struggle pitting powerless workers against hard-hearted owners.**

Their grievances went beyond the scuffle. They complained that with just one exception, only Greeks became waiters at 3 Guys. They challenged the sole Mexican waiter, Salomon Paniagua, a former Mexican army officer who, everyone agreed, looked Greek, to stand with them.

But on the day the labor group picketed the restaurant, Paniagua refused to put down his order pad. A handful of demonstrators carried signs on Madison Avenue for a short while before Zannikos and his partners reluctantly agreed to settle.

Zannikos said he felt betrayed. "When I see these guys, I see myself when I started, and I always try to help them," he said. "I didn't do anything wrong."

The busboy and the Mexican who intervened were paid several thousand dollars and the owners promised to promote a current Mexican employee to waiter within a month. But that did not end the turmoil.

Fearing that the other Mexicans might try to get back at him, Paniagua decided to strike out on his own. After asking Zannikos for advice, he bought a one-third share of a Greek diner in Jamaica, Queens. He said he put it in his father's name because the older man had become a legal resident after the 1986 amnesty.

After Paniagua left, 3 Guys went without a single Mexican waiter for ten months, despite the terms of the settlement. In March, an eager Mexican busboy with a heavy accent who had worked there for four years got a chance to wear a waiter's tie.

Peralta ended up having to leave 3 Guys around the same time as Paniagua. Zannikos's partners suspected he had sided with the labor group, he said, and started to criticize his work unfairly. Then they cut back his schedule to five days a week. After he hurt his ankle playing soccer, they told him to go home until he was better. When Peralta came back to work about two weeks later, he was fired.

Zannikos confirms part of the account but says the firing had nothing to do with the scuffle or the ensuing dispute. "If he was good, believe me, he wouldn't get fired," he said of Peralta.

Peralta shrugged when told what Zannikos said. "I know my own work and I know what I can do," he said. "There are a lot of restaurants in New York, and a lot of workers."

When 3 Guys fired Peralta, another Mexican replaced him, just as Peralta replaced a Mexican at the Greek diner in Queens where he went to work next.

This time, though, there was no Madison Avenue address, no elaborate menu of New Zealand mussels or designer mushrooms. In the Queens diner a bowl of soup with a buttered roll cost two dollars, all day. If he fried burgers and scraped fat off the big grill for ten hours a day, six days a week, he might earn about as much as he did on Madison Avenue, at least for a week.

His schedule kept changing. Sometimes he worked the lunch and dinner shift, and by the end of the night he was worn out, especially since he often found himself arguing with the Greek owner. But he did not look forward to going home. So after the night manager lowered the security gate, Peralta would wander the streets.

One of those nights he stopped at a phone center off Roosevelt Avenue to call his mother. "Everything's okay," he told her. He asked how she had spent the last $100 he sent, and whether she needed anything else. There is always need in Huamuxtitlán.

Still restless, he went to the Scorpion, a shot-and-beer joint open till 4 A.M. He sat at the long bar nursing vodkas with cranberry juice, glancing at the soccer match on TV and the busty Brazilian bartender who spoke only a little Spanish. When it was nearly eleven, he called it a night.

Back home, he quietly opened the door to his room. The lights were off, the television murmuring. His family was asleep in the bunk bed that the store had now threatened to repossess. Antony was curled up on the top, Matilde and Heidi cuddled in the bottom. Peralta moved the plastic stool out of the way and dropped his mattress to the floor.

The children did not stir. His wife's eyes fluttered, but she said nothing. Peralta looked over his family, his home.

"This," he said, "is my life in New York."

Not the life he imagined, but his life. In early March 2005, just after Heidi's third birthday, he quit his job at the Queens diner after yet another heated argument with the owner. In his mind, preserving his dignity is one of the few liberties he has left.

"I'll get another job," he said while babysitting Heidi at home a few days after he quit. The rent is already paid till the end of the month and he has friends, he said. People know him. To him, jobs are interchangeable—just as he is to the jobs. If he cannot find work as a grillman, he will bus tables. Or wash dishes. If not at one diner, then at another.

"It's all the same," he said.

It took about three weeks, but Peralta did find a new job as a grillman at another Greek diner in a different part of New York. His salary is roughly the same, the menu is roughly the same (one new item, Greek burritos, was a natural), and he sees his chance for a better future as being roughly the same as it has been since he got to America.

A LONG DAY CLOSES

It was now dark again outside 3 Guys. About 9:00 P.M. John Zannikos asked his Mexican cook for a small salmon steak, a little rare. It had been another busy ten-hour day for him, but a good one. Receipts from the morning alone exceeded what he needed to take in every day just to cover the $23,000 a month rent.

He finished the salmon quickly, left final instructions with the lone Greek waiter still on duty, and said good night to everyone else. He put on his light tan corduroy jacket and the baseball cap he picked up in Florida.

"'Night," he said to the lone table of diners.

Outside, as Zannikos walked slowly down Madison Avenue, a self-made man comfortable with his own hard-won success, the bulkhead doors in front of 3 Guys clanked open. Faint voices speaking Spanish came from below. A young Mexican who started his shift ten hours earlier climbed out with a bag of garbage and heaved it onto the sidewalk. New Zealand mussel shells. Uneaten bits of portobello mushrooms. The fine grounds of decaf cappuccino.

One black plastic bag after another came out until Madison Avenue in front of 3 Guys was piled high with trash.

"Hurry up!" the young man shouted to the other Mexicans. "I want to go home, too."

DISCUSSION

1. DePalma begins his essay by presenting a list of the powerful or famous people who frequent the 3 Guys café. Why do you think he does this? What sort of framework does this introduction provide for the experiences of the Mexican workers whom the essay goes on to profile?

2. According to DePalma, the workplace portrait sketched here is a "template of the class divisions in America." How accurate does this claim seem to you? In what ways does the essay's depiction of work also function as a commentary on the ideals of class mobility?

3. How would you define the ideal working environment? What kinds of jobs or roles? How does this hypothetical world compare to or differ from the one depicted in this essay?

WRITING

4. This essay draws a clear connection between work and immigration, exploring the ways that the contemporary landscape for temporary workers threatens to rewrite what DePalma calls the "classic immigrant success story." Write an essay in which you assess the validity of this claim. What is the "classic immigrant success story"? What is its typical plot line, its traditional roles? How does this conventional script compare to the immigrant story DePalma relates about either Juan Manuel Peralta or John Zannikos? How closely does this example resemble the ideal?

5. Make a list of the different jobs Peralta performs during his years in the United States. Write an essay in which you describe the particular role you think these jobs script for the workers who undertake them. What is the profile of the typical person who performs these jobs? How accurate and fair do you think these descriptions are? Why?

6. How much of DePalma's discussion here reminds you of what Louis Uchitelle (p. 370) says about the kinds of psychic harm job-related struggles can inflict? Write a review of DePalma's essay that you think Uchitelle might offer. To what extent would Uchitelle's review find parallels in the social and economic hardships profiled here and his argument regarding the emotional costs of unemployment?

MATTHEW B. CRAWFORD

The Case for Working with Your Hands

In our hyperactive, information-based economy, it's easy to assume that any work involving manual skill has become obsolete. According to Matthew B. Crawford, however, ours may well be the moment where precisely such work is most urgently needed. Taking a critical look at current cultural conceits about "knowledge work," he offers a spirited defense of what he calls "working with your hands." Crawford lives in Richmond, Virginia, and is a fellow at the Institute for Advanced Studies in Culture at the University of Virginia. He is the author of the book *Shop Class as Soulcraft: An Inquiry into the Value of Work* (2009). The following essay appeared in the May 21, 2009, issue of the *New York Times Magazine*.

THE TELEVISION SHOW *DEADLIEST CATCH* DEPICTS COMMERCIAL crab fishermen in the Bering Sea. Another, *Dirty Jobs*, shows all kinds of grueling work; one episode featured a guy who inseminates turkeys for a living. The weird fascination of these shows must lie partly in the fact that such confrontations with material reality have become exotically unfamiliar. Many of us do work that feels more surreal than real. Working in an office, you often find it difficult to see any tangible result from your efforts. What exactly have you accomplished at the end of any given day? Where the chain of cause and effect is opaque and responsibility diffuse, the experience of individual agency can be elusive. *Dilbert, The Office* and similar portrayals of cubicle life attest to the dark absurdism with which many Americans have come to view their white-collar jobs.

Is there a more "real" alternative (short of inseminating turkeys)?

High-school shop-class programs were widely dismantled in the 1990s as educators prepared students to become "knowledge workers." The imperative of the last 20 years to round up every warm body and send it to college, then to the cubicle, was tied to a vision of the future in which we somehow take leave of material reality and glide about in a pure information economy. This has not come to pass. To begin with, such work often feels more enervating than gliding. More fundamentally, now as ever, somebody has to actually do things: fix our cars, unclog our toilets, build our houses.

When we praise people who do work that is straightforwardly useful, the praise often betrays an assumption that they had no other options.

We idealize them as the salt of the earth and emphasize the sacrifice for others their work may entail. Such sacrifice does indeed occur—the hazards faced by a lineman restoring power during a storm come to mind. But what if such work answers as well to a basic human need of the one who does it? I take this to be the suggestion of Marge Piercy's poem "To Be of Use," which concludes with the lines "the pitcher longs for water to carry/and a person for work that is real." Beneath our gratitude for the lineman may rest envy.

This seems to be a moment when the useful arts have an especially compelling economic rationale. A car mechanics' trade association reports that repair shops have seen their business jump significantly in the current recession: people aren't buying new cars; they are fixing the ones they have. The current downturn is likely to pass eventually. But there are also systemic changes in the economy, arising from information technology, that have the surprising effect of making the manual trades—plumbing, electrical work, car repair—more attractive as careers. The Princeton economist Alan Blinder argues that the crucial distinction in the emerging labor market is not between those with more or less education, but between those whose services can be delivered over a wire and those who must do their work in person or on site. The latter will find their livelihoods more secure against outsourcing to distant countries. As Blinder puts it, "You can't hammer a nail over the Internet." Nor can the Indians fix your car. Because they are in India.

If the goal is to earn a living, then, maybe it isn't really true that 18-year-olds need to be imparted with a sense of panic about getting into college (though they certainly need to learn). Some people are hustled off to college, then to the cubicle, against their own inclinations and natural bents, when they would rather be learning to build things or fix things. One shop teacher suggested to me that "in schools, we create artificial learning environments for our children that they know to be contrived and undeserving of their full attention and engagement. Without the opportunity to learn through the hands, the world remains abstract and distant, and the passions for learning will not be engaged."

A gifted young person who chooses to become a mechanic rather than to accumulate academic credentials is viewed as eccentric, if not self-destructive. There is a pervasive anxiety among parents that there is only one track to success for their children. It runs through a series of gates controlled by prestigious institutions. Further, there is wide use of drugs to medicate boys, especially, against their natural tendency toward action, the better to "keep things on track." I taught briefly in a public high school and would have loved to have set up a Ritalin fogger in my classroom. It is a rare person, male or female, who is naturally inclined to sit still for 17 years in school, and then indefinitely at work.

The trades suffer from low prestige, and I believe this is based on a simple mistake. Because the work is dirty, many people assume it is also stupid. This is not my experience. I have a small business as a motorcycle mechanic in Richmond, Virginia, which I started in 2002. I work on Japanese and European motorcycles, mostly older bikes with some "vintage" cachet that makes people willing to spend money on them. I have found the satisfactions of the work to be very much bound up with the intellectual challenges it presents. And yet my decision to go into this line of work is a choice that seems to perplex many people.

After finishing a Ph.D. in political philosophy at the University of Chicago in 2000, I managed to stay on with a one-year postdoctoral fellowship at the university's Committee on Social Thought. The academic job market was utterly bleak. In a state of professional panic, I retreated to a makeshift workshop I set up in the basement of a Hyde Park apartment building, where I spent the winter tearing down an old Honda motorcycle and rebuilding it. The physicality of it, and the clear specificity of what the project required of me, was a balm. Stumped by a starter motor that seemed to check out in every way but wouldn't work, I started asking around at Honda dealerships. Nobody had an answer; finally one service manager told me to call Fred Cousins of Triple O Service. "If anyone can help you, Fred can."

I called Fred, and he invited me to come to his independent motorcycle-repair shop, tucked discreetly into an unmarked warehouse on Goose Island. He told me to put the motor on a certain bench that was free of clutter. He checked the electrical resistance through the windings, as I had done, to confirm there was no short circuit or broken wire. He spun the shaft that ran through the center of the motor, as I had. No problem: it spun freely. Then he hooked it up to a battery. It moved ever so slightly but wouldn't spin. He grasped the shaft, delicately, with three fingers, and tried to wiggle it side to side. "Too much free play," he said. He suggested that the problem was with the bushing (a thick-walled sleeve of metal) that captured the end of the shaft in the end of the cylindrical motor housing. It was worn, so it wasn't locating the shaft precisely enough. The shaft was free to move too much side to side (perhaps a couple of hundredths of an inch), causing the outer circumference of the rotor to bind on the inner circumference of the motor housing when a current was applied. Fred scrounged around for a Honda motor. He found one with the same bushing, then used a "blind hole bearing puller" to extract it, as well as the one in my

> *A gifted young person who chooses to become a mechanic rather than to accumulate academic credentials is viewed as eccentric, if not destructive.*

397

motor. Then he gently tapped the new, or rather newer, one into place. The motor worked! Then Fred gave me an impromptu dissertation on the peculiar metallurgy of these Honda starter-motor bushings of the mid-'70s. Here was a scholar.

Over the next six months I spent a lot of time at Fred's shop, learning, and put in only occasional appearances at the university. This was something of a regression: I worked on cars throughout high school and college, and one of my early jobs was at a Porsche repair shop. Now I was rediscovering the intensely absorbing nature of the work, and it got me thinking about possible livelihoods.

As it happened, in the spring I landed a job as executive director of a policy organization in Washington. This felt like a coup. But certain perversities became apparent as I settled into the job. It sometimes required me to reason backward, from desired conclusion to suitable premise. The organization had taken certain positions, and there were some facts it was more fond of than others. As its figurehead, I was making arguments I didn't fully buy myself. Further, my boss seemed intent on retraining me according to a certain cognitive style—that of the corporate world, from which he had recently come. This style demanded that I project an image of rationality but not indulge too much in actual reasoning. As I sat in my K Street office, Fred's life as an independent tradesman gave me an image that I kept coming back to: someone who really knows what he is doing, losing himself in work that is genuinely useful and has a certain integrity to it. He also seemed to be having a lot of fun.

Seeing a motorcycle about to leave my shop under its own power, several days after arriving in the back of a pickup truck, I don't feel tired even though I've been standing on a concrete floor all day. Peering into the portal of his helmet, I think I can make out the edges of a grin on the face of a guy who hasn't ridden his bike in a while. I give him a wave. With one of his hands on the throttle and the other on the clutch, I know he can't wave back. But I can hear his salute in the exuberant "bwaaAAAAP!" of a crisp throttle, gratuitously revved. That sound pleases me, as I know it does him. It's a ventriloquist conversation in one mechanical voice, and the gist of it is "Yeah!"

After five months at the think tank, I'd saved enough money to buy some tools I needed, and I quit and went into business fixing bikes. My shop rate is $40 per hour. Other shops have rates as high as $70 per hour, but I tend to work pretty slowly. Further, only about half the time I spend in the shop ends up being billable (I have no employees; every little chore falls to me), so it usually works out closer to $20 per hour—a modest but decent wage. The business goes up and down; when it is down I have supplemented it with writing. The work is sometimes frustrating, but it is never irrational.

And it frequently requires complex thinking. In fixing motorcycles you come up with several imagined trains of cause and effect for manifest symptoms, and you judge their likelihood before tearing anything down. This imagining relies on a mental library that you develop. An internal combustion engine can work in any number of ways, and different manufacturers have tried different approaches. Each has its own proclivities for failure. You also develop a library of sounds and smells and feels. For example, the backfire of a too-lean fuel mixture is subtly different from an ignition backfire.

As in any learned profession, you just have to know a lot. If the motorcycle is 30 years old, from an obscure maker that went out of business 20 years ago, its tendencies are known mostly through lore. It would probably be impossible to do such work in isolation, without access to a collective historical memory; you have to be embedded in a community of mechanic-antiquarians. These relationships are maintained by telephone, in a network of reciprocal favors that spans the country. My most reliable source, Fred, has such an encyclopedic knowledge of obscure European motorcycles that all I have been able to offer him in exchange is deliveries of obscure European beer.

There is always a risk of introducing new complications when working on old motorcycles, and this enters the diagnostic logic. Measured in likelihood of screw-ups, the cost is not identical for all avenues of inquiry when deciding which hypothesis to pursue. Imagine you're trying to figure out why a bike won't start. The fasteners holding the engine covers on 1970s-era Hondas are Phillips head, and they are almost always rounded out and corroded. Do you really want to check the condition of the starter clutch if each of eight screws will need to be drilled out and extracted, risking damage to the engine case? Such impediments have to be taken into account. The attractiveness of any hypothesis is determined in part by physical circumstances that have no logical connection to the diagnostic problem at hand. The mechanic's proper response to the situation cannot be anticipated by a set of rules or algorithms.

There probably aren't many jobs that can be reduced to rule-following and still be done well. But in many jobs there is an attempt to do just this, and the perversity of it may go unnoticed by those who design the work process. Mechanics face something like this problem in the factory service manuals that we use. These manuals tell you to be systematic in eliminating variables, presenting an idealized image of diagnostic work. But they never take into account the risks of working on old machines. So you put the manual away and consider the facts before you. You do this because ultimately you are responsible to the motorcycle and its owner, not to some procedure.

Some diagnostic situations contain a lot of variables. Any given symptom may have several possible causes, and further, these causes may interact with one another and therefore be difficult to isolate. In deciding how to proceed, there often comes a point where you have to step back and get a larger gestalt. Have a cigarette and walk around the lift. The gap between theory and practice stretches out in front of you, and this is where it gets interesting. What you need now is the kind of judgment that arises only from experience; hunches rather than rules. For me, at least, there is more real thinking going on in the bike shop than there was in the think tank.

Put differently, mechanical work has required me to cultivate different intellectual habits. Further, habits of mind have an ethical dimension that we don't often think about. Good diagnosis requires attentiveness to the machine, almost a conversation with it, rather than assertiveness, as in the position papers produced on K Street. Cognitive psychologists speak of "metacognition," which is the activity of stepping back and thinking about your own thinking. It is what you do when you stop for a moment in your pursuit of a solution, and wonder whether your understanding of the problem is adequate. The slap of worn-out pistons hitting their cylinders can sound a lot like loose valve tappets, so to be a good mechanic you have to be constantly open to the possibility that you may be mistaken. This is a virtue that is at once cognitive and moral. It seems to develop because the mechanic, if he is the sort who goes on to become good at it, internalizes the healthy functioning of the motorcycle as an object of passionate concern. How else can you explain the elation he gets when he identifies the root cause of some problem?

This active concern for the motorcycle is reinforced by the social aspects of the job. As is the case with many independent mechanics, my business is based entirely on word of mouth. I sometimes barter services with machinists and metal fabricators. This has a very different feel than transactions with money; it situates me in a community. The result is that I really don't want to mess up anybody's motorcycle or charge more than a fair price. You often hear people complain about mechanics and other tradespeople whom they take to be dishonest or incompetent. I am sure this is sometimes justified. But it is also true that the mechanic deals with a large element of chance.

I once accidentally dropped a feeler gauge down into the crankcase of a Kawasaki Ninja that was practically brand new, while performing its first scheduled valve adjustment. I escaped a complete tear-down of the motor only through an operation that involved the use of a stethoscope, another pair of trusted hands, and the sort of concentration we associate with a bomb squad. When finally I laid my fingers on that feeler gauge, I felt as if I had cheated death. I don't remember ever feeling so alive as in the hours that followed.

Often as not, however, such crises do not end in redemption. Moments of elation are counterbalanced with failures, and these, too, are vivid, taking place right before your eyes. With stakes that are often high and immediate, the manual trades elicit heedful absorption in work. They are punctuated by moments of pleasure that take place against a darker backdrop: a keen awareness of catastrophe as an always-present possibility. The core experience is one of individual responsibility, supported by face-to-face interactions between tradesman and customer.

Contrast the experience of being a middle manager. This is a stock figure of ridicule, but the sociologist Robert Jackall spent years inhabiting the world of corporate managers, conducting interviews, and he poignantly describes the "moral maze" they feel trapped in. Like the

> **There probably aren't many jobs that can be reduced to rule-following and still be done well.**

mechanic, the manager faces the possibility of disaster at any time. But in his case these disasters feel arbitrary; they are typically a result of corporate restructurings, not of physics. A manager has to make many decisions for which he is accountable. Unlike an entrepreneur with his own business, however, his decisions can be reversed at any time by someone higher up the food chain (and there is always someone higher up the food chain). It's important for your career that these reversals not look like defeats, and more generally you have to spend a lot of time managing what others think of you. Survival depends on a crucial insight: you can't back down from an argument that you initially made in straightforward language, with moral conviction, without seeming to lose your integrity. So managers learn the art of provisional thinking and feeling, expressed in corporate doublespeak, and cultivate a lack of commitment to their own actions. Nothing is set in concrete the way it is when you are, for example, pouring concrete.

Those who work on the lower rungs of the information-age office hierarchy face their own kinds of unreality, as I learned some time ago. After earning a master's degree in the early 1990s, I had a hard time finding work but eventually landed a job in the Bay Area writing brief summaries of academic journal articles, which were then sold on CD-ROMs to subscribing libraries. When I got the phone call offering me the job, I was excited. I felt I had grabbed hold of the passing world—miraculously, through the mere filament of a classified ad—and reeled myself into its current. My new bosses immediately took up residence in my imagination, where I often surprised them with my hidden depths. As I was shown to my cubicle, I felt a real sense of being honored. It seemed more than spacious enough. It was my desk, where I would think my thoughts—my unique contribution to a common enterprise, in a real company with hundreds of employees. The regularity of the cubicles made me feel I had found a place in the order of things. I was to be a knowledge worker.

But the feel of the job changed on my first day. The company had gotten its start by providing libraries with a subject index of popular magazines like *Sports Illustrated*. Through a series of mergers and acquisitions, it now found itself offering not just indexes but also abstracts (that is, summaries), and of a very different kind of material: scholarly works in the physical and biological sciences, humanities, social sciences, and law. Some of this stuff was simply incomprehensible to anyone but an expert in the particular field covered by the journal. I was reading articles in *Classical Philology* where practically every other word was in Greek. Some of the scientific journals were no less mysterious. Yet the categorical difference between, say, *Sports Illustrated* and *Nature Genetics* seemed not to have impressed itself on the company's decision makers. In some of the titles I was assigned, articles began with an abstract written by the author. But even in such cases I was to write my own. The reason offered was that unless I did so, there would be no "value added" by our product. It was hard to believe I was going to add anything other than error and confusion to such material. But then, I hadn't yet been trained.

My job was structured on the supposition that in writing an abstract of an article there is a method that merely needs to be applied, and that this can be done without understanding the text. I was actually told this by the trainer, Monica, as she stood before a whiteboard, diagramming an abstract. Monica seemed a perfectly sensible person and gave no outward signs of suffering delusions. She didn't insist too much on what she was telling us, and it became clear she was in a position similar to that of a veteran Soviet bureaucrat who must work on two levels at once: reality and official ideology. The official ideology was a bit like the factory service manuals I mentioned before, the ones that offer procedures that mechanics often have to ignore in order to do their jobs.

My starting quota, after finishing a week of training, was 15 articles per day. By my 11th month at the company, my quota was up to 28 articles per day (this was the normal, scheduled increase). I was always sleepy while at work, and I think this exhaustion was because I felt trapped in a contradiction: the fast pace demanded complete focus on the task, yet that pace also made any real concentration impossible. I had to actively suppress my own ability to think, because the more you think, the more the inadequacies in your understanding of an author's argument come into focus. This can only slow you down. To not do justice to an author who had poured himself into the subject at hand felt like violence against what was best in myself.

The quota demanded, then, not just dumbing down but also a bit of moral re-education, the opposite of the kind that occurs in the heedful absorption of mechanical work. I had to suppress my sense of responsibility to the article itself, and to others — to the author, to begin with, as well as to the hapless users of the database, who might naïvely suppose that my abstract reflected the author's work. Such detachment was made easy by the fact there was no immediate consequence for me; I could write any nonsense whatever.

Now, it is probably true that every job entails some kind of mutilation. I used to work as an electrician and had my own business doing it for a while. As an electrician you breathe a lot of unknown dust in crawl spaces, your knees get bruised, your neck gets strained from looking up at the ceiling while installing lights or ceiling fans, and you get shocked regularly, sometimes while on a ladder. Your hands are sliced up from twisting wires together, handling junction boxes made out of stamped sheet metal, and cutting metal conduit with a hacksaw. But none of this damage touches the best part of yourself.

You might wonder: Wasn't there any quality control? My supervisor would periodically read a few of my abstracts, and I was sometimes corrected and told not to begin an abstract with a dependent clause. But I was never confronted with an abstract I had written and told that it did not adequately reflect the article. The quality standards were the generic ones of grammar, which could be applied without my supervisor having to read the article at hand. Rather, my supervisor and I both were held to a metric that was conjured by someone remote from the work process — an absentee decision maker armed with a (putatively) profit-maximizing calculus, one that took no account of the intrinsic nature of the job. I wonder whether the resulting perversity really made for maximum profits in the long term. Corporate managers are not, after all, the owners of the businesses they run.

At lunch I had a standing arrangement with two other abstracters. One was from my group, a laconic, disheveled man named Mike whom I liked instantly. He did about as well on his quota as I did on mine, but it didn't seem to bother him too much. The other guy was from beyond the parti-

> **A good job requires a field of action where you can put your best capacities to work and see an effect in the world.**

tion, a meticulously groomed Liberian named Henry who said he had worked for the C.I.A. He had to flee Liberia very suddenly one day and soon found himself resettled near the office parks of Foster City, California. Henry wasn't going to sweat the quota. Come 12:30, the three of us would hike to the food court in the mall. This movement was always thrilling. It involved traversing several "campuses," with ponds frequented by oddly real seagulls, then the lunch itself, which I always savored. (Marx writes that under conditions of estranged labor, man "no longer feels himself to be freely active in any but his animal functions.") Over his burrito, Mike would recount the outrageous things he had written in his abstracts. I could see my own future in such moments of sabotage—the compensating pleasures of a cubicle drone. Always funny and gentle, Mike confided one day that he was doing quite a bit of heroin. On the job. This actually made some sense.

How was it that I, once a proudly self-employed electrician, had ended up among these walking wounded, a "knowledge worker" at a salary of $23,000? I had a master's degree, and it needed to be used. The escalating demand for academic credentials in the job market gives the impression of an ever-more-knowledgeable society, whose members perform cognitive feats their unschooled parents could scarcely conceive of. On paper, my abstracting job, multiplied a millionfold, is precisely what puts the futurologist in a rapture: we are getting to be so smart! Yet my M.A. obscures a more real stupidification of the work I secured with that credential, and a wage to match. When I first got the degree, I felt as if I had been inducted to a certain order of society. But despite the beautiful ties I wore, it turned out to be a more proletarian existence than I had known as an electrician. In that job I had made quite a bit more money. I also felt free and active, rather than confined and stultified.

A good job requires a field of action where you can put your best capacities to work and see an effect in the world. Academic credentials do not guarantee this.

Nor can big business or big government—those idols of the right and the left—reliably secure such work for us. Everyone is rightly concerned about economic growth on the one hand or unemployment and wages on the other, but the character of work doesn't figure much in political debate. Labor unions address important concerns like workplace safety and family leave, and management looks for greater efficiency, but on the nature of the job itself, the dominant political and economic paradigms are mute. Yet work forms us, and deforms us, with broad public consequences.

The visceral experience of failure seems to have been edited out of the career trajectories of gifted students. It stands to reason, then, that those who end up making big decisions that affect all of us don't seem to have much sense of their own fallibility, and of how badly things can go wrong even with the best of intentions (like when I dropped that feeler gauge down into the Ninja). In the boardrooms of Wall Street and the corridors of Pennsylvania Avenue, I don't think you'll see a yellow sign that says "Think Safety!" as you do on job sites and in many repair shops, no doubt because those who sit on the swivel chairs tend to live remote from the consequences of the decisions they make. Why not encourage gifted students to learn a trade, if only in the summers, so that their fingers will be crushed once or twice before they go on to run the country?

There is good reason to suppose that responsibility has to be installed in the foundation of your mental equipment—at the level of perception and habit. There is an ethic of paying attention that develops in the trades through hard experience. It inflects your perception of the world and your habitual responses to it. This is due to the immediate feedback you get from material objects and to the fact that the work is typically situated in face-to-face interactions between tradesman and customer.

An economy that is more entrepreneurial, less managerial, would be less subject to the kind of distortions that occur when corporate managers' compensation is tied to the short-term profit of distant shareholders. For most entrepreneurs, profit is at once a more capacious and a more concrete thing than this. It is a calculation in which the intrinsic satisfactions of work count—not least, the exercise of your own powers of reason.

Ultimately it is enlightened self-interest, then, not a harangue about humility or public-spiritedness, that will compel us to take a fresh look at the trades. The good life comes in a variety of forms. This variety has become difficult to see; our field of aspiration has narrowed into certain channels. But the current perplexity in the economy seems to be softening our gaze. Our peripheral vision is perhaps recovering, allowing us to consider the full range of lives worth choosing. For anyone who feels ill suited by disposition to spend his days sitting in an office, the question of what a good job looks like is now wide open.

DISCUSSION

1. What are some of the stereotypes we are taught to associate with "working with your hands"? What are the social scripts that teach us to define and evaluate this type of labor? In your view, are these attitudes accurate or fair? Why or why not?

2. For Crawford, cultural norms around work are intimately entwined with cultural norms around school. "Some people," he writes, "are hustled off to college, then to the cubicle, against their own inclinations and natural bents, when they would rather be learning to build things or fix things." In your view, is Crawford correct? Do you agree that there exists a bias within our educational system against manual labor? And do you share Crawford's sense that this educational script needs to be rewritten? Why or why not?

3. "Ultimately," Crawford writes, "it is enlightened self-interest, then, not a harangue about humility or public-spiritedness, that will compel us to take a fresh look at the trades." Do you agree? In your view, is it ultimately in our better interests — whether individually or societally — to change our public attitudes toward manual work? If so, how?

WRITING

4. Part of Crawford's argument in favor of "hand work" rests on the claims he makes about "mind work." In a brief essay, explore what characterizes white-collar or "mind" work. What rules dictate what this kind of labor is supposed to look like and what it is supposed to be for? What specific forms of work does it involve? What skills does it require? Next, explain what, specifically, Crawford finds wanting or problematic about this type of work. Do you agree?

5. Write an essay in which you apply Crawford's analysis to your own experiences with work. How do you define the ideal job? Does this ideal resemble or differ from Crawford's portrait of his own work? Does your ideal confirm or challenge the claims Crawford makes about hands-on versus knowledge work? How or how not?

6. Crawford, like Robert Sullivan (p. 407), is interested in challenging his readers to think about work and jobs in ways that deviate from the conventional social scripts. Write an assessment of how the messages in these two essays compare with one another. Does Sullivan's ironic description of "jobs that won't make you rich" remind you in any way of the types of hands-on employment Crawford showcases? Do these essays invite their readers to measure the value of work in ways that are similar? Different? How?

ROBERT SULLIVAN

How to Choose a Career That Will Not Get You Rich No Matter What Anyone Tells You

When it comes right down to it, what really is the best way to define a worthwhile job? And how do our personal standards compare to those we are taught by our larger culture? In this satiric piece, Robert Sullivan turns our conventional thinking on its head. Compiling a list of "non-Big-Buck-making careers," he skewers the long-standing norm in our culture that pegs the worthiness of a job solely to its profitability. Sullivan is a contributing editor to *Vogue* and a frequent contributor to the *New York Times.* His work has appeared in publications such as *Condé Nast Traveler* and the *New York Times Magazine.* He has sometimes been called a nature writer, but Sullivan has said, "If you're from New York or New Jersey, I didn't think you were allowed to be a nature writer." He lives in Hastings-on-Hudson, New York, and his book *Rats* (2004) examines the history of a New York City pest. Among his other books are *How Not to Get Rich, or Why Being Bad Off Isn't So Bad* (2005), from which this selection comes; *Cross Country* (2006); and, most recently, *The Thoreau You Don't Know* (2009).

CHOOSING A CAREER PATH IS ESSENTIAL TO IMPLEMENTING A SPOT that is not in the top 2 percent of American incomes or anywhere near it, and an essential part of choosing the right career is choosing the right kind of education. These days, a good education is a must if you are planning on working your entire life and ending up with little or nothing. History tells us that at one time only the wealthiest Americans had a college education, and the people who did not go to college made money working in factory jobs that today no longer exist. Now you need a college education to work on the line in one of the few remaining auto plants, if you can afford a college education, that is. If you do manage to wrangle the absurdly large loans necessary to fund a trip to college, then, to not succeed financially, you will want to choose a field of study that will be personally rewarding

> **You will want to choose a field of study that will be personally rewarding but have no apparent application in the real world.**

but have no apparent application in the real world. Here are just a few possibilities:

Medieval literature. This is a wonderful area of essentially not-for-profit study, and, indeed, a study of just medieval poetry will only reinforce the improbability of retiring on what you will earn, even though you may see the world as a more beautiful place, and, through the sight of such beauty, you will be stock-poor but soul-enhanced. In addition to translating wonderful but sensationally obscure poems that could never be valued in accordance with their aesthetic worth, other areas of unprofitable expertise would include the study of medieval literary figures themselves, such as Alcuin, the once world-renowned and now not-so-well-known tutor to Charlemagne, who, excitingly, had a school of scholars translating and copying ancient texts in medieval France, and who reignited interest in Greek and Roman classics in Europe, giving us a glimpse back into a time when the world was smaller and you could retire to your kids' villa, rather than be forced to begin to apply to assisted-living places when you are in your forties in hopes of getting a spot that you probably won't be able to afford one day. Alcuin, who also tutored Pippin, the son of Charlemagne, rediscovered Socratic dialogue as a teaching method, so that the following questions might be offered to the following responses in the eighth century A.D.:

PIPPIN: What is a letter?

ALCUIN: The guardian of history.

PIPPIN: What is a word?

ALCUIN: The expositor of the mind.

PIPPIN: What produces a word?

ALCUIN: The tongue.

PIPPIN: What is the tongue?

ALCUIN: The whip of the air.

PIPPIN: What is the air?

ALCUIN: The guardian of life.

PIPPIN: What is life?

ALCUIN: The joy of the blessed, the sorrow of the miserable, the expectation of death.

PIPPIN: What is death?

ALCUIN: The inevitable issue, an uncertain pilgrimage, the tears of the living, the thief of man.

PIPPIN: What is man?

ALCUIN: The possession of death, a transient wayfarer, a guest.

PIPPIN: How is man situated?

ALCUIN: Like a lantern in the wind.

Magnificent, and it notably does not end the way a financial investment company's commercials typically end. You know the financial investment company commercials I'm referring to. They feature a long, sentimental, and joyful montage of images that portray the imaginary life you would have if you had nothing to worry about money-wise: sailing, croquet on the lawn of the beach house, sentimental gazes between well-dressed family members. Then, the ad ends with the logo of the financial invest-ment company, the message being something along the lines of this: *Don't you want to have a really amazing life, as far as material goods go, or do you have some kind of a problem?*

If you should actually go into medieval studies, then your only real worry is that a huge movie star—say he has his car parked by the guy you sat next to in the waiting room of the downtown health clinic—hears about your obscure area of expertise, becomes enamored with Alcuin while on location in France, gets a kind of over-glamorized view of what it was like to run a medieval school of classical scholarship during the Holy Roman Empire, shows up with his entourage at your library cubicle one afternoon, lunches you, hires you as a consultant, makes a film in which the scene that you worked hardest on (where rows of robed schol-ars sat quietly copying ancient texts) is cut, after which you appear on a public television talk show to praise the movie's accuracy, after which you are offered your own television show on cable, which subsequently spawns best-selling books and CD-ROMs and a Wednesday spot on the *Today* show that features you translating French medieval lyrics for the viewers at home. Granted, that scenario is not incredibly likely, but it's a possibility, and to live the not-rich life completely, you have to stay on your toes.

Wildlife biologist. As far as not making it big goes, studies of flora and fauna are especially unlucrative, despite that flora and fauna are seemingly the most related to the world, or at least the living, breathing world. Why? Because they investigate an area that the economic system considers unprofitable—i.e., natural life. If you played your cards "right," you could spend years in graduate school studying biology and then finally manage to cobble together grant money to pursue your area of interest—Pacific-coast sea otters *(Enhydra lutris),* let's say, hunted into near extinction in the eighteen hundreds for their pelts despite being, as can unprofitably be noted, one of the few mammals besides humans to use tools.[1] You will live in a tent in the cold watching a small radar screen indicating the location of the sea otter that you have forcibly but lovingly tagged, and you will make important discoveries about the animal's migratory patterns, and then your studies will be discounted by cruise ship and real estate interests. (Caution: Oil companies sometimes hire wildlife biologists, decorating oil-interested company reports with otter-friendly statistics that are subsequently ignored when drilling time comes.)

Traditional music. This is an excellent area of unprofitable possibilities, especially in light of today's popular music, which can, in many instances, be explained as multimillion-dollar marketing set to a computer-generated sound track—which is to say the sound track of a corporation raking it in. In some ways, someone choosing to become a professional hammer dulcimer player is the opposite of someone choosing a career that statistics indicate will manage to keep him or her alive—careers such as health care, education, and engineering, all of which are recommended by career planners and require advanced degrees that you will be paying for over many, many years.[2] Have you ever seen a mandolin player with a yacht? Do you know many full-time jug-band members with 401(k) plans? Is there in America today a professional pennywhistle player who has two homes and a condo on Central Park West in Manhattan? Do people who make their living as accordionists fly first-class out of LAX? No, in fact people with accordions

> **Have you ever seen a mandolin player with a yacht?**

are the butt of jokes even from other traditional musicians, implying a lowest-man-on-the-lowest-totem-pole status that can be applauded in the area of not getting fantastically rich. Some gratuitous accordion joke examples are as follows:

Q: What's the difference between an onion and an accordion?

A: People cry when they chop up onions.

Q: What do you call ten accordions at the bottom of the ocean?

A: A good start.

Q: If you drop an accordion, a set of bagpipes, and a viola off a twenty-story building, which one lands first?

A: Who cares?[3]

There are, of course, an infinite number of non-wealth-producing careers to choose from. There's public broadcasting, wherein the person involved attempts to create radio and television programs that will attract viewers interested in a broad range of subjects that may not titillate advertisers, the core audience, it sometimes seems, for non-public broadcasting. There are more obvious examples, such as teaching, which has to do with the joy of learning and with the education of the next generation of adults, as well as the future of the economy and of the world. There is art that has no wide commercial appeal. There is commerce that has no wide commercial appeal but works on a limited basis in a limited area for a limited number of people until a chain store hears about it and comes in and takes over, putting everyone else out of business. In other words, the options for non-Big-Buck-making careers are wide-ranging. The one universally important thing to keep in mind when choosing a career that will not be making you loaded is to choose a field of study and expertise that interests you, to follow your passions—and unless your passion is making lots of money, you will be fairly assured of not getting rich. Ralph Waldo Emerson said, "The reward of doing a thing well is to have done it," and he had a point, though he is not factoring in the cost of child care, studio space, and gas, or even parking, all of which really add up.

NOTES

[1] Sea otters smash abalone shells on their chest using a small rock, and they tie themselves to the seafloor with kelp to sleep securely through the night, not that it matters to the stock market. I find sea otters fascinating: their hands, their apparent jocularity even in the face of tremendous waves and storms and currents. Sea otters also faced great dangers from hunters who wanted their valuable coats; they were hunted so heavily in the eighteenth and nineteenth centuries that they had to be placed on the U.S. government endangered species list. Today, the populations have come back to a large extent, but conservationists would like to continue to protect them. Fishermen would like them off the endangered species list to protect the abalone harvest, but not me. I could watch a sea otter all day and not get bored—or rich, for that matter.

[2] According to the U.S. Department of Labor, two of the fastest-growing occupations between 2002 and 2012 are expected to be physician's assistants and network systems and data communications analysts. Both of these jobs require bachelor's

degrees and both are expected to pay in the highest anticipated wage category, which is $41,820 and up. As bad luck would have it, many of the fastest-growing occupations that do not require college are also in the lowest-earning category. Home health aide is an example of the latter category, and the demand for home health aides is expected to grow by 50 percent. Other examples of jobs that will be in the highest demand in the lowest wage-earning category are maids and personal aides, categories that are expected to grow by 40 percent. The lowest expected earnings category is up to $19,600 a year—nobody seems to want to pay maids a lot of money.

[3] A traditional joke regarding the moneymaking abilities of traditional musicians is as follows:

Q: How do you make a million dollars as a traditional musician?

A: Start with two million.

I heard this joke at a traditional-music festival. I heard it told by David Jones, an exquisite singer of old folk songs, ballads, and sea shanties, who sings regularly at the South Street Seaport in New York City, and at various folk festivals along the East Coast.

As far as I know, David Jones is not raking it in singing folk songs. I should also note, with reference to the idea of mandolin players owning a yacht, that the late Johnny Carson, who was a drummer, once asked, rhetorically, "Is that the banjo player's Porsche?"

DISCUSSION

1. Take a moment to evaluate the title of this essay. What is your immediate reaction? In what ways does the advice it proffers seem odd, even abnormal?

2. "To not succeed financially," writes Sullivan, "you will want to choose a field of study that will be personally rewarding but have no apparent application in the real world." How do you understand the distinction between personal reward and real-world applicability? To what extent in our culture are we taught to use this distinction in making our career choices? Is it valid to do so?

3. These days, notes Sullivan, the idea that one would choose a "non-lucrative" career over a financially profitable one has become close to unthinkable. According to the standards of our culture, what is it exactly that supposedly makes "Big-Buck-making" jobs so much more preferable than the alternatives? Can you think of advantages or benefits to a "non-lucrative" job that this kind of cultural logic overlooks?

WRITING

4. Sullivan concludes his essay by quoting Ralph Waldo Emerson's well-known dictum: " 'The reward of doing a thing well is to have done it.' " Write an essay in which you assess the particular ways Emerson's statement challenges the norms by which we are taught to measure the value of work. To what extent does this statement encourage us to use a different set of values or priorities when it comes to making our own career choices? What might a job modeled along these different lines look like? What sorts of tasks would it involve? What large goal or purpose would it be dedicated to? What rewards or benefits would it bring?

5. Sullivan uses satire to comment on the monetary value of work. Write your own satirical response to Sullivan in which you espouse the merits of *not* choosing a career that will leave you poor.

6. How do you think Sullivan would respond to the critique of Goldman Sachs advanced by Matt Taibbi (p. 416)? Given what his essay has to say about status, success, and money, do you think Sullivan would react sympathetically to Taibbi's scathing attack on Wall Street "greed"? Does Sullivan's satiric portrait of "non-remunerative careers" share anything in common with Taibbi's indictment of modern American capitalism? If so, what specifically?

Then and Now: *Dressing for Success*

The rules establishing proper workplace attire have changed markedly over the years. But are these changes merely cosmetic? Or do they tell us something about the ways our attitudes toward work, or perhaps even our social or cultural attitudes, have changed? To be sure, there is a long and storied history in America of treating workplace wardrobe as a kind of societal barometer. In the case of the 1950s office worker, for example, the "gray flannel suit" came to be widely viewed as a metaphor for the corporate standardization, political conformity, and social conservatism that for many defined American life during this period. For countless commentators, this unadorned and anonymous business uniform not only captured the supposedly faceless, robotic nature of 1950s office work, but it also symbolized a pervasive hostility in midcentury America toward individuality, creativity, and dissent.

Designed for modern living

Plateau—smooth 100% worsted—the suit with the "weightless feel"

Plan to spend the fall in Plateau—that rich-surfaced 100% worsted suit with its countless built-in features! Pre-based in the loom to remove tension... marvelously comfortable to wear, never bulky. Since it is all worsted, it stays well-groomed, hour after hour. Plateau, with balanced tailoring by Timely Clothes, in single- and double-breasted styles, at fine stores everywhere. For the name of the store in your city, write Timely Clothes, Dept. L50, Rochester 7, N. Y.

Free Booklet! Valuable information about worsteds and woolens. Drop a card to Pacific Mills, Worsted Division, Dept. L50, 261 Fifth Avenue, New York 16, N. Y.

Timely Clothes
PLATEAU
FABRIC BY
Pacific Mills

It's a PACIFIC Worsted BY PACIFIC MILLS ... WEAVERS OF FINE WOOLENS, WORSTEDS, COTTONS, RAYONS

When compared to the corporate dress codes that prevail today, it's hard not to feel we've come a long way from this buttoned-down, bygone era. Nowadays the drab uniformity of gray flannel has given way to the more flexible and informal wardrobe norms of so-called business casual — a shift, we are told, that proves how much more liberated, freewheeling, and creative office work has become. No longer the faceless drone of yore, the corporate employee of the twenty-first century (at least according to what we see in countless commercials) plies his or her trade in an environment where individuality and diversity are prized, a world in which employees are members of teams, professional colleagues are also personal friends, and creativity rather than conformity is the rule of thumb.

But is this actually true? Does this shift in dress code really prove how much more liberated office life — or life in general — has become? In answering this question, we might begin by pointing out a paradox: Despite its emphasis on nonconformity and individual choice, business casual is nonetheless still a *style*, a wardrobe standard established for and marketed to us. Just because we get to wear khakis and sandals to the office these days doesn't automatically mean we're now using clothes to express our individuality — particularly when we may well have gotten the idea for this outfit by paging through a clothing catalog. Even when an office wardrobe is informal, it isn't necessarily any less of an office uniform. What the rise of business casual may well demonstrate, in fact, is not how nonconformist modem American culture has become, but rather how the terms defining such conformity have simply changed. It certainly seems a stretch to claim that white-collar work is no longer hierarchical or rigidly organized, or that the contemporary business landscape has grown any less "corporate." Perhaps this shift toward casualness is best understood not as a movement beyond conformity than as a compensation for conformity: a style change designed to add a gloss of informality and autonomy to a work world still largely dictated by scripts we ourselves do not write.

WRITING

1.   Write an essay in which you analyze what sorts of norms about work are conveyed by the style of dress in these two examples. What, if anything, seems to have changed between the depictions of work dress in the 1950s versus today? In your opinion, which example seems more typical of the concepts of work and career? Why?

2.   One of the biggest differences between white-collar and blue-collar work is the difference in dress. How do you think Anthony DePalma (p. 381) would respond to the idea of business casual dress? In your opinion, does the idea of business casual highlight or diminish the differences between white- and blue-collar work? Why?

MATT TAIBBI
The Great American Bubble Machine

In the midst of the worst economic downturn in decades, media headlines are filled with accounts of corporate misbehavior, incompetence, and greed. But do we really take these cautionary tales to heart? And what do we put at risk when we fail to heed these warnings? Posing precisely these questions, Matt Taibbi offers readers a scathing account of how one such corporate titan gamed the system and, in the process, helped to usher in the current financial crisis. Taibbi is a political reporter who writes the "Road Rage" and "Low Post" columns for *Rolling Stone,* for which he won a National Magazine Award in 2008. He is also a blogger for the news website *True/Slant*. His most recent book is *The Great Derangement: A Terrifying True Story of War, Politics, and Religion at the Twilight of the American Empire* (2008).

THE FIRST THING YOU NEED TO KNOW ABOUT GOLDMAN SACHS IS that it's everywhere. The world's most powerful investment bank is a great vampire squid wrapped around the face of humanity, relentlessly jamming its blood funnel into anything that smells like money. In fact, the history of the recent financial crisis, which doubles as a history of the rapid decline and fall of the suddenly swindled dry American empire, reads like a Who's Who of Goldman Sachs graduates.

By now, most of us know the major players. As George Bush's last Treasury secretary, former Goldman CEO Henry Paulson was the architect of the bailout, a suspiciously self-serving plan to funnel trillions of Your Dollars to a handful of his old friends on Wall Street. Robert Rubin, Bill Clinton's former Treasury secretary, spent 26 years at Goldman before becoming chairman of Citigroup—which in turn got a $300 billion taxpayer bailout from Paulson. There's John Thain, the asshole chief of Merrill Lynch who bought an $87,000 area rug for his office as his company was imploding; a former Goldman banker, Thain enjoyed a multibilliondollar handout from Paulson, who used billions in taxpayer funds to help Bank of America rescue Thain's sorry company. And Robert Steel, the former Goldmanite head of Wachovia, scored himself and his fellow executives $225 million in golden parachute payments as his bank was self-destructing. There's Joshua Bolten, Bush's chief of staff during the bailout, and Mark Patterson, the current Treasury chief of staff, who was a Goldman lobbyist just a year ago, and Ed Liddy, the former Goldman director whom Paulson put in charge of bailed-out insurance giant AIG, which forked over $13 billion to Goldman after Liddy came on board. The heads of the Canadian and Italian national banks are Goldman alums, as is the head of the World Bank, the head of the New York Stock Exchange, the last two heads of the Federal Reserve Bank of New York—which, incidentally, is now in charge of overseeing Goldman—not to mention. . . .

But then, any attempt to construct a narrative around all the former Goldmanites in influential positions quickly becomes an absurd and pointless exercise, like trying to make a list of everything. What you need to know is the big picture: If America is circling the drain, Goldman Sachs has found a way to be that drain—an extremely unfortunate loophole in the system of Western democratic capitalism, which never foresaw that in a society governed passively by free markets and free elections, organized greed always defeats disorganized democracy.

The bank's unprecedented reach and power have enabled it to turn all of America into a giant pump-and-dump scam, manipulating whole economic sectors for years at a time, moving the dice game as this or that market collapses, and all the time gorging itself on the unseen costs that are breaking families everywhere—high gas prices, rising consumer credit rates, half-eaten pension funds, mass layoffs, future taxes to pay off bailouts. All that money that you're losing, it's going somewhere, and in both a literal and a figurative sense, Goldman Sachs is where it's going: The bank is a huge, highly sophisticated engine for converting the useful, deployed wealth of society into the least useful, most wasteful and insoluble substance on Earth—pure profit for rich individuals.

They achieve this using the same playbook over and over again. The formula is relatively simple: Goldman positions itself in the middle of a speculative bubble, selling investments they know are crap. Then they hoover up vast sums from the middle and lower floors of society with the aid of a crippled and corrupt state that allows it to rewrite the rules in exchange for the relative pennies the bank throws at political patronage. Finally, when it all goes bust, leaving millions of ordinary citizens broke and starving, they begin the entire process over again, riding in to rescue us all by lending us back our own money at interest, selling themselves as men above greed, just a bunch of really smart guys keeping the wheels greased. They've been pulling this same stunt over and over since the 1920s—and now they're preparing to do it again, creating what may be the biggest and most audacious bubble yet.

If you want to understand how we got into this financial crisis, you have to first understand where all the money went—and in order to understand that, you need to understand what Goldman has already gotten away with. It is a history exactly five bubbles long—including last year's strange and seemingly inexplicable spike in the price of oil. There were a lot of losers in each of those bubbles, and in the bailout that followed. But Goldman wasn't one of them.

BUBBLE #1: THE GREAT DEPRESSION

Goldman wasn't always a too-big-to-fail Wall Street behemoth, the ruthless face of kill-or-be-killed capitalism on steroids—just almost always. The bank was actually founded in 1869 by a German immigrant named Marcus Goldman, who built it up with his son-in-law Samuel Sachs. They were pioneers in the use of commercial paper, which is just a fancy way of saying they made money lending out short-term IOUs to small-time vendors in downtown Manhattan.

You can probably guess the basic plot line of Goldman's first 100 years in business: plucky, immigrant-led investment bank beats the odds, pulls itself up by its bootstraps, makes shitloads of money. In that ancient history there's really only one episode that bears scrutiny now, in light of more recent events: Goldman's disastrous foray into the speculative mania of precrash Wall Street in the late 1920s.

This great Hindenburg of financial history has a few features that might sound familiar. Back then, the main financial tool used to bilk investors was called an "investment trust." Similar to modern mutual funds, the trusts took the cash of investors large and small and (theoretically, at least) invested it in a smorgasbord of Wall Street securities, though the securities and amounts were often kept hidden from the public. So a regular guy could invest $10 or $100 in a trust and feel like he was a big player. Much as in the 1990s, when new vehicles like day trading and e-trading attracted reams of new suckers from the sticks who wanted to feel like big shots, investment trusts roped a new generation of regular-guy investors into the speculation game.

Beginning a pattern that would repeat itself over and over again, Goldman got into the investment trust game late, then jumped in with both feet and went hog wild. The first effort was the Goldman Sachs Trading Corporation; the bank issued a million shares at $100 apiece, bought all those shares with its own money, and then sold 90 percent of them to the hungry public at $104. The trading corporation then relentlessly bought shares in itself, bidding the price up further and further. Eventually it dumped part of its holdings and sponsored a new trust, the Shenandoah Corporation, issuing millions more in shares in that fund—which in turn sponsored yet another trust called the Blue Ridge Corporation. In this way, each investment trust served as a front for an endless investment pyramid: Goldman hiding behind Goldman hiding behind Goldman. Of the 7,250,000 initial shares of Blue Ridge, 6,250,000 were actually owned by Shenandoah—which, of course, was in large part owned by Goldman Trading.

The end result (ask yourself if this sounds familiar) was a daisy chain of borrowed money, one exquisitely vulnerable to a decline in performance anywhere along the line. The basic idea isn't hard to follow. You take a dollar and borrow nine against it; then you take that $10 fund and borrow $90; then you take your $100 fund and, so long as the public is still lending, borrow and invest $900. If the last fund in the line starts to lose value, you no longer have the money to pay back your investors, and everyone gets massacred.

In a chapter from *The Great Crash, 1929* titled "In Goldman Sachs We Trust," the famed economist John Kenneth Galbraith held up the Blue Ridge and Shenandoah trusts as classic examples of the insanity of leverage-based investment. The trusts, he wrote, were a major cause of the market's historic crash; in today's dollars, the losses the bank suffered totaled $475 billion. "It is difficult not to marvel at the imagination which was implicit in this gargantuan insanity," Galbraith observed, sounding like Keith Olbermann in an ascot. "If there must be madness, something may be said for having it on a heroic scale."

BUBBLE #2: TECH STOCKS

Fast-forward about 65 years. Goldman not only survived the crash that wiped out so many of the investors it duped, it went on to become the chief underwriter to the country's wealthiest and most powerful corporations. Thanks to Sidney Weinberg, who rose from the rank of janitor's assistant to head the firm, Goldman became the pioneer of the initial public offering, one of the principal and most lucrative means by which companies raise money. During the 1970s and 1980s, Goldman may not have been the planet-eating Death Star of political influence it is today, but it was a top-drawer firm that had a reputation for attracting the very smartest talent on the Street.

It also, oddly enough, had a reputation for relatively solid ethics and a patient approach to investment that shunned the fast buck; its executives were trained to adopt the firm's mantra, "long-term greedy." One former Goldman banker who left the firm in the early Nineties recalls seeing his superiors give up a very profitable deal on the grounds that it was a long-term loser. "We gave back money to 'grownup' corporate clients who had made bad deals with us," he says. "Everything we did was legal and fair—but 'long-term greedy' said we didn't want to make such a profit at the clients' collective expense that we spoiled the marketplace."

But then, something happened. It's hard to say what it was exactly; it might have been the fact that Goldman's cochairman in the early Nineties, Robert Rubin, followed Bill Clinton to the White House, where he directed the National Economic Council and eventually became Treasury secretary. While the American media fell in love with the story line of a pair of baby boomer, Sixties child, Fleetwood Mac yuppies nesting in the White House, it also nursed an undisguised crush on Rubin, who was hyped as without a doubt the smartest person ever to walk the face of the Earth, with Newton, Einstein, Mozart, and Kant running far behind.

The bank is a huge, highly sophisticated engine for converting the useful, deployed wealth of society into . . . pure profit for rich individuals.

Rubin was the prototypical Goldman banker. He was probably born in a $4,000 suit, he had a face that seemed permanently frozen just short of an apology for being so much smarter than you, and he exuded a Spock-like, emotion-neutral exterior; the only human feeling you could imagine him experiencing was a nightmare about being forced to fly coach. It became almost a national cliché that whatever Rubin thought was best for the economy—a phenomenon that reached its apex in 1999, when Rubin appeared on the cover of *Time* with his Treasury deputy, Larry Summers, and Fed chief Alan Greenspan under the headline *The Committee To Save The World*. And "what Rubin thought," mostly, was that the American economy, and in particular the financial markets, were over-regulated and needed to be set free. During his tenure at Treasury, the Clinton White House made a series of moves that would have drastic consequences for the global economy—beginning with Rubin's complete and total failure to regulate his old firm during its first mad dash for obscene short-term profits.

The basic scam in the Internet Age is pretty easy even for the financially illiterate to grasp. Companies that weren't much more than pot-fueled ideas scrawled on napkins by up-too-late bong smokers were taken public via IPOs, hyped in the media, and sold to the public for mega-millions. It was as if banks like Goldman were wrapping ribbons around watermelons, tossing them out 50-story windows, and opening the phones for bids. In this game you were a winner only if you took your money out before the melon hit the pavement.

It sounds obvious now, but what the average investor didn't know at the time was that the banks had changed the rules of the game, making the deals look better than they actually were. They did this by setting up what was, in reality, a two-tiered investment system—one for the insiders who knew the real numbers, and another for the lay investor who was invited to chase soaring prices the banks themselves knew were irrational. While Goldman's later pattern would be to capitalize on changes in the regulatory environment, its key innovation in the Internet years was to abandon its own industry's standards of quality control.

"Since the Depression, there were strict underwriting guidelines that Wall Street adhered to when taking a company public," says one prominent hedge-fund manager. "The company had to be in business for a minimum of five years, and it had to show profitability for three consecutive years. But Wall Street took these guidelines and threw them in the trash." Goldman completed the snow job by pumping up the sham stocks: "Their analysts were out there saying Bullshit.com is worth $100 a share."

The problem was, nobody told investors that the rules had changed. "Everyone on the inside knew," the manager says. "Bob Rubin sure as hell knew what the underwriting standards were. They'd been intact since the 1930s."

Jay Ritter, a professor of finance at the University of Florida who specializes in IPOs, says banks like Goldman knew full well that many of the public offerings they were touting would never make a dime. "In the early Eighties, the major underwriters insisted on three years of profitability. Then it was one year, then it was a quarter. By the time of the Internet bubble, they were not even requiring profitability in the foreseeable future."

Goldman has denied that it changed its underwriting standards during the Internet years, but its own statistics belie the claim. Just as it did with the investment trust in the 1920s, Goldman started slow and finished crazy in the Internet years. After it took a little-known company with weak financials called Yahoo! public in 1996, once the tech boom had already begun, Goldman quickly became the IPO king of the Internet era. Of the 24 companies it took public in 1997, a third were losing money at the time of the IPO. In 1999, at the height of the boom, it took 47 companies public, including stillborns like Webvan and eToys, investment offerings that were in many ways the modern equivalents of Blue Ridge and Shenandoah. The following year, it underwrote 18 companies in the first four months, 14 of which were money losers at the time. As a leading underwriter of Internet stocks during the boom, Goldman provided profits far more volatile than those of its competitors: in 1999, the average Goldman IPO leapt 281 percent above its offering price, compared to the Wall Street average of 181 percent.

How did Goldman achieve such extraordinary results? One answer is that they used a practice called "laddering," which is just a fancy way of saying they manipulated the share price of new offerings. Here's how it works: Say you're Goldman Sachs, and Bullshit.com comes to you and asks you to take their company public. You agree on the usual terms: You'll price the stock, determine how many shares should be released, and take the Bullshit.com CEO on a "road show" to schmooze investors, all in exchange for a substantial fee (typically six to seven percent of the amount raised). You then promise your best clients the right to buy big chunks of the IPO at the low offering price—let's say Bullshit.com's starting share price is $15—in exchange for a promise that they will buy more shares later on the open market. That seemingly simple demand gives you inside knowledge of the IPO's future, knowledge that wasn't disclosed to the daytrader schmucks who only had the prospectus to go by: You know that certain of your clients who bought X amount of shares at $15 are also going to buy Y more shares at $20 or $25, virtually guaranteeing that the price is going to go to $25 and beyond. In this way, Goldman could artificially jack up the new company's price, which of course was to the bank's benefit—a six percent fee of a $500 million IPO is serious money.

Goldman was repeatedly sued by shareholders for engaging in laddering in a variety of Internet IPOs, including Webvan and NetZero. The deceptive practices also caught the attention of Nicholas Maier, the syndicate manager of Cramer & Co., the hedge fund run at the time by the now-famous chattering television asshole Jim Cramer, himself a Goldman alum. Maier told the SEC that while working for Cramer between 1996 and 1998, he was repeatedly forced to engage in laddering practices during IPO deals with Goldman.

"Goldman, from what I witnessed, they were the worst perpetrator," Maier said. "They totally fueled the bubble. And it's specifically that kind of behavior that has caused the market crash. They built these stocks upon an illegal foundation—manipulated up—and ultimately, it really was the small person who ended up buying in." In 2005, Goldman agreed to pay $40 million for its laddering violations—a puny penalty relative to the enormous profits it made. (Goldman, which has denied wrongdoing in all of the cases it has settled, refused to respond to questions for this story.)

> **Its executives were trained to adopt the firm's mantra, "long-term greedy."**

Another practice Goldman engaged in during the Internet boom was "spinning," better known as bribery. Here the investment bank would offer the executives of the newly public company shares at extra-low prices, in exchange for future underwriting business. Banks that engaged in spinning would then undervalue the initial offering price—ensuring that those "hot" opening-price shares it had handed out to insiders would be more likely to rise quickly, supplying bigger first-day rewards for the chosen few. So instead of Bullshit.com opening at $20, the bank would approach the Bullshit.com CEO and offer him a million shares of his own company at $18 in exchange for future business—effectively robbing all of Bullshit's new shareholders by diverting cash that should have gone to the company's bottom line into the private bank account of the company's CEO.

In one case, Goldman allegedly gave a multimillion-dollar special offering to eBay CEO Meg Whitman, who later joined Goldman's board, in exchange for future i-banking business. According to a report by the House Financial Services Committee in 2002, Goldman gave special stock offerings to executives in 21 companies that it took public, including

Yahoo! cofounder Jerry Yang and two of the great slithering villains of the financial-scandal age—Tyco's Dennis Kozlowski and Enron's Ken Lay. Goldman angrily denounced the report as "an egregious distortion of the facts"—shortly before paying $110 million to settle an investigation into spinning and other manipulations launched by New York state regulators. "The spinning of hot IPO shares was not a harmless corporate perk," then-attorney general Eliot Spitzer said at the time. "Instead, it was an integral part of a fraudulent scheme to win new investment-banking business."

Such practices conspired to turn the Internet bubble into one of the greatest financial disasters in world history: Some $5 trillion of wealth was wiped out on the NASDAQ alone. But the real problem wasn't the money that was lost by shareholders, it was the money gained by investment bankers, who received hefty bonuses for tampering with the market. Instead of teaching Wall Street a lesson that bubbles always deflate, the Internet years demonstrated to bankers that in the age of freely flowing capital and publicly owned financial companies, bubbles are incredibly easy to *inflate,* and individual bonuses are actually bigger when the mania and the irrationality are greater.

Nowhere was this truer than at Goldman. Between 1999 and 2002, the firm paid out $28.5 billion in compensation and benefits—an average of roughly $350,000 a year per employee. Those numbers are important because the key legacy of the Internet boom is that the economy is now driven in large part by the pursuit of the enormous salaries and bonuses that such bubbles make possible. Goldman's mantra of "long-term greedy" vanished into thin air as the game became about getting your check before the melon hit the pavement.

The market was no longer a rationally managed place to grow real, profitable businesses: It was a huge ocean of Someone Else's Money where bankers hauled in vast sums through whatever means necessary and tried to convert that money into bonuses and payouts as quickly as possible. If you laddered and spun 50 Internet IPOs that went bust within a year, so what? By the time the Securities and Exchange Commission got around to fining your firm $110 million, the yacht you bought with your IPO bonuses was already six years old. Besides, you were probably out of Goldman by then, running the U.S. Treasury or maybe the state of New Jersey. (One of the truly comic moments in the history of America's recent financial collapse came when Governor Jon Corzine of New Jersey, who ran Goldman from 1994 to 1999 and left with $320 million in IPO-fattened stock, insisted in 2002 that "I've never even heard the term 'laddering' before.")

For a bank that paid out $7 billion a year in salaries, $110 million fines issued half a decade late were something far less than a deterrent—they were a joke. Once the Internet bubble burst, Goldman had no incentive to reassess its new, profit-driven strategy; it just searched around for another bubble to inflate. As it turns out, it had one ready, thanks in large part to Rubin.

BUBBLE #3: THE HOUSING CRAZE

Goldman's role in the sweeping global disaster that was the housing bubble is not hard to trace. Here again, the basic trick was a decline in underwriting standards, although in this case the standards weren't in IPOs but in mortgages. By now almost everyone knows that for decades mortgage dealers insisted that home buyers be able to produce a down payment of 10 percent or more, show a steady income and good credit rating, and possess a real first and last name. Then, at the dawn of the new millennium, they suddenly threw all that shit out the window and started writing mortgages on the backs of napkins to cocktail waitresses and ex-cons carrying five bucks and a Snickers bar.

None of that would have been possible without investment bankers like Goldman, who created vehicles to package those shitty mortgages and sell them en masse to unsuspecting insurance companies and pension funds. This created a mass market for toxic debt that would never have existed before; in the old days, no bank would have wanted to keep some addict ex-con's mortgage on its books, knowing how likely it was to fail. You can't write these mortgages, in other words, unless you can sell them to someone who doesn't know what they are.

Goldman used two methods to hide the mess they were selling. First, they bundled hundreds of different mortgages into instruments called Collateralized Debt Obligations. Then they sold investors on the idea that, because a bunch of those mortgages would turn out to be OK, there was no reason to worry so much about the shitty ones: The CDO, as a whole, was sound. Thus, junk-rated mortgages were turned into AAA-rated investments. Second, to hedge its own bets, Goldman got companies like AIG to provide insurance—known as credit default swaps—on the CDOs. The swaps were essentially a racetrack bet between AIG and Goldman: Goldman is betting the ex-cons will default, AIG is betting they won't.

There was only one problem with the deals: All of the wheeling and dealing represented exactly the kind of dangerous speculation that federal regulators are supposed to rein in. Derivatives like CDOs and credit swaps had already caused a series of serious financial calamities: Procter & Gamble and Gibson Greetings both lost fortunes, and Orange County, California, was forced to default in 1994. A report that year by the Government Accountability Office recommended that such financial instruments be tightly regulated—and in 1998, the head of the Commodity Futures Trading Commission, a woman named Brooksley Born, agreed. That May, she circulated a letter to business leaders and the Clinton administration suggesting that banks be required to provide greater disclosure in derivatives trades, and maintain reserves to cushion against losses.

More regulation wasn't exactly what Goldman had in mind. "The banks go crazy—they want it stopped," says Michael Greenberger, who worked for Born as director of trading and markets at the CFTC and is now a law professor at the University of Maryland. "Greenspan, Summers, Rubin and [SEC chief Arthur] Levitt want it stopped."

Clinton's reigning economic foursome—"especially Rubin," according to Greenberger—called Born in for a meeting and pleaded their case. She refused to back down, however, and continued to push for more regulation of the derivatives. Then, in June 1998, Rubin went public to denounce her move, eventually recommending that Congress strip the CFTC of its regulatory authority. In 2000, on its last day in session, Congress passed the now-notorious Commodity Futures Modernization Act, which had been inserted into an 11,000-page spending bill at the last minute, with almost no debate on the floor of the Senate. Banks were now free to trade default swaps with impunity.

But the story didn't end there. AIG, a major purveyor of default swaps, approached the New York State Insurance Department in 2000 and asked whether default swaps would be regulated as insurance. At the time, the office was run by one Neil Levin, a former Goldman vice president, who decided against regulating the swaps. Now freed to underwrite as many housing-based securities and buy as much credit-default protection as it wanted, Goldman went berserk with lending lust. By the peak of the housing boom in 2006, Goldman was underwriting $76.5 billion worth of mortgage-backed securities—a third of which were subprime—much of it to institutional investors like pensions and insurance companies. And in these massive issues of real estate were vast swamps of crap.

> **The market . . . was a huge ocean of Someone Else's Money.**

Take one $494 million issue that year, GSAMP Trust 2006S3. Many of the mortgages belonged to second mortgage borrowers, and the average equity they had in their homes was 0.71 *percent*. Moreover, 58 percent of the loans included little or no documentation—no names of the borrowers, no addresses of the homes, just zip codes. Yet both of the major ratings agencies, Moody's and Standard & Poor's, rated 93 percent of the issue as investment grade. Moody's projected that less than 10 percent of the loans would default. In reality, 18 percent of the mortgages were in default *within 18 months*.

Not that Goldman was personally at any risk. The bank might be taking all these hideous, completely irresponsible mortgages from beneath-gangster-status firms like Countrywide and selling them off to municipalities and pensioners—old people, for God's sake—pretending the whole time that it wasn't grade D horseshit. But even as it was doing so, it was taking short positions in the same market, in essence betting against the same crap it was selling. Even worse, Goldman bragged about it in public. "The mortgage sector continues to be challenged," David Viniar, the bank's chief financial officer, boasted in 2007. "As a result, we took significant markdowns on our long inventory position. . . . However, our risk bias in that market was to be short, *and that net short position was profitable.*" In other words, the mortgages it was selling were for chumps. The real money was in betting against those same mortgages.

"That's how audacious these assholes are," says one hedgefund manager. "At least with other banks, you could say that they were just dumb—they believed what they were selling, and it blew them up. Goldman knew what it was doing."

I ask the manager how it could be that selling something to customers that you're actually betting against—particularly when you know more about the weaknesses of those products than the customer—doesn't amount to securities fraud.

"It's exactly securities fraud," he says. "It's the *heart* of securities fraud."

Eventually, lots of aggrieved investors agreed. In a virtual repeat of the Internet IPO craze, Goldman was hit with a wave of lawsuits after the collapse of the housing bubble, many of which accused the bank of withholding pertinent information about the quality of the mortgages it issued. New York state regulators are suing Goldman and 25 other underwriters for selling bundles of crappy Countrywide mortgages to city and state pension funds, which lost as much as $100 million in the investments. Massachusetts also investigated Goldman for similar misdeeds, acting on behalf of 714 mortgage holders who got stuck holding predatory loans. But once again, Goldman got off virtually scot-free, staving off prosecution by agreeing to pay a paltry $60 million—about what the bank's CDO division made in a day and a half during the real estate boom.

The effects of the housing bubble are well known—it led more or less directly to the collapse of Bear Stearns, Lehman Brothers, and AIG, whose toxic portfolio of credit swaps was in significant part composed of the insurance that banks like Goldman bought against their own housing portfolios. In fact, at least $13 billion of the taxpayer money given to AIG in the bailout ultimately went to Goldman, meaning that the bank made out on the housing bubble twice: It fucked the investors who bought their horseshit CDOs by betting against its own crappy product, then it turned around and fucked the taxpayer by making him pay off those same bets.

And once again, while the world was crashing down all around the bank, Goldman made sure it was doing just fine in the compensation department. In 2006, the firm's payroll jumped to $16.5 billion—an average of $622,000 per employee. As a Goldman spokesman explained, "We work very hard here."

But the best was yet to come. While the collapse of the housing bubble sent most of the financial world fleeing for the exits, or to jail, Goldman boldly doubled down—and almost single-handedly created yet another bubble, one the world still barely knows the firm had anything to do with.

BUBBLE #4: $4 A GALLON

By the beginning of 2008, the financial world was in turmoil. Wall Street had spend the past two and a half decades producing one scandal after another, which didn't leave much to sell that wasn't tainted. The terms *junk bond, IPO, subprime mortgage,* and other once-hot financial fare were now firmly associated in the public's mind with scams; the terms *credit swaps* and *CDOs* were about to join them. The credit markets were in crisis, and the mantra that had sustained the fantasy economy throughout the Bush years—the notion that housing prices never go down—was now a fully exploded myth, leaving the Street clamoring for a new bullshit paradigm to sling.

Where to go? With the public reluctant to put money in anything that felt like a paper investment, the Street quietly moved the casino to the physical-commodities market—stuff you could touch: corn, coffee, cocoa, wheat, and, above all, energy commodities, especially oil. In conjunction with a decline in the dollar, the credit crunch and the housing crash caused a "flight to commodities." Oil futures in particular skyrocketed, as the price of a single barrel went from around $60 in the middle of 2007 to a high of $147 in the summer of 2008.

That summer, as the presidential campaign heated up, the accepted explanation for why gasoline had hit $4.11 a gallon was that there was a problem with the world oil supply. In a classic example of how Republicans and Democrats respond to crises by engaging in fierce exchanges of moronic irrelevancies, John McCain insisted that ending the moratorium on offshore drilling would be "very helpful in the short term," while Barack Obama in typical liberal-arts yuppie style argued that federal investment in hybrid cars was the way out.

But it was all a lie. While the global supply of oil will eventually dry up, the short-term flow has actually been increasing. In the six months before prices spiked, according to the U.S. Energy Information Administration, the world oil supply rose from 85.24 million barrels a day to 85.72 million. Over the same period, world oil demand dropped from 86.82 million barrels a day to 86.07 million. Not only was the short-term supply of oil rising, the demand for it was falling—which, in classic economic terms, should have brought prices at the pump down.

So what caused the huge spike in oil prices? Take a wild guess. Obviously Goldman had help—there were other players in the physical commodities market—but the root cause had almost everything to do with the behavior of a few powerful actors determined to turn the once solid market into a speculative casino. Goldman did it by persuading pension funds and other large institutional investors to invest in oil futures—agreeing to buy oil at a certain price on a fixed date. The push transformed oil from a physical commodity, rigidly subject to supply and demand, into something to bet on, like a stock. Between 2003 and 2008, the amount of speculative money in commodities grew from $13 billion to $317 billion, an increase of 2,300 percent. By 2008, a barrel of oil was traded 27 times, on average, before it was actually delivered and consumed.

> **"At least with other banks, you could say that they were just dumb . . . Goldman knew what it was doing."**

As is so often the case, there had been a Depression-era law in place designed specifically to prevent this sort of thing. The commodities market was designed in large part to help farmers: A grower concerned about future price drops could enter into a contract to sell his corn at a certain price for delivery later on, which made him worry less about building up stores of his crop. When no one was buying corn, the farmer could sell to a middleman known as a "traditional speculator," who would store the grain and sell it later, when demand returned. That way, someone was always there to buy from the farmer, even when the market temporarily had no need for his crops.

In 1936, however, Congress recognized that there should never be more speculators in the market than real producers and consumers. If that happened, prices would be affected by something other than supply and demand, and price manipulations would ensue. A new law empowered the Commodity Futures Trading Commission—the very same body that would later try and fail to regulate credit swaps—to place limits on speculative trades in commodities. As a result of the CFTC's oversight, peace and harmony reigned in the commodities markets for more than 50 years.

All that changed in 1991 when, unbeknownst to almost everyone in the world, a Goldman-owned commodities trading subsidiary called J. Aron wrote to the CFTC and made an unusual argument. Farmers with big stores of corn, Goldman argued, weren't the only ones who needed to hedge their risk against future price drops—Wall Street dealers who made big bets on oil prices *also* needed to hedge their risk, because, well, they stood to lose a lot too.

This was complete and utter crap—the 1936 law, remember, was specifically designed to maintain distinctions between people who were buying and selling real tangible stuff and people who were trading in paper alone. But the CFTC, amazingly, bought Goldman's argument. It issued the bank a free pass, called the "Bona Fide Hedging" exemption, allowing Goldman's subsidiary to call itself a physical hedger and escape virtually all limits placed on speculators. In the years that followed, the commission would quietly issue 14 similar exemptions to other companies.

Now Goldman and other banks were free to drive more investors into the commodities markets, enabling speculators to place increasingly big bets. That 1991 letter from Goldman more or less directly led to the oil bubble in 2008, when the number of speculators in the market—driven there by fear of the falling dollar and the housing crash—finally overwhelmed the real physical suppliers and consumers. By 2008, at least three quarters of the activity on the commodity exchanges was speculative, according to a congressional staffer who studied the numbers—and that's likely a conservative estimate. By the middle of last summer, despite rising supply and a drop in demand, we were paying $4 a gallon every time we pulled up to the pump.

What is even more amazing is that the letter to Goldman, along with most of the other trading exemptions, was handed out more or less in secret. "I was the head of the division of trading and markets, and Brooksley Born was the chair of the CFTC," says Greenberger, "and neither of us knew this letter was out there." In fact, the letters only came to light by accident. Last year, a staffer for the House Energy and Commerce Committee just happened to be at a briefing when officials from the CFTC made an offhand reference to the exemptions.

"I had been invited to a briefing the commission was holding on energy," the staffer recounts. "And suddenly in the middle of it, they start saying, 'Yeah, we've been issuing these letters for years now.' I raised my hand and said, 'Really? You issued a letter? Can I see it?' And they were like, 'Duh, duh.' So we went back and forth, and finally they said, 'We have to clear it with Goldman Sachs.' I'm like, 'What do you mean, you have to clear it with Goldman Sachs?'"

The CFTC cited a rule that prohibited it from releasing any information about a company's current position in the market. But the staffer's request was about a letter that had been issued 17 *years* earlier. It no longer had anything to do with Goldman's current position. What's more, Section 7 of the 1936 commodities law gives Congress the right to any information it wants from the commission. Still, in a classic example of how complete Goldman's capture of government is, the CFTC waited until it got clearance from the bank before it turned the letter over.

Armed with the semi-secret government exemption, Goldman had become the chief designer of a giant commodities betting parlor. Its Goldman Sachs Commodities Index—which tracks the prices of 24 major commodities but is overwhelmingly weighted toward oil—became the place where pension funds and insurance companies and other institutional investors could make massive long-term bets on commodity prices. Which was all well and good, except for a couple of things. One was that index speculators are mostly "long only" bettors, who seldom if ever take short positions—meaning they only bet on prices to rise. While this kind of behavior is good for a stock market, it's terrible for commodities, because it continually forces prices upward. "If index speculators took short positions as well as long ones, you'd see them pushing prices both up and down," says Michael Masters, a hedgefund manager who has helped expose the role of investment banks in the manipulation of oil prices. "But they only push prices in one direction: up."

Complicating matters even further was the fact that Goldman itself was cheerleading with all its might for an increase in oil prices. In the beginning of 2008, Arjun Murti, a Goldman analyst, hailed as an "oracle of oil" by *The New York Times,* predicted a "super spike" in oil prices, forecasting a rise to $200 a barrel. At the time Goldman was heavily invested in oil through its commodities trading subsidiary, J. Aron; it also owned a stake in a major oil refinery in Kansas, where it warehoused the crude it bought and sold. Even though the supply of oil was keeping pace with demand, Murti continually warned of disruptions to the world oil supply, going so far as to broadcast the fact that he owned two hybrid cars. High prices, the bank insisted, were somehow the fault of the piggish American consumer; in 2005, Goldman analysts insisted that we wouldn't know when oil prices would fall until we knew "when American consumers will stop buying gas-guzzling sport utility vehicles and instead seek fuel-efficient alternatives."

But it wasn't the consumption of real oil that was driving up prices—it was the trade in paper oil. By the summer of 2008, in fact, commodities speculators had bought and stockpiled enough oil futures to fill 1.1 billion barrels of crude, which meant that speculators owned more future oil on paper than there was real, physical oil stored in all of the country's commercial storage tanks and the Strategic Petroleum Reserve combined. It was a repeat of both the Internet craze and the housing bubble, when Wall Street jacked up present-day profits by selling suckers shares of a fictional fantasy future of endlessly rising prices.

In what was by now a painfully familiar pattern, the oil-commodities melon hit the pavement hard in the summer of 2008, causing a massive loss of wealth; crude prices plunged from $147 to $33. Once again the big losers were ordinary people. The pensioners whose funds invested in this crap got massacred: CalPERS, the California Public Employees' Retirement System, had $1.1 billion in commodities when the crash came. And the damage didn't just come from oil. Soaring food prices driven by the commodities bubble led to catastrophes across the planet, forcing an estimated 100 million people into hunger and sparking food riots throughout the Third World.

Now oil prices are rising again: They shot up 20 percent in the month of May and have nearly doubled so far this year. Once again, the problem is not supply or demand. "The highest supply of oil in the last 20 years is now," says Rep. Bart Stupak, a Democrat from Michigan who serves on the House energy committee. "Demand is at a 10-year low. And yet prices are up."

Asked why politicians continue to harp on things like drilling or hybrid cars, when supply and demand have nothing to do with the high prices, Stupak shakes his head. "I think they just don't understand the problem very well," he says. "You can't explain it in 30 seconds, so politicians ignore it."

BUBBLE #5: RIGGING THE BAILOUT

After the oil bubble collapsed last fall, there was no new bubble to keep things humming—this time, the money seems to be really gone, like worldwide-depression gone. So the financial safari has moved elsewhere, and the big game in the hunt has become the only remaining pool of dumb, unguarded capital left to feed upon: taxpayer money. Here, in the biggest bailout in history, is where Goldman Sachs really started to flex its muscle.

It began in September of last year, when then-Treasury secretary Paulson made a momentous series of decisions. Although he had already engineered a rescue of Bear Stearns a few months before and helped bail out quasi-private lenders Fannie Mae and Freddie Mac, Paulson elected to let Lehman Brothers—one of Goldman's last real competitors—collapse without intervention. ("Goldman's superhero status was left intact," says market analyst Eric Salzman, "and an investment banking competitor, Lehman, goes away.") The very next day, Paulson greenlighted a massive, $85 billion bailout of AIG, which promptly turned around and repaid $13 billion it owed to Goldman. Thanks to the rescue effort, the bank ended up getting paid in full for its bad bets: By contrast, retired auto workers awaiting the Chrysler bailout will be lucky to receive 50 cents for every dollar they are owed.

Immediately after the AIG bailout, Paulson announced his federal bailout for the financial industry, a $700 billion plan called the Troubled Asset Relief Program, and put a heretofore unknown 35-year-old Goldman banker named Neel Kashkari in charge of administering the funds. In order to qualify for bailout monies, Goldman announced that it would convert from an investment bank to a bank-holding company, a move that allows it access not only to $10 billion in TARP funds, but to a whole galaxy of less conspicuous, publicly backed funding—most notably, lending from the discount window of the Federal Reserve. By the end of March, the Fed will have lent or guaranteed at least $8.7 trillion under a series of new bailout programs—and thanks to an obscure law allowing the Fed to block most congressional audits, both the amounts and the recipients of the monies remain almost entirely secret.

Converting to a bank-holding company has other benefits as well: Goldman's primary supervisor is now the New York Fed, whose chairman at the time of its announcement was Stephen Friedman, a former co-chairman of Goldman Sachs. Friedman was technically in violation of Federal Reserve policy by remaining on the board of Goldman even as he was supposedly regulating the bank; in order to rectify the problem, he applied for, and got, a conflict-of-interest waiver from the government. Friedman was also supposed to divest himself of his Goldman stock after Goldman became a bank-holding company, but thanks to the waiver, he was allowed to go out and buy 52,000 *additional* shares in his old bank, leaving him $3 million richer. Friedman stepped down in May, but the man now in charge of supervising Goldman—New York Fed president William Dudley—is yet another former Goldmanite.

The collective message of all this—the AIG bailout, the swift approval for its bank-holding conversion, the TARP funds—is that when it comes to Goldman Sachs, there isn't a free market at all. The government might let other players on the market die, but it simply will not allow Goldman to fail under any circumstances. Its edge in the market has suddenly become an open declaration of supreme privilege. "In the past it was an implicit advantage," says Simon Johnson, an economics professor at MIT and former official at the International Monetary Fund, who compares the bailout to the crony capitalism he has seen in Third World countries. "Now it's more of an explicit advantage."

Once the bailouts were in place, Goldman went right back to business as usual, dreaming up impossibly convoluted schemes to pick the American carcass clean of its loose capital. One of its first moves in the post-bailout era was to quietly push forward the calendar it uses to report its earnings, essentially wiping December 2008—with its $1.3 billion in pretax losses—off the books. At the same time, the bank announced a highly suspicious $1.8 billion profit for the first quarter of 2009—which apparently included a large chunk of money funneled to it by taxpayers via the AIG bailout. "They cooked those first quarter results six ways from Sunday," says one hedgefund manager. "They hid the losses in the orphan month and called the bailout money profit."

Two more numbers stand out from that stunning first-quarter turnaround. The bank paid out an astonishing $4.7 billion in bonuses and compensation in the first three months of this year, an 18 percent increase over the first quarter of 2008. It also raised $5 billion by issuing new shares almost immediately after releasing its first quarter results. Taken together, the numbers show that Goldman essentially borrowed a $5 billion salary payout for its executives in the middle of the global economic crisis it helped cause, using half-baked accounting to reel in investors, just months after receiving billions in a taxpayer bailout.

Even more amazing, Goldman did it all right before the government announced the results of its new "stress test" for banks seeking to repay TARP money—suggesting that Goldman knew exactly what was coming. The government was trying to carefully orchestrate the repayments in an effort to prevent further trouble at banks that couldn't pay back the money right away. But Goldman blew off those concerns, brazenly flaunting its insider status. "They seemed to know everything that they needed to do before the stress test came out, unlike everyone else, who had to wait until after," says Michael Hecht, a managing director of JMP Securities. "The government came out and said, 'To pay back TARP, you have to issue debt of at least five years that is not insured by FDIC—which Goldman Sachs had already done, a week or two before."

And here's the real punch line. After playing an intimate role in four historic bubble catastrophes, after helping $5 trillion in wealth disappear from the NASDAQ, after pawning off thousands of toxic mortgages on pensioners and cities, after helping to drive the price of gas up to $4 a gallon and to push 100 million people around the world into hunger, after securing tens of billions of taxpayer dollars through a series of bailouts overseen by its former CEO, what did Goldman Sachs give back to the people of the United States in 2008?

Fourteen million dollars.

That is what the firm paid in taxes in 2008, an effective tax rate of exactly one, read it, one percent. The bank paid out $10 billion in compensation and benefits that same year and made a profit of more than $2 billion—yet it paid the Treasury less than a third of what it forked over to CEO Lloyd Blankfein, who made $42.9 million last year.

How is this possible? According to Goldman's annual report, the low taxes are due in large part to changes in the bank's "geographic earnings mix." In other words, the bank moved its money around so that most of its earnings took place in foreign countries with low tax rates. Thanks to our completely fucked corporate tax system, companies like Goldman can ship their revenues offshore and defer taxes on those revenues indefinitely, even while they claim deductions upfront on that same untaxed income. This is why any corporation with an at least occasionally sober accountant can usually find a way to zero out its taxes. A GAO report, in fact, found that between 1998 and 2005, roughly two-thirds of all corporations operating in the U.S. paid no taxes at all.

This should be a pitchfork-level outrage—but somehow, when Goldman released its post-bailout tax profile, hardly anyone said a word. One of the few to remark on the obscenity was Rep. Lloyd Doggett, a Democrat from Texas who serves on the House Ways and Means Committee.

"With the right hand out begging for bailout money," he said, "the left is hiding it offshore."

BUBBLE #6: GLOBAL WARMING

Fast-forward to today. It's early June in Washington, D.C. Barack Obama, a popular young politician whose leading private campaign donor was an investment bank called Goldman Sachs—its employees paid some $981,000 to his campaign—sits in the White House. Having seamlessly navigated the political minefield of the bailout era, Goldman is once again back to its old business, scouting out loopholes in a new government-created market with the aid of a new set of alumni occupying key government jobs.

Gone are Hank Paulson and Neel Kashkari; in their place are Treasury chief of staff Mark Patterson and CFTC chief Gary Gensler, both former Goldmanites. (Gensler was the firm's cohead of finance.) And instead of credit derivatives or oil futures or mortgage-backed CDOs, the new game in town, the next bubble, is in carbon credits—a booming trillion dollar market that barely even exists yet, but will if the Democratic Party that it gave $4,452,585 to in the last election manages to push into existence a groundbreaking new commodities bubble, disguised as an "environmental plan," called cap-and-trade.

The new carbon credit market is a virtual repeat of the commodities-market casino that's been kind to Goldman, except it has one delicious new wrinkle: If the plan goes forward as expected, the rise in prices will be government-mandated. Goldman won't even have to rig the game. It will be rigged in advance.

Here's how it works: If the bill passes, there will be limits for coal plants, utilities, natural-gas distributors, and numerous other industries on the amount of carbon emissions (a.k.a. greenhouse gases) they can produce per year. If the companies go over their allotment, they will be able to buy "allocations" or credits from other companies that have managed to produce fewer emissions. President Obama conservatively estimates that about $646 billion worth of carbon credits will be auctioned in the first seven years; one of his top economic aides speculates that the real number might be twice or even three times that amount.

The feature of this plan that has special appeal to speculators is that the "cap" on carbon will be continually lowered by the government, which means that carbon credits will become more and more scarce with each passing year. Which means that this is a brand new commodities market where the main commodity to be traded is guaranteed to rise in price over time. The volume of this new market will be upwards of a trillion dollars annually; for comparison's sake, the annual combined revenues of all electricity suppliers in the U.S. total $320 billion.

Goldman wants this bill. The plan is (1) to get in on the ground floor of paradigm-shifting legislation, (2) make sure that they're the profitmaking slice of that paradigm, and (3) make sure the slice is a big slice. Goldman started pushing hard for cap-and-trade long ago, but things really ramped up last year when the firm spent $3.5 million to lobby climate issues. (One of their lobbyists at the time was none other than Patterson, now Treasury chief of staff.) Back in 2005, when Hank Paulson was chief of Goldman, he personally helped author the bank's environmental policy, a document that contains some surprising elements for a firm that in all other areas has been consistently opposed to any sort of government regulation. Paulson's report argued that "voluntary action alone cannot solve the climate change problem." A few years later, the bank's carbon chief, Ken Newcombe, insisted that cap-and-trade alone won't be enough to fix the climate problem and called for further public investments in research and development. Which is convenient, considering that Goldman made early investments in wind power (it bought a subsidiary called Horizon Wind Energy), renewable diesel (it is an investor in a firm called Changing World Technologies), and solar power (it partnered with BP Solar), exactly the kind of deals that will prosper if the government forces energy producers to use cleaner energy. As Paulson said at the time, "We're not making those investments to lose money."

> *It wasn't the consumption of real oil that was driving up prices—it was the trade in paper oil.*

The bank owns a 10 percent stake in the Chicago Climate Exchange, where the carbon credits will be traded. Moreover, Goldman owns a minority stake in Blue Source LLC, a Utah-based firm that sells carbon credits of the type that will be in great demand if the bill passes. Nobel Prize winner Al Gore, who is intimately involved with the planning of cap-and-trade, started up a company called Generation Investment Management with three former bigwigs from Goldman Sachs Asset Management, David Blood, Mark Ferguson, and Peter Harris. Their business? Investing in carbon offsets. There's also a $500 million Green Growth Fund set up by a Goldmanite to invest in greentech . . . the list goes on and on. Goldman is ahead of the headlines again, just waiting for someone to make it rain in the right spot. Will this market be bigger than the energy futures market?

"Oh, it'll dwarf it," says a former staffer on the House energy committee.

Well, you might say, who cares? If cap-and-trade succeeds, won't we all be saved from the catastrophe of global warming? Maybe—but cap-and-trade, as envisioned by Goldman, is really just a carbon tax structured so that private interests collect the revenues. Instead of simply imposing a fixed government levy on carbon pollution and forcing unclean energy producers to pay for the mess they make, cap-and-trade will allow a small tribe of greedy-as-hell Wall Street swine to turn yet another commodities market into a private tax collection scheme. This is worse than the bailout: It allows the bank to seize taxpayer money *before it's even collected*.

"If it's going to be a tax, I would prefer that Washington set the tax and collect it," says Michael Masters, the hedgefund director who spoke out against oil futures speculation. "But we're saying that Wall Street can set the tax, and Wall Street can collect the tax. That's the last thing in the world I want. It's just asinine."

Cap-and-trade is going to happen. Or, if it doesn't, something like it will. The moral is the same as for all the other bubbles that Goldman helped create, from 1929 to 2009. In almost every case, the very same bank that behaved recklessly for years, weighing down the system with toxic loans and predatory debt, and accomplishing nothing but massive bonuses for a few bosses, has been rewarded with mountains of virtually free money and government guarantees—while the actual victims in this mess, ordinary taxpayers, are the ones paying for it.

It's not always easy to accept the reality of what we now routinely allow these people to get away with; there's a kind of collective denial that kicks in when a country goes through what America has gone through lately, when a people lose as much prestige and status as we have in the past few years. You can't really register the fact that you're no longer a citizen of a thriving first-world democracy, that you're no longer above getting robbed in broad daylight, because like an amputee, you can still sort of feel things that are no longer there.

But this is it. This is the world we live in now. And in this world, some of us have to play by the rules, while others get a note from the principal excusing them from homework till the end of time, plus 10 billion free dollars in a paper bag to buy lunch. It's a gangster state, running on gangster economics, and even prices can't be trusted anymore; there are hidden taxes in every buck you pay. And maybe we can't stop it, but we should at least know where it's all going.

DISCUSSION

1. Early in the essay, Taibbi makes a point of highlighting some of the most lavish expenses incurred by and compensation paid to Wall Street CEOs. Why do you think he gives this information such prominent attention? What view of these CEOs does it encourage us to form? And how does this view relate to the larger argument about Wall Street, high finance, and the economic recession Taibbi is trying to make?

2. Despite Taibbi's scathing criticism, investment banking has stood for years as one of the most sought-after careers in our culture. Why do you think this is? What, according to prevailing cultural norms, makes this industry so attractive? What are some of the rewards we have been taught to associate with it? Do you share this view? And how does Taibbi attempt to challenge or discredit this image?

3. For Taibbi, the story of Goldman Sachs is purely and simply a tale about greed. But where does ambition end and greed begin? Where do the cultural norms and social scripts in our world encourage us to draw this line? In your view, is this line drawn where it should be?

WRITING

4. Here is how Taibbi characterizes the role played by investment firms like Goldman Sachs: "The bank is a huge, highly sophisticated engine for converting the useful, deployed wealth of society into the least useful, most wasteful and insoluble substance on Earth — pure profit for rich individuals." Write an essay in which you provide a critical close reading of this passage. In your view, does it offer an accurate or an inaccurate description of the norm and scripts that define success in this world? Why or why not?

5. Our airwaves are replete these days with reality and scripted shows that present us with the flip side of Taibbi's portrait. They celebrate the achievements and acumen of America's business elite. Choose one such example and write an essay in which you contrast the central differences between its depiction and Taibbi's essay. How does this show depict the corporate executive? What qualities, skills, and accomplishments does it emphasize? And how do these differ from the picture of corporate behavior Taibbi draws?

6. Taibbi's essay about Wall Street malfeasance couldn't offer a more divergent portrait of work than the one presented by Matthew B. Crawford (p. 395). As a shorthand description, "working with your hands" stands at the opposite end of the spectrum from the information-based "knowledge work" Taibbi examines. In an essay, discuss the ways that Crawford's defense of manual labor compares to Taibbi's critique of Wall Street. Does Crawford's critique of white-collar work seem similar to Taibbi's indictment of Goldman Sachs? To what extent does Crawford's portrait of "hands-on" labor offer an effective or appealing alternative?

LYNETTE CLEMETSON
Work vs. Family, Complicated by Race

When it comes to debates over motherhood and work, it's easy to assume that the issues revolve entirely around gender. This, however, says Lynette Clemetson, may well be a social norm in need of a second look. Profiling the experiences and viewpoints of African American professional women, Clemetson sheds light on the role that race plays in shaping this debate. Clemetson is managing editor of the *Root,* a website of news and social commentary for the African American community. Its editor-in-chief is noted scholar Henry Louis Gates Jr. Clemetson has also written about race and society for *Newsweek* and the *New York Times,* where the following selection appeared on February 9, 2006.

THE SUBJECT, YET AGAIN, WAS MOTHERHOOD AND WORK. OVER TEA and hors d'oeuvres in this affluent Washington suburb, a cluster of well-educated women gathered to discuss the work-life debate. Most in the roomful of lawyers, technology experts, corporate managers, and entrepreneurs had read dispatches from the so-called "mommy wars," the books and articles grounded in the gulch between working and stay-at-home mothers.

But for the women in attendance—all of them black—those discussions inevitably fell short. "They don't speak to my reality," said Robin Rucker Gaillard, 41, a lawyer and mother of two. "We don't generally have the time or luxury for the guilt and competition that some white mothers engage in."

Around the country black women are opting out of the "opt-out" debate, the often-heated exchange about the compatibility of motherhood and work. Steeped in issues like working versus staying at home, nannies versus day care, and the benefits or garish excess of $800 strollers, the discussion has become a hot topic online, in newspapers, and in book publishing.

It is not that black mothers do not wrestle with some of the same considerations as white mothers. But interviews with more than two dozen women suggest that the discussions as portrayed in books and the news media often lack the nuances and complexities particular to their experience.

For professional black women, debates about self-fulfillment can seem incomprehensibly narrow against the need to build sustainable wealth and security for their families. The discussions also pale in comparison to worries about shielding sons and daughters from the perils that black children face growing up, and overlook the practical pull of extended families in need of financial support.

Ms. Gaillard and others had gathered to broaden the working-mother debate by discussing a new book, *I'm Every Woman: Remixed Stories of Marriage, Motherhood, and Work.*

Equal parts memoir, history lesson, and cultural critique, the book, by Lonnae O'Neal Parker, a reporter for the *Washington Post* and

> *For professional black women, debates about self-fulfillment can seem incomprehensibly narrow against the need to build sustainable wealth and security for their families.*

a mother of three, celebrates the balancing act practiced by black women. Published in November [2005] by Amistad, an imprint of HarperCollins, it takes a sometimes wrenching, sometimes joyful look at black mother-hood from slavery and the great migration to suburbia, the corporate workplace, and the ascendancy of hip-hop. And since it came out, Ms. O'Neal Parker has been invited to gatherings around the country by black women eager to talk about motherhood on their own terms.

"It was a breath of fresh air to have a conversation that resonated with me," said Pamela Walker, 41, a professor at Northwestern Business College in Chicago. A married mother of six, she attended a reading of *I'm Every Woman* at Sensual Steps, a shoe boutique in the predominantly black Bronzeville section on the South Side of Chicago. "My family can afford expensive things, but why would I think about spending hundreds on a stroller when I could help a cousin buy textbooks for college? That is not my world."

Black mothers have traditionally worked in higher percentages than white women. And educated black mothers are still more likely to work than their white counterparts. According to census data from March 2005, 83.7 percent of college-educated black women with children under 18 are in the labor force, compared to 74 percent of college-educated white mothers.

Census figures from 2005 also show that college-educated black women earn slightly more than their white counterparts, largely because they are more likely to stay in the work force and work longer hours than white women after having children.

The commitment of black women to work is in large part economi-cally driven. They have lower marriage rates than white women, meaning they are more likely to be single parents. Those who are married are more likely than their white counterparts to earn more than their husbands, census figures show.

But for black middle-class women from Mary Church Terrell, a charter member of the N.A.A.C.P., to Coretta Scott King, working has also been a matter of choice. For generations black women have viewed work as a means for elevating not only their own status as women, but also as a crucial force in elevating their family, extended family, and their entire race.

DISCUSSION

1. Take a closer look at the title of this essay. Do you agree that race "complicates" public conversations about work and family? To what extent do prevailing social scripts around these two questions leave issues of race and racial difference out of the equation?

2. "For generations," Clemetson writes, "black women have viewed work as a means for elevating not only their own status as women, but also as a crucial force in elevating their family, extended family, and their entire race." What point is she trying to make here about the importance of work? To what extent does this characterization challenge established norms regarding how and why we are supposed to think about work?

3. One of the unspoken messages in this essay is that we need to rethink the social norm that teaches us to reflexively associate work with self-fulfillment. Do you agree? Is there something problematic about expecting a job to fulfill us personally? Why or why not?

WRITING

4. "It is not," Clemetson writes, "that black mothers do not wrestle with some of the same considerations as white mothers. But interviews with more than two dozen women suggest that the discussions as portrayed in books and the news media often lack the nuances and complexities particular to their experience." Choose a pop culture text (a book, magazine, website, TV show, etc.) that offers a representation of the black family experience. In a brief essay, assess the ways this representation compares with the ways a white family typically gets represented in our pop culture. Does this comparison bear out the observation made by Clemetson? Are there key differences in the ways these respective family experiences get depicted?

5. According to one of the interviewees profiled here, African American mothers tend to opt out of the conventional debates over motherhood because they don't "have the time or luxury for the guilt and competition" these debates typically involve. Write a response to this claim. In your view, do the typical "mommy war" debates either foster or cater to guilt and competition? If so, how? Do you find the attitude toward motherhood and work profiled here a preferable alternative? Why or why not?

6. Does Clemetson's essay give us a different way to think about Judith Warner's (p. 441) argument regarding motherhood and work? Write an essay in which you reflect on the ways that Clemetson's essay helps us see more clearly some of the underlying assumptions at work in Warner's piece. In light of what Clemetson has to say about work, motherhood, and race, how does your view of Warner's argument change? Does it make you more sympathetic to the points she raises? Less? And how?

JUDITH WARNER

This Mess

We often hear that we now live in an era in which all of the old restrictions and prejudices around work — especially those regarding gender — have fallen away. But how much of this conceit is truth and how much is fantasy? Taking up this question, Judith Warner examines how motherhood — long idealized as a refuge from the world of work — has grown into one of the most intensively regulated, micromanaged, and anxiety-ridden "jobs" in our entire culture. Sharing insights culled from hundreds of interviews of working moms, she offers a sobering assessment of the expectations that frame the parenting choices available today. Warner is the author of the bestselling biography *Hillary Clinton: The Inside Story* (1993), and she collaborated with Howard Dean to write *You Have the Power: How to Take Back Our Country and Restore Democracy in America* (2004). A former special correspondent for *Newsweek* in Paris, she has also published articles on politics and women's issues for the *New Republic* and *Elle,* and wrote the "Domestic Disturbances" blog for the *New York Times*. "This Mess" is an excerpt from her book *Perfect Madness: Motherhood in the Age of Anxiety* (2005). Her most recent book is *We've Got Issues: Children and Parents in the Age of Medication* (2010).

I LISTENED TO MY FRIENDS, LISTENED TO TALK RADIO, TO THE MOTHERS on the playground, and to my daughter's nursery school teachers, and I found it all—the general culture of motherhood in America—oppressive. The pressure to perform, to attain levels of perfect selflessness was insane. And it was, I thought, as I listened to one more anguished friend wringing her hands over the work-family "balance," and another expressing her guilt at not having "succeeded" at breast-feeding, driving American mothers crazy.

Myself along with them.

It took very little time on the ground in America before I found myself becoming unrecognizable. I bought an SUV. I signed my unathletic elder daughter up for soccer. Other three-year-olds in her class were taking gymnastics, too, and art, and swimming and music. I signed her up for ballet. I bought a small library of pre-K skill books. I went around in a state of quiet panic.

The financial burden of trying to set up a life similar to the one I'd had in France was overwhelming. The calculation was grim: the way things were going, if I wanted to keep on writing, working at home, and seeing my children, I would have to take out a home-equity loan to pay my babysitter. Was it worth it? Was I really a good enough writer to justify the sacrifice? Or should I, at long last, just hang it up? The problem was, I wasn't all that good at being a stay-at-home mom.

I started to drink Calvados in the evenings.

At social events, the men and women separated out into two groups, the men discussing sports and stock prices and the women talking about their children. On vacation, the fathers took advantage of "their time" away from work to disappear for whole afternoons of fishing. The mothers continued their daily grind in a new locale.

This reversion to what I would once have termed 1950s-style sex roles wasn't necessarily so different from what I had witnessed among couples with young children in France. Yet there was one significant difference: in America, when couples found themselves sliding back into traditional "masculine" and "feminine" roles, a new power dynamic tended to fall into place as well, with the men distinctly coming out ahead. This was much less true in France—partly, I think, because many more mothers did work full-time and partly because, even in families where the husband was the sole wage earner, the cultural context that was leading American husbands to lord it over their wives was largely missing. Workaholism was frowned upon. Vacation was sacred, as were weekends and holidays. And no matter how hard they worked, no matter how much they tended to distance themselves from the drudgery of diapers and laundry, French men (unless they were the kinds of uncultured boors routinely mocked in movies and TV ads) did not permit themselves to retreat from domestic concerns altogether. They weighed in, as a matter of course, on areas that affected their quality of life: like food and home décor. "We are more 'feminine' than American men," a French diplomat in Washington mused to me. Whether or not that's so, it is true that the "feminine" realm in France is not routinely denigrated, as it is in the United States. And perhaps that's why, for French women my age, inhabiting a traditional "feminine" role as a mother doesn't feel like a tragedy.

Doing so in the States came as a shock to me. Ozzie and Harriet sex roles just weren't what I had expected to find back in America. I was a child of the 1970s, a feminist formed by the 1980s, a product of the girls-can-be-anything school of socialization, which rested on the idea that not only was biology not destiny, it was largely irrelevant. And I had truly believed, gazing back at my country from France, that American feminists had managed to secure for American women a sex-free public space in which they could operate with dignity as people first and women

> **Ozzie and Harriet sex roles just weren't what I had expected to find back in America.**

second. I remembered American women as smiling, sympathetic souls, self-possessed and forward-striding. Their prospects, I'd thought, were as unlimited as the blue sky that thrilled my eyes each time I came home and touched down at Kennedy Airport. American women, I'd thought, didn't have to fit into the gray landscape of Old World–style categories like wives or mothers. They were free to be themselves.

Some of this rosy view had been, no doubt, the symptom of a more general nostalgia for home. Some of it was fed by the only images of American women I had access to then: visions derived from CNN, where every woman, from Christian Amanpour to Janet Reno, looked, from a distance, like an action hero. Women politicians and TV personalities in France all too often were the wives or mistresses of more powerful men, and French movies were filled with sultry consumptives and tooth-baring madwomen. The American movies I saw on the Champs-Élysées in those years were full of virile female stars: Demi Moore as G.I. Jane and a kickboxing Ashley Judd and a blackbelt René Russo breaking heads while pregnant and a whole slew of new women warriors looking fabulous as they ran around with walkie-talkies and guns. I'd leave the theater after watching these American Amazons, see the French women lighting their cigarettes, tugging on their male companions' arms, and pouting their way off into the night, and I'd think: God Bless America. We're doing something right.

Now, back in the United States, I was belatedly realizing that there was a big difference between my memory of young womanhood, my faith in the far-reaching changes wrought by feminism, and the reality of motherhood in America. There was also a big gap between the virility projected by actresses on-screen and the vulnerability felt by the women who watched them. Indeed, I had a new take now on why there had been such a spate of hard-fighting comic book heroines on the American screen during the years I'd been away, the years in which my generation of women had fully come of age professionally and embarked upon motherhood. It wasn't for a sense of identification, not at all. It was to escape—from the feeling of powerlessness brought on by a society that made superhuman demands. To escape the impossible demands of motherhood in particular, just as men had always escaped via superhero movies from impossible demands for power and productivity.

I wondered: How did two generations of feminism bring us here? Why did life feel so difficult? Why, with all our rights and privileges, with all our opportunities and, for some, riches, hadn't we achieved a decent quality of life—that is to say, a life that included time for ourselves and some sense of satisfaction?

In the Spring of 2001, an editor at the *Washington Post's* "Outlook" section asked me to write a first-person piece comparing ideals of women's equality in France and America. After turning the topic around in my head for a number of weeks, I ended up writing about how my own ideas on the nature of real-life equality had changed: whereas once I'd mocked the French culture of "*différence*" and seduction and had believed that American women were more politically and socially evolved, since moving back to America as a mother I'd come to agree with many European observers that American women, despite their surface equality, lived "dogs' lives." It was time, I suggested, to shift the focus of our political debates away from parochial notions of equality and concentrate more on working to guarantee us all—men, women, and children alike—a decent quality of life.

In the days following the article's publication, I received dozens and dozens of e-mails from readers. Some women wrote me to protest the depiction of their mothering styles as "dogs' lives." But they were surprisingly few. Many more wrote to agree with me—and to ask for more. Why wasn't anybody else writing about this? they asked. Why wasn't anyone else focusing on the issue of quality of life? Could they tell me their stories? Could we keep in touch? Meet for coffee? Did I plan to write a book?

Over and over again, I heard the same refrain: You're right. There's a problem. Life doesn't have to be this way. It's time to take a step back and figure out how to make things better.

Over the course of the next year, I interviewed close to 150 women about their experience of motherhood in America. I talked to equal numbers of working and stay-at-home moms. About half the women were from Washington and its suburbs and the rest were from all around the United States. The majority were white. Many were African-American. Most were American, although a fair number either had grown up overseas or were from families that had only recently settled in the U.S. Almost all were college-educated. Some were well off, others struggled to make ends meet, and most were somewhere in the middle. Their children ranged in age from babies to young teenagers.

I tried not to interview women who were super-superwealthy—the social X-ray types ridiculed in *The Nanny Diaries* or the "New Economy Parents," with their $60,000-a-year nannies, kiddie limo services, and "family chaos consultants" featured in *Business Week*. I also did not interview working-class or poor women—not because I wasn't interested in them, but because I quickly saw that giving sufficient attention and understanding to their experiences was beyond the scope of what I could do with this book.

My goal was to write about the middle class. I soon realized, however, that it is very hard to write about the middle class in America *without* excessively focusing on the upper middle class. (Every other book on "American" motherhood that I have read, from *The Feminine Mystique* to

Jessie Bernard's *The Future of Motherhood* to Naomi Wolf's *Misconceptions*, suffers the same fate.) And that is because the influence of the upper middle class is disproportionate in American culture. It is upper-middle-class homes that we see in movies, upper-middle-class lifestyles that are detailed in our magazines, upper-middle-class images of desirability that grace the advertising destined for us all. The upper middle class is our reference point for what the American good life is supposed to look like and contain. This has always been true in America, but became more so in the late 1990s, when the "luxury fever" of the boom years pushed everyone—rich and not-so-rich—to mimic the spending patterns, the ambitions, and the competitive keeping-up-with-the-Joneses of the wealthy. It is because of our overidentification with the upper middle class that so many of us came out of the boom years of the late 1990s so terribly in debt. It is also why so many of us turn ourselves inside out trying to parent to perfection, so that our children will be "winners."

The ways of the upper-middle-class affect everyone—including, to their detriment, the working class and the poor. And this is because our politicians hail, almost exclusively, from the upper-income reaches of our society. Thus to understand the conflicts and, I would say, the *pathologies* of upper-middle-class thinking is to understand the often perplexing state of family politics in America. As a woman who worked with Hillary Rodham Clinton on child care put it to me, "The whole problem of the upper class making policy is that they have choices and they're conflicted about their choices. The women have the conflict about whether they want to stay home or go to work and the men have the conflict of wanting women to have choices but also wanting their wives to stay home. The people making the policy are not the people enjoying the policy, so they're just conflicted for themselves and making policy for people who don't have the choice."

The middle-class and upper-middle-class women I interviewed for this book were strikingly similar in their attitudes toward motherhood, whatever their race, cultural background, or geographic location in America may have been. On the big issues there were no real differences between working and nonworking mothers, either—a fact that, though it flies in the face of received wisdom about the Mommy Wars, didn't surprise me, given my own experience of having moved between the worlds of working and stay-at-home motherhood.

It wasn't just that the working mothers and stay-at-home moms I interviewed felt similarly about motherhood. It was that they *went about it in much the same ways*. The "stay-at-home" moms very often worked part-time, either from their homes or in an office. Like the working mothers, they were dependent on child care. Indeed, one study I read about actually showed that *one-third* of "nonworking" mothers were *putting their kids in day care for an average of eighteen hours a week by the time they were twelve months old.* And the "working mothers," very often, worked only part-time. Meaning that if their kids were of school age, they saw them for about the same number of hours each day as did the stay-at-home moms.

Many studies have borne these similarities out. At the turn of the millennium, for example, we commonly heard that 64 percent of American mothers worked. In reality, though, just a minority of those mothers were working full-time. Only a third of married mothers with children under six were working full-time year-round, and fully two-thirds of mothers were working less than forty hours a week during their key career years. Indeed, the definition of "working" used to derive the Department of Labor percentages for "working mothers" in America is so all-embracing that it catches many women who would probably consider themselves stay-at-home moms. It includes mothers who work part-time (sometimes as little as one hour a week), mothers who work only seasonally (as little as one week out of the year), mothers who work from home part-time, or mothers who work part-time without pay for a family business.

Clearly, the mothers we see represented in the media replays of the Mommy Wars—the militant stay-at-home moms and the round-the-clock workaholics—are very much the exception to the rule. Yet their images—and their alleged conflicts—tend to dominate our notions of contemporary motherhood. And the pressure to live up to their extreme examples inspires much of the sense of inadequacy that plagues us all. One of my most treasured goals for this book is to put the notion that mothers are profoundly divided—in calling, "values," and style of life—to rest.

> **The mothers we see represented in the media replays of the Mommy Wars . . . are very much the exception to the rule.**

Race, geographic location, self-identification as a working or stay-at-home mother—none of this made a real difference in the attitudes and mothering styles of the women I interviewed. What did matter, however, was something more intangible: a kind of personal philosophy. The more women bought into the crazy competitiveness of our time, the more they tended to suffer as mothers. Those who, in one way or another, managed to step outside of the parenting pressure cooker tended to have a greater degree of peace of mind and to mother with a greater level of sanity. They did not push themselves or their children to be "winners"—and so seemed to me to be winning out in terms of happiness and quality of life.

I "spoke" with about half of the women I interviewed for this book via the Internet—sending out questionnaires that they answered in essay form. I interviewed the other half in person. We would meet in the evenings, in groups of eight or ten, everyone "playing hooky" from their families, grinning complicitously and chortling pleasantly at the sound of the on-duty dad putting our hostess's kids to bed upstairs. (Meetings in my own home were the exception; my husband worked nights.)

The enthusiasm and excitement were incredible. Total strangers opened their homes to me, invited friends, and put out food for conversations that stretched as late into the night as the next morning's wakeup time allowed. Friends passed the word on to their friends, who spoke to their friends, until, by the end, I had to stop interviewing for sheer lack of time and the mental and physical resources necessary to transcribe and digest all the material.

When our conversations took off, it was exhilarating. It was exhausting. It felt, I imagined, like the consciousness-raising groups of the early days of the second-wave feminist movement (groups that, as a four- or five-year-old, I would not have attended and which took place, in any case, in universes far from my home). The women came to my groups with a sense of mission. They were going to get at the roots of the problems that plague mothers today. (Which some of them called "guilt," some of them called the Mommy Wars, and one of them, a working-mom-turned-stay-at-home, called "feeling like Alice down the rabbit hole.") They were going to find a way out. I always started off the sessions by telling the women about my move from France to America, and about how my shock at how difficult motherhood was here had grown into my book. Sometimes, toward the end of the evening, the tables turned, and they would ask me for some answers. What was the solution? they'd ask. How could we all calm down, feel better, and parent with the relative ease and insouciance that I'd felt as a mother in France?

I heard the questions with a kind of shame. I knew there were some mothers who managed to rise above the excessive nonsense of our times and work out ways to parent with reason and balance. Some of them came to my groups: the successful working mother with the stay-at-home husband, the stay-at-home mother of four who braved universal disdain to put her youngest children (twins) in part-time day care, the mother who stood out on her front lawn with bubbles and toys until the neighborhood kids stopped, and stayed, and enough trust was built among the parents that they started letting their kids run house to house. But I was not one of them.

In fact, as my time back in America lengthened from months into years, I became more and more bound up in all the aspects of motherhood I'd once found strange. The more I reconnected to the world I'd known as a young adult before leaving for France, the more I grew back into the person I'd always been here—a relatively typical, if quirky, would-be overachiever—and the worse I felt about myself as a mother.

In Paris, I'd felt very good about myself just for mothering according to my inclinations. Since I was an American, those inclinations were far more hands-on than those of the women around me, and so I'd easily enjoyed a somewhat smug sense of superiority. Simply by doing things I *enjoyed*—reading to my daughter for hours on end, taking her out to lunch and telling her stories, sitting on the edge of the sandbox in my sneakers, rather than perching peevishly on a park bench and smoking—*just by smiling*—I felt I was earning a perpetual merit badge for Good Motherhood. I had no qualms about eliminating those activities I found needlessly boring or stupid—like the lap-sit story hour at the nearby American Library, with the fish-out-of-water mommies clutching little plastic bags of Cheerios. If it wasn't fun, I figured, what was the point? If my daughter and I were doing some kind of added-value activity together and it wasn't a pleasure, then why bother?

In ever-smiling America, I was learning, it was actually a lot harder to maintain my sense of fun in motherhood. This was in part, for me, because the things I'd considered the simple pleasures of motherhood were harder and harder to come by. Things like pushing the stroller somewhere pretty for a walk—alone or with a friend. There was too much suburban sprawl and our lives were too atomized. Or things like spending lazy weekend days in the park or with another family. Everyone was too busy with "activities." It was hard to spend time just sort of vegetating in the sun because our kids, overstimulated by daily story hours and Gymboree, couldn't just play in the sandbox, or run around the flagpole, or climb without running to us every five minutes. Without our having constantly to explain, interpret, *facilitate* the world for them. ("*What that lady is saying is, she would really prefer you not empty your bucket of sand over her little boy's head. Is that okay with you, honey?*")

Maybe our children could have run off and played. If we'd let them. But we didn't. There was so much pressure to always be *doing* something with or for them. And doing it right. And I was increasingly feeling that I was doing everything wrong. As a mother. As a woman. As a human being.

> **Maybe our children could have run off and played. If we'd let them. But we didn't. There was so much pressure to always be doing something with or for them.**

A year went by and I could not find a reliable babysitter. I put my elder daughter in a D.C. public school and watched the light in her eyes go dim. (Her kindergarten teacher there told me he'd put all his kids in private school.) I did not have a pediatrician available for human contact in an emergency (being given the "opinion of the practice" by one of his nameless nurses when my younger daughter cut her face open just didn't do the trick). I felt like all responsibility for my daughters' care, health, and education resided within our family. Often enough, it seemed to rest on my shoulders alone.

Sometimes now, when I berated myself for any one of my many shortcomings as a mother (I did not do enough ball-playing; I did not have a sufficient variety of arts-and-crafts supplies; I had not [yet] converted my basement into the requisite playroom), I was reminded of the way a friend in Paris—an American married to a Frenchman—had laughed at me when I'd once expressed guilt about sending my toddler daughter off to six hours a week of preschool. "Do you have a mini arts studio in your home?" she'd asked. "Do you have a playhouse and a variety of tricycles? Can you provide new sources of fun and stimulation every day?" The answers were, obviously, no on all counts. The mere idea of having all that equipment at home had seemed absurd. In fact, when she put things that way, it began to seem absurd to keep a child at home when so many wonderful opportunities existed on the outside.

But in Washington, everything was different. The homes around me *were* equipped like mini arts studios. Many people had backyard equipment that rivaled public parks. And there was a sense that whatever was done at home was best. Anything "institutional," as people put it, was far lesser—a sad replacement for the at-home loving care a good mother could provide by herself.

I tried to do it all myself: be mommy and camp counselor and art teacher and prereading specialist (and somehow, in my off-hours, to do my own work). I tried my absolute best. And like so many of the moms around me, I started to go a little crazy.

I spent night after night arranging toys by color and type in the basement and lining up children's books in size order on the bookshelves.

I spent hours on the phone with other mothers, arranging play dates and negotiating birthday party days.

People said I was "organized."

Sometimes, for no apparent reason, I broke out into hives.

Everything was spinning out of control.

DISCUSSION

1. What do you make of the conventional distinction in our culture that divides work and family into two entirely separate categories? To what extent does it make sense to think of each as its own form of work? And how might doing so challenge or rewrite the dominant scripts by which women's roles are currently defined?

2. "Ozzie and Harriet sex roles just weren't what I had expected to find back in America. I was a child of the 1970s, a feminist formed by the 1980s, a product of the girls-can-be-anything school of socialization, which rested on the idea that not only was biology not destiny, it was largely irrelevant." In your experience, how much of this promise seems to have been fulfilled? Does it seem to you that we now live in a world where biology is no longer destiny?

3. How does the work of motherhood, which Warner itemizes, compare to the tasks that — according to the myths or ideals of our culture — are supposed to more typically define this role? How do the two sets of tasks compare? Which seems more accurate?

WRITING

4. Warner spends much of this essay critiquing what she calls the "culture of total motherhood": entrenched attitudes and expectations that, even in this day and age, continue to demand that women commit themselves first and foremost to the needs of their children. Write an essay in which you assess the kind of "work" you think the "culture of total motherhood" does in our culture. What specific roles does it script for women? How does it frame the choices mothers confront when pursuing careers outside the home?

5. According to Warner, there is a plethora of material — from parenting advice books to ballet lessons for three-year-olds — that encourages us to view motherhood as a structured and formalized type of job. Choose an example that Warner lists and write an assessment of the ways it defines the job of being a "proper" mother. What kind of work does it assign? What expectations and attitudes does it proscribe as mandatory? And what sort of payoff or reward does it suggest makes this work worthwhile?

6. Choose one of the interviews Warner excerpts in this essay. What story does it relate? What problem does it identify? Then, cast yourself in the role of one of the writers featured in this chapter. What kind of suggestions would he or she offer for solving the challenges or dilemmas of work that Warner describes? What solution would you recommend? And what, in your view, makes it most preferable?

FRANK DEFORD

Awful Injustice: It's Time to Pay Revenue-Earning College Athletes

Few norms are more enduring in the academic world than the idea of the "student athlete." But it is well past time, argues sportswriter Frank Deford, to retire this old cliché. Arguing that the culture of amateurism is hopelessly obsolete, he calls for the adoption of a new campus role for athletes, one in which their endeavors in the gym or on the field are treated and compensated as a type of job. Deford is an author, a commentator for National Public Radio, and a correspondent for HBO's *Real Sports with Bryant Gumbel.* His books include *The Old Ball Game* (2005) and *The Entitled* (2007). He is also a senior contributing writer to *Sports Illustrated,* where this column was originally published on January 2, 2008.

SOME THINGS IN SPORT, AS SOME THINGS IN LIFE, NEVER REALLY GET changed, even when they are indefensible. We say: life is unfair and move on. Sports, though, are supposed to be altogether fair. Ah, the level playing field! But, alas, that's only so when referees are around.

Still, every now and then, it's worth bringing up some glaring inequity, even if it's pointless to do so. So now, when college basketball is in full swing and college football is at its climax, with bowls jammed with high-paying customers, with television revenue pouring in—not to mention all the money that hotels and airlines and restaurants and souvenir salesmen and announcers and sportswriters and coaches and athletic directors are raking in—yes, now is a good time to lament anew that, my gracious, isn't it interesting that the only people not making money are the people actually playing the games.

It is perfectly unconscionable that big-time college football and basketball players go unpaid. They are employees, and deserve to be paid based on the National Labor Relations Act.

First, a little history is in order. When college football become a popular sensation more than a hundred years ago, the concept of amateurism was in full sway. Okay. All Olympic athletes, for example, had to live by what was always called "the amateur ideal." But all that has changed. The most popular Olympic sports have all gone pro. Today, in all the world, amongst big-ticket spectator sports, virtually the only athletes who are not paid are our college football and basketball players—whose numbers, ironically, include so many poor African-Americans.

That this should be so in the United States, bastion of both freedom and capitalism, makes it even worse. That this should remain the case when college sports charge Broadway ticket prices and pay their coaches literally millions of dollars, makes it even more shameful.

Moreover, colleges always emphasize that football and basketball make so much money that they pay for the entire athletic program. To me, this only adds to the cynicism. Not only do poor black kids get no remuneration for their work, they are expected to carry all these other coaches and players and teams on their backs with their unpaid labor. Basically, a scholarship boils down to a device to keep the players on the premises where they can perform their services for free. Okay, they get a lot of perks. They live well. They're the equivalent of what we used to call "kept women."

> *A scholarship boils down to a device to keep the players on the premises where they can perform their services for free.*

Besides, why is it only athletes who must perform for the so-called love of the game? Nobody cares if college kids who are actors or musicians or writers or dancers can make a buck using their talent. Why is an athlete any different?

But, at the end of the day, it isn't an economic issue so much as a moral one. It's absolutely evil that only here in the United States do we allow this unscrupulous nineteenth-century arrangement to continue to exist—and nobody anymore hardly even bothers to bring up this awful injustice.

DISCUSSION

1. As Deford acknowledges, the idea of paying college athletes challenges a long-standing educational norm that continues to treat such athletes exclusively as students. "It is perfectly unconscionable," he writes, "that big-time college football and basketball players go unpaid." Do you find Deford convincing? Why or why not? How would paying "big-time" athletes alter the norms we use to think about higher education and college athletics? In your view, would these changes be for the better? How or how not?

2. Deford likens students who are given athletic scholarships to "kept women." What do you make of this analogy? What larger point about college athletes and the schools for which they play does Deford use this comparison to make? In your view, is this comparison accurate? Fair? Why or why not?

3. How does Deford make his proposal to pay college athletes both an economic and a moral issue? Do you agree with him? Is Deford correct in labeling the rules against paying student athletes as "evil"? Why or why not?

WRITING

4. "Why," asks Deford, "is it only athletes who must perform for the so-called love of the game? Nobody cares if college kids who are actors or musicians or writers or dancers can make a buck using their talent. Why is an athlete any different?" In a brief essay, offer a response to Deford's question. Do you agree with his suggestion that, when it comes to "making a buck," athletes are held to a different standard, are expected to follow a different social script? And if so, what, in your view, should be done about this?

5. According to Deford, the ideal of "amateurism" that prevailed in athletics a century ago has become hopelessly obsolete. Write an argument either in favor of or against a return to this amateur ideal. What might its advantages or benefits be? Its dangers or downsides? And how would such a return to amateurism alter the ways we typically think about sports?

6. How do you think Robert Sullivan (p. 407) would respond to Deford's call to pay college athletes? Does his satirical portrait of "non-money-making professions" remind you in any way of Deford's description of non-money-making student athletes? Given what Sullivan seems to be saying about the cultural norms around wealth, status, and money, do you think he would be sympathetic to Deford's plan? How or how not?

Scenes and Un-Scenes: *A Woman's Work*

For decades, if not centuries, Americans have been encouraged not only to draw firm boundaries between men's work and women's work, but also to *value* these kinds of work in radically different ways. As many of us know firsthand, gender stereotypes continue to play a prominent role in scripting the ways we are taught to think about and evaluate life on the job. Whether measured in terms of annual income, social prestige, or professional clout, we know, for example, that we are supposed to view being a kindergarten teacher and being a corporate CEO very differently. We know how to assess and rank these respective occupations because our culture has supplied us with a set of ready-made and highly gendered assumptions (for example, about the kind of person who is the most natural fit for the job, about the rewards and respect such a jobholder is allowed to expect, and so on).
But do these assumptions really offer us an accurate guide? Do they frame choices or script norms that actually "work" for us? And if they don't, to what extent can they be challenged or revised? Each of the following images presents us with an image that rewrites stereotypical scripts by which we have been taught to segregate men's work from women's work. What do these acts of revision involve? What particular norms do their portraits of women and work seem to parody or critique? And what new norms do they posit in their place?

>> *An image initially created as part of a government-led effort during World War II to recruit women into industries that had lost their all-male workforces to overseas fighting, Rosie the Riveter was originally intended to represent the country's short-term employment crisis. One of the most iconic work images of the twentieth century, Rosie the Riveter stands as a pointed rebuke to the ways Americans have traditionally been taught to think about "women's work."*

>> *Other cultural texts have built on Rosie's legacy in different ways. Unlike its preceding counterparts, this image works much more clearly to redirect traditional gender stereotypes toward nontraditional ends. Rather than a sexist shorthand used to marginalize the contributions of working women, the phrase* girltalk *— uttered here by a female executive — gets transformed into a sly joke, one that inverts conventional gender hierarchies by making men the object of humor.*

▲ *In the 1980 film* 9 to 5, *three women office workers end up running their company when, through a series of comic misunderstandings, they end up holding their boss hostage. Over the last few decades, our airwaves have been filled with movies and television shows that attempt the very Rosie-like feat of placing women within positions of workplace authority traditionally occupied by men. However, this sort of role reversal has often been undertaken for comic effect: a way of poking fun at conventional gender norms and gender hierarchies by turning them upside down. In the end, though, how much of the film's comedy rests on the assumption that a woman running a company is inherently funny?*

"What do you say, gentlemen—ready for some girltalk?"

▲▲ *In 2007, Representative Nancy Pelosi (D-Calif.) became the first woman*
Speaker of the U.S. House of Representatives. Is there anything about the
composition of this news photo that could be said to be reminiscent of the
depiction of Rosie the Riveter from the 1940s? In what ways does it differ?

DISCUSSION

1. How does the Rosie the Riveter image seem to define the ideal job? What kinds of work? What particular roles? And to what extent does this definition challenge or rewrite conventional gender stereotypes?

2. How accurately do the work portraits presented above capture or comment on your experiences on the job? Do they convey messages or model norms that would be considered acceptable within the work environments you know personally? How or how not?

3. How valid do you think the distinction between men's work and women's work is in this day and age? Is it a distinction that continues to exert influence in our culture? Does it present a script we are still encouraged to use?

WRITING

4. Choose the image above that you think most directly reinforces the connection between work and self-worth. Write an essay in which you assess the merits and/or flaws of this depiction. In what ways does this image encourage viewers to forge a connection between their work and their self-worth? What, in your view, are the implications of embracing this message? Of using it as the basis for living one's own life?

5. In addition to the distinction between men's and women's work, the examples above also underscore certain differences between white-collar and blue-collar jobs. What are the scripts in our culture by which we are taught to differentiate these two types of employment? Choose one of the images above and write an essay in which you analyze how particular gender stereotypes influence the depiction of white- or blue-collar work. What gender roles or gender scripts get associated with this kind of work? How does the photo convey them? Does this portrayal seem accurate? Fair? How or how not?

6. In "This Mess," Judith Warner (p. 441) writes about motherhood as a full-time job. How do you think she would respond to the images you have just seen, all of which depict women in stereotypically male-dominated types of work? What images can you think of from popular culture that might be added to the preceding set that would corroborate Warner's view of motherhood as a type of career?

Putting It into Practice: *Working Hard or Hardly Working?*

Now that you've read the chapter selections, try applying your conclusions to your own life by completing the following exercises.

BUILDING THE PERFECT WORK ENVIRONMENT   The selections in this chapter cover many different types of jobs, but they also describe, sometimes indirectly, different work *environments*. Write an essay in which you describe the different environments in two or three of these selections. What are the standards of dress or behavior you think these environments condone? What isn't allowed? What type of work environment do you believe is most suited to your personality? Why? What does your ideal "office" (whether or not it's a traditional workspace) look like? What are the standards of conduct you would implement?

EVALUATING SALARIES   The U.S. Department of Labor Bureau and Labor Statistics has compiled a list of mean salaries for 800 jobs (www.bls.gov/oes/current/oes_nat.htm). Select several different occupations and see how each one compares in terms of its related salary. Write an essay in which you discuss what salary tells us about the "value" of work. What sorts of skills or training seem to lead to larger salaries? In your opinion, do the higher-earning jobs truly merit their larger salaries? Why or why not? If you could reassign rank to the jobs you've chosen, how would your list compare with the real salaries for the jobs you've chosen?

PUT YOUR BEST FOOT FORWARD   Bedford/St. Martin's *Re:Writing* website (bedfordstmartins.com/rewriting) has several models of effective résumés, which you can access by clicking the "See sample documents in design" link on the front page and then clicking "Business and Technical Writing." Think about a job or career path that you are interested in pursuing, and use these resources to write a résumé for an entry-level job (or one commensurate with your experience) in this field.

6 How We

CHANGE

Introduction

"So, What's New with You?"

This book began by asking you to take a closer look at your own underlying beliefs: what they are, where they come from, and what role they play in shaping how you think, talk, and act. In doing so, as you no doubt recall, you also found yourself confronting a number of larger questions: What is our relationship to the larger culture? In what ways does our culture actively teach us what to believe? By ending with a chapter entitled "How We Change," this book concludes by asking you to consider the flip side of this equation. Not just "How does culture endeavor to shape us?" but "How are we able to shape culture?" This chapter invites you to take seriously the proposition that we are more than just the passive recipients of our culture's rules and scripts. It helps you to appreciate the many ways we are the *makers* of these things as well.

You have received this same invitation, of course, throughout the book. Our investigation into the societal rules and public roles, cultural norms and social scripts has consistently been underwritten by a healthy belief in our own agency: the power and prerogative to make our own decisions, choose our own path — even in the face of a culture bent on making these choices for us. We have come to see that the views, values, attitudes, and actions promoted in our world as norms — what everybody, everywhere accepts as simply "the way things are" — are not timeless verities set in stone but social constructs: the products of particular forces in particular times and places. And as we have also come to see, if these are things that have been written out for us, then they can be rewritten as well.

Everybody Knows That...

❝Things do not change; we change."

— *Henry David Thoreau*

Writers are change agents, often whether they intend to be or not. The act of recording our impressions about the world around us creates a record not only of how we see ourselves in relation to society, but also a reverse negative that shows our perfect, ideal world. When Henry David Thoreau decided to forsake the world for a simpler life at Walden Pond, the act in itself did not change the world. Rather, it was his writing about that experience in *Walden* that made sense of his endeavor, that set forth his principles for a perfect life, and that passed down his set of beliefs for future generations to discover and contend with. As Thoreau proved, good writing has the potential to bend the arc of society in ever new directions. As you practice your own writing, think about how you are re-scripting the rules you live by.

CHANGE WE CAN BELIEVE IN

Change, as the old saying goes, is the
one constant in life. But what this
well-worn cliché doesn't tell us is how, exactly,
change comes about. What are the factors
and forces that cause one collection of
rules, one set of norms, one body of scripts
to be replaced by another? And to what
extent do we, as individual actors within
our culture, participate in this process?
"How We Change" offers an opportunity to
begin answering these questions. It does so not only by presenting us with
examples of individuals whose own assumptions and actions differ from
the prevailing norm, but also by encouraging us to use these examples as
role models for how we might go about challenging or rethinking norms
and conventions in our own lives. On a personal level, of course, change
is a natural, even inevitable feature of our lives. As circumstances around
us change, as we forge new connections, find ourselves in new settings,
confront new obligations and opportunities, so too do our underlying
ideas, views, and values change. But this is true not only for individuals; it
is equally true for the broader culture as well. Just as our own views and
values change with the passage of time, so too do the views and values
that set the norms around public life. Societies, like people, are not static.
They transform and grow. Whether it be new trends in fashion or music, new
political movements, or new technological breakthroughs, every generation
comes of age in an era defined by its own priorities and concerns: different
assumptions about what is and isn't "normal."

   As you read and write about the act of change (and being changed),
take note of the different levels at which change occurs in our society. A
good place to start examining the conversation about change is to think
about the different rites and occasions in our culture that usher in change at
the personal level. It seems that for every major milestone in our lives, there
exists some ceremony designed to celebrate it: from births to graduations to
marriage, there are few thresholds that are passed without notice. When you
think about the ways you have changed throughout the course of your life,
consider how you and those around you made these changes public.

   Think, for instance, about the attitudes and assumptions about work
and family that passed for the norm fifty years ago. In an age where the
workforce remained predominantly male, where most households divided the
labor along sharply drawn gender roles, where the middle-class suburban
model was promoted as the ideal, the prevailing model of the ideal family
was far narrower than it is today. Likewise for civil and sexual rights. Prior

Everybody Knows That...

to the social revolutions of the 1960s, the mainstream American public held a very different view about whose voices, in public affairs or political policy, should be heard.

In the face of such momentous change, how are we to understand the roles we play? Does cultural change drive personal change? Or vice versa? Are our own beliefs — our private inventory of ideas, views, and values — simply a reflection of the changing norms around us? A by-product of the political, social, technological, and economic forces reshaping our society? Or are these norms and forces the product of changes that we instigate ourselves? Following on the heels of such questions is another, equally important, consideration: Is change always for the good? Does different automatically mean better? We are quite accustomed to seeing change as "progress," but this very view is itself a cultural norm and perhaps a fundamental one that we ought to rethink.

The selections assembled in this chapter revolve around precisely these questions. Taking aim at a particular social or cultural norm — from the definition of gender identity to the notion of community — each of these essays showcases the ways individual people negotiate and remake this norm to suit their own purposes. The goal behind these selections is to lay out the range of possibilities for responding to such change. What new choices do people make in the face of rapidly changing circumstances and times? Do they respond to such change with anxiety and trepidation? Do they embrace it with confidence and gusto? And how, in acting on such change, do they find themselves changed in the process? William Deresiewicz and Jared Keller both examine how social technology has fostered important changes in the way we socialize and connect with each other, for better or worse. Joel Kotkin explores a new trend, as economic downturn has meant a return to hometowns for many Americans, perhaps in an attempt to reclaim familiarity and comfort. However, Peter Lovenheim writes about how he discovered just how little he knows about his neighbors and how he plans to change that for the good of his community, while Julie Bosman presents a portrait of the last homeless man resisting New York City's push to relocate him from Times

Square. Exposing how we change, react to, and shape the world around us, Frances Moore Lappé pleads for a political discourse that dispenses with characterizing one side as "good" and the other as "evil." Steven Kurutz looks at an anticonsumerist trend that just might bring us closer together. And finally, transgender activist Julia Serano addresses change from a personal angle in an essay about how her decision to change her gender was about claiming who she really is.

"EVERYBODY KNOWS THAT" EXERCISE

Choose one of the images or quotations featured in the margins on the preceding pages and answer the following questions:

1. What does this image or quotation ask you to believe?
2. What are the particular ideas, values, or attitudes it invites us to accept as *normal*?
3. What would it feel like to act on or act out these norms in our personal lives?

Rule *Maker* >>>>>>>>>>>> Rule *Breaker*

> When I hear the cynical talk that blacks and whites and Latinos can't join together and work together, I'm reminded of the Latino brothers and sisters I organized with and stood with and fought with side by side for jobs and justice on the streets of Chicago. So don't tell us change can't happen.
>
> When I hear that we'll never overcome the racial divide in our politics, I think about that Republican woman who used to work for Strom Thurmond, who is now devoted to educating inner-city children and who went out into the streets of South Carolina and knocked on doors for this campaign. Don't tell me we can't change.
>
> Yes, we can. Yes, we can change. Yes, we can."
>
> — PRESIDENT BARACK OBAMA,
> COLUMBIA, SC, JANUARY 28, 2008

> [Joe] Wilson's wasn't the only disruption, though it was the most extreme. Throughout the speech, Republican members of Congress repeatedly held up stacks of papers that appeared to represent ideas they had for the bill.
>
> Rep. Louie Gohmert (R-Texas) held signs that read 'What Bill?' and 'What Plan?'
>
> When Obama told the chamber that the 'death panel' lie was, in fact, a lie, a Republican member said loudly enough to be heard in the press gallery, 'Read the bill' — a common refrain at August's angry town hall meetings."
>
> — RYAN GRIM,
> *THE HUFFINGTON POST*, ON THE OUTBURSTS
> DURING PRESIDENT OBAMA'S SPEECH TO
> CONGRESS ON HEALTHCARE,
> SEPTEMBER 9, 2009

"YES WE CAN!" VS. "YOU LIE!"

Over the last few years, the word *change* has enjoyed a remarkable resurgence in both popularity and social clout. Once little more than a neutral descriptor, an objective and unobjectionable way to reference the new developments and trends taking place within society at large, *change* has transformed into one of the most potent, pointed, and volatile political catchphrases of our time. For partisans of all stripes, being for or against change has become the signature strategy for staking out one's position on the most controversial and topical debates of the day. From politicians to pundits, corporate lobbyists to grassroots activists, everyone with a stake in the political process, it seems, has turned to *change* as the term of art for articulating and advocating their particular views.

In 2008, for example, the concept of change was so central to supporters of Barack Obama that it came to stand as a virtual trademark for the campaign itself: "Change We Can Believe In." For legions of Obama followers, "believing in change" not only crystallized their disdain for the outgoing administration, it also served as useful shorthand for the many new policies they hoped Obama's election would quickly usher in. Following the election, *change* continued to perform much the same role, supplying administration officials with a term for promoting the broad range of reform initiatives they hoped to pass: from the economic recovery act to healthcare overhaul to financial regulation to efforts to address climate change. During this same period, however, *change* came to fulfill a quite different purpose for Obama opponents. In their eyes, *change* was a political epithet, a rallying cry uniting them in furious opposition to what they derisively termed the "Obama agenda." From Republican South Carolina representative Joe Wilson's shouted accusation "You lie!" during a joint address of Congress (seen in this photo) to the Tea Party's steadfast insistence that this change is no less than a slide into socialism or worse, the modern political landscape of late is littered with just as many declarations that turn *change* into a harbinger of doom rather than a symbol of hope.

FIND THE RULES: Choose a current political issue that revolves around the concept of change (examples include healthcare or financial reform, environmental legislation, or bailouts and economic stimulus). First, write about how this issue gets debated within our current political culture. What makes this issue controversial? What different groups does it pit against each other? And how do their views and values differ? Next, analyze the ways these differences can be understood in terms of change more specifically. To what extent does this debate involve competing visions of what change means?

MAKE YOUR OWN RULES: Imagine that you are a political strategist tasked with creating a new campaign to market "change" to the American public. First, write a description of the specific strategies this campaign would entail. Would you define change broadly or connect it to specific ideas or initiatives? What particular tactics would you use to represent such change in the most appealing ways? What groups or constituencies would you target specifically? What groups or constituencies would you not target? When you're done, write an assessment of why you made these particular choices. What, in your view, makes these strategies particularly effective?

WILLIAM DERESIEWICZ

Faux Friendship

The explosive growth and burgeoning popularity of online social networking sites raise important questions about the ways we are redefining friendship. It is beyond dispute that these new technologies have reconfigured the ways we think about, talk to, and define our friends. Less clear, however, is whether these changes are for the better. Taking up this question, William Deresiewicz offers a pointed critique lamenting the demise of more traditional models of friendship while asking us to consider whether making communication easier and more accessible has opened up new possibilities for connection and understanding as well. Deresiewicz was associate professor of English at Yale University and is a well-respected literary critic whose work has appeared in the *Nation,* the *American Scholar,* and the *Chronicle of Higher Education*, where the following essay was published in March of 2010.

"[A] numberless multitude of people, of whom no one was close, no one was distant. . . ." — War and Peace

"Families are gone, and friends are going the same way." — In Treatment

W E LIVE AT A TIME WHEN FRIENDSHIP HAS BECOME BOTH ALL AND nothing at all. Already the characteristically modern relationship, it has in recent decades become the universal one: the form of connection in terms of which all others are understood, against which they are all measured, into which they have all dissolved. Romantic partners refer to each other as boyfriend and girlfriend. Spouses boast that they are each other's best friends. Parents urge their young children and beg their teenage ones to think of them as friends. Adult siblings, released from competition for parental resources that in traditional society made them anything but friends (think of Jacob and Esau), now treat one another in exactly those terms. Teachers, clergymen, and even bosses seek to mitigate and legitimate their authority by asking those they oversee to regard them as friends. We're all on a first-name basis, and when we vote for president, we ask ourselves whom we'd rather have a beer with. As the anthropologist Robert Brain has put it, we're friends with everyone now.

Yet what, in our brave new mediated world, is friendship becoming? The Facebook phenomenon, so sudden and forceful a distortion of social space, needs little elaboration. Having been relegated to our screens, are our friendships now anything more than a form of distraction? When they've shrunk to the size of a wall post, do they retain any content? If we have 768 "friends," in what sense do we have any? Facebook isn't the whole of contemporary friendship, but it sure looks a lot like its future. Yet Facebook—and MySpace, and Twitter, and whatever we're stamped-ing for next—are just the latest stages of a long attenuation. They've accelerated the fragmentation of consciousness, but they didn't initiate it. They have reified the idea of universal friendship, but they didn't invent it. In retrospect, it seems inevitable that once we decided to become friends with everyone, we would forget how to be friends with anyone. We may pride ourselves today on our aptitude for friendship—friends, after all, are the only people we have left—but it's not clear that we still even know what it means.

How did we come to this pass? The idea of friendship in ancient times could not have been more different. Achilles and Patroclus, David and Jonathan, Virgil's Nisus and Euryalus: Far from being ordinary and universal, friendship, for the ancients, was rare, precious, and hard-won. In a world ordered by relations of kin and kingdom, its elective affinities were exceptional, even subversive, cutting across established lines of allegiance. David loved Jonathan despite the enmity of Saul; Achilles' bond with Patroclus outweighed his loyalty to the Greek cause. Friendship was a high calling, demanding extraordinary qualities of character—rooted in virtue, for Aristotle and Cicero, and dedicated to the pursuit of goodness and truth. And because it was seen as superior to marriage and at least equal in value to sexual love, its expression often reached an erotic intensity. Jonathan's love, David sang, "was more wondrous to me than the love of women." Achilles and Patroclus were not lovers—the men shared a tent, but they shared their beds with concubines—they were something greater. Achilles refused to live without his friend, just as Nisus died to avenge Euryalus, and Damon offered himself in place of Pythias.

The rise of Christianity put the classical ideal in eclipse. Christian thought discouraged intense personal bonds, for the heart should be turned to God. Within monastic communities, particular attachments were seen as threats to group cohesion. In medieval society, friendship entailed specific expectations and obligations, often formalized in oaths. Lords and vassals employed the language of friendship. "Standing surety"—guaranteeing a loan, as in *The Merchant of Venice*—was a chief institution of early modern friendship. Godparenthood functioned in Roman Catholic society (and, in many places, still functions) as a form of alliance between families, a relationship not between godparent and godchild, but godparent and parent. In medieval England, godparents were "godsibs"; in Latin America, they are "compadres," co-fathers, a word we have taken as synonymous with friendship itself.

The classical notion of friendship was revived, along with other ancient modes of feeling, by the Renaissance. Truth and virtue, again, above all: "Those who venture to criticize us perform a remarkable act of friendship," wrote Montaigne, "for to undertake to wound and offend a man for his own good is to have a healthy love for him." His bond with Étienne, he avowed, stood higher not only than marriage and erotic attachment, but also than filial, fraternal, and homosexual love. "So many coincidences are needed to build up such a friendship, that it is a lot if fortune can do it once in three centuries." The highly structured and, as it were, economic nature of medieval friendship explains why true friendship was held to be so rare in classical and neoclassical thought: precisely because relations in traditional societies were dominated by interest. Thus the "true friend" stood against the self-interested "flatterer" or "false friend," as Shakespeare sets Horatio—"more an antique Roman than a Dane"—against Rosencrantz and Guildenstern. Sancho Panza begins as Don Quixote's dependent and ends as his friend; by the close of their journey, he has come to understand that friendship itself has become the reward he was always seeking.

Are our friendships now anything more than a form of distraction?

Classical friendship, now called romantic friendship, persisted through the 18th and 19th centuries, giving us the great friendships of Goethe and Schiller, Byron and Shelley, Emerson and Thoreau. Wordsworth addressed his magnum opus to his "dear Friend" Coleridge. Tennyson lamented Hallam—"My friend . . . My Arthur . . . Dear as the mother to the son"—in the poem that became his masterpiece. Speaking of his first encounter with Hawthorne, Melville was unashamed to write that "a man of deep and noble nature has seized me." But meanwhile, the growth of commercial society was shifting the very grounds of personal life toward the conditions essential for the emergence of modern friendship. Capitalism, said Hume and Smith, by making economic relations impersonal, allowed for private relationships based on nothing other than affection and affinity. We don't know the people who make the things we buy and don't need to know the people who sell them. The ones we do know—neighbors, fellow parishioners, people we knew in high school or college, parents of our children's friends—have no bearing on our economic life. One teaches at a school in the suburbs, another works for a business across town, a third lives on the opposite side of the country. We are nothing to one another but what we choose to become, and we can unbecome it whenever we want.

Add to this the growth of democracy, an ideology of universal equality and inter-involvement. We are citizens now, not subjects, bound together directly rather than through allegiance to a monarch. But what is to bind us emotionally, make us something more than an aggregate of political monads? One answer was nationalism, but another grew out of the 18th-century notion of social sympathy: friendship, or at least, friend-liness, as the affective substructure of modern society. It is no accident that "fraternity" made a third with liberty and equality as the watch-words of the French Revolution. Wordsworth in Britain and Whitman in America made visions of universal friendship central to their democratic vistas. For Mary Wollstonecraft, the mother of feminism, friendship was to be the key term of a renegotiated sexual contract, a new domestic democracy.

Now we can see why friendship has become the characteristically modern relationship. Modernity believes in equality, and friendships, unlike traditional relationships, are egalitarian. Modernity believes in individualism. Friendships serve no public purpose and exist inde-pendent of all other bonds. Modernity believes in choice. Friendships, unlike blood ties, are elective; indeed, the rise of friendship coincided with the shift away from arranged marriage. Modernity believes in self-expression. Friends, because we choose them, give us back an image of ourselves. Modernity believes in freedom. Even modern marriage entails contractual obligations, but friendship involves no fixed commitments. The modern temper runs toward unrestricted fluidity and flexibility, the endless play of possibility, and so is perfectly suited to the informal, improvisational nature of friendship. We can be friends with whomever we want, however we want, for as long as we want.

Social changes play into the question as well. As industrialization uprooted people from extended families and traditional communities and packed them into urban centers, friendship emerged to salve the anonymity and rootlessness of modern life. The process is virtually instinctive now: You graduate from college, move to New York or L.A., and assemble the gang that takes you through your 20s. Only it's not just your 20s anymore. The transformations of family life over the last few decades have made friendship more important still. Between the rise of divorce and the growth of single parenthood, adults in contemporary households often no longer have spouses, let alone a traditional extended family, to turn to for support. Children, let loose by the weakening of parental authority and supervision, spin out of orbit at ever-earlier ages. Both look to friends to replace the older structures. Friends may be "the family we choose," as the modern proverb has it, but for many of us there is no choice but to make our friends our family, since our other families—the ones we come from or the ones we try to start—have fallen apart. When all the marriages are over, friends are the people we come back to. And even those who grow up in a stable family and end up creating another one pass more and more time between the two. We have yet to find a satisfactory name for that period of life, now typically a decade but often a great deal longer, between the end of adolescence and the making of definitive life choices. But the one thing we know is that friendship is absolutely central to it.

Inevitably, the classical ideal has faded. The image of the one true friend, a soul mate rare to find but dearly beloved, has completely disappeared from our culture. We have our better or lesser friends, even our best friends, but no one in a very long time has talked about friendship the way Montaigne and Tennyson did. That glib neologism "bff," which plays at a lifelong avowal, bespeaks an ironic awareness of the mobility of our connections: Best friends forever may not be on speaking terms by this time next month. We save our fiercest energies for sex. Indeed, between the rise of Freudianism and the contemporaneous emergence of homosexuality to social visibility, we've taught ourselves to shun expressions of intense affection between friends—male friends in particular, though even Oprah was forced to defend her relationship with her closest friend—and have rewritten historical friendships, like Achilles' with Patroclus, as sexual. For all the talk of "bromance" lately (or "man dates"), the term is yet another device to manage the sexual anxiety kicked up by straight-male friendships—whether in the friends themselves or in the people around them—and the typical bromance plot instructs the callow bonds of youth to give way to mature heterosexual relationships. At best, intense friendships are something we're expected to grow out of.

As for the moral content of classical friendship, its commitment to virtue and mutual improvement, that, too, has been lost. We have ceased to believe that a friend's highest purpose is to summon us to the good by offering moral advice and correction. We practice, instead, the nonjudg-mental friendship of unconditional acceptance and support—"therapeu-tic" friendship, in Robert N. Bellah's scornful term. We seem to be terribly fragile now. A friend fulfills her duty, we suppose, by taking our side—val-idating our feelings, supporting our decisions, helping us to feel good about ourselves. We tell white lies, make excuses when a friend does something wrong, do what we can to keep the boat steady. We're busy people; we want our friendships fun and friction-free.

Yet even as friendship became universal and the classical ideal lost its force, a new kind of idealism arose, a new repository for some of friendship's deepest needs: the group friendship or friendship circle. Companies of superior spirits go back at least as far as Pythagoras and Plato and achieved new importance in the salons and coffeehouses of the 17th and 18th centuries, but the Romantic age gave them a fresh impetus and emphasis. The idea of friendship became central to their self-conception, whether in Wordsworth's circle or the "small band of true friends" who witness Emma's marriage in Austen. And the notion of superiority acquired a utopian cast, so that the circle was seen—not least because of its very emphasis on friendship—as the harbinger of a more advanced age. The same was true, a century later, of the Bloomsbury Group, two of whose members, Woolf and Forster, produced novel upon novel about friendship. It was

> **Best friends forever may not be on speaking terms by this time next month.**

the latter who famously enunciated the group's political creed. "If I had to choose between betraying my country and betraying my friend," he wrote, "I hope I should have the guts to betray my country." Modernism was the great age of the coterie, and like the legendary friendships of antiquity, modernist friendship circles—bohemian, artistic, transgressive—set their face against existing structures and norms. Friendship becomes, on this account, a kind of alternative society, a refuge from the values of the larger, fallen world.

The belief that the most significant part of an individual's emotional life properly takes place not within the family but within a group of friends began to expand beyond the artistic coterie and become general during the last half of the 20th century. The Romantic-Bloomsburyan prophecy of society as a set of friendship circles was, to a great extent, realized. Mary McCarthy offered an early and tart view of the desirability of such a situation in *The Group*; Barry Levinson, a later, kinder one in *Diner*. Both works remind us that the ubiquity of group friendship owes a great deal to the rise of youth culture. Indeed, modernity associates friendship itself with youth, a time of life it likewise regards as standing apart from false adult values. "The dear peculiar bond of youth," Byron called friendship, inverting the classical belief that its true practice demands maturity and wisdom. With modernity's elevation of youth to supreme status as the most vital and authentic period of life, friendship became the object of intense emotion in two contradictory but often simultaneous directions. We have sought to prolong youth indefinitely by holding fast to our youthful friendships, and we have mourned the loss of youth through an unremitting nostalgia for those friendships. One of the most striking things about the way the 20th century understood friendship was the tendency to view it through the filter of memory, as if it could be recognized only after its loss, and as if that loss were inevitable.

The culture of group friendship reached its apogee in the 1960s. Two of the counterculture's most salient and ideologically charged social forms were the commune—a community of friends in self-imagined retreat from a heartlessly corporatized society—and the rock'n'roll "band" (not "group" or "combo"), its name evoking Shakespeare's "band of brothers" and Robin Hood's band of Merry Men, its great exemplar the Beatles. Communes, bands, and other 60s friendship groups (including Woodstock, the apotheosis of both the commune and the rock concert) were celebrated as joyous, creative places of eternal youth—havens from the adult world. To go through life within one was the era's utopian dream; it is no wonder the Beatles' break-up was received as a generational tragedy. It is also no wonder that 60s group friendship began to generate its own nostalgia as the baby boom began to hit its 30s. *The Big Chill*, in 1983, depicted boomers attempting to recapture the magic of a late-60s friendship circle. ("In a cold world," the movie's tagline reads, "you need your friends to keep you warm.") *Thirtysomething,* taking a step further, certified group friendship as the new adult norm. Most of the characters in those productions, though, were married. It was only in the 1990s that a new generation, remaining single well past 30, found its own images of group friendship in *Seinfeld, Sex and the City,* and, of course, *Friends.* By that point, however, the notion of friendship as a redoubt of moral resistance, a shelter from normative pressures and incubator of social ideals, had disappeared. Your friends didn't shield you from the mainstream, they were the mainstream.

And so we return to Facebook. With the social-networking sites of the new century—Friendster and MySpace were launched in 2003, Facebook in 2004—the friendship circle has expanded to engulf the whole of the social world, and in so doing, destroyed both its own nature and that of the individual friendship itself. Facebook's very premise—and promise—is that it makes our friendship circles visible. There they are, my friends, all in the same place. Except, of course, they're not in the same place, or, rather, they're not my friends. They're simulacra of my friends, little dehydrated packets of images and information, no more my friends than a set of baseball cards is the New York Mets.

I remember realizing a few years ago that most of the members of what I thought of as my "circle" didn't actually know one another. One I'd met in graduate school, another at a job, one in Boston, another in Brooklyn, one lived in Minneapolis now, another in Israel, so that I was ultimately able to enumerate some 14 people, none of whom had ever met any of the others. To imagine that they added up to a circle, an embracing and encircling structure, was a belief, I realized, that violated the laws of feeling as well as geometry. They were a set of points, and I was wandering somewhere among them. Facebook seduces us, however, into exactly that illusion, inviting us to believe that by assembling a list, we have conjured a group. Visual juxtaposition creates the mirage of emotional proximity. "It's like they're all having a conversation," a woman I know once said about her Facebook page, full of posts and comments from friends and friends of friends. "Except they're not."

Friendship is devolving, in other words, from a relationship to a feeling—from something people share to something each of us hugs privately to ourselves in the loneliness of our electronic caves, rearranging the tokens of connection like a lonely child playing with dolls. The same path was long ago trodden by community. As the traditional face-to-face community disappeared, we held on to what we had lost—the closeness, the rootedness—by clinging to the word, no matter how much we had to water down its meaning. Now we speak of the Jewish "community" and the medical "community" and the "community" of readers, even though none of them actually is one. What we have, instead of community, is, if we're lucky, a "sense" of community—the feeling without the structure; a private emotion, not a collective experience. And now friendship, which arose to its present importance as a replacement for community, is going the same way. We have "friends," just as we belong to "communities." Scanning my Facebook page gives me, precisely, a "sense" of connection. Not an actual connection, just a sense.

What purpose do all those wall posts and status updates serve? On the first beautiful weekend of spring this year, a friend posted this update from Central Park: "[So-and-so] is in the Park with the rest of the City." The first question that comes to mind is, if you're enjoying a beautiful day in the park, why don't you give your iPhone a

> **Facebook seduces us . . . to believe that by assembling a list, we have conjured a group.**

rest? But the more important one is, why did you need to tell us that? We have always shared our little private observations and moments of feeling—it's part of what friendship's about, part of the way we remain present in one another's lives—but things are different now. Until a few years ago, you could share your thoughts with only one friend at a time (on the phone, say), or maybe with a small group, later, in person. And when you did, you were talking to specific people, and you tailored what you said, and how you said it, to who they were—their interests, their personalities, most of all, your degree of mutual intimacy. "Reach out and touch someone" meant someone in particular, someone you were actually thinking about. It meant having a conversation. Now we're just broadcasting our stream of consciousness, live from Central Park, to all 500 of our friends at once, hoping that someone, anyone, will confirm our existence by answering back. We haven't just stopped talking to our friends as individuals, at such moments, we have stopped thinking of them as individuals. We have turned them into an indiscriminate mass, a kind of audience or faceless public. We address ourselves not to a circle, but to a cloud.

It's amazing how fast things have changed. Not only don't we have Wordsworth and Coleridge anymore, we don't even have Jerry and George. Today, Ross and Chandler would be writing on each other's walls. Carrie and the girls would be posting status updates, and if they did manage to find the time for lunch, they'd be too busy checking their BlackBerrys to have a real conversation. *Sex* and *Friends* went off the air just five years ago, and already we live in a different world. Friendship (like activism) has been smoothly integrated into our new electronic lifestyles. We're too busy to spare our friends more time than it takes to send a text. We're too busy, sending texts. And what happens when we do find the time to get together? I asked a woman I know whether her teenage daughters and their friends still have the kind of intense friendships that kids once did. Yes, she said, but they go about them differently. They still stay up talking in their rooms, but they're also online with three other friends, and texting with another three. Video chatting is more intimate, in theory, than speaking on the phone, but not if you're doing it with four people at once. And teenagers are just an early version of the rest of us. A study found that one American in four reported having no close confidants, up from one in 10 in 1985. The figures date from 2004, and there's little doubt that Facebook and texting and all the rest of it have already exacerbated the situation. The more people we know, the lonelier we get.

The new group friendship, already vitiated itself, is cannibalizing our individual friendships as the boundaries between the two blur. The most disturbing thing about Facebook is the extent to which people are willing— are eager—to conduct their private lives in public. "hola cutie-pie! i'm in town on wednesday. lunch?" "Julie, I'm so glad we're back in touch. xoxox." "Sorry for not calling, am going through a tough time right now." Have these people forgotten how to use e-mail, or do they actually prefer to stage the emotional equivalent of a public grope? I can understand "[So-and-so] is in the Park with the rest of the City," but I am incapable of comprehending this kind of exhibitionism. Perhaps I need to surrender the idea that the value of friendship lies precisely in the space of privacy it creates: not the secrets that two people exchange so much as the unique and inviolate world they build up between them, the spider web of shared discovery they spin out, slowly and carefully, together. There's something faintly obscene about performing that intimacy in front of everyone you know, as if its real purpose were to show what a deep person you are. Are we really so hungry for validation? So desperate to prove we have friends?

But surely Facebook has its benefits. Long-lost friends can reconnect, far-flung ones can stay in touch. I wonder, though. Having recently moved across the country, I thought that Facebook would help me feel connected to the friends I'd left behind. But now I find the opposite is true. Reading about the mundane details of their lives, a steady stream of trivia and ephemera, leaves me feeling both empty and unpleasantly full, as if I had just binged on junk food, and precisely because it reminds me of the real sustenance, the real knowledge, we exchange by e-mail or phone or face-to-face. And the whole theatrical quality of the business, the sense that my friends are doing their best to impersonate themselves, only makes it worse. The person I read about, I cannot help feeling, is not quite the person I know.

As for getting back in touch with old friends—yes, when they're people you really love, it's a miracle. But most of the time, they're not. They're someone you knew for a summer in camp, or a midlevel friend from high school. They don't matter to you as individuals anymore, certainly not the individuals they are now, they matter because they made up the texture of your experience at a certain moment in your life, in conjunction with all the other people you knew. Tear them out of that texture—read about their brats, look at pictures of their vacation—and they mean nothing. Tear out enough of them and you ruin the texture itself, replace a matrix of feeling and memory, the deep subsoil of experience, with a spurious sense of familiarity. Your 18-year-old self knows them. Your 40-year-old self should not know them.

Facebook holds out a utopian possibility: What once was lost will now be found. But the heaven of the past is a promised land destroyed in the reaching. Facebook, here, becomes the anti-madeleine, an eraser of memory. Carlton Fisk has remarked that he's watched the videotape of his famous World Series home run only a few times, lest it overwrite his own recollection of the event. Proust knew that memory is a skittish creature that peeks from its hole only when it isn't being sought. Mementos, snapshots, reunions, and now this—all of them modes of amnesia, foes of true remembering. The past should stay in the heart, where it belongs.

Finally, the new social-networking Web sites have falsified our understanding of intimacy itself, and with it, our understanding of ourselves. The absurd idea, bruited about in the media, that a MySpace profile or "25 Random Things About Me" can tell us more about someone than even a good friend might be aware of is based

> **The most disturbing thing about Facebook is the extent to which people are willing . . . to conduct their private lives in public.**

on desiccated notions about what knowing another person means: First, that intimacy is confessional—an idea both peculiarly American and peculiarly young, perhaps because both types of people tend to travel among strangers, and so believe in the instant disgorging of the self as the quickest route to familiarity. Second, that identity is reducible to information: the name of your cat, your favorite Beatle, the stupid thing you did in seventh grade. Third, that it is reducible, in particular, to the kind of information that social-networking Web sites are most interested in eliciting, consumer preferences. Forget that we're all conducting market research on ourselves. Far worse is that Facebook amplifies our longstanding tendency to see ourselves ("I'm a Skin Bracer man!") in just those terms. We wear T-shirts that proclaim our brand loyalty, pique ourselves on owning a Mac, and now put up lists of our favorite songs. "15 movies in 15 minutes. Rule: Don't take too long to think about it."

So information replaces experience, as it has throughout our culture. But when I think about my friends, what makes them who they are, and why I love them, it is not the names of their siblings that come to mind, or their fear of spiders. It is their qualities of character. This one's emotional generosity, that one's moral seriousness, the dark humor of a third. Yet even those are just descriptions, and no more specify the individuals uniquely than to say that one has red hair, another is tall. To understand what they really look like, you would have to see a picture. And to understand who they really are, you would have to hear about the things they've done. Character, revealed through action: the two eternal elements of narrative. In order to know people, you have to listen to their stories.

But that is precisely what the Facebook page does not leave room for, or 500 friends, time for. Literally does not leave room for. E-mail, with its rapid-fire etiquette and scrolling format, already trimmed the letter down to a certain acceptable maximum, perhaps a thousand words. Now, with Facebook, the box is shrinking even more, leaving perhaps a third of that length as the conventional limit for a message, far less for a comment. (And we all know the deal on Twitter.) The 10-page missive has gone the way of the buggy whip, soon to be followed, it seems, by the three-hour conversation. Each evolved as a space for telling stories, an act that cannot usefully be accomplished in much less. Posting information is like pornography, a slick, impersonal exhibition. Exchanging stories is like making love: probing, questing, questioning, caressing. It is mutual. It is intimate. It takes patience, devotion, sensitivity, subtlety, skill—and it teaches them all, too.

They call them social-networking sites for a reason. Networking once meant something specific: climbing the jungle gym of professional contacts in order to advance your career. The truth is that Hume and Smith were not completely right. Commercial society did not eliminate the self-interested aspects of making friends and influencing people, it just changed the way we went about it. Now, in the age of the entrepreneurial self, even our closest relationships are being pressed onto this template. A recent book on the sociology of modern science describes a networking event at a West Coast university: "There do not seem to be any singletons—disconsolately lurking at the margins—nor do dyads appear, except fleetingly." No solitude, no friendship, no space for refusal—the exact contemporary paradigm. At the same time, the author assures us, "face time" is valued in this "community" as a "high-bandwidth interaction," offering "unusual capacity for interruption, repair, feedback and learning." Actual human contact, rendered "unusual" and weighed by the values of a systems engineer. We have given our hearts to machines, and now we are turning into machines. The face of friendship in the new century.

DISCUSSION

1. Deresiewicz organizes much of his argument regarding "faux friendship" around a focus on the popular website Facebook. In your view, does Facebook offer an accurate case study of how online technologies have reshaped how we define and think about friendship? In your view, have these changes been for better or worse? How?

2. Deresiewicz devotes considerable time in this essay to a historical overview of older models of friendship. What does this discussion contribute to his argument? How do these older models compare to your own definition of friendship? Do you still define friendship in ways that resemble what Deresiewicz calls the "classical models" of friendship?

3. One possible counterargument to Deresiewicz's critique of modern friendship is to see online technologies as instruments or aids for creating closer and more meaningful connections in the so-called real world. How do you respond to this idea? Is it valid to think of the virtual connections we forge online as a supplement to the actual connections we forge face to face? And if so, how might this impact the overall effectiveness of Deresiewicz's argument?

WRITING

4. For Deresiewicz, current cultural norms around friendship stand as a particularly revealing symbol of modernity itself. "We can see," he writes, "why friendship has become the characteristically modern relationship. Modernity believes in equality, and friendships, unlike traditional relationships, are egalitarian. Modernity believes in individualism. Friendships serve no public purpose and exist independent of all other bonds. Modernity believes in choice." Write an essay in which you assess the key claims Deresiewicz makes here. Do you agree that modern definitions of friendship reflect our more widespread cultural celebration of individualism and independence? If so, is this a good thing? How or how not?

5. One of the key objections Deresiewicz levels against social networking sites is that they erode our belief in the value of personal privacy. In a brief essay, present a discussion that makes clear where you stand on this issue. Do you agree that we live in an age where privacy is at risk of becoming an outdated or obsolete idea? In your view, is this kind of change something we should worry about or work against?

6. Peter Lovenheim (p. 494) is another writer interested in exploring the ways modern American culture might be fostering habits of social and emotional disconnection. Write an essay in which you speculate about how Lovenheim might respond to the argument Deresiewicz is advancing about "faux friendship." Do you think Lovenheim would find much commonality between this argument and the portrait of contemporary "neighbor relations" his essay presents? How or how not?

STEVEN KURUTZ
Not Buying It

At first glance, it seems clear how we are supposed to think about consumer waste, the mountains of disposable stuff we throw away on a day-to-day basis. As the term itself suggests, waste is worthless stuff: forgotten leftovers we are more than free to ignore. But what happens, Steven Kurutz asks, when we rethink this assumption? When we start to think about these leftovers not as trash but as a rich trove of valuable and usable things? Kurutz is a contributor to the *New York Times,* where this piece was published on June 21, 2007. His writing has also appeared in *Spin, Details,* and *W.* He is the author of the book *Like a Rolling Stone: The Strange Life of a Tribute Band* (2008).

ON A FRIDAY EVENING LAST MONTH, THE DAY AFTER NEW YORK University's class of 2007 graduated, about 15 men and women assembled in front of Third Avenue North, an N.Y.U. dormitory on Third Avenue and 12th Street. They had come to take advantage of the university's end-of-the-year move-out, when students' discarded items are loaded into big green trash bins by the curb.

New York has several colleges and universities, of course, but according to Janet Kalish, a Queens resident who was there that night, N.Y.U.'s affluent student body makes for unusually profitable Dumpster diving. So perhaps it wasn't surprising that the gathering at the Third Avenue North trash bin quickly took on a giddy shopping-spree air, as members of the group came up with one first-class find after another.

Ben Ibershoff, a dapper man in his 20s wearing two bowler hats, dug deep and unearthed a Sharp television. Autumn Brewster, 29, found a painting of a Mediterranean harbor, which she studied and handed down to another member of the crowd.

Darcie Elia, a 17-year-old high school student with a half-shaved head, was clearly pleased with a modest haul of what she called "random housing stuff"—a desk lamp, a dish rack, Swiffer dusters—which she spread on the sidewalk, drawing quizzical stares from passers-by.

Ms. Elia was not alone in appreciating the little things. "The small thrills are when you see the contents of someone's desk and find a book of stamps," said Ms. Kalish, 44, as she stood knee deep in the trash bin examining a plastic toiletries holder.

A few of those present had stumbled onto the scene by chance (including a janitor from a nearby homeless center, who made off with a working iPod and a tube of body cream), but most were there by design, in response to a posting on the Web site freegan.info.

The site, which provides information and listings for the small but growing subculture of anticonsumerists who call themselves freegans—the term derives from vegans, the vegetarians who forsake all animal products, as many freegans also do—is the closest thing their movement has to an official voice. And for those like Ms. Elia and Ms. Kalish, it serves as a guide to negotiating life, and making a home, in a world they see as hostile to their values.

Freegans are scavengers of the developed world, living off consumer waste in an effort to minimize their support of corporations and their impact on the planet, and to distance themselves from what they see as out-of-control consumerism. They forage through supermarket trash and eat the slightly bruised produce or just-expired canned goods that are routinely thrown out, and negotiate gifts of surplus food from sympathetic stores and restaurants.

They dress in castoff clothes and furnish their homes with items found on the street; at freecycle.org, where users post unwanted items; and at so-called freemeets, flea markets where no money is exchanged. Some claim to hold themselves to rigorous standards. "If a person chooses to live an ethical lifestyle it's not enough to be vegan, they need to absent themselves from capitalism," said Adam Weissman, 29, who started freegan.info four years ago and is the movement's de facto spokesman.

Freeganism dates to the mid-'90s, and grew out of the antiglobalization and environmental movements, as well as groups like Food Not Bombs, a network of small organizations that serve free vegetarian and vegan food to the hungry, much of it salvaged from food market trash. It also has echoes of groups like the Diggers, an anarchist street theater troupe based in Haight-Ashbury in San Francisco in the 1960's, which gave away food and social services.

According to Bob Torres, a sociology professor at St. Lawrence University in Canton, N.Y., who is writing a book about the animal rights movement—which shares many ideological positions with freeganism—the freegan movement has become much more visible and increasingly popular over the past year, in part as a result of growing frustrations with mainstream environmentalism.

Environmentalism, Mr. Torres said, "is becoming this issue of, consume the right set of green goods and you're green," regardless of how much in the way of natural resources those goods require to manufacture and distribute.

"If you ask the average person what can you do to reduce global warming, they'd say buy a Prius," he added.

There are freegans all over the world, in countries as far afield as Sweden, Brazil, South Korea, Estonia, and England (where much has been made of what *The Sun* recently called the "wacky new food craze" of trash-bin eating), and across the United States as well.

In Southern California, for example, "you can find just about anything in the trash, and on a consistent basis, too," said Marko Manriquez, 28, who has just graduated from the University of California at San Diego with a bachelor's degree in media studies and is the creator of "Freegan Kitchen," a video blog that shows gourmet meals being made from trash-bin ingredients. "This is how I got my futon, chair, table, shelves. And I'm not talking about beat-up stuff. I mean it's not Design Within Reach, but it's nice."

But New York City in particular—the financial capital of the world's richest country—has emerged as a hub of freegan activity, thanks largely to Mr. Weissman's zeal for the cause and the considerable free time he has to devote to it. (He doesn't work and lives at home in Teaneck, N.J., with his father and elderly grandparents.)

Freegan.info sponsors organize Trash Tours that typically attract a dozen or more people, as well as feasts at which groups of about 20 people gather in apartments around the city to share food and talk politics.

In the last year or so, Mr. Weissman said, the site has increased the number and variety of its events, which have begun attracting many more first-time participants. Many of those who have taken part in one new program, called Wild Foraging Walks—workshops that teach people to identify edible plants in the wilderness—have been newcomers, he said.

> **"If a person chooses to live an ethical life-style it's not enough to be vegan, they need to absent themselves from capitalism."**

The success of the movement in New York may also be due to the quantity and quality of New York trash. As of 2005, individuals, businesses, and institutions in the United States produced more than 245 million tons of municipal solid waste, according to the E.P.A. That means about 4.5 pounds per person per day. The comparable figure for New York City, meanwhile, is about 6.1 pounds, according to statistics from the city's Sanitation Department.

"We have a lot of wealthy people, and rich people throw out more trash than poor people do," said Elizabeth Royte, whose book *Garbage Land* (Little, Brown, 2005) traced the route her trash takes through the city. "Rich people are also more likely to throw things out based on style obsolescence—like changing the towels when you're tired of the color."

At the N.Y.U. Dorm Dive, as the event was billed, the consensus was that this year's spoils weren't as impressive as those in years past. Still, almost anything needed to decorate and run a household—a TV cart, a pillow, a file cabinet, a half-finished bottle of Jägermeister—was there for the taking, even if those who took them were risking health, safety, and a $100 fine from the Sanitation Department.

Ms. Brewster and her mother, who had come from New Jersey, loaded two area rugs into their cart. Her mother, who declined to give her name, seemed to be on a search for laundry detergent, and was overjoyed to discover a couple of half-empty bottles of Trader Joe's organic brand. (Free and organic is a double bonus.) Nearby, a woman munched on a found bag of Nature's Promise veggie fries.

As people stuffed their backpacks, Ms. Kalish, who organized the event (Mr. Weissman arrived later), demonstrated the cooperative spirit of freeganism, asking the divers to pass items down to people on the sidewalk and announcing her finds for anyone in need of, say, a Hoover Shop-Vac.

"Sometimes people will swoop in and grab something, especially when you see a half-used bottle of Tide detergent," she said. "Who wouldn't want it? But most people realize there's plenty to go around." She rooted around in the trash bin and found several half-eaten jars of peanut butter. "It's a never-ending supply," she said.

Many freegans are predictably young and far to the left politically, like Ms. Elia, the 17-year-old, who lives with her father in Manhattan. She said she became a freegan both for environmental reasons and because "I'm not down with capitalism."

There are also older freegans, like Ms. Kalish, who hold jobs and appear in some ways to lead middle-class lives. A high school Spanish teacher, Ms. Kalish owns a car and a two-family house in Queens, renting half of it as a "capitalist landlord," she joked. Still, like most freegans, she seems attuned to the ecological effects of her actions. In her house, for example, she has laid down a mosaic of freegan carpet parcels instead of replacing her aging wooden floor because, she said, "I'd have to take trees from the forest."

Not buying any new manufactured products while living in the United States is, of course, basically impossible, as is avoiding everything that requires natural resources to create, distribute, or operate. Don't freegans use gas or electricity to cook, for example, or commercial products to brush their teeth?

"Once in a while I may buy a box of baking soda for toothpaste," Mr. Weissman said. "And, sure, getting that to market has negative impacts, like everything." But, he said, parsing the point, a box of baking soda is more ecologically friendly than a tube of toothpaste, because its cardboard container is biodegradable.

These contradictions and others have led some people to suggest that freegans are hypocritical, making use of the capitalist system even as they rail against it. And even Mr. Weissman, who is often doctrinaire about the movement, acknowledges when pushed that absolute freeganism is an impossible dream.

Mr. Torres said: "I think there's a conscious recognition among freegans that you can never live perfectly." He added that generally freegans "try to reduce the impact."

It's not that freeganism doesn't require serious commitment. For freegans, who believe that the production and transport of every product contributes to economic and social injustice, usually in multiple ways, any interaction with the marketplace is fraught. And for some freegans in particular—for instance, Madeline Nelson, who until recently was living an upper-middle-class Manhattan life with all the attendant conveniences and focus on luxury goods—choosing this way of life involves a considerable, even radical, transformation.

Ms. Nelson, who is 51, spent her 20s working in restaurants and living in communal houses, but by 2003 she was earning a six-figure salary as a communications director for Barnes & Noble. That year, while demonstrating against the Iraq war, she began to feel hypocritical, she said, explaining: "I thought, isn't this safe? Here I am in my corporate job, going to protests every once in a while. And part of my job was to motivate the sales force to sell more stuff."

After a year of progressively scaling back—no more shopping at Eileen Fisher, no more commuting by means other than a bike—Ms. Nelson, who had a two-bedroom apartment with a mortgage in Greenwich Village, quit her job in 2005 to devote herself full-time to political activism and freeganism.

She sold her apartment, put some money into savings, and bought a one-bedroom in Flatbush, Brooklyn, that she owns outright.

"My whole point is not to be paying into corporate America, and I hated paying a big loan to a bank," she said while fixing lunch in her kitchen one recent afternoon. The meal—potato and watercress soup and crackers and cheese—had been made entirely from refuse left outside various grocery stores in Manhattan and Brooklyn.

The bright and airy prewar apartment Ms. Nelson shares with two cats doesn't look like the home of someone who spends her evenings rooting through the garbage. But after some time in the apartment, a visitor begins to see the signs of Ms. Nelson's anticonsumerist way of life.

An old lampshade in the living room has been trimmed with fabric to cover its fraying parts, leaving a one-inch gap where the material ran out. The ficus tree near the window came not from a florist, Ms. Nelson said, but from the trash, as did the CD rack. A 1920s loveseat belonged to her grandmother, and an 18th-century, Louis XVI-style armoire in the bedroom is a vestige of her corporate life.

The kitchen cabinets and refrigerator are stuffed with provisions—cornmeal, Pirouline cookies, vegetarian cage-free eggs—appropriate for a passionate cook who entertains often. All were free.

She longs for a springform pan in which to make cheesecakes, but is waiting for one to come up on freecycle.org. There are no new titles on the bookshelves; she hasn't bought a new book in six months. "Books were my impulse buy," said Ms. Nelson, whose short brown hair and glasses frame a youthful face. Now she logs onto bookcrossing.

For freegans . . . any interaction with the marketplace is fraught.

com, where readers share used books, or goes to the public library.

But isn't she depriving herself unnecessarily? And what's so bad about buying books, anyway? "I do have some mixed feelings," Ms. Nelson said. "It's always hard to give up class privilege. But freegans would argue that the capitalist system is not sustainable. You're exploiting resources." She added, "Most people work 40-plus hours a week at jobs they don't like to buy things they don't need."

Since becoming a freegan, Ms. Nelson has spent her time posting calendar items and other information online and doing paralegal work on behalf of bicyclists arrested at Critical Mass anticar rallies. "I'm not sitting in the house eating bonbons," she said. "I'm working. I'm just not working for money."

She is also spending a lot of time making rounds for food and supplies at night, and has come to know the cycles of the city's trash. She has learned that fruit tends to get thrown out more often in the summer (she freezes it and makes sorbet), and that businesses are a source for envelopes. A reliable spot to get bread is Le Pain Quotidien, a chain of bakery-restaurants that tosses out six or seven loaves a night. But Ms. Nelson doesn't stockpile. "The sad fact is you don't need to," she said. "More trash will be there tomorrow."

By and large, she said, her friends have been understanding, if not exactly enthusiastic about adopting freeganism for themselves. "When she told me she was doing this I wasn't really surprised—Madeline is a free spirit," said Eileen Dolan, a librarian at a Manhattan law firm who has known Ms. Nelson since their college days at Stony Brook. But while Ms. Dolan agrees that society is wasteful, she said that going freegan is not something she would ever do. "It's a huge time commitment," she said.

One evening a week after the Dorm Dive, a group of about 20 freegans gathered in a sparely furnished, harshly lit basement apartment in Bushwick, Brooklyn, to hold a feast. It was an egalitarian affair with no one officially in charge, but Mr. Weissman projected authority, his blue custodian-style work pants and fuzzy black beard giving him the air of a Latin American revolutionary as he wandered around, trailed by a Korean television crew.

Ms. Kalish stood over the sink, slicing vegetables for a stir-fry with a knife she had found in a trash bin at N.Y.U. A pot of potatoes simmered on the stove. These, like much of the rest of the meal, had been gathered two nights earlier, when Mr. Weissman, Ms. Kalish, and others had met in front of a Food Emporium in Manhattan and rummaged through the store's clear garbage bags.

The haul had been astonishing in its variety: sealed bags of organic vegetable medley, bagged salad, heirloom tomatoes, key limes, three packaged strawberries-and-chocolate-dip kits, carrots, asparagus, grapes, a carton of organic soy milk (expiration date: July 9), grapefruit, mushrooms, and, for those willing to partake, vacuum-packed herb turkey breast. (Some freegans who avoid meat will nevertheless eat it rather than see it go to waste.)

As operatic music played on a radio, people mingled and pitched in. One woman diced onions, rescuing pieces that fell on floor. Another, who goes by the name Petal, emptied bags of salad into a pan. As rigorous and radical as the freegan world view can be, there is also something quaint about the movement, at least the version that Mr. Weissman promotes, with its embrace of hippie-ish communal activities and its household get-togethers that rely for diversion on conversation rather than electronic entertainment.

Making things last is part of the ethos. Christian Gutierrez, a 33-year-old former model and investment banker, sat at the small kitchen table, chatting. Mr. Gutierrez, who quit his banking job at Matthews Morris & Company in 2004 to pursue filmmaking, became a freegan last year, and opened a free workshop on West 36th Street in Manhattan to teach bicycle repair. He plans to add lessons in fixing home computers in the near future.

Mr. Gutierrez's lifestyle, like Ms. Nelson's, became gradually more constricted in the absence of a steady income. He lived in a Midtown loft until last year, when, he said, he got into a legal battle with his landlord over a rent increase—a relationship "ruined by greed," he said. After that, he lived in his van for a while, then found an illegal squat in SoHo, which he shares with two others. Mr. Gutierrez had a middle-class upbringing in Dallas, and he said he initially found freeganism off-putting. But now he is steadfastly devoted to the way of life.

As people began to load plates of food, he leaned in and offered a few words of wisdom: "Opening that first bag of trash," he said, "is the biggest step."

DISCUSSION

1. What are some of the images or ideas you typically associate with the term *scavenging*? Does it evoke a vision of a particular setting? A particular kind of person? And does this essay challenge or reinforce these stereotypes?

2. How does freeganism compare to its analog veganism? In your view, do these two practices share much in common? What are the key similarities and differences? What are the aspects of our culture that these movements seek to change?

3. "The freegan movement," Kurutz notes, "has become much more visible and increasingly popular over the past year, in part as a result of growing frustrations with mainstream environmentalism." In your view, does it make sense to think of freeganist practices in terms of environmental activism? Is it valid to see freeganism as a better or more effective form of environmentalism? In what ways does freeganism adopt and perhaps improve on the norms that conventionally underlie the environmental movement?

WRITING

4. "Freegans," Kurutz writes, "are scavengers of the developed world, living off consumer waste in an effort to minimize their support of corporations and their impact on the planet, and to distance themselves from what they see as out-of-control consumerism." In an essay, analyze the particular ways this practice can be read as an effort to challenge and/or rewrite the social scripts around consumerism.

5. As Kurutz notes, the rules around such freegan activities as dumpster diving are deliberately vague. But should they be? If you were in charge of writing the rules around the freegan activities Kurutz outlines, what would they look like? And what purpose would they be designed to serve? Write an essay that addresses these specific questions. What boundaries or limits would you set around practices like dumpster diving?

6. Among other things, Kurutz's portrait of freeganism gives us a different way to think about community and the norms that define relations among people who are neighbors. How does this portrait compare on this point to Peter Lovenheim's essay (p. 494)? How does Lovenheim's focus on the changing norms around community and neighborliness compare to Kurutz's discussion of freeganism? Does freeganism stand, in your view, as an example of the changes Lovenheim identifies? How or how not?

JOEL KOTKIN
There's No Place Like Home

It has become a cliché in recent years to observe that Americans are more and more disconnected from each other. But how much truth does this old saw actually contain? Taking a closer look at some of the data that belies this assumption, Joel Kotkin sketches a portrait of what he calls the "new localism": a trend, increasingly prevalent, that finds more and more people settling down, establishing roots, finding themselves more and more invested in the people and places around them. Kotkin frequently writes on the economy, politics, and society. He is the author of the books *The City: A Global History* (2006) and *The Next Hundred Million: America in 2050* (2010). He is Distinguished Presidential Fellow in Urban Futures at Chapman University in Orange, California, and an Adjunct Fellow with the Legatum Institute based in London. The following article originally appeared in the October 9, 2009, edition of *Newsweek*.

ON ALMOST ANY NIGHT OF THE WEEK, CHURCHILL'S RESTAURANT IS hopping. The 10-year-old hot spot in Rockville Centre, Long Island, is packed with locals drinking beer and eating burgers, with some customers spilling over onto the street. "We have lots of regulars—people who are recognized when they come in," says co-owner Kevin Culhane. In fact, regulars make up more than 80 percent of the restaurant's customers. "People feel comfortable and safe here," Culhane says. "This is their place."

Thriving neighborhood restaurants are one small data point in a larger trend I call the new localism. The basic premise: the longer people stay in their homes and communities, the more they identify with those places, and the greater their commitment to helping local businesses and institutions thrive, even in a downturn. Several factors are driving this process, including an aging population, suburbanization, the Internet, and an increased focus on family life. And even as the recession has begun to yield to recovery, our commitment to our local roots is only going to grow more profound. Evident before the recession, the new localism will shape how we live and work in the coming decades, and may even influence the course of our future politics.

Perhaps nothing will be as surprising about 21st-century America as its settledness. For more than a generation Americans have believed that "spatial mobility" would increase, and, as it did, feed an inexorable trend toward rootlessness and anomie. This vision of social disintegration was perhaps best epitomized in Vance Packard's 1972 bestseller *A Nation of Strangers*, with its vision of America becoming "a society coming apart at the seams." In 2000, Harvard's Robert Putnam made a similar point, albeit less hyperbolically, in *Bowling Alone*, in which he wrote about the "civic malaise" he saw gripping the country. In Putnam's view, society was being undermined, largely due to suburbanization and what he called "the growth of mobility."

Yet in reality Americans actually are becoming less nomadic. As recently as the 1970s as many as one in five people moved annually; by 2006, long before the current recession took hold, that number was 14 percent, the low-

> **The longer people stay in their homes and communities, the more they identify with those places.**

est rate since the census starting following movement in 1940. Since then tougher times have accelerated these trends, in large part because opportunities to sell houses and find new employment have dried up. In 2008, the total number of people changing residences was less than those who did so in 1962, when the country had 120 million fewer people. The stay-at-home trend appears particularly strong among aging boomers, who are largely eschewing Sunbelt retirement condos to stay tethered to their suburban homes—close to family, friends, clubs, churches, and familiar surroundings.

The trend will not bring back the corner grocery stores and the declining organizations—bowling leagues, Boy Scouts, and such—cited by Putnam and others as the traditional glue of American communities. Nor will our car-oriented suburbs replicate the close neighborhood feel so celebrated by romantic urbanists like the late Jane Jacobs. Instead, we're evolving in ways congruent with a postindustrial society. It will not spell the demise of Wal-Mart or Costco, but will express itself in scores of alternative institutions, such as thriving local weekly newspapers, a niche that has withstood the shift to the Internet far better than big-city dailies.

Our less mobile nature is already reshaping the corporate world. The kind of corporate nomadism described in Peter Kilborn's recent book, *Next Stop, Reloville: Life Inside America's Rootless Professional Class*, in which families relocate every couple of years so the breadwinner can reach the next rung on the managerial ladder, will become less common in years ahead. A smaller cadre of corporate executives may still move from place to place, but surveys reveal many executives are now unwilling to move even for a good promotion. Why? Family and technology are two key factors working against nomadism, in the workplace and elsewhere.

Family, as one Pew researcher notes, "trumps money when people make decisions about where to live." Interdependence is replacing independence. More parents are helping their children financially well into their 30s and 40s; the numbers of "boomerang kids" moving back home with their parents has also been growing as job options and the ability to buy houses has decreased for the young. Recent surveys of the emerging millennial generation suggest this family-centric focus will last well into the coming decades.

> **We are seeing a return to placeness, along with more choices for individuals, families, and communities.**

Nothing allows for geographic choice more than the ability to work at home. By 2015, suggests demographer Wendell Cox, there will be more people working electronically at home full time than taking mass transit, making it the largest potential source of energy savings on transportation. In the San Francisco Bay Area and Los Angeles, almost one in 10 workers is a part-time tele-commuter. Some studies indicate that more than one quarter of the U.S. workforce could eventually participate in this new work pattern. Even IBM, whose initials were once jokingly said to stand for "I've Been Moved," has changed its approach. Roughly 40 percent of the company's workers now labor at home or remotely from a client's location.

These home-based workers become critical to the localist economy. They will eat in local restaurants, attend fairs and festivals, take their kids to soccer practices, ballet lessons, or religious youth-group meetings. This is not merely a suburban phenomenon; localism also means a stronger sense of identity for urban neighborhoods as well as smaller towns.

Could the new localism also affect our future politics? Ever greater concentration of power in Washington may now be all the rage as the federal government intervenes, albeit often ineffectively, to revive the economy. But throughout our history, we have always preferred our politics more on the home-cooked side. On his visit to America in the early 1830s, Alexis de Tocqueville was struck by the de-centralized nature of the country. "The intelligence and the power are dispersed abroad," he wrote, "and instead of radiating from a point, they cross each other in every direction."

This is much the same today. The majority of Americans still live in a patchwork of smaller towns and cities, including many suburban towns within large metropolitan regions. There are well over 65,000 general-purpose governments, and with so many "small towns," the average local jurisdiction population in the United States is 6,200, small enough to allow nonprofessional politicians to have a serious impact.

After decades of frantic mobility and homogenization, we are seeing a return to placeness, along with more choices for individuals, families, and communities. For entrepreneurs like Kevin Culhane and his workers at Churchill's, it's a phenomenon that may also offer a lease on years of new profits. "We're holding our own in these times because we appeal to the people around here," Culhane says. And as places like Long Island become less bedroom community and more round-the-clock locale for work and play, he's likely to have plenty of hungry customers.

DISCUSSION

1. How do you understand the term *placeness*? How do you define this concept? Does it, in your view, suggest a value or ideal that you consider important? How or how not?

2. Much of Kotkin's argument rests on recent statistical findings regarding what he calls the "stay-at-home trend" in American life. How convincing do you find this argument to be? In your view, do these statistics effectively prove his thesis that Americans are becoming more connected to each other? Can you think of a counter-trend in American life that might lead to the opposite conclusion?

3. Counter to popular thinking, according to Kotkin, advances in technology are actually leading more Americans to become rooted within and committed to a single place. To what extent does this view challenge the norms we typically use to think about technology?

WRITING

4. "For more than a generation," Kotkin writes, "Americans have believed that 'spatial mobility' would increase, and, as it did, feed an inexorable trend toward rootlessness." Is Kotkin right in suggesting that this trend has been overstated? In an essay, make clear your own views on this question of rootlessness in modern American life. Can you think of a context or setting in which the rules, norms, and scripts produce a sense of disconnection? Can you, conversely, think of an example in which the rules, norms, and scripts produce the opposite? Which, in your view, is representative of American life more generally?

5. Choose a specific technology such as e-mail, texting, or BlackBerry. Write a one-page essay in which you argue for the ways this example either fosters or inhibits greater connection among people. Does this technology, in your view, render us closer to each other? Or does it serve, rather, to make us more alone? In either case, how?

6. Write an essay in which you evaluate how Kotkin's examination of home and roots compares to William Deresiewicz's discussion of online friendship (p. 470). Does Deresiewicz's essay, in your view, confirm or complicate the conclusions Kotkin draws about Americans' increasing commitment to place and each other?

PETER LOVENHEIM
Won't You Be My Neighbor?

In a "wired" age often celebrated for its interactivity and interconnected-ness, it may come as a surprise to hear how disconnected from each other so many of us have become. For Peter Lovenheim, this disconnec-tion has become the signature condition of our times. Reflecting on how this has come to be and what it means, he offers some suggestions — at once both unorthodox and commonsensical — about how to ameliorate the loneliness at the heart of modern life. Lovenheim is the author of *In the Neighborhood: The Search for Community on an American Street, One Sleepover at a Time* (2010), the culmination of a project he discusses in the following essay, originally published in the *New York Times* on June 23, 2008. He teaches writing at Rochester Institute of Technology and is also the author of *Portrait of a Burger as a Young Calf: The Story of One Man, Two Cows, and the Feeding of a Nation* (2002).

THE ALARM ON MY CELLPHONE RANG AT 5:50 A.M., AND I AWOKE to find myself in a twin bed in a spare room at my neighbor Lou's house.

Lou was 81. His six children were grown and scattered around the country, and he lived alone, two doors down from me. His wife, Edie, had died five years earlier. "When people learn you've lost your wife," he told me, "they all ask the same question. 'How long were you married?' And when you tell them 52 years, they say, 'Isn't that wonderful!' But I tell them no, it isn't. I was just getting to know her."

Lou had said he gets up at six, but after 10 more minutes, I heard nothing from his room down the hall. Had he died? He had a heart ail-ment, but generally was in good health. With a full head of silver-gray hair, bright hazel-blue eyes, and a broad chest, he walked with the con-fident bearing of a man who had enjoyed a long and satisfying career as a surgeon.

The previous evening, as I'd left home, the last words I heard before I shut the door had been, "Dad, you're crazy!" from my teenage daughter. Sure, the sight of your 50-year-old father leaving with an overnight bag to sleep at a neighbor's house would embarrass any teenager, but "crazy"? I didn't think so.

There's talk today about how as a society we've become fragmented by ethnicity, income, city versus suburb, red state versus blue. But we also divide ourselves with invisible dotted lines. I'm talking about the property lines that isolate us from the people we are physically closest to: our neighbors.

It was a calamity on my street, in a middle-class suburb of Rochester, several years ago that got me thinking about this. One night, a neighbor shot and killed his wife and then himself; their two middle-school-age children ran screaming into the night. Though the couple had lived on our street for seven years, my wife and I hardly knew them. We'd see them jogging together. Sometimes our children would carpool.

Some of the neighbors attended the funerals and called on relatives. Someone laid a single bunch of yellow flowers at the family's front door, but nothing else was done to mark the loss. Within weeks, the children had moved with their grandparents to another part of town. The only indication that anything had changed was the "For Sale" sign on the lawn.

A family had vanished, yet the impact on our neighborhood was slight. How could that be? Did I live in a community or just in a house on a street surrounded by people whose lives were entirely separate? Few of my neighbors, I later learned, knew others on the street more than casually; many didn't know even the names of those a few doors down.

According to social scientists, from 1974 to 1998, the frequency with which Americans spent a social evening with neighbors fell by about one-third. Robert Putnam, the author of *Bowling Alone*, a groundbreaking study of the disintegration of the American social fabric, suggests that the

> *Why is it that in an age of cheap long-distance rates, discount airlines, and the Internet . . . we often don't know the people who live next door?*

decline actually began 20 years earlier, so that neighborhood ties today are less than half as strong as they were in the 1950s.

Why is it that in an age of cheap long-distance rates, discount airlines, and the Internet, when we can create community anywhere, we often don't know the people who live next door?

Maybe my neighbors didn't mind living this way, but I did. I wanted to get to know the people whose houses I passed each day—not just what they do for a living and how many children they have, but the depth of their experience and what kind of people they are.

What would it take, I wondered, to penetrate the barriers between us? I thought about childhood sleepovers and the insight I used to get from waking up inside a friend's home. Would my neighbors let me sleep over and write about their lives from inside their own houses?

A little more than a year after the murder-suicide, I began to telephone my neighbors and send e-mail messages; in some cases, I just walked up to the door and rang the bell. The first one turned me down, but then I called Lou. "You can write about me, but it will be boring," he

495

warned. "I have nothing going on in my life—nothing. My life is zero. I don't do anything."

That turned out not to be true. When Lou finally awoke that morning at 6:18, he and I shared breakfast. Then he lay on a couch in his study and, skipping his morning nap, told me about his grandparents' immigration, his Catholic upbringing, his admission to medical school despite anti-Italian quotas, and how he met and courted his wife, built a career, and raised a family.

Later, we went to the Y.M.C.A. for his regular workout; he mostly just kibitzed with friends. We ate lunch. He took a nap. We watched the business news. That evening, he made us dinner and talked of friends he'd lost, his concerns for his children's futures, and his own mortality.

Before I left, Lou told me how to get into his house in case of an emergency, and I told him where I hide my spare key. That evening, as I carried my bag home, I felt that in my neighbor's house lived a person I actually knew.

I was privileged to be his friend until he died, just this past spring.

Remarkably, of the 18 or so neighbors I eventually approached about sleeping over, more than half said yes. There was the recently married young couple, both working in business; the real estate agent and her two small children; the pathologist married to a pediatrician who specializes in autism.

Eventually, I met a woman living three doors away, the opposite direction from Lou, who was seriously ill with breast cancer and in need of help. My goal shifted: could we build a supportive community around her—in effect, patch together a real neighborhood? Lou and I and some of the other neighbors ended up taking turns driving her to doctors' appointments and watching her children.

Our political leaders speak of crossing party lines to achieve greater unity. Maybe we should all cross the invisible lines between our homes and achieve greater unity in the places we live. Probably we don't need to sleep over; all it might take is to make a phone call, send a note, or ring a bell. Why not try it today?

DISCUSSION

1. For Lovenheim, the relations among the neighbors on his street become a barometer of how "community" has come to be defined in our culture. "Did I live in a community," he asks, "or just in a house on a street surrounded by people whose lives were entirely separate?" Do you share Lovenheim's concerns? In your view, does a belief in the importance of community constitute one of our culture's vanishing norms?

2. How would you define the ideal neighborhood? What kinds of relationships among neighbors would you most like to see? Why?

3. Many of his neighbors, Lovenheim observes, didn't seem to mind living next door to people they barely knew. How do you think you would feel? Would you find this kind of anonymity acceptable? Troubling? Why?

WRITING

4. "There's talk today," writes Lovenheim, "about how as a society we've become fragmented by ethnicity, income, city versus suburb, red state versus blue. But we also divide ourselves with invisible dotted lines. I'm talking about the property lines that isolate us from the people we are physically closest to: our neighbors." Write an essay in which you respond to this claim. Is Lovenheim correct? Do the physical barriers in our lives divide us from each other as deeply as do social differences in income, age, ethnicity, or gender? How or how not?

5. How well do you know your neighbors? And how well do they, in turn, know you? In a two-page essay, reflect on how much of Lovenheim's argument about neighborliness and community applies to your experiences. Based on your interactions with the people who live in your neighborhood, would you say Lovenheim's insights are valid? In what ways do your experiences either confirm or challenge his insights?

6. In many ways, Lovenheim's response to the crisis of neighborliness could be read as a commentary on what William Deresiewicz (p. 470) terms "faux friendship": the way modern communications technology has rendered us, paradoxically, more distanced from each other than ever before. Write an essay in which you identify and assess the parallels connecting Lovenheim's examination of neighborhoods and Deresiewicz's discussion of friendship.

Then and Now: *The Hero Monster*

In the long, storied history of horror movies, few monsters have haunted the public imagination quite so enduringly as the vampire. To a great extent, the vampire, beginning with the publication of Bram Stoker's *Dracula* in 1897, has always been a Victorian creation, a manifestation of our simultaneous sexual temptation and fear. For example, the first film representation of the vampire is the ugly, misshapen creature seen in the iconic 1922 film *Nosferatu*. The vampire manages to be an alluring figure, but his allure is undoubtedly menacing and to be avoided.

However, as our attitudes about sex and romance have changed, vampires have experienced a measure of cultural reevaluation, even rehabilitation, as seen by vampires like Bill in HBO's series *True Blood*. No longer the weird, monstrous villain of old, the modern vampire has morphed into one of our era's most representative romantic heroes — an object not of dread but of desire. Handsome yet mysterious, alluring yet elusive, this figure now traverses the pop culture landscape as a potent, if undead, sex symbol. Now, it seems, the monster can also be the good guy.

And yet, has that much changed? Although the vampire's sexuality is at the forefront of current popular representations, in the two most popular depictions of vampires — in *True Blood* and in Stephenie Meyer's *Twilight* series — vampires struggle with "going straight," that is, giving up human blood as food in favor of less horrific alternatives. In terms of our cultural taboos, what might this blood represent? Does it, in effect, sanitize and "de-fang" the vampire? And, if so, is today's vampire really much different from yesteryear's *Nosferatu*?

WRITING

1. What are some of the ways our popular culture portrays something or someone as good or bad? Pick some examples from film or television and think about them in the context of where they fit on this scale. What cultural fears or ideals do these examples embody? Do you have trouble categorizing them? Why might that be?

2. Frances Moore Lappé (p. 503) writes about the "good guy vs. bad guy" distinction. Why do you think our culture, even in its entertainment, is drawn to making this distinction? Do you think the lines are blurring? How or how not? In your opinion, what does this say about the way our culture is evolving?

JULIA SERANO
Vice Versa

Sex is assigned at birth, but for some people sex and gender identity do not match. People's experiences of gender range across an exceptionally wide spectrum. But are we, as a culture, ready to acknowledge and accept this fact? What is it like to want to change your physical sex to match your gender identity? Taking up these questions, Julia Serano, a transgender activist and writer with a PhD in biochemistry and molecular biophysics, presents us with the portrait of a relationship that defies the cultural norms that typically define what it means to be a man or a woman. She is the author of *Whipping Girl: A Transsexual Woman on Sexism and the Scapegoating of Femininity* (2007). Her writing has appeared in many feminist and transgender publications. The following essay was published in the *Big Ugly Review* in the fall of 2004.

ALMOST FORGOT ABOUT HER, BURIED ALIVE IN THE BACK OF MY MIND. At the time, I was a 26-year-old closet case, a self-described occasional crossdresser. And she was just like me only vice versa.

I met her in Kansas City at my first transgender support group meeting. The chairs were set up in a circle and most of the seats were filled with middle-aged transvestites in their 40s and 50s. They were painstakingly dressed, wearing Sunday's best, floral prints and muted pinks with just a hint of five o'clock shadow. Looking strangely sweet, almost equal parts aunt and uncle. And she seemed so out of place there, the only one in t-shirt and jeans. And genetically speaking, she was the only girl in the room. And chronologically we were the only two in our 20s.

After the meeting's minutes and a guest speaker from Mary Kay offering make-up tips, she introduced herself to me. She told me her name was Joan; I told her mine was Tom. And after a bit of random chit-chat, she asked if I wanted to hang out some time. I said "sure," and a week later we did.

I drove to Topeka where she lived. I remember the two of us were sitting on her bed listening to Tom Lehrer on her portable cassette player when I asked her what her deal was. She said she wasn't sure what to call herself exactly. She wanted to be male but was also attracted to men. . . . I told her that I knew what she meant, because I was just like her, only lesbian.

And so I told her, the first time I told anyone, about when I was in the 7th grade and had the biggest crush on Kathy Patterson. And every pre-teen fantasy I had about her began with me being turned into a girl somehow. And only afterwards would we run away together.

Then Joan told me about her high school boyfriend who told her he was gay. And she replied that she wasn't surprised and that she liked him that way.

And we told our gender histories like we were swapping war stories. Experiences we couldn't share with our families or friends, because they were never there and they would never understand. But that night, sitting on Joan's bed, for the first time in my life I didn't feel quite so much like an alien.

And the last time I saw her was a Saturday evening we spent watching a *Star Trek Next Generation* re-run—the episode where Beverly Crusher falls in love with a trill. And we both sat still on her couch next to one another. And when our bodies touched, it was the first human contact that either of us had in a while. And at one point, I put my arm around her and she leaned into me. It felt like we were pretending that I was the he and she was the she.

> **And we told our gender histories like we were swapping war stories.**

And for a moment, I thought one thing might lead to another. Maybe we would make out on her sofa and wake up naked next to one another. And somehow it almost made sense, like we were each other's long lost complement, the way that two odd numbers add up to make an even. But the problem was, we weren't really a perfect match, we were more like exact replicas—the same only vice versa. And while there was definitely some mutual attraction, nothing ever happened, because I wasn't a gay man and she wasn't a lesbian.

Now it's eight years later and I'm not in Kansas anymore. I'm a woman living in Oakland. And that bedroom in Topeka literally feels like a lifetime ago. And every now and again, when I find myself feeling alone, I think about Joan and wonder how he's doing.

DISCUSSION

1. What does the term *transgender* suggest to you? What associations does it conjure? Where do they come from? And to what extent does Serano's portrait challenge or alter these associations?

2. "We told our gender histories," Serano writes, "like we were swapping war stories." What does Serano mean by this statment? What does it say about gender — about how cultural expectations around it get defined and enforced — that Serano would liken it to the experience of combat?

3. "I almost forgot about [Joan]," Serano confesses at the outset, "buried alive in the back of my mind." What do you make of this opening formulation? Why do you think Serano introduces us to Joan by describing her as "buried alive"? In what ways does this metaphor capture Joan's particular relationship to the dominant social scripts around gender?

WRITING

4. In this account, Serano draws a distinction between assigned sex and gender identity. How do you understand the relationship between these two categories? To what extent, in your view, can or should one's biological sex determine one's experience of oneself as a "man" or a "woman"?

5. One of the underlying contentions of this essay is that gender is far from a singular or monolithic category. How has reading this brief essay challenged your idea about what gender is? In your view, does this expanded understanding give us a better way to think about gender? How or how not?

6. In many ways, Serano's account of her encounter with Joan can be read as another of this chapter's many investigations into the changing nature of friendship in contemporary society. Write an essay in which you assess how this essay's portrait of friendship compares to the portrait presented in another selection from this chapter. What are the commonalities? The differences?

FRANCES MOORE LAPPÉ

Let's Drop the Good Guys vs. Bad Guys Talk. We Need to Grow Up as a Species

From political debates to blockbuster movies, we are taught over and over to divide the world neatly into two opposed camps: *us* and *them*. While utterly familiar, this tendency may also reflect an underdeveloped, even immature, understanding of the problems confronting us — or so says Frances Moore Lappé. A prolific writer and activist, Lappé's work addresses poverty, hunger, and the environment. She is the author of eighteen books, including the bestseller *Diet for a Small Planet* (1971), a groundbreaking book about our food system. The following essay was posted on Alternet on March 20, 2010.

PRESIDENT OBAMA HAS GIVEN US A HUGE GIFT. IT'S SO BIG WE MAY have trouble getting our arms around it, but it's potentially life-changing.

In 2008, even though I knew better, I fell for the notion that a more intelligent, reflective, and progressive president could deflect our country's, even our world's, downward spin. Apparently a lot of people shared my frame of mind, or, dare I say, my hope.

It's tempting to blame the president for letting us down, or even easier to blame his opponents. But doing that would deny us his gift. Obama's gift is that the very failure we're witnessing—failure to reform the financial system at the root level necessary to avoid the next calamity or the failure to convince Americans that health insurance reform now is an immediate, moral, and economic necessity—exposes a deeper truth. If President Obama's first year had been more successful, maybe we'd have missed it.

The truth is simply this: Bad people are not the root cause of our problems and "better people" can't make everything right.

Many think of conservatives, long wrapped in "family values," as the moralists, but the tendency to blame shortcomings of character for our problems shows up across the political spectrum. Economist Joseph Stiglitz, in his newest book, *Freefall*, talks of a "moral deficit" at the heart of our financial industry's woes, and Nomi Prins rails against "greed" on Wall Street in *It Takes a Pillage*.

Right and Left appear to share at least one common frame: The problem is defects in those people in power. If true, it's easy to believe that changing the people will solve a lot. As long as we believe this, we're in big trouble.

Really accepting Obama's gift starts with letting go of this frame and facing truths about ourselves we'd rather avoid. But the work is worth it. Only with an evidence-based take on ourselves can we move toward the saner, healthier world most people want.

> *Bad people are not the root cause of our problems and "better people" can't make everything right.*

The first part of this frame adjustment is fairly easy to swallow: More and more neuroscience confirms that we are indeed hardwired to care about each other, so we can't legitimately claim great moral victory when we're good. We just can't help it. Cooperation, it turns out, stimulates pleasure centers that are similar to what happens when we eat chocolate! Babies cry at the sound of other babies' cries but typically not at recordings of their own cries. In recent charming experiments, toddlers scurry to help clueless adults, without being asked and with no reward. And in another study, subjects ended up happier by buying a gift for someone else rather than indulging themselves.

Berkeley anthropologist Sarah Blaffer Hrdy brings us the greatest news of all. We probably didn't evolve in the same line with extant great apes. Whew. They can be really brutal. We likely evolved our uniquely cooperative nature through eons of distinctive "cooperative breeding," caring for each others' babies, which developed empathy, trust, and the capacity to read each others' feelings. But there's more, and here's where it gets touchy.

History and lab experiments provide undeniable proof that *most* of us, not a handful of bad guys, will commit horrible deeds in the wrong conditions.

Have most of us, for example, really taken in the truth that the Holocaust was not the work of one madman but carried out by millions of ordinary people? And other genocides? The same truth. Like the one in the Congo today, ignored by the world but arguably resulting in even more deaths by everyday people than Hitler's death camps.

To solid historical evidence we can add compelling results from psychological experiments. One is the infamous 1971 Stanford prison experiment, which Dr. Philip Zimbardo had to halt early because his young subjects who'd tested "normal" were abusing each other in ways eerily similar to what happened at Abu Ghraib.

Taking all this in—truly accepting the good, the bad, and the ugly in ourselves—we can drop the false and failing good-guys-vs.-bad-guys frame. We can grow up as a species. Accepting who we really are, we can identify the conditions shown to bring out the worst. They seem pretty clear. My short list includes concentrated unaccountable power, anonymity and lack of transparency, and scapegoating others.

Whether you would pick these conditions or others, my point is that we can begin to redirect the trajectory we're on—decimating 100 species a day and causing a billion of our own species to go hungry despite vast abundance—*only* if we take this big step: Only if we are determined to stop blaming and create the social conditions now proven to bring out the best in us, the pro-social needs and capacities we know are in there.

> **Most of us . . . will commit horrible deeds in the wrong conditions.**

How?

By working to flip the conditions proven to bring out the worst in us. We can begin by dispersing power—by creating new power as we ourselves step up as community problem solvers and by challenging the concentration of power by, for example, getting democracy-killing money out of politics. Only then can we create rules to ensure wealth's dispersion and to hold decision makers accountable.

Helping us to let go of illusion and get a grip on an evidence-based path to democratic solutions could be the real gift of Obama's presidency. Let's grab it.

DISCUSSION

1. Take a moment to reflect on the plea embedded within the essay's title. Do you agree that such talk is prevalent in our society, and, if so, what are some examples? In your estimation, what would be useful or beneficial about dropping the "good guys vs. bad guys" model for thinking about societal problems? Can you think of any instances where using this framework has done us more harm than good?

2. The idea that individuals are responsible for the political, social, and economic ills that beset us is, according to Lappé, an "illusion." Do you agree? Can you think of a particular problem or crisis that, in your view, was caused by individual misbehavior?

3. "Truly accepting the good, the bad, and the ugly in ourselves," Lappé contends, is about "grow[ing] up as a species." Why do you think she chooses this phrase to describe the goal behind her vision? Do you agree with this contention?

WRITING

4. "More and more neuroscience," Lappé writes, "confirms that we are indeed hardwired to care about each other, so we can't legitimately claim great moral victory when we're good. We just can't help it." In an essay, find examples in Lappé's argument and evaluate the ways this kind of scientific framing challenges the conventional ways we are taught to think about morality. Do you agree with Lappé? How does the proposition that we are hardwired to act ethically rewrite the established social scripts that tell us how to distinguish being good from being bad?

5. "We can begin," Lappé declares, "to redirect the trajectory we're on — decimating 100 species a day and causing a billion of our own species to go hungry despite vast abundance — *only* if we take this big step: Only if we are determined to stop blaming and create the social conditions now proven to bring out the best in us, the pro-social needs and capacities we know are in there." Write an essay in which you address Lappé's contention directly. Do you share her concerns as outlined in her essay? In your view, is the change in tone she identifies as necessary truly the *only* way to begin effecting meaningful social change? Are there alternative solutions that Lappé's argument overlooks? If so, what?

6. Lappé, like Peter Lovenheim (p. 494), is interested in helping us move beyond social attitudes that divide the world into opposed camps of *us* and *them*. How do you think Lappé would respond to Lovenheim's plan for bridging the divide that separates the people in his neighborhood from each other? Would she regard his "sleepover" plan as an example of or an exception to her vision for moving beyond the paradigm of "good guys vs. bad guys"?

JULIE BOSMAN

In Times Square, One Last Homeless Holdout

What does it mean to be "homeless"? Few segments of the population are the object of more pervasive stereotyping and greater misunderstanding than the homeless. Julie Bosman's surprising portrait of the last homeless man living in Times Square shows us someone defiant to change, who may very well be redefining what it means to feel like you belong to a place. Bosman is a reporter for the *New York Times,* where this story was published on March 29, 2010. She writes on politics and topics relating to New York City, and her work has also appeared in the *Wall Street Journal* and *Slate*.

A S LONG AS THERE HAVE BEEN HOMELESS PEOPLE SLEEPING IN TIMES Square, there have been social workers and city officials trying to persuade them to leave.

In the past, the homeless were offered a free ride to one of the city's warehouse-like shelters. These days, workers for nonprofit groups help people move into apartments, keeping track as the number of the chronically homeless in Times Square goes down.

According to their records, by 2005, there were only 55. Last summer, it was down to 7.

Now there is one.

His name is Heavy, and he has lived on the streets of Times Square for decades. Day after day, he has politely declined offers of housing, explaining that he is a protector of the neighborhood and cannot possibly leave, said the workers who visit him every day.

Yet they are determined to get through to Heavy, the last homeless holdout in Times Square.

"I just have this dream that all of a sudden something will snap, and he'll say, 'I'd love to have housing,'" said Amie Pospisil, an associate director at Common Ground Community, a nonprofit that conducts street outreach. "I don't rule out that it could happen."

Little is known about Heavy, even his full name. Heavy is a nickname, part of his last name, a fact he surrendered after more than a year of daily visits from workers. He declined to be interviewed.

According to neighbors and social workers, he is a gentle presence, possibly delusional and mentally ill, a quiet man who does not harass passers-by or panhandle aggressively. An employee in a deli on Eighth

507

Avenue said that he usually gave Heavy a few pieces of bread at lunchtime. Neighbors bring him hot coffee, loose change, and warm clothing in the winter.

"He is a sweetheart," said an 82-year-old woman who gave her name as Nanny and stopped to talk near her home on 48th Street, where she has lived for 44 years. "He sees me coming and says, 'Hi, Mommy,' and I say, 'Hi, honey.' And I give him his quarter, and I go on with my business."

The most recent annual estimate of the number of homeless people sleeping on the streets of New York showed an increase, but Times Square has been an exception. Heavy is the last member of what social workers called the Times Square Seven, the only homeless people remaining last summer out of the dozens they had been placing in housing for years.

Of the seven, three men were regularly sleeping on the steps of churches. All of them had been homeless for a long time—on average, 17 years. One man, a middle-aged Southerner, had been homeless for 40 years.

One by one, from last September to January, the men were convinced to accept housing.

Except Heavy.

"I think it's fair to say that we gave all seven people the same attention and effort," Ms. Pospisil said. "Heavy is still there."

The outreach teams had long since memorized his location and his habits. For a long stretch, he had been camped out on Seventh Avenue, until a city sanitation crew disposed of his belongings, which had become an eyesore on the sidewalk. Then he found a new spot nearby, under the fire escape of a theater. Now he is usually seen around the corner of 48th Street and Seventh Avenue, a block or two from the heart of Times Square.

During the day, Heavy is typically seen wearing a red knit cap, sipping coffee and smoking a cigarette, sitting on a makeshift chair near his black-and-red suitcase. At night, outreach workers often find him nestled within a thin cardboard box, near the scaffolding of a building under construction.

Heavy was far from alone on the streets of Times Square in the 1990s, when he began sleeping there frequently in the midst of a roiling mess of drug dealing, prostitution, and crime.

"Times Square has always been this signpost for whatever's going on in New York City, for good or ill, and when there was a very heavy homeless population, it all contributed to a larger perception that New York City had lost control of the public realm," said Tim Tompkins, the president of the Times Square Alliance. "I think there was a time at the very beginning of the homelessness issue when it was like, let's squeeze the balloon and get them out of the way."

But tactics changed. Nonprofit groups began sharing information about the homeless people who were anchored in Times Square, gathering names, ages, medical conditions, and the personal issues that might be keeping them homeless.

The street outreach teams from Common Ground and the Goddard Riverside Community Center, another nonprofit group, began maintaining close ties with the Times Square Alliance and the Police Department. More units of supportive housing and specialized shelter beds were opened up to the chronically homeless, as an alternative to the sometimes-unruly and intimidating general shelter system. And the more commercial, safer, and more tourist-friendly Times Square slowly became less comfortable for the street homeless.

> *"We're devising a strategy to encourage people not to support him in his homelessness."*

"Whether by accident or not, certainly over the last 10 or 15 years, the cleaning up of Times Square and the street traffic in Times Square may have been an issue," said Stephan Russo, the executive director of Goddard Riverside. "It can be a little daunting for them."

The area still attracts its share of panhandlers, especially during the day, and a few emotionally disturbed people who occasionally draw the attention of security employees of the Times Square Alliance. This month, for example, they intervened when a man began tearing flowers out of a planter.

The social workers at Common Ground said they have no intention of pressuring Heavy to leave the streets. But Tim Marx, the executive director, said neighbors might not be helping in the long term by giving Heavy food and clothing. Directors at Common Ground are considering posting one of their outreach workers to stay with Heavy all day, study his habits and movements, and talk to neighbors about what is best for him.

"We're devising a strategy to encourage people not to support him in his homelessness," Mr. Marx said.

Rosanne Haggerty, the president of Common Ground, says she has known Heavy since at least 1990, early in the days when she was working to end homelessness in Times Square. In those days, there were more than 70 people sleeping in the area on a typical night.

"He's kind of iconic," Ms. Haggerty said. "He would leave for periods and then return, and some days we would actually succeed in getting him inside. But he has this fascination with the life in Times Square."

She added, "We are continuing to plug away to find the right housing solution for Heavy."

DISCUSSION

1. What, in your estimation, might account for Heavy's refusal to be moved into conventional housing? Do any of these explanations offer a plausible justification for his decision?

2. One of our most ingrained cultural norms has to do with what is sometimes called the "myth of self-reliance": the belief that, whatever the obstacles, we are all personally responsible for whatever befalls us. To what extent does Bosman's portrait of Heavy challenge this norm? To what extent does it confirm this norm?

3. Although Heavy is homeless, Bosman notes, he is far from alone. A number of people, from neighbors to social workers, keep in regular contact with and take an active interest in Heavy's day-to-day life. In your view, is this fact significant? To what extent does the existence of an ad hoc community influence your view of Heavy's decision to remain homeless?

WRITING

4. As Bosman reports, there is something surprising, even unnatural, in the example of a homeless person who chooses to remain living on the streets. What are the particular assumptions about and stereotypes of the homeless that Heavy's story challenges? To what extent does this portrait give you a different way of understanding the issue of homelessness altogether? And, in your view, are these differences for the better? How or how not?

5. Write an essay in which you argue for or against Heavy continuing to live in Times Square. What are the arguments for and against him moving to subsidized housing? Does his story represent a man standing up to social change around him? How or how not?

6. How do you think Joel Kotkin (p. 490) would react to Bosman's portrait of Heavy? In your estimation, does this account of Heavy's refusal to "budge" from Times Square correspond to Kotkin's discussion of "placeness"? What are the specific similarities and differences in the way each of these essays showcases a person's relationship to place?

JARED KELLER

Twitter Is Forever

In a world where we are increasingly surrounded, even overrun, with "chatter," no technology stands out more vividly than Twitter. In a stunningly short period, Twitter has emerged as one of the most widely used and widely discussed communications tools in existence. So rapidly has it ascended, in fact, that very little consensus yet exists about how, when, and why it should be used. Does Twitter represent an important change in the way we share information, or is it yet another example of the decline of communication? Jared Keller offers some thoughts on this quintessentially modern technology and its implications for how we communicate. Keller writes for an online feature of the *Atlantic*, the *Atlantic Wire,* where this story was originally posted on April 15, 2010. He is the editor of MySecretBoston.com and has written for Boston's *Weekly Dig*, an alternative newspaper.

THE LIBRARY OF CONGRESS ANNOUNCED WEDNESDAY VIA ITS official Twitter feed that it would be adding tweets to its inventory of published works. The addition of the vast body of public tweets sent since Twitter's founding in March 2006 is the latest step in the Library of Congress' effort to incorporate digitally published works into its archives. With an official press release forthcoming, the Library posted a teaser on its blog.

Expect to see an emphasis on the scholarly and research implications of the acquisition. I'm no Ph.D., but it boggles my mind to think what we might be able to learn about ourselves and the world around us from this wealth of data. And I'm certain we'll learn things that none of us now can possibly conceive.

Just a few examples of important tweets in the past few years include the first-ever tweet from Twitter co-founder Jack Dorsey (http://twitter .com/jack/status/20), President Obama's tweet about winning the 2008 election (http://twitter.com/barackobama/status/992176676), and a set of two tweets from a photojournalist who was arrested in Egypt and then freed because of a series of events set into motion by his use of Twitter (http://twitter.com/jamesbuck/status/786571964) and (http://twitter.com/ jamesbuck/status/787167620). . . .

So if you think the Library of Congress is "just books," think of this: The Library has been collecting materials from the web since it began harvesting congressional and presidential campaign websites in 2000. Today we hold more than 167 terabytes of web-based information, including legal blogs, websites of candidates for national office, and websites of Members of Congress.

Twitter cofounder Biz Stone explained the decisions as part of the service's ongoing commitment to openness. "The open exchange of information can have a positive global impact," he wrote on Twitter's official blog.

The announcement has elicited plenty of Internet chatter, particularly from tech and social media bloggers. Nancy Scola at TechPresident pondered the long-term feasibility of the project. "Is this going to be a continuously updated tweet archive? Will it be searchable by researchers? Will it track retweets and responses? Why not archive Facebook?" Marshall Kirkpatrick at ReadWriteWeb inquired into some of the specifics. "Will the archive include friend/follower connection data? Will it be usable for commercial purposes? Will there be a web interface for searching it and will that change the face of Twitter search for good?"

But while the blogosphere buzzes with curiosity over the logistics, a larger question looms: is including Twitter in the Library of Congress a good idea, at all?

If the goal of the Library of Congress is to create a cultural snapshot of a given moment in American history, capturing and archiving the totality of Twitter might be the most earnest way to do it.

I, for one, find myself somewhere between confusion and revulsion. The Library of Congress, founded in 1800, was intended to be a repository for America's cultural history, a permanent record of our country's progress and a resource for historians and researchers. Initially, I found it somewhat irksome that 140-character spurts should have the same significance as written works. Of course, remanding the task of determining cultural and literary significance to a set group of individuals is equally problematic, but while *Twilight* may find a place on the Library's shelves, the more scattershot or vulgar contributions to the Twitterverse don't necessarily stack up. Do short-form spats between Aimee Mann and Ice T really share the same cultural gravitas as *How The Other Half Lives*? And what insights will future historians gain into the nature of American society based on my joke tweets about my own neurosis?

Then again, including the entire history of Twitter—no matter how banal, trivial, or purely disgusting the content may be—seems to fall within the goals of the Library of Congress. In its efforts to capture the nation's cultural development, the Library receives copies of every book, pamphlet, map, print, and piece of music registered in the U.S. through the United States Copyright Office. The movement to collect, archive, and disseminate online works is the logical continuation of this mission, especially as online publishing—via blogs or social networks—becomes increasingly egalitarian.

The Pew Internet and American Life Project released a study in October 2009 stating that 19 percent of Americans on the Internet use Twitter to share content, up from 11 percent the previous April. Today, Twitter users send a total of 55 million tweets a day. TechCrunch's Jason Kincaid reports that Twitter boasts over 100 million registered users, with 300,000 new users joining daily. The rapid growth of the microblogging service and its social media competitors suggests that no end is in sight for the explosion of personalized online publishing.

If the goal of the Library of Congress is to create a cultural snapshot of a given moment in American history, capturing and archiving the totality of Twitter might be the most earnest way to do it. Most long-form written works tend to be highly structured, methodically executed, and stylistically packaged, and while their content certainly refines and articulates specific cultural perceptions, their contemplative origins create a disconnect between the experiences lived and expressed.

Twitter's perpetual narrative captures the mundane and extraordinary with equal measure. President Obama's first tweet may be a "historic" moment for technology and American government, but my brother's musings on the decline of Blockbuster provide an equally important insight into the minds of average Americans. What seems trivial to us—from the feverish anticipation of the newest Justin Bieber album to a declaration of one's intent to purchase milk and eggs—is part of the constantly metamorphosing character of American culture.

What lesson can the average Twitter user glean from this occasion? Twitter is forever; make your tweets count.

DISCUSSION

1. Take a closer look at this essay's title. Is there anything surprising, even incongruous, in the proposition that what gets generated via Twitter will last "forever"? Does this prospect seem in line with or contrary to the norms that have grown around this particular communication technology? How?

2. Do you have any personal experience with Twitter? How does this type of writing compare to other types with which you are familiar? How do the norms around tweeting compare with those defining more conventional forms of communication? Would you say there are goals for which Twitter is particularly, even uniquely, suited?

3. Keller worries that Twitter is fast becoming a tool for generating and disseminating "trivia." Do you agree? Can you think of a use for Twitter that would complicate, even contradict, this claim?

WRITING

4. Write an essay in which you outline the rules for how Twitter should best be used. What are the proper settings or contexts in which it is best to tweet? What are the goals or purposes for which this type of technology could best be used? Which subject or topics are best to raise? Which are best to avoid? When you're done, write an additional paragraph in which you reflect on the particular rules you chose to outline. Why did you script the uses of Twitter in this particular way? What rationale underlay your choices?

5. For Keller, the idea of archiving tweets elicits a reaction "somewhere between confusion and revulsion." Write an essay in which you reflect on your own reaction to the Library of Congress decision. Do you share Keller's dismay? If so, why? Or are you more sanguine about this change? Again, if so, why?

6. Like Facebook, Twitter is the product of our new digital age. How do you think William Deresiewicz (p. 470) would react to the decision to archive tweets? Given his argument about the ways digital technologies are giving rise to "faux friendship," do you think he would regard this decision as an encouraging sign of progress? A worrisome step backwards? Why?

Scenes and Un-Scenes: *"Hello, Neighbor"*

It has become cliché to bemoan the demise of community in contemporary life. But what exactly do we mean by the term *community*? Ritually invoked by politicians and pundits, commentators and educators, community stands as one of the most frequently lauded, and yet chronically unspecified, ideals in public life — defined as much by what it's not and where it's missing as by anything else. To speak of community is, on some level, to pose the questions "What do we have in common? What interests or sympathies, experiences or background, bind us to one another?" To watch the news and listen to pundits, one is always hearing declarations that the nature of community is changing and, by many accounts, eroding. But do you agree?

How we answer such questions depends in large measure on where we stand. Different vantages generate different notions of community. This, in the broadest sense, is what the images assembled here make clear. Sampling some of the more representative perspectives on community within our culture, these visuals show us the extent to which our definitions of community are determined by our given perspective.

▶▶ *An iconic figure in American pop culture, Mr. Rogers embodied for generations of American children what it means to be part of a community. The gentle invitation with which he opened every show — "Won't you be my neighbor?" — grew over the years into one of the most universally recognized and endlessly imitated phrases in all of television. In its own way, this phrase encapsulated the conception of community that guided the entire show. To be a "neighbor" meant joining a community that placed no restrictions on belonging, a world in which differences of race and class, gender and age, were dissolved in the vision of an all-inclusive "neighborhood" in which all were recognized as equals. What do you make of this ethic? Does such acceptance and inclusiveness still constitute a norm in our society? (See next page.)*

▼▼ *When we think of community, many of us think of the physical*
space we inhabit. Looking at a community from a distance, how
does our idea of it change? How is this space dependent on who lives
inside it? Does an image like this say "community" to you? When
looking at an aerial image, does community still evoke the same
communal ideals?

▲▲ *What happens when community goes online? In the wake of technologies that now allow us to invent, control, or even fabricate our chosen community, we have seen the emergence of an entirely new set of rules and norms around how this ideal can be defined. Virtual relationships, those that exist nowhere except online, now routinely fall within the category of community. But should they? What are the differences between an online and a so-called real-world community? Are communities we create online any less authentic than those we join in our everyday lives?*

"NOW THAT WE'VE LEARNED TO TALK, WE'D BETTER ESTABLISH SOME LOCAL COMMUNITY STANDARDS."

◄◄ *This cartoon takes a tongue-in-cheek look at the idea of communal living, namely that we collaborate on rules by which we live. But it also skewers this notion. How does it do that? What does this cartoon seem to say about the existence of community standards? Are they good or bad?*

GIVE. ADVOCATE. VOLUNTEER.
LIVE UNITED. United Way
Ad Council Want to make a difference? Find out how at LIVEUNITED.ORG.

For many, the term community *is a rallying cry, a call to tackle and redress a pressing social problem. In this context, community denotes less a specific group or place than a program or plan for implementing some type of policy. This United Way campaign is designed to advocate for community involvement in urban areas. What ideas about community are present in this image? Which are missing?*

DISCUSSION

1. Which of these images most resembles your notion of community? Why is that?

2. Which of these images seems most foreign to you? How does its depiction of community or community ideals fail to relate to your experience?

3. Do you think any images are missing from this portfolio? What would they be? How would they represent your opinion on the way community is changing?

WRITING

4. Pick one of the images in this portfolio and write a brief essay in which you evaluate how well it reflects your notion of what community ideals are. Be sure to focus on specific aspects of the image in your critique. If anything, what might you change about this image to bring it in line with your own experience of community?

5. Do the images in this portfolio represent fundamental changes in the nature of community? Write an essay in which you argue how they do or do not.

6. Peter Lovenheim (p. 494) writes about bygone ideals of community. Write an essay in which you use his definition of community to evaluate the images shown in this portfolio. Do any images in particular fit his ideal? Would he find any of them undesirable? Why or why not?

Putting It into Practice: *The More Things Change . . .*

Now that you've read the chapter selections, try applying your conclusions to your own life by completing the following exercises.

DESIGNING YOUR IDEAL COMMUNITY   Write a one-page description of the community in which you live, whether it represents your school, home, church, or other institution. Be as specific as possible about what essential elements you think make this a distinct community. Then write another page in which you evaluate what about this community does not meet the ideal. Is this a good or bad thing? What aspects about this community would you change to make it fit your ideal of community?

ADVOCATING FOR CHANGE   Think of a social issue that interests you and research groups in your community that advocate for change in this area. What are their goals, and how do they go about achieving them? If possible, interview a member of one organization and find out what about this group appeals to him or her. Using all the information you have collected, write a summary report that profiles the organization you have chosen.

BE THE CHANGE   Write a personal reflection in which you examine the ways you feel that you have changed over the course of your life, both physically (see Julia Serano, p. 500) or in terms of your outlook or beliefs (like Peter Lovenheim, p. 494). How have these changes come about? Have they been positive or negative? Since change is a never-ending process, how would you like aspects of yourself to change in years to come? How might these changes happen?

Acknowledgments (continued from copyright page)

Julie Bosman, "Times Square Homeless Holdout, Not Budging" from *The New York Times*, Metropolitan Section, 3/30/2010 issue, page A1. Reprinted by permission.

Po Bronson and Ashley Merryman, "See Baby Discriminate" from *Newsweek* 9/5/2009 issue, page A1. Reprinted by permission.

David Brooks, "People Like Us." *Atlantic Monthly*, September 2003. Reprinted by permission.

Buy Nothing Christmas homepage. Reprinted by permission of Adbusters.org.

Lynette Clemetson, "Work vs. Family, Complicated by Race" from *The New York Times*, Fashion and Style Section, 2/9/2006 issue. Reprinted by permission.

Michael B. Crawford, "The Case for Working with Your Hands," from *Shop Class as Soulcraft*. Reprinted by permission of The Susan Rabiner Literary Agency, Inc.

A.M. Cusac, 2005. "Watching Torture in Prime Time." *The Progressive*. 69(8): 34, 36. This piece was originally written for *The Progressive* magazine, 409 E. Main St., Madison, WI 53703. www.progressivemediaproject.org.

Frank Deford, "Awful Injustice: It's Time to Start Paying Revenue-Earning College Athletes." *Sports Illustrated*. January 2, 2008. Reprinted by permission.

Anthony DePalma, "Fifteen Years on the Bottom Rung" from "Class Matters" from *The New York Times*, Science Section, 5/26/2005 issue. Reprinted by permission.

William Deresiewicz, "Faux Friendship." *The Chronicle Review*, December 6, 2009. Reprinted by permission of the author.

Sara Dickerman, "Food Fright," from Slate 9/15/2004 issue. Reprinted by permission.

Debra J. Dickerson, "The Great White Way." From *Mother Jones*, September/October 2005. Copyright © 2005 by the Foundation for National Progress. Reprinted by permission.

Michael Dyson, *Frames of Reference: Class, Caste, Culture and Cameras from Come Hell or High Water: Hurricane Katrina and the Color of Disaster*. Copyright © 2006. Reprinted by arrangement with Basic Civitas, a Member of The Perseus Books Group. All rights reserved.

Barbara Ehrenreich, excerpt from *Bright-Sided: How Positive Thinking Is Undermining America*. © 2010 Picador. Reprinted by permission.

Jason Fagone, excerpt from *Horsemen of the Esophagus: Competitive Eating and the Big Fat American Dream*, copyright © 2006 by Jason Fagone. Used by permission of Crown Publishers, a division of Random House, Inc.

John Taylor Gatto, "Against School." Originally appeared in *Harper's*, September 2003. Reprinted by permission of the author. For more info: www.johntaylorgatto.com.

Makenna Goodman, "Ever Wonder if You Could Kill What You Eat? We Did the Other Night." Originally appeared in AlterNet (August 28, 2009). Reprinted by permission of Chelsea Green Publishing.

Mathew Honan, "I Am Here: One Man's Experiment with the Location-Aware Lifestyle." Reprinted by permission of the author.

bell hooks, "Learning in the Shadow of Race and Class." *The Chronicle of Higher Education*, 11/17/2000, pp. 14–16. Reprinted by permission of the author.

Harriet McBryde Johnson, "Unspeakable Conversations" from *The New York Times*, Magazine Section, 2/16/2003 issue, page 50. Reprinted by permission.

Frederick Kaufman, "They Eat What We Are" from *The New York Times* 9/2/2007 issue, page 20. Reprinted by permission.

Jared Keller, "Twitter Is Forever." *The Atlantic*, April 15, 2010. Reprinted by permission.

Naomi Klein, "Patriarchy Gets Funky," from *No Logo*, Picador, 2002. Reprinted by permission.

Caroline Knapp, "Add Cake, Subtract Self-Esteem" from *Appetites: Why Women Want*. © 2004 Counterpoint Press. Reprinted by permission of Counterpoint Press, a division of The Perseus Books Group.

John West, except from *The Last Goodnights: Assisting My Parents with Their Suicides*. © 2010 Counterpoint Press. Reprinted by permission of Counterpoint Press, a division of The Perseus Books Group.

Photo Credits

Index of Authors and Titles